Ninth edition

Published in November 2004
Alastair Sawday Publishing Co. Ltd
The Home Farm Stables,
Barrow Gurney, Bristol BS48 3RW
Tel: +44 (0)1275 464891
Fax: +44 (0)1275 464887
E-mail: info@specialplacestostay.com
Web: www.specialplacestostay.com

The Globe Pequot Press
P.O. Box 480, Guilford,
Connecticut 06437, USA
Tel: +1 203 458 4500
Fax: +1 203 458 4601
E-mail: info@globepequot.com
Web: www.globepequot.com

Design:
Caroline King

Maps & Mapping:
Bartholomew Mapping, a division of HarperCollins, Glasgow

Printing:
Pims, UK

UK Distribution:
Penguin UK, 80 Strand, London

US Distribution:
The Globe Pequot Press, Guilford, Connecticut

A catalogue record for this book is available from the British Library.

ISBN 1-901970-48-5

Printed in UK on Revive Silk: 75% de-inked post-consumer waste, 25% mill broke and virgin fibres.

ALASTAIR SAWDAY'S
SPECIAL PLACES TO STAY

FRENCH BED & BREAKFAST

Contents

Guide entries

Back

Index by département

Photo Sara Allan

Alastair Sawday Publishing

We began by chance, in 1993, seeking a job for a friend. On my desk was a file: a miscellany of handsome old houses in France, some that could provide a bed, and some a meal, to strangers.

I ran a small travel company at the time, taking people off the beaten track; these places were our 'finds'. No chain hotels for us, no tourist restaurants if we could possibly visit old manor houses, farms and châteaux whose owners would breathe new life into our enthusiasm for France.

So Jane set off with a file under her arm and began to turn it into a book. We were then innocent enough to ignore advice and print 'far too many' – 10,000. We sold them all, in six months – and a publishing company was born.

We exhorted readers to enjoy a 'warm welcome, wooden beams, stone walls, good coffee' and nailed our colours firmly to the mast: 'We are not impressed by TVs, mini-bars and trouser-presses'. We urged people to enjoy simplicity and authenticity and railed against the iniquities of corporate travel. Little has changed.

Although there are now more than 25 of us working out here in our rural idyll, publishing about 20 books, we are holding tightly to our original ethos and gradually developing it. Our first priority is to publish the best books in our field and to nourish a reputation for integrity. It is critically important that readers trust our judgement.

Our next priority is to sell them – fortunately they sell themselves, too, such is their reputation for reliability and for providing travellers with memorable experiences and friendships.

However, publishing and selling books is not enough. It raises other questions: what is our impact on the world around us? How do we treat ourselves and other people? Is not a company just people working together with a shared focus? So we have begun to consider our responses to those questions and thus have generated our Ethical Policy.

There is little intrinsically ethical about publishing travel guides, but there are ways in which we can improve. First, we use recycled paper and seek the most eco-friendly printing methods. Secondly, we are promoting local economies and encouraging good work. We seek beauty and are providing an alternative to the corporate culture that has done so much damage. Thirdly, we celebrate the use of locally-sourced and organic food

Who are we?

among our owners and have launched a pilot Fine Breakfast scheme in our British B&B guide.

But the way we function as a company matters too. We treat each other with respect and affection. An easy-going but demanding office atmosphere seems to work for us. But for these things to survive we need to engage all the staff, so we are split into three teams: the Green team, the Better Business team and the Charitable Trust team.

Each team meets monthly to advise the company. The Green team uses our annual Environmental Audit as a text and monitors progress. The Better Business team ponders ethical issues such as flexible working, time off in lieu/overtime, and other matters that need a deep airing before decisions are made. The Trust team allocates the small sum that the company gives each year to charities, and raises extra money.

A few examples of our approach to company life: we compost our waste, recycle the recyclable, run a shared car to work, run a car on LPG and another on a mix of recycled cooking oil and diesel, operate a communal organic food ordering system, use organic or local food for our own events, take part in Bike to Work day, use a 'green' electricity supplier, partially bank with Triodos (the ethical bank in Bristol), have a health insurance scheme that encourages alternative therapies, and sequester our carbon emissions.

Especially exciting for us is an imminent move to our own eco offices; they will conserve energy and use little of it. But I have left to the end any mention of our most tangible effort in the ethical field: our Fragile Earth series of books. There are The Little Food Book, The Little Earth Book and The Little Money Book – hugely respected and selling solidly – look out for new titles in the Fragile Earth series.

Perhaps the most vital element in our growing Ethical Policy is the sense of engagement that we all have. It is not only stimulating to be trying to do the right thing, it is an important perspective for us all at work. And that can only help us to continue to produce beautiful books.

Alastair Sawday

Photo Paul Groom

Acknowledgements

This was our first book, and it is still a 'flagship'. This ninth edition is huge, packed with fascinating places and people, and thousands of people depend on it. So Emma Carey carries a great responsibility, and she does so with a rare cheerfulness and easy efficiency. Always kind, always patient, she has put together this latest edition with great sensitivity to the nuances of French people and French places. The results are spectacular – by far the best book of its kind. And she has been working on her own in Leeds, far from her usual daily support system. She has our admiration and gratitude.

Behind the scenes there has been a grand supporting cast of inspectors, readers, proofers, assistants and producers. Emma's first line of support has been Philippa Rogers, who has been knowledgeable and loyal, and undaunted by the weight of 'admin.' The others are too numerous to mention, but we owe our customary vote of thanks to Ann Cooke-Yarborough for her writing and her good judgement.

Alastair Sawday

Series Editor
Alastair Sawday

Editor
Emma Carey

Assistant to Editor
Philippa Rogers

Editorial Director
Annie Shillito

Production Manager
Julia Richardson

Web & IT
Russell Wilkinson, Matt Kenefick

Production
Rachel Coe, Paul Groom, Allys Williams

Copy Editor Jo Boissevain

Editorial
Roanne Finch, Danielle Williams

Sales & Marketing & PR
Siobhan Flynn, Paula Brown, Sarah Bolton

Accounts
Sheila Clifton, Bridget Bishop, Christine Buxton, Jenny Purdy, Sandra Hassell

Writing
Ann Cooke-Yarborough, Jo Boissevain

Inspections
Richard & Linda Armspach, Helen Barr, Alyson & Colin Browne, Jill Coyle, Meredith Dickinson, Sue Edrich, John & Jane Edwards, Valerie Foix, Georgina Gabriel, Giselle Genillard, Denise Goss, Diana Harris, Jo-Bell Moore, Joanna Morris, Clarissa Novak, Elizabeth Yates.
And many thanks to those people who did just a few inspections.

A word from Alastair Sawday

I once feared that, with almost 800 places to keep an eye on in France, we would lose our grip. Staleness, a creeping loss of 'standards', seemed likely.

But this latest edition is the most colourful, the most tantalising ever – one wants to visit them all. The book just gets better and better; a phrase oft-repeated but it could be a good leitmotif? French artistry, elegance and flair run riot on these pages. We hear of wild excesses of hospitality: a friend of mine, upon declaring himself as such, became the object of ravishing, unstoppable and embarrassing generosity. We hear of countless, continuing, friendships forged between our readers and French owners. Good relationships depend on some emotional exchange, so it must be happening, despite what countless writers and pundits have said about our 'English reserve'. Sir Isaiah Berlin even said it of the French; after many long holidays in France, he complained to a friend that the French doled out their emotions in thimbles-full. Had he been able to flourish this book on his travels he might have thought differently.

Now that the stream of English house-buyers to France has become a flood we may rightly fear the creation of thousands of isles of Englishness all over France. So don't forget, you newly-proud house-owners, to flex your French en route and to seize the friendships which this book can inspire.

We have become, to our great satisfaction, purveyors of pleasure on a grand scale.

Alastair Sawday

Photo Paul Groom

Introduction

THOUGHTFUL HUMAN TOUCHES THAT MAKE A STAY MEMORABLE

What to expect and how we choose our Special Places

In the 10 years since the first edition of this guide, B&B in France has flourished and evolved. Created to boost the rural economy, *chambres d'hôtes* originally brought visitors to stay with French farming families. Since when the ranks of those who offer chambres d'hôtes have broadened to include hosts whose living is not directly linked to the land, those living in châteaux and manoirs and, more recently, their urban cousins. These days townhouses, restoration projects and the odd *monument historique* rub shoulders with real farmhouses.

Since we began, we have visited hundreds of houses every year and chosen only those that strike us as special – ones whose atmosphere, warmth and value really sparkle. This specialness is as crucial as it ever was and we still love those places run by people with traditional lifestyles, whether simple or not so, where little has changed for 50 years. But, we are also keen to reflect the best of the new variations on the theme. So, read carefully to know whether a particular place is going to be right for you. This book is an open invitation to stay in real homes, sampling a different way of life, and 'getting under the skin' of an area.

You will increasingly find places where you have independence; separate entrances, private sitting areas and door keys are useful and give guests, and host families, more freedom. And overall there is now more sophistication in the decoration, furnishing, mattresses, bed linen and towels than before; the standard of plumbing has greatly improved, too! (Though we're not at all put off by rusticity or by quirky arrangements.)

Photo above Bastide de la Roquette, entry 731
Photo opposite Cephas Picture Library / Alamy

Introduction

Above all we seek enthusiastic, generous-spirited hosts; we see no point in recommending a fabulous château if the welcome is chilly. It's the thoughtful, human touches that make a stay memorable, such as a sprig of rosemary on the pillow, a glass of homemade wine on arrival, or an owner who gets up early to toss fresh pancakes.

We receive reams of letters from happy readers who have been touched by exceptional kindnesses: efforts to solve the mystery of a missing passport, the care of a sick guest, the rescue from a broken-down car on a snowy night. In turn the owners often say how "interesting, courteous and civilised" their 'Sawday' guests are. Friendships have flourished, sometimes with just a few words of French/English, lots of sign language and broad smiles. People often go back year after year and are greeted as old friends.

Photo Les Bournais, entry 403

French and non-French owners

Our main aim is to guide you to fruitful encounters with French families in their homes, so non-French owners have a smaller chance of being chosen. We receive a great number of requests from non-French owners to be in the guide but we have, reluctantly, to disappoint many.

However, many of you have written to say how restful it can be, after several evenings of valiant French conversation, to have a 'day off' and relax in your native tongue. B&B owners are changing too: there are more escapees from the 9-5 grind, those seeking warmer, or cooler, climes. Your host might be a wildlife photograher from Zimbabwe, a yoga teacher from Yorkshire - we choose interesting, integrated people who will make your stay special.

Many of our French owners from the early years are still with us; some have passed on the baton to the next generation and they have been joined by others. The people in this guide come from all walks of life – aristocrats and artisans, painters and paysans, teachers, writers, retired globetrotters and those francophile' newcomers': so many opportunities for enriching encounters. And although most of our owners are down-to-earth, friendly individuals living in reliably French houses, they all have a touch of originality, are passionate about their area and want you to discover its treasures.

Choosing the right place for you

There is a wider-than-ever variety of places and prices in this edition but we seek good value for money whatever the price. *Chambres d'hôtes* still offers exceptional value for money. Where else can you stay in a château, sleep in one tower, bath in another and breakfast on home-hive honey and brioche for less than £50 for two

Remember to interpret what you see and read in this book. If you opt for a working farm, expect cockerels to crow or tractors to set off at dawn. If you choose a 'rambling château with old-fashioned bathrooms', there could be some draughty corridors and idiosyncratic plumbing. If 'antique beds' sounds seductively authentic, remember they are liable to be antique sizes, too (190cm long, doubles 140cm wide, singles 80 or 90cm wide). Check on anything that is really important to you before confirming your booking, eg. whether the swimming pool will be ready to use at Easter, whether the bicycles have been booked by others. We celebrate authentic B&Bs with a family welcome. We won't exclude a superb farmhouse with a genuine welcome because of a few cobwebs or a bit of family chaos. Instead, we write honestly so that you can decide for yourselves.

"For the hostess, nothing was too much trouble, and she made everyone feel really at home. Who cares about the odd speck of dust with such a welcome," wrote one reader.

B&Bs are not hotels

If you are expecting anonymity or hotel-like services then *chambres d'hôtes* are not for you! We all run our homes differently and so do our hosts, so expect to fit in with their norm, however informal and family-orientated.

Photo La Fournière, entry 515

You may expect to feel a privileged guest and to gain a fascinating glimpse of a French way of life, but don't expect your beds to be made or your towels to be changed daily, your children's toys to be gathered or your late request for a vegetarian meal to produce anything more exciting than an omelette. Let your hosts know of any special needs well ahead and take your own tea bags if you are fussy. Owners love guests to stay more than one night and it's really worth doing so for genuine contact, but they often expect you to be out during the day - they have their own lives to lead and cannot be on hand all the time. If they are happy for you to be around, check which parts of the house or garden you may use during the day.

Photo above Manoir de Kerledan, entry 272
Photo opposite Mas de l'Amandier, entry 625
(©Dominique Bernard)

Problems

Do discuss any problem with your hosts at the time. They are the ones who can do something about it immediately and would be mortified to discover, too late, that you were, for example, cold in bed when extra blankets could easily have been provided.

If you find anything we say misleading (things can change in the lifetime of a guide), or you think we miss the point – if, for example, you thought you'd chosen a child-friendly house and were surprised by white carpets and ornaments at toddler height – please let us know.

Breakfast

The range of what you might be given for breakfast is becoming more diverse. You may 'just' be offered *pain de campagne* with apricot jam and a bowl of coffee but more choice has crept in as one reader discovered. "His breakfasts were 'to die for'! He offered the best choice of things to eat: homemade orange and apple juice, cereal, brioche, pain au raisin, homemade jams and marmalades as well as three different kinds of bread."

Dinner – table d'hôtes

Again, this varies hugely: from simple farmhouse recipes to four courses cooked by a professionally-trained chef. *Table d'hôtes* is a

wonderful opportunity to eat honest, even gourmet, food in an authentic family atmosphere. Don't expect a choice: *table d'hôtes* means the same food for all and absolutely must be booked ahead, so do say what your dietary needs are when you book. The number and type of courses you will be offered varies and we have not attempted to go into details, although price may be a guide. Meals probably won't be available every day, and may only be prepared for a minimum number of guests, but do turn up if you have booked – it's distressing to prepare a meal that no one comes to enjoy. Few places offer lunch but occasionally picnics can be provided.

Sadly, changing lifestyles mean that fewer people are prepared to do evening meals. Do make the most of those that are available.

Photo Casteyre, entry 572

Meals: en famille or not?

Traditionally they would be, but practically, there are good reasons why they won't always be. Two of these reasons will make sense to a lot of you:

- the owners' young children need their parents' presence at dinner and for homework time and/or are not considered 'civilised' enough to dine with guests
- Your hostess is minding her figure!

If there is no *table d'hôtes*, we give an idea of other places to eat, but beware: rural restaurants stop taking orders at 9pm and close at least one day a week.

Including wine

When wine is included this can mean a range of things, from a standard quarter-litre carafe per person to a barrel of table wine; from a decent bottle of local wine to an excellent estate wine. Whatever it is, it is usually good value but please do not abuse your hosts' *vin à volonté* (unlimited wine with meals). And do check prices – some estates may use meals to showcase their wines and this can make for an expensive meal.

Do be considerate about keeping hosts up late... some simply love to stay and chat; others find it hard to say when they feel they should be turning in. (The boot can, of course, be on the other foot!).

How to use this book

Bedrooms and how we describe them:

- double: one double bed
- twin: two single beds
- twin/double: two single beds that can become a large double
- triple or 'family room': any mix of beds (sometimes sofabeds) for 3, 4 or more people
- 'suite': either one large room with a sitting area or two or more interconnecting rooms, plus one or more bathrooms
- 'apartment': similar to a suite but with an independent entrance and often a small kitchen
- 'studio': bedroom, bathroom, sitting and cooking areas

Extra beds and cots for children, at an extra cost, can often be provided; ask when booking.

Bathrooms

There is a wonderful array of washing arrangements in French homes. We've done our best to make the layouts clear: if a room has no bathroom details mentioned, you can assume that the bath/shower room is directly off the bedroom; we only mention shared or separate bathrooms. Most, but not all baths have shower attachments. Bathrooms are generally good but if you are wary of quirky arrangements go for the modernised places (which are probably more expensive).

Prices

The prices in this book are not guaranteed, but are presumed to be for 2005. Check our web site for those up-dates that we have received from owners.

Many places offer reductions for longer stays; good half-board rates, special prices for children: ask when you book.

There is a €/£/$ conversion table at the back of the book.

Symbols

Symbols and their explanations are listed on the last page of the book. Use them as a guide rather than an unequivocal statement of fact and double-check anything that is important to you.

Photo Le Moulin L'Étang, entry 400

Our symbol shows where children are welcome with no age restrictions. Elsewhere, they may be welcome with restrictions as indicated in italics at the end of the description. eg. babies only, because of an unfenced pool.

Our symbol tells you which houses generally welcome pets but you must check whether this includes the size and type of your pet. Your hosts will expect animals to be well-behaved and you to be responsible for them at all times.

Our symbol shows the houses where there's no smoking anywhere indoors.

Photo above Moulin de la Follaine, entry 397
Photo opposite La Ferme de l'Oudan, entry 201

Practical Matters

Types of houses

For a definition of château, bastide, mas, see 'French words & expressions' on page 451.

Telephoning/faxing/e-mailing

All phone numbers in France have ten digits,
eg. (0)5 05 25 35 45.
You should know that:

- the zero (bracketed above) is for use when telephoning from inside France only, eg. dial 05 15 25 35 45 from any private or public telephone;
- when dialling from outside France use the international access code, then the country code for France (33) then the last 9 digits of the number you want, eg. 00 33 5 15 25 35 45;
- numbers beginning (0)6 are mobile phone numbers;
- to telephone from France
to Great Britain: 00 44 then the number without the first 0;
to North America: 00 1 then the number without the first 0.

Télécartes (phone cards) are widely available in France and there are plenty of telephone boxes, even in the countryside (they often only take cards).

Don't automatically expect a rapid response to e-mails, particularly at busy times of the year.

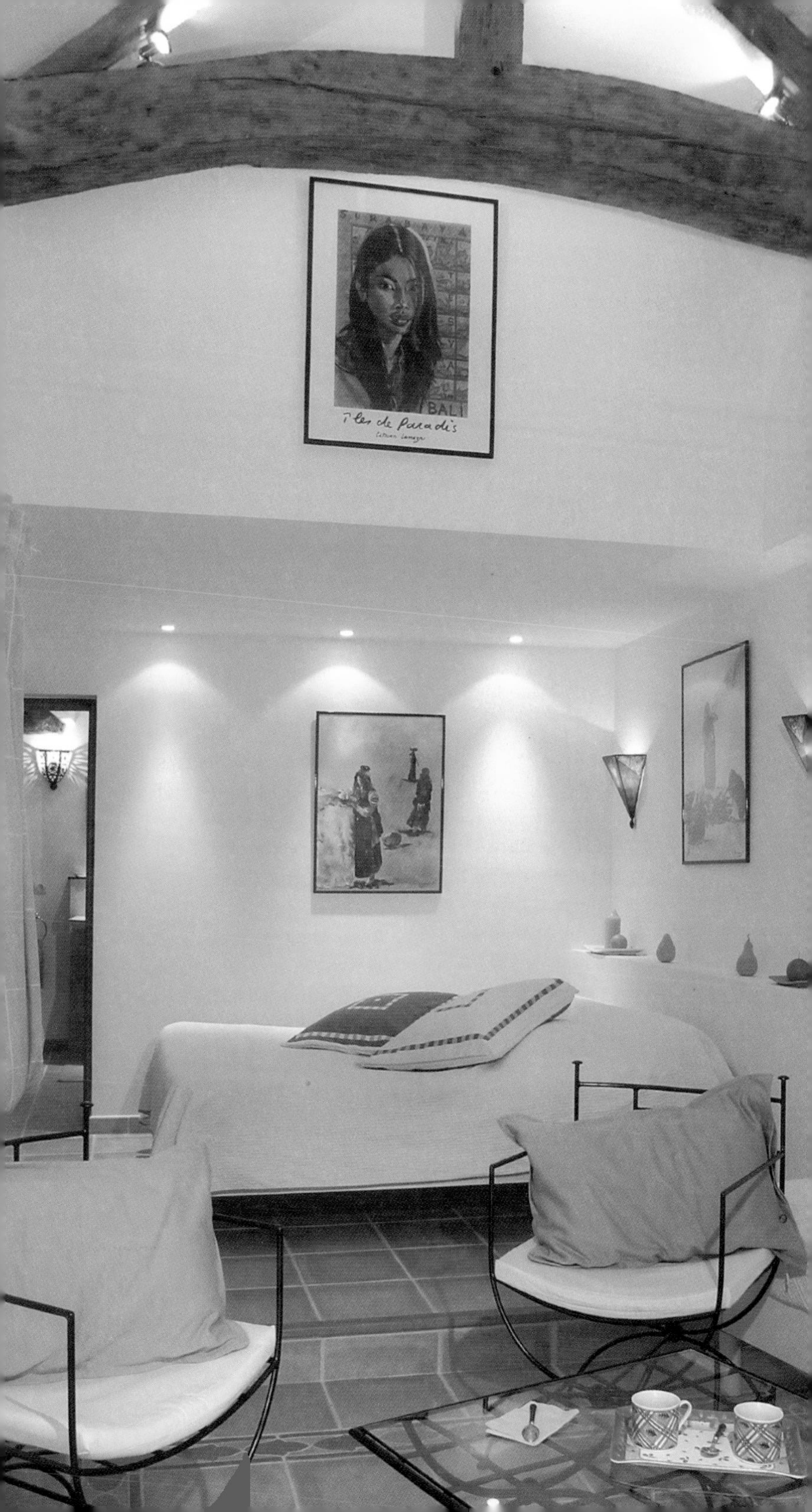
SURABAYA
BALI
Îles de Paradis

Travel to and from France

We hope it proves easy, and entertaining, to choose your Special Place to stay in France using this book. But getting there can be expensive and the poor person to whom the organisational task falls can have a horrible – and bewildering – time getting ferries and/or trains sorted out. So, hoping to make things easier – and cheaper – for you, we have linked up with Bonnes Vacances. They are a small, family-run company in Surrey who have gradually built up a reputation for decent, personal service and good prices.

They are not the biggest fish in the pond but by all accounts they do a marvellous job and will treat you like human beings. Best of all, they will save you from those frustrating phone calls to ferry companies in your quest for the best route and best deal. They have a page at the back of this book with phone numbers etc. Note that in order to use them you have to have a booking at a Special Place. The ball is in your court.

Photo La Louveterie, entry 718

Booking

There is a bilingual Booking Form at the back of this book. It is essential to book well ahead for July and August, and wise for other months. You may receive a *Contrat de Location* (Tenancy Contract) as confirmation. It must be filled in and returned, probably with a deposit, and commits both sides to the arrangement.

Remember not to telephone any later than 9pm or 9.30pm at the latest – you may disturb those that go early to bed - and that Ireland and the UK are one hour behind the rest of Europe. And please remember that owners count on you to stay as long as you have booked for. If you don't, they may feel justified in applying a cancellation charge.

Deposits

Some owners ask for a deposit. Many readers have found it difficult or ridiculously expensive to do this by direct transfer but you can send an ordinary cheque which the owner will destroy when you arrive (so no one pays the charges); when you leave, they will ask you for cash for your whole stay.

Paying

Most B&B owners do not take credit cards but those who do have our credit card symbol. Virtually all ATMs in France take Visa and MasterCard. Euro travellers' cheques should be accepted, other currency cheques are unpopular because of commission charges.

Taxe de séjour

This is a small tax that local councils can levy on all visitors paying for accommodation. Some councils do, some don't: you may find your bill increased by a euro or two per person per day.

to Autrefois St Fortunat, entry 673

Tipping

B&B owners would be taken aback by a tip but if you encounter unusual kindness you may feel a thank-you letter, Christmas card or small gift would be appropriate.

Arriving

Most owners expect you to arrive between 5pm and 7pm. If you come earlier, rooms may not be ready or your hosts may still be at work. If you are going to be late (or early, unavoidably), please telephone and say so.

No-shows

Owners hope you will treat them as friends by being sensitive and punctual. It's obviously upsetting for them to prepare rooms, even meals, and to wait up late for 'guests' who give no further sign of life. So if you find you are not going to take up a booking, telephone right away.

There is a tacit agreement among some B&B owners that no-show + no-call by 8pm, even 6pm in some cases, can be taken as a refusal of the booking and they will re-let the room if another guest turns up.

Subscriptions

Owners pay to appear in this guide. Their fee goes towards the high costs of a sophisticated inspection system and producing an all-colour book. We only include places and

owners that we find positively special. It is not possible for anyone to buy his/her way into our guides.

Internet

www.specialplacestostay.com
Our web site has online entries for all the places featured here and in our other books, with up-to-date information and direct links to their own e-mail addresses and web sites. You'll find more about the site at the back of this book.

Disclaimer

We make no claims to pure objectivity in choosing our Special Places to Stay. They are here because we like them. Our opinions and tastes are ours alone and this book is a statement of them; we hope that you will share them. A huge Thank You to those of you who take the time and trouble to write to us about your *chambres d'hôtes* experiences – good and bad – or to recommend new places. This is what we do with them:

- Do bear with us at busy times; it's difficult to respond immediately.
- Poor reports are followed up with the owners in question: we need to hear both sides of the story. Really bad reports lead to incognito visits, after which we may exclude a place.
- Owners are informed when we receive substantially positive reports about them.
- Recommendations are followed up with inspection visits where appropriate. If your recommendation leads us to include a place, you receive a free copy of the edition in which it first appears.

We have done our utmost to get our facts right but apologise unreservedly for any mistakes that may have crept in. We would be grateful to hear of any errors that you find.

You should know that we do not check such things as fire alarms, swimming pool security or any other regulation with which owners of properties receiving paying guests should comply. This is the responsibility of the owners.

And finally

Feedback from you is invaluable and we always act upon comments. With your help and our own inspections we can maintain our reputation for dependability.

We value your letters and comments which make a real contribution to this book, be they on our report form, by letter or by e-mail to info@sawdays.co.uk. Or you can visit our web site and write to us from there.

Bon Voyage – Happy Travelling!

Emma Carey

Photo opposite Premium/arcaid.co.uk

General Map

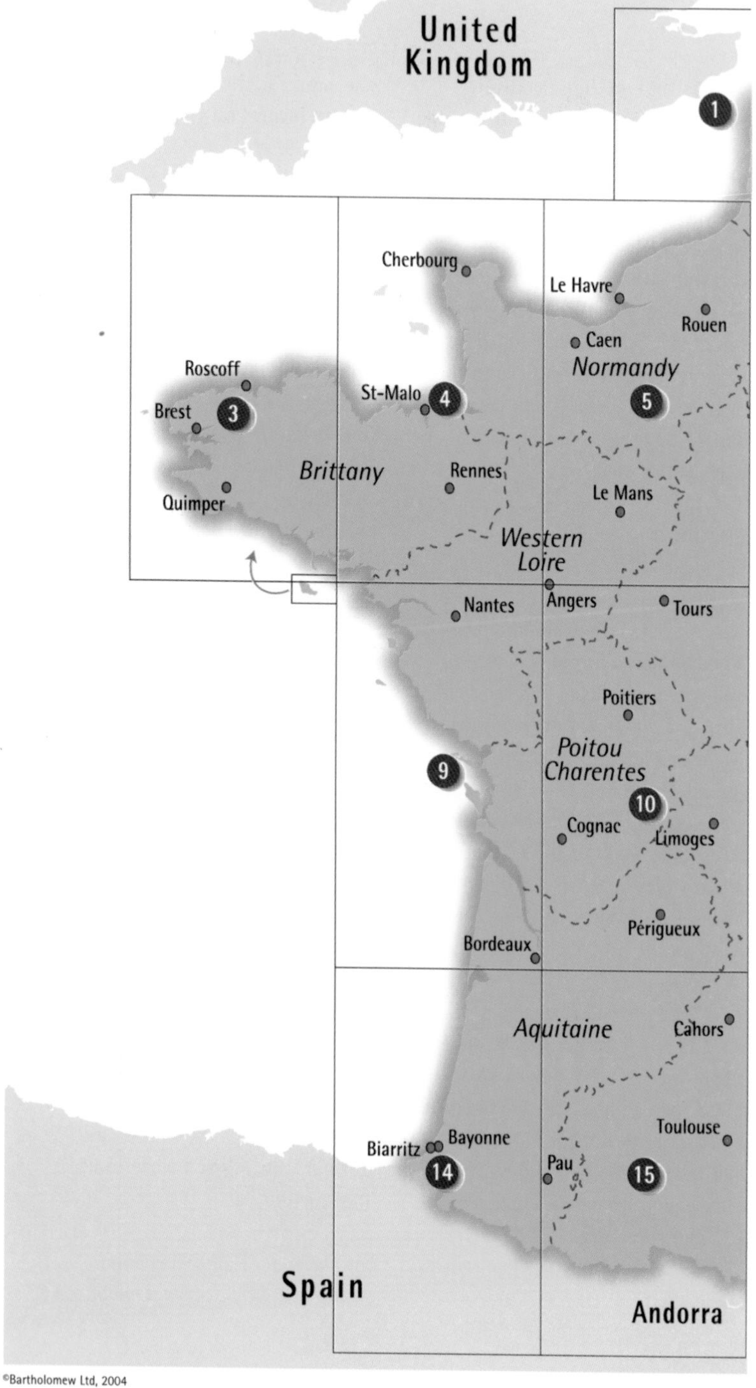
United Kingdom
1
Cherbourg
Le Havre
Rouen
Caen
Normandy
Roscoff
Brest
3
St-Malo
4
5
Brittany
Rennes
Le Mans
Quimper
Western Loire
Nantes
Angers
Tours
Poitiers
Poitou Charentes
9
10
Cognac
Limoges
Périgueux
Bordeaux
Aquitaine
Cahors
Toulouse
Biarritz
Bayonne
Pau
14
15
Spain
Andorra

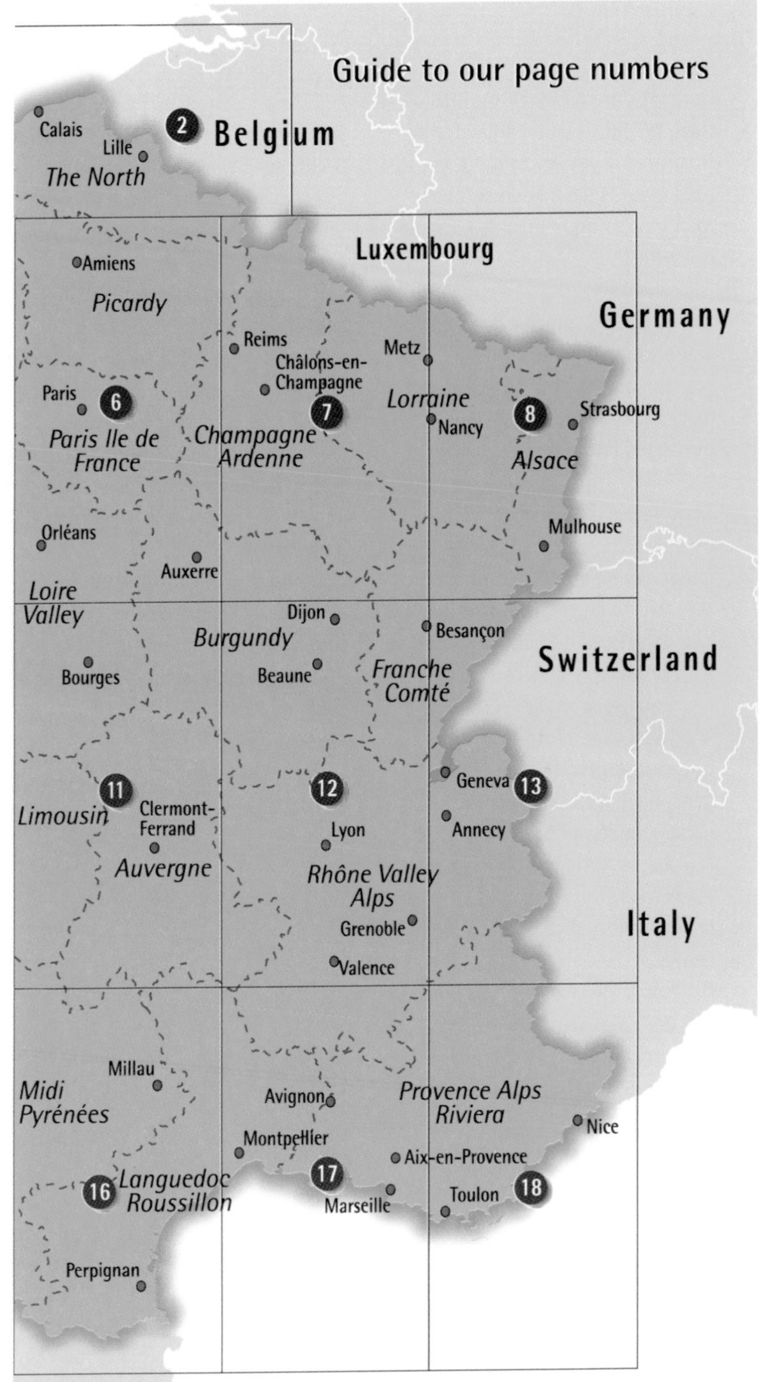
Guide to our page numbers
Calais
Lille
2
Belgium
The North
Amiens
Picardy
Luxembourg
Germany
Reims
Châlons-en-Champagne
Metz
Paris
6
7
Lorraine
8
Strasbourg
Nancy
Paris Ile de France
Champagne Ardenne
Alsace
Mulhouse
Orléans
Auxerre
Loire Valley
Dijon
Besançon
Burgundy
Switzerland
Bourges
Beaune
Franche Comté
Geneva
13
11
12
Limousin
Clermont-Ferrand
Lyon
Annecy
Auvergne
Rhône Valley Alps
Grenoble
Italy
Valence
Millau
Midi Pyrénées
Avignon
Provence Alps Riviera
Nice
Montpellier
Aix-en-Provence
17
16
Languedoc Roussillon
Marseille
Toulon
18
Perpignan

How to use our maps

Our maps are designed for B&B flagging only – you will be deeply frustrated if you try to use them as road maps! Take a good detailed road map or atlas such as Michelin or Collins.

The numbered flags have no pointers and are simply indications of position on the ground, not accurate markers. You will find specific directions in the relevant entry.

Reading our directions:

Except in the case of two-way motorway junctions, our directions take you to each house from one side only. French roads are identified with the letters they carry on French maps and road signs:

A = Autoroute. Motorways (mostly toll roads) with junctions that generally have the same name/number on both sides.

N = Route Nationale. The old trunk roads that are still fairly fast, don't charge tolls and often go through towns.

D = Route Départementale. Smaller country roads with less traffic.

Our directions are as succinct as possible.

For example: From A7 exit Valence Sud A49 for Grenoble; exit 33; right D538a for Beaumont 2.5km; right again at sign 800m; house on right.

Interpretation: Take A7 motorway going north or south; leave at junction named 'Valence Sud' and get onto motorway A49 going towards Grenoble; leave this road at junction 33 and turn right onto road D538a (the 'a' means there are probably roads numbered 538b, 538c... in the vicinity) towards Beaumont for 2.5km until you meet a meaningful sign (often 'Chambres d'Hôtes', the name of the house or a pictogram of a bed under a roof); turn right at this sign; the house is 800 metres down this road on the right.

Remember –

Our maps are for guidance only; use a good quality road map for navigation.

Map 1

Scale 1: 1,600,000

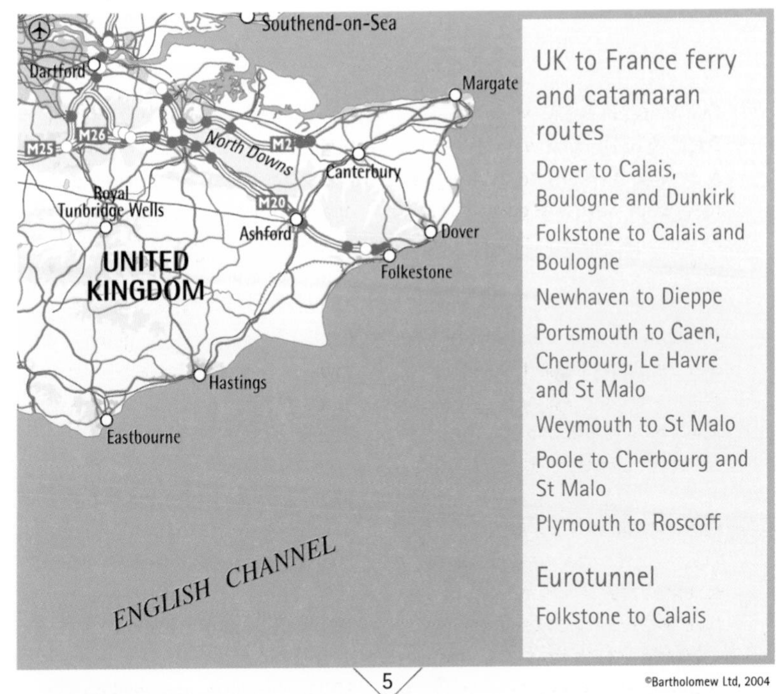

Map 2

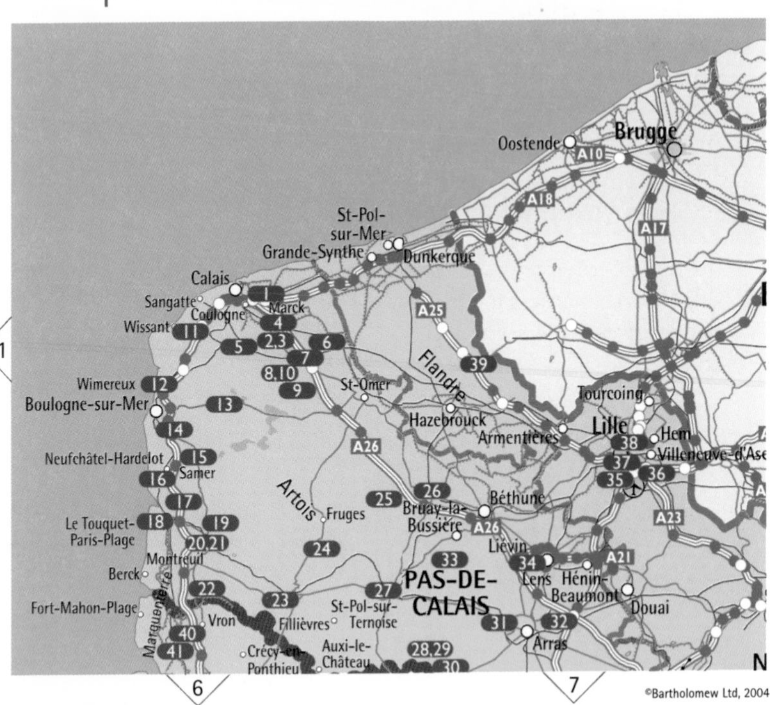

Map 3

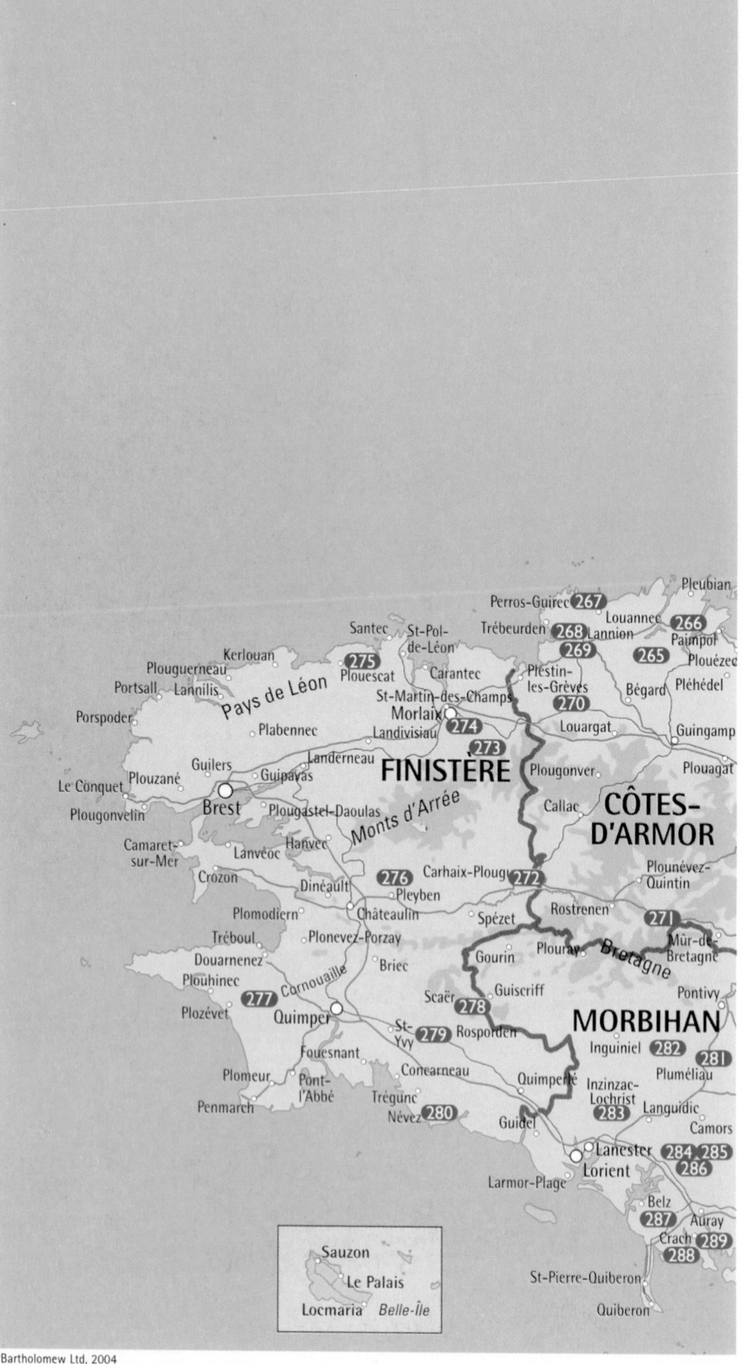
Pleubian
Perros-Guirec 267
Louannec
266
Trébeurden 268 Lannion
Paimpol
Santec
St-Pol-de-Léon
269
Kerlouan
275
265
Plouézec
Plouguerneau
Plouescat
Carantec
Plestin-les-Grèves
Portsall
Lannilis
Pays de Léon
St-Martin-des-Champs
Bégard
Pléhédel
270
Porspoder
Morlaix
Plabennec
Landivisiau 274
Louargat
Guingamp
273
Guilers
Landerneau
FINISTÈRE
Plougonver
Plouagat
Le Conquet
Plouzané
Guipavas
Brest
Callac
CÔTES-D'ARMOR
Plougonvelin
Plougastel-Daoulas
Monts d'Arrée
Camaret-sur-Mer
Hanvec
Lanvéoc
Plounévez-Quintin
Crozon
276
Carhaix-Plouguer 272
Dinéault
Pleyben
Plomodiern
Châteaulin
Spézet
Rostrenen
271
Tréboul
Plonevez-Porzay
Mûr-de-Bretagne
Douarnenez
Briec
Gourin
Plouray
Bretagne
Plouhinec
Cornouaille
Guiscriff
Pontivy
277
Scaër 278
Plozévet
Quimper
MORBIHAN
St-Yvy 279
Rosporden
Inguiniel 282
Fouesnant
281
Concarneau
Quimperlé
Pluméliau
Plomeur
Pont-l'Abbé
Inzinzac-Lochrist
Trégunc
283
Languidic
Penmarch
Névez 280
Guidel
Camors
Lanester
284, 285
286
Lorient
Larmor-Plage
Belz
287
Auray
Crach 289
288
Sauzon
Le Palais
Locmaria
Belle-Île
St-Pierre-Quiberon
Quiberon

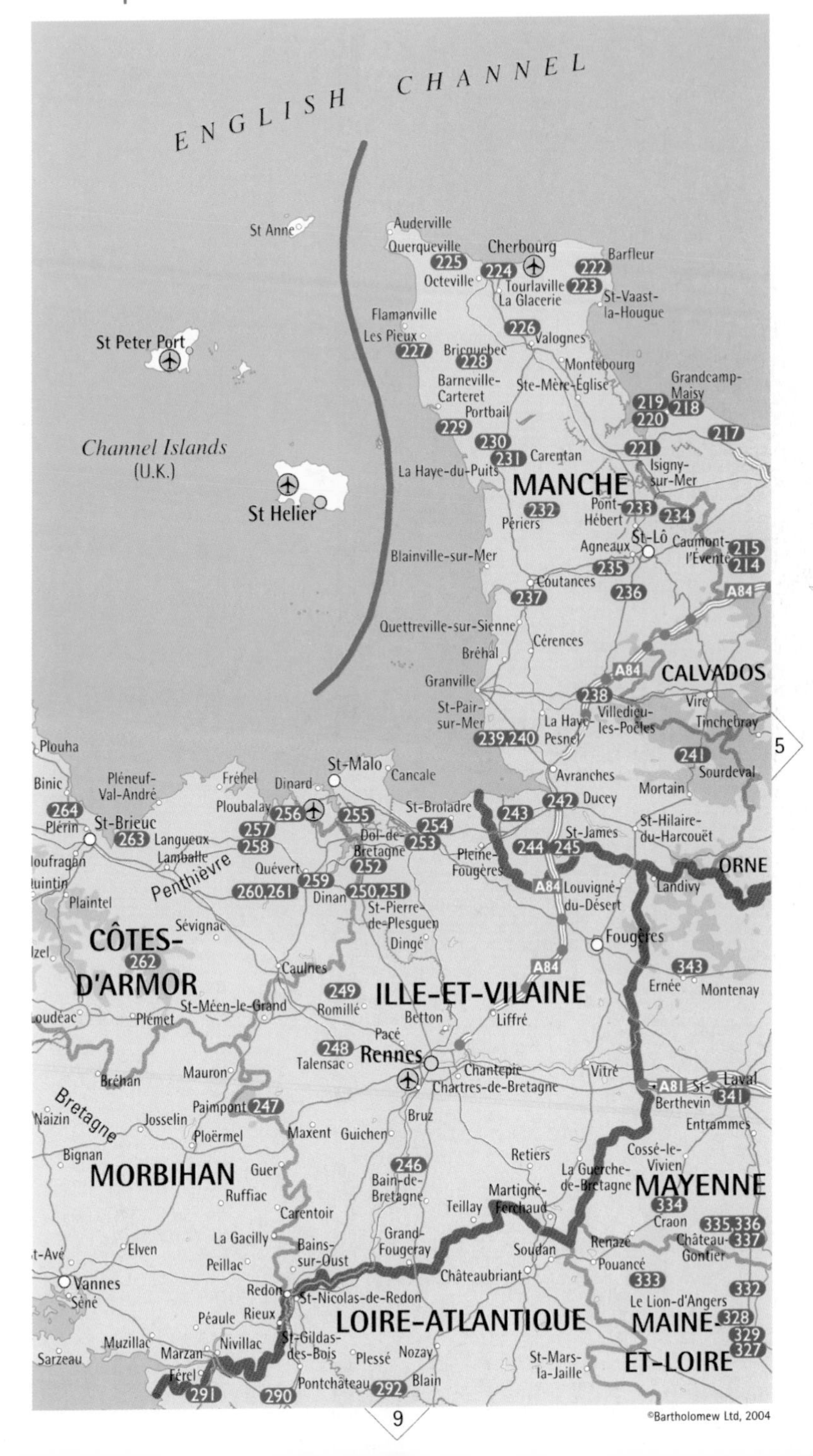
ENGLISH CHANNEL
Channel Islands
(U.K.)
St Anne
St Peter Port
St Helier
Auderville
Querqueville
Cherbourg
Barfleur
225
224
222
223
Octeville
Tourlaville
La Glacerie
St-Vaast-
la-Hougue
Flamanville
Les Pieux
226
Valognes
227
Bricquebec
228
Montebourg
Barneville-
Carteret
Ste-Mère-Église
Grandcamp-
Maisy
219
218
220
Portbail
229
217
230
231
Carentan
221
Isigny-
sur-Mer
La Haye-du-Puits
MANCHE
Pont-
Hébert
233
234
232
Périers
St-Lô
Caumont-
l'Eventé
215
214
Agneaux
Blainville-sur-Mer
235
Coutances
236
237
A84
Quettreville-sur-Sienne
Cérences
Bréhal
A84
CALVADOS
Granville
238
Vire
St-Pair-
sur-Mer
La Haye-
Pesnel
Villedieu-
les-Poêles
Tinchebray
239,240
5
241
Sourdeval
Plouha
St-Malo
Cancale
Avranches
Mortain
Binic
Pléneuf-
Val-André
Fréhel
Dinard
264
Plérin
St-Brieuc
Ploubalay
256
255
St-Broladre
242
Ducey
243
St-Hilaire-
du-Harcouët
254
263
Langueux
Lamballe
257
258
Dol-de-
Bretagne
253
St-James
Pleine-
Fougères
244
245
Penthièvre
Quévert
252
ORNE
Landivy
259
260,261
Dinan
250,251
A84
Louvigné-
du-Désert
Plaintel
St-Pierre-
de-Plesguen
Sévignac
CÔTES-
D'ARMOR
262
Dingé
Fougères
A84
343
Caulnes
249
ILLE-ET-VILAINE
Ernée
Montenay
St-Méen-le-Grand
Plémet
Romillé
Betton
Liffré
Pacé
248
Talensac
Rennes
Chantepie
Vitré
Bréhan
Mauron
Chartres-de-Bretagne
A81
St-
Berthevin
Laval
341
Bretagne
Paimpont
247
Naizin
Josselin
Ploërmel
Bruz
Entrammes
Maxent
Guichen
Bignan
246
Retiers
Cossé-le-
Vivien
MORBIHAN
Guer
Bain-de-
Bretagne
La Guerche-
de-Bretagne
MAYENNE
Ruffiac
Martigné-
Ferchaud
334
Carentoir
Teillay
Craon
335,336
La Gacilly
Bains-
sur-Oust
Grand-
Fougeray
Renazé
Château-
Gontier
337
Elven
Peillac
Soudan
Pouancé
Vannes
Châteaubriant
333
Séné
Redon
St-Nicolas-de-Redon
332
Le Lion-d'Angers
Péaule
Rieux
LOIRE-ATLANTIQUE
MAINE-
328
Muzillac
Nivillac
St-Gildas-
des-Bois
329
Sarzeau
Marzan
Plessé
Nozay
St-Mars-
la-Jaille
ET-LOIRE
327
Férel
Pontchâteau
292
Blain
291
290
9

Map 5

ENGLISH CHANNEL
SOMME
Le Tréport
Criel-sur-Mer
Eu
Penly
Gamaches
Dieppe
Neuville-lès-Dieppe
St-Valery-en-Caux
St-Pierre-en-Port
Fécamp
Cany-Barville
Longueville-sur-Scie
Neufchâtel-en-Bray
SEINE-MARITIME
Pays de Bray
Étretat
Héricourt-en-Caux
Yerville
St-Saëns
Goderville
Pavilly
Barentin
Forges-les-Eaux
Montivilliers
Bolbec
Ste-Adresse
Harfleur
Le Havre
Gonfreville-l'Orcher
Mont-St-Aignan
Rouen
Honfleur
Seine
Le Grand-Quevilly
Trouville-sur-Mer
Roumois
St-Étienne-du-Rouvray
Dives-sur-Mer
Ouistreham
Hérouville-St-Clair
Cormeilles
Elbeuf
Louviers
Les Andelys
Pays d'Auge
Lieuvin
Brionne
Tilly-sur-Seulles
Caen
Mondeville
Lisieux
Le Neubourg
Gaillon
Mézidon-Canon
Bernay
EURE
Vernon
St-Pierre-sur-Dives
Évreux
Broglie
Potigny
CALVADOS
Orbec
Breuilpont
Clécy
Falaise
Conches-en-Ouche
Guichainville
Condé-sur-Noireau
Vimoutiers
Le Sap
Pont-d'Ouilly
Ézy-sur-Eure
Chambois
Exmes
Glos-la-Ferrière
Breteuil
St-Lubin-des-Joncherets
Flers
Gacé
L'Aigle
Bourth
Dreux
Écouché
Argentan
Verneuil-sur-Avre
La Ferrière-aux-Etangs
ORNE
Ste-Gauburge-Ste-Colombe
Brézolles
Vernouillet
Mortrée
Maillebois
Domfront
La Ferté-Macé
Sées
Thymerais
Couterne
Châteauneuf-en-Thymerais
Ceaucé
Mortagne-au-Perche
Longny-au-Perche
Digny
Jouy
Damigny
Chartres
Alençon
La Loupe
Ambrières-les-Vallées
Bellême
Bretoncelles
Lucé
Luisant
EURE-ET-LOIR
Oisseau
Maine
Mamers
Berd'huis
Igé
Mayenne
Nogent-le-Rotrou
Bais
Le Theil
Loir
Sillé-le-Guillaume
Marolles-les-Braults
MAYENNE
La Ferté-Bernard
Brou
Évron
Céton
Bonnétable
Authon-du-Perche
Bonneval
La Bazoge
Conlie
SARTHE
Arrou
Logron
La Milesse
Châteaudun
Vaiges
Chassillé
Coulaines
Droué
Courtalain
St-Mars-la-Brière
Le Mans
Dunois
Bouloire
Meslay-du-Maine
Brûlon
Allonnes
Mondoubleau
Cloyes-sur-le-Loir
Auvers-le-Hamon
Arnage
Mulsanne
Épuisay
Ouzouer-le-Marché
St-Calais
Morée
Noyen-sur-Sarthe
Sablé-sur-Sarthe
Savigny-sur-Braye
St-Ouen
Oucques
Daon
Vendôme
Aubigné-Racan
Château-du-Loir
Durtal
LOIR-ET-CHER
La Flèche
Vaas
MAINE-ET-LOIRE
Le Lude
Herbault
Gâtine
Château-la-Vallière
Château-Renault
Blois
Vineuil
Avrillé
Angers
Baugé
Noyant
INDRE-ET-LOIRE
A29
A151
A131
A13
A84
A28
A11
A81
A85
A10
1
4
10

Map 6

NORD
SOMME
PAS-DE-CALAIS
AISNE
OISE
VAL-D'OISE
PARIS
SEINE-ST-DENIS
HAUTS-DE-SEINE
VAL-DE-MARNE
SEINE-ET-MARNE
MARNE
ESSONNE
EURE-ET-LOIR
LOIRET
YONNE
AUBE
LOIR-ET-CHER
CHER
NIÈVRE
SEINE-MARITIME
Abbeville
Amiens
Beauvais
Compiègne
Soissons
Laon
St-Quentin
Cambrai
Creil
Senlis
Meaux
Pontoise
Cergy
Versailles
Boulogne-Billancourt
Nanterre
St-Denis
Marne-la-Vallée
Créteil
Évry
Melun
Fontainebleau
Étampes
Provins
Sens
Auxerre
Orléans
Montargis
Gien
Nemours
Coulommiers
Château-Thierry
Noyon
Péronne
Montdidier
©Bartholomew Ltd, 2004

Map 7

2
BELGIUM
Plateau de l'Ardenne
LUXEMBOURG
Diekirch
Arlon
Hargnies
Fumay
Revin
Fourmies
Anor
Hirson
Thiérache
Signy-le-Petit
Nouzonville
Charleville-Mézières
AISNE
Liart
Signy-l'Abbaye
Sedan
Montcornet
Dizy-le-Gros
Mouzon
ARDENNES
Rethel
Montmédy
Stenay
Esch-sur-Alzette
Nouart
Longuyon
MOSELLE
Thionville
Guignicourt
Buzancy
Côtes de Meuse
Audun-le-Roman
Mazagran
Vouziers
Lorraine
Bazancourt
Sivry-sur-Meuse
Fameck
Amnéville
Bétheny
Pontfaverger-Moronvilliers
Autry
Argonne
Étain
Briey
Reims
St-Hilaire-le-Grand
Verdun
Metz
Montigny-lès-Metz
Suippes
Ste-Menehould
Marly
Ay
Futeau
Clermont-en-Argonne
Dieue-sur-Meuse
Épernay
Auve
Ars
Châlons-en-Champagne
St-Memmie
Villotte-sur-Aire
St-Mihiel
Blénod-lès-Pont-à-Mousson
Champagne Pouilleuse
Nettancourt
Sampigny
Villeseneux
MARNE
6
Pargny-sur-Saulx
Bar-le-Duc
MEUSE
Commercy
Liverdun
Fère-Champenoise
Connantre
Vitry-le-François
Tronville-en-Barrois
Écrouves
Toul
Ligny-en-Barrois
Void-Vacon
Perthois
Ancerville
St-Dizier
Neuves-Maisons
St-Ouen-Domprot
Eurville-Bienville
Vaucouleurs
MEURTHE-ET-MOSELLE
Arcis-sur-Aube
Montiers-sur-Saulx
Chevillon
Champagne Humide
Vaudémont
St-Mesmin
Savières
AUBE
Lesmont
Montier-en-Der
Joinville
Coussey
Piney
Vallage
Neufchâteau
Liffol-le-Grand
Châtenois
Troyes
Beurville
Froncles
Andelot-Blancheville
Bourmont
Contrexéville
Bar-sur-Aube
Bologne
HAUTE-MARNE
VOSGES
St-Phal
Chaumont
Martigny-les-Bains
Bar-sur-Seine
Lamarche
Laferté-sur-Aube
Val-de-Meuse
Seine
Châteauvillain
Rolampont
Bassigny
Mussy-sur-Seine
Molesmes
Vix
Marac
Melay
Corre
Châtillon-sur-Seine
Langres
Chaudenay
Tonnerre
Tanlay
Laignes
Auberive
Chalindrey
Arbecey
Ancy-le-Franc
CÔTE-D'OR
Cintrey
YONNE
Praslay
Chassigny-Aisey
Port-sur-Saône
Nuits
Aisy-sur-Armançon
Nitry
Châtel-Gérard
Baigneux-les-Juifs
Minot
Champlitte
HAUTE-SAÔNE
Montbard
Selongey
Sacquenay
Membrey
Dampierre-sur-Salon
Is-sur-Tille
Venarey-les-Laumes
Chanceaux
Semur-en-Auxois
Gray
12
A4
A34
A203
A6
A13
A3
A30
A26
A5
A31
63
66
67
68
71
72
74
75
77
78
87
117
118
119
122
123

Map 8

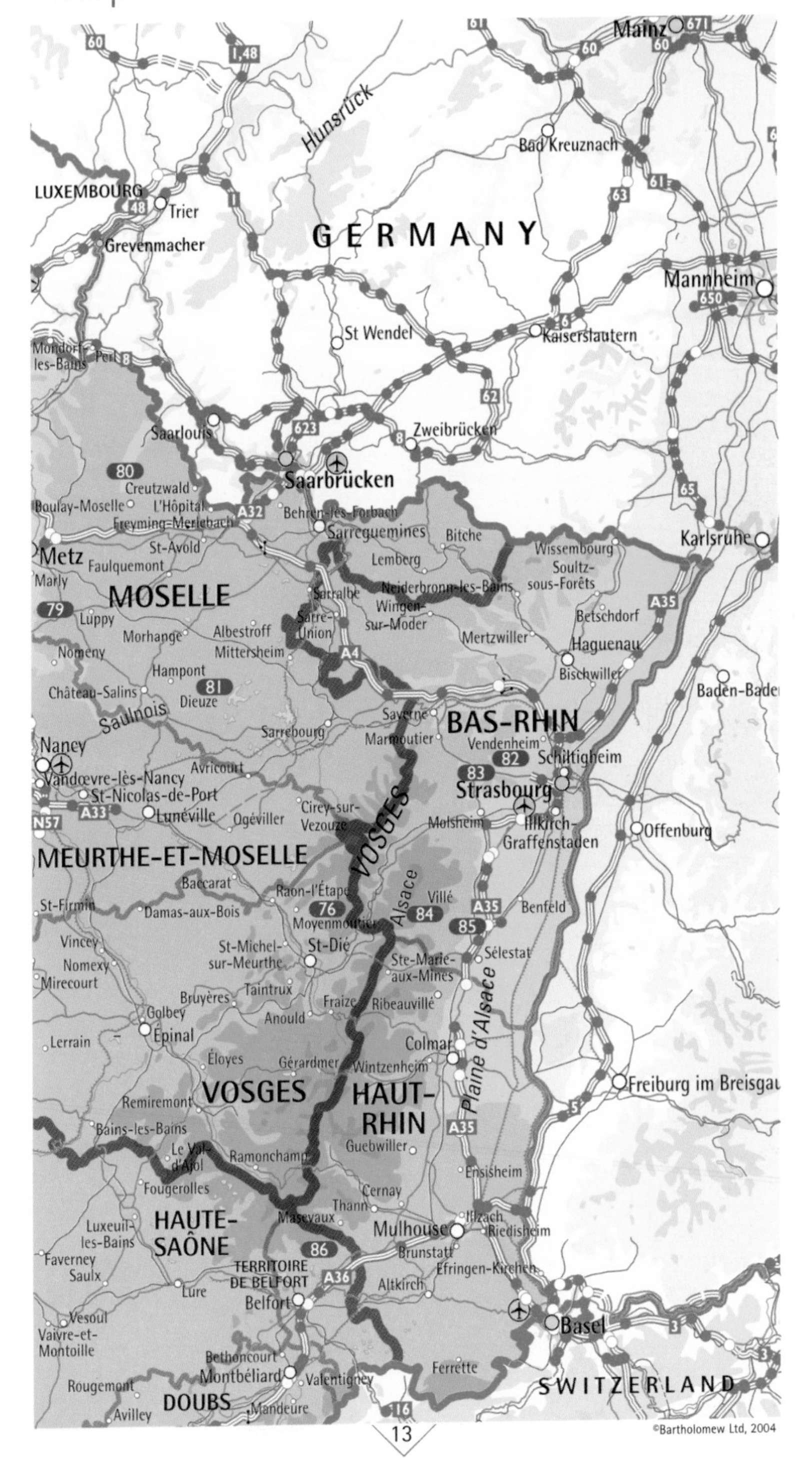

Mainz
Hunsrück
Bad Kreuznach
LUXEMBOURG
Trier
GERMANY
Grevenmacher
Mannheim
St Wendel
Kaiserslautern
Mondorf-les-Bains
Perl
Saarlouis
Zweibrücken
Saarbrücken
Creutzwald
Boulay-Moselle
L'Hôpital
Freyming-Merlebach
Behren-lès-Forbach
Sarreguemines
Bitche
Karlsruhe
Metz
St-Avold
Faulquemont
Lemberg
Wissembourg
Soultz-sous-Forêts
Marly
MOSELLE
Sarralbe
Niederbronn-les-Bains
Wingen-sur-Moder
Betschdorf
Luppy
Sarre-Union
Morhange
Albestroff
Mertzwiller
Haguenau
Nomeny
Mittersheim
Hampont
Bischwiller
Baden-Baden
Château-Salins
Dieuze
Saulnois
Saverne
BAS-RHIN
Sarrebourg
Marmoutier
Vendenheim
Nancy
Schiltigheim
Vandœvre-lès-Nancy
Avricourt
Strasbourg
St-Nicolas-de-Port
Lunéville
Ogéviller
Cirey-sur-Vezouze
Molsheim
Illkirch-Graffenstaden
Offenburg
MEURTHE-ET-MOSELLE
VOSGES
Baccarat
Alsace
Raon-l'Étape
Villé
St-Firmin
Damas-aux-Bois
Moyenmoutier
Benfeld
Vincey
St-Michel-sur-Meurthe
St-Dié
Sélestat
Nomexy
Ste-Marie-aux-Mines
Mirecourt
Bruyères
Taintrux
Fraize
Ribeauvillé
Golbey
Épinal
Anould
Plaine d'Alsace
Lerrain
Colmar
Éloyes
Gérardmer
Wintzenheim
Freiburg im Breisgau
Remiremont
VOSGES
HAUT-RHIN
Bains-les-Bains
Le Val-d'Ajol
Ramonchamp
Guebwiller
Ensisheim
Fougerolles
Cernay
Thann
Illzach
Luxeuil-les-Bains
HAUTE-SAÔNE
Masevaux
Mulhouse
Riedisheim
Faverney
Saulx
TERRITOIRE DE BELFORT
Brunstatt
Efringen-Kirchen
Lure
Altkirch
Belfort
Vesoul
Basel
Vaivre-et-Montoille
Bethoncourt
Ferrette
Rougemont
Montbéliard
Valentigney
SWITZERLAND
DOUBS
Mandeure
Avilley
©Bartholomew Ltd, 2004

13

Map 9

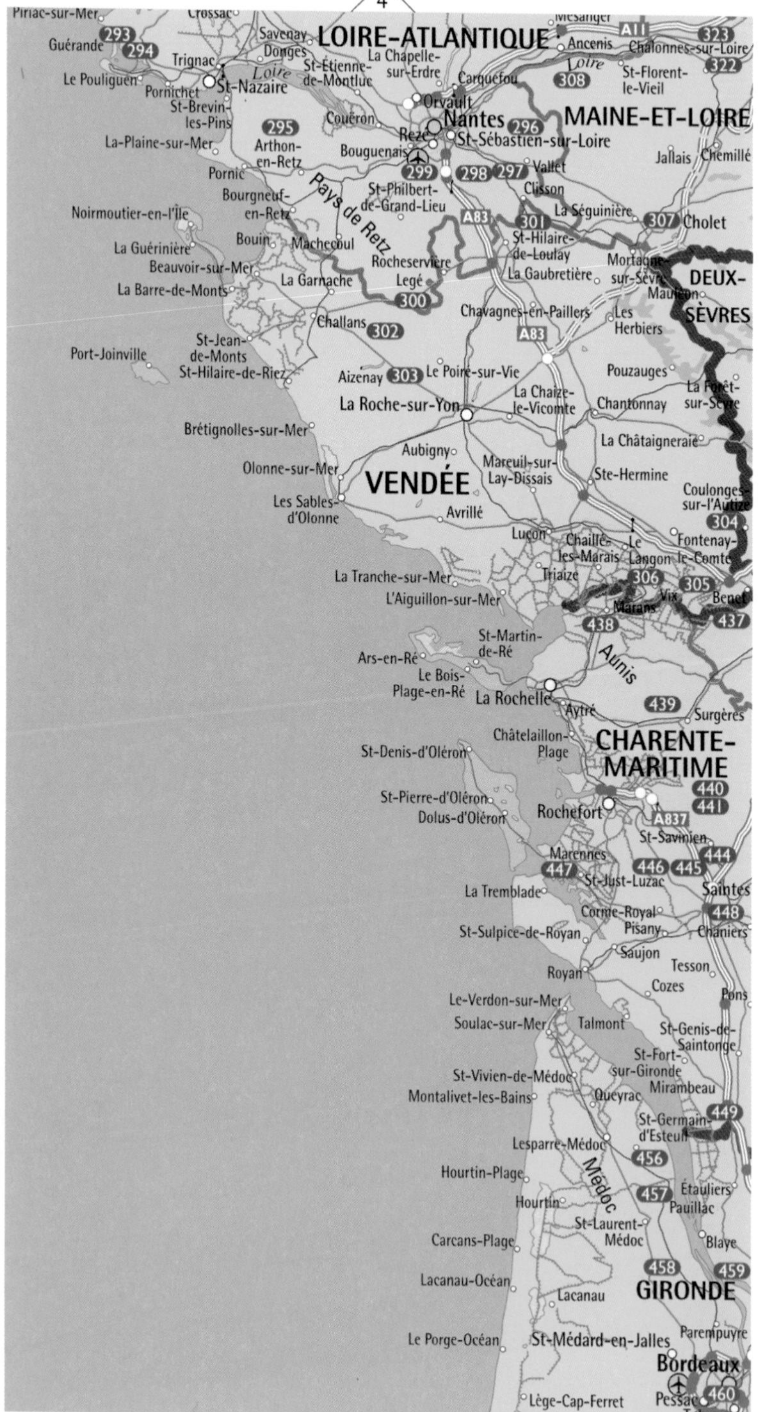
4
LOIRE-ATLANTIQUE
MAINE-ET-LOIRE
DEUX-SÈVRES
VENDÉE
CHARENTE-MARITIME
GIRONDE
Guérande
Le Pouliguen
Pornichet
Trignac
St-Nazaire
Savenay
Donges
St-Étienne-de-Montluc
La Chapelle-sur-Erdre
Carquefou
Ancenis
Chalonnes-sur-Loire
St-Florent-le-Vieil
Orvault
Nantes
Couëron
Rezé
St-Sébastien-sur-Loire
Bouguenais
St-Brevin-les-Pins
La-Plaine-sur-Mer
Arthon-en-Retz
Pornic
Bourgneuf-en-Retz
Pays de Retz
St-Philbert-de-Grand-Lieu
Vallet
Clisson
Jallais
Chemillé
La Séguinière
Cholet
Noirmoutier-en-l'Île
La Guérinière
Bouin
Machecoul
Beauvoir-sur-Mer
La Barre-de-Monts
La Garnache
Rocheservière
Legé
St-Hilaire-de-Loulay
La Gaubretière
Mortagne-sur-Sèvre
Mauléon
Challans
Chavagnes-en-Paillers
Les Herbiers
Port-Joinville
St-Jean-de-Monts
St-Hilaire-de-Riez
Aizenay
Le Poiré-sur-Vie
Pouzauges
La Forêt-sur-Sèvre
La Roche-sur-Yon
La Chaize-le-Vicomte
Chantonnay
Brétignolles-sur-Mer
Aubigny
La Châtaigneraie
Olonne-sur-Mer
Mareuil-sur-Lay-Dissais
Ste-Hermine
Coulonges-sur-l'Autize
Les Sables-d'Olonne
Avrillé
Luçon
Chaillé-les-Marais
Le Langon
Fontenay-le-Comte
La Tranche-sur-Mer
Triaize
L'Aiguillon-sur-Mer
Marans
Vix
Benet
St-Martin-de-Ré
Aunis
Ars-en-Ré
Le Bois-Plage-en-Ré
La Rochelle
Aytré
Surgères
Châtelaillon-Plage
St-Denis-d'Oléron
St-Pierre-d'Oléron
Dolus-d'Oléron
Rochefort
St-Savinien
Marennes
St-Just-Luzac
La Tremblade
Saintes
Corme-Royal
Pisany
Chaniers
St-Sulpice-de-Royan
Saujon
Tesson
Royan
Cozes
Pons
Le-Verdon-sur-Mer
Soulac-sur-Mer
Talmont
St-Genis-de-Saintonge
St-Fort-sur-Gironde
St-Vivien-de-Médoc
Mirambeau
Montalivet-les-Bains
Queyrac
St-Germain-d'Esteuil
Lesparre-Médoc
Médoc
Hourtin-Plage
Hourtin
Étauliers
Pauillac
St-Laurent-Médoc
Carcans-Plage
Blaye
Lacanau-Océan
Lacanau
Le Porge-Océan
St-Médard-en-Jalles
Parempuyre
Bordeaux
Lège-Cap-Ferret
Pessac
Loire
A11
A83
A837
293
294
295
296
298
297
299
300
301
302
303
304
305
306
307
308
322
323
437
438
439
440
441
444
445
446
447
448
449
456
457
458
459
460
14

Map 10

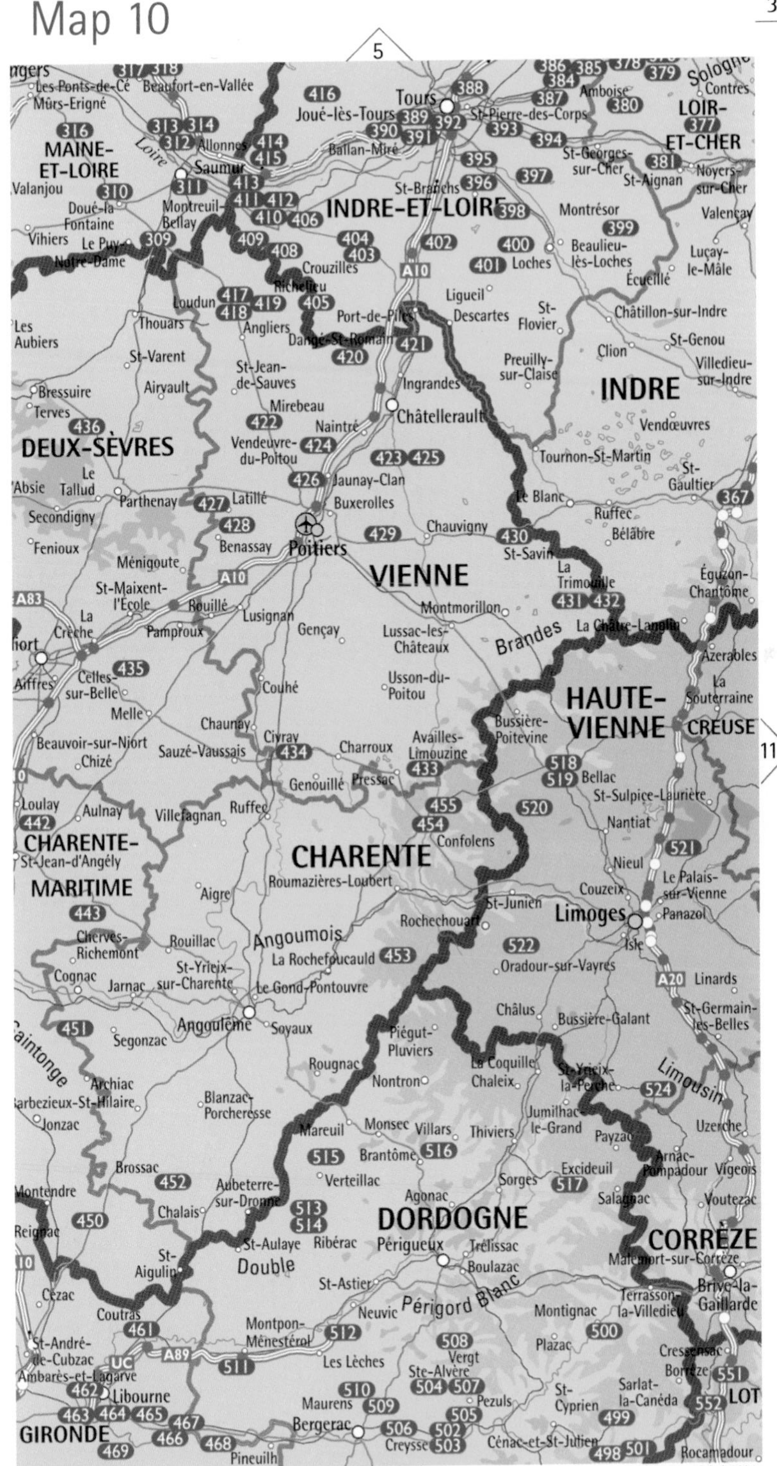
5
Les-Ponts-de-Cé
Beaufort-en-Vallée
Mûrs-Erigné
MAINE-ET-LOIRE
Valanjou
Loire
Allonnes
Saumur
Doué-la-Fontaine
Montreuil-Bellay
Vihiers
Le Puy-Notre-Dame
Joué-lès-Tours
Tours
Ballan-Miré
St-Pierre-des-Corps
Amboise
Sologne
Contres
LOIR-ET-CHER
St-Georges-sur-Cher
St-Aignan
Noyers-sur-Cher
Valençay
St-Branchs
INDRE-ET-LOIRE
Montrésor
Beaulieu-lès-Loches
Loches
Crouzilles
Richelieu
Écueillé
Luçay-le-Mâle
Loudun
Ligueil
Descartes
St-Flovier
Châtillon-sur-Indre
Les Aubiers
Thouars
Angliers
Port-de-Piles
Dangé-St-Romain
St-Genou
St-Varent
St-Jean-de-Sauves
Preuilly-sur-Claise
Clion
Villedieu-sur-Indre
Airvault
Bressuire
Terves
Mirebeau
Ingrandes
INDRE
Châtellerault
Naintré
Vendœuvres
DEUX-SÈVRES
Vendeuvre-du-Poitou
Tournon-St-Martin
L'Absie
Le Tallud
Jaunay-Clan
St-Gaultier
Parthenay
Latillé
Buxerolles
Le Blanc
Secondigny
Ruffec
Bélâbre
Fenioux
Benassay
Poitiers
Chauvigny
St-Savin
Ménigoute
VIENNE
La Trimouille
Éguzon-Chantôme
St-Maixent-l'École
Rouillé
Lusignan
Montmorillon
La Crèche
Pamproux
Gençay
Lussac-les-Châteaux
Brandes
La Châtre-Langlin
Niort
Azerables
Celles-sur-Belle
Aiffres
Couhé
Usson-du-Poitou
La Souterraine
HAUTE-VIENNE
CREUSE
Melle
Chaunay
Bussière-Poitevine
Beauvoir-sur-Niort
Civray
Charroux
Availles-Limouzine
11
Chizé
Sauzé-Vaussais
Bellac
Genouillé
Pressac
St-Sulpice-Laurière
Loulay
Aulnay
Villefagnan
Ruffec
Nantiat
CHARENTE-MARITIME
St-Jean-d'Angély
CHARENTE
Confolens
Nieul
Le Palais-sur-Vienne
Roumazières-Loubert
Aigre
Couzeix
St-Junien
Limoges
Panazol
Rochechouart
Isle
Cherves-Richemont
Rouillac
Angoumois
La Rochefoucauld
Oradour-sur-Vayres
Linards
Cognac
Jarnac
St-Yrieix-sur-Charente
Le Gond-Pontouvre
Châlus
Bussière-Galant
St-Germain-les-Belles
Angoulême
Soyaux
Saintonge
Segonzac
Piégut-Pluviers
Rougnac
La Coquille
Chaleix
St-Yrieix-la-Perche
Limousin
Archiac
Nontron
Barbezieux-St-Hilaire
Jonzac
Blanzac-Porcheresse
Jumilhac-le-Grand
Uzerche
Mareuil
Monsec
Villars
Thiviers
Payzac
Brantôme
Arnac-Pompadour
Vigeois
Brossac
Verteillac
Excideuil
Montendre
Aubeterre-sur-Dronne
Agonac
Sorges
Salagnac
Voutezac
Chalais
DORDOGNE
Reignac
St-Aulaye
Ribérac
Périgueux
Trélissac
CORRÈZE
St-Aigulin
Double
Boulazac
Malemort-sur-Corrèze
St-Astier
Brive-la-Gaillarde
Cézac
Coutras
Neuvic
Périgord Blanc
Montignac
Terrasson-la-Villedieu
Montpon-Ménestérol
St-André-de-Cubzac
Plazac
Cressensac
Les Lèches
Vergt
Ambarès-et-Lagarve
Ste-Alvère
Borrèze
Libourne
Maurens
Pezuls
St-Cyprien
Sarlat-la-Canéda
LOT
GIRONDE
Bergerac
Creysse
Cénac-et-St-Julien
Pineuilh
Rocamadour
A10
A83
A89
A20
15

Map 11

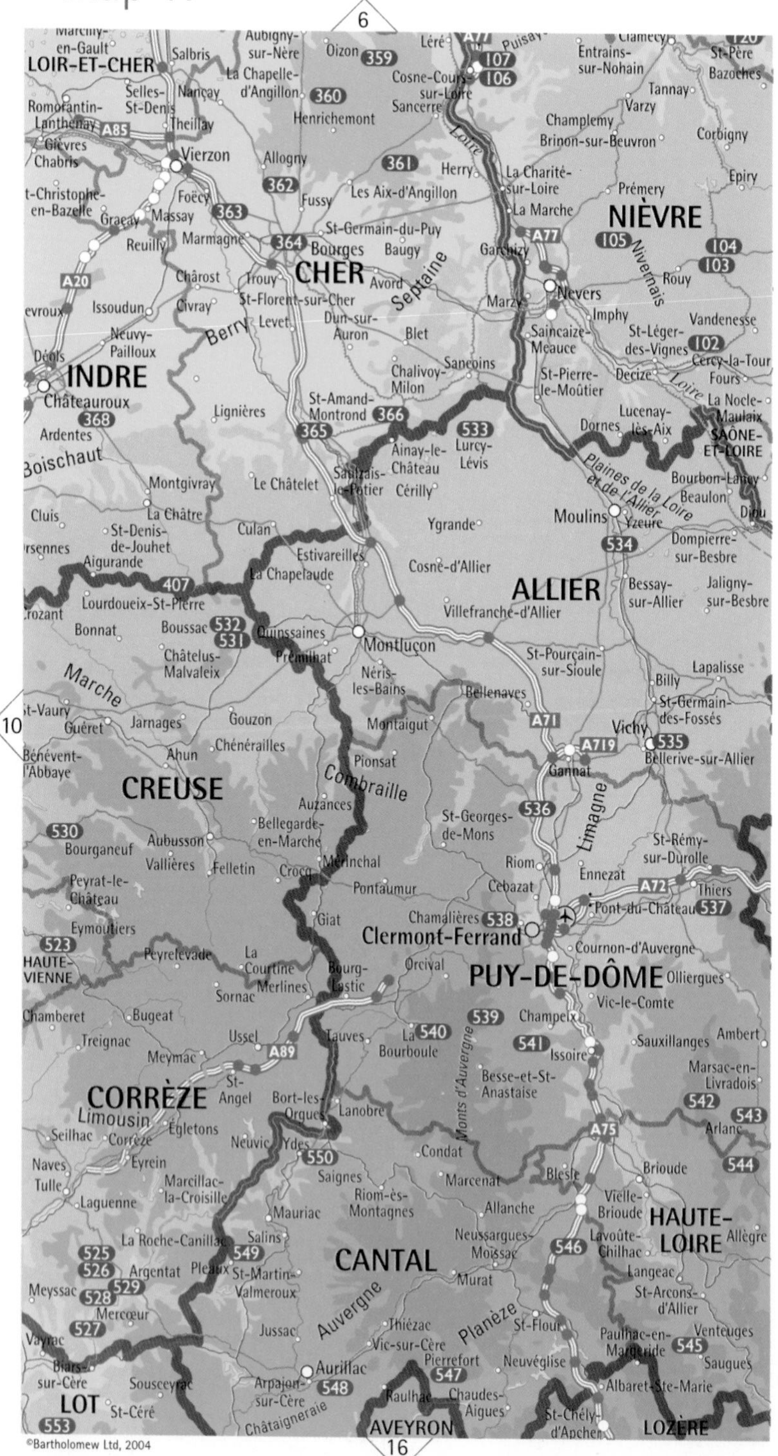
6
10
16
LOIR-ET-CHER
en-Gault
Salbris
Aubigny-sur-Nère
Oizon
359
Léré
A77
107
106
Puisaye
Clamecy
Entrains-sur-Nohain
St-Père
Bazoches
Selles-St-Denis
Nançay
La Chapelle-d'Angillon
360
Cosne-Cours-sur-Loire
Sancerre
Tannay
Varzy
Romorantin-Lanthenay
A85
Theillay
Henrichemont
Champlemy
Brinon-sur-Beuvron
Corbigny
Gièvres
Chabris
Vierzon
Allogny
361
Herry
Loire
La Charité-sur-Loire
Epiry
St-Christophe-en-Bazelle
362
Foëcy
Fussy
Les Aix-d'Angillon
Prémery
Graçay
Massay
363
La Marche
NIÈVRE
Reuilly
Marmagne
364
St-Germain-du-Puy
Bourges
Baugy
A77
105
Nivernais
104
103
A20
Chârost
Trouy
CHER
Avord
Septaine
Garchizy
Nevers
Rouy
Issoudun
Civray
St-Florent-sur-Cher
Marzy
Imphy
Vandenesse
Levet
Dun-sur-Auron
Neuvy-Pailloux
Berry
Blet
Saincaize-Meauce
St-Léger-des-Vignes
102
Cercy-la-Tour
Déols
INDRE
Sancoins
Chalivoy-Milon
St-Pierre-le-Moûtier
Decize
Fours
Châteauroux
St-Amand-Montrond
366
La Nocle-Maulaix
368
Lignières
Lucenay-lès-Aix
Dornes
Ardentes
365
533
Lurcy-Lévis
SAÔNE-ET-LOIRE
Boischaut
Ainay-le-Château
Plaines de la Loire et de l'Allier
Montgivray
Le Châtelet
Saulzais-le-Potier
Cérilly
Bourbon-Lancy
Beaulon
La Châtre
Moulins
Digoin
Cluis
Culan
Ygrande
Yzeure
St-Denis-de-Jouhet
534
Dompierre-sur-Besbre
Aigurande
Estivareilles
Cosne-d'Allier
La Chapelaude
407
ALLIER
Bessay-sur-Allier
Jaligny-sur-Besbre
Lourdoueix-St-Pierre
Villefranche-d'Allier
Bonnat
Boussac
532
531
Quinssaines
Montluçon
Prémilhat
Châtelus-Malvaleix
St-Pourçain-sur-Sioule
Lapalisse
Néris-les-Bains
Billy
Marche
Bellenaves
St-Germain-des-Fossés
Guéret
Jarnages
Gouzon
Montaigut
A71
Vichy
A719
535
Bénévent-l'Abbaye
Chénérailles
Ahun
Gannat
Bellerive-sur-Allier
Pionsat
CREUSE
Combraille
Limagne
Auzances
536
Bellegarde-en-Marche
St-Georges-de-Mons
530
St-Rémy-sur-Durolle
Bourganeuf
Aubusson
Vallières
Felletin
Crocq
Mérinchal
Riom
Ennezat
Peyrat-le-Château
Pontaumur
Cébazat
A72
Thiers
Pont-du-Château
537
Giat
Chamalières
538
Eymoutiers
Clermont-Ferrand
523
Cournon-d'Auvergne
HAUTE-VIENNE
Peyrelevade
La Courtine
Merlines
Bourg-Lastic
Orcival
PUY-DE-DÔME
Olliergues
Sornac
Vic-le-Comte
Chamberet
Bugeat
539
Champeix
Treignac
Ussel
Tauves
La Bourboule
540
Monts d'Auvergne
541
Issoire
Sauxillanges
Ambert
Meymac
A89
St-Angel
Besse-et-St-Anastaise
Marsac-en-Livradois
CORRÈZE
Bort-les-Orgues
542
543
Limousin
Lanobre
A75
Arlanc
Seilhac
Corrèze
Égletons
Neuvic
Ydes
550
Condat
544
Naves
Eyrein
Saignes
Marcenat
Blesle
Brioude
Tulle
Marcillac-la-Croisille
Riom-ès-Montagnes
Vieille-Brioude
Laguenne
Mauriac
Allanche
HAUTE-LOIRE
Allègre
La Roche-Canillac
Salins
Neussargues-Moissac
Lavoûte-Chilhac
525
526
Argentat
Pleaux
549
St-Martin-Valmeroux
CANTAL
546
Langeac
Meyssac
528
529
Murat
St-Arcons-d'Allier
Mercœur
Auvergne
527
Thiézac
Planèze
St-Flour
Vayrac
Jussac
Vic-sur-Cère
Paulhac-en-Margeride
Venteuges
545
Pierrefort
Neuvéglise
Saugues
Biars-sur-Cère
Aurillac
547
Sousceyrac
Arpajon-sur-Cère
548
Raulhac
Chaudes-Aigues
Albaret-Ste-Marie
LOT
St-Céré
Châtaigneraie
St-Chély-d'Apcher
553
AVEYRON
LOZÈRE

Map 12

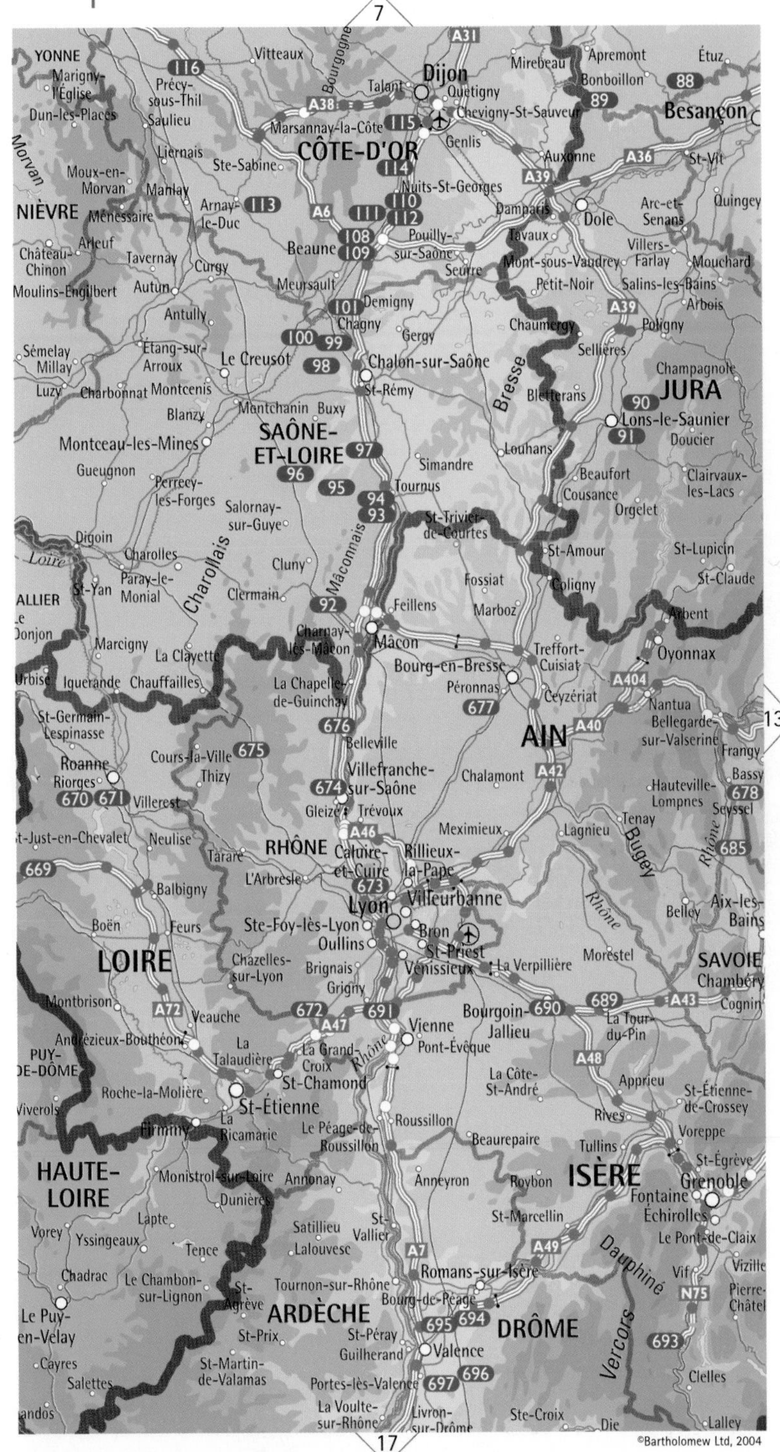
7
YONNE
Vitteaux
Bourgogne
A31
Dijon
Mirebeau
Apremont
Étuz
Marigny-l'Église
Précy-sous-Thil
116
Talant
Quetigny
Bonboillon
88
89
Dun-les-Places
Saulieu
A38
Chevigny-St-Sauveur
Besançon
Marsannay-la-Côte
115
Genlis
Morvan
Liernais
CÔTE-D'OR
Ste-Sabine
Auxonne
A36
St-Vit
Moux-en-Morvan
Manlay
114
A39
NIÈVRE
Ménessaire
Arnay-le-Duc
113
Nuits-St-Georges
110
Dampans
Dole
Arc-et-Senans
Quingey
A6
111
112
Château-Chinon
Arleuf
108
Pouilly-sur-Saône
Tavaux
Villers-Farlay
Mouchard
Tavernay
Beaune
109
Curgy
Seurre
Mont-sous-Vaudrey
Salins-les-Bains
Moulins-Engilbert
Autun
Meursault
Petit-Noir
Arbois
Antully
101
Demigny
A39
Poligny
Chagny
Gergy
Chaumergy
Sémelay
Millay
Étang-sur-Arroux
Le Creusot
100
99
Sellières
98
Chalon-sur-Saône
Bresse
Champagnole
Luzy
Charbonnat
Montcenis
St-Rémy
Bletterans
JURA
90
Blanzy
Montchanin
Buxy
Lons-le-Saunier
SAÔNE-ET-LOIRE
91
Doucier
Montceau-les-Mines
97
Louhans
Simandre
96
Gueugnon
Beaufort
Clairvaux-les-Lacs
95
Tournus
Perrecy-les-Forges
Cousance
Salornay-sur-Guye
94
93
Orgelet
St-Trivier-de-Courtes
Digoin
Mâconnais
Loire
Charolles
St-Amour
St-Lupicin
Cluny
Charollais
Fossiat
Paray-le-Monial
St-Claude
St-Yan
Coligny
ALLIER
Clermain
92
Feillens
Marboz
Arbent
Le Donjon
Charnay-lès-Mâcon
Mâcon
Treffort-Cuisiat
Oyonnax
Marcigny
La Clayette
Bourg-en-Bresse
Urbise
Iguerande
Chauffailles
La Chapelle-de-Guinchay
Péronnas
A404
Ceyzériat
Nantua
677
St-Germain-Lespinasse
Bellegarde-sur-Valserine
13
676
A40
Belleville
AIN
Frangy
Roanne
Cours-la-Ville
675
Thizy
Riorges
Villefranche-sur-Saône
Chalamont
A42
Bassy
670
671
674
Hauteville-Lompnes
678
Villerest
Gleizé
Trévoux
Seyssel
Tenay
St-Just-en-Chevalet
Neulise
A46
Meximieux
Lagnieu
Bugey
Rhône
RHÔNE
Caluire-et-Cuire
Rillieux-la-Pape
685
Tarare
669
L'Arbresle
673
Rhône
Balbigny
Lyon
Villeurbanne
Aix-les-Bains
Belley
Boën
Feurs
Ste-Foy-lès-Lyon
Bron
Oullins
St-Priest
Morestel
SAVOIE
LOIRE
Chazelles-sur-Lyon
Brignais
Vénissieux
La Verpillière
Chambéry
Grigny
Montbrison
A72
689
A43
Cognin
Veauche
672
691
Bourgoin-Jallieu
690
La Tour-du-Pin
A47
Vienne
Andrézieux-Bouthéon
La Talaudière
La Grand-Croix
Pont-Évêque
PUY-DE-DÔME
A48
Rhône
St-Chamond
La Côte-St-André
Apprieu
Roche-la-Molière
St-Étienne-de-Crossey
Viverols
St-Étienne
Roussillon
Rives
La Ricamarie
Firminy
Le Péage-de-Roussillon
Beaurepaire
Voreppe
Tullins
St-Égrève
HAUTE-LOIRE
Monistrol-sur-Loire
Annonay
Anneyron
Roybon
ISÈRE
Grenoble
Dunières
Fontaine
Échirolles
Lapte
St-Vallier
St-Marcellin
Satillieu
Vorey
Yssingeaux
Le Pont-de-Claix
Tence
Lalouvesc
Dauphiné
A7
A49
Vizille
Chadrac
Le Chambon-sur-Lignon
St-Agrève
Tournon-sur-Rhône
Romans-sur-Isère
Vif
Le Puy-en-Velay
N75
Pierre-Châtel
ARDÈCHE
Bourg-de-Péage
694
DRÔME
Vercors
St-Prix
St-Péray
695
693
Guilherand
Valence
Cayres
St-Martin-de-Valamas
696
Salettes
Portes-lès-Valence
697
Clelles
La Voulte-sur-Rhône
Livron-sur-Drôme
Ste-Croix
Die
Lalley
17

Map 13

8
Delémont
Rigz
Pont-de-Roide
A36
Baume-les-Dames
Seignelégier
Thise
Aïssey
Maîche
Solothurn
Saône
Laviron
Le Noirmont
Mamirolle
Valdahon
Le Russey
DOUBS
Ornans
Morteau
20
Neuchâtel
BERN
Éternoz
JURA
Doubs
Levier
Pontarlier
Frasne
La Cluse-et-Mijoux
Fribourg
Bonnevaux
Métabief
Sirod
SWITZERLAND
Lausanne
BERNER ALPEN
Morez
Les Rousses
St-Cergue
LAC LÉMAN
Divonne-les-Bains
Thonon-les-Bains
681
Gex
680
Sion
AIN
Genève
Annemasse
Morzine
St-Julien-en-Genevois
Faucigny
Cluses
12
La Roche-sur-Foron
682
HAUTE-SAVOIE
Vallorcine
679
Argentière
Cruseilles
Passy
Chamonix-Mont-Blanc
Alpi Pennine
Sallanches
Seynod
Annecy
683
684
Megève
St-Gervais-les-Bains
27
Talloires
686
St-Jorioz
Savoie
Crest-Voland
Doussard
Hauteluce
Aosta
A5
Faverges
Ugine
Mercury
Albertville
La Bâthie
Bourg-St-Maurice
Séez
687
ITALY
Chambéry
A430
Aime
688
Peisey-Nancroix
La Ravoire
Tarentaise
A43
Moûtiers
Tignes
Ivrea
Chapareillan
SAVOIE
Pontcharra
A43
A41
St-Pierre-d'Allevard
St-Martin-de-Belleville
Crolles
Val-Thorens
Termignon
Ciriè
A4
Froges
St-Jean-de-Maurienne
Val-Cenis
Belledonne
Maurienne
Modane
Torino
A32
Valloire
L'Alpe-d'Huez
A21
ISÈRE
Oisans
Les Deux-Alpes
Montgenèvre
Le Périer
St-Chaffrey
Airasca
La Bérarde
Briançon
Carmagnola
HAUTES-ALPES
Dauphiné
Valgaudemar
La Roche-de-Rame
A6
Bra
Freissinières
St-Véran
18

Map 14

9
Andernos-les-Bains
Cestas
Léognan
Arcachon
Gujan-Mestras
Biganos
La Teste
A660
Guyenne
Le Barp
Salles
A63
Hostens
Landes
Biscarrosse-Plage
Le Tuzan
Saugnacq-et-Muret
St-Symphorien
Biscarrosse
Pays de Born
Moustey
Belhade
Ychoux
Pissos
Sore
Ste-Eulalie-en-Born
Pontenx-les-Forges
Luxey
Mimizan
Labouheyre
Bias
473
Sabres
Escource
Solférino
Mézos
Onesse-et-Laharie
Aquitaine
St-Julien-en-Born
Uza
Morcenx
474
Brocas
Ygos-St-Saturnin
Lévignacq
Lesperon
475
Vielle-St-Girons
Rion-des-Landes
Gascogne
Mont-de-Marsan
Linxe
LANDES
Léon
Marensin
Tartas
Messanges
Azur
Herm
Soustons
St-Paul-lès-Dax
Souprosse
St-Sever
479
A63
476
Narrosse
Capbreton
Dax
Bénesse-Maremne
477
Pomarez
Tarnos
Pouillon
Amou
Momuy
478
Habas
Boucau
A641
Biarritz
Morlanne
Bayonne
485
Orthez
St-Jean-de-Luz
Bardos
Salies-de-Béarn
Donostia - San Sebastián
480
482
483
484
Oraàs
Cambo-les-Bains
Sauveterre-de-Béarn
A64
15
Urrugne
481
486
Mourenx
Itxassou
St-Palais
Navarrenx
A8
Pays Basque
Béarn
Ossès
PYRÉNÉES-ATLANTIQUES
Oloron-Ste-Marie
488
St-Jean-Pied-de-Port
487
Bidos
Urepel
PYRENEES
CORDILLERA CANTÁBRICA
Laruns
A15
Etsaut
Pamplona
SPAIN
Logroño
A15
A68
Huesca
©Bartholomew Ltd, 2004

Map 15

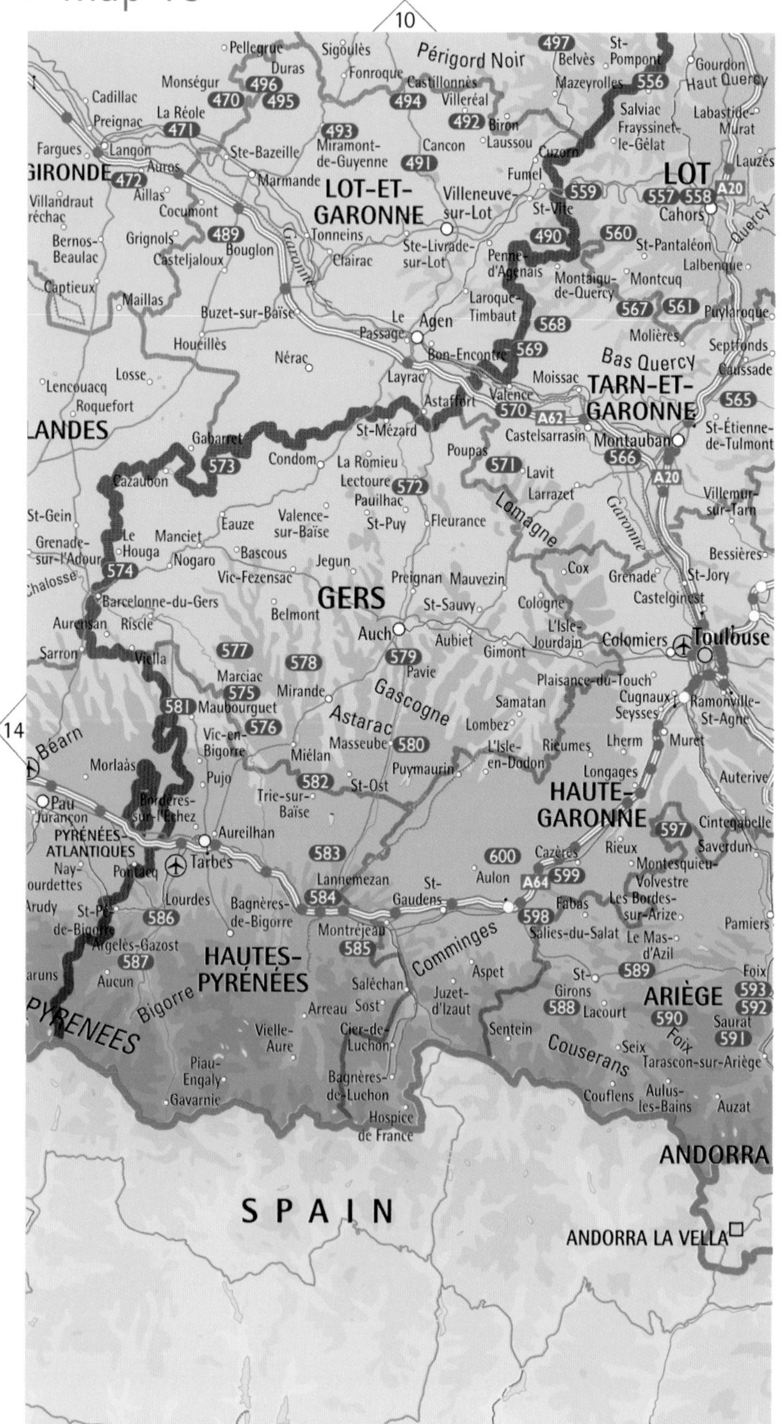
10
14
Périgord Noir
GIRONDE
LOT-ET-GARONNE
LOT
TARN-ET-GARONNE
LANDES
GERS
HAUTE-GARONNE
HAUTES-PYRÉNÉES
PYRÉNÉES-ATLANTIQUES
ARIÈGE
ANDORRA
ANDORRA LA VELLA
SPAIN
PYRENEES
Bas Quercy
Lomagne
Gascogne
Astarac
Comminges
Couserans
Bigorre
Béarn
Chalosse
Garonne
Quercy
Foix
Agen
Toulouse
Tarbes
Pau
Auch
Montauban
Cahors
Marmande
Villeneuve-sur-Lot
Condom
Lourdes
St-Gaudens
Muret
Colomiers
Moissac
Castelsarrasin
Valence
Fumel
Nérac
Mirande
Lectoure
Fleurance
Eauze
Nogaro
Riscle
Marciac
Maubourguet
Lannemezan
Bagnères-de-Bigorre
Bagnères-de-Luchon
Argelès-Gazost
Langon
Cadillac
La Réole
Duras
Monségur
Sigoulès
Castillonnès
Villeréal
Biron
Belvès
Gourdon
Cazères
Rieux
Saverdun
Pamiers
Foix
St-Girons
Aspet
Samatan
Lombez
Gimont
L'Isle-Jourdain
Grenade
Castelginest
Seysses
Longages
Auterive
Cintegabelle
A20
A62
A64
470
471
472
489
490
491
492
493
494
495
496
497
556
557
558
559
560
561
565
566
567
568
569
570
571
572
573
574
575
576
577
578
579
580
581
582
583
584
585
586
587
588
589
590
591
592
593
597
598
599
600

Map 16

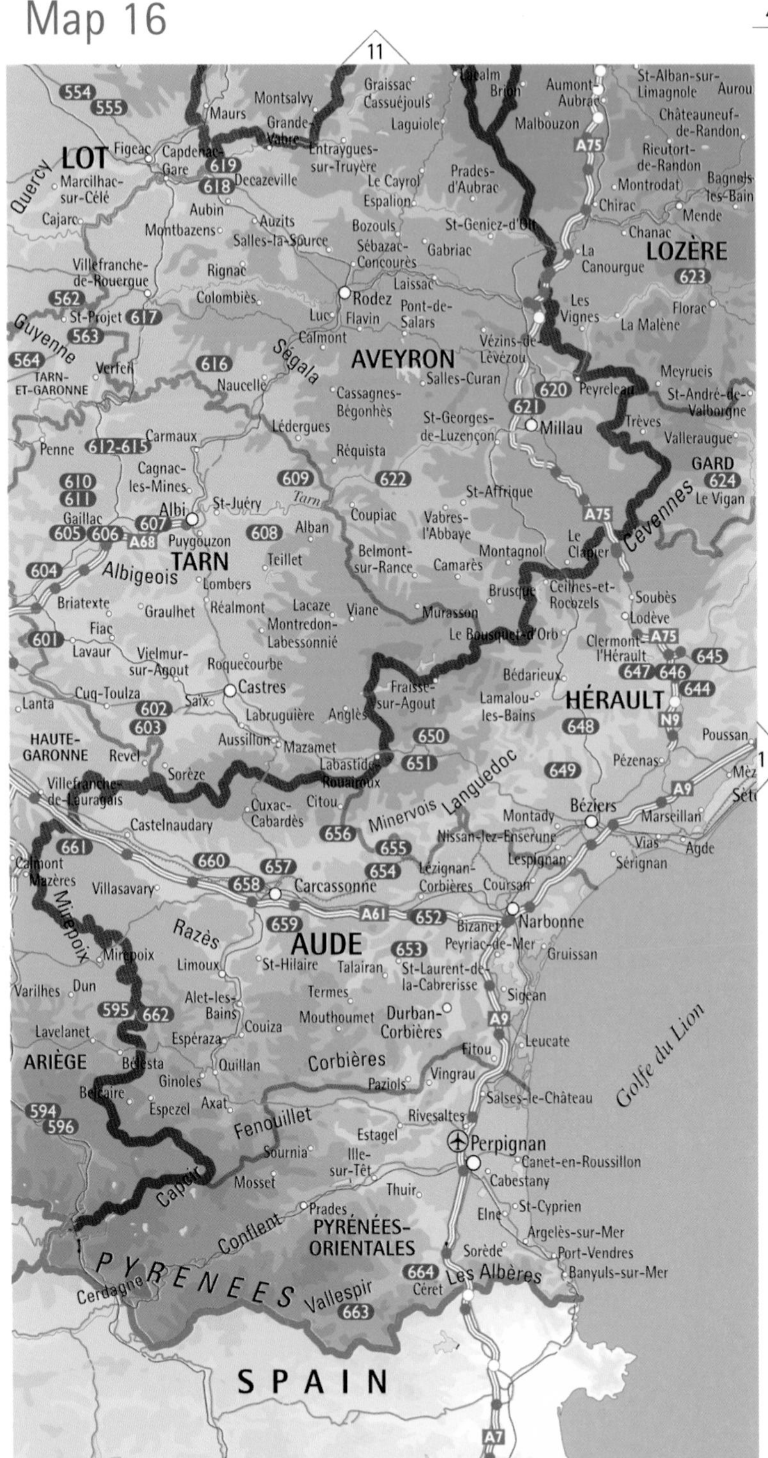

©Bartholomew Ltd, 2004

Map 17

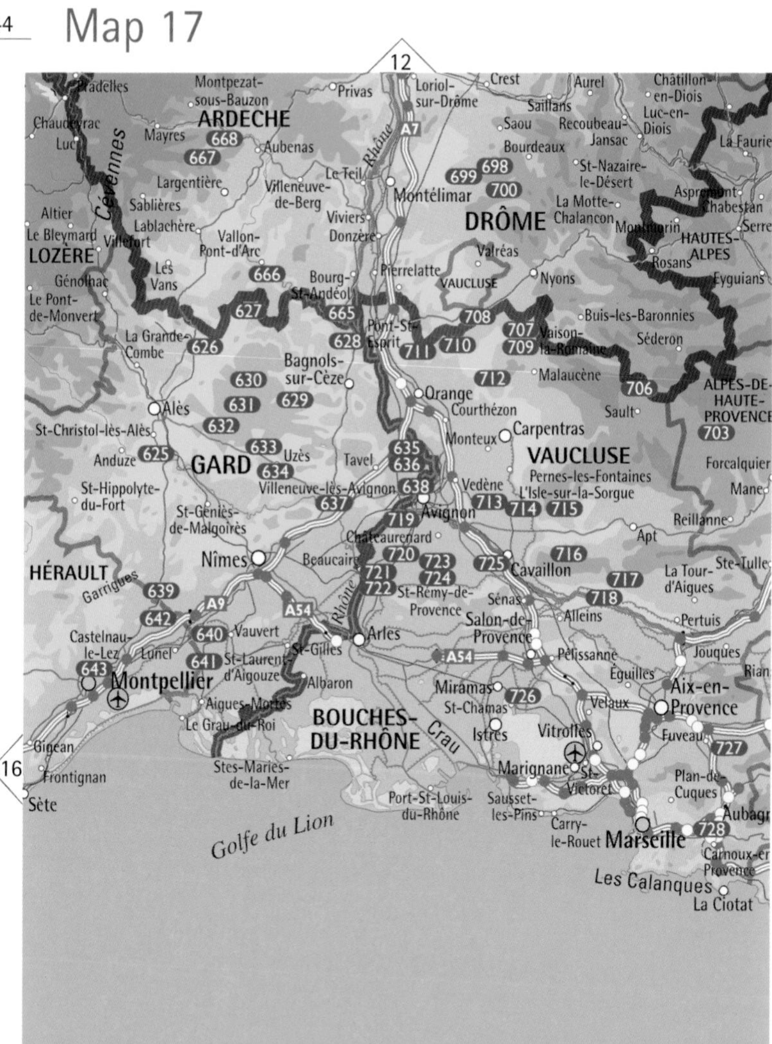
12
16
Pradelles
Montpezat-sous-Bauzon
Privas
Loriol-sur-Drôme
Crest
Aurel
Châtillon-en-Diois
Saillans
Luc-en-Diois
Chaudeyrac
ARDECHE
Saou
Recoubeau-Jansac
Mayres
668
Aubenas
A7
Rhône
Bourdeaux
La Faurie
667
Cévennes
St-Nazaire-le-Désert
Largentière
Le Teil
699
698
Villeneuve-de-Berg
Montélimar
700
La Motte-Chalancon
Aspremont
Altier
Sablières
Viviers
Chabestan
Le Bleymard
Lablachère
Vallon-Pont-d'Arc
Donzère
DRÔME
Montmorin
Serre
LOZÈRE
Villefort
HAUTES-ALPES
Valréas
Rosans
Génolhac
Les Vans
666
Bourg-St-Andéol
Pierrelatte
VAUCLUSE
Nyons
Eyguians
Le Pont-de-Monvert
627
665
708
Buis-les-Baronnies
La Grande-Combe
626
628
Pont-St-Esprit
711
710
707
709
Vaison-la-Romaine
Séderon
Bagnols-sur-Cèze
712
Malaucène
630
631
629
Orange
706
ALPES-DE-HAUTE-PROVENCE
Alès
Courthézon
Sault
632
Carpentras
703
St-Christol-lès-Alès
633
Monteux
Uzès
Tavel
635
636
VAUCLUSE
Anduze
625
GARD
634
Forcalquier
Vedène
Pernes-les-Fontaines
St-Hippolyte-du-Fort
Villeneuve-lès-Avignon
638
L'Isle-sur-la-Sorgue
Mane
637
713
714
715
St-Geniès-de-Malgoirès
Avignon
719
Reillanne
Apt
Châteaurenard
Nîmes
720
723
716
Beaucaire
Ste-Tulle
HÉRAULT
721
724
725
Cavaillon
Garrigues
722
St-Rémy-de-Provence
717
La Tour-d'Aigues
639
A9
718
A54
Sénas
Rhône
Alleins
642
Salon-de-Provence
Pertuis
Castelnau-le-Lez
Vauvert
Arles
640
St-Gilles
Jouques
Lunel
643
A54
Pélissanne
641
St-Laurent-d'Aigouze
Éguilles
Rians
Montpellier
Albaron
Miramas
Aix-en-Provence
726
Aigues-Mortes
St-Chamas
BOUCHES-DU-RHÔNE
Le Grau-du-Roi
Crau
Istres
Vitrolles
Fuveau
Gigean
727
Stes-Maries-de-la-Mer
Marignane
St-Victoret
Plan-de-Cuques
Frontignan
Aubagne
Sète
Port-St-Louis-du-Rhône
Sausset-les-Pins
Golfe du Lion
Carry-le-Rouet
Marseille
728
Carnoux-en-Provence
Les Calanques
La Ciotat

Map 18

13

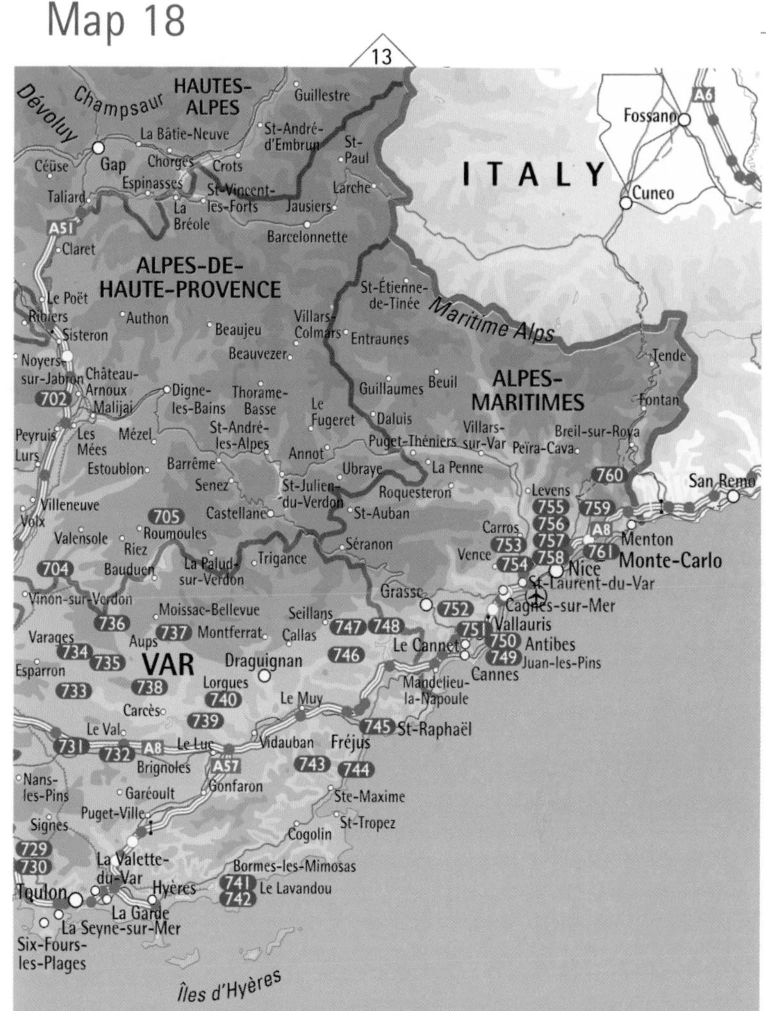

HAUTES-ALPES
Dévoluy
Champsaur
Guillestre
La Bâtie-Neuve
St-André-d'Embrun
St-Paul
Céüse
Gap
Chorges
Crots
Espinasses
St-Vincent-les-Forts
Larche
Taliard
La Bréole
Jausiers
Barcelonnette
A51
Claret
ITALY
Fossano
Cuneo
A6
ALPES-DE-HAUTE-PROVENCE
Le Poët
Ribiers
Sisteron
Authon
Beaujeu
Villars-Colmars
Entraunes
St-Étienne-de-Tinée
Maritime Alps
Beauvezer
Noyers-sur-Jabron
Château-Arnoux
Malijai
702
Digne-les-Bains
Thorame-Basse
Le Fugeret
Guillaumes
Beuil
ALPES-MARITIMES
Tende
Fontan
Daluis
Peyruis
Lurs
Les Mées
Mézel
St-André-les-Alpes
Annot
Puget-Théniers
Villars-sur-Var
Peïra-Cava
Breil-sur-Roya
Estoublon
Barrême
Senez
Ubraye
La Penne
St-Julien-du-Verdon
Roquesteron
Levens
760
San Remo
Villeneuve
Volx
705
Castellane
St-Auban
755
759
756
757
758
A8
761
Menton
Monte-Carlo
Valensole
Roumoules
Riez
Carros
753
754
Séranon
Vence
Nice
704
Bauduen
La Palud-sur-Verdon
Trigance
St-Laurent-du-Var
Vinon-sur-Verdon
Grasse
752
Cagnes-sur-Mer
Moissac-Bellevue
Seillans
747
748
751
Vallauris
736
Aups
737
Montferrat
Callas
750
Antibes
Varages
734
735
VAR
Draguignan
746
Le Cannet
749
Juan-les-Pins
Esparron
733
738
Lorgues
740
Cannes
Mandelieu-la-Napoule
Le Muy
Carcès
739
Le Val
745
St-Raphaël
731
732
Le Luc
Vidauban
Fréjus
Brignoles
A57
743
744
Nans-les-Pins
Garéoult
Gonfaron
Ste-Maxime
Puget-Ville
St-Tropez
Signes
Cogolin
729
730
La Valette-du-Var
Bormes-les-Mimosas
Toulon
Hyères
741
742
Le Lavandou
La Garde
La Seyne-sur-Mer
Six-Fours-les-Plages
Îles d'Hyères

photo Michael Busselle

the north–picardy

Manoir du Meldick

Tranquil Meldick, a gorgeous 1930s house, is extremely smart behind its electronic gates. The long dining room windows look across the empty garden to pond and fields – hard to imagine that two terrible wars were waged here but one of Madame's fascinating treasures is a real collection of wartime medals and badges. She has huge energy, colour-codes each of her big, panelled, beamed bedrooms for flower names, arranges her many pictures and *objets* with artistic care – you could admire them for hours – and really appreciates guests who respond to this level of chic, this mix of warm home and personal museum.

rooms	5: 2 doubles, 2 twins, 1 quadruple.
price	€55 for two.
meals	Good restaurant 5km.
closed	Rarely.
directions	From A16 exit 19 for Marck; 2nd roundabout exit Le Fort Vert; through Marck; right D119; house 1km on right.

Jean & Danièle Houzet
Manoir du Meldick,
Le Fort Vert,
62730 Marck, Pas-de-Calais
tel +33 (0)3 21 85 74 34
fax +33 (0)3 21 85 74 34
e-mail jeandaniele.houzet@free.fr

Les Draps d'Or

The 'Cloths of Gold' has been an inn since 1640 and Christine's open and vivacious welcome fits the tradition – she adores receiving guests, the youngest included. She uses colour joyfully too: the warm, bright little dayroom in the guest wing is a reflection of her dynamic personality. Bedrooms upstairs – blue, yellow, green, white – are equally fresh and bright; the twin has bedheads festooned in muslin, studded with fairy lights, gathered with red raffia. All give onto the cobbled street but Ardres, a delightful little town, is quiet at night while the perfect town garden gives a country feel at the back.

rooms	3: 1 twin, 2 doubles, all with shower & separate wc; extra twin for children.
price	€48 for two.
meals	Restaurants within walking distance.
closed	Rarely.
directions	From Calais A16, exit 17; N43 to Ardres; right after church; house on corner.

Christine & François Borel
Les Draps d'Or,
62610 Ardres, Pas-de-Calais
tel +33 (0)3 21 82 20 44
fax +33 (0)3 21 82 20 44
e-mail christine@drapsdor.com
web www.drapsdor.com

Le Manoir de Bois en Ardres

After 200 years of conversions, this house of history and unusual character stands, connected by glazed arches, cloister-like round its sheltered, intimate garden and old stone pond. Beyond, ponies graze beneath the mature trees of the 10-acre park: come to commune with nature. Inside, strikingly attractive cottage-contemporary rooms are a hymn to Françoise's stencil and furniture-painting skills and the fruit of Thierry's collecting flair (his antiques and bric-à-brac shop occupies an old stable), the whole atmosphere an echo of this warm, eager couple's joie de vivre. Breakfasts are a delight.

rooms	5: 2 suites for 4; 2 triples (1 with separate wc on floor below); 1 twin.
price	€59-€64 for two.
meals	Restaurant 1km.
closed	Rarely.
directions	From Calais A16, exit 17 for St Omer N43. Pass Les Attaques, Pont d'Ardres, 1st r'bout at Bois en Ardres; before 2nd r'bout left Rue de St Quentin for 1km; green gate.

Françoise & Thierry Roger
Le Manoir de Bois en Ardres,
62610 Ardres, Pas-de-Calais

tel	+33 (0)3 21 85 97 78
fax	+33 (0)3 21 36 48 07
e-mail	roger@aumanoir.com
web	www.aumanoir.com

Map 2 Entry 3

Les Fuchsias

There is something touchingly mixed-up-Victorian about this unusual house with its gingerbread cutouts, variegated roofs and copsy garden of woodland thrown against lawns and fields with quantities of migrating birds flying past. Monsieur is chatty (in English), charming and informative; Madame is quieter but very attentive: ever busy with needle or paintbrush, she tends her house with loving care and embroidered samplers. Guests have their own cosy colourful sitting and breakfast rooms. Bedrooms have fresh modern furnishings – pretty duvets, wicker armchairs – and simple washing arrangements.

rooms	3: 1 suite for 4; 1 twin, 1 family room sharing separate wc.
price	€43-€47 for two.
meals	Good choice of restaurants at Ardres, 2km.
closed	Rarely
directions	A16 exit 17; N43 for Ardes & St Omer. In Bois en Ardres, 2nd left after r'bout; house on this road.

Bernadette Balloy
Les Fuchsias,
62610 Bois en Ardres, Pas-de-Calais

tel	+33 (0)3 21 82 05 25
fax	+33 (0)3 21 82 05 25
e-mail	lesfuchsias@aol.com
web	www.lesfuchsias-ardres.fr.fm

Map 2 Entry 4

La Bohême

Extrovert Sonia loves music, painting, cooking and spoiling her guests. White walls, dark wooden doors, floors and beams, solid, good-looking furniture – it's 'French rustique'. The bedroom under the eaves is prettily decorated in red *toile de Jouy* and looks onto the garden; the suite, in stylish white and grey with a good big bathroom, is in a separate building and perfect for a family (but watch the stairs). You'll adore the garden, bursting with life, full of secret corners. This is walking and pony-trekking country and if you'd like to trade car for horse, Sonia's daughter will happily organise rides.

rooms	3: 2 doubles, 1 family suite.
price	€45-€50 for two.
meals	Dinner with wine €19, book ahead.
closed	Rarely.
directions	From A26 exit 2 for Ardres; N43; 1st left for Zutkerque - Château de Cocove; signposted.

Sonia Benoît
La Bohême,
62370 Zutkerque,
Pas-de-Calais

tel	+33 (0)3 21 35 70 25
fax	+33 (0)3 21 35 70 25
e-mail	sonia-benoit-la-boheme@wanadoo.fr

La Motte Obin

Madame Breton is irreplaceable: a lovely old lady in a genuine old farmhouse, she talks lots, in French, and otherwise relies on radio and telly for company. Hers is an intriguing, piecemeal family house with comfortable old furniture, masses of photographs (a tribe of grandchildren) and very steep stairs. Rooms are country attractive: simple décor, good beds and windows to fields of peace. Madame loves cooking country dishes for visitors and readers have praised her hospitality. Ask to see the exquisite vaulted stables – built for cows and carthorses, fit for thoroughbreds and prizewinners.

rooms	2: 1 double, 1 family room.
price	€37 for two.
meals	Dinner with wine €17, book ahead.
closed	November-March.
directions	From A26 exit 2 for Tournehem, over N43, follow to Muncq Nieurlet, on for Ruminghem. House on left, about 1.5km after leaving Muncq Nieurlet, at sign.

Mme Françoise Breton
La Motte Obin,
62890 Muncq Nieurlet,
Pas-de-Calais

tel	+33 (0)3 21 82 79 63

La Ferme de Wolphus

The softly impressive park belonged to Jean-Jacques's grandfather's château, destroyed in the war – the lake, old trees, sheep and peacocks hug both farmhouse and separate guesthouse. All is straightforward and simple, breakfast is in your own quarters (or the family kitchen for very early starts), where basic pine furniture and slatting grace the smallish, under-the-eaves rooms and some windows give onto the garden. The closeness to ferry ports is seductive, though the nearby main road may disturb some people. The open intelligent family, who do wine-tastings and will sell you wine and honey, are delightful.

rooms	3: 2 triples, both with shower, sharing wc on floor below; 1 quadruple.
price	€38-€42 for two; €49-€54 for three; €64 for four; €12 extra bed.
meals	Restaurants nearby.
closed	Rarely.
directions	From A26 exit 2 onto N43 for Calais. Wolphus on left 1km after junction, with woods beside road. Be careful turning in.

Jean-Jacques Behaghel
La Ferme de Wolphus,
62890 Zouafques,
Pas-de-Calais

tel	+33 (0)3 21 35 61 61
fax	+33 (0)3 21 35 61 61
e-mail	ferme.de.wolphus@wanadoo.fr
web	perso.wanadoo.fr/ferme-wolphus

Map 2 Entry 7

Le Manoir

Sylvie is restoring her old house, painstakingly and very well. Built in 1839 and known in the village as le château, it's not really big but, with so many original details intact, it's an architectural historian's delight. Stained glass, marble fireplaces, trompe l'œil wall paintings on the stairs, superb green and white tiling in the kitchen, original colours. The feel is French-traditional and wooden-floored and some of the bedrooms have spectacular carved wardrobes and beds. This is a comfortable house with a great atmosphere, good *table d'hôtes* dinners and a delightful young family.

rooms	5: 3 doubles, 1 triple, 1 suite for 4.
price	€58 for two; €85 for four.
meals	Dinner with wine €25-€40, book ahead.
closed	Rarely.
directions	From A26 exit 2; left D217 for Zouafques, Tournehem then Bonningues; house on right just after entering village.

Sylvie & Pierre Breemersch
Le Manoir,
62890 Bonningues lès Ardres,
Pas-de-Calais

tel	+33 (0)3 21 82 69 05
fax	+33 (0)3 21 82 69 05
e-mail	pierre.breemersch@wanadoo.fr
web	www.lemanoirdebonningues.com

Map 2 Entry 8

27 route de Guémy

It's new, brand new. So is the garden. But Madame, a long-standing B&B owner, will soon bring her young house to life, inside and out. Quiet and confident, she simply loves having guests. You have the run of the upper floor, where all rooms look long and far over green hills, are fairly minimalist in décor with white walls and clothes racks, and share a big spanking bathroom. Downstairs, a conservatory for a good friendly breakfast and rooms full of light. It's excellent value, so come and watch as the trees begin to grow and the house learns to breathe under Madame's ministrations.

rooms	1 suite for 2-6.
price	€39 for two.
meals	Choice of restaurants 5-10km.
closed	Rarely.
directions	From Calais A26 for Paris; exit Licques; left D217 for Zouafques & Clerques; right opp. church in Clerques for La Chapelle St Louis 500m; house with columns.

Christiane Devines
27 route de Guémy,
62890 Clerques,
Pas-de-Calais
tel +33 (0)3 21 82 40 65
fax +33 (0)3 21 82 40 65

La Ferme de Beaupré

This organic dairy farm is run with passion by your hosts who receive you in their gorgeous old house at the end of the tree-lined drive and ply you with fine, home-grown food (breakfast jams are the best). Lut, from Belgium, is a gracious and unpretentiously warm mother of two boys – her genuine welcome will touch you. Your perfect, peaceful bedroom is a study in taupes and off-whites, papered in *toile de Jouy*; a tiny room off it has a bed for a child, and a useful fridge. You get sole use of the living room, and the garden bursts with peonies, lupins, roses and cherries. An adorable, very special place.

rooms	1 double.
price	€49 for two.
meals	Dinner with wine €18, book ahead.
closed	Rarely.
directions	From A26 exit 2 for Licques; through Tournehem & Bonningues lès Ardres; left after village to farm.

Lut & Jean-Michel Louf-Degrauwe
La Ferme de Beaupré,
62890 Bonningues lès Ardres,
Pas-de-Calais
tel +33 (0)3 21 35 14 44
fax +33 (0)3 21 35 57 35
e-mail lut.degrauwe@nordnet.fr

La Leulène

Your dark, lively hostess will flash her quick smile and lead you into her house of surprises. The little low frontage opens onto a most unexpected double-height living space where modern and family pieces – a superb table made from a convent door, a baby grand piano, an immensely high carved bridal armoire – sit comfortably together and a picture window brings the garden indoors for breakfast. Upstairs, a gallery leads to immaculate attic bedrooms where floors are parquet, colours are strong and the style classic rustic French. Sit out in summer on curly wrought-iron chairs in the equally charming garden.

rooms	3: 1 double, 1 triple, 1 suite for 4.
price	€49-€57 for two.
meals	Good restaurants 3-5km.
closed	Christmas & New Year.
directions	From A16 Boulogne, exit 8 for Hervelinghen on D244. There, house on right before church.

Catherine & Jean-Marc Petitprez
La Leulène,
62179 Hervelinghen,
Pas-de-Calais

tel	+33 (0)3 21 82 47 30
e-mail	laleulene@aol.com
web	catherine.petitprez.free.fr

Map 2 Entry 11

La Goélette

A great place from which to explore the 'Opal Coast', made fashionable by the British in the Thirties, or to spend your first or last night of a trip to France. *Monsieur Hulot's Holiday* is a perfect image of the little seaside town and this ravishingly exuberant house on the front. Mary's décor is soberly luxurious, in keeping with the period: white linen, wooden floors, carefully chosen fabrics and furniture, lots of books. She speaks excellent English and may offer you tea in the beautiful room looking out to sea. Her huge, delicious breakfast takes place here too. One room is tiny and only two have sea views.

rooms	4: 2 doubles, 2 twins.
price	€60-€96 for two.
meals	Dinner with wine €29, book ahead.
closed	Rarely.
directions	From A16 exit 3 to Wimereux. There, go to sea front. House about halfway along promenade, 100m left of Hôtel Atlantic (with your back to sea).

Mary Avot
La Goélette,
62930 Wimereux, Pas-de-Calais

tel	+33 (0)3 21 32 62 44
fax	+33 (0)3 21 33 77 54
e-mail	lagoelette@nordnet.fr
web	www.lagoelette.com

Map 2 Entry 12

60 impasse de Bouillets

Ideal for families. You could spend hours exploring the woods and meadows that surround this place, there's a sheltered spot for picnics, barbecues, slides and swings (to share with the owners' three lovely children) and guest rooms are relatively independent. Madame teaches part-time; Monsieur, warm and outgoing, serves you croissants, jams and cheeses, homemade tarts and fresh juices at superb breakfasts before a huge fire. The bedrooms are plainer with great dark beams, white walls and traditional French country décor – florals and twiddly bits; one has a proper kitchen. And it's all marvellously quiet.

rooms	2 family suites for 3, 1 with kitchen.
price	€43-€45 for two.
meals	Restaurant 3km. Self-catering in one suite.
closed	Rarely.
directions	From Boulogne N42 for St Omer; right D206 for Henneveux; left D253 for Desvres; left D253E2 for Brunembert; through wood, at top, house on left.

Philippe & Marie-Christine Fastrez
60 impasse de Bouillets,
62142 Henneveux, Pas-de-Calais
tel +33 (0)3 21 83 97 31
fax +33 (0)3 21 83 97 31
e-mail mcfastrez@aol.com
web www.lehautchamp.com

Rue de l'Église

The golden stone of the oldest farmhouse in the village is easy on the eye. Flowers flourish to the front, the garden and orchard run down to the stream, and the retired horses are happy in their stables (the stud farm is further away). Madame is discreetly friendly and obliging, and gives you delicious breakfasts at marble-topped tables. The bedrooms, in an outbuilding that looks out onto the courtyard and wooded hills, have straightforward modern décor; the new triple sports a wrought-iron four-poster with leopard-skin cover, and a bathroom pretty with mosaics. The living room, too, is spotless and cosy.

rooms	5: 2 doubles, 2 twins, 1 triple.
price	€40-€50 for two.
meals	Auberge in village.
closed	Christmas-January.
directions	From Boulogne D940 to St Léonard; at 2nd lights, left on small road to Echinghen (no sign); in village centre, left in tiny street immed. after sharp bend; left 1st gateway.

Jacqueline & Jean-Pierre Boussemaere
Rue de l'Église,
62360 Echinghen,
Pas-de-Calais
tel +33 (0)3 21 91 14 34
fax +33 (0)3 21 91 06 41
e-mail jp-boussemaere@wanadoo.fr

127 rue du Breuil

The shield on the front is a *notaire's* badge of office: his is a house of generous proportions with original 18th-century features and a courtyard at the back that opens into a lovely garden. Matching your hosts' quiet good breeding, a certain old-world formality clings to the heavy dark antiques downstairs; upstairs, the big, prettily traditional French rooms are lighter with more antiques and good rugs on wooden floors. There's a highly original attic salon for guests with all the furniture gathered in the centre. A chance to experience a valuable bourgeois facet of France in an unspoilt village.

rooms	3: 2 twins, 1 family room.
price	€45-€60 for two. Minimum stay 2 nights.
meals	Good restaurant 5km.
closed	Rarely.
directions	From Boulogne N1 S for St Léonard & Montreuil approx. 15km. In Samer, take road that goes down to right of church; house on left, near top of hill.

Joëlle Maucotel
127 rue du Breuil,
62830 Samer,
Pas-de-Calais
tel +33 (0)3 21 87 64 19
fax +33 (0)3 21 87 64 19

Le Moulin

The wheel has to be repaired, so no more milling, but the lake is there and it's good to throw open a window and watch the ducks. This is a classically French B&B with massive black leather sofas in the sitting room, a padded velvet chair or two in the bedrooms and a painted white table against blue or pink-and-white striped walls. The dining room has old cherry-wood pieces.
All very neat and comfortable in this big, square handsome old house, built in 1855. Christine is reserved and friendly and gives you a comfortable welcome and a good breakfast, shared with gîte guests. Utterly reliable and great value.

rooms	3 doubles.
price	€50-€55 for two.
meals	Restaurants 5km.
closed	Rarely.
directions	A16 exit Neufchâtel Hardelot & Ste Cécile; D940 for Boulogne & Le Touquet; house near church on entering Dannes.

Christine Lécaille
Le Moulin,
62187 Dannes, Pas-de-Calais
tel +33 (0)3 21 33 74 74
fax +33 (0)3 21 33 74 74
e-mail christine.lecaille@free.fr
web lecaille@au-moulin.com

La Longue Roye

This fabulous set of buildings was a Cistercian farm and the 13th-century barn – a 'harvest cathedral' – is worth the detour alone. Old arches spring, the brickwork dazzles, the courtyard focuses properly on its duckpond, the guest quarters – bedrooms, log-fired dayroom with separate tables, garden with its furniture – are in a beamy outbuilding and the place still breathes monastic peace. Your hosts work hard to maintain their precious legacy, breeding pheasants as well as caring attentively for guests. Madame loves decorating the cosy, harmonious rooms and has plenty of time to chat over breakfast.

rooms	6: 4 doubles, 2 twins.
price	€55 for two.
meals	Restaurants nearby.
closed	Rarely.
directions	From Calais A16 for Amiens; exit 25, N1 for Montreuil; left for Longvillers; signposted.

Anne & Jean-Philippe Delaporte
La Longue Roye,
62630 Longvillers, Pas-de-Calais
tel +33 (0)3 21 86 70 65
fax +33 (0)3 21 86 71 32
e-mail longue-roye@la-longue-roye.com
web www.la-longue-roye.com

Birdy Land

These two are fabulously alive, attentive and cultivated. Georges, a painter, is a majestic figure, well able to talk at the same time as charming Marie... an irresistible double act. The well-proportioned house is an architectural flourish, the contents a classic mix of antique and modern, and there's a new dayroom/bar for guests. Two bedrooms share a balcony terrace and a separate entrance, the third is smaller; all are cosily cossetting with chintz quilts and the odd antique. The landscaped crescents and avenues are restful, the sea is 10 minutes away, the garden tended and beautiful. Perfect for families.

rooms	3: 1 double, 1 twin, 1 triple.
price	€75 for two.
meals	Wide choice of restaurants within walking distance.
closed	Rarely.
directions	From A16 Le Touquet exit; through Étaples; follow signs for Le Touquet centre. After 4th lights, 2nd right for Holiday Inn. 2nd house on right opp. telephone box.

Georges & Marie Versmée
Birdy Land,
62520 Le Touquet,
Pas-de-Calais
tel +33 (0)3 21 05 31 46
fax +33 (0)3 21 05 95 07
e-mail georges.versmee@wanadoo.fr

Le Vert Bois

It's very grand for a farm – the 200-year-old house, outbuildings and courtyard are immaculate. Étienne and Véronique and their family are delightful, warm and generous; they grow cereals, keep cows and may offer you a guided tour of the place. You'll sleep well in your converted cowshed; rooms are white-walled, parquet-floored, spotless. The twin is particularly pretty with its pale beams and fresh blue and white colours. The old rampart town of Montreuil sur Mer is minutes away for shops, restaurants and "astonishing points of view". Ancient peace, lovely people, fields as far as the eye can see.

rooms	2: 1 double, 1 twin.
price	€45 for two.
meals	Choice of restaurants nearby.
closed	Rarely.
directions	From Montreuil, arriving in Neuville, right opp. antique shop, 1.5km; left at roadside cross; signposted.

Étienne & Véronique Bernard
Le Vert Bois,
62170 Neuville sous Montreuil,
Pas-de-Calais
tel +33 (0)3 21 06 09 41
fax +33 (0)3 21 06 09 41
e-mail etienne.bernard6@wanadoo.fr
web gite.montreuil.online.fr

L'Overgne

A calm unaffected welcome and not even a cockerel to disturb the peace. Madame is as self-assured and down-to-earth as you would expect of someone who brought up nine children on the farm. The farmhouse, built in 1724, has a natural family feel. Rooms are simple and dated, shower rooms basic. The twin in the main house has country fabrics and a wooden floor; the double in the old stables is more intimate. Good breakfasts include cheese and homemade jam on fresh baguettes and croissants. Madame is a fount of local knowledge and loves getting to know her guests properly. Best in summer.

rooms	2: 1 double, 1 twin.
price	€45-€50 for two.
meals	Restaurants in Montreuil sur Mer 3km.
closed	December-February.
directions	From A16 exit 26 to Montreuil; D349 for Hesdin; through Beaumerie St Martin; 1st right at signpost.

Francis & Jeanne-Marie Locqueville
L'Overgne,
62170 Beaumerie St Martin,
Pas-de-Calais
tel +33 (0)3 21 81 81 87
e-mail jmarie.locqueville@wanadoo.fr

77 rue Pierre Ledent

Behind the pretty face hides the wonder of an extraordinary free-standing wooden staircase, a local speciality in the 17th century. Two gracious rooms up here: high ceilings, parquet floors, space and no clutter – the primrose-and-moss twin over the street has elegant original cupboards; the double over the back is cosily alcoved. Families will like the privacy of the snugger room across the yard: pretty blue head cushions and duvet-clothed bunks. The baths could fill more speedily but the breakfasts are brilliant (they used to run a bistro) and Madame is the jolliest, laughingest hostess we know.

rooms	3: 1 double, 1 twin, 1 family room.
price	€55 for two.
meals	Restaurant 50m.
closed	Rarely.
directions	In Montreuil, drive to top, Place Darnétal; house on right facing square.

Mme Louchez
77 rue Pierre Ledent,
62170 Montreuil sur Mer,
Pas-de-Calais
tel +33 (0)3 21 81 54 68
e-mail louchez.anne@wanadoo.fr

Ferme du Saule

Readers have called La Saule's breakfast cakes and compote their best in France. And we know that the Trunnets' smiles are genuine, their converted outbuilding handsome and perfectly finished (down to mosquito nets on windows), if a touch characterless, the beds excellent and the dayroom proud of its beautiful armoire. Monsieur is only too happy to show you the flax production process (it's fascinating), while Madame will be baking yet another superb cake for tomorrow's breakfast. Proclaimed "the best cowshed I've ever stayed in" by one happy guest.

rooms	4: 1 double, 3 triples.
price	€50 for two.
meals	Restaurants in Montreuil, 6km.
closed	Rarely.
directions	From A16 exit Montreuil; just before town right at lights; left D349 to Brimeux; left at junction, pass church, house on right, sign. From N39 exit Campagne les Hesdin.

M & Mme Germain Trunnet
Ferme du Saule,
62170 Brimeux,
Pas-de-Calais
tel +33 (0)3 21 06 01 28
fax +33 (0)3 21 81 40 14
web perso.wanadoo.fr/fermedusaule

La Hotoire

Bedrooms round the pretty courtyard have wonky timbers, cream tiled floors, pastel colours and modern bathrooms – a joint effort: Madame's ideas executed by Monsieur. The Garrels left lively Lille for the calm of the country, exchanging staying in B&Bs for running their own. They love meeting guests, both young and old, and children from the village play in their yard. The family suite snugly holds all you'll need, with toys, books and twin beds tucked beneath eaves – a dream den. Walk in the hills and woods behind and spot the wild deer – one of the delightful donkeys will happily accompany you.

rooms	3: 1 double, 1 suite for 4, both with kitchenette; 1 double.
price	€46 for two; €68 for four.
meals	Restaurants 3-4km; self-catering possible; BBQ.
closed	Rarely.
directions	From Hesdin D928 for St Omer; st left D913 through Huby St Leu to Guisy; signposted.

Martine & Marc-Willam Garrel
La Hotoire,
62140 Guisy,
Pas-de-Calais
tel +33 (0)3 21 81 00 31
fax +33 (0)3 21 81 00 31
e-mail a.la.hotoire@wanadoo.fr
web perso.wanadoo.fr/a.la.hotoire/

La Gacogne

The excitement starts in the tower living room (1750): it is crammed with things, from armoured reminders of the Battle of Agincourt (1415) to hats, statues and teddy bears. You may be bowled over, you may hear the clanking of swords and see medieval knights passing – that's just your hosts on their way to re-enact a battle. Passionate about local history and tales of ghosts, archers and horses, they are also exceedingly generous hosts. The atmospheric bedrooms, dark-beamed, heavy-draped, are in an even older outbuilding with a log-fired dayroom. Huge theatrical fun, a wonderful place for a real change.

rooms	4: 3 doubles, 1 triple, all with shower & wc (1 behind curtain).
price	€50 for two.
meals	Restaurant 1km; choice 6-15km.
closed	Rarely.
directions	From St Omer D928 for Abbeville. At Ruisseauville left for Blangy-Tramecourt; at next x-roads, left for Tramecourt; house 100m along.

Patrick & Marie-José Fenet
La Gacogne,
62310 Azincourt,
Pas-de-Calais
tel +33 (0)3 21 04 45 61
fax +33 (0)3 21 04 45 61
e-mail fenetgeoffroy@aol.com

Les Cohettes

In calm countryside with neither cockerels nor dogs to alarm your early morning, here are a genuine, unpretentious hostess and house. It's fun too. There are garden games, *pétanque* tournaments in summer, informal wine-tastings, an outbuilding where you may cook. Bedrooms are colour coded; we preferred the fabrics and antiques of the three in the attic of this long low farmhouse (mind your head up there!). The new garden room is snug with its own little patio. Gina cares deeply that everyone should be happy, adores her guests and creates a really homely atmosphere. *Themed weekends.*

rooms	6: 3 doubles, 2 family rooms, 1 suite for 6.
price	€45-€48 for two.
meals	Dinner with wine €19.50, book ahead.
closed	Rarely.
directions	From Calais A26, exit 4 to Thérouanne; D341 to Auchy au Bois, 12km. Right at Le Vert Dragon restaurant. 1st left; 2nd house on right after church.

Gina Bulot
Les Cohettes,
62190 Auchy au Bois,
Pas-de-Calais

tel	+33 (0)3 21 02 09 47
fax	+33 (0)3 21 02 81 68
e-mail	temps-libre-evasion@wanadoo.fr
web	perso.wanadoo.fr/gina.lescohettes

Ferme de la Vallée

This is a real farm, so don't expect pretty-pretty – but Madame's welcome is top class. It was recommended by one of our readers who has been back many a time for the atmosphere... and the food. Furniture has been handed down or gleaned from careful perusal of local brocantes and is set off by impeccably French wallpaper. Good bedding, too. Small boys – and bigger ones – will love the 1950s table football. Or there's billiards and various other games to keep you occupied before supper, which will be delicious and probably all grown a stone's throw from the kitchen. A good, French place to stop.

rooms	3: 1 twin, 1 triple, 1 suite.
price	€42 for two.
meals	Dinner with wine €16, book ahead.
closed	Rarely.
directions	Exit Thérouanne from A26; then D341 for Arras; after 'Vert Dragon' r'bout, 1st on right.

Brigitte de Saint Laurent
Ferme de la Vallée,
62190 Auchy au Bois,
Pas-de-Calais

tel	+33 (0)3 21 25 80 09
fax	+33 (0)3 21 25 80 09
e-mail	brigitte.de-saint-laurent@wanadoo.fr
web	www.fermedelavallee

Le Loubarré

What an exciting building. The period of each piece shows on its face so you expect the elegantly coffered ceilings, the deeply carved woodwork, the vast Louis XIII dresser – but nothing prepares you for the '1830s-medieval' fireplace! In the converted stables, guest rooms are simple and modern, each with pretty fabrics, some old furniture, a neat shower room. Madame loves telling tales of the house and its contents, has a few goats in the quiet garden (a weekend racetrack in the valley, though), and will do anything for her guests. Both your hosts work constantly on their beloved house – good people.

rooms	5: 2 doubles, 3 twins.
price	€44 for two.
meals	Restaurants within walking distance; self-catering possible.
closed	Rarely.
directions	From St Pol sur Ternoise, D343 NW for Fruges. Just after entering Gauchin Verloingt, right Rue de Troisvaux; right Rue des Montifaux. House on right.

Marie-Christine & Philippe Vion
Le Loubarré,
62130 Gauchin Verloingt,
Pas-de-Calais
tel +33 (0)3 21 03 05 05
fax +33 (0)3 21 41 26 76
e-mail mcvion.loubarre@wanadoo.fr
web www.loubarre.com

3 rue de l'Église

Hugging the hollyhocks of its 'curate's garden', this low house behind the church is a charmer and Madame is shyly proud of it. With their air of family history, the bedrooms are a delightful mix of modern and old: spriggy wallpaper among the timbers, an unusual old desk in the ground-floor room, an amazing armchair/desk/bookcase on the red-carpeted salon/landing, a corner bed said to have belonged to Jules Verne, well-fitted bathrooms. The blithe florality up here contrasts with the quiet dimness downstairs where owls abound – stuffed, china, wooden, pictured – and Madame serves a generous, imaginative breakfast.

rooms	3: 2 doubles; 1 twin with separate shower.
price	€35 for two.
meals	Basic bar/restaurant 5km.
closed	Rarely.
directions	From Arras N25 towards Doullens. At Bac du Sud right on D66 to Gouy en Artois & Fosseux. House near church.

Geneviève Delacourt
3 rue de l'Église,
62810 Fosseux,
Pas-de-Calais
tel +33 (0)3 21 48 40 13
fax +33 (0)3 21 48 40 13

Château de Grand Rullecourt

An exceptional mix of place and people. After 12 years, this dynamic family, all eight of them, have almost finished rebuilding their monumental château and brightening their escutcheon while being publishers in Paris and brilliant socialites – fascinating people, phenomenal energy, natural hospitality that makes up for any residual damp or slight winter chill. Built in 1745, the château has striking grandeur: come play lord and lady in chandeliered, ancestored salons, discover an aristocratic bedroom with big windows and walk the rolling green parkland as if it were your own. Enter another world.

rooms	4 twins/doubles.
price	€90 for two.
meals	Two restaurants within 4km.
closed	Rarely.
directions	From Arras N39 for St Pol & Le Touquet 5km; left D339 to Avesnes le Comte; D75 for Doullens & Grand Rullecourt 4km. Château in village square; sign.

Patrice & Chantal de Saulieu
Château de Grand Rullecourt,
62810 Grand Rullecourt,
Pas-de-Calais
tel +33 (0)3 21 58 06 37
fax +33 (0)1 41 27 97 30
e-mail saulieu@routiers.com
web www.saulieu.com/chateau/

Château de Saulty

The re-lifted stately face looks finer than ever in its great park and apple orchards. Inside, it's a warm, embracing country house with a panelled breakfast room, a perfectly amazing, museum-worthy, multi-tiled gents cloakroom and, up the wide old stairs, delightful bedrooms, some very big, mostly done with fresh pine furniture and good strong colours on wooden floors with old fireplaces or mirrored armoires. Quiet and intelligent, Sylvie will make you feel deeply welcome in her redecorated rooms while serenely managing her young family.

rooms	5: 1 double, 2 triples, 2 suites for 4.
price	€50 for two; €75 for four.
meals	Choice of restaurants 5-9km.
closed	January.
directions	From Doullens N25 towards Arras 17km. In L'Arbret, 1st left to Saulty; follow signs.

Emmanuel & Sylvie Dalle
Château de Saulty,
62158 Saulty,
Pas-de-Calais
tel +33 (0)3 21 48 24 76
fax +33 (0)3 21 48 18 32
e-mail chateaudesaulty@nordnet.fr

Le Clos Grincourt

Madame is warmly relaxed and attentive, and is passionate about interior design: beautifully made curtains, gently matched papers and fabrics, old-fashioned touches (crochet, carving) and modern details in good bedrooms in the guests' quarters. Monsieur's domain, the lush sheltered garden going down to the little river, is splendid (swings for the children too) and the lime trees are a fitting backdrop to this imposing old manor built in soft grey stone. It originally belonged to the château next door and the drive is still flanked by a fine laurel hedge. Reassuringly, comfortingly French.

rooms	2: 1 double, 1 family suite, both with separate wc.
price	€49 for two.
meals	Choice of restaurants 4-7km.
closed	Rarely.
directions	From Arras, N39 for Le Touquet. After 6km under r'way bridge, 1st left along D56 to Duisans. House 1st on left.

Annie & Patrick Senlis
Le Clos Grincourt,
62161 Duisans,
Pas-de-Calais
tel +33 (0)3 21 48 68 33
fax +33 (0)3 21 48 68 33

17 rue Paul Verlaine

A lovely surprise as you turn into the big farmyard: the old house is as splendid as the 19th-century brewery across the road with its curious double swastika emblem, and the people are simple, warm and gentle. Their children have grown and flown, they no longer farm and visibly enjoy good company. The homely décor is without pretension, the attic bedrooms are basic but perfectly adequate with their roof windows, screened-off showers (one outside the room), old timbers and floorboards; the welcome is family-friendly. A good-value stopover or base for a day trip to fascinating old Arras.

rooms	5: 3 doubles, 1 twin, 1 quadruple, sharing 2 wcs.
price	€33 for two.
meals	Restaurants 5km.
closed	Christmas & New Year.
directions	From A26 exit 7 on N50 for Lille to Gavrelle then Fampoux; in village follow Chambres d'Hôtes signs; house on right.

Dominique & Marie-Thérèse Peugniez
17 rue Paul Verlaine,
62118 Fampoux,
Pas-de-Calais
tel +33 (0)3 21 55 00 90
fax +33 (0)3 21 55 00 90

La Maison de Champagne

After years as a school librarian, Madame has thrown herself into encouraging local tourism: a member of numerous associations – theatre, library, tourism – she loves taking guests on walks and visits; Monsieur is mayor of the village. Many people drive straight through this area – take the chance to know it better with people who belong. You enter through the conservatory and every window looks onto flowers and meadows beyond. One room has doors to the garden, the other is upstairs, simple but welcoming. Children love it here – farm trips are possible – and you will enjoy some genuine French cooking.

rooms	2: 1 double with separate wc; 1 family suite.
price	€40 for two.
meals	Dinner with wine €20, book ahead.
closed	Rarely.
directions	From Calais A26, exit 6, on N41 for Bruay La Buissière, Le Touquet. In Divion D341 left to Houdain; right D86 to Magnicourt en Comté. Follow signs 'Mairie, École'.

Jacqueline Guillemant
La Maison de Champagne,
62127 Magnicourt en Comté,
Pas-de-Calais
tel +33 (0)3 21 41 51 00
fax +33 (0)3 21 04 79 76
e-mail Jguillemant@hotmail.com
web www.lamaisondecampagne.com

Ferme du Moulin

Terraced houses in front, a perfect little farmyard behind, the friendliest of hosts within – it's a privilege to meet such splendid human beings, retired farmers of old-fashioned simple good manners, he silently earthy, tending his garden, she comfortably maternal, delighting in her freedom to indulge her wanderlust at last. Their pretty, old-fashioned French farmers' house is stuffed with collections of bric-à-brac; their genuine *chambres d'hôtes* are family-furnished, floral-papered, draped with all sorts and conditions of crochet. Home-cooking is delicious and you are perfectly placed for those battlefields.

rooms	2: 1 double, 1 triple, each with shower & separate bath, sharing wc.
price	€35 for two.
meals	Dinner with wine €13, book ahead.
closed	Rarely.
directions	A26 from Calais, exit Aix-Noulette for Liévin. Head for 'centre ville'; for Givenchy. House 300m past little park.

M & Mme François Dupont
Ferme du Moulin,
62800 Liévin,
Pas-de-Calais
tel +33 (0)3 21 44 65 91

59 rue Faidherbe

Chantal's feminine touch colours the whole of this bright little modern town house: the snug and pleasing bedrooms are cosily furnished, florally papered, fitted with carpet or parquet and there's a little guest kitchen. The big uncluttered living room – plain white or brick walls, plants, mementos – has a fine window onto a little flower-filled garden where you can relax with the birds by the fountain after exploring the treasures of Lille. Chantal, bright, energetic and typically French, speaks perfect English. Yves has good English too and may breakfast with you – they both enjoy having an open house and it shows.

rooms	3: 2 doubles, 1 twin.
price	€40-€50 for two. Minimum stay 2 nights.
meals	Restaurants within walking distance.
closed	Rarely.
directions	From Calais & Dunkerque A25 for Lille exit 4 1.5km; right at lights to Wattignies; straight on 3km; left for C.R.E.P.S/village centre; pass church on left, house on right.

Yves & Chantal Le Bot
59 rue Faidherbe,
59139 Wattignies,
Nord
tel +33 (0)3 20 60 24 51
e-mail lebot.yves@wanadoo.fr

Ferme de la Noyelle

The 17th-century archway leads into a typical enclosed farmyard where you feel sheltered and welcomed. Guest rooms in the old stables – the standard conversion job includes a kitchen – are in simple cottagey style with careful colour matches and remarkably wide showers. Another wing houses the Pollets' new venture, a little country restaurant open at weekends; on weekdays, enjoy nourishing Flemish specialities at their family table. These attentive dairy farmers love having guests, including children (they have three of their own) and serve a heart-warming breakfast. Ideal for families, real value.

rooms	4: 1 double, 1 twin, 1 triple, 1 family room.
price	€41 for two.
meals	Dinner with wine €14, book ahead.
closed	Rarely.
directions	From A1 for Lille onto A22 for Valenciennes exit 'Cité Scientifique' for Cysoing. In Sainghin follow Chambres d'Hôtes signs.

Dominique & Nelly Pollet
Ferme de la Noyelle,
59262 Sainghin en Mélantois,
Nord
tel +33 (0)3 20 41 29 82
fax +33 (0)3 20 79 06 99
e-mail dominique-nelly.pollet@wanadoo.fr
web perso.wanadoo.fr/dpollet

28 rue des Hannetons

Jeanine Hulin's townhouse reflects her warm, colourful, informal personality and painter's eye. Bright kitchen, snug salon and flowering conservatory – step by step towards the little garden – show masterly use of colour; old tiles, stripped pine doors, masses of plants add atmosphere. Sprightly and dynamic, she adores receiving guests and is a mine of tips for antique and brocante trawlers. Bedrooms are interestingly unsmart: matching sleigh bed, wardrobe and desk, antique bed linen and mirrors, claw-footed bath downstairs for the double (bathrobes supplied). *Will collect from railway station.*

rooms	2: 1 double with separate bath downstairs, 1 twin with shower, both sharing wc on floor below.
price	€48 for two.
meals	Choice of restaurants in town.
closed	15 July-end of first week of September.
directions	From A1 exit 20 on D917 for Fâches Ronchin & Lille for 4km. At lights (Boulangerie Paul on corner) left; 200m, 1st right is Rue des Hannetons.

Jeanine Hulin
28 rue des Hannetons,
59000 Lille,
Nord
tel +33 (0)3 20 53 46 12
fax +33 (0)3 20 53 46 12
e-mail janinehulin@wanadoo.fr

Map 2 Entry 37

Château de Courcelette

From a small-town back street you enter unexpected 18th-century elegance – pilasters, panelling, marble, medallions – then cross a beautiful brick and cobble terrace into an acre of superb walled garden: bliss on the doorstep of Lille and the oldest château left standing in the area. Your hosts will enchant you with their courtesy and deep love for Courcelette, their energy in preserving its classical forms, their care for your comfort; Madame bubbles and chats, Monsieur charms quietly. Pale bedrooms with original doors and handsome antiques set the tone for this quietly luxurious and deeply civilised house.

rooms	4: 2 doubles, 1 twin/double, 1 suite for 4.
price	€82 for two.
meals	Dinner with wine €30, book ahead.
closed	1-20 August.
directions	A22 exit Roubaix Est. for Wattrelos; left at 2nd r'bout to Lys Lez Lannoy; after 100m left to Lannoy; at cross roads follow 'les orchidées'. Right into blind alley.

Famille Brame
Château de Courcelette,
59390 Lannoy,
Nord
tel +33 (0)3 20 75 45 67
fax +33 (0)3 20 75 45 67
e-mail contact@chateau-de-courcelette.com
web chateau-de-courcelette.com

Map 2 Entry 38

340 rue de la Gare

Helped by the innate character of the solid old house, Béatrice has applied her artist's talent to the interiors. Tempting ground-floor rooms brim with pictures, antique porcelains, original frieze and pieces handed down from previous generations; bedrooms sing with bright but gentle colours. All are light and harmonious with marble fireplaces, hand-painted furniture and big shower rooms. Roger is as relaxed and generous as his wife; their three teenagers are well-mannered, their dinners are based on real Flemish specialities. The garden is bustling-English-landscape style with formal touches.

rooms	4: 2 doubles, 2 triples.
price	€70 for two.
meals	Dinner with wine €25, book ahead.
closed	Rarely.
directions	From A25 exit 28 on N225 & A25 for Lille; exit 13 on D948 for Poperinghe; immed. right to Goderwaersveld; D139 to Boeschepe; house on left - just after windmill.

Roger & Béatrice Maerten
340 rue de la Gare,
59299 Boeschepe,
Nord
tel +33 (0)3 28 49 45 73
fax +33 (0)3 28 49 45 73
e-mail info@boeschepe.com
web www.boeschepe.com

La Bergerie

That simple face hides character and riches: a pink, beamed living room, marble floor, old fireplace and some good antiques; an overwhelmingly pretty breakfast room full of *objets trouvés* and plants; two smart, mostly pink bedrooms, one reached by a steep spiral outside stair, which can also be a suite: fine linen, good bathrooms, beams and views over the 12th-century church and the large lush garden. Your hosts are a touch French-formal yet terrifically friendly and interesting. Outside, a summer kitchen/diner, an avenue of poplars swishing, a pony grazing, bantams scuttling – what a picture!

rooms	2 doubles both with extra single beds.
price	€59 for two.
meals	Good restaurants 5km.
closed	Rarely.
directions	From Paris A16 exit 24 (25 from Calais); N1 for Montreuil 25km; in Vron left to Villers; right Rue de l'Église (opp. café); at end of road, left unpaved lane; house left up poplar tree avenue.

Pierre & Sabine
Singer de Wazières
La Bergerie,
80120 Villers sur Authie,
Somme
tel +33 (0)3 22 29 21 74
fax +33 (0)3 22 29 39 58
e-mail alabergerie@wanadoo.fr

Le Thurel

The open mansion and enclosed farmyard (horses welcome) announce gentle contrasts and that deceptively simple sobriety that turns every patch of colour, every rare object into a rich reward. The minimalist basics of your delightful artistic hosts are white, ivory, sand; floors are pine with ethnic rugs by big new beds; blue, ginger or red details shine out, the setting sun fills a round window, great-grandfather's Flemish oil paintings are perfect finishing touches. Drink in the white-panelled, open-hearthed, brown-leather sitting room, revel in the pale, uncluttered dining room, good food – and a games room.

rooms	4: 3 doubles, 1 suite for 4.
price	€85-€150 for two.
meals	Dinner €29, book ahead; wine €8-€35.
closed	1-15 January.
directions	From A16 exit 24 for Boulogne through Bernay en Ponthieu then 1st left; through Arry; 1km beyond, left to Le Thurel after great barn.

Claudine & Patrick
van Bree-Leclef
Le Thurel,
80120 Rue, Somme

tel	+33 (0)3 22 25 04 44
fax	+33 (0)3 22 25 79 69
e-mail	lethurel.relais@libertysurf.fr
web	www.lethurel.com

Map 2 Entry 41

Château des Alleux

An exquisite horn of plenty. The potager gives artichokes, asparagus, peaches and pears, the farmyard chickens, the fields lamb, the woods game... and Élisabeth makes her own cider. The château, in the family since the Revolution, was gutted by fire but is being properly restored... elegant guest rooms will soon be reached via a 16th-century tower. Rooms in the cottage are modern, low-ceilinged and softly lit; both have kitchenettes; the suite has sitting room and log fire. Dense trees protect from distant motorway hum; dinners and wines, shared in the château with your very engaging hosts, are a treat.

rooms	3: 2 doubles, 1 family suite.
price	€55-€65 for two.
meals	Dinner with wine €20, book ahead.
closed	Rarely.
directions	From Calais A16 for Abbeville onto A28 for Rouen 4km; exit Monts Caubert 3; right at Stop sign; D928 to Croisettes; right for Les Alleux not Béhen.f

René-François & Élisabeth
de Fontanges
Château des Alleux,
80870 Béhen,
Somme

tel	+33 (0)3 22 31 64 88
fax	+33 (0)3 22 31 64 88

Map 6 Entry 42

Château de Foucaucourt

A genuine northern château, but above all a family house. Madame, mother of four lovely-mannered children and lover of things outdoor – dogs, horses, gardening – reigns with energy and a refreshingly natural attitude: what matter if a little mud walks into the hall? In pleasing contrast is the beautifully atmospheric dining room with its vast table, family silver and chandeliers (and first-class food). Up the brilliant ginger-clothed staircase, the rooms may seem slightly worn: they are slowly being rejuvenated. Come for lively hospitality not smart château bedrooms, and a house to be shared.

rooms	4: 1 double, 1 suite for 4; 2 doubles sharing bath.
price	€54-€61 for two.
meals	Dinner €17, book ahead; wine €10.
closed	Rarely.
directions	From Abbeville N28 for Rouen. At St Maxent, D29 to Oisemont; D25 for Sénarpont. Sign on edge of Foucaucourt.

Mme Élisabeth de Rocquigny
Château de Foucaucourt,
80140 Oisemont,
Somme
tel +33 (0)3 22 25 12 58
fax +33 (0)3 22 25 15 58
e-mail chateau.defoucaucourt@wanadoo.fr
web www.chateaudefoucaucourt.com

3 rue d'Inval

It feels imposing, this very fine house with its extraordinary staircase, but you soon relax into the homely atmosphere created by your calm, hospitable, country hosts – the first in the Somme to open their house for B&B. Aart grows thousands of tulips and dahlias in serried ranks, honey, cider and calvados in superb vaulted cellars. Dorette was mayor for 24 years. Her big uncluttered bedrooms (smaller on the second floor) are comfortable, shower rooms big enough for a third bed, views peaceful, the panelled dining room a proper setting for a good breakfast. A great place to stay, with fishing on the lake.

rooms	4: 1 double; 3 triples, all with shower & basin, sharing wc.
price	€40-€45 for two; €60 for three.
meals	BBQ & guest kitchen available; good restaurants 12km.
closed	Rarely.
directions	From Abbeville A28 for Rouen, 28km, exit 5; left at Bouttencourt D1015 to Sénarpont; D211 for Le Mazis, 4.5km; follow Chambres d'Hôtes signs.

Dorette & Aart Onder de Linden
3 rue d'Inval,
80430 Le Mazis,
Somme
tel +33 (0)3 22 25 90 88
fax +33 (0)3 22 25 76 04
e-mail onderdelinden@wanadoo.fr

1 rue de l'Église

The garden and ancient farmhouse here glow from the loving attention they receive: Françoise 'learned gardens' in England and has made a timbered shrubby delight of the sloping site, Francis loves working with wood and his respectful creativity shines through the gable-end windows. Their lovely big sitting room with its vast fireplace may be your first stop, then up the steep and narrow stairs to pretty white rooms, not huge but uncluttered, fresh and timbered, with floral quilts and compact bathrooms; one wraps itself round a vast chimney breast. A place of friendly peace with an Érard grand piano in the hall.

rooms	3: 1 triple, 2 family rooms.
price	€46-€48 for two. Triple €54. Family room €60.
meals	Restaurant 6km.
closed	Rarely.
directions	From A16 exit 18 to Quévauvillers; right on D38 & D51 through Bussy lès Poix. Last house on left.

Francis & Françoise Guérin
1 rue de l'Église,
80290 Bussy lès Poix,
Somme
tel +33 (0)3 22 90 06 73
e-mail guerin.francis@free.fr

26 rue Principale

This enclosed paradise is made yet more heavenly by its gentle, poised, artistic creator's eye for detail: exquisitely framed prints, pretty cushions, antique kilims, choice bantams among perfect flower beds, an all-organic breakfast, both beautiful and good, in her lovely old beamed and gorgeously furnished house. Each bedroom has its own door from the garden. White all over with pools of colour in *Jouy* bed hangings, rugs, old oils and dark polished antiques, the double has a stunning antique-fitted bathroom; the suite is another delight, its sporty blue and white twin leading to a caressingly soft yellow double.

rooms	2: 1 double, 1 suite for 4.
price	€50-€65 for two. Suite €90 for four.
meals	Restaurant 5km; choice 8km.
closed	November-March.
directions	From Amiens, N29 for Poix; left on D162 to Creuse; signposted.

Mme Monique Lemaître
26 rue Principale,
80480 Creuse,
Somme
tel +33 (0)3 22 38 91 50
fax +33 (0)3 22 38 91 50

L'Herbe de Grâce

You will get a warm northern welcome. Once a social worker, Madame is at ease with all sorts and has the most infectious laugh. Monsieur, a big-hearted, genuine, chatty countryman, is good company too, though they don't breakfast with guests. Bedrooms, each with separate entrance and a sitting area, are furnished with panache, personality and all modernities including good kitchenettes and bathrooms. The big room under the rafters in the *grenier* is splendid; the other has a veranda onto the lush garden with its wrought-iron furniture, lily pond and hens scratching in a large pen behind the flowers.

rooms	2 triples, each with kitchenette.
price	€42-€48 for two.
meals	Many good restaurants in Amiens.
closed	November-April, except by arrangement.
directions	From Amiens for Conty on D210.N1 S to Hébécourt 8km. Opp. church follow 'Chambre d'Hôtes' signs to Plachy Buyon.

Mme Jacqueline Pillon
L'Herbe de Grâce,
80160 Plachy Buyon,
Somme
tel +33 (0)3 22 42 12 22
fax +33 (0)3 22 42 04 42

Les Aulnaies

The emphasis here is on country family hospitality and Madame, uncomplicated and several times a grandmother, gives guests a wonderful welcome. The rambling garden has stone love-seats and two ponds, swings and a playhouse – a paradise for children – while the old manor house has the feel of an adventure story. Your quarters are nicely independent beyond the hall and your living room leads down to the bedroom; there's plenty of space, a draped bed, and big square French pillows. Most of European history is at your doorstep, from Gothic Amiens to the battlefields of the First World War.

rooms	1 suite for 2-4.
price	€50 for two; €65 for four.
meals	Auberge 6km.
closed	December-March.
directions	From Amiens D929 for Albert. At Pont Noyelles, D115 left for Contay; signs in Bavelincourt.

M & Mme Noël Valengin
Les Aulnaies,
80260 Bavelincourt,
Somme
tel +33 (0)3 22 40 51 51
e-mail francois-xavier.valengin@wanadoo.fr

Château d'Omiécourt

On a working estate, Omiécourt is a proudly grand 19th-century château and elegant family house (the Thézys have four teenage children), with tall slender windows and some really old trees. Friendly if formal, communicative and smiling, your hosts have worked hugely to restore their inheritance and create gracious French château guest rooms, each with an ornate fireplace, each named and furnished for a different period and upholstered in *Jouy*. Fine workmanship shines through oak staircase and carved fireplaces, too. A house of goodwill where you will be very comfortable.

rooms	4: 2 doubles, 1 family room, 1 suite for 4.
price	€58 for two.
meals	Light supper €10-15, book ahead. Restaurants in Roye, 12km.
closed	Rarely.
directions	From A1 south for Paris; exit 13 onto N29 for St Quentin; in Villers-Carbonnel right at lights onto N17 for 9km to Miécourt; right in village, château on right.

Dominique & Véronique de Thézy
Château d'Omiécourt,
80320 Omiécourt,
Somme
tel +33 (0)3 22 83 01 75
fax +33 (0)3 22 83 09 56
e-mail thezy@terre-net.fr
web www.chateau-omiecourt.com

1 rue Génermont

A dazzling house whose hill-shaped roof becomes a timbered vault way above swathes of natural stone floor. The Picardy sky pours in and fills the vast minimally-furnished living space and your hostess shows pleasure at your amazement... then serves you superb food and intelligent conversation. Bedrooms are pure and peaceful: white walls, patches of colour, stone floors, excellent beds and design-conscious bathrooms, 1930s antiques and touches of fun. Civilised seclusion... and modern European history and the First World War battlefields at your door. *Gourmet weekends can be arranged.*

rooms	4: 2 twins, 1 family room, 1 suite for 4.
price	€48-€50 for two.
meals	Dinner with wine €20-€22, book ahead.
closed	Rarely.
directions	From A1 exit 13 on N29 for St Quentin; in Villers-Carbonnel, right at lights on N17 for 5km to Fresnes Mazancourt; house next to church.

Martine Warlop
1 rue Génermont,
80320 Fresnes Mazancourt,
Somme
tel +33 (0)3 22 85 49 49
fax +33 (0)3 22 85 49 59
e-mail martine.warlop@wanadoo.fr
web www.maison-warlop.com

3 rue de la Mare

Such gentle, kind, chatty folk who love tending their orchard and kitchen garden after a lifetime of farming in this picture-book pretty countryside where cows graze the fields and fruits fall from the trees. All is neat and spotless inside and out. Furniture and décor in various colours, textures and styles have been carefully chosen and placed. Classic French country guest rooms in the modern ground-floor extension have good repro pieces on honey-coloured parquet and immaculate crochet bedcovers. Monsieur is proud to have been a proper 'natural' farmer, Madame is the perfect country hostess.

rooms	2 doubles.
price	€42 for two.
meals	3 restaurants within 2km.
closed	Rarely.
directions	From Beauvais for Le Tréport to Troissereux; D133 to Songeons; D143 for Gournay en Bray. 1st village on leaving forest is Buicourt; house near church.

Eddy & Jacqueline Verhoeven
3 rue de la Mare,
60380 Buicourt,
Oise
tel +33 (0)3 44 82 31 15

Map 6 Entry 51

La Ferme du Colombier

In a typical big farmyard in a timber-old village stands a round dovecote. Tradition and roses cling to the place, guest rooms in the old bakery are made of space, simple furniture, an Indian cotton throw at each bedhead, magnificent roof timbers and sober carpets – plus two pretty breakfast rooms. Dinner with your active, quietly humorous hosts in their lovely open-plan farmhouse room is time to enjoy the simplicity, soak in the human warmth. There's masses to see in this ancient land – Gothic cathedrals, medieval villages, thriving markets: you may need a week.
20 minutes from Paris-Beauvais airport.

rooms	4: 2 doubles, 1 triple, 1 quadruple.
price	€40-€42 for two; €50 for three.
meals	Dinner with wine €14, book ahead.
closed	Rarely.
directions	From Beauvais N31 for Rouen. Leaving Beauvais follow to Savignies. Farm in village, 50m from church.

Annick & Jean-Claude Leturque
La Ferme du Colombier,
60650 Savignies, Oise
tel +33 (0)3 44 82 18 49
fax +33 (0)3 44 82 53 70
e-mail ferme.colombier@wanadoo.fr
web ferme.colombier.free.fr

Map 6 Entry 52

La Pointe

King of concrete in 1927, Auguste Perret added a piece of design history to a pretty 18th-century house: an immense living room of squares in squares – panels, shelving, tiles, table; above is the green and puce Perret-panelled bedroom with a flourish of columns, super 1930s furniture, terrace and vast view. Other rooms have lovely ethnic fabrics, much light, sophisticated bathrooms. Madame, who is Scottish, loves her house and enjoys sharing its delights. Monsieur is mad about horses; their pasture is part of the sweeping view. And the train can carry you straight from the village to Paris… and back again.

rooms	3: 1 double, 1 triple, 1 quadruple.
price	€55 for two.
meals	Dinner with wine €25, book ahead.
closed	Rarely.
directions	From Calais A16 exit 13 (Méru) for Chaumont en Vexin. In Loconville, left to Liancourt St Pierre; right to post office & follow left into Rue du Donjon (no through road); high gate on left.

Fiona & Luc Gallot
La Pointe,
60240 Liancourt St Pierre, Oise
tel +33 (0)3 44 49 32 08
fax +33 (0)3 44 49 32 08
e-mail lucgallot@aol.com
web www.la-pointe.com

Le Clos

The sprucest of farmhouses, whitewashed and Normandy-beamed, sits in the lushest, most secret of gardens, reached via a door in the wall. Inside, a remarkably fresh, open-plan and modernised interior, with a comfortable sitting room to share. Three bedrooms are in the old hayloft, one up, two down, all cosy-cottage fresh and prettily colourful. The fourth room, clean, neat, uncluttered, warm, is above the garage. Dine with your informative hosts by the old farm fireplace on *tarte aux pommes du jardin* – Monsieur loves to cook while Madame keeps you gentle company. A peaceful spot, close to Paris.

rooms	4: 1 double, 2 triples, 1 single.
price	€48 for two.
meals	Dinner with wine €23, book ahead.
closed	Rarely.
directions	From A16 exit 13 for Gisors & Chaumont en Vexin about 20km; after Fleury left to Fay les Étangs; 2nd left; house on left.

Philippe & Chantal Vermeire
Le Clos,
60240 Fay les Étangs,
Oise
tel +33 (0)3 44 49 92 38
fax +33 (0)3 44 49 92 38
e-mail philippe.vermeire@wanadoo.fr

Le Château de Fosseuse

Your window looks over the great landscaped park fading away to wooded hillside (with railway), beneath you is the soft grandeur of 16th-century brick. The grand staircase flounces up to big canopied glorious-viewed bedrooms that are château-worthy (one looks over the private lake) but not posh. The sweetest is the double over the library/breakfast room: open the panelling to find the secret stair. Your hosts are a fascinating, cultured marriage of exquisite French manners and Irish warmth who labour on to save their family home and genuinely enjoy sharing it and their insights into regional history with guests.

rooms	3: 2 doubles, 1 quadruple.
price	€72-€75 for two; €120 for four.
meals	Good choice of restaurants 2-10km.
closed	Rarely.
directions	From A16 exit 13 for Esches D923; in Fosseuse, château gate on right at traffic lights.

Shirley & Jean-Louis Marro
Le Château de Fosseuse,
60540 Fosseuse, Oise
tel +33 (0)3 44 08 47 66
fax +33 (0)3 44 08 47 66
e-mail infos@chateau-de-fosseuse.com
web www.chateau-de-fosseuse.com

Château de Saint Vincent

An enchantment for garden lovers who want real old château style but not plush bathrooms. Madame is still repairing her 200-year-old family home and garden, her great love – complete with stream and island – and a work of art. The house is elegantly well-worn, you breakfast in a darkly handsome room, sit in a totally French oak-panelled salon, sleep in 210cm-long antique sleigh beds. The second bedroom is simpler, and the washing arrangements, with continental bath, not American standard. But Madame's passion for house and garden will convince you. *Children over 10 welcome.*

rooms	2: 1 twin; 1 twin with basin & wc, sharing bath. Child's room available.
price	€100 for two.
meals	Good auberge 3km; Senlis 8km.
closed	15 October-15 May.
directions	From Senlis D330 for Borest & Nanteuil for 8km; right at cemetery; 1st right; across Place du Tissard towards big farm; left Rue de la Ferme; gates at bottom: No 1.

Hélène Merlotti
Château de Saint Vincent,
60300 Borest,
Oise
tel +33 (0)3 44 54 21 52
fax +33 (0)3 44 54 21 52

La Gaxottière

The high walls look daunting? Fear not, they protect a secret garden, a goldfish pond, lots of intriguing mementos and a merry laughing lady – a retired chemist who loves her dogs, travelling and contact with visitors. In the old house, the two mellow, beamed, fireplaced rooms are like drawing rooms with old pieces and exquisite fabrics (and kettle etc); the fine new suite is above. Madame lives in the brilliantly converted barn; all is harmony and warmth among the family antiques. Drink it all in with this great soul's talk of France and the world. Sleep in peace, wake to the dawn chorus and breakfast in the sunshine.

rooms	3: 1 double, 1 twin, 1 family suite.
price	€50-€55 for two.
meals	Restaurants 4-6km.
closed	Rarely, please book ahead.
directions	From A1 exit 10 for Compiègne, 4km. By caravan yard right at small turning for Jaux. 1st right to Varanval, over hill. House on right opp. château gates.

Françoise Gaxotte
La Gaxottière,
60880 Jaux Varanval,
Oise
tel +33 (0)3 44 83 22 41
fax +33 (0)3 44 83 22 41
e-mail lagaxottiere@tele2.fr

Ferme de Ressons

At Ressons, you enter the home of a dynamic, intelligent couple who, after a hard day's work running this big farm (Jean-Paul) or being an architect (Valérie) and tending three children, will ply you in apparently leisurely fashion with champagne, excellent dinner and vibrant conversation; they also hunt. The deeply-carved Henri III furniture is an admirable family heirloom; rooms are airy and colour-coordinated, beds are beautiful, views roll for miles and sharing facilities seems easy. Bring rod and permit and you can fish in the little lake. An elegant, sophisticated house of comfort and relaxed good manners.

rooms	5: 1 double, 1 twin, both with bath, sharing wc; 2 doubles, 1 twin, sharing bath & 2 wcs.
price	€46-€48 for two.
meals	Dinner €17, book ahead; wine €13, champagne €18.
closed	Rarely.
directions	From Fismes D967 for Fère en Tardenois & Château Thierry 4km. Don't go to Mont St Martin, on 800m beyond turning; white house on left.

Valérie & Jean-Paul Ferry
Ferme de Ressons,
02220 Mont St Martin,
Aisne
tel +33 (0)3 23 74 71 00
fax +33 (0)3 23 74 28 88

Domaine de Montaigu

This inviting 18th-century house has, in its vast 1950s extension, a living room heaving with furniture, fabric flowers, an overpowering stone fireplace, some exquisite collections and antiques. There are books, films, music for a relaxing evening with your delightful, gentlemanly hosts, Philippe retired from business, Christian from the army. Montaigu's periods are reflected in three antique-furnished, frilled and furbelowed rooms in pure French style, another done with the heavy wealth of the George V hotel, and *Colette*, an extraordinary 1950s collector's set of mirror-fronted furniture.

rooms	5: 4 doubles, 1 suite for 4.
price	€75-€85 for two.
meals	Restaurant 5km.
closed	Rarely
directions	From Paris north on A1; exit 9 to Compiegne; N31 for Soissons. 5km after Jauzy right onto D943 to Le Soulier (don't take 1st turning to Ambleny). Signposted to Domaine.

Philippe de Reyer
Domaine de Montaigu,
02290 Ambleny, Aisne

tel	+33 (0)3 23 74 06 62
fax	+33 (0)3 23 74 06 62
e-mail	info@domainedemontaigu.com
web	www.domainedemontaigu.com

Map 6 Entry 59

La Quincy

Longing to sleep a castle tower? This one is octagonal, in a delicious *troubadour* château, its wonderful great double room and child's room across the landing imaginatively set in the space – all airy and chintzily minimalist. The family have been here for five generations and are likely to remain, given your hosts' tribe of exquisitely-behaved children. Shrubs hug the feet of the château, the garden slips into meadow, summer breakfast and dinner (book ahead) are in the enchanting orangery. The old family home, faded and weary, timeless and romantic, is well loved and lived in by these delightful people.

rooms	1 suite for 3.
price	€55 for two.
meals	Dinner with good wine €18, book ahead.
closed	Rarely.
directions	From A26 exit 13 for Laon; Laon bypass for Soissons; N2 approx 15km; left D423; through Nanteuil for La Quincy; château on right outside village.

Jacques & Marie-Catherine Cornu-Langy
La Quincy,
02880 Nanteuil la Fosse, Aisne

tel	+33 (0)3 23 54 67 76
fax	+33 (0)3 23 54 72 63
e-mail	laquincy@caramail.com

Hello

Map 6 Entry 60

Le Clos

Authentic country hospitality and generosity are yours in the big old house. It's welcoming and warmly tatty with mix 'n' not-match wallpapers, funny old prints in bedrooms, comforting clutter in the living room by the old family furniture and grandfather clock. The energetic owners are great fun and love their dinner parties where Monsieur is MC and guests of all nations communicate as the wine flows. They wouldn't dream of changing a thing for the sake of modern sanitising fashions – may they prosper! The rooms are simple and good; one has a ship's shower room, all look onto green pastures.

rooms	4: 1 double, 1 twin, 2 suites for 4.
price	€35-€50 for two.
meals	Dinner with wine €20, book ahead. Restaurant in village.
closed	20 October-February, except by arrangement.
directions	From A26-E17 exit 13 on N2 for Laon; 2nd left to Athies sur Laon; D516 to Bruyères & M. 7km; left D967 for Fismes; Chérêt sign leaving Bruyères; house on left entering Chérêt.

Mme Monique Simonnot
Le Clos,
02860 Chérêt,
Aisne
tel +33 (0)3 23 24 80 64
e-mail leclos.cheret@club-internet.fr
web www.lecloscheret.com

La Commanderie

Up on the hill is a Templar hamlet and a millenium of history: an enclosed farmyard, a ruined medieval chapel that frames the sunrise, a magnificent tithe barn with leaping oak timbers – and this 30-year-old house. Marie-José, an unhurried grandmother of generous spirit, welcomes genuinely and cooks her own produce deliciously. Perfectly clean and equipped bedrooms are in plain farm style but open the window and you fall into heaven, the view soars away on all sides of the hill, even to Laon cathedral. Bathrooms are old-fashioned too and a converted old house on the hill has brought water scarcities.

rooms	3: 1 double, 1 family suite for 4, 1 family suite for 3.
price	€38-€41 for two.
meals	Dinner with wine €15, book ahead.
closed	Rarely.
directions	From Calais A26 for Reims, exit 12 to Pont à Bucy; 1st left to Nouvion & Catillon; D26 right for La Ferté Chevresis, 4km; small lane left up hill to Catillon. Drive through farm on left. Signposted.

José-Marie Carette
La Commanderie,
02270 Nouvion et Catillon,
Aisne
tel +33 (0)3 23 56 51 28
fax +33 (0)3 23 56 50 14
e-mail carette.jm@wanadoo.fr

photo Michael Busselle

champagne-ardenne

5 rue du Paradis

The Harlauts are great company, love entertaining and are keen to provide good value and, even though they produce their own marque of champagne and bottles are for sale, it is for the first-class food and the atmosphere that guests return. Dinner en famille is either in the dining room or on the terrace overlooking the garden. There are steep narrow stairs up to the warm, wood-floored, uncluttered guest rooms, two of which share a loo – a minor concern as everything is spotless and they make a good family suite. Great views over the plains of Reims, and you must try the champagne cakes.

rooms	3: 1 double, 1 suite for 2-4, 1 family room with kitchenette.
price	€44-€48 for two.
meals	Dinner with wine €23, book ahead.
closed	January & Easter.
directions	From A26 exit 15 (Reims La Neuvillette) onto N44 for Laon 2km; left to St Thierry; house in village.

Évelyne & Remi Harlaut
5 rue du Paradis,
51220 St Thierry, Marne

tel +33 (0)3 26 03 13 75
fax +33 (0)3 26 03 03 65
e-mail contact@champagne-harlaut.fr
web www.champagne-harlaut.fr

Champagne Ariston Fils

Independent champagne growers, the Aristons delight in showing guests round vineyards and cellars (tastings included). Indeed Madame, a wonderful person, started doing B&B for champagne buyers who did not want to leave after tasting! Through the flower-filled courtyard and up a private stair to lovely, light, airy, attic bedrooms with fresh white walls, beams, matching curtains and covers; one has its own kitchenette and the showers are excellent. Breakfast is served in the characterful old family house. A treat to be so near Reims.
Latest bookings taken at 7pm.

rooms	4: 3 doubles, 1 family room with kitchenette.
price	€48-€52 for two; €75 for three. Minimum stay 2 nights in family room.
meals	Choice of restaurants in Fismes, 11km.
closed	3rd week in August.
directions	From A4 exit 22 on N31 Fismes to Jonchery sur Vesle; left D28 to Savigny sur Ardres; right D386 to Crugny 3km; left D23 to Brouillet; house on right, sign.

Remi & Marie Ariston
Champagne Ariston Fils,
51170 Brouillet, Marne

tel +33 (0)3 26 97 43 46
fax +33 (0)3 26 97 49 34
e-mail contact@champagne-aristonfils.com
web www.champagne-aristonfils.com

Ferme du Grand Clos

A neat and utterly French-pretty place, the old family farmhouse, rebuilt in the 1920s after war destruction, has guest rooms and a deep terrace round the quiet courtyard. You can't hear the road, only the two running springs, so sleep till 11 if you like – that's the latest Nathalie serves fresh fruit juice and croissants in her country-furnished living room or on the terrace in summer. Each big, plain-walled, flower- or geometry-draped bedroom is blessed with a sitting area and all have shining modern shower rooms. With their three teenagers, the Lelarges are a delightful young family, welcoming, available and friendly.

rooms	4 suites for 3-4.
price	€50 for two; €75 for four.
meals	Restaurant in village.
closed	Rarely.
directions	From Reims D980 SW to Ville en Tardenois 20km; house in town centre opp. Crédit Agricole bank.

Nathalie & Éric Lelarge
Ferme du Grand Clos,
51170 Ville en Tardenois,
Marne
tel +33 (0)3 26 61 83 78
fax +33 (0)3 26 50 01 32

189 rue Ferdinand Moret

This courageous, endearing couple have flung their rich welcome out into the woods with five newly-redone cottage-cosy bedrooms on top of the lovely big room in their own house 2km away. Éric is a creative handyman, both are ardent trawlers of brocante stalls, the results are an exquisite personal mix of antique styles set against pastel paints, polished floorboards and gorgeously dressed beds. There's a handsome old-fitted kitchen/diner, too, in the house in the woods, plus piano, bar billiards and a big new garden. Sylvie and Éric bend over backwards to bring you delicious, fresh meals and their sparkling presence.

rooms	5: 1 double, with separate bath & wc; 2 doubles, 1 twin/double, 1 suite for 4 in separate house.
price	€53-€60 for two; €90-€95 for four.
meals	Choice of restaurants nearby.
closed	Rarely.
directions	From Épernay, Place de la République, D3 for Châlons; at Chouilly r'bout, right for Avize 500m; 1st right for Cramant.

Sylvie & Éric Charbonnier
189 rue Ferdinand Moret,
51530 Cramant,
Marne
tel +33 (0)3 26 57 95 34
e-mail eric-sylvie@wanadoo.fr
web www.ericsylvie.com

Le Vieux Cèdre

The façade and trees are grand, the interior is gorgeous – the huge, original-panelled dining room looks straight through its 'fireplace window' to a grassy slope – the atmosphere is hospitably informal, a mix of old and new, French and English, champagne and motor-biking. With flair and drive, Imogen has created brilliant bedrooms: two have space, light and luxurious sitting/bathrooms; the smaller has a richly canopied bed, an oriental air, a great claw-footed bath. She is a lively mother of two and an excellent cook; Didier makes the champagne and continues his fine restoration work.

rooms	3: 2 doubles, 1 twin.
price	€52 for two.
meals	Dinner with wine €28, book ahead.
closed	2 weeks in September & Christmas.
directions	From Calais A26 to Reims; N51 to Épernay; follow for Châlons en Champagne then to Avize; head for Lycée Viticole, house opp. lycée.

Imogen & Didier Pierson Whitaker
Le Vieux Cèdre,
51190 Avize, Marne
tel +33 (0)3 26 57 77 04
fax +33 (0)3 26 57 97 97
e-mail champagnepiersonwhitaker@club-internet.fr

La Madeleine

The quiet is so deep that the grandfather clock ticking inside – and the doves cooing in the trees outside – can seem deafening. A timeless feel wafts through the new house from that clock, the pretty, traditionally decorated bedrooms (sleigh beds and Louis Philippe furniture), the piano and a lovely old sideboard. Huguette and her husband, who runs the dairy farm, are generous hosts offering traditional unpretentious farmhouse hospitality; they take gîte guests, too. You can opt for champagne from their son-in-law's nearby vineyard, with a meal to match the quality of the wine and the welcome.

rooms	3: 2 doubles, 1 triple.
price	€45 for two.
meals	Dinner with wine €20, book ahead; champagne €30.
closed	Rarely.
directions	From Châlons en Champagne D933 to Bergères (29km); right D9 through Vertus; left, follow signs to La Madeleine 3km.

Huguette Charageat
La Madeleine,
51130 Vertus, Marne
tel +33 (0)3 26 52 11 29
fax +33 (0)3 26 59 22 09
e-mail charageat.la.madeleine@wanadoo.fr

Ferme de Bannay

Bannay bustles with hens, ducks, guinea fowl, turkeys, donkey, sheep, cows, goats… the chatter starts at 6am. Children love this working farm, and its higgledy-piggledy buildings too; school groups come to visit. The house brims with beams, the rooms dance in swags, flowers and antique bits; the piano swarms with candles and photographs and one bathroom is behind a curtain. Our readers have loved the house, the family and the food. Little English is spoken but the welcome is so exceptional, the generosity so genuine, that communication is easy. Superb outings in the area for all.

rooms	3: 2 doubles, 1 suite.
price	€46-€55 for two.
meals	Dinner with wine €26; with champagne €32; book ahead.
closed	Rarely.
directions	From Épernay D51 for Sézanne; at Baye, just before church, right D343; at Bannay right; farm before small bridge.

Muguette & Jean-Pierre Curfs
Ferme de Bannay,
51270 Bannay,
Marne
tel +33 (0)3 26 52 80 49
fax +33 (0)3 26 59 47 78

Ferme de Désiré

A strong, brave woman of character and hidden humour will welcome you to this majestic double-yarded 17th-century farm where she still grows 360 acres of cereals as well as providing real hospitality and good food. It is all simple and real. In the converted stables, guests have a living room with original mangers, log fire and kitchenette, then steep stairs up to two simply decorated, warmly carpeted, roof-lit rooms. You breakfast next to the kitchen but dine at the big old table in the family salon on home-grown vegetables, eggs, poultry and fruit. Fabulous walks to be had in the great Forêt du Gault nearby.

rooms	2: 1 double, 1 twin.
price	€42 for two.
meals	Dinner with wine €19, book ahead.
closed	Rarely.
directions	From Calais A26 to St Quentin; D1 to Montmirail; D373 for Sézanne, 7km. On leaving Le Gault left at silo; sign.

Famille Boutour
Ferme de Désiré,
51210 Le Gault Soigny, Marne
tel +33 (0)3 26 81 60 09
fax +33 (0)3 26 81 67 95
e-mail domaine_de_desire@yahoo.fr

5 rue St Bernard

Natural, unsophisticated country folk in deep rural France: Madame fun and an excellent cook (lots of organic and farm-grown ingredients); Monsieur a whizz on local history; both proud of their country heritage, wonderful with children, deeply committed to 'real B&B'. In a sleepy village, they chose this roadside house to retire to, did the guest rooms in brave youthful colours that perfectly set off the mix of old and new furniture on lino floors, fitted lovely linen, good mattresses, clean-cut bathrooms. Two rooms have their own ground-floor entrance, the third is upstairs in their 'wing'. All plain sailing.

rooms	3: 1 double, 1 suite for 4, 1 quadruple.
price	€37-€40 for two.
meals	Dinner with wine €15, book ahead.
closed	Rarely.
directions	From A4 exit Ste Menehould D982 (382 on some maps) to Givry en Argonne; left D54 to Les Charmontois (9km).

M & Mme Bernard Patizel
5 rue St Bernard,
51330 Les Charmontois, Marne
tel +33 (0)3 26 60 39 53
fax +33 (0)3 26 60 39 53
e-mail nicole.patizel@wanadoo.fr
web www.chez.com/patizel

Les Épeires

This was the château family's summer house for two centuries and has been their main house for one: Madame will show you the family books, lovely old furniture and mementos and tell you the stories (of Louis XIV's envoy to Peter the Great who was an ancestor...) in incredibly fast French. She does her own bookbinding, adores her rose garden – a jungle of perfume and petals – and has a couple of horses in the paddock; there are racehorses elsewhere. A blithe and extrovert soul, she serves delightful, ever-so-French dinners before a log fire, and offers you a simple bedroom as country-cosy as the old house.

rooms	1 triple.
price	€45 for two; €56 for three.
meals	Dinner with wine €20; champagne €26, book ahead.
closed	Rarely.
directions	A26 to junc. 22 (Troyes); N19 to Bar sur Aube; D384 to Ville sur Terre. Follow for Fuligny. House on long main street.

Nicole Georges-Fougerolle
Les Épeires,
10200 Fuligny,
Aube
tel +33 (0)3 25 92 77 11
fax +33 (0)3 25 92 77 11

Domaine du Moulin d'Eguebaude

The secluded old buildings house two owner families, a fish-tasting restaurant, several guest rooms and 50 tons of live fish – it's a fish farm! Fishers may gather on Sundays to catch trout in the spring water that feeds the ponds. Delicious breakfast and *table d'hôtes* are shared with your enthusiastic hosts, who created this place from an old mill 40 years ago; groups come for speciality lunches. Bedrooms under the eaves are compact, small-windowed, simply furnished, prettily decorated in rustic or granny style, the larger annexe rooms are more modern. Great fun for children, and good English spoken.

rooms	6: 2 doubles, 1 twin, 1 triple, 2 family rooms.
price	€60-€70 for two.
meals	Dinner with wine €20, book ahead.
closed	Rarely.
directions	From Paris A5 exit 19 on N60 to Estissac; right on to Rue Pierre Brossolette; mill at end of lane.

Édouard-Jean & Chantal Mesley
Domaine du Moulin d'Eguebaude,
10190 Estissac,
Aube
tel +33 (0)3 25 40 42 18
fax +33 (0)3 25 40 40 92
e-mail eguebaude@aol.com

Domaine de Boulancourt

This large and splendid farmhouse is irresistible. For fishermen there's a river, for bird-watchers a fine park full of wildlife (come for the cranes in spring or autumn); for architecture buffs, the half-timbered churches are among the "100 most beautiful attractions in France". Bedrooms are comfortable and attractive; afternoon tea is served in the elegant panelled salon; dinner, possibly home-raised boar or carp, is eaten communally or separately but not with your hosts, delightful as they are: they live in another wing and prefer to concentrate on their good *cuisine maison. Children over seven welcome.*

rooms	5: 2 doubles, 2 twins, 1 suite.
price	€53-€60 for two. Suite €92 for two.
meals	Dinner with wine €25, book ahead.
closed	Rarely.
directions	From Troyes D960 to Brienne; D400 for St Dizier; at Louze D182 to Longeville; D174 for Boulancourt; house on left at 1st crossroads, sign 'Le Désert'.

Philippe & Christine Viel-Cazal
Domaine de Boulancourt,
Longeville sur la Laines,
52220 Montier en Der,
Haute-Marne
tel +33 (0)3 25 04 60 18
fax +33 (0)3 25 04 60 18

Massin Perrette

While restoring the old house, the Poopes were enchanted to 'meet' the former owners in the shape of old photographs in the attic. These inspired the décor of each plush and classically French bedroom; Évelyne and Michel adore doing B&B, are natural hosts and do all they can to make you feel at home. Breakfast, served at separate tables, is deeply local: yogurt from the farm, honey from the village and Évelyne's jam; dinner in the pastel-panelled dining room is wonderful value. Michel is chief pastry-cook, lawn-mower and hedge-cutter; the garden, too, is impeccably tended.

rooms	5: 1 double, 1 twin, 2 triples, 1 suite for 4.
price	€50-€55 for two.
meals	Dinner with wine €15, book ahead.
closed	Christmas.
directions	From A31 exit 7 to north Langres; N19 for Vesoul for 40km. Right at Chambres d'Hôtes sign to Pressigny; just after pond on left.

Évelyne & Michel Poope
Massin Perrette,
52500 Pressigny,
Haute-Marne
tel +33 (0)3 25 88 80 50
fax +33 (0)3 25 88 80 49
e-mail e.m.poope@wanadoo.fr

Meals, booking and cancelling

Dinner

Do remember that table d'hôtes is a fixed-price set menu that has to be booked. Very few owners offer dinner every day. Once you have booked dinner, it is a question of common courtesy to turn up and partake of the meal prepared for you. Dining in can be a wonderful opportunity to experience both food and company in an authentic French family atmosphere. Or it may be more formal and still utterly French. Some owners no longer eat with their guests for family and waistline reasons.

Rooms

We have heard of chambres d'hôtes hopefuls arriving unannounced at 7pm and being devastated to learn that the house was full. For your own sake and your hosts', do ring ahead: if they can't have you, owners can usually suggest other places nearby. But arriving without warning at the end of the day is asking for disappointment.

Cancelling

As soon as you realise you are not going to take up a booking, even late in the day, please telephone immediately. The owners may still be able to let the room for that night and at least won't stay up wondering whether you've had an accident and when they can give up and go to bed.

By the same token, if you find you're going to arrive later than planned, let your hosts know so that they won't worry unnecessarily or… let your room to someone else.

photo Michael Busselle

lorraine–alsace–franche comté

Les Champs Grandmère

Utter country quiet, inside and out (no telly, many books), views sailing away to the Vosges hills behind, across Judith's lovely rose arbour, herb beds, rock garden and reed-ringed lake in front (fancy a swim with the trout?). She sells her own herb-scented soaps. The 1960s chalet, open-plan downstairs, carpeted up, is spotless throughout. Here, it's bed, breakfast and afternoon tea and cake… and apparently the cake is superb. Bedrooms have good repro furniture typical of the region and new beds. Breakfast can be French, German or English – you choose. Supremely peaceful house, place and person.

rooms	2 doubles, sharing bath & wc.
price	€53.50 for two.
meals	Good restaurant nearby.
closed	Rarely.
directions	From Strasbourg A352 & N420 to St Blaise la Roche 45km; right D424 14km to La Petite Raon; right after church for Moussey; 3rd left after café on to Rue Gen. Leclerc up steep hill; then left, left & left to house.

Judith Lott
Les Champs Grandmère,
88210 La Petite Raon,
Vosges
tel +33 (0)3 29 57 68 08
fax +33 (0)3 29 57 68 83
e-mail judelott@aol.com

Le Clos du Pausa

The lively, dynamic owners are justifiably proud of their deeply-adapted stables, built two centuries ago in local stone. Out with the horses, in with the big, plush guest rooms: the suite has its own telly and phone. They are all done with taste and quality, and there's a new sauna. Dinner is superb, a chance to sample some of the region's best dishes, course after course, wine after wine; Madame will join you for dessert and a chat. In the forest, an 'artist's path' to explore; in the garden, a golf practice area. An excellent stopover in a pretty, peaceful village between the ferries and Germany.

rooms	3: 2 triples, 1 suite.
price	€70-€90 for two.
meals	Dinner with wine €26, book ahead.
closed	Rarely.
directions	From Reims A4 exit 'Voie Sacrée' N35 for Bar le Duc; at Chaumont sur Aire D902 left to Longchamps sur Aire; D121 left to Thillombois; house next to château.

Lise Tanchon
Le Clos du Pausa,
55260 Thillombois,
Meuse
tel +33 (0)3 29 75 07 85
fax +33 (0)3 29 75 00 72
e-mail leclosdupausa@wanadoo.fr

Villa des Roses

Monsieur's seemingly endless restoration of these venerable buildings – one house 400, the other 300 years old – is finished, and very nicely too: fine woodwork, stylish furniture, an intriguing gas chandelier in the dining room, elegant terraces and a super garden with a children's play area. Madame is charmingly lively, her attractive rooms have goodnight chocolates, kettle kits, smallish shower rooms and lots of religion on view (bedside Bibles are French Catholic, not American Gideon). Hers is a genuine welcome.

rooms	4: 2 doubles, 1 twin, 1 family room.
price	€50-€75 for two.
meals	Restaurants 300m; self-catering possible.
closed	Rarely.
directions	From A4 exit Ste Menehould; N3 for Verdun-Chalons; sign in La Vignette, hamlet before Les Islettes; 1st building on left.

M & Mme Léopold Christiaens
Villa des Roses,
Les Islettes,
55120 Clermont en Argonne, Meuse
tel +33 (0)3 26 60 81 91
fax +33 (0)3 26 60 23 09
e-mail gites-christiaens@wanadoo.fr

Ferme de Haute-Rive

History weighs heavy in these ancient stones: the tower was part of the 13th-century defensive ring around Metz. It is now a typical farmhouse with 110 acres of cereal fields. Brigitte relishes her role as hostess, does it with great talent, makes friends easily and keeps goats, rabbits, a donkey and a dog. The bedrooms are in a separate building, filled with her paintings and beautiful hand-painted furniture. A handsome breakfast room with great beams, a wonderful family and a friendly peaceful village, despite the by-pass being built as discreetly as possible in a cutting on the other side of the river.

rooms	3: 1 double, 1 triple, 1 twin.
price	€55 for two.
meals	Restaurants 4km.
closed	November-March.
directions	From A31 exit 29 for Féy; right at junction; continue for Cuvry; farm on edge of village past Mairie; signposted.

Brigitte & Jean-François Morhain
Ferme de Haute-Rive,
57420 Cuvry,
Moselle
tel +33 (0)3 87 52 50 08
fax +33 (0)3 87 52 60 20
e-mail mbm21@wanadoo.fr

51 rue Lorraine

Alina came from Poland with a bundle of talents: a professional gardener, she paints, embroiders, decorates; Gérard, a retired French architect, has won a prize for his brilliant conversion of this dear little 200-year-old house; their skills and taste for contemporary and ethnic styles shine through the house, their thoughtful, artistic personalities enliven the dinner table, their environmentalist passion informs their lives. Expect superb vegetarian food if you ask for it (delicious meaty things too), pretty rooms with excellent beds and linen, a lovely garden and patio, relaxed and unpretentious intelligence.

rooms	2: 1 double, 1 triple.
price	€50-€52 for two.
meals	Dinner with wine €20 (meat or fish) or €17 (vegetarian), book ahead.
closed	Rarely.
directions	From Metz D3 NE for Bouzonville approx. 21km; right on D53a to Burtoncourt. On left in main street.

Alina & Gérard Cahen
51 rue Lorraine,
57220 Burtoncourt, Moselle

tel	+33 (0)3 87 35 72 65
fax	+33 (0)3 87 35 72 65
e-mail	ag.cahen@wanadoo.fr
web	www.perso.wanadoo.fr/burtoncourt/

Château d'Alteville

A solidly reassuring family château in a peaceful, privileged setting. Bedrooms are *vieille France*; not large, bar the twin, with the patina of long history in carved armoires, Voltaire armchairs, and the softness of bygone days in bedhead draperies, pastel fabrics and plush. Bathrooms are endearingly Fifties. The real style is in the utterly French many-chaired salon and the dining room – reached through halls and hunting trophies – with its huge square table. Here you may share elegant meals with your charming, entertaining hosts: he a mine of local history, she skilfully attentive to all. And always fresh flowers.

rooms	5: 4 doubles, 1 twin.
price	€68-€91 for two.
meals	Dinner €31-€38.50; wine €10, book ahead.
closed	15 October-15 April.
directions	From Nancy N74 for Sarreguemines & Château Salins. At Burthecourt x-roads D38 to Dieuze; D999 south 5km; left on D199F; right D199G to château.

Livier & Marie Barthélémy
Château d'Alteville,
57260 Dieuze,
Moselle

tel	+33 (0)3 87 86 92 40
fax	+33 (0)3 87 86 02 05
e-mail	chateau.alteville@caramail.com

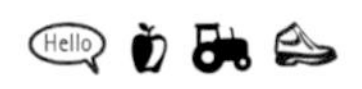

La Maison du Charron

In a separate house, these gentle-mannered people have converted stables and barns into neat little sleeping spaces, fitting showers ingeniously into corners, hanging pretty patchwork pieces, carving stairs, delicately painting the eaves – Monsieur's pride is his woodwork, it feels almost like a play house – with room for a couple of real ponies. The quiet courtyard has a garden walled off from the busy road. Breakfast, with fresh juice and a fine array of homemade jams and cake, is at the long table headed by Monsieur. English-speaking offspring are home after 8pm but please don't ring too late.

rooms	5: 3 doubles, 2 family rooms, all with shower (1 behind curtain) & wc.
price	€42-€51 for two.
meals	Restaurants Pfettisheim 2-3km; self-catering in family rooms.
closed	Rarely.
directions	From A4 exit 49; N63 for Vendenheim & Strasbourg; D64 for Lampertheim to Pfulgriesheim; right D31 to Pfettisheim. In village follow main road; signposted.

Marie-Célestine Gass
La Maison du Charron,
67370 Pfettisheim,
Bas-Rhin

tel	+33 (0)3 88 69 60 35
fax	+33 (0)3 88 69 85 45
e-mail	mdc67@free.fr
web	www.maisonducharron.com

Map 8 Entry 82

86 rue du Général de Gaulle

A real old Alsatian farmhouse in the wine-growing area where you can be in a bustling village street one minute and your own peaceful little world the next. It is on a fairly busy main road but bedrooms, in the separate guest wing, are at the back; they are simple, small, comfortable. Your friendly hosts retired from milk and wine production to enjoy having more time for guests. Marie-Claire still teaches German; Paul serves breakfast in the garden or in the dining room. A great place to know at the start of the Route des Vins: so close to gorgeous, expensive Strasbourg, it is great value.

rooms	3 doubles.
price	€33-€36 for two.
meals	Traditional restaurant 200m.
closed	Rarely.
directions	From Saverne A4, exit 45 onto N404 & N4 for Strasbourg, 16km. Farm in middle of Marlenheim on left, before post office.

Paul & Marie-Claire Goetz
86 rue du Général de Gaulle,
67520 Marlenheim,
Bas-Rhin

tel	+33 (0)3 88 87 52 94

Map 8 Entry 83

Maison Fleurie

Bubbling, friendly and generous, Doris has been receiving guests for years: she learnt the art at her mother's knee and will greet you with the warmest welcome. Her peaceful chalet is a real home, surrounded by breathtaking views of the mountains and forests. Both she and her husband are upholsterers so furnishings in the neat, traditional bedrooms are... perfect, strong colours giving depth to modernity. Guests have their own quarters, with a log fire in the breakfast room, tables laden with goodies in the morning – try the homemade organic fruit jams and Alsace cake – and geraniums cascading.

rooms	3: 2 doubles, 1 twin.
price	€48-€52 for two.
meals	Choice of restaurants nearby.
closed	Rarely.
directions	From Colmar A35 & N83 Sélestat (exit 17); N59 & D424 to Villé; D697 to Dieffenbach au Val. Careful: ask for exact address as two other Engels do B&B!

Doris Engel-Geiger
Maison Fleurie,
Dieffenbach au Val,
67220 Villé, Bas-Rhin
tel +33 (0)3 88 85 60 48
fax +33 (0)3 88 85 60 48
e-mail infos@lamaisonfleurie.com
web www.lamaisonfleurie.com

34 rue Maréchal Foch

At the centre of a working vineyard in gorgeous old Dambach is a typical, geranium-dripping Alsatian house, built by the first Ruhlmann wine-grower in 1688. Wine buffs enjoy visiting the wine cellar and non-drinkers can taste the sweet water springing from the Vosges hills. The charming rooms, in the guest wing under the sloping roof, have new carpets and old family furniture (there are two less exciting overflow rooms; in use, all share one wc); no sitting room, but a huge relic-filled guest dayroom: a wine press, a grape basket, a superb ceramic stove. Your friendly hostess speaks excellent English.

rooms	2 doubles, both with shower, sharing wc.
price	€40 for two.
meals	6 restaurants within walking distance.
closed	December-March.
directions	From Sélestat N on D35, 8km. House in village centre, about equidistant between town gates on main road.

Jean-Charles & Laurence Ruhlmann
34 rue Maréchal Foch,
67650 Dambach la Ville, Bas-Rhin
tel +33 (0)3 88 92 41 86
fax +33 (0)3 88 92 61 81
e-mail vins@ruhlmann-schutz.fr
web www.ruhlmann-schutz.fr

Le Montanjus

The house is a gallery for Madame's hand-painted stencils (she'll teach you if you like). She and her artistic daughter often paint quietly on the landing. The top-floor pine-clad sitting room is a delight – you feel you are in a boat; bedrooms are big and cosy, the suite in a separate building. Dinner with your hosts and possibly their grown children is a model of conviviality… and Madame should charge extra for her conversation! "Lucky is the traveller who stops here," said one reader. The garden leads out to forest, deer, red squirrels; nearby are golf, skiing and the *Ballons des Vosges* Regional Park.

rooms	3: 1 double, 1 suite, 1 suite for 4.
price	€52 for two. Suite €74 for four.
meals	Dinner with wine €21, book ahead.
closed	Rarely.
directions	From A36 exit 14 N83 for Mulhouse; in Les Errues left for Anjoutey & Étueffont; at r'bout right for Rougemont; left at 1st bend; house at end.

Astride & Daniel Elbert
Le Montanjus,
90170 Étueffont,
Territoire-de-Belfort

tel +33 (0)3 84 54 68 63
e-mail daniel.elbert@wanadoo.fr
web perso.wanadoo.fr/chambres-tourisme

Le Château

As part of its vast 100m2 suite, this château has one of the most extra-ordinary bathrooms this side of the Saône: panels hung with old engravings, a sunken bath and an Italian chandelier making an atmosphere of exceptionally elegant luxury; bedroom and sitting room are just as amazing. All this and a family feel. Antiques, attention to detail, a charming hostess with an easy laugh, make it a very special place. Dinner, carefully chosen to suit guests' tastes (if you want snails, you'll have to ask), is exquisitely presented on Gien porcelain, on the terrace in summer. Untouched 18th-century living.

rooms	1 suite for 3.
price	€68 for two.
meals	Dinner with wine €18; light supper €8; book ahead.
closed	September-mid-May.
directions	From A36 exit 3 D67 to Gray 35km; entering Gray right D474; fork left D13 to Beaujeu & Motey sur Saône; left to Mercey; signposted in village.

Bernadette Jantet
Le Château,
70130 Mercey sur Saône,
Territoire-de-Belfort

tel +33 (0)3 84 67 07 84

Les Egrignes

Refinement, loving care and high craftsmanship: you are welcomed to this house of exquisite taste by an inspired couple who have breathed new life into the lovely old stones and mouldings. Quiet Roland combs the auctions for fine rugs, old mirrors and modern paintings; bubbly Fabienne puts thick curtains, pretty desks, carved armoires and soft sofas in vast pale-walled bedrooms and deluxe bathrooms. He gardens his acres passionately (the half-wheel potager is breathtaking), she cooks brilliantly. Remarkable hosts, interior designers of much flair, they are fun and excellent company. Here is value indeed.

rooms	3: 1 double with 2 extra beds, 2 suites (2nd double in each is a sofabed).
price	€70 for two; €120 for four. Minimum stay 2 nights June-August.
meals	Dinner with wine €25, book ahead.
closed	Rarely.
directions	From Troyes A31 exit 6 Langres-Sud through Longeau; D67 through Gray for Besançon. Cult on right 21km after Gray; signposted in village.

Mme Fabienne Lego-Deiber
Les Egrignes,
70150 Cult,
Haute-Saône

tel	+33 (0)3 84 31 92 06
fax	+33 (0)3 84 31 92 06
e-mail	lesegrignes@wanadoo.fr
web	les-egrignes.com

Map 12 Entry 88

La Maison Royale

The gaunt exterior, part of the town's 15th-century fortress, imposes – but wait. Guy, novelist, traveller and collector, bought the two-metre-thick walls and built a house within them – his pride and joy. The huge ground-floor rooms, open to the public, are gorgeous; the breakfast room is suspended from the ceiling of the salon; bedrooms, all artistically marvellous, have luxy bathrooms and great views – it's like sleeping in a modern palace. It could be overwhelming but Guy and Lydie are such a super couple that it is, in fact, unforgettably moving. *Children over five welcome.*

rooms	6: 4 doubles, 1 twin, 1 triple.
price	€65-€70 for two.
meals	Restaurants 2 minutes' walk.
closed	Mid-October-mid-March.
directions	From A36 exit 2 onto D475 to Pesmes, 20km. House at top of village on left.

M & Mme Guy Hoyet
La Maison Royale,
70140 Pesmes,
Haute-Saône

tel	+33 (0)3 84 31 23 23
fax	+33 (0)3 84 31 23 23

Hello

Map 12 Entry 89

L'Arché au Logie

We were thrilled to hear from the owners of this astonishing house, for it has one of the most exquisitely crafted arched doorways in Europe, let alone France. The interlocking stones are unique to this old village and archeologists and historians will mind not one jot that the house has no roof, for there is much to please the eye and even more to satisfy the curious. Why the indented lintel and that miniscule, unfinished window opening? It appears to have been carved from the very rock - quite magnificient.

rooms: One 'space', with room enough for most of a body. Legs may have to be accommodated separately.
price: Contributions to upkeep welcome - bring a chisel.
meals: Many many restaurants within a hundred miles or so.
closed: Never - not for the last few millenia, at least.
directions: On arrival at Petits Murs, look out for a series of small walls... follow them to their intersection. Parking may invlove caves.

M. Le Grand Patron
L'Arché au Logie,
00000 Petits Murs,

tel: 0
fax: 0
e-mail: reception@beaucoup.bc
web: www.arche-au-logie.beaucoup.bc

Map 0 Entry 90

Rose Art

The gentlest, most generous couple live here with all the time in the world for you and a delightful art gallery in their vaulted basement: Madame embroiders but shows other artists' paintings and their son holds wine-tasting sessions. It's a fairly average old wine merchant's house but that welcome, the rooms under the roof, a lovely view of orchards and meadows, a brook to sing you to sleep after a fine meal, make it special. Plus a particularly pretty village full of old winemerchants' homes of character, a tempting garden with a playhouse for children, a piano anyone may play – or golf down the road.

rooms: 2: 1 twin, 1 suite for 4.
price: €45 for two.
meals: Dinner €12, book ahead; wine €10-€12 a bottle.
closed: Rarely.
directions: In Lons le Saunier for Chalon; right before SNCF station D117 for Macournay; D41 to Vernantois; left before houses & follow signs.

Monique & Michel Ryon
Rose Art,
39570 Vernantois,
Jura

tel: +33 (0)3 84 47 17 28
fax: +33 (0)3 84 47 17 28
e-mail: rose.art@wanadoo.fr

Map 12 Entry 91

photo Michael Busselle

burgundy

Le Tinailler d'Aléane

The lovely stones and cascading geraniums outside, the silk flowers, frilly lampshades and polished furniture inside have an old-world charm. The breakfast room is cosily stuffed with bric-à-brac, bedrooms are family-simple. Madame was a florist: she arranges her rooms as if they were bouquets, is always refreshing them and might put a paper heart on your pillow wishing you *bonne nuit*. She doesn't refuse children but may well be happier if you arrive with a little dog under your arm. She or her husband can do winery visits for non-French speakers. Ask for one of the larger rooms; the smallest feels cramped.

rooms	3 doubles.
price	€40-€48 for two.
meals	Choice of restaurants 3-5km.
closed	Sundays in winter.
directions	From A6-N79 exit La Roche Vineuse. Left to Charnay & Mâcon; after 500m left at r'bout for Sommeré (not into Roche Vineuse); up hill follow EH signs, house at top on left, bell by gate.

Éliane Heinen
Le Tinailler d'Aléane,
71960 La Roche Vineuse,
Saône-et-Loire
tel +33 (0)3 85 37 80 68
fax +33 (0)3 85 37 80 68

Map 12 Entry 92

Le Tinailler

Come backstage. Jean-Paul runs a theatre company with the local actor-winegrowers and he and Régine, a musician, combine their farmhouse B&B with a thriving summer theatre and permanent art gallery. Busy, artistic people who live in the main house, they create an atmosphere of relaxed energy, take their B&B seriously and offer attractive, cosy rooms in the converted tithe barn over the theatre and gallery: good beds, original beams, modern pale wood décor and, generously, Grand-père's excellent cubist paintings.
A friendly welcome at all times and theatrical novelty in June and July.

rooms	5: 4 doubles, 1 twin.
price	€50-€55 for two.
meals	Restaurants 6km.
closed	November-February.
directions	From A6 exit Tournus; D56 for Lugny. 3km after Chardonnay right on D463 & follow signs to Chambres d'Hôtes & Théâtre Champvent.

Régine & Jean-Paul Rullière
Le Tinailler,
71700 Chardonnay,
Saône-et-Loire
tel +33 (0)3 85 40 50 23
fax +33 (0)3 85 40 50 18

Map 12 Entry 93

Le Pré Ménot

Open-minded and wise after years abroad, a man of many parts and full of mirth who punctuates his phrases with a bemused chuckle and a puff of tobacco, Monsieur appears to read unspoken wishes – and cannot put enough out for breakfast. In deep wine-growing country, his traditional Mâconnais house, thrown open for conviviality, appears to wear typical French décor, then you notice the contemporary paintings, tapestries, pottery, antique African sculpture – fascinating. Bedrooms and bathrooms have the same heart-warming mix of ancient, modern and attention to detail. The church is a Romanesque jewel.

rooms	2 doubles.
price	€48 for two.
meals	Excellent restaurant nearby, 5km.
closed	Rarely.
directions	From Tournus D14 for Cormatin 12km; left D163 for Grévilly 200m; right to Grévilly; across T-junc.; house 100m on left, outside village, just below church.

Claude Depreay
Le Pré Ménot,
71700 Grévilly,
Saône-et-Loire
tel +33 (0)3 85 33 29 92
fax +33 (0)3 85 33 02 79

Château de Nobles

A place to die for – oceans of history behind it (a prehistoric *menhir* stands in the grounds) and charming owners bursting with more restoration ideas and passionate about it. Monsieur cultivates the vines and the wine: wine production started here in the 10th century. The bedrooms, in a renovated building near the main 13th-15th-century château, are fresh and unfussy in the stylish way so many are in France – the bigger one is a gem, with its superb beams, vast mezzanine, little veranda, huge new bath. Breakfast is in the château, a delightfully lived-in listed monument. Irresistible.

rooms	3: 1 double, 1 triple, 1 family room.
price	€76 for two.
meals	Restaurants within 5km.
closed	November-March.
directions	From Tournus D14 for Cormatin. Passing Brancion on right continue on main road for 1.5km. Towers opposite on bend.

Bertrand & Françoise de Cherisey
Château de Nobles,
71700 La Chapelle sous Brancion,
Saône-et-Loire
tel +33 (0)3 85 51 00 55
e-mail cheriseyb@free.fr

La Ferme

Children love it here: they can watch the goats being milked in the clean, enclosed farmyard, even help if they (and the nannies) like. There are horses too. Your hard-working hosts, with three children of their own and sensitive to the needs of families, have made a large family room at the top of the old stone farmhouse. Bathrobes are provided for grown-ups, so everyone feels cared for. All six rooms are sparkling and charmingly simple. People return, not only for the relaxing experience but also to stock up on the homemade cheeses, mouthwatering jams and local wines that the family make and sell.

rooms	6: 2 doubles sharing shower & wc; 2 twins; 2 family suites with kitchen.
price	€53-€60 for two.
meals	Self-catering in suites; restaurant nearby.
closed	Rarely.
directions	From Tournus D14 for Cluny. At Chapaize, D314 to Bissy sous Uxelles. House next to church.

Pascale & Dominique de La Bussière
La Ferme,
71460 Bissy sous Uxelles,
Saône-et-Loire
tel +33 (0)3 85 50 15 03
fax +33 (0)3 85 50 15 03
e-mail dominique.de-la-bussiere@wanadoo.fr
web www.m-fjsolutions.com/BB/

Abbaye de la Ferté

Immense grandeur with no trace of original Cistercian austerity: the abbot's palace is all that's left of the former abbey and you may glimpse the oversized staircase on your way to family breakfast in the 'small dining room'. Guests sleep in the highly original pigeon loft with its amazing round nest-holed bathroom or in the new and enchanting coach house suite done with old materials and tremendous flair. Both suites have log fires and tea trays, art books and a bottle of local wine. It's a short walk to breakfast where your young hosts, the easiest of people, make it all pleasingly eccentric and fun.

rooms	2: 1 suite for 4 sharing bath & wc; 1 suite for 2-4.
price	€61 for two; €95 for four.
meals	Dinner with wine €25, July-August, book ahead. Restaurant 6-8km.
closed	Rarely.
directions	From A6 exit Chalon south, N6 for Varrennes le Grand; D6 for Le Lac de Laives to La Ferté; at crossroads marked La Ferté, press intercom at large iron gates.

Jacques & Virginie Thenard
Abbaye de la Ferté,
71240 St Ambreuil,
Saône-et-Loire
tel +33 (0)3 85 44 17 96
fax +33 (0)3 85 44 17 96
e-mail abbayedelaferte@aol.com
web www.abbayeferte.com

Manoir du Clos de Vauvry

A fantastic ceramic stove as big as two men dominates the panelled breakfast room of this 17th-century royal hunting lodge. And summer breakfasts are on the terrace... The whole place has an air of exaggeration: over-generous stairs, ingenious double windows, highly voluptuous decoration, all totally French with floral wallpapers and embroidered bedcovers in magnificent bedrooms, 1930s tiled bathrooms (one whirlpool) and stained-glass panels. Marie knows everyone in wine growing and will help you all she can over another cigarette. And Burgundy has so much to offer, as well as superb wines.

rooms	3: 1 twin, 2 suites (1 for 4, 1 for 5).
price	€65-€76 for two. Suite €122-€140 for four.
meals	Dinner with wine €25, book ahead.
closed	Rarely.
directions	From Chalon sur Saône motorway exit 26, N80 for Montceau les Mines 9km; exit 31 on D981 for Givry; follow Complexe Sportif signs; 2nd on left.

Marie & Daniel Lacroix-Mollaret
Manoir du Clos de Vauvry,
71640 Givry Poncey,
Saône-et-Loire
tel +33 (0)3 85 44 40 83
fax +33 (0)3 85 44 40 83
e-mail daniel.mollaret@wanadoo.fr
web www.multimania.com/closdevauvry

La Griottière

That pale ochre stone warms this converted barn inside as well – exposed walls among the lime-washed plaster, a delicious bathroom alcove – giving the house an air of serenity. A few well-matched colours help: château grey, rich beige, various reds, all fresh and clean with soft quilts and draped bedheads but nothing riotous in the inviting rooms. Generous and jovial, Monsieur helps a wine-grower friend and willingly takes you wine-tasting. Madame quietly cares for her house and pretty stream-fed garden. Fontaines has a remarkable collection of 19th-century public washhouses.

rooms	2: 1 double, 1 twin/double.
price	€75-€89 for two.
meals	Dinner with wine €28, book ahead.
closed	Rarely
directions	From A6 Paris to Lyon exit Chalon sur Saône Nord; for Autun 5km to Fontaines; signposted.

Serge Doumenc
La Griottière,
71150 Fontaines,
Saône-et-Loire
tel +33 (0)3 85 91 48 47
e-mail lagriottiere@infonie.fr
web www.griottiere.com

La Messalière

Done with passion and panache, the variegated bedrooms – classic, mock medieval, Provençal, Jouy-romantic – in the venerable wine-grower's house (some of it 600 years old) are part of a full French experience. Your hostess, a friendly outgoing person who loves to chat with guests, used to have a dress shop: the old wedding-gowned models in some bedrooms and changing-room swing doors in the smallish bathrooms (one is low if you're tall) were part of this past life. She does it all herself and you will be intrigued by curios in the heavily-draped salon, tempted by genuine Burgundy dinners and candlelight.

rooms	4: 3 doubles, 1 suite for two.
price	€70-€130 for two.
meals	Dinner with wine €30, book ahead.
closed	November-March.
directions	From A6 for Autun exit Chalon N; at St Léger sur Dheune; 1st right in centre of village for Santenay & Chagny.

Mireille Marquet
La Messalière,
71510 St Léger sur Dheune,
Saône-et-Loire
tel +33 (0)3 85 45 35 75
fax +33 (0)3 85 45 40 96
e-mail reservations@saintlegersurdheune.com
web www.saintlegersurdheune.com

La Maison Chaudenay en Bourgogne

Bruce and Anne have settled with gusto, new fittings and French lessons into the ancient vibrations of 17th-century winepress, well-planned cellars, functioning bread oven and fantastic (horseless) stables that surround their gracious bourgeois house. It came complete with veranda, œils de bœuf, parquet and a superb garden. Bedrooms, pale and rich, cream and floral, have taste, antiques and modern bathrooms, the fine sitting room rejoices in a beautiful carved fireplace, deep sofas, books and a stock of games. Elegant restraint and enthusiasm near one of France's best restaurants.

rooms	5: 3 doubles, 1 twin, 1 suite for 4.
price	€88-€138 for two. Minimum stay 2 nights.
meals	Wide choice of restaurants nearby.
closed	December-January.
directions	From village centre for Demigny; past Mairie; after 200m traffic island; white gate on right, not signposted.

Anne & Bruce Leonard
La Maison Chaudenay en Bourgogne
71150 Chaudenay,
Saône-et-Loire
tel +33 (0)3 85 87 35 98
fax +33 (0)3 85 87 09 56
e-mail info@maisonchaudenay.com
web www.maisonchaudenay.com

La Marquise

The Perreaus are wonderful folk, full of joie de vivre, who may even greet you with a glass of something special. They breed cattle and horses and summer foals dance in the buttercup meadows – a lovely backdrop to the terrace and swimming pool. They also have a sideline in organic vegetables – Madame, who is a delight, loves her big potager, and you will love its fruits. You stay in the big loft of the old farmhouse where bright, finely furnished bedrooms share a large sitting room and a sweet little breakfast room. A tremendous place for enjoying the good things in life.

rooms	3: 2 doubles, 1 suite.
price	€50 for two.
meals	Dinner with wine €20, book ahead.
closed	Rarely.
directions	From Nevers D978 towards Château Chinon. 3km before Châtillon right on D10 for Alluy. In St Gratien left on C3 to La Marquise; 800m on right.

Huguette & Noël Perreau
La Marquise,
58340 St Gratien Savigny,
Nièvre
tel +33 (0)3 86 50 01 02
fax +33 (0)3 86 50 07 14
e-mail hcollot@aol.com
web perso.wanadoo.fr/la-marquise

Bouteuille

This modest, friendly couple clearly enjoy sharing their fine old 1690s house and its great park, dovecote and all; in sunflower season, it's surrounded by them for ever and beyond. Inside the immaculately restored house are a big antique-filled sitting room, a cheery breakfast room with antique plates and small tables, elegant bedrooms with interesting wallpaper and stupendously curtained bathrooms. Your hosts are happy to advise on châteaux, canalside walks, pony rides. And Monsieur is keen to flex his English-language muscles with any willing talkers – he has an impressive Burgundy accent!

rooms	3 doubles.
price	€52-€60 for two.
meals	Self-catering possible; restaurant 5km.
closed	Rarely.
directions	From Château Chinon D978 through Châtillon en Bazois for Nevers 4km (not to Alluy); after service station, right D112 for Bernière 1.5km; house on left.

Colette & André Lejault
Bouteuille,
58110 Alluy,
Nièvre
tel +33 (0)3 86 84 06 65
fax +33 (0)3 86 84 03 41
e-mail lejault.c@wanadoo.fr
web perso.wanadoo.fr/bouteuille

Hello

Fleury La Tour

The peace is palpable as the sun sets over sweeping garden and still lake. Next day, borrow the owners' small boat and row, fish, canoe or windsurf, there's a private beach you can swim from – perfect for children. Breakfast at the scrubbed farmhouse table includes home-grown honey; big, bright, unpretentious rooms have that inimitable French air of gilt-framed mirrors, round tables in modern bathrooms and French Rustic wallpaper. Your lovely hosts, she level-headed, he quietly cheerful, create a relaxed family atmosphere. Madame is learning English but her genuine welcome transcends any language barrier.

rooms	2: 1 double, 1 triple.
price	€43-€46 for two.
meals	Self-catering possible; restaurants 10km.
closed	Rarely.
directions	From Nevers D978 to Rouy; D132 to Tintury, right on D112 to Fleury (aka Fertrève); 1st right after village, up to lake, turn right; signposted.

Michel & Marie-France Guény
Fleury La Tour,
58110 Tintury, Nièvre
tel +33 (0)3 86 84 12 42
fax +33 (0)3 86 84 12 42
e-mail fleurylatour@wanadoo.fr
web perso.wanadoo.fr/fleurylatour

Domaine des Perrieres

Make the most of seasonal *produits de ferme* and traditional French food: the visitors' book is plump with praise. Madame the farmer's wife loves cooking (delectable patisserie and jams) and making folk feel at home. Wheat fields wave to the horizon, farm and cows are next door, this is deepest France. Inside, simple, straightforward rooms, green friezed walls, a bathroom in blue; all is airy and light, cheerful and double-glazed. No sitting room to share, but after a day on horses or bikes (the cross-country trails are inspiring) and a long, leisurely supper, most guests retire gratefully to bed.

rooms	2: 1 double, 1 twin.
price	€50 for two.
meals	Dinner with wine €15, book ahead.
closed	Rarely.
directions	From Clamecy D34. Right on D958 at Premery; 4km after St Reverier; signposted on left.

Pascale Cointe
Domaine des Perrieres,
58330 Les Perrières Crux-La-Ville, Nièvre
tel +33 (0)3 86 58 34 93
fax +33 (0)3 86 58 26 00
e-mail pascale.benoit.cointe@wanadoo.fr
web perso.wanadoo.fr/domainedesperrieres

Habitation Beauvilliers

You can do a day's canoeing on the Loire and disembark at the bottom of the garden for aperitifs and boules beneath the plane trees – classy. Your hosts leave you the run of their fine French garden – box hedges and central pond – and classically symmetrical house with its unusual double stairway. Casually elegant and a whizz at interiors, Madame came from Switzerland to study fine art and loves living here. Bedrooms are light and airy, one of them with a dreamy river view and a step-down bathroom disguised as a cupboard. Breakfast is in the super kitchen, decorated with printed teacloths.

rooms	3 suites.
price	€60-€75 for two.
meals	Dinner with wine €20, book ahead.
closed	Rarely.
directions	From Cosne sur Loire for Bourges; at r'bout in front of bridge take exit after exit for Bourges (do not cross river); on for 30m; right; on for 50m; left following river upwards; after 3km road turns to left; follow wall on right; gate on right.

Marianne & Daniel Perrier
Habitation Beauvilliers,
Port Aubry,
58200 Cosne sur Loire,
Nièvre
tel +33 (0)3 86 28 41 37
e-mail habitationbeauvilliers@hotmail.com

Chez Elvire

Language no obstacle, the Duchets are easy communicators and natural hosts. Their cottagey old farmhouse in the depths of Burgundy is full of character and space beneath its sweeping roof – exposed beams and old tiles are part of Monsieur's fine renovation job. Madame, who is Portuguese, is a charming hostess, keen to provide her guests with authentic country hospitality. Breakfast (homemade jams) and dinner are eaten with the family and Madame will make her national specialities if asked – a real treat. Rooms, traditionally decorated and comfortable, include a pleasant living room with books and games.

rooms	2: 1 double, 1 triple.
price	€50 for two; €63 for three.
meals	Dinner with wine €22, book ahead.
closed	November-Easter.
directions	From Cosne sur Loire, D114 towards St Loup; left on D114; Chauffour between St Loup & St Vérain; follow Musée de la Machine Agricole then Chambres d'Hôtes signs.

Elvire & René Duchet
Chez Elvire,
58200 St Loup,
Nièvre
tel +33 (0)3 86 26 20 22

14 avenue Charles Jaffelin

Bruno and Fabienne and their three children have recently taken over this former cooper's house just outside the ramparts of the old town. Peeping over high walls, it has two creeper-clad wings joined by a tower and your hosts are planning how to redecorate it while preserving its graciously cosy atmosphere. Relaxed and charming, they have lived abroad (Japan and America) and are sincerely happy to share their interests with other travellers. The pretty walled garden behind has a child-safe pool and it's a short walk to the centre of town and all its delights: Beaune is the 'crossroads of Europe'. *Japanese spoken.*

rooms	2: 1 double, 1 family suite for 4.
price	€100-€120 for two.
meals	Dinner €25, book ahead; wine list from €15.
closed	Rarely.
directions	On one-way road round ramparts of Beaune, exit for Auxerre (RN, not m'way); house on right after 200m, big white gates.

Fabienne & Bruno Guillemin
14 avenue Charles Jaffelin,
21200 Beaune,
Côte-d'Or
tel +33 (0)3 80 22 38 89
fax +33 (0)3 80 24 79 37
e-mail bruno.b-and-b-beaune.com
web www.bed-and-breakfast-beaune.com

Les Planchottes

If you find yourself in the Mecca of Wine, surely you should stay with a famous family of winegrowers like the Bouchards – and sip your aperitif in the courtyard looking out over the vineyards of the Côtes de Beaune. Then a private wine-tasting? Cécile can arrange it. Her newly refurbished townhouse looks rather 18th-century colonial from the outside; inside all is spotless but in no way sterile. The craftsmanship of the new oak and stone, the quiet good taste of the old white paint, the space in the comfortable bedrooms and the fittings in the bathrooms – they all beat most three-star hotels into a cocked hat.

rooms	2: 1 double, 1 twin.
price	€95 for two.
meals	Restaurants 100m.
closed	January-February.
directions	On one-way road round ramparts of Beaune, 200m after War Memorial, right at 2nd traffic light; Rue Sylvestre Chauvelot starts at Peugeot garage.

Christophe & Cécile Bouchard
Les Planchottes,
21200 Beaune,
Côte-d'Or
tel +33 (0)3 80 22 83 67
fax +33 (0)3 80 22 83 67
e-mail lesplanchottes@voila.fr
web lesplanchottes.free.fr

Les Hêtres Rouges

A pretty old Burgundian hunting lodge, 'Copper Beeches' stands in a walled garden full of centenarian trees and has an unexpected air of Provence inside: beautifully judged colour schemes (Madame paints and knows about colour), fine furniture, numerous *objets* and the odd sprig of flowers: soothing and reviving. Your hosts extend a warm, genuine yet ungushing welcome to the weary traveller – lots of towels, superb bed linen, breakfast that has the savour of yesteryear: yogurt, fresh bread and homemade jam. The guest cottage is a deliciously independent blue hideaway with a working fireplace.

rooms	3: 1 double, 2 twins.
price	€85-€173 for two.
meals	Wide choice of restaurants 10km.
closed	Rarely.
directions	From A31 exit 1 on D35 for Seurre 3km; right to Quincey then Antilly, 4km. House on right.

Jean-François & Christiane Bugnet
Les Hêtres Rouges,
21700 Argilly, Côte-d'Or
tel +33 (0)3 80 62 53 98
fax +33 (0)3 80 62 54 85
e-mail leshetresrouges2@wanadoo.fr
web www.leshetresrouges.com

Maison des Abeilles

Madame, a genuine Burgundian with family in all the surrounding villages, believes in simplicity, quality and conviviality, and is gradually renovating all her rooms in the 19th-century barn and adjacent workers' cottages. Each has an outside door, two are up an outside stair, bathrooms are snug, some with half baths, and the décor is getting brighter by the month: newly-whitewashed stone walls, fresh fabrics, wooden ceilings and floors, some bits of rustic rough plaster. Breakfast is at one big table in the broad open kitchen looking onto hollyhocks and a fig tree: super atmosphere, excellent value.

rooms	6: 3 doubles, 1 twin, 1 family suite for 4, 1 suite for 4.
price	€43-€46 for two.
meals	Dinner with wine €20, book ahead.
closed	Rarely.
directions	From A6 exit for Beaune St Nicholas; N74 for Dijon. In Serrigny left at Chemist for Magny les Vilier; in village, 1st left opposite you with blue windows. If you reach Marne you've gone too far!

Jocelyne Gaugey
Maison des Abeilles,
21700 Magny lès Villers,
Côte-d'Or
tel +33 (0)3 80 62 95 42
e-mail joel.gaugey@wanadoo.fr

Place de l'Église

Ancient rafters, white-swathed roof windows, little florals, and a beamy salon on the landing. The bedrooms, one with a ladder up to the simple children's mezzanine, are sweetly French-traditional, just like the wide rose-bordered terrace where breakfast is served on fine days. The Dufouleur wine is pretty good too – they are one of the old wine-growing families. This house stands on the remains of the Duke of Burgundy's 13th-century castle (he was Hugues de Quincey) and the little church is floodlit at night. Perfect for country- and wine-lovers. *Children over 12 welcome.*

rooms	3: 2 doubles, 1 triple; mezzanine for children.
price	€65 for two.
meals	Choice of restaurants 1-3km.
closed	Rarely.
directions	From A31 exit Nuits St Georges for Gerland-Seurre 3km; right to Quincey; house opposite church.

Chantal Dufouleur
Place de l'Église,
21700 Quincey,
Côte-d'Or
tel +33 (0)3 80 61 13 23
fax +33 (0)3 80 61 13 23
e-mail dufouleurchantal@wanadoo.fr
web perso.wanadoo.fr/gite.nuits-saint-georges/

La Monastille

Do pancakes or gingerbread for breakfast sound tempting? Traditionalists can stick to fresh bread and homemade jam. Supper might be *pot-au-feu*, with chicken from the farm next door, followed by cheese and a freshly-baked tart. Françoise will be happy to chat as she makes it, she is passionate about history, antiques and cooking and enjoys seeing her guests happy and relaxed. She is doing up La Monastille herself. It's old, built in 1750 as a wealthy farmhouse. Bedrooms are a soothing mix of muted walls, dark old furniture and crisp yellow and white, or perhaps flowery pink bed covers. Delightful.

rooms	4 doubles.
price	€60 for two.
meals	Dinner with wine €25, book ahead.
closed	Rarely.
directions	From Beaune D970 to Bligny sur Ouche; after village left to Êcutigny; right to Thomirey; house with terracotta flower pots by church.

Françoise Moine
La Monastille,
21360 Thomirey,
Côte-d'Or
tel +33 (0)3 80 20 00 80
fax +33 (0)3 80 20 00 80
e-mail moine.francoise@wanadoo.fr
web www.monastille.com

Hello

La Closerie de Gilly

The generous warmth of the green-shuttered façade reaches indoors, too, where a beautiful Alsatian ceramic stove stands beside huge plants in the sunny breakfast room and the guest rooms are airy and florally friezed. Interesting prints on the walls too. Your hosts are chatty and friendly. Monsieur teaches economics, Madame gave up a high-powered marketing job to care for two small children and the visitors she so enjoys receiving. The entrance to the fine gardens and house may seem narrow but don't get it wrong: you are very welcome and can always leave the car outside.

rooms	5: 1 triple, 1 twin, 2 doubles, 1 family suite, with kitchen corner.
price	€75-€85 for two.
meals	Restaurant 1km.
closed	Rarely.
directions	From A31 exit Nuits St Georges; N74 for Dijon; at Vougeot r'bout head for Gilly centre; 1st right after station.

André & Sandrine Lanaud
La Closerie de Gilly,
Gilly lès Cîteaux,
21640 Vougeot, Côte-d'Or

tel	+33 (0)3 80 62 87 74
fax	+33 (0)3 80 62 87 74
e-mail	informations@closerie-gilly.com
web	www.closerie-gilly.com

34 rue de Mazy

You cannot forget the lifeblood of Burgundy: wine buffs will love the twisting drive along the *Route des Vins* into the gravelled courtyard of this fine old wine-grower's house. Your courteous host knows a lot about wine and loves to practise his English, so sample an aperitif in his atmospheric stone-arched cellar; there are locally-pressed fruit juices too. The house has a classic stone staircase and generous windows, the comfortable and homely bedrooms are reached by outside steps, the breakfast room has flagstones and ochre-coloured walls. In summer, breakfast is in the well-kept, willow-draped garden.

rooms	3: 1 double, 1 twin, 1 family room.
price	€50-€56 for two.
meals	Excellent restaurant 300m.
closed	Rarely.
directions	From Lyon N on A6 exit Nuits St Georges; N74 for Dijon. After approx. 13km left to Marsannay.

Jean-Charles & Brigitte Viennet
34 rue de Mazy,
21160 Marsannay la Côte,
Côte-d'Or

tel	+33 (0)3 80 59 83 63
fax	+33 (0)3 80 59 83 28
e-mail	viennet.jean-charles@wanadoo.fr
web	perso.wanadoo.fr/gite.marsannay

Château de Beauregard

A brief history of France, 17th-century Beauregard was built on a medieval stronghold overlaying a fifth-century Gallo-Roman settlement – and owned by one of Napoleon's generals who left a couple of sphinxes. The delightful, sociable Bonorons have been restoring the grand old house, its roofs piled high with old tiles, and the beautiful, sadly neglected garden for 15 years. They're also passionate about local wine-growing. Rooms are superb: fairly floral, proper old-style France with copies of original colours and wallpapers, and the suite has a bath you could swim in. A splendid place.

rooms	4: 1 twin, 2 doubles, 1 suite.
price	€100-€130 for two.
meals	Restaurant nearby 5km.
closed	Rarely.
directions	From A6 exit at Bierre lès Semur; right for Précy sous Thil; D170 left for Dijon. At tile factory with large chimney right. Signposted.

Nicole Bonoron
Château de Beauregard,
21390 Nan sous Thil, Côte-d'Or
tel +33 (0)3 80 64 41 08
fax +33 (0)3 80 64 47 28
e-mail beauregard.chateau@wanadoo.fr
web perso.wanadoo.fr/beauregard.chateau

Villa le Clos

French country hospitality by the bucket, meals you will remember for ever (people copy Madame's recipes), a sun trap by the summer house for your own barbecue, stupendous valley views over historic Alésia where Caesar fought Vercingétorix in 52BC (brush up your Asterix), great walks, medieval villages and a modern house set among bright tulips, terraced features and birdsong. Inside, beyond the alpine mural, you find spotless rooms, good mattresses and bathrooms, a colourful chintzy décor – all endearingly French. But above all, you will remember these generous, honest and open people.

rooms	2: 1 double, 1 twin, both with curtained shower, sharing wc.
price	€45 for two.
meals	Dinner with wine €20, book ahead.
closed	November-Easter, except by arrangement.
directions	From Dijon N71 for Châtillon sur Seine; after Courceau D6 left & follow signs; house on D19A near junction with D6. (50km from Dijon.)

Claude & Huguette Gounand
Villa le Clos,
21150 Darcey, Côte-d'Or
tel +33 (0)3 80 96 23 20
fax +33 (0)3 80 96 23 20
e-mail claude.gounand@libertysurf.fr
web perso.wanadoo.fr/claude.gounand/

Manoir de Tarperon

Tarperon is uniquely French and an ageless charm breathes from the ancient turrets, fine antiques, paintings and prints. Soisick is modern and good fun, with her sense of humour and her unstuffy formality – if you can't find her, walk in and make yourself at home, she's not far. The rooms are full of family furniture in an uncontrived, fadedly elegant, lived-in décor; the bathrooms are family style, with lots of unusual bits. Dinner, superbly cooked by Claudine and Soisick, is a treat. Also: lovely gardens, fly-fishing (€25 a day), painting courses. *Whole house can be rented for weekend or week.*

rooms	5: 3 doubles, 1 twin, 1 suite for 3.
price	€62-65 for two; €82-90 for three. Minimum stay 2 nights.
meals	Dinner with wine €25, book ahead.
closed	2 November-March.
directions	From Dijon N71 for Châtillon sur Seine, 62km; D901 right for Aignay le Duc. Tarperon sign on D901.

Soisick de Champsavin
Manoir de Tarperon,
21510 Aignay le Duc,
Côte-d'Or
tel +33 (0)3 80 93 83 74
fax +33 (0)3 80 93 83 74
e-mail manoir.de.tarperon@wanadoo.fr

Rue Hoteaux

A master stone mason built this house in the 19th century and left many marks of his consummate skill in stairs and fireplaces as well as his quarry at the back where the Escots have made a sheltered flower-filled rock garden, Madame's passion. They are a relaxed, generous couple, she bubbly and proud of her many grandchildren, he shyer but a mine of information; both love having people to stay. In the converted barn, the big ground-floor stable room has a finely clothed bed, white slatted walls and good green wallpaper, or climb the lovely winding stairs to the pretty pink and beamed attic room.

rooms	2: 1 family room, 1 triple.
price	€75 for two; €90 for three.
meals	Restaurants 3-7km.
closed	16 November-April.
directions	From Montbard D980 for Chatillon; right in village of Puits. House on right next to large tree.

Gilberte & Jean Escot
Rue Hoteaux,
21400 Puits,
Côte-d'Or
tel +33 (0)3 80 93 14 83
e-mail gilbertemichel@free.fr
web chambrepuits.free.fr

Cabalus

Was it Cabalus that made Monsieur the character he is? Or has he made it? It's a case of perfect osmosis. Ancient and atmospheric, this old pilgrims' hospice stands in the shadow of the revered Basilica. A gallery of quietly intriguing, tempting objects and a much-loved coffee shop occupy the 12th-century vaulted hall but guests have that vast fireplace to themselves for breakfast. Rooms are simple, authentic, with good beds. Eccentric, Swiss and slightly shuffling, Monsieur Cabalus is the perfect gentleman with a fine sense of humour, Madame a most welcoming artist. An inimitable house.

rooms	4: 2 doubles; 2 doubles, both with shower, sharing wcs.
price	€75 for two.
meals	Dinner with wine €20, book ahead.
closed	Rarely.
directions	In Vézelay centre main street up to Basilica. Park, walk down main street, ring at 2nd door on right.

M Cabalus
Cabalus,
89450 Vézelay,
Yonne

tel +33 (0)3 86 33 20 66
fax +33 (0)3 86 33 38 03
e-mail contact@cabalus.com
web www.cabalus.com

Le Moulinot

The handsome millhouse, surrounded by herons, kingfishers and a rushing river, is reached via a narrow, private bridge. Wander the beautiful grounds or settle yourself in the most inviting sitting room, complete with roaring log fire when it's cold. Leigh and Cinda are charming hosts who delight in sharing their watery world. There's a canoe and a lake where Leigh has sunk a brilliant natural-looking swimming pool; and balloon flights can be arranged. The big, light bedrooms are freshly decorated with good bathrooms and the mill race is generally noisier than the road. Wonderful. *Children eight and over welcome.*

rooms	6: 5 doubles, 1 twin.
price	€55-€80 for two.
meals	Restaurants close by.
closed	Rarely.
directions	From Auxerre N6 for Avallon, 22km; just before Vermenton village sign, sharp right, double back & over bridge.

Leigh & Cinda Wootton
Le Moulinot,
89270 Vermenton,
Yonne

tel +33 (0)3 86 81 60 42
fax +33 (0)3 86 81 52 21
e-mail lemoulinot@aol.com
web www.moulinot.com

Le Calounier

These young owners have brought vitality to their handsome old house with a clever conversion that lets in stacks of light – perfect for exhibiting artists' work. Busy Corinne, full of plans, has created comfortable, colour coordinated bedrooms and good bathrooms; the suite, with inter-connecting rooms, has a sitting room downstairs. Meals are worth booking, there are courses for groups interested in traditional French cooking, and you may choose from Pascal's Yonne wines (not cheap!). A sail provides welcome shade in the pretty little garden. The village is tiny, the peace a balm.

rooms	4: 1 double, 1 twin, 1 family room, 1 suite for 4.
price	€58 for two.
meals	Dinner €23, book ahead; wine €13-€26.
closed	Rarely.
directions	From A6 exit Nitry for Tonnerre for 7km, right at x-roads sign Chambres d'Hôtes 1.5km; left for Môlay to Arton; house opposite 'lavoir' (wash hut).

Corinne & Pascal Collin
Le Calounier,
89310 Môlay,
Yonne

tel	+33 (0)3 86 82 67 81
fax	+33 (0)3 86 82 67 81
e-mail	info@lecalounier.fr
web	www.lecalounier.fr

Map 7 Entry 122

Le Moulin

Following their philosophy of life, this couple are creating the harmony and space for the communication they believe in: no TV, no rat race, just a mill race... that still generates power; they are proud to preserve this vestige of a vanishing era. Jean-Louis, an expansive reformed globetrotter, did the renovation himself, Marie-Pierre, an artist, decorated the interior to honour the light that rises from the water: big pale living room with lots of windows, bedrooms with pretty papers, stained glass, exposed stone and space. Spin off on bikes – explore! *Watch children with unfenced water.*

rooms	5: 1 double, 1 quaduple, 2 suites, 1 suite for 4-5.
price	€61-€130 for two.
meals	Restaurants nearby 2km.
closed	Rarely.
directions	From A6 exit 20 for Montbord; through Ancy le Franc; just before leaving village, right; house between bridge over river & bridge over canal.

Jean-Louis & Marie-Pierre Guiennot
Le Moulin,
89160 Ancy le Franc, Yonne

tel	+33 (0)3 86 75 02 65
fax	+33 (0)3 86 75 17 97
e-mail	info@moulin-ancy.com
web	www.moulin-ancy.com

Map 7 Entry 123

La Maison d'Aviler

On each floor, eight tall windows look down on the fine mature garden that shelters Aviler from noise. At the back is the Yonne where barges peacefully ply. The house was originally a workhouse – destitution in 18th-century France had its compensations. The Barrés were interior decorators by trade and collectors by instinct, so expect a riot of sumptuous colour in your bedroom and advice on the best local auctions. Monsieur will even help you bid – he's eager and good fun. Sens has a memorable cathedral, a tempting market, and the shops and restaurants of this lovely town simply yell 'quality'.

rooms	3: 2 doubles, 1 twin.
price	€66-€77 for two.
meals	Restaurants in Sens.
closed	Rarely.
directions	From A19 exit St Denis lès Sens; at river Yonne, follow road on right bank to No. 43.

Bernard Barré
La Maison d'Aviler,
89100 Sens,
Yonne

tel	+33 (0)3 86 95 49 25
e-mail	daviler@online.fr
web	www.daviler.online.fr

Map 6 Entry 124

Les Feuillles Volantes

Roof gardens are all the rage in Cuba; in fact there are gardens up the wall almost everywhere you look in Havana, and the city could feed itself therefrom, some suggest. The Cubans, too, are at it with vigour. Here in deepest Burgundy the idea has caught on and produced one of the most luxuriant versions of the technique anywhere, so effectively that the owners have gone to live elsewhere, driven out by the unexpected wildlife: woodpeckers and ants. But the house is a gem of stonework and simplicity, worth a detour – as Michelin would have it.

rooms	None – space can be cleared by guests with decent bivouac-building skills.
price	Free, but worth every cent.
meals	Vegetarian only, leaf-based. Best suited to sloths or other tree-dwellers.
closed	During overgrowth.
directions	Follow A77 to Nevers, then follow signs for Nulle Part until road becomes impassable due to leaf *débris*.

Mme Sylvi Culture
Les Feuillles Volantes,
Rue Branche, 111111 La Forêt, Aude

tel	01 01 01 01
fax	10 10 10 10
e-mail	sylvi@feuilles-volantes.not.fr
web	www.feuilles-volantes.not.fr

Map 0 Entry 124a

photo Quentin Craven

paris–île de france

Le Logis d'Arnières

Several centuries shaped this old hunting lodge, then it was determinedly 'modernised' in the 1920s Art Deco style: high-windowed, fully-panelled dining room with extraordinary dressers, fabulous bathroom fittings. It is exuberantly sober and shapely with Versailles parquet and fine fireplaces as well. Tae, from Chile, uses her perfect sense of style and colour to include these respected elements in her décor alongside richly baroque Chinese chairs and lots of South American pieces and paintings. Quiet spot, vast natural garden, joyous hosts, perfect for Chartres, Paris, Versailles.

rooms	2 suites for 5.
price	€70 for two; €100 for four.
meals	Good restaurant 200m.
closed	Rarely.
directions	From A10 exit 10 to toll gate, right after toll; right again on D27 to St Cyr; continue for Arpajon; first house on left.

Claude & Tae Dabasse
Le Logis d'Arnières,
91410 St Cyr sous Dourdan,
Essonne

tel +33 (0)1 64 59 14 89
fax +33 (0)1 64 59 07 46
e-mail taedabasse@aol.com

Map 6 Entry 125

Ferme de la Grange Rouge

Madame's delightful serenity must be fed by the natural air of farm life wafting in from the great wheat fields. Tractors come and go, the old horse grazes in the meadow, the children play in the sandpit, the dog dances in its pen. The Desforges have done an excellent barn conversion. You climb the steep stairs to the lofty raftered dayroom where breakfast is served (tea-making equipment, an old dresser, a comfortable sofa), and the simply pretty, good-size bedrooms. One is furnished with grandmother's richly-carved, if short-bedded, Breton bridal suite, one with grandfather's brass bed; wardrobes are old, mattresses new.

rooms	5: 3 doubles, 2 twins.
price	€40 for two.
meals	Choice of restaurants in Milly, 3km; picnic possible.
closed	Last two weeks in August & Mid-December-January.
directions	From A6 exit Cély en Bière for Milly La Forêt. At Milly, 1st r'bout for Étampes; next r'bout, for Gironville, right. Farm 2km on right.

Sophie & Jean-Charles Desforges
Ferme de la Grange Rouge,
91490 Milly la Forêt,
Essonne

tel +33 (0)1 64 98 94 21
fax +33 (0)1 64 98 77 68

Map 6 Entry 126

L'Atalante

Cocooned behind the garden walls and beneath the fruit trees, your ivy-hugged hideaway leads straight off the garden. The uncluttered, open-plan space is fresh and bright in its cool cream floors, nautical stripes and pale walls – bliss for a family. There's a curtain to divide it up if needed and a huge new shower. Stretch out on the flower-freckled lawn or curl up in front of the open fire. You can use the kitchenette if you want to be independent or simply cross the garden and join your relaxed, interesting and chatty hosts for dinner – they know about martial arts, among other things.

rooms	1 suite with double, single, sofabed and separate shower & wc.
price	€55 for two.
meals	Dinner with wine €20, book ahead.
closed	Rarely.
directions	From A5 exit 17 on D210 for Provins 2km; right D133 1km; left for Gardeloup. Left to Grand Buisson.

Florence & Georges Manulelis
L'Atalante,
77148 Laval en Brie,
Seine-et-Marne
mobile +33 (0)6 86 18 54 98
fax +33 (0)1 45 82 94 02
e-mail florence.manulelis@worldonline.fr
web latalante.free.fr

Ferme de Vert St-Père

Cereals and beets grow in wide fields and show-jumpers add a definite touch of elegance to the landscape. A generous farmyard surrounded by beautiful warm stone buildings encloses utter quiet and a genuine welcome from hosts and labradors alike, out here where Monsieur's family has come hunting for 200 years (his great-grandfather was a surgeon with Napoleon's army). Family furniture (the 1900s ensemble is most intriguing) in light-filled rooms, spotless mod cons and a vast sitting room for guests with piano and billiard table. Your hosts are excellent tour advisers who can direct you to little-known treasures.

rooms	1 + 2 apartments: 1 triple; 2 apartments for 4 with mini-kitchen.
price	€52 for two; €87 for four.
meals	Auberge in village (3 Michelin stars).
closed	Christmas week.
directions	From A5 exit 15 on N36 towards Meaux, 200m; 2nd right to Crisenoy after TGV bridge, through village for 'Tennis/Salle des Fêtes'; 1.5km to farm.

Philippe & Jeanne Mauban
Ferme de Vert St-Père,
77390 Crisenoy,
Seine-et-Marne
tel +33 (0)1 64 38 83 51
fax +33 (0)1 64 38 83 52
e-mail mauban.vert@wanadoo.fr
web vert.saint.pere.free.fr

Le Portail Bleu

The high blue doors open onto a pair of low stone buildings round a narrow courtyard, the apse of the medieval church can be peeped over the wall. The Laurents are friendly, easy-going, generous with ever a new project to hand (the marble bathroom is not their doing!). They have two children who adopt stray cats, keep miniature ponies and will do all they can to make your stay peaceful and fruitful. Flexible breakfasts are served in a bistro-like breakfast room, and bedrooms are 1930-style and inviting. Pleasing bric-a-brac, paintings and old lace at windows; one room has doors to the garden.

rooms	4: 1 triple, 1 suite for 4 with kitchen, 1 suite for 5, 1 suite for 6.
price	€56-€65 for two; €77 for three. Suites €97-€137.
meals	Restaurants 2km.
closed	Rarely.
directions	From A4 exit 13 to Villeneuve le Comte; right on D96 through Neufmoutiers to Châtres. House in village centre to left of church.

Dominique & Pierre Laurent
Le Portail Bleu,
77610 Châtres,
Seine-et-Marne

tel	+33 (0)1 64 25 84 94
fax	+33 (0)1 64 25 84 94
e-mail	leportailbleu@voila.fr
web	perso.wanadoo.fr/leportailbleu/

Map 6 Entry 129

Manoir de Beaumarchais

It's charmingly bourgeois, and the welcome is warmly French. The house is an architectural cuckoo: an 'Anglo-Norman' face concealing an unspoilt 1920s interior. Fascinating (great arched windows, crested tiles), elegant, comfortable, beautifully furnished. Views are of stretching pastures. Your suite is as untouched as the aqua-panelled salon: pretty, intimate and stylish, with a boudoir sitting room in the tower. Big breakfasts appear at the long dining table; in good English, your retired hosts enjoy telling the history of grandfather's hunting lodge (they still organise shoots).

rooms	1 suite.
price	€130 for two.
meals	Variety of restaurants nearby.
closed	Rarely.
directions	From A4 exit 13 to Villeneuve le C.; right D96 for Tournan; after Neufmoutiers, 1st left small road 1.5km; white gates on left.

Hubert & Francine Charpentier
Manoir de Beaumarchais,
77610 Les Chapelles Bourbon,
Seine-et-Marne

tel	+33 (0)1 64 07 11 08
fax	+33 (0)1 64 07 14 48
e-mail	hubert.charpentier@wanadoo.fr
web	www.le-manoir-de-beaumarchais.com

Map 6 Entry 130

Bellevue

The big informal garden merges into fields: don't worry about those new houses, there's green space for everyone. Space in the high-beamed dayroom too, and at the magnificent breakfast table made of ancient oak. Upstairs, the simple, softly-coloured rooms, each with two beds on a mezzanine, are ideal for families. A dash of colour adds character, and shower rooms are cleverly designed. The two temptingly independent lodges are quietly stylish, with antique mirrors, modern checks and terraces. Isabelle and Patrick have all the time in the world for their guests and speak English well.

rooms 5: 1 triple, 4 quadruples.
price €55-€74 for two; €70-€89 for three; €85-€104 for four.
meals Choice of restaurants 4km.
closed Rarely.
directions From A4 exit 13 to Villeneuve le Comte; follow signs to Neufmoutiers en Brie then Chambres d'Hôtes signs.

Isabelle & Patrick Galpin
Bellevue,
77610 Neufmoutiers en Brie,
Seine-et-Marne
tel +33 (0)1 64 07 11 05
fax +33 (0)1 64 07 19 27
e-mail bellevue@fr.st
web www.bellevue.fr.st

Map 6 Entry 131

Le Clos de la Rose

For birdwatchers and garden lovers (masses of roses, age-old trees), history vultures and cheese tasters (Brie on the doorstep, lovely Provins nearby), Jean-Paul's gorgeous green retreat from crazed Paris is cool, quiet, elegantly homely and has been restored with fine respect for an old flint house: limewash, wood, terracotta and a great collection of books, paintings, prints. He works from home and looks after guests with care and intelligence, Martine still works in town. Bedrooms have pretty colours and mixed-style furniture, a big new apartment is planned, the adorable cottage (with kitchen) is ideal for a longer stay.

rooms 1 + 2: 1 double; 1 apartment for 2, 1 cottage for 2.
price €67-€117 for two. Minimum stay 2 nights.
meals Good restaurant 5 mins by car.
closed Rarely.
directions From Paris A4 for Reims; exit 18 to La Ferté sous Jouarre; D407 for Montmirail; through woodland to Montapeine (6 km from r'bout in La Ferté); D68 for St Ouen; 1.8 km right; 400m to black gate.

Martine & Jean-Paul Krebs
Le Clos de la Rose,
L'Hermitière,
77750 St Cyr sur Morin,
Seine-et-Marne
tel +33 (0)1 60 44 81 04
fax +33 (0)1 60 24 40 84
e-mail infos@rosa-gallica.fr
web www.rosa-gallica.fr

Map 6 Entry 132

Châtelet district

You will be staying with a most civilised couple, she bubbly and interested, he quiet and studious, a university professor, in their very personal, gently refined apartment where original timbers, saved from the renovator's axe, divide the living room and two friendly cats proclaim the cosiness. It is beautifully done, like a warm soft nest, antique-furnished, lots of greenery, interesting art. Madame greatly enjoys her guests and is full of tips on Paris. The attractive, compact guest quarters down the corridor are nicely private with good storage space, pretty quilts and lots of light.

rooms	1 twin.
price	€80 for two. Minimum stay 2 nights.
meals	This is Paris!
closed	Summer holidays.
directions	Metro: Châtelet (1, 4, 7, 11) or Pont-Neuf (7) (between Louvre & Notre-Dame). Parking: Conforama car park, via Rue du Pont Neuf then Rue Boucher. Lift to 3rd floor.

Mme Mona Pierrot
75001 Paris
tel +33 (0)1 42 36 50 65

Latin Quarter

Quiet, a little shy, and most helpful, Madame sets tea in a silver pot before the roofs and domes of Paris: she treats her guests properly. The compact salon also houses two sofas, an upright piano and a collection of curiosities, well worth investigating, and some glorious sunsets. Bedrooms are simpler and perfectly comfortable with yet more interesting pictures and new beds. This is a trendy area with the colourful Rue Mouffetard for shopping, the Mosque for tea and hammam, the magnificent modern Institut du Monde Arabe for culture and the peaceful Jardin des Plantes for the Natural History Museum.

rooms	2: 1 double sharing bath; 1 triple with shower; both sharing wc.
price	€75-€83 for two; €98 for three. Minimum stay 2 nights.
meals	This is Paris!
closed	Rarely.
directions	Metro: Austerlitz (5, 10). Parking: Rue Censier. Lift to 8th floor.

Mme Lélia Cohen-Scali
75005 Paris
tel +33 ((0)1 43 36 51 62)
fax +33 ((0)1 45 87 94 16)
e-mail lelia1@noos.fr

Latin Quarter

Wildlife photographer and writer, lively, intense and intelligent, Nadine is good company. Sink into a soft purple sofa, look past shimmering green silk curtains to pale old stone and blue sky beyond and hear about Paris, aboriginal art (she has some) and her wide-ranging pursuit of endangered species. The small guest room, white with exotic touches like the rest of this delicious apartment, looks over a tiny courtyard where only the birds of the Jardin des Plantes are heard; the little shower room is perfect. The natural history museum, Sunday markets and venerable learning are all around – breathe deep.

rooms	1 double.
price	€100 for two.
meals	Dinner with wine €20, book ahead.
closed	August.
directions	Metro: Place Monge (7). Metro/RER: St Michel-Notre Dame. Parking: Place Monge. Lift to 3rd floor.

Nadine Saunier
75005 Paris
tel +33 (0)1 43 31 09 88
e-mail nadine@nungara.com
web www.nungara.com

Notre Dame district

At the end of the street are the river, the island and the glory of Notre Dame, her Gothic buttresses flying through centuries of history. In a grand old building, the unpretentious, tall-windowed rooms, separated by one flight of 17th-century stone staircase, look down to a little garden and peace. The low-mezzanined family room has a bathroom off the private landing where simple breakfast is served beside a spiral staircase. Madame is polyglot, active in the city, and eager to help when she can – she and her daughter enjoy guests and the variety of contact they bring. *House to rent in Provence.*

rooms	2: 1 double, 1 room for 2-4 with separate bathroom.
price	€75-€90 for two.
meals	Many restaurants nearby.
closed	Rarely.
directions	Metro: Maubert-Mutualité (10). RER/Metro: St Michel-Notre Dame. Book parking ahead.

Mme Brigitte Chatignoux
75005 Paris
tel +33 (0)1 43 25 27 20
e-mail brichati@hotmail.com

Hello

National Assembly/Invalides district

Classy dressed stone outside, intelligence, sobriety and style inside. Madame takes you into her vast, serene apartment: no modern gadgets or curly antiques, just a few good pieces, much space and light-flooded parquet floors. Beyond the dining room, the cosy guest room gives onto the big, silent, arcaded courtyard. Your hosts have lived all over the world; Monsieur, a retired engineer, spends his days studying. Madame, as quietl and genuine as her surroundings, enjoys renovating her old mill near Chartres and the company of like-minded visitors: worth getting to know, she makes tea in the afternoon.

rooms	1 twin/double.
price	€80 for two.
meals	Choice of restaurants within 5 minutes' walk; St Germain des Prés 10 minutes away.
closed	Rarely.
directions	Metro: Solférino (12), Assemblée Nationale (12) or Invalides (8). Parking: Invalides. Lift to 2nd floor.

Mme Élisabeth Marchal
75007 Paris
tel +33 (0)1 47 05 70 21/ (0)2 37 23 38 19

Map 6 Entry 137

Montparnasse district

Filled with books, paintings and objects from all over the world, the Monbrisons' intimate little flat is fascinating. Lively American Cynthia, an art-lover, and quintessentially French Christian, knowledgeable about history, wine and cattle-breeding, offer great hospitality and will take guests on special evening tours to historical landmarks. Their guest room, quiet, sunny, snug, has a king-size bed and its own bathroom. Twice a week, the street market brings the real food of France to your doorstep; shops, cafés and restaurants abound; you can walk to the Luxembourg Gardens. *Ask about their B&B in south-west France. Please call during European daylight hours.*

rooms	1 twin/double.
price	€79 for two.
meals	Occasionally, book ahead; varying prices.
closed	August.
directions	Metro: Edgar Quinet (6) or Montparnasse (4, 6, 12, 13). Airport buses from Orly & Charles de Gaulle to Montparnasse (5 minutes' walk).

Christian & Cynthia de Monbrison
75014 Paris
tel +33 (0)1 43 35 20 87

Map 6 Entry 138

Montparnasse district

A little white blue-shuttered house in a cobbled alley? Just behind Montparnasse? It's not a dream and Janine, a fascinating live-wire cinema journalist who has lived in Canada, will welcome you of an evening to her pretty wood-ceilinged kitchen/diner (she's a night bird so breakfast will be laid for you to do your own). The guest room across the book-lined hall is a good, square room with a highly pleasing mix of warm fabrics, honeycomb tiles, white walls, old chest and contemporary paintings. The new white and pine bathroom has space, all mod cons and good cupboards. Ideal. *German spoken.*

rooms	1 double.
price	€54 for two. Minimum stay 2 nights.
meals	This is Paris!
closed	July-September.
directions	Metro: Gaîté (13). RER: Denfert-Rochereau. Airport buses nearby. Bus: 28 58.

Janine Euvrard
75014 Paris
tel +33 (0)1 43 27 19 43
fax +33 (0)1 43 27 19 43
e-mail euvrard@club-internet.fr

Montparnasse-Luxembourg

Artily elegant, fascinatingly cosmopolitan, Maria happily shares her incredible light/dark flat. Light: the single with the Man Ray table or Maria's own double with wall hangings, view across the internal balcony and out to trees and skyscraper. Dark: the vast double-height salon bounded by two carved Renaissance doorways and matching monumental fireplace, leftovers from a film set, but genuine. Plus sculpted corbels, shades of Great Men, a vibrant blue dining room, masses of art and carpets, a highly personal mix of *objets* and a unique, zinging atmosphere. *Flat to rent on Normandy coast.*

rooms	1 double or 1 single.
price	€100 for two. Singles €65.
meals	Good restaurant down the street.
closed	June-August.
directions	Metro: Raspail (4, 6).

Maria Bilz
75014 Paris
tel +33 (0)1 43 20 22 82
fax +33 (0)2 31 88 83 89

Passy-Trocadero

A vivacious, well-travelled photographer, Anne has her eyrie up a small private stair in the upper-class peace of Passy where she lays breakfast for you in her pretty kitchen with the Eiffel Tower View. Your big room has sitting and sleeping sections, oriental draperies, family antiques and a window to the quiet white courtyard where pigeons (sorry, no eagles) may lay eggs in the oleander pot. In the sitting room, Anne's photographs and those of her late husband are superb illustrations to fascinating travellers tales, told in fluent English. *Also self-catering family house for rent near Poitiers. German & Italian spoken.*

rooms	1 suite sharing bath.
price	€85 for two.
meals	Plenty of restaurants within walking distance.
closed	Rarely.
directions	Metro: Rue de la Pompe (9). Bus: 63, 52. RER: Henri Martin.

Anne de Henning
11 rue de Siam,
75016 Paris
tel +33 (0)1 45 04 50 06
fax +33 (0)1 45 04 50 06
e-mail dehenni@club-internet.fr

Porte Champerret district

Touches of humour lift the great living space of this fine 1890s townhouse: a rustic oak cupboard on graceful parquet, a couple of amateur oils hung beneath nobly high ceilings. And the gorgeous rarity of a garden in Paris for summer breakfast with scrumptious things from the bakery. Pure minimalist bedrooms in restful white, beige and sand, finely subtle fabrics, good bedding, brand new bright white showers – and one loo for three rooms (you won't share with strangers). Your young hosts are intelligently attentive and anxious to please; their little girl brings freshness and light to the big house.

rooms	2: 1 double, 1 suite for 2-3, sharing separate wc.
price	€100 for two.
meals	Many restaurants in the area.
closed	Occasionally.
directions	Metro: Pereire (3). RER/Metro: Porte Champerret. Bus: 84 92 93.

Sophie & Damien Vandewynckele
75017 Paris
tel +33 (0)1 40 54 83 89

Montmartre

Wow! Gently and firmly, Hélène leads you from a little blue-shuttered courtyard to a superb modern kitchen/diner guarded by an eclectic collection of brocante and art, including her own, whence you fall into the pool then out into the terraced garden – a Parisian dream house. The three ground-floor bedrooms – one in the shrubbery, sweet and snug, the two suites, one formal, the other a great open loft – are superb; all have perfect shower rooms and simple, personal décor done with auction trophies. Hélène's lively talents – sculpture, breakfast, music, conversation – will inform your stay.

rooms	5: 2 doubles, 2 suites, 1 single.
price	€90-€120 for two. Singles €60-€80. Suite €130-€150 for three-four. Minimum stay 2 nights.
meals	Breakfast €8 p.p. Restaurants 10 minutes' walk.
closed	Rarely.
directions	Metro: Anvers Sacré Cœur (2); Château Rouge (4); Barbès Rochechouart (4, 2). Bus: 30, 54, 31, 85. Car park: Rue Feutrier.

Hélène Bignon
75018 Paris
fax +33 (0)1 42 55 95 16
e-mail helene-bignon@wanadoo.fr
web www.paris-oasis.com

Montmartre

In the 'village' of Montmartre – few cars, many birds – barrister Valérie and her architect husband have created a super studio room off their charming courtyard. It has space and height for a second double bed on a low-ceilinged 'balcony' over the master bed, both dressed in dramatic dark red against the white walls; the dining table is an oval antique, the kitchen space a little pine and steel gem, the shower generous, the mirror framed in red. Valérie's discreet decorative flourishes speak for her calm, positive personality and her interest in other lands. A delicious Paris hideaway you can call your own.

rooms	1 studio for 2-3 with kitchenette.
price	€90 for two per night; €540 per week. Minimum stay 2 nights.
meals	Breakfast not included. Self-catering possible. Restaurants nearby.
closed	Rarely.
directions	Metro: Anvers (2), Château Rouge (4). Metro/ RER: Gare du Nord. Bus: 30, 31, 54, 85. Car park: Rue Feutrier.

Valérie Zuber
14 rue André del Sarte,
75018 Paris
fax +33 (0)1 42 58 47 40
e-mail studiodamelie@wanadoo.fr
web www.paris-oasis.com

Belleville district

The street throbs with a motley, multicultural crowd but from the top of this clean modern block you can stretch your eyes across Paris to the scintillating towers of La Défense or the Parc de Belleville, a surprising green hillside above the city. Your pretty room lets in fabulous sunsets over the Eiffel Tower and no noise. The flat is all white walls, modern parquet floors and fine old family furniture, lots from Provence where your very proper elderly hostess used to live. Madame serves fresh pastries at breakfast and tells you all about everything with great verve.

rooms	1 double.
price	€69 for two. Minimum stay 2 nights.
meals	Wide choice of restaurants.
closed	Rarely.
directions	Metro: Belleville (2, 11) 200m: 15 mins to centre. Parking & directions: ask owners. Lift to 9th floor.

Danièle de La Brosse
75019 Paris
tel +33 (0)1 42 41 99 59
fax +33 (0)1 42 41 99 59
e-mail dan.delabrosse@tiscali.fr

Belleville district

Sabine, artist and art therapist, "feeds people with colours". Jules makes the organic bread with a dazzling smile and big, beautiful Taquin, his guide dog, loves people. Kindly and artistic, they live calmly in the bit of genuine old Paris between two tiny gardens and a tall house. The simple guest room, with good double bed and flame-covered sleigh-bed divan, a welcome tea-maker and an old-fashioned bathroom, shares a building with Sabine's studio. Healthfoody continental breakfast is in the cosy family room in the main house or outside under the birdsung tree. Such peace in Paris is rare.

rooms	1 triple.
price	€66 for two. Minimum stay 2 nights.
meals	Choice of restaurants within walking distance.
closed	July-August.
directions	Metro: Jourdain (11) or Place des Fêtes (11). Parking: Place des Fêtes. Bus: 26, 48, 60.

Sabine & Jules Aïm
75019 Paris
tel +33 (0)1 42 08 23 71
fax +33 (0)1 42 40 56 04
e-mail jules.aim@wanadoo.fr

10 rue Denfert Rochereau

You can be close to the centre of Paris but still relax in a sweet, gnomy garden under the gazebo. Cecilia is Anglo-French and loves having people to stay in her comfortable 1950s suburban house. She enjoys a chat over the breakfast table, helping you plan the day ahead. Green is clearly her favourite colour. Rooms open directly to the garden and are light and airy with replica tapestry wall hangings, chintzy curtains with net drapes, onyx figurine bedside lamps, potted plants and, I need hardly say, green carpets. *You may subtract your breakfast & do your own. Italian spoken. 6 minutes from centre of Paris by train.*

rooms	2 triples, both with kitchenette.
price	€70 for two; €90 for three. Minimum stay 2 nights.
meals	Self-catering possible; restaurants nearby.
closed	Occasionally.
directions	From Paris Bd Périphérique exit Porte d'Asnières through Levallois, across Seine. Ask for map. Train: from St Lazare, *Banlieue* direct train to Bécon Les Bruyères.

M & Mme Bobrie
10 rue Denfert Rochereau,
92600 Asnières sur Seine,
Hauts-de-Seine
tel +33 (0)1 47 93 53 60
fax +33 (0)1 47 93 53 60
e-mail ceciliasguesthouse@hotmail.com

Map 6 Entry 147

Villa Mansart

Wind up the handsome staircase and push open the attic door. Your sitting room has sunny walls, mustard sofas and ethnic rugs on polished floors. Slim, arched bedrooms are blue or vanilla and orange with family furniture and windows that peep over the rooftops. Breakfast is in the elegant dining room or on the terrace; marble steps, rescued from a local demolition, sweep down to a huge, immaculate lawn, a curtain of trees shields you from the suburbs – all is peace and calm yet only 20 minutes from the centre of Paris. *Garage available.*

rooms	2: 1 double, 1 triple; single bed in lounge available for groups of 6.
price	€76 for two; €99 for three; €190 for six. Singles €53. Minimum stay 2 nights March-Oct.
meals	10 restaurants close by.
closed	Rarely.
directions	From Paris A4; exit 5 for Pont de Nogent; at exit keep left, don't take tunnel; along viaduct; at 2nd lights under bridge; Av. L. Rollin for Le Perreux centre; next lights straight on; 2nd left 200m.

Françoise Marcoz
Villa Mansart,
94170 Le Perreux sur Marne,
Val-de-Marne
tel +33 (0)1 48 72 91 88
fax +33 (0)1 43 24 93 78
e-mail francoisemarcoz@hotmail.com
web www.chambresdhotes.fr.fm

Map 6 Entry 148

Château de Poigny

From Indonesia, Morocco and reddest America, this great traveller has amassed carvings great and small, artefacts ancient and modern, inlays and filigrees in brass, lacquer and wood, and filled his family mansion. Here is love of life, and bedrooms are an exuberant feast: the Coca Cola room is devastatingly… Coke, the Indonesian bed overwhelmingly rich. Your host is very good company and on weekdays his delightful assistant Taïeb will take excellent care of you. There is also a loo/library and a three-legged cat, exotic fowl, stone boars… and a vast number of honeys and jams for breakfast.

rooms	6: 5 doubles, 1 suite for 5.
price	€60-€68 for two.
meals	3 restaurants in village.
closed	Rarely.
directions	From N10 north of Rambouillet D937; D936 for Poigny la Forêt, 5km; left on D107 to Poigny; left up road by church; house on right.

François Le Bret
Château de Poigny,
78125 Poigny la Forêt,
Yvelines
tel +33 (0)1 34 84 73 42
fax +33 (0)1 34 84 74 38
e-mail lemanoirdepoigny@wanadoo.fr

7 rue Gustave Courbet

Behind the modest façade – on this lush, private housing estate – is a generous interior where Madame's interesting paintings (she once taught art) stand in pleasing contrast to elegant antiques and feminine furnishings. Picture windows let the garden in and the woods rise beyond. The larger guest room is soberly classic in blue, with a fur throw and big bathroom; the smaller one with skylight and bathroom across the landing is excellent value. Madame, charming and communicative, sings as well as she paints and enjoys cooking refined dinners for attentive guests; she is very good company. Usefully close to Paris.

rooms	2 doubles.
price	€50-€65 for two.
meals	Dinner with wine €18, book ahead.
closed	Rarely.
directions	From Paris A13 on A12 for St Quentin en Yvelines; exit N12 for Dreux; exit to Plaisir Centre; 1st exit off r'bout for Plaisir Les Gâtines, 1st left for 400m; right into Domaine des Gâtines; consult roadside plan.

Mme Hélène Castelnau
7 rue Gustave Courbet,
78370 Plaisir,
Yvelines
tel +33 (0)1 30 54 05 15
fax +33 (0)1 30 54 05 15
e-mail hcastelnau@club-internet.fr

27 rue de Beauvau

The new owners of this townhouse have brought it new, gorgeously minimalist white life. Their three well-mannered teenagers add to the lively atmosphere; all happily chat to guests with comfortable informality. The one smallish second-floor guest room is as uncomplicated as the rest with honey-coloured floorboards, red/beige *Jouy* curtains and bedcover and two deep red lampshades to focus the eye. In the big double salon original mouldings and fireplaces gleam palely, its one painting a modern splash of colour. A sumptuous breakfast and intimate garden finish the picture.

rooms	1 double with separate wc.
price	€77 for two. Minimum stay 2 nights.
meals	Wide choice of restaurants nearby.
closed	Rarely.
directions	From Paris A13 for Rouen; after 7km exit for Versailles on D186 & Bvd St Antoine to r'bout: Place de la Loi; opp. rue Colonel de Bauge; right at lights, 3rd right, rue Beauvau; house 3rd on right.

Philippe & Christine Agostini
27 rue de Beauvau,
78000 Versailles,
Yvelines
tel +33 (0)1 39 50 16 43
fax +33 (0)1 39 50 16 43
e-mail p.agostini1@libertysurf.fr

Château d'Hazeville

Utterly original, a meld of brimming creativity and scholarship, Hazeville dazzles. Your artist host uses his fine château-farm, dated 1400s to 1600s, as a living show of his talents: huge abstract paintings, hand-painted plates and tiles, a stunning 'Egyptian' reception room (and loos) and now, photography. The old stables house hi-tech artisans. Beautifully finished guest rooms in the *pigeonnier* are deeply luxurious; generous breakfasts come on china hand-painted by Monsieur to match the wall covering; he also knows the secret treasures of the Vexin. *Children over seven welcome. Hot-air ballooning possible.*

rooms	2: 1 double, 1 twin.
price	€125 for two.
meals	Wide choice of restaurants 5-10km.
closed	Weekdays & school term time.
directions	From Rouen N14 for Paris. 20km before Pontoise, at Magny en Vexin, right D983 to Arthies; left D81 through Enfer; château on left.

Guy & Monique Deneck
Château d'Hazeville,
95420 Wy dit Joli Village,
Val-d'Oise
tel +33 (0)1 34 67 06 17
fax +33 (0)1 34 67 17 82
e-mail guy.deneck@free.fr

La Ferme des Tourelles

A straightforward welcome, an unpretentious house with that friendly, lived-in air – what matter if sometimes it's the oilcloth on the table. These amiable, down-to-earth farmers lead a sociable life and love having grandchildren and guests around. Low-beamed bedrooms are modest but comfortable with imitation parquet floors and very good mattresses. In summer, meals can be taken under canvas in the flower-filled courtyard. Readers have told of hilarious evenings in approximate French and English over honest, family meals, often made with home-grown vegetables. Usefully near Paris.

rooms	2 doubles.
price	€44 for two.
meals	Dinner with wine €18, book ahead.
closed	Rarely.
directions	From Dreux N12 to Broué; D305 to La Musse (La Musse between Boutigny & Prouais); Chambres d'Hôtes signs.

Serge & Jeanne-Marie Maréchal
La Ferme des Tourelles,
La Musse,
28410 Boutigny Prouais,
Eure-et-Loir
tel +33 (0)2 37 65 18 74
fax +33 (0)2 37 65 18 74
e-mail la-ferme.des-tourelles@wanadoo.fr

Map 5 Entry 153

Les Chandelles

Horses and clubs share the quiet style of the Simons' converted farmhouse behind its high gates: Jean-Marc teaches golf to all ages and levels; Catherine has the friendliest mare imaginable and a horse-blanket laundry service. She is full of infectious enthusiasm and advice for visitors. They, their son and two big sloppy dogs receive you with alacrity in the old beamed kitchen then send you up steep barn stairs to simple white rooms where patches of bright colour punctuate the space. The two lovely new rooms, bigger, higher and more luxurious in fabric and fitting, are good for families.

rooms	5: 1 double, 2 twins, 2 family rooms.
price	€60-€80 for two. Family room €115 for four.
meals	Restaurants in Nogent le Roi & Maintenon.
closed	Rarely.
directions	From Paris A13, A12, N12, exit Gambais for Nogent le Roi. Entering Coulombs, left at lights for Chandelles; left at x-roads 1.5km; house on right.

Catherine & Jean-Marc Simon
Les Chandelles,
Chandelles,
28130 Villiers le Morhier,
Eure-et-Loir
tel +33 (0)2 37 82 71 59
fax +33 (0)2 37 82 71 59
e-mail info@chandelles-golf.com
web www.chandelles-golf.com

Map 5 Entry 154

Château de Jonvilliers

Delightful hosts: Virginie beautifully French, Richard a gentle Europeanised American and their two young sons. Down a wooded drive and set in a big leafy garden, the family house has tall windows, fine proportions and the air of a properly lived-in château: elegance and deep armchairs by the marble fireplace under crystal chandeliers. The top floor has been converted into five good rooms with sound-proofing, big beds, masses of hot water, rich, bright colour schemes... and just the right amount of family memorabilia: oils, engravings, lamps, old dishes. It feels easy, intelligent and fun.

rooms	5: 4 doubles, 1 triple.
price	€60-€70 for two.
meals	Restaurants 5km.
closed	Rarely, but book ahead.
directions	From A11 exit Ablis on N10 for Chartres. At Essars, right to St Symphorien, Bleury & Ecrosnes. There right & immed. left to Jonvilliers, 2.5km. White château gates straight ahead.

Virginie & Richard Thompson
Château de Jonvilliers,
28320 Jonvilliers,
Eure-et-Loir
tel +33 (0)2 37 31 41 26
fax +33 (0)2 37 31 56 74
e-mail information@chateaudejonvilliers.com
web www.chateaudejonvilliers.com

Regional food styles

À l'Alsacienne: With sauerkraut and sausage.

À l'Américaine: A corruption of à l'Armoricaine from Armor, Celtic for Britanny – with shallots and tomatoes (see also Bretonne).

À l'Anglaise: Plain boiled.

À l'Ardennaise: With juniper berries.

À l'Auvergnate: With cabbage and bacon bits.

À la Basquaise: With onions, rice, sweet peppers and possibly Bayonne cured ham.

À la Bretonne: With leeks, celery, beans (see also Américaine).

À la Dauphinoise: With cream, garlic and sometimes cheese.

À la Dijonnaise: With mustard sauce.

À la Flamande: Flemish – cooked in beer or vinegar.

À la Lyonnaise: With onions, wine, vinegar and often sausage.

À la Niçoise: With anchovies and olives.

À la Normande: With cream.

À la Périgourdine: With goose liver and truffles.

À la Provençale: With tomatoes, garlic, olive oil.

À la Savoyarde: With cream and cheese.

And four supra-regional methods:

À la Bonne Femme: Good Woman style – with white wine, shallots and mushrooms.

À la Bourgeoise: Townswoman style – with a carrot, onion and bacon sauce.

À la Ménagère: Housewife style – with onions, carrots, turnips, peas.

À la Paysanne: Peasant/Country Woman style – with vegetables!

photo Michael Busselle

normandy

Prieuré Sainte Croix

Built in 1850 as part of the Château d'Eu, one of Louis Philippe's residences, this is where all the king's horses and all the king's men were stabled and lodged. Guests are in a creeper-clad L enclosing a courtyard with the other L where Romain was born and he and Nicole live. Bedrooms are elegant with strong colours and bold flowers that are most definitely French. At breakfast, guests from each room have their own table, their own flowers and their own coffee machine. You can walk into Le Tréport along the towpath but in the garden of Sainte Croix you could well be in the countryside.

rooms	5: 4 doubles, 1 twin.
price	€45-€57 for two.
meals	Restaurants in Le Tréport, 2km.
closed	Rarely.
directions	From Dieppe D925 for Le Tréport; at Étalondes left at r'bout for Le Tréport; at 2nd r'bout 1st right; 100m, signposted.

Romain & Nicole Carton
Prieuré Sainte Croix,
76470 Le Tréport,
Seine-Maritime

tel	+33 (0)2 35 86 14 77
fax	+33 (0)2 35 86 14 77
e-mail	carton.nicole@wanadoo.fr
web	prieuresaintecroix.free.fr

Manoir de Beaumont

In the old hunting lodge: a vast, boar- and stag's-headed dayroom with log fire, chandelier and beds for ten – ideal for parties; in the main house: the huge room for three; from the garden: wide hilltop views. Monsieur manages the Port and is a mine of local knowledge, Madame tends house, garden and guests, masterfully. Proud of their region, they are keen to advise on explorations: nature, hiking, historical visits, wet days, dry days... A delightful, welcoming couple of natural generosity, elegance and manners. Legend has it that Queen Victoria 'stopped' at this very gracious house.

rooms	2 + 1: 1 double, 1 triple; 1 apartment for 5.
price	€47 for two.
meals	In Eu 2km, Le Tréport 4km; self-catering in apartment.
closed	Rarely.
directions	D49 to Eu. Before Eu left for Forest of Eu & Route de Beaumont. House 3km on right.

Catherine & Jean-Marie Demarquet
Manoir de Beaumont,
76260 Eu,
Seine-Maritime

tel	+33 (0)2 35 50 91 91
e-mail	catherine@demarquet.com
web	www.demarquet.com

Le Clos Mélise

Madame is smart, stylish and chatty and has a definite artistic flair, as her oil paintings prove. Her dear little village house with its tiny garden overlooking the village green and a bigger one behind is modestly, authentically itself and her sense of colour has been well used in her charmingly pretty rooms with their pleasing furniture and fresh fabrics. Two rooms are in a little building by the main house. The other, bright and young, is up a steep stair to the attic. The house is spotlessly clean, cosy and neat, the welcome attentive and genuine. *"Très cosy"* say the English.

rooms	3 doubles.
price	€42 for two.
meals	Restaurant in village.
closed	Rarely.
directions	From Le Tréport D925 for Dieppe 15km; in Biville sur Mer right Rue de l'Église, No. 14 faces you in middle of fork in road.

Marie-José Klaes
Le Clos Mélise,
76630 Biville sur Mer,
Seine-Maritime
tel +33 (0)2 35 83 14 71
e-mail closmelise@wanadoo.fr

Château Le Bourg

Luxury and sophistication are the nouns, friendly and intelligent the adjectives. Leonora's refined mix of English mahogany and French fabrics is as high-class as her sumptuous dinners. Having finished the soberly elegant bedrooms and scintillating bathrooms of her grand 19th-century mansion, she is turning her attention to the garden: it will undoubtedly delight. A brilliant hands-on hostess, she is independent and generous, talks with passionate knowledge about art and has a mass of books for you to browse through on your return from walking the old railway line or exploring the coastal cliffs.

rooms	2: 1 double, 1 family suite for 4.
price	€70-€100 for two.
meals	Dinner with wine €20-€45, book ahead.
closed	Rarely.
directions	A16 from Calais to A28, exit 6 for Londinières. D12 for 8km to Bures en Bray. House opposite church, with high iron gates between red & white brick pillars.

Leonora Macleod
Château Le Bourg,
76660 Bures en Bray,
Seine-Maritime
tel +33 (0)2 35 94 09 35
fax +33 (0)2 35 94 09 35
e-mail leonora.macleod@wanadoo.fr

Château du Mesnil Geoffroy

This gloriously restored 1640 château is surrounded by gardens designed by a pupil of Lenôtre's: a hornbeam maze, lime tree avenues and 2,457 perfectly tended roses. The Prince (Syrian father, French mother) knows every one of them; the Princess makes rose-petal jelly for breakfast. She is also a devotee of 17th-century dishes. Bedrooms are dreamy with fireplaces and panelling, canopies and lavender, fat duvets and fine linen, while dressing closets have been transformed into bathrooms. A sophisticated dining room, an elegant sitting room, and a lovely log fire (perhaps even a cat) to keep you company.

rooms	5: 2 doubles, 1 twin, 2 suites.
price	€89-€139 for two.
meals	Dinner with wine €42, on Saturday, book ahead. Restaurants 7km.
closed	Rarely.
directions	From A13 exit 25 Pont de Bretonne & Yvetot. Through Yvetot for St Valéry en Caux. 2km after Ste Colombe, right for Houdetot. Château 2km on left.

Prince & Princesse Kayali
Château du Mesnil Geoffroy,
76740 Ermenouville,
Seine-Maritime

tel	+33 (0)2 35 57 12 77
fax	+33 (0)2 35 57 10 24
e-mail	contact@chateau-mesnil-geoffroy.com
web	www.chateau-mesnil-geoffroy.com

179 Chemin du Bel Évent

Informal elegance, old French charm from 1864, a dose of American antiques and masses of warmly impressionistic paintings: Boston-born Daniel adopted France, married Virginie, had three children and chose these two houses, one for B&B, one for the family, in an area they both love; then his mother, a prolific painter, joined them. They put books everywhere and create a youthful, easy atmosphere. The guest-house dining, sitting and music rooms are grand: superb floors, high ceilings, views to the delicious period garden (tennis court too); bedrooms are generous and work progresses on the details.

rooms	4 doubles.
price	€48-€55 for two.
meals	Good bistro-épicerie in village.
closed	Rarely.
directions	From Dieppe D925 for St Valéry en Caux; 3.5km after Le Bourg Dun, left for La Chapelle sur Dun; opp. church, left at café go to end; enter on left.

Daniel Westhead
179 Chemin du Bel Évent,
76740 La Chapelle sur Dun,
Seine-Maritime

tel	+33 (0)2 35 57 08 44
fax	+33 mobile(0)6 11 10 00 80
e-mail	info@chaletdubelevent.com
web	www.chaletdubelevent.com

La Ferme de la Rue Verte

The 300-year-old house stands in a classic, poplar-sheltered Seine-Maritime farmyard, its worn old stones and bricks and the less worn flints bearing witness to its age, as does the fine timberwork inside. Otherwise it has been fairly deeply modernised, but your retired farmer hosts and the long lace-clothed breakfast table before the winter log fire are most welcoming. Madame was born here, has a winning smile and loves to talk – in French. Her pleasant rooms are in good, rural French style and the only sounds are the occasional lowing of the herd and the shushing of the poplars.

rooms	4: 1 double, 1 triple; 2 doubles sharing shower & wc.
price	€40-€42 for two.
meals	Auberge 1km. Restaurant 4km.
closed	Rarely.
directions	From Dieppe N27 for Rouen 29km; right N29 through Yerville, continue 4.5km; left D20 to Motteville; right to Flamanville. Rue Verte behind church. Farm 300m on left; signposted.

Yves & Béatrice Quevilly Baret
La Ferme de la Rue Verte,
76970 Flamanville,
Seine-Maritime
tel +33 (0)2 35 96 81 27

Manoir de Captot

Gracious living is declared at the pillared gates, the drive curves through slow horse pastures to a serene 18th-century mansion, the forest behind may ring with the stag's call, the heads and feet of his kin decorate the hall. Peacefully formal, it is a fine classic French interior: gorgeous primrose yellow dining room with an oval mahogany table for breakfast, collection-filled drawing room, one superb high bedroom with the right curly antiques and pink *Jouy* draperies, one attic twin plus little twin for children. Madame cherishes her mansion and resembles it: gently friendly with impeccable manners.

rooms	3: 1 double, 1 twin/double, 1 children's twin.
price	€70-€75 for two. Children's twin €35.
meals	Restaurants nearby.
closed	Rarely.
directions	From Rouen D982, north side of river Seine going west 8km to Cantelen on left. D351 for Sahurs. Entrance on right 900m after church. Big iron gates.

Mme Michèle Desrez
Manoir de Captot,
76380 Canteleu,
Seine-Maritime
tel +33 (0)2 35 36 00 04
fax +33 (0)2 35 36 00 04
web www.captot.com

22 rue Hénault

The elegant, black-doored face hides a light, stylish interior with soul-lifting views across old Rouen to the spires of the cathedral. Dominique, a cultured Egyptologist and delightful hostess, has a flair for decoration – as her paintings, coverings and mix of contemporary and country furniture declare. Oriental rugs on parquet floor, French windows to balcony and garden, bedrooms feminine but not frilly. Nothing standard, nothing too studied, a very personal home and leisurely breakfasts brimming with homemade surprises. The house's hillside position in this attractive suburb is equally special. Such value!

rooms	3: 1 double; 2 doubles, both with bath, sharing wc.
price	€50 for two.
meals	Restaurant 1km.
closed	October-November.
directions	In Rouen follow Gare SNCF signs; Rue Rochefoucault right of station; left Rue des Champs des Oiseaux; over 2 traffic lights into Rue Vigné; fork left Rue Hénault; black door on left.

Dominique Gogny
22 rue Hénault,
76130 Mont St Aignan,
Seine-Maritime
tel +33 (0)2 35 70 26 95
e-mail chambreavecvue@online.fr
web chambreavecvue.online.fr

Map 5 Entry 164

Le Brécy

Patricia has happy childhood holiday memories of this 17th-century manor house and the atmosphere is palpable. She and Jérôme moved here 10 years ago to be with her grandmother, who had been living alone in a few rooms for years. A long path flanked by willows leads down to the Seine: perfect for an evening stroll. Your suite (twin room, small sitting room) is on the ground floor, in classically French coral and cream, with windows opening to the walled garden. Breakfast is whenever it takes your fancy: brioche, walnuts and fresh fruit in a pretty green-panelled room. Ask Patricia about the Abbey.

rooms	1 suite with kitchenette.
price	€70 for two.
meals	Choice of restaurants 5km.
closed	Rarely.
directions	From A13 exit 24 'Maison Brulée' for La Bouille-Bas to Sahurs; left for St Martin de Boscherville; after Quevillon, 2nd left for Le Brécy; signposted.

Jérôme & Patricia Lanquest
Le Brécy,
76840 St Martin de Boscherville,
Seine-Maritime
tel +33 (0)2 35 32 69 92
fax +33 (0)2 35 32 00 30
e-mail jlanquest@tele2.fr
web home.tele2.fr/lebrecy

Map 5 Entry 165

45 rue aux Ours

You are in a privileged position in the heart of old Rouen, 100m from the cathedral. This building of character, built around a cobbled courtyard, is maintained like a museum, its beamed and passaged interior a treasure trove of curios and antiques, ethnic pieces, ecclesiastical art and salvage and family memorabilia. Once he has warmed to you, wry Monsieur enjoys sharing – in English, German or Norman – the history of Rouen. Bedrooms are dated but warm, bathrooms just adequate, breakfast generous and good, and Madame kindly attentive. *Car park a short walk from house.*

rooms	4: 1 double, 1 apartment for 5 (double, twin, single) & kitchen.
price	€55 for two.
meals	Vast choice of restaurants.
closed	Rarely.
directions	On Cathedral-side embankment: at Théâtre des Arts, take Rue Jeanne d'Arc; Rue aux Ours 2nd on right but NO parking: leave car in Bourse or Pucelle car park & walk.

Philippe & Annick Aunay-Stanguennec
45 rue aux Ours,
76000 Rouen,
Seine-Maritime
tel +33 (0)2 35 70 99 68

Map 5 Entry 166

Le Clos Jouvenet

It is a privilege to stay in these refined city surroundings, safely inside a serene walled garden above the towers of Rouen (from one bath you can gaze at the cathedral spire). The garden is as elegantly uncomplicated as the house and its Belgian owners, the décor classic sophisticated French to suit the gentle proportions: there are pretty pictures and prints, lots of books, handsome antique furniture and on cold mornings breakfast is served in the kitchen, warmed by slate and oak. Madame is charming, Monsieur enjoys guests too, and you wake to birdsong and church bells.

rooms	4: 2 double, 2 twins/doubles.
price	€78-€85 for two.
meals	Restaurants within walking distance.
closed	Rarely.
directions	From train station for Boulevard de L'Yser for Boulogne-Amiens; take Neufchatel road in same direction, first right rue du Champ du Pardon; rue Jouvenet; left at lights; second right.

Catherine de Witte
Le Clos Jouvenet,
76000 Rouen, Seine-Maritime
tel +33 (0)2 35 89 80 66
fax +33 (0)2 35 98 37 65
e-mail cdewitte@club-internet.fr
web www.leclosjouvenet.com

Map 5 Entry 167

Château de Fleury la Forêt

A huge place that breathes comfort – and a huge challenge for the young Caffins: half the château's 65 rooms have yet to be restored. They live in one wing, you in another, a museum sits in between. The handsome guest suite is pale-panelled and red-brocaded, with a separate twin room for children; the double elegantly and creamily draped; the guest sitting room serenely sage. There are stylish lawns to the front and majestic trees; stables for the show-jumpers and a maize-fashioned maze for the visitors. Breakfast is at a vast table in a kitchen hung with a tapestry and a hundred copper pans.

rooms	2: 1 double, 1 family suite.
price	€65 for two. Suite €110 for four.
meals	Choice of restaurants 6km.
closed	Rarely.
directions	From Gournay en Bray N31 for Rouen 17km; left D921 to Lyons la Forêt; D6 for Étrépagny; 1st left for Château de Fleury; left at fork; 5km, house on right, signposted.

Kristina Caffin
Château de Fleury la Forêt,
27480 Lyons la Forêt,
Eure

tel	+33 (0)2 32 49 63 91
fax	+33 (0)2 32 49 71 67
web	www.chateau-fleury-la-foret.com

Les Ombelles

The cottagey garden runs down to the clean, cool River Epte which Monet diverted at nearby Giverny (35km) for his famous ponds – it bestows the same serenity here. The old house is beautifully furnished with family antiques and Madame, a strong, intelligent and elegant person, willingly shares her great knowledge of all things Norman, including food. She has even devised her own detailed tourist circuits. One bedroom has a majestic Art Deco brass bed designed by *Grand-père* and a hand-painted carved armoire, both have original paintings and individuality.

rooms	3: 1 double, 1 twin; 1 double with separate bath & wc.
price	€55-€60 for two.
meals	Dinner with wine €20, book ahead.
closed	15 November-14 March.
directions	From Dieppe D915 to Gisors. Cross Gisors; D10 for Vernon. In Dangu, rue du Gué is beside River Epte.

Nicole de Saint Père
Les Ombelles,
27720 Dangu, Eure

tel	+33 (0)2 32 55 04 95
fax	+33 (0)2 32 55 59 87
e-mail	vextour@aol.com
web	vextour.ifrance.com

La Réserve

Big and beautiful, old and new, refined, relaxed and unpretentious. The Brunets, as delightful as their house, have the lightness of touch to combine the fresh best of modern French taste with an eye for authenticity, in a brand new house. Light floods in through recycled château windows on both sides of the classically narrow *maison de campagne*; soft limewash walls hemmed by lavender outside, matt grey woodwork inside, handsome rugs on polished floors, gorgeous fabrics by fine antiques all add up to the château feel. Exquisite style, massive comfort, perfect hosts – and wild deer on occasional visits.

rooms	5: 2 doubles, 3 twins.
price	€95-€155 for two.
meals	Restaurants 1.5km-4km.
closed	December-March, except by arrangement.
directions	From A13 exit 16 to Giverny; left Rue Claude Monet; after church & Hotel Baudy, 1st left Rue Blanche Hoshedé Monet 1.2km; left on white arrow, immed. right on track 800m, left to house.

Didier & Marie Lorraine Brunet
La Réserve,
27620 Giverny, Eure

tel	+33 (0)2 32 21 99 09
fax	+33 (0)2 32 21 99 09
e-mail	ml1reserve@aol.com
web	giverny.org/hotels/brunet/

L'Aulnaie

Michel and Éliane invested seven years and much natural good taste in restoring this lovely 19th-century farmhouse in a particularly pretty village. Guests share a self-contained part of the house with its own dayroom and breakfast area, and there's lots of space to settle in, with books, music and open fire. Bedrooms are gentle, quiet, fresh, with *toile de Jouy* fabrics, plain walls and honey-coloured floors. Naturally elegant Éliane is an amateur painter and passionate gardener, pointing out the rich and the rare; lawns sweep down to a stream that meanders beneath high wooded cliffs.

rooms	2: 1 double, 1 twin.
price	€60 for two.
meals	Choice of restaurants nearby.
closed	Rarely.
directions	A13 exit 16 for Cocherel; after 10km to Chambray; left at monument; left after 100m to Fontaine sous Jouy. In centre right Rue de l'Ancienne Forge for 800m; Rue de l'Aulnaie on right.

Éliane & Michel Philippe
L'Aulnaie,
27120 Fontaine sous Jouy, Eure

tel	+33 (0)2 32 36 89 05
fax	+33 (0)2 32 36 89 05
e-mail	emi.philippe@worldonline.fr
web	chambre-fontaine.chez.tiscali.fr

Clair Matin

Handsomely carved Colombian furniture, strong colours and interesting prints create an unusual atmosphere inside this 18th-century manor with its Norman cottage face and surprising turret. Your charming Franco-Spanish hosts spent over 20 years and raised five children in South America before renovating their French home – it vibrates with echoes of faraway places. Bedrooms aren't huge but are solidly comfortable with immaculate bathrooms. There are fresh breads and homemade jams at the huge Andean cedar breakfast table, a quiet, pretty garden and good conversation.

rooms	3: 1 double, 1 family room, 1 suite.
price	€45-€55 for two; €65 for four.
meals	Auberges 6km.
closed	Rarely.
directions	From A13 exit 17 for Gaillon D316 for Évreux through Autheuil, St Vigor & up hill 11km; right to Reuilly; house on road, 200m past Mairie on right.

Jean-Pierre & Amaia Trevisani
Clair Matin,
27930 Reuilly,
Eure
tel +33 (0)2 32 34 71 47
fax +33 (0)2 32 34 97 64
e-mail clair_matin@compuserve.com

Domaine de Broc Fontaine

The highlight of Broc Fontaine is the lovely tailored, immaculate garden, and the star turn, the remarkable colour-coded organic potager where Deborah grows blue leeks, scarlet chard and masses of berries. In the 300-year-old farmhouse, your friendly hosts entertain together and treasure their contact with guests. Bedrooms, with a fine personal mix of antique furniture and fabrics, are welcoming and private; the pretty garden cottage with its kitchen is perfect for families. American Deborah adopted France and French food 25 years ago and is an excellent cook who now gives courses.

rooms	3: 1 twin, 1 suite for 3-6, 1 suite in cottage for 4.
price	€75-€95 for two.
meals	Dinner with wine €25-€30, book ahead.
closed	Rarely.
directions	From Rouen A13 for Paris; exit 18 for Louviers; A154 for 7km; N154 for 3km; exit Acquigny; D61 7km; D52 to Brosville. 1st house after bakery on right.

Deborah Pivain
Domaine de Broc Fontaine,
27930 Brosville, Eure
tel +33 (0)2 32 34 61 78
fax +33 (0)2 32 24 14 72
e-mail brocfontaine@aol.com
web giverny.org/hotels/pivain

Manoir de la Boissière

Madame cooks great Norman dishes with home-grown ingredients served on good china; also, tomato and banana jam for breakfast – be brave, it's worth trying. She has been doing B&B for years, is well organised and still enjoys meeting new people when she's not too busy. Guest quarters, independent of the house, have pretty French-style rooms, good bedding and excellent tiled shower rooms while the caringly-restored, listed 15th-century farmhouse, the duck pond, the peacocks and the furniture – each item carefully chosen, some tenderly hand-painted – all give it character. And it's excellent value. *Games room.*

rooms	5: 2 doubles, 2 twins, 1 triple.
price	€46 for two; €60 for three.
meals	Dinner with cider €21, book ahead.
closed	Rarely.
directions	From Rouen N15 for Paris 40km; at Gaillon right D10 for La Croix St Leufroy about 7km; in La Boissaye, Chambres d'Hôtes signs.

Clotilde & Gérard Sénécal
Manoir de la Boissière,
27490 La Croix St Leufroy,
Eure
tel +33 (0)2 32 67 70 85
fax +33 (0)2 32 67 03 18
e-mail chambreslaboissiere@wanadoo.fr

4 sente de l'Abreuvoir

The big garden runs down to the banks of the Eure: peace reigns in this privileged spot. Smiley Bernard keeps lawns mown and borders clipped; sweet Madeleine devotes herself to home and guests. The old farmhouse is as neat as a new pin, bedrooms soberly pretty and inviting. The parquet-floored double has French windows to the garden; the suite, papered and friezed in pale green, has a sitting area under the eaves. Refined breakfast is served on antique lace in a dining room with garden views. Woods and water for walking, canoeing, fishing; gentle people; Giverny and Rouen a half-hour drive. A form of perfection.

rooms	2: 1 double, 1 suite for 3.
price	€47-€53 for two.
meals	Choice of restaurants 5km.
closed	Rarely.
directions	A13 exit 19 for Louviers & Évreux; 2nd exit N154 to Acquigny; D71 through Heudreville for Cailly to La Londe; left; house on right.

Madeleine & Bernard Gossent
4 sente de l'Abreuvoir,
27400 Heudreville sur Eure,
Eure
tel +33 (0)2 32 40 36 89
e-mail madeleine.gossent@online.fr
web www.lalonde.online.fr

Manoir d'Hermos

The sedately old-French panelled rooms with refreshing colours, good antiques and windows to the gentle world outside are up the grand staircase of this 16th-century house where brick and sandstone sit in peace by birdy orchard, pastoral meadows and spreading lake. Madame is a most welcoming hostess, full of spontaneous smiles, who puts flowers everywhere and whose family has owned the house for 100 years. She also organises seminars (not when B&B guests are here), cares for two teenagers and gardens brilliantly: trees are being planted to Napoleonic plans discovered in the archives...

rooms	2: 1 quadruple, 1 triple.
price	€46-€62 for two; €64-€80 for three; €98 for four. Singles €42-€57.
meals	Choice of restaurants 2-8km.
closed	Rarely.
directions	From A13 exit Maison Brulée N138 for Bourgthéroulde & Brionne. 8km after Bourgthéroulde D83 left to Le Gros Theil; enter village, sharp right D92 & follow signs for 2km.

Béatrice & Patrice Noël-Windsor
Manoir d'Hermos,
27800 St Éloi de Fourques,
Eure
tel +33 (0)2 32 35 51 32
fax +33 (0)2 32 35 51 32
e-mail manoirhermos@lemel.fr
web www.hermos.fr.st

Les Aubépines

That lovely timber frame embraces a heart-warming antique clutter spread with great taste over original bricks, beams, tiles and carved family furniture. Guests share this marvellous space as family; Madame welcomes and cooks with delight (maybe over an open fire) and tends the intimate paradise of her garden whence views glide over forested hills; Monsieur smiles, charms and mends everything. The delicious bedrooms are subtly lit by dormer windows, country furnished, pastel hued and comfortably bathroomed; the suite has steep rafters and a smart new shower room. A dream of a place, they deserve a medal.

rooms	3: 2 twins/doubles, 1 suite for 4.
price	€50-€55 for two.
meals	Dinner with wine €20, book ahead.
closed	October-March, except by arrangement.
directions	From Paris A13 exit 26 for Pont Audemer D89; at 'Médine' r'bout. on for Évreux &Appeville-Annebault 4km; left immed. after Les Marettes sign, follow Chambres d'Hôtes signs.

Françoise & Yves Closson Maze
Les Aubépines,
27290 Appeville dit Annebault,
Eure
tel +33 (0)2 32 56 14 25
fax +33 (0)2 32 56 14 25
e-mail clossonmaze@wanadoo.fr
web perso.wanadoo.fr/lesaubepines

8 Allée des Châteaux

From the cliff, gasp as the Seine sweeps curvaceously on to the sea below the helter-skelter Second Empire villa. Darkly atmospheric, opulent rooms wear gilt, oils, marbles, ivories and some original clothes – 1875 (stern dark wallpapers, decorative floor tiles), the 70s (gift-wrapped walls)... Madame has added flashes of exuberance and humour: thick vibrant throws, big floral fabrics, a dog-headed ancestor. Her forebears made history, she moves among artists and intellectuals, a generous and rather mysterious figure who loves a house full of children and animals – in matchless style.

rooms: 3: 1 double, 2 suites for 6.
price: €100-€120 for two. Minimum stay 2 nights.
meals: Dinner with wine €30, book ahead.
closed: Rarely.
directions: From Paris A13 exit 24 Maison Brulée onto N175 & then telephone.

Laurence Scherrer
8 Allée des Châteaux,
27310 Caumont,
Eure
tel: +33 (0)2 35 18 03 11
fax: +33 (0)1 45 01 23 57

Map 5 Entry 178

Les Sources Bleues

A privileged setting on the banks of the Seine just below Rouen... once every four years the great armada comes sailing by. The garden is 50m from the water's edge and there are binoculars for birdwatching – this is a Panda (WWF) house (the owners live in the cottage next door). Bedrooms, though in need of a lick of paint, are old-fashioned and charming, with family rooms squeezed into the attic. You get beams and panelling and windows onto that stunning view, a kitchen/diner, a surprisingly elegant sitting room. Monsieur cooks and Madame has all the time in the world for you.

rooms: 4: 2 suites for 3, 2 quadruples.
price: €51-€63 for two.
meals: Dinner €18, book ahead; wine-list €11-€13 or cider €5.
closed: Rarely.
directions: From Pont Audemer D139 NE for 10km to Bourneville & D139 to Aizier. There, left at Mairie for Vieux Port, D95; on right.

Yves & Marie-Thérèse Laurent
Les Sources Bleues,
27500 Aizier,
Eure
tel: +33 (0)2 32 57 26 68
fax: +33 (0)2 32 57 42 25

Map 5 Entry 179

L'Aufragère

This generous couple run food-and-wine breaks and cookery courses: you'll eat very well. Nicky is English and a Cordon Bleu cook, Régis is French with great taste in all departments, and there's nothing nicer than waking up in one of the sedate, antique-furnished rooms of their superbly renovated farmhouse (those in the attic are more ethnic in flavour). The dining room has a long table and fine panelling, the sitting room wraparound red sofas and a gentle black lab, and the grassed farmyard just gets prettier, strutted by poultry and mown by black-headed sheep. Come and indulge in everything.

rooms	5: 2 doubles, 3 twins.
price	Half-board only: €107 for two. Minimum stay 2 nights.
meals	Breakfast & dinner included.
closed	Rarely.
directions	In Fourmetot turn for Corneville by church for 1km; 50m after small r'bout left through 2 round brick pillars.

Régis & Nicky Dussartre
L'Aufragère,
27500 Fourmetot,
Eure
tel +33 (0)2 32 56 91 92
e-mail regis@laufragere.com
web www.laufragere.com

Le Coquerel

Jean-Marc overflows with ideas for varied stays, love for his garden, modern art and lingering dinners with guests. He has transformed the old cottage, surrounded by soft pastures, into a country gem, and the garden is exuberant with flowers. Inside, a mix of the sober, the cultivated, the frivolous and the kitsch: old and modern pieces, rustic revival and leather, paintings and brocante. Bedrooms stand out in their uncomplicated good taste, bathrooms are irreproachable, but it's your host who makes the place; duck in cider, strawberry soup and laughter, butterflies alighting on the table at breakfast.

rooms	5: 1 twin, 1 double, 1 triple, 2 family.
price	€53-€56 for two.
meals	Dinner with wine €20, book ahead; picnic possible.
closed	Rarely.
directions	From Pont Audemer D810 for Bernay 12km; right through St Siméon; up hill for Selles; house on left at top.

Jean-Marc Drumel
Le Coquerel,
27560 St Siméon, Eure
tel +33 (0)2 32 56 56 08
fax +33 (0)2 32 56 56 08
e-mail moreau-drumel@wanadoo.fr
web perso.wanadoo.fr/chambreshotes/

La Charterie

One of the most delicious houses we know, with the bonus of fine *table d'hôtes*. It is the new-found delight of your courteous and endearing hosts, ex-Parisiens. Hidden amid the fields of the Normandy plains, the 18th-century *maison de maître* stands in a dream of a garden, overgrown here, brought to heel there, flanked by a majestic walnut and age-old pears, filled with shrub roses; the odd forgotton bench adds to the Flaubertian charm. Inside, Marie-Hélène, bright-eyed and eager, has used *Jouy* cloth and elegant colours to dress the country-French bedrooms that fill the first floor. Enchanting.

rooms	4: 2 doubles, 1 twin, 1 triple.
price	€55 for two.
meals	Dinner with wine €20, book ahead.
closed	Rarely.
directions	From Évreux N13 for Lisieux 50km; entering Duranville right D41 for St Aubin de Scellon 2.5km; drive on right.

Marie-Hélène François
La Charterie,
27230 St Aubin de Scellon, Eure
tel +33 (0)2 32 45 46 52
mobile +33 (0)6 20 39 08 63
e-mail la.charterie@wanadoo.fr
web monsite.wanadoo.fr/la.charterie

Map 5 Entry 182

Château du Grand Bus

A many-shuttered house of sturdy grandeur, it feels like a family home inside: up the monumental oak staircase to big comfortably French bedrooms with family furniture (old washstands, carved wardrobes, a billiard table...), views of grazing cattle and Madame's own wallpapering. Tall, sophisticated, relaxed and welcoming, she finds it normal that everyone sit together in the ochre and scarlet breakfast room. There's a family-friendly common room with picnic table and refrigerator. No finery, a touch of faded grandeur and all-pervasive warmth characterise this splendidly unsmart house of friendship.

rooms	4: 1 double, 1 twin, 2 family rooms.
price	€48 for two.
meals	Choice of restaurants in Orbec.
closed	Rarely.
directions	From Lisieux N13 for Évreux 18km to Thiberville; D145 for Orbec 10km. On right about 50m after sign 'Le Grand Bus'.

Bruno & Laurence de Préaumont
Château du Grand Bus,
27230 Thiberville, Eure
tel +33 (0)2 32 44 71 14
fax +33 (0)2 32 46 45 81
e-mail chambrepreaumont@libertysurf.fr
web perso.libertysurf.fr/depreaumont

Map 5 Entry 183

Le Vieux Château

Alone on its tiny island, the 'ancient' fortress is 40 years old and the rickety rail-less bridge made of 60s sleepers; goats and fowl roam the courtyard. Downstairs, a collector's clutter of pictures, porcelain and old shoes. Up a corkscrew staircase in the tower to classic bedrooms, irreproachably clean, with starched linen and lace. Madame, extraordinary and bohemian, changes from scatty gardener to lady-at-gracious-candlelit-dinner – enjoy conversation about the arts illuminated with flashes of outrageous humour. One loo between three rooms is a small price to pay for such fun.

rooms	3: 2 doubles, 1 twin, all with bath or shower, sharing wc.
price	€61-€65 for two.
meals	Dinner with wine €23, book ahead.
closed	January-February.
directions	From Breteuil D141 for Rugles; through forest; at Bémécourt, left 300m after lights into Allée du Vieux Château.

Mme Maryvonne Lallemand-Legras
Le Vieux Château,
27160 Bémécourt,
Eure
tel +33 (0)2 32 29 90 47

Map 5 Entry 184

Château de la Grande Noë

Trompe-l'œil marble and Wedgwood mouldings inherited from an Adam-inspired ancestor; chamber music in the log-fired drawing room; breakfast in the dining room wrapped in oak panelling inlaid with precious woods; elegant, alcoved bedrooms full of antiques, books, ancestral portraits, much soft comfort and a loo in a tower: it's a fascinating, human place. And the delightful Longcamps are a civilised, friendly couple, she vivaciously cultured and musical, he a top-class Camembert-maker who mows his acres on Sundays. Come and belong briefly to this wonderful world. Walks start 2km away.

rooms	3: 1 twin, 2 doubles.
price	€100-€115 for two.
meals	2 good restaurants within 5km.
closed	December-March, except by arrangement.
directions	From Verneuil sur Avre, N12 SW 24km to Carrefour Ste Anne. Left D918 for Longny au Perche for 4.5km; left D289 for Moulicent. House 800m on right.

Jacques & Pascale de Longcamp
Château de la Grande Noë,
61290 Moulicent, Orne
tel +33 (0)2 33 73 63 30
fax +33 (0)2 33 83 62 92
e-mail grandenoe@wanadoo.fr
web www.chateaudelagrandenoe.com

Map 5 Entry 185

La Simondrière

Your English hosts take great care of you in the Percheron farmhouse they have rescued and restored – and enjoy sharing their enthusiasm for this beautiful, undiscovered, horse-breeding region. Feel free to potter on their land or to venture further afield, then come back to a friendly cup of tea and a truly delicious supper in the farmhouse kitchen. Bedrooms are beamy, cosy and uncomplicated, with good mattresses, warm duvets and floral linen. In the big square sitting room, books, maps and voluminous easy chairs. A super country place on the edge of the forest, and Rex and Helen wonderful company.

rooms	2: 1 twin, 1 triple.
price	€50 for two.
meals	Dinner with wine €25, book ahead. Restaurants within 10km.
closed	December.
directions	From Mortagne au Perche D931 for Mamers for 8km; right on D650 for Coulimer at small x-roads. House 800m on left, last of small hamlet of houses.

Helen Barr
La Simondrière,
61360 Coulimer,
Orne
tel +33 (0)2 33 25 55 34
fax +33 (0)2 33 25 49 01
e-mail helenbarr@wanadoo.fr

Le Tertre

Pilgrims have trudged past towards Mont St Michel since the 1500s and the search for inner peace continues: groups come for yoga, tai chi and meditation but never overlap with B&B. Anne talks brilliantly about her exotic travels, is active in the village and also pours her creative energy into her house, with the help of an excellent restorer. Each room has its own clear personality, good beds and sitting space, antiques, soft colours and privacy. One has a six-seater jacuzzi, another a fine set of ivory-backed brushes, the third an impressive bureau. Super breakfast in the big kitchen, served with love.

rooms	3: 2 doubles, 1 twin.
price	€65-€130 for two.
meals	Choice of restaurants 6km.
closed	February
directions	From Alençon D311 for Mamers, left for Contilly & Montgaudry D113, 5km. Follow signs.

Anne Morgan
Le Tertre,
61360 Montgaudry, Orne
tel +33(0)2 33 25 59 98
fax +33 (0)2 33 25 56 96
e-mail annemorgan@wanadoo.fr
web www.french-country-retreat.com

Le Marnis

This is Barbara's "corner of paradise" and her delight is contagious. In utter peace among the cattle-dotted Norman pastures, here is one brave, outspoken woman, her horses, dogs and cats in a low-lying farmhouse, beautifully rebuilt "from a pile of stones", where old and new mix easily and flowers rampage all around. The lovely sloping garden is all her own work too – she appears to have endless energy. The pastel guest rooms, one upstairs, one on the ground floor with doors to the garden, are pleasantly floral. Come by horse, or walk. *Children over 10 welcome.*

rooms 2: 1 double, 1 twin.
price €50 for two.
meals Restaurant in village, 1.5km.
closed Rarely.
directions From Courtomer, past Mairie right after last building for Tellières. Left at crossroads for Le Marnis. 2nd lane on right.

Barbara Goff
Le Marnis,
61390 Courtomer,
Orne
tel +33 (0)2 33 27 47 55
e-mail barbara.goff@wanadoo.fr

La Bussière

It's angular inside too, the staircase elbowing its way right up to the top guest-room floor where the sky rushes in. Grandmother's hobby-camel stands here in its 1905 skin: the house was built by her parents in 1910 in open-plan American style. Sliding glass partitions give grandly generous dining and sitting rooms; bedrooms are excellent, much-windowed, soft-coloured and -bedded, marble-fireplaced, old-mirrored. Impeccable and full of personality, the house is the pride and joy of your intelligent hostess who laughs easily and manages her home, four children and guests expertly. *Please arrive after 6pm.*

rooms 2: 1 twin, 1 suite for 4.
price €56 for two.
meals Dinner with wine €24, book ahead.
closed December-February.
directions From Argentan N26 E for 37km. Entrance 4km after Planches on right by small crucifix; long lime-bordered drive.

Antoine & Nathalie Le Brethon
La Bussière,
61370 Ste Gauburge Ste Colombe,
Orne
tel +33 (0)2 33 34 05 23
fax +33 (0)2 33 34 71 47

Les Gains

There's homemade elderflower cordial if you arrive on a hot day or the wonderful smell of hot bread may greet you: this converted manor farm with its pigeon tower and duck stream has a lived-in family atmosphere. Your hosts have 800 sheep, 300 apple trees, work hard and are thoroughly integrated, as are their daughters. Bedrooms in the old dairy are light, soberly furnished with touches of *fantaisie* and Diana's very decorative stencils. Breakfast is superb, dinner should be an occasion to linger over and remember; both happen under the pergola in fine weather. Watch the steep stairs.

rooms	3: 1 double, 1 twin, 1 triple.
price	€50-€55 for two.
meals	Dinner with wine €25, book ahead.
closed	December-February.
directions	From Vimoutiers D916 for Argentan. Just outside Vimoutiers fork left D16 for Exmes; D26 for Survie & Exmes.

Diana & Christopher Wordsworth
Les Gains,
61310 Exmes, Orne
tel +33 (0)2 33 36 05 56
fax +33 (0)2 33 35 03 65
e-mail lesgains@tiscali.fr
web www.lesgains.tk

Château de La Maigraire

Built in 1870, it stands in pretty grounds with its own little carp-filled lake. Monsieur (an interior designer) fell for it, took it on (with his cousin) and did a brilliant restoration. You get an elegant drawing room with a rosewood baby grand, a cosy sitting room filled with books, and three sunny bedrooms furnished with antiques, one with its own terrace. Bathrooms come with oodles of towels "for the English"; croissants and homemade jams are presented on antique Limoges: Monsieur loves to please. Guests are encouraged to lounge around during the day, and you may picnic in the grounds.

rooms	2: 1 double, 1 suite for 2-3.
price	€85-€105 for two.
meals	Several good restaurants in the area.
closed	Rarely.
directions	From D962, between Flers & Domfront, D260 for Forges de Varennes & Champsecret for 1.5km; left into La Maigraire hamlet.

Jean Fischer
Château de La Maigraire,
61700 St Bômer les Forges, Orne
tel +33 (0)2 33 38 09 52
fax +33 (0)2 33 38 09 52
e-mail la.maigraire@wanadoo.fr
web chateaudelamaigraire.monsite.wanadoo.fr

La Maison du Vert

Debbie and Daniel, artistic young landscape gardeners fairly new to the world of B&B, are enthusiastic about it all – welcoming their guests to their pretty, unfussy rooms, improving the bathrooms, devising and preparing vegetarian menus that look and taste wonderful, redesigning the mature garden with its great old trees to include areas for scent, colour and feel, developing the organic vegetable patch (free-range hens too). They have decorated the place with creative good taste, provide varied, healthy breakfasts and dinners and will take great care of your comfort and well-being.

rooms	3: 2 doubles, 1 triple.
price	€61-€77 for two.
meals	Dinner with wine €25, book ahead.
closed	December-February.
directions	D579 from Lisieux to Vimoutiers; D979 for Alençon for 5km; left D12 for L'Aigle. In Ticheville, left opp. church, house 20m on right.

Debbie & Daniel Armitage
La Maison du Vert,
61120 Ticheville,
Orne
tel +33 (0)2 33 36 95 84
e-mail mail@maisonduvert.com
web www.maisonduvert.com

Le Prieuré St Michel

An atmospheric time warp for the night: the timbered 14th-century monks' storeroom (you are on the St Michel pilgrim route here) with tapestry wall covering and antiques, or the old dairy or perhaps a converted stable; a huge 15th-century cider press for breakfast in the company of the Ulrichs' interesting choice of art; a chapel for yet more art, a tithe barn in magnificent condition for fabulous receptions, perfectly stupendous gardens (to rival Giverny?). Your hosts are totally devoted to their fabulous domain and its listed buildings and deeply happy to share it with guests who appreciate their historical value.

rooms	5: 2 doubles, 1 twin, 2 suites for 3.
price	€95-€135 for two.
meals	Dinner €25, book ahead; wine list €17-€31.
closed	Rarely.
directions	From Lisieux D579 for Livarot & Vimoutiers. D916 for d'Argentan. Right 3km after Vimoutiers D703 for Crouttes. Le Prieuré is 500m after village.

Jean-Pierre & Viviane Ulrich
Le Prieuré St Michel,
61120 Crouttes, Orne
tel +33 (0)2 33 39 15 15
fax +33 (0)2 33 36 15 16
e-mail leprieuresaintmichel@wanadoo.fr
web www.prieure-saint-michel.com

Les Hauts de la Côte Ransue

Light bounces off the symmetry of this pretty 19th-century farmhouse in its large landscaped setting: quiet harmony outside, striking colour and style inside. Your charming Anglo-French hosts have done a super renovation bringing the original woodwork to life with careful toning, as well as having a baby. Even on grey days the sun shines at breakfast in the airy yellow dining room/kitchen... especially with Catherine's hawthorn berry coulis on fromage frais. Bedrooms are country comfortable in pale green or blue and cream, little sweets appear daily and Catherine's artistic talent is clear.

rooms	2: 1 double, 1 family suite for 4.
price	€60 for two.
meals	Dinner with wine €25, book ahead.
closed	Rarely.
directions	N175 to Pont l'Evêque; exit Beuzeville, D109 to Quetteville; turn right for 'Les Anglais' & follow road for 3km.

Catherine & Robert Wall
Les Hauts de la Côte Ransue,
14130 Quetteville, Calvados
tel +33 (0)2 31 64 69 95
fax +33 (0)2 31 64 69 95
e-mail catherinegruvel@hotmail.com

Château des Parcs Fontaine

A dream of a place for children: five acres of trees, bushes, rides; a 200-year-old lime tree whose branches sweep the ground in a corner of the walled garden, ideal for making a den; join Monsieur at croquet, he's a fiendish player, or badminton, table tennis, billiards, darts, the piano... These are outgoing, enthusiastic, interesting people, she an English teacher, he a journalist. In the breakfast room awash with sunlight, you are struck by an enormous Art Deco tiled panel surveying a veritable feast. Bedrooms have the deep luxury of thick carpets, good decor and colour schemes and old-fashioned bathrooms.

rooms	4: 3 doubles, 1 twin.
price	€60-€75 for two.
meals	Restaurants nearby 5km.
closed	Rarely.
directions	Autoroute exit Pont l'Evêque, to Lisieux. After 5km, sign on left for property.

M & Mme Rouet
Château des Parcs Fontaine,
14130 Fierville les Parcs,
Calvados
tel +33 (0)2 31 65 49 70
e-mail rouetch@wanadoo.fr

Clos St Hymer

The approach is down a leafy lane, dotted with primroses in spring. Françoise and Michel have been doing B&B for years, and are ever ready to welcome guests to their typically Norman house where space is well organised and you won't feel crowded in. In the sitting/dining room is a roaring, open-doored woodburning stove, in the double bedroom a patchwork quilt and Louis XIII wardrobe, in the triple an *armoire de mariage* and cupboards stocked with towels. Both bedrooms look onto the pretty garden, complete with table tennis. Utterly French, and friendly.

rooms	2: 1 double, 1 triple.
price	€60-€68 for two.
meals	Dinner with wine €25, book ahead.
closed	Rarely.
directions	From Pont l'Évêque D579 for Lisieux. At Le Breuil en Auge r'bout D264 to Le Torquesne. 1st right after church, Chemin des Toutains. House 500m on.

Françoise Valle
Clos St Hymer,
14130 Le Torquesne, Calvados
tel +33 (0)2 31 61 99 15
fax +33 (0)2 31 61 99 15
e-mail f.valle@free.fr

La Baronnière

The Baron moved on but left a fine house, superb grounds and a stream-fed lake – enchanting. Pet geese gabble, birds triumph, children rejoice (dens in trees, games on lawns, bikes). Christine, who is English, is in heaven caring for the old house and chatting with her guests; her French husband cooks subtle regional meals served in the pretty conservatory. The room in the old pantry has a Louis XIV bed and painted furniture on original honeycomb tiles, the other, up an outside staircase in the handsome timbered barn, is just as pretty. *Watch children with unfenced water.*

rooms	2 doubles.
price	€60 for two. Minimum stay 2 nights.
meals	Dinner with wine €30-€38, book ahead.
closed	Rarely.
directions	From Liseux N13 for Evreux; D145 at Thiberville to la Chapelle Hareng. Follow signs, do not go into Cordebugle.

Christine Gilliatt-Fleury
La Baronnière,
14100 Cordebugle, Calvados
tel +33 (0)2 32 46 41 74
fax +33 (0)2 32 44 26 09
web www.labaronniere.connectfree.co.uk

Côté Jardin

Behind the urbanity of this fine house in the centre of old Orbec (timbers, thatch, cider orchards), you discover the stableyard with the guest rooms, a pretty garden and a lively little stream. Your hosts came back from African jobs in 2002 and the atmosphere over breakfast in the family kitchen is warm and friendly: they enjoy life and laugh a lot. The coachhouse room has an African theme, *naturellement*, and a splendid tiled shower; up a steep outside staircase, the coachman's room is pale green and floral; the other two are equally thoughtful. *Watch children with unfenced water.*

rooms 4: 2 doubles, 2 family rooms.
price €50-€60 for two.
meals Choice of restaurants in Orbec.
closed Rarely.
directions Orbec 19km south of Lisieux on D519. Turn into village; house on main street on left next to L'Orbecquoise restaurant.

Georges & Véronique Lorette
Côté Jardin,
14290 Orbec,
Calvados
tel +33 (0)2 31 32 77 99
fax +33 (0)2 31 32 77 99
e-mail georges.lorette@wanadoo.fr
web www.cotejardin-france.be

Manoir de Cantepie

It may have a make-believe face, among the smooth green curves of racehorse country, but it is genuine early 1600s; it's amazing from all sides. Inside is an equally astounding dining room built by one Mr Swann and resplendently carved, panelled and painted. Bedrooms have a sunny feel, and are delightful: one with white-painted beams and green *toile de Jouy*, another in yellows, a third with a glorious valley view. All are incredible value. Madame, a beautiful Swedish lady, made the curtains and covers. She and her husband are well-travelled, polyglot, cultured and make their B&B doubly special.

rooms 3: 2 doubles, 1 twin.
price €60 for two.
meals Restaurant 1km.
closed 15 November-February.
directions From Caen N13 for Lisieux 25km; at Carrefour St Jean, D50 (virtually straight on) for Cambremer; 5km from junc., house on right; sign.

Christine & Arnauld Gherrak
Manoir de Cantepie,
14340 Cambremer,
Calvados
tel +33 (0)2 31 62 87 27
fax +33 (0)2 31 62 87 27

Manoir du Lieu Rocher

That beautiful 17th-century symmetry is home to a fascinating couple. Born in Bulgaria, Madame is a polyglot classical singer, Monsieur accompanies her on the piano, they are widely travelled, enthusiastic and have a fine sense of humour (recitals are sometimes held here). Their exceptional house, all set about with beams and timbers and bursting with antiques, paintings and portraits, has its original oak stair. Bedrooms are in keeping: big, soft welcoming feel, antiques, lovely views; the suite is perfect for families. The ancient village church peeks into the garden, and rose fans visit in June.

rooms	3: 1 double, 1 twin, 1 suite for 2-5.
price	€65-€80 for two. Suite €130-€150.
meals	Restaurants 5km.
closed	Rarely.
directions	From St Pierre sur Dives D4 for Livarot, 7km; at Boissy D154 to Veux Pont; continue on D154 towards church. Manoir on right.

M & Mme Grigaut
Manoir du Lieu Rocher,
14140 Vieux Pont en Auge,
Calvados
tel +33 (0)2 31 20 53 03
fax +33 (0)2 31 20 59 03
e-mail manoirlieurocher@wanadoo.fr
web www.castlenormandy.com

La Ferme de l'Oudon

Madame has hugely enjoyed rescuing this old house, making the modern blend with the ancient, and her enthusiasm is infectious. Her husband is a decorator – it helps. Come and chat in the kitchen conservatory, mingle with this lively couple, admire the potager. Rooms are delightful; one under the eaves, up a worn spiral past the old pigeon niches, has sun-filled roof windows; another has fine beams, a mezzanine and several big desert pictures. Décor is strong green and yellow, warm terracotta or dainty floral; bathrooms are excellent with careful detail and colour splashes. Dining here must be delicious and fun.

rooms	3 doubles.
price	€55-€75.
meals	Dinner with wine €28, Mondays & Fridays, book ahead.
closed	January.
directions	A13 exit 29a for La Haie Tondue; D16 to Carrefour St Jean; N13 to Crévecoeur (for 3km); D16 to St Pierre sur Dives; from St Pierre sur Dives, D40 to Berville. La Ferme at last x-roads, on left.

Patrick & Dany Vesque
La Ferme de l'Oudon,
14170 Berville L'Oudon,
Calvados
tel +33 (0)2 31 20 77 96
fax +33 (0)2 31 20 67 13
e-mail contact@fermedeloudon.com
web www.fermedeloudon.com

Ferme la Croix

England's last conqueror lived in Falaise until he left in 1066 to cross the water, but this typical house in its quiet little Norman village is young, only built in the 1600s. Monsieur's family have owned it for 100 years: he was born here and married a local girl who is now mayor. They are a sweet couple, quietly and unobtrusively attentive, and you will feel well tended, like the much-loved garden with its flowery bower holding a stone table. The pretty dining room has some superb family furniture, country French at its best; the pastel bedrooms have more antiques, crinkly pink lights and little bits of brocante.

rooms	2: 1 double + extra single, 1 suite for 4.
price	€38 for two.
meals	Restaurants Falaise, 3km; BBQ & picnic possible.
closed	Rarely.
directions	From Falaise D63 for Trun, 2km; 2nd left for Villy lez Falaise 1km; in village, farm first on right after stop sign.

Alice & Gilbert Thomas
Ferme la Croix,
14700 Villy lez Falaise,
Calvados
tel +33 (0)2 31 90 19 98
mob (0)6 74 46 84 92

Arclais

Such very special people, quietly, uncomplicatedly intelligent: what the house lacks in years is made up for tenfold by their timeless, down-to-earth Norman hospitality. Close to all things natural, they plough their big veg patch with the cob in harness, share organic dinners made to old forgotten recipes, offer good rooms where you wake to soul-lifting views over the hushed hills of *La Suisse Normande*. Nothing gushy or corny, these are independent, strong, comforting people who take you to their bosom and genuinely care for your well-being and that of the land.

rooms	3: 1 double, 1 twin, 1 suite.
price	€40 for two.
meals	Dinner with cider €16, book ahead.
closed	Rarely.
directions	From Caen D562 for Flers, 35km; at Le Fresne D1 for Falaise, 4km; house on right, sign.

Roland & Claudine Lebatard
Arclais,
14690 Pont d'Ouilly,
Calvados
tel +33 (0)2 31 69 81 65
fax +33 (0)2 31 69 81 65

Les Fontaines

Just about impossible to fault this big, elegant mansion with lovely, half-kempt garden and pool (unfenced), games room with drums, and excellent meals. Quite often Andrew cooks on the grand open fire, and is a relaxed host; dynamic Elizabeth is present at weekends. Up the lovely elm stair to sleeping and sitting rooms with generous light, glowing parquet, French and English antiques against pale walls; the big new attic bedroom is wonderful for families. The breakfast room is unusually frescoed, the dining room oak-beamed, and both have seriously big tables. Comfortable, civilised, easy.

rooms	5: 2 doubles, 3 family rooms, 1 single.
price	€65 for two.
meals	Dinner with wine €23, book ahead.
closed	Christmas & New Year.
directions	From Caen ring road exit 13 for Falaise; 9km, right to Bretteville sur Laize; continue to Barbery. House behind field on right, with high, green gates.

Elizabeth & Andrew Bamford
Les Fontaines,
14220 Barbery,
Calvados
tel +33 (0)2 31 78 24 48
fax +33 (0)2 31 78 24 49
e-mail information@lesfontaines.com
web www.lesfontaines.com

Château des Riffets

The square-set château stands handsome still as the park recovers from the 1999 storm. Taste the "world's best cider" (says Monsieur), admire yourself in myriad gilded mirrors, luxuriate in a jacuzzi, bare your chest to a power shower, play the piano, appreciate Madame's superb cooking, and lie at last in an antique bed in one of the great, deep-tinted bedrooms. Take a stroll in the 40-acre wooded park, hire a nearby horse or a canoe, hone your carriage-driving skills. Period ceilings, tapestries and furniture make Riffets a real château experience; the people make it very human.

rooms	4: 2 doubles, 2 suites.
price	€95-€145 for two.
meals	Dinner with wine & calvados €45, book ahead.
closed	Rarely.
directions	From Caen N158 for Falaise; at La Jalousie, right D23; right D235 just before Bretteville; signposted.

Anne-Marie & Alain Cantel
Château des Riffets,
14680 Bretteville sur Laize,
Calvados
tel +33 (0)2 31 23 53 21
fax +33 (0)2 31 23 75 14
e-mail acantel@free.fr
web www.jeanluc.de/riffets

Manoir de la Marjolaine

The Parisian burgher who built Marjolaine in 1850 designed a toes-in-the-water holiday retreat – then the sea retreated 300 metres. So peace reigns here behind the dunes, yet beach and village are within easy walking distance. Your friendly host is genuinely interested in people, chatting easily in his antique-furnished, tapestry-curtained dining room. He has created four good bedrooms with two exotic moods – African (with great balcony views) and Asian (with oriental marriage wardrobe) – and two classic French. Excellent jacuzzi bathrooms, a good feel of bourgeois comfort all over.

rooms	4: 2 doubles, 1 family room, 1 suite for 3.
price	€80-€120 for two; €130 for three.
meals	Good restaurants 200m.
closed	Rarely.
directions	From Caen D513 to Cabourg; after Peugeot garage, right into chemin de Cailloue; 100m stop; left, house signposted on left.

Éric Faye
Manoir de la Marjolaine,
14390 Le Home Varaville,
Calvados
tel +33 (0)2 31 91 70 25
fax +33 (0)2 31 91 77 10
e-mail eric.faye@orange.fr
web manoirdelamarjolaine.free.fr

La Malposte

It's just plain lovely, this little group of stone buildings with wooden footbridge over the rushing river, trees and flowers and hens. There's the age-old converted mill for the family and the 'hunting lodge' for guests, where Madame's talented decoration marries nostalgic past (antiques, old prints, photographs) and designer-hued present. A spiral stair winds to a sitting/dining room with your own kitchen and homemade jams; sun pours into the suite at the top. Woods for nut-gathering, beaches nearby, table tennis here and that playful stream. Your hosts are sweet and love having families.

rooms	3: 1 double; 1 double, 1 twin sharing shower & wc.
price	€58 for two.
meals	Restaurants 2-3km; self-catering possible.
closed	Rarely.
directions	From Ouistreham D35 through Douvres & Tailleville; over D404; right at r'bout entering Reviers; 2nd Chambres d'Hôtes on left.

Patricia & Jean-Michel Blanlot
La Malposte,
14470 Reviers,
Calvados
tel +33 (0)2 31 37 51 29
fax +33 (0)2 31 37 51 29

Le Clos St Bernard

It was the second farmhouse to be built in the village – and named, 400 years later, in honour of the Vandons' dog. Madame loves her house and its history, her family and her guests – and delights in concocting Breton breakfasts of *tergoule*, crêpes, homemade juice, rice pudding. Bedrooms are lovely, with pretty bedcovers and cushions and interesting antiques, showers have embroidered towels and the beamy two-bedroom suite is worth the climb. There's a big guest dining salon (and a kichenette where the hens once lived) that opens to a garden terraced against salt breezes. Charming, and great value.

rooms	3: 2 doubles, 1 family suite.
price	€45 for two. Singles €35. Minimum stay 2 nights.
meals	Restaurants 4-5km.
closed	15 December-15 January.
directions	From Caen ring-road north; exit 5 for Douvres la Délivrande; 8km, for Courseulles & Mer; at 6th x-roads D35 left to Reviers; straight over at r'bout; 1st left into rue de l'Église; house no. 36 at top of road with white gate.

Nicole Vandon
Le Clos St Bernard,
14470 Reviers,
Calvados

tel	+33 (0)2 31 37 87 82
fax	+33 (0)2 31 37 87 82
e-mail	nicole.vandon@free.fr
web	www.le-clos-st-bernard.ifrance.com

Le Mas Normand

Your young hosts have done a great job on their lovely 18th-century house at the end of the lane. Old stonework and beams, modern showers, decent beds and a modern-rustic style. Mylène has brought Provençal fabrics and handmade soaps from her native Drôme and bedrooms are sheer delight: the sunny yellow double on the ground floor, the charming suite, with *armoire de mariage*, across the yard. Christian is Norman and trained as a chef. Chicken, apples, calvados and laughter at dinner; at breakfast, perfect brioche and jams. Ducks, geese and hens roam; there are bikes, fridge and barbecue to borrow.

rooms	2: 1 double, 1 suite for 3-4.
price	€50-€65 for two. Suite €85 for three; €90 for four.
meals	Dinner with wine €25-€30, book ahead.
closed	Rarely, please book ahead.
directions	From Caen D7 for Douvres 8km; left D404 5.5km; D79 to Courseulles sur Mer; D514 to Ver sur Mer; at village entrance 1st left Av. Provence; 1st right; 1st left cul-de-sac; at end on right.

Christian Mériel & Mylène Gilles
Le Mas Normand,
14114 Ver sur Mer,
Calvados

tel	+33 (0)2 31 21 97 75
fax	+33 (0)2 31 21 97 75
e-mail	lemasnormand@wanadoo.fr
web	perso.wanadoo.fr/lemasnormand

Manoir des Doyens

The lovely old house of golden stone is the warmly natural home of interesting people: a fascinating military historian who takes battlefield tours (don't be daunted, you'll learn lots) and willingly shares his passion for the dramas that took place here, and his gentle lady who directs things masterfully and serves her own jams for breakfast. Stone stairs lead to big, comfortably casual guest rooms and good, clean bathrooms – nothing flashy. The courtyard houses several tribes of animal and a games room. Here is space and a genuine family-friendly welcome just 15 minutes' walk from the Cathedral.

rooms	3: 1 double, 2 triples.
price	€55 for two.
meals	Choice of restaurants in Bayeux, 1km.
closed	Rarely.
directions	On Bayeux bypass, at Campanile Hotel left on D572 for St Lô; second right; follow signs to arched gateway.

Lt-Col & Mrs Chilcott
Manoir des Doyens,
14400 Bayeux,
Calvados
tel +33 (0)2 31 22 39 09
fax +33 (0)2 31 21 97 84
e-mail chilcott@mail.cpod.fr

Le Relais de la Vignette

Back to our roots. A Celtic chieftain was buried here 2100 years ago; then the Romans stayed a bit; the present house is 11th century, rebuilt in 1801. Its brass-railed staircase and salon are gracious but the dining room, relaxed in its yellow and green garb with huge fireplace and modern bar, is the hub of life where a warm, jolly family take you naturally into their circle. Madame uses colour and style well, mixing bright with soft, antiques with artificial flowers. The comfortable, fluffy bedrooms, raftered in the attic, fireplaced below, look onto wide fields and the 'Norman' dinners have been praised to the skies.

rooms	4 doubles.
price	€50 for two.
meals	Dinner with wine €22, book ahead.
closed	Rarely.
directions	From Bayeux for Cherbourg 4km; at r'bout to Tour en Bessin; through village, left D100 for Crouay 1km; house on right.

Catherine & Bertrand Girard
Le Relais de la Vignette,
Tour en Bessin,
14400 Bayeux, Calvados
tel +33 (0)2 31 21 52 83
fax +33 (0)2 31 21 52 83
e-mail relais.vignette@wanadoo.fr
web perso.wanadoo.fr/relais.vignette/

13 rue aux Coqs

This delicious couple, she softly-spoken and twinkling, he jovial and talkative, have retired from farming and moved into Bayeux – you can glimpse the cathedral spires from their creamy-coloured townhouse which was probably part of the former bishop's palace. Beyond the wisteria, the door opens onto a lofty beamed living room rejoicing in good antiques and a monumental fireplace – through (yes) another is the kitchen. Upstairs, the pretty guest rooms, with excellent new bedding and pastel-tiled bathrooms, look quietly over the pocket-handkerchief back garden. An ideal town address.

rooms	3: 2 doubles, 1 twin.
price	€56 for two.
meals	Restaurant 50m.
closed	Rarely.
directions	From Caen N13 to Bayeux; for Gare SNCF; right after traffic lights; over 1st crossroads & traffic lights, park on left; house 50m on right, signposted.

Louis & Annick Fauvel
13 rue aux Coqs,
14400 Bayeux,
Calvados
tel +33 (0)2 31 22 52 32

Map 5 Entry 212

La Londe

Come through the wood and across the stream and with that timeless quality of solid country dwellers, the Ameys will wrap you in blue-eyed smiles – their unpretentious welcome is full of comfort and warmth. You find simple country furnishings, bar two superb Norman armoires; walls are pastel, curtains lace, bathroom pink, towels small. Breakfast brings incomparably good farm milk and butter; later you may be offered a glass of home-brewed *pommeau* and cider. The simplest, friendliest place you could imagine: lovely people, excellent value, and the wisteria blooms.

rooms	3 doubles, all with basin, sharing bath & separate wc.
price	€35-€37 for two.
meals	Good restaurants 3km.
closed	Rarely.
directions	From Caen A84 for Mt St Michel, exit 46 'Noyers Bocage'. Right D83 for Cheux 1.5km; left to Tessel; signposted.

Paul & Éliane Amey
La Londe,
14250 Tessel,
Calvados
tel +33 (0)2 31 80 81 12
fax +33 (0)2 31 80 81 57
e-mail paul.amey@wanadoo.fr

Map 5 Entry 213

Le Mesnil de Benneville

You could scarcely find easier, friendlier hosts than Joseph and Marie-Thé who have quantities of local lore and advice to communicate, will join you for a farm supper at the long table in the fresh-flowered guests' dayroom, with its log fire in winter, and create a generally fun-loving, relaxed atmosphere. There are animals for children, table football and volleyball for teenagers, *pétanque* for all. They are simple, genuine people, as are their gently-hued rooms and their welcome. This is superb value and far enough from the road not to suffer from much traffic noise.

rooms	2: 1 double; 1 suite for 3-4, with kitchen.
price	€37 for two; €45 for three; €54 for four.
meals	Dinner with wine €15, book ahead.
closed	Rarely.
directions	From A84 & E401 exit 42 on N175 for Cahagnes 2km; right & follow Chambres d'Hôtes signs to farm.

Joseph & Marie-Thé Guilbert
Le Mesnil de Benneville,
14240 Cahagnes,
Calvados
tel +33 (0)2 31 77 58 05
fax +33 (0)2 31 77 37 84
e-mail ferme.benneville@wanadoo.fr

La Suhardière

Up the drive, across the cleanest ever farmyard to this totally French house to be met by a charmingly hospitable owner. She delights in gardening and cooking while her husband runs the dairy farm. Beyond the dinky little hall, the salon, with its high-backed chairs, beams and antimacassars, is a good place for a quiet read. The big sunny bedrooms are cosily frilly with quantities of lace, country furniture and gentle morning views over the garden dropping down to the pond. Special extras are the pond for fishing, paths for walking, homemade yoghurt and cider – and pillows for the asking. *Small dogs welcome.*

rooms	3: 2 doubles, 1 suite.
price	€43 for two.
meals	Dinner with wine €20, book ahead.
closed	Rarely.
directions	From Caen A13 for Cherbourg, exit Carpiquet & Caumont l'Éventé; 500m before Caumont, left at Chambres d'Hôtes sign.

Alain & Françoise Petiton
La Suhardière,
14240 Livry,
Calvados
tel +33 (0)2 31 77 51 02
fax +33 (0)2 31 77 51 02
e-mail petiton.alain@wanadoo.fr

Le Mesnil

There are fresh flowers everywhere and your hosts, retired farmers, offer good country hospitality. Peace is the norm not the exception in this deeply rural spot, racehorses graze in the pasture and you are unhesitatingly received into a warm and lively family. Two rooms are in a converted outbuilding and have an appropriately rustic air with beams, old wardrobes and mini-kitchens. The upstairs room is bigger and lighter, the ground-floor room has a little private garden. The suite, ideal for families, is in the main house. Breakfast is at the family table. Children are welcome to visit their son's farm next door.

rooms	3: 2 doubles, both with kitchenette; 1 suite for 4.
price	€40 for two.
meals	Restaurant 5km; self-catering in 2 rooms.
closed	Rarely.
directions	From Argentan N158 for Caen; after sign 'Moulin sur Orne', left; house 800m on left; sign (3.5km from Argentan).

Janine & Rémy Laignel
Le Mesnil,
61200 Occagnes,
Orne
tel (0)2 33 67 11 12

Le Mouchel

A charming couple, she natural, strong and brave, he softly spoken and communicative, with three courteous, smiling sons, they have been enjoying B&B for 20 years now as well as running a large dairy herd. Their 300-year-old farmhouse contains two of the guest rooms; the family room is in the more recent extension with the breakfast room that leads onto the pretty patio. There's also a largish grassy area for run-around children. Rooms are floral, shiny floorboarded and have excellent beds and shower rooms. This is a good, reliable place to stay with a delightful family.

rooms	3: 1 double, 1 triple, 1 family suite for 4.
price	€44 for two. Suite €61-€70 for four.
meals	Restaurants St Laurent sur Mer, 4km.
closed	Rarely.
directions	From Cherbourg N13 S 76km; exit Formigny for St Laurent sur Mer; after church right 800m: entrance on left.

Odile & Jean-Claude Lenourichel
Le Mouchel,
14710 Formigny,
Calvados
tel +33 (0)2 31 22 53 79
fax +33 (0)2 31 21 56 55
e-mail odile.lenourichel@libertysurf.fr

Le Château

At the end of the road stands the original old old château, built in 1580. Here, two beamy bedrooms give onto the arched outbuildings round the yard, restored to tremendous shape and character and now a garden area for guests. In the main house, as well as two other rooms, you can admire the astounding roof timbers through a trap window. Rooms are pretty, pastelly, restful and private. Madame is a warm, well-read person, Monsieur is a trawler master, they travel lots, speak good English, love having guests and can discourse at fascinating length about the Vikings, the Inuits, the Dukes of Normandy...*Italian spoken.*

rooms	4: 2 doubles, 1 twin, 1 suite for 5.
price	€70-€85 for two.
meals	Good choice of restaurants walking distance.
closed	1 November-15 March.
directions	From Cherbourg N13; D514; exit for Grandcamp Maisy; at edge of village continue on D514 for Vierville sur Mer; just after water tower & football field, right (signposted tennis club). House at end of lane, 400m.

Dominique Marion
Le Château,
14450 Grandcamp Maisy, Calvados

tel	+33 (0)2 31 22 66 22
fax	+33 (0)2 31 22 25 77
e-mail	marionbandb@wanadoo.fr
web	perso.wanadoo.fr/alain.marion/gbindex.html

Ferme-Manoir de la Rivière

Breakfast by the massive fireplace may be candle or oil-lamp-lit on dark mornings in this ancient fortress of a farm. It also has a stupendous tithe barn and a little watchtower turned into a perfect gîte for two. Madame is proud of her family home, its flagstones worn smooth with age, its fine country antiques so suited to the sober, immensely high second-floor rooms – one has a shower in a tower, another looks over the calving field. Her energy is boundless and she is ever redecorating, cooking imaginative Norman cuisine, improving her rooms, much supported by her cattle-farmer husband – a great team.

rooms	3: 2 triples, 1 double.
price	€55-€57 for two.
meals	Dinner with cider or wine €20, during low-season, book ahead. Restaurants 4km.
closed	Rarely.
directions	From Bayeux N13 30km west; exit on D514 to Osmanville & on for Grandchamp, 5km; left for Géfosse Fontenay; house 800m on left before church.

Gérard & Isabelle Leharivel
Ferme-Manoir de la Rivière,
14230 Géfosse Fontenay, Calvados

tel	+33 (0)2 31 22 64 45
fax	+33 (0)2 31 22 01 18
e-mail	leharivel@wanadoo.fr
web	www.chez.com/manoirdelariviere

L'Hermerel

Some sort of perfection? A round pigeon tower and a private chapel complete the picture of this charming fortified working farm, parts of which are 15th century. The lofty beamed rooms and vast fireplaces have been carefully restored and it all feels unpretentiously stylish with a friendly, relaxed atmosphere. Up the old worn stone stair of the interconnecting wing to green velvet armchairs, taffeta drapes and vases of wild flowers: these bedrooms have been decorated quite beautifully. Breakfasts of compotes, special jams and *viennoiserie*, a walled garden to share and the sea a short walk away.

rooms	4: 1 double, 1 twin, 1 suite, 1 family room.
price	€60 for two.
meals	Choice of restaurants in Grandcamp Maisy.
closed	November-March.
directions	From Bayeux N13 30km west; exit on D514 to Osmanville & on for Grandcamp 4km; left D199a for Géfosse Fontenay 400m; follow yellow signs on right.

François & Agnès Lemarié
L'Hermerel,
14230 Géfosse Fontenay,
Calvados
tel +33 (0)2 31 22 64 12
fax +33 (0)2 31 22 76 37
e-mail lemariehermerel@aol.com

Château de Vouilly

Previously renovated in the 16th and 18th centuries... the glorified farm has 30 rooms with fabulous tiled and parquet floors and classic French décor. At its centre, the grand panelled dining room has sun pouring in from both sides and views across the moat, over the formal garden with its swings and myriad plants, down to the orangery. Breakfast is at separate tables here. The whole house is littered with woodcarvings and furniture made by Monsieur's father and bedrooms are, of course, splendidly, classically French. Madame is a gracious and outgoing hostess. *Pets by arrangement.*

rooms	5 doubles.
price	€65-€75 for two.
meals	Choice of restaurants 7-12km.
closed	December-March.
directions	From Cherbourg N13 to Isigny; right D5 for Le Molay; left near Vouilly church; château on right.

Marie-José & James Hamel
Château de Vouilly,
14230 Isigny sur Mer, Calvados
tel +33 (0)2 31 22 08 59
fax +33 (0)2 31 22 90 58
e-mail chateau.vouilly@wanadoo.fr
web www.chateau-vouilly.com

Le Manoir

Lush lawns, myriad flowers and white geese soften nature's wildness here where great swaying pines and a wild coast have stood guard for over 800 years – the English burnt the first castle in 1346. The 16th-century manor's stern granite face hides a warm, elegant welcome in rooms with good beds, superb fireplaces, big windows to let in the light and utterly personal decoration: pictures, antiques and books (breakfast is in the library). Madame, charming and knowledgeable, will enthrall you with tales of Norman history and has detailed maps for hikers; Monsieur is a jovial ex-teacher. Bask in it all.

rooms	2: 1 double, 1 suite for 3.
price	€65 for two. Suite €85 for three.
meals	Auberge walking distance.
closed	Rarely.
directions	From Cherbourg D901 to Barfleur; D1 for St Vaast. After end of Barfleur sign, 2nd right, 1st left.

Mme Claudette Gabroy
Le Manoir,
50760 Montfarville,
Manche
tel +33 (0)2 33 23 14 21

La Fèvrerie

One of our very best. Your blithe, beautiful, energetic hostess is a delight. Her shyly chatty ex-farmer husband now breeds racehorses while she indulges her passion for interior decoration: her impeccable rooms are a festival of colours, textures, antiques, embroidered linen. It's a heart-warming experience to stay in this wonderful old building where they love having guests; the great granite hearth is always lit for the delicious breakfast which includes local specialities on elegant china; there is a richly-carved 'throne' at the head of the long table. A stupendous place, very special people.

rooms	3: 2 doubles, 1 twin; children's room available.
price	€58-€68 for two.
meals	Good choice of restaurants in Barfleur, 3km.
closed	Rarely.
directions	From Cherbourg D901; after Tocqueville right, D10; 1st left.

Marie-France & Maurice Caillet
La Fèvrerie,
50760 Ste Geneviève,
Manche
tel +33 (0)2 33 54 33 53
fax +33 (0)2 33 22 12 50
e-mail caillet.manoirlafevrerie@wanadoo.fr

Manoir Saint Jean

Standing on the Normandy coastal hiking path, the old stone manor looks proudly across the town and out to sea. It is spotless, not over-modernised and furnished in pure French Formal style – all velvet, floral linen and marble-topped chests. Retired from farming, the sociable Guérards welcome guests with French courtesy and happily point them towards the cliff walks, the nearby blue-green granite château of Ravalet and other hidden sights. You are in quiet country, just 6km from the ferries – the separate room with its own outside entrance is ideal for early ferry-catchers.

rooms	3: 1 double, 1 twin; 1 triple with own entrance.
price	€47-€52 for two.
meals	Restaurants 3km.
closed	Rarely.
directions	From Cherbourg D901 to Tourlaville & for St Pierre Église. Right at lights for Chât. Ravalet & Ham. St Jean; up hill to 'Centre Aéré', follow Chambre d'Hôtes signs (3km from lights).

Mme Guérard
Manoir Saint Jean,
50110 Tourlaville,
Manche
tel +33 (0)2 33 22 00 86

Map 4 Entry 224

Eudal de Bas

Old-fashioned hospitality in a modern house. You are just a mile from the (often) glittering sea and Michel, who makes submarines, is happy to share his passion for sailing and might even take you coast-hopping. His shipbuilding skill is evident here: the attic space has been cleverly used to make two snug rooms with showers (one with a kitchenette for evening meals); the landing makes a pleasant sitting area. A brilliantly quiet position, simple décor, spotless rooms and an open, chatty hostess who will rise early for dawn ferry-catchers make it ideal for beach holidays and channel crossing alike.

rooms	2: 1 double, 1 triple.
price	€42 for two.
meals	Two restaurants within 2km; self-catering.
closed	Rarely.
directions	From Cherbourg D901 then D45 W 13km to Urville Nacqueville; 1st left by Hôtel Le Beau Rivage; up hill D22 for 2km; 2nd left; sign.

Michel & Éliane Thomas
Eudal de Bas,
50460 Urville Nacqueville, Manche
tel +33 (0)2 33 03 58 16
fax +33 (0)2 33 03 58 16
e-mail thomas.eudal@wanadoo.fr
web www.chez.com/lahague/hebergem/hote/urville1.htm

Map 4 Entry 225

Manoir de Bellaunay

Even the smallest bathroom oozes atmosphere through its oeil de boeuf. The youngest piece of this fascinating house is over 400 years old, its predecessor stood on the site of a monastery, the fireplace in the lovely *Medieval* bedroom carries the coat of arms of the original owners and your farmer hosts share their energy enthusiastically between a large beef herd, their ancient house and the guests they love to share it with. They have sought carved marriage wardrobes, lace canopies, footstools for the rooms – and hung tapestry curtains at the windows. Sheer comfort among warm old stones.

rooms	3: 2 doubles, 1 suite for 3.
price	€50-€70 for two.
meals	Choice of restaurants 4km.
closed	November-March.
directions	On RN13 exit at Valognes; follow Route de Quettehou D902; house 3km after Valognes, number 11.

Christiane & Jacques Allix-Desfauteaux
Manoir de Bellaunay,
50700 Tamerville, Manche
tel +33 (0)2 33 40 10 62
fax +33 (0)2 33 40 10 62
e-mail bellauney@wanadoo.fr
web www.bellauney.com

Le Château

The amazingly wonderful granite château with fairytale towers, crinkly walls and perfect outbuildings round the courtyard has spanned the centuries as wild breakers crashed on the endless beach 1km away. No wonder its owners worship it! Hosts and furnishings are irreproachably French and civilised – books, fine china, panelling, gilt mirrors, plush chairs, engravings. Your suite has ancient floor tiles, new bedding, a loo in a tower. Stay a while, make your own breakfast with homemade jam and fresh eggs and you may use the grand dining room, and get to know your literary *châtelaine*.

rooms	1 suite for 2-4.
price	€76 for two; €115 for four.
meals	Restaurants 2-3km.
closed	Rarely.
directions	From Cherbourg D904 for Carteret; 3km after Les Pieux, right D62 to Le Rozel; right D117 into village; house just beyond village; signposted.

Josiane & Jean-Claude Grandchamp
Le Château,
50340 Le Rozel,
Manche
tel +33 (0)2 33 52 95 08
fax +33 (0)2 33 02 00 35

La Lande

A laughing, talkative couple with taste and manners, your hosts give you "the best of France, the best of England" in their fabulous old Norman house. Antiques from both countries and English china inside, wild French hares and owls outside. The (smallish) twin and double are enticing, the studio room under the eaves big and full of light, all have deep comfort and oodles of towels. Seductive dining, sitting and reading rooms, too. Linda varies her menus, napkin colours and china; Ted, an expert on WWII, will take you round the landing beaches. A tremendous atmosphere of friendship and goodwill.

rooms	3: 2 doubles, 1 twin.
price	€55-€65 for two.
meals	Dinner with wine; picnics available; book ahead.
closed	Rarely.
directions	From Cherbourg S for Caen; D900 to Bricquebec via Le Pont; on for Valognes, past Intermarché, left at T-junc., left after 'Sapeurs Pompiers' for Les Grosmonts; on right after 400m.

Ted & Linda Malindine
La Lande,
50260 Bricquebec,
Manche

tel	+33 (0)2 33 52 24 78
fax	+33 (0)2 33 52 24 78
e-mail	la.lande@wanadoo.fr

Map 4 Entry 228

La Roque de Gouey

Madame is the same honest, open character as ever and Monsieur, retired, has time to spread his modest farmer's joviality. Two of our favourite owners, they have carefully restored an old *longère* on the edge of this pretty fishing town – spanking new lime-washed walls, bedding and floral prints. Your side of the house has its own entrance, dayroom with vast old fireplace, good furniture and little kitchen. Old beams and family photographs flourish. The two rooms up the steepish outside stairs are small but welcoming, the ground floor room is larger – and these people are remarkable hosts.

rooms	4: 1 twin, 1 double, 1 family room for 3, 1 family suite for 5.
price	€42 for two; €55 for three.
meals	Choice of restaurants 500m; self-catering possible.
closed	Rarely.
directions	From St Sauveur le Vicomte D15 to Portbail; right just before church Rue R. Asselin; over old railway; house 250m on right.

Bernadette Vasselin
La Roque de Gouey,
50580 Portbail,
Manche

tel	+33 (0)2 33 04 80 27
fax	+33 (0)2 33 04 80 27

Map 4 Entry 229

La Ferme de l'Église

The simple charm of the Clays' welcome is in harmony with the gentle marshes of the bird-rich Regional Park; an excellent circular walk and cycle path runs past farmhouse and church. In the well-converted house you climb the handsome, worn stone stairs to big, beamed or raftered, beautifully furnished, peaceful rooms (even 7am church bells are in keeping). The Clays put everyone at their ease, share their television, serve great breakfasts (homemade jams, own eggs) in front of an open fire, make their own cider. Children love the goats, ducks and hens – and the sandy beaches a 10-minute drive.

rooms	2: 1 double, 1 triple.
price	€40 for two.
meals	Restaurants 5-15km.
closed	Rarely.
directions	From La Haye du Puits, D903 for Barneville Carteret. At Bolleville, right on D127 to St Nicolas; left before church; house on right after cemetery.

Richard & Jay Clay
La Ferme de l'Église,
50250 St Nicolas de Pierrepont,
Manche
tel +33 (0)2 33 45 53 40
fax +33 (0)2 33 45 53 40
e-mail theclays@wanadoo.fr
web perso.wanadoo.fr/normandie-cottages-bed-and-breakfast

Village de Haut

After travelling the world, John and Valerie moved from Australia to this bird-lovers' haven (marsh, coastal and woodland species protected by the nature reserve) and are thoroughly integrated in their rural community. A lively, interesting and attentive couple, they understand home comforts and guests easily join them for coffee and chat. Leading off the kitchen, the gently-coloured ground-floor guest room is generous enough for some old-style Normandy furniture, a hand-made quilt and two extra beds. It looks over the pretty garden where chirruping peace is a constant and the sun shines a lot.

rooms	1 double with 2 extra children's beds.
price	€40 for two.
meals	Dinner €20, book ahead.
closed	Rarely
directions	From Cherbourg to Valognes take N13; left to Gorges; follow D97. First small lane on right.

Valerie & John Armstrong
Village de Haut,
50430 La Haye du Puits,
Manche
tel +33 (0)2 33 45 63 86
e-mail the.armstrong@free.fr

Le Pont Sanson

So old it's almost venerable: timbers dated 1400s, a spiral staircase up to big bedrooms full of antiques, personality and paintings, a Vielle Cuisine where fresh orange juice is served before a giant fireplace. Another 'wow' is the garden, planted for a brilliant effect of colour and perspective and sporting a delicious summer room for guests and the Monet-Grouvel Bridge – sense of humour too. Your hosts, she Scottish, he French, enthusiastic about their lovely home, who welcome you with real pleasure and give the guided tour to anyone interested in history, architecture and gardens.

rooms	2: 1 double, 1 twin/double with separate bath.
price	€75-€85 for two.
meals	Auberge 3km.
closed	Rarely.
directions	From Periers or St Lô D900 take D57 to Feugères; in village left D142 then D533 for Lozon. White gates on right.

Baron & Baronne Grouvel
Le Pont Sanson,
50190 Periers,
Manche

tel +33 (0)2 33 07 79 00
fax +33 (0)2 33 07 79 00

La Virmonderie

Sigrid's big country kitchen and crackling fire are the heart of this fine 18th-century granite house and you know instantly you are sharing her home: the built-in dresser carries pretty china, her pictures and ornaments bring interest to the salon and its Normandy fireplace, and she proudly tells how she rescued the superb elm staircase. A fascinating person, for years a potter in England, she has retired to France and vegetarian happiness. Bedrooms have colour and lace, unusual antiques and original beams. Five acres of garden mean plenty of space for children and grown-ups alike. Great value.

rooms	3 doubles.
price	€45 for two. Minimum stay 2 nights.
meals	Dinner with wine from €20; light supper €10; picnic baskets from €5; book ahead.
closed	January-February.
directions	From Carentan N174 to St Lo. for 12-13km; before major r'bout D377 for Cavigny; fourth house on right.

Sigrid Hamilton
La Virmonderie,
50620 Cavigny,
Manche

tel +33 (0)2 33 56 01 13
fax +33 (0)2 33 56 41 32
e-mail sigihamilton12@hotmail.com
web perso.wanadoo.fr/sigrid.hamilton

Le Suppey

The younger Franco-American Buissons have given a thorough internal facelift to this 18th-century farmhouse with its old stables and outbuildings flanking a flowered courtyard. Rooms are sprigged in peach or green, beds have new mattresses, the rustic furniture is locally made with marble tops, the watercolours are done by an aunt. It is all simple, sunny and most welcoming. Jean works during the week; Nancy, perfectly bilingual, is very present and loving her B&B activity. There's a green and secluded garden for picnics, and a small spring that has great damming-up potential for little ones!

rooms	2 doubles.
price	€40 for two.
meals	Restaurants in St Lô 5km.
closed	Rarely.
directions	From Cherbourg, N13 & N174 to St Lô. At St Georges-Montcocq, D191 to Villiers Fossard. In village, right on C7; house 800m on right.

Jean & Nancy Buisson
Le Suppey,
50680 Villiers Fossard,
Manche
tel +33 (0)2 33 57 30 23
e-mail nancy.buisson@wanadoo.fr
web perso.wanadoo.fr/nancy.buisson/

Saint Léger

The totally French farmhouse, 19th-century without, modern within, is colourful, neat and immaculate. One room is pink-flavoured, the other blue, each with bits of crochet, a carved armoire (one *charbourgoise*, the other from St Lô) and a clean, compact shower room; the gloriously ostentatious blue bathroom is also yours for the asking – giant tub and plants rampaging. But most special of all is the charming, elegant Madame Lepoittevin, full of smiles and laughter, and actively involved in a walking group in summer – why not join in? You can picnic in the garden or cook your own on the barbecue.

rooms	2: 1 double; 1 double with shower & separate wc.
price	€38 for two.
meals	Choice of restaurants 2-10km.
closed	1st two weeks of March.
directions	From St Lô D972 for Coutances, through St Gilles; house sign on left, 4km after St Gilles, on D972.

Jean & Micheline Lepoittevin
Saint Léger,
50570 Quibou,
Manche
tel +33 (0)2 33 57 18 41
fax +33 (0)2 33 57 18 41

La Rhétorerie

Here is old-style, down-to-earth, French country hospitality. Madame, an elderly live wire, full of smiles, humorous chat and spontaneous welcome, plays the organ in the village church. Monsieur, a retired farmer, is quietly interested. Their bedrooms have old family furniture (admire *grand-mère's* elaborately crocheted bedcover), really good mattresses, simple washing arrangements. It is all spotless and guests have a biggish, colourful dayroom with massive beams, lots of plants and a kitchen in the old cider press – the great stone is now a flower feature outside.

rooms	3: 1 double; 1 twin, 1 double, both with shower, sharing 2 wcs.
price	€38.50 for two.
meals	Restaurant 1km; choice St Lô 4km; self-catering possible.
closed	Rarely.
directions	From St Lô D999 for Percy, exit 5, 3km; right D38 for Canisy. House 1km along on right.

Marie-Thérèse & Roger Osmond
La Rhétorerie,
50750 St Ébremond de Bonfossé,
Manche
tel +33 (0)2 33 56 62 98

Les Hauts Champs

This place is so French: rich carpeting on floors and walls, highly floral linen, toiletries, bathrobes and bonbons. Monsieur breeds horses and riding is possible for experienced riders; the less horsey can visit the stables which have produced great show jumpers. Madame cooks the food, including bread and croissants, and serves you special meals in the beamed and colombaged kitchen. She and her husband are wonderful hosts, it is all snug and homey (one room up steep wooden stairs), the setting is charming, among hills, woods and fields. Perfect for winter visits, too.

rooms	2: 1 double, 1 twin.
price	€40 for two.
meals	Dinner with wine €20, book ahead.
closed	Rarely.
directions	From Coutances D971 for Granville; fork quickly left D7 for Gavray for 1.5km; left D27 to Nicorps; through village; 1st right; house on left, signposted.

M & Mme Posloux
Les Hauts Champs,
50200 Nicorps,
Manche
tel +33 (0)2 33 45 30 56
fax +33 (0)2 33 07 60 21

Château des Boulais

There is space and grandeur in this mixed-period château and Madame and her Dutch partner have bravely taken up the colour challenge: the red and cream sitting room is vast, bedrooms have big colourful paintings and strong plain walls alongside old wooden floors and fireplaces – it's almost minimalist yet great fun and the views sail out of those big windows across copses and woods for miles. Your hostess, a strong, easy-going, independent woman with a fine sense of humour, adores meeting new people and hearing about their lives, her four teenagers are a delight and her meals delicious.

rooms	3 doubles.
price	€50-€70 for two.
meals	Dinner €15, book ahead; wine €10.
closed	Christmas & New Year.
directions	From Villedieu les P. N175 & D524 for Vire 1.5km; right D999 for Brécey. After Chérencé le H. left through St Martin le Bouillant to sawmill; follow signs to Loges sur Brécey; house 2km, 2nd left after wood.

Nathalie de Drouas
Château des Boulais,
50800 St Martin le Bouillant,
Manche
tel +33 (0)2 33 60 32 20
fax +33 (0)2 33 60 45 20

Map 4 Entry 238

Belleville

They say there are as many horses as inhabitants in the area: your hosts train racehorses and are also bringing up five children in this deep country spot by the sea – Mont St Michel can be seen from the roof windows. They are energetic and sociable, have lots of time for guests and really enjoy doing B&B. Your rooms and bathrooms are refreshingly minimalist in their white paint and duvets with simple country or wicker furniture. In the morning, you go through an immaculate kitchen to the simply furnished yellow and blue dining room for a generous breakfast.

rooms	2: 1 double, 1 twin.
price	€58 for two.
meals	Restaurants 3km.
closed	Rarely.
directions	From A13 & N176 exit Avranches for Granville; over bridge; left D911 for Jullouville; in Dragey right before petrol station 1km; left for Dragey l'Église; house 800m on left.

Florence & Olivier Brasme
Belleville,
Dragey l'Église,
50530 Sartilly, Manche
tel +33 (0)2 33 48 93 96
fax +33 (0)8 25 18 74 48
e-mail belleville@mt-st-michel.net
web www.mt-st-michel.net

Map 4 Entry 239

La Haute Gilberdière

Generous, artistic and young in spirit, the Champagnacs are a privilege to meet. Their 18th-century *longère* bathes in a floral wonderland: roses climb and tumble, narrow paths meander and a kitchen garden grows your breakfast – wander and revel or settle down in a shady spot. Inside, bedrooms are perfect with handsome antiques, pretty bed linen and polished floors or modern with pale wood and bucolic views. The honey-coloured breakfast room is warmly contemporary – all timber and exposed stone – pots of homemade jam roost between the beams. A deeply romantic place to stay.

rooms	2 + 1: 2 doubles; 1 apartment with double & twin sharing bath & wc.
price	€78-€150 for two. Minimum stay 2 nights.
meals	Good restaurants 5-25km.
closed	November-March.
directions	From Avranches D973 for Granville & Sartilly; left at end of village D61 for Carolles; after 800m house on left.

Édith & Pierre Champagnac
La Haute Gilberdière,
50530 Sartilly,
Manche
tel +33 (0)2 33 60 17 44
e-mail champagnac@libertysurf.fr
web www.champagnac-farmhouse.com

Map 4 Entry 240

Le Val

These are solid, earthy, farming folk, part of deeply rural France. Monsieur was born in this 200-year-old house and Madame, who is a bit shy, has a lovely sunny smile. She keeps lots of poultry and always encourages guests to visit Sourdeval on Tuesdays to see the cattle market in full swing. Their rooms are unpretentiously simple with candlewick bedcovers, old floor tiles, wooden wardrobes and views of the farmyard or the valley. The family room has a mezzanine for children and a modern bathroom. Guests breakfast at one long table and are welcome to watch the milking. Real people, real value.

rooms	2 + 1: 1 double, 1 triple sharing shower & separate wc. 1 cottage with family room.
price	€31 for two.
meals	Choice of restaurants 5km.
closed	Rarely.
directions	From Sourdeval D977 for Vire 6km. Just before 'end of Manche' sign right for Le Val. 2km on right.

Jeanne & Raymond Desdoits
Le Val,
50150 Sourdeval,
Manche
tel +33 (0)2 33 59 64 16
fax +33 (0)2 33 69 36 99

Hello

Map 4 Entry 241

Les Blotteries

Monsieur, formerly a fire officer, is proud of his restoration of the old farm (the B&B is his project, Madame works in town). He is an attentive, positive host, full of smiles and jokes, and has done a good job. Old granite glints as you pass into the softly-curtained entrance; an original hay rack hangs above. One bedroom is on the first floor, another is in the former stable, a third in the old bakery: a ground-floor family room whose large windows overlook the courtyard. The cream breakfast room is simple and elegant and the fields around are open to all so no need to worry about the road at the front.

rooms	3: 1 double, 2 family rooms.
price	€58 for two.
meals	Restaurants in Juilley, 1km.
closed	Rarely.
directions	From A84 exit 33; right at r'bout & uphill for about 300m to next r'bout; left then left again D998 for St James; house on right after 5km.

Laurence & Jean-Malo Tizon
Les Blotteries,
50220 Juilley, Manche
tel +33 (0)2 33 60 84 95
fax +33 (0)2 33 60 84 95
e-mail bb@les-blotteries.com
web www.les-blotteries.com

Le Petit Manoir

Three big rooms and a dayroom face Mont St Michel! And that view is definitely worth the detour; you can walk to the Mount in two hours. The Gédouins keep cows and pigs; Annick, who used to teach, makes jams, crêpes and delicious breakfast rice pudding (a Breton speciality); Jean is Mayor. Rooms are French country style, without frills or soft touches, but spotless clean; one has wheelchair access. In the courtyard are passion fruit and figs; two large cider presses brim with geraniums. All is rural peace in this tiny village by the marshes.

rooms	5: 1 double, 1 twin, 1 triple, 2 family rooms.
price	€38-€45 for two.
meals	Restaurants 500m-2km.
closed	15 November-7 February.
directions	From A84 exit 33 for St Malo & Pontorson on N175 for 9km; right to Servon; at church right for 500m; farm on left.

Annick, Jean & Valérie Gédouin
Le Petit Manoir,
50170 Servon,
Manche
tel +33 (0)2 33 60 03 44
fax +33 (0)2 33 60 17 79
e-mail agedouinmanoir@tiscali.fr

La Ferme de l'Étang

An authentic farm B&B in a glorious setting. Ivy on walls, beamed attic bedrooms with fresh flowers, woodland walks, lake and château across the way – and a proper farming family. Jean-Paul and Brigitte are friendly, interested people, travel a lot and talk well. He is a dairy farmer and arbitrator, she collects copper and brass. Country meals (quite delicious) are taken round the big table in the dining room with its huge fireplace. A splendid staircase leads you up to the good, snug, cottagey yet unfussy guest rooms. Children love it – there are games galore, swings in the garden and cows all around.

rooms	4: 2 doubles, 2 family rooms.
price	€43-€45 for two.
meals	Dinner with wine €15, book ahead.
closed	Rarely.
directions	From Cherbourg A84 exit 34 for Mt St Michel & St Malo 600m; exit for Mt St Michel & Rennes D43 for Rennes. At r'bout D40 for Rennes, 5.5km; D308 left; signposted.

Jean-Paul & Brigitte Gavard
La Ferme de l'Étang,
Vergoncey,
50240 St James, Manche
tel +33 (0)2 33 48 34 68
fax +33 (0)2 33 48 48 53
e-mail jpgavard@club-internet.fr

La Gautrais

The old granite stable block, built in 1622, was modernised in the 1970s: polished floors and easy furnishings, cots in the attic rooms and a kitchenette – ideal for families. It is all clean and comfortable in solid farmhouse style and guests may use the beamy sitting room. The Balcony Room is in a league of its own with exposed timbers and… a (glassed-in) balcony. Madame is quietly friendly, "makes a superb soufflé" and mouthwatering Norman cuisine – she loves it. The poetically-named but perfectly ordinary Two Estuaries motorway now provides quick access 1km away.

rooms	4: 1 double, 1 twin, 1 triple, 1 quadruple.
price	€40 for two.
meals	Dinner with wine €15, book ahead.
closed	Rarely.
directions	From A84 exit 32 at St James then D12, following signs for Super U store for Antrain, 900m. On right.

François & Catherine Tiffaine
La Gautrais,
50240 St James,
Manche
tel +33 (0)2 33 48 31 86
fax +33 (0)2 33 48 58 17
e-mail catherine.tiffaine@wanadoo.fr

photo Michael Busselle

brittany

Épineu

Fear not, the farm mess is forgotten once you reach the cottage and the long, rural views beyond. Through that timbered porch, a sprightly, brave and unpretentious lady will lead you into her big, wood-floored and -ceilinged country dining room – warmed in winter by the old granite fireplace, it is uncluttered and soberly French. Bedrooms are simple and unfussy too, with sloping ceilings and soft rugs, roof windows or dormers; the garden is tended with love and pride and produces vegetables for dinner, when you can enjoy intelligent and wide-ranging conversation (in French) with an interesting companion.

rooms	3: 1 triple; 1 double, 1 single sharing small bath & separate wc.
price	€46 for two; €61 for three.
meals	Dinner €16, book ahead; wine €9.50.
closed	Rarely.
directions	From Rennes N137 S exit Poligné D47 for Bourg des Comptes for 4km; left to L'Aubrais; right into & across farmyard, down lane 20m, cottage on right.

Yvette Guillopé
Épineu,
35890 Bourg des Comptes,
Ille-et-Vilaine
tel +33 (0)2 99 52 16 84

Manoir de la Ruisselée

Here be a genuine welcome and… wizards. Brocéliande forest, just 500m away, was Merlin's home. The enchantment continues. The suite has two real little round windows and some magic ones in the amazing, soft-coloured murals. Madame's good taste and new ideas in handling her lovely big old manor house give it huge originality; old it is, mainly 1760s with some 15th-century bits, rambling organically round the courtyard. Comfortable but not lavish rooms, beautiful woodwork, fresh juice in the log-warmed breakfast room, a most unusual, interesting companion – one feels at peace here.

rooms	3: 2 doubles, 1 suite for 4.
price	From €50 for two.
meals	Choice of restaurants 1-5km.
closed	Rarely.
directions	From Rennes N24 to Plélan le Gr.; right at church D59 for St Malon sur M.; 1st left: Ch. des Châteaux 1km; house on top of small hill, entrance behind on left.

Mme Christine Hermenier
Manoir de la Ruisselée,
35380 Paimpont,
Ille-et-Vilaine
tel +33 (0)2 99 06 85 94

Hello

Château du Pin

Watercolourist and photographer, the brave, artistic Ruans have launched with passionate enthusiasm into renovating a small château with its ruined chapel, stables and thrilling atmosphere. Their sense of space and colour will triumph. The original staircase curves up to the 'literary' guest rooms: mauve/silver *Proust*, ochre/gold *George Sand*, theatrical suite *Victor & Juliette*; each shower is behind a great rafter; the vastly magnificent drawing/billiard room wears rich reds – it's brilliant, and great fun. Your gentle hosts love cooking – then sharing dinner and stimulating talk with you.

rooms	3: 1 twin, 2 family suites for 4.
price	€58-€65 for two; €100-€111 for four.
meals	Dinner with wine €23, book ahead.
closed	Rarely.
directions	From Rennes N12 west to Bédée 23km; D72 to Montfort sur Meu; D125 for St Méen le Grand; château 4km on left.

Catherine & Luc Ruan
Château du Pin,
35370 Iffendic près de Montfort,
Ille-et-Vilaine

tel	+33 (0)2 99 09 34 05
fax	+33 (0)2 99 09 34 05
e-mail	luc.ruan@wanadoo.fr
web	www.chateau_du_pin_broceliande.com

Château du Quengo

Two fascinating generations of an ancient Breton family welcome you open-armed to their inimitable house where history, atmosphere and silence rule: private chapel, fishing pond and rare trees outside, monumental oak staircase, Italian mosaic floor, 1900s wallpaper, about 30 rooms inside. Madame Mère sparkles and tells you myriad tales of ancestors (one royalist exile is buried near Waterloo Station); Anne plys you with homemade delights or teaches you wickerwork; Alfredo builds organs (there may be piano recitals...). The bathroom has a claw-footed bath and bedrooms are properly old-fashioned.

rooms	5: 3 doubles, 2 quadruples. Kitchen available.
price	€47-€70 for two.
meals	Choice of restaurants 1.5-5km.
closed	Rarely.
directions	From N12 for St Brieuc exit at Bédée D72 to Irodouer; 1st right before church to Romillé; château entrance 600m on left, signposted.

Anne & Alfred
du Crest de Lorgerie
Château du Quengo,
35850 Irodouer,
Ille-et-Vilaine

tel	+33 (0)2 99 39 81 47
e-mail	lequengo@hotmail.com
web	www.chateauduquengo.com

Le Pont Ricoul

The little lakeside cottage in the old bakery is a dream, far enough from the main house to feel secluded… it is snugly romantic, utterly seductive. The suite off the big house is larger and as pretty, its split levels twinned by a blue-painted stair. Cane chairs, sunny curtains, a granite handbasin, rugs on parquet: a dreamy décor in a bucolic setting. If your need for intimacy is deep, then Catherine will deliver breakfast and dinner (course by course, and delicious) to your hideaway. Nicer still to join them at their artistic table; they are young and delightful and we have received nothing but praise.

rooms	2: 1 suite for 4 with salon; 1 suite in cottage with salon.
price	€45-€56 for two; €71-€82 for four.
meals	Dinner with wine €20, book ahead.
closed	Rarely.
directions	From St Malo N137 to St Pierre de Plesguen; by church D10 for Lanhelin 1.5km; signposted on right.

Catherine & François Grosset
Le Pont Ricoul,
35720 St Pierre de Plesguen,
Ille-et-Vilaine
tel +33 (0)2 99 73 92 65
fax +33 (0)2 99 73 94 17
e-mail pontricoul@aol.com
web www.pontricoul.com

Le Petit Moulin du Rouvre

Leave the modern world behind and come a while to this 17th-century watermill. Régis has taken over from his grandmother and is an excellent host – professional yet charmingly easy-going. Bedrooms are all special in some way: one overlooks the swishing wheel (fear not, it's turned off at night), another has an enormous window, its own staircase and front door, another looks over the lake and all those lily pads. They are dressed in satin and lace, country and antique furniture and have excellent beds, good bathrooms and homely bits and pieces dotted around. And we believe he's a good cook.

rooms	5: 3 doubles, 2 triples.
price	€60-€63 for two.
meals	Dinner with wine €23, book ahead.
closed	Rarely.
directions	From Rennes-St Malo N137, exit St Pierre de Plesguen; D10 for Lanhélin: right for 2.5km; signposted.

Régis Maillard
Le Petit Moulin du Rouvre,
35720 St Pierre de Plesguen,
Ille-et-Vilaine
tel +33 (0)2 99 73 85 84
fax +33 (0)2 99 73 71 06
e-mail maillard.regis@aumoulindurouvre.com
web www.aumoulindurouvre.com

Manoir de Launay-Blot

All the salty history of Brittany's seafaring adventurers is stored in the granite and oak of this handsome old mariner's manor where a heavy four-poster, a light brass bed, a gentle canopy echo the changing moods of man and nature. The heavily-papered dining room is an endearing backdrop of formal and faded grandeur for meals served at separate tables. Your hosts and their adult children, all eager to help if somewhat shy and who live in another wing, are restoring the sitting room in the traditional style. It is Breton-grand yet relaxed and welcoming and the bigger rooms are excellent value.

rooms	5: 2 doubles, 1 triple, 2 family suites for 4.
price	€61-€78 for two.
meals	Dinner with wine €19, book ahead.
closed	Rarely.
directions	From Dol de Britagne D676 for Dinon; at last r'bout D119 for Baguer Morvan; after village, 2nd left after cemetery.

M & Mme Mabile
Manoir de Launay-Blot,
35120 Dolde-Bretagne,
Ille-et-Vilaine
tel +33 (0)2 99 48 07 48
fax +33 (0)2 99 80 94 47
e-mail launay.blot@cergiv.cernet.fr
web www.pays-de-dol.com

La Hamelinais

Old bones: the largest mammoth skeleton ever discovered in Europe was found at Mont Dol; old stones: Mont St Michel is so close. But it's Marie-Madeleine who makes this place special: up before breakfast to lay the fire and, in summer, giving her all to garden and orchard. Gentle, bright-eyed Jean says that, tied to the farm, he "travels through his guests". Of course the wear and tear of returning guests shows in some of the linen – so what? Rooms are good, the fireplace huge, your hosts know and love their region intimately and the sea is just 3km away. *Stays of 2 nights or more preferred.*

rooms	3: 2 doubles, 1 triple.
price	€43 for two.
meals	Choice of restaurants in Dol de Bretagne 4km.
closed	Rarely.
directions	From St Malo N137 for Rennes 15km; exit N176 for Mt St Michel 12km. At Dol de Bretagne D80 for St Broladre 3km; left D85 for Cherrueix; house sign on right before 3rd little bridge.

Jean & Marie-Madeleine Glémot
La Hamelinais,
35120 Cherrueix,
Ille-et-Vilaine
tel +33 (0)2 99 48 95 26
fax +33 (0)2 99 48 89 23

Le Presbytère

Solid granite, earth energy: inside its walled garden, the vast old priest's house is warm, reassuring and superbly restored: fine old timbers, antiques, panelling, hangings. Dotted around the house, each bedroom has character... perhaps a sleigh bed or a canopy, a staircase straight or spiral, pretty fabrics, white bedcovers, a garden view; our favourites are those with private entrances. There's a sense of its never ending, there's even a classy mobile home. Breakfast is a feast and Madame, a lovely energetic and warmly attentive person, loves cooking. You will leave with new friends in your address book.

rooms	5: 1 double, 1 twin sharing bath; 1 suite for 3, 2 triples.
price	€40-€46.
meals	Dinner €17-€20, book ahead; wine list.
closed	15-31 January.
directions	From Pontorson D219 to Vieux-Viel; follow signs for 'Chambres d'Hôte Vieux-Viel'; next to church.

Madeleine Stracquadanio
Le Presbytère,
35610 Vieux-Viel,
Ille-et-Vilaine
tel +33 (0)2 99 48 65 29
fax +33 (0)2 99 48 61 29
e-mail madeleine.stracquadanio@voila.fr
web www.vieux-viel.com

Les Mouettes

House and owner are imbued with the calm of a balmy summer's morning, whatever the weather – timeless simplicity reigns inside, modernity bustles on the village street. Isabelle's talent seems to touch the very air that fills her old family house. There is nothing superfluous: simple carved pine furniture, an antique wrought-iron cot, dhurries on scrubbed plank floors, palest yellow or mauve walls to reflect the ocean-borne light, harmonious striped or gingham curtains. Starfish and many-splendoured pebbles keep the house sea-connected. The unspoilt seaside village is worth the trip alone.

rooms	5: 4 doubles, 1 twin.
price	€46 for two.
meals	Choice of restaurants in village.
closed	Rarely.
directions	From St Malo, N137 for Rennes. 6km after St Malo, right on D117 to St Suliac (3km from N137 exit to village entrance). Road leads to Grande Rue down to port; house at top on right.

Isabelle Rouvrais
Les Mouettes,
35430 St Suliac,
Ille-et-Vilaine
tel +33 (0)2 99 58 30 41
fax +33 (0)2 99 58 39 41
e-mail contact@les-mouettes-saint-suliac.com
web www.les-mouettes-saint-suliac.com

Le Clos Saint Cadreuc

New to B&B, your shy eager hostess plans to put generous, Breton dishes on your plate and her husband, who works in town, to pour good organic wines – they create a welcoming atmosphere in their stone farmhouse. The stylish, very French rooms in the converted stables are enlivened by primitive West Indian paintings and there's more colour and garden lushery along the long slow steps through the rockery to the terrace outside your windows. Great bathrooms, a small guest sitting room, real peace in this quiet hamlet just 2km from the coast and a stone's throw from Mont St Michel.

rooms	3 + 1 apartment: 2 doubles, 1 twin; 1 apartment for 4-5.
price	€56 for two.
meals	Dinner with wine €20, book ahead. Good restaurants 4km.
closed	January.
directions	From St Malo D168 for St Brieuc. At 1st r'bout after Ploubalay D26 for Plessix Balisson for 4km to hamlet; house on right, signposted.

Brigitte & Patrick Noël
Le Clos Saint Cadreuc,
22650 Ploubalay, Côtes-d'Armor

tel	+33 (0)2 96 27 32 43
fax	+33 (0)2 96 27 32 43
e-mail	clos-saint-cadreuc@wanadoo.fr
web	www.clos-saint-cadreuc.com

La Belle Noé

Vibrant and energetic, Chantal does everything: gardening (she grows summer flowers for sale beyond the zinc planters), restoration (her father helps with the carpentry), decorating (every room has its own arrangement of dried mushrooms, eggs, moss, paintings), furniture renovation – it's a festival of style, flair and impeccable finish. You sleep on new mattresses in fine old beds beneath the beams of cottagey bedrooms on polished wood floors, wash in generous basins on marble tops in big soft bathrooms, eat in the tangerine dining room. Then borrow a bike to a Breton adventure.

rooms	3: 1 double, 2 family rooms.
price	€54-€84 for two. Minimum stay 3 nights.
meals	Dinner with wine €22, book ahead.
closed	Rarely.
directions	From St Malo for Rance; D768 for St Brieuc & Plancoët. At r'bout, for Crehen; continue for 2.5km; 1st road on right.

Chantal Bigot
La Belle Noé,
22130 Crehen, Côtes-d'Armor

tel	+33 (0)2 96 84 08 47
fax	+33 (0)2 96 80 41 88
e-mail	info@crehen.com
web	www.crehen.com

La Pastourelle

Here is a long, low Breton house built on hard Breton granite, guarded by a soft Breton spaniel and kept by a relaxed and generous Breton woman whose family has owned it for generations and who lives in the little house. Small bedrooms are off the corridor upstairs, and old pine is everywhere – ceilings, wardrobes, beams, beds; there are fabrics and fancies: gingham cloths, floral curtains, lace cushions. Breakfasts and good suppers (which must be booked ahead) are cooked on a wood-fired range and served on attractive rough pottery at separate tables in the guests' dining room. Great for those on a budget.

rooms	6: 3 doubles, 1 twin, 1 triple, 1 double & bunks.
price	€40-€42 for two.
meals	Dinner with wine €16.50, book ahead.
closed	Rarely.
directions	From Dinard, D168 to Ploubalay & D768 to Plancoët; D19 to St Lormel; left opp. school at far end of village; follow signs for 1.5km.

Évelyne Ledé
La Pastourelle,
22130 Plancoët,
Côtes-d'Armor
tel +33 (0)2 96 84 03 77
fax +33 (0)2 96 84 03 77

53/55 rue de Coëtquen

Sheer delight for lovers of the utterly personal, even eccentric. In this miniature museum of a house where the orange-draped dining room leads to an elegant yellow salon, the warm and vibrant Rhona will introduce you to her wiggly Chinese sofa, her husband's regimental drum and her remarkable collection of 18th-century looking-glasses. Unsurpassed hospitality, a new little conservatory, comfortable bedrooms (you may prefer the one without the barely screened-off loo), a generous and elegant breakfast, and the tiniest Yorkie in France. Make time for Dinan, a lovely place.

rooms	2 doubles.
price	€58-€62 for two.
meals	Wide choice of restaurants close by.
closed	Occasionally.
directions	From town centre square, Place du Guesclin, towards Port, past tourist office. 100yds right through Port. St Louis gate 2nd left into Rue Coëtquen.

Rhona Lockwood
53/55 rue de Coëtquen,
22100 Dinan,
Côtes-d'Armor
tel +33 (0)2 96 85 23 49
fax +33 (0)2 96 87 51 44

La Corbinais

The grand old family house, a 15th-century Breton *longère*, has a cosy, farm atmosphere, utterly delightful owners who are generous with their time and talk, plus a nine-hole golf course and all the trappings (clubhouse, lessons, socialising), carp ponds for those with rods and imaginative decoration. Madame, who paints, has a flair for interiors and uses velvet and florals, plants, paintings, sculptures and photographs – her rooms are appealingly personal and very comfortable. The old Breton bread oven is working again for the baking of bread and the birds cavort in the trees.

rooms	3: 2 doubles, 1 family room.
price	€52 for two.
meals	Good restaurant 4km.
closed	Rarely.
directions	From Dinan N176 for St Brieuc; at Plélan le Petit D19 right to St Michel de Plélan; 1km after village, follow golf sign to left.

Odile & Henri Beaupère
La Corbinais,
22980 St Michel de Plélan,
Côtes-d'Armor
tel +33 (0)2 96 27 64 81
fax +33 (0)2 96 27 68 45
e-mail corbinais@corbinais.com
web www.corbinais.com

Malik

The everyday becomes remarkable in these people's hands: we seldom consider modern houses but sensitively-designed Malik sailed in. Clad in red cedar, open-plan to provide space for six children, its wood, metal and sliding glass doors are in harmony with the dense trees, and every detail is taken care of. Plain white covers on good beds, eastern-style cushions and wall hangings on plain walls, monogrammed towels and lovely soaps. Breakfast, *un peu brunch*, is carefully attended to, and breads and jams homemade. Lovely people and an exquisitely serene house that seems to hug its garden to its heart.

rooms	2: 1 suite with salon, 1 suite for 4 (2 bedrooms).
price	€59 for two; €77 for three; €90 for four.
meals	Restaurants within walking distance.
closed	December-March.
directions	From Dinan N176 W for St Brieuc for about 12km. Exit right to Plélan le Petit. Follow signs to Centre & Mairie; at Mairie right for St Maudez then 2nd right.

Martine & Hubert Viannay
Malik,
22980 Plélan le Petit,
Côtes-d'Armor
tel +33 (0)2 96 27 62 71
e-mail bienvenue@malik-bretagne.com
web www.malik-bretagne.com

La Ville Lieu de Fer

The energetic Richardsons bought this luxuriously renovated manor-farm complex from the American designer who created its international look in 1998 and plan to mix B&B in the main house and self-catering in the two cottages. The décor uses *Jouy* wall fabrics in cool blue or lively red and plain quilted bedcovers; there are antiques and attractive modern bathrooms (just one loo upstairs and one down), a vast great living room with an enormous table and a blazing fire in winter. It's a lovely spot and the unsung medieval towns of inland Brittany deserves attention. A high price for a high standard.

rooms	3: 1 double, 2 twins; 2 separate wcs.
price	€100 for two.
meals	Restaurants nearby.
closed	Rarely.
directions	From N176 for Jugon les Lacs; for Plenée-Jugon & Le Gouray D792; in Le Gouray, keep church on right, bear right at bottom of hill, right fork, right at sign for Chapel St Roch, iron gates at top of hill.

Mike & Gaile Richardson
La Ville Lieu de Fer,
22330 Collinée,
Côtes-d'Armor

tel	+33 (0)2 96 34 95 30
fax	+33 (0)2 96 34 95 30
e-mail	richardson.michael@wanadoo.fr

Château de Bonabry

Incomparable: an extraordinary old château, built in 1373 by the Viscount's ancestor, the sea at the bottom of the drive, vastly wonderful bedrooms, a lively, lovable couple of aristocratic hosts bent on riding, hunting and entertaining you – do come on horseback. Breakfast is in your room or in the dining room with the family silver and antiques. Madame is using her energy and taste in renovating some of the 30 rooms. One suite is pink, another blue and yellow. Beds are draped, windows tall, portraits ancestral, rugs cotton, chapel 18th century, roses myriad – atmosphere unreal yet utterly alive.

rooms	3: 2 suites, 1 double.
price	€85-€130 for two.
meals	Good choice of restaurants 5km.
closed	October-Easter.
directions	From St Brieuc N12 for Lamballe, exit Yffigniac-Hillion; left D80 to Hillion; D34 for Morieux, 200m to roadside cross on left by château gates.

Vicomtesse Louis
du Fou de Kerdaniel
Château de Bonabry,
22120 Hillion, Côtes-d'Armor

tel	+33 (0)2 96 32 21 06
fax	+33 (0)2 96 32 21 06
e-mail	bonabry@wanadoo.fr
web	www.bonabry.fr.st

56 rue de la Ville Éveque

A wonder at every turn: a life-size bronze panther, seahorses flowing up the oakstair, a zebra-covered throne for an Arab prince, the stone, bronze and marble works of sculptor Pierre Roche whose summer retreat this was. Yours now, in all its Breton austerity, and its superb gardens falling away to the bluebell wood, its private lane to the shore, its owners' eclectic collection of furniture, *objets* and art, Monsieur's amazing Egyptian photographs, its quilty, lacey bedrooms on different themes. Ask your hosts about the history of the house and its previous occupants: they'll regale and delight you.

rooms	4: 3 doubles, 1 family room.
price	€70-€100 for two.
meals	Good restaurants 2-4km.
closed	Rarely.
directions	RN12 west of St Brieuc; D768, exit Les Rampes for Pordic; at 2nd r'bout for Pordic centre; right at church; left at r'bout past Mairie, 700m; 3rd right; 1st left.

Isabelle & Jean-Yves Le Fevre
56 rue de la Ville Éveque,
22590 Pordic,
Côtes-d'Armor

tel	+33 (0)2 96 79 17 32
e-mail	keryos@wanadoo.fr
web	www.keryos.com

Château de Kermezen

A very special place, aristocratic Kermezen has been in the family for 600 years and feels as if it will stand for ever in its granite certainty. Its 17th-19th-century 'modernisation' is a masterpiece of understated elegance: high ceilings, generous windows, a granite-hearthed, tapestried guest sitting room where old books and family portraits remind you this is "just an ordinary family house". Madame, dynamic and adorable, loves her visitors. All the bedrooms, from traditional to timber-strewn to yellow-panelled, are fascinating. Plus lovely garden, private chapel, old mill... Worth every penny.

rooms	5: 3 doubles, 2 twins.
price	€85-€100 for two.
meals	Crêperie in village; excellent restaurant nearby.
closed	Rarely.
directions	From St Brieuc N12 to Guingamp; D8 for Tréguier; at Pommerit Jaudy left at lights; signposted.

Comte & Comtesse de Kermel
Château de Kermezen,
22450 Pommerit Jaudy,
Côtes-d'Armor

tel	+33 (0)2 96 91 35 75
fax	+33 (0)2 96 91 35 75
e-mail	micheldekermel@kermezen.com

Manoir de Coat Gueno

The 15th-century manor house, only a few minutes' drive from the fishing ports, headlands and long sandy beaches, is cocooned in countryside. Wrapped in a rich fluffy towel, gaze out of your lavishly furnished bedroom onto the lawns below and know your privilege. You may hear the crackling of the log fire in the vast stone hearth downstairs, lit by your perfectionist host, the splash and laughter of guests in the pool, the crack of billiard balls echoing upwards to the tower. The games room is in a separate building in the grounds. *Gosford Park*, à la Bretonne. *Children over 8 welcome.*

rooms	3: 1 double, 1 suite for 3, 1 suite for 4.
price	€85-€95 for two. Suite €115-€140. Minimum stay 2 nights.
meals	Dinner €25, book ahead; wine €15. Restaurants nearby.
closed	September-April.
directions	From Paimpol for Lézardrieux; after bridge left to Pleudaniel; right for Pouldouran; through Prat Collet & Passe Porte to sign for Croas Guezou; left; 1st track right 800m.

Christian de Rouffignac
Manoir de Coat Gueno,
22740 Pleudaniel,
Côtes-d'Armor
tel +33 (0)2 96 20 10 98
e-mail coatguen@aol.com
web mapage.noos.fr/coatgueno

41 rue de la Petite Corniche

Enter and you will understand why we chose this modernised house: the ever-changing light of the great bay shimmers in through vast swathes of glass. In guest rooms too you can sit in your armchair and gaze as boats go by. Or take 10 minutes and walk to Perros. Guy chose the house so he could see his small ship at anchor (lucky guests may be taken for a sail) and Marie-Clo has enlivened the interior with her patchwork and embroidery. It is calm, light, bright; they are attentive, warm and generous and breakfast is seriously good. Great for family holidays by the sea, but note steep steps on arrival.

rooms	2 doubles, both with sitting area.
price	€55-€60 for two.
meals	Restaurants 600-800m.
closed	Christmas.
directions	From Lannion D788 N to Perros Guirec; follow signs to Port; coastal road round bay for approx. 1km; left at sign. (Will fax map or collect you from railway station.)

Marie-Clo & Guy Biarnès
41 rue de la Petite Corniche,
22700 Perros Guirec, Côtes-d'Armor
tel +33 (0)2 96 23 28 08
fax +33 (0)2 96 23 28 08
e-mail guy.biarnes@wanadoo.fr
web perso.wanadoo.fr/corniche/

Manoir du Launay

A fine beech avenue leads to the reconstructed *maison bourgeoise*, the original stone family crest above its front door. Your very welcoming hosts renovated the old place superbly, then rag-rolled and stencilled each airy room. Bedrooms are colour themed and serene; a painted fireplace, a mistletoe-sprigged duvet, a simple armoire; luxurious bathrooms ooze big fluffy towels. In the peachy dining room plenteous breakfasts are served at three tables before an impressive stone fireplace: *far breton* cake, crêpes, homemade jams. There's a games room for children and a salon for you.

rooms	5: 4 doubles, 1 suite for 4.
price	€75-€105 for two.
meals	Good choice of restaurants nearby.
closed	Rarely.
directions	From Lannion D65 for Trébeurden; at r'bout signs for Servel, 3km; right into wooded driveway; signposted.

Florence & Ivan Charpentier
Manoir du Launay,
22300 Servel, Côtes-d'Armor
tel +33 (0)2 96 47 21 24
fax (0)2 96 47 26 04
e-mail manoirdulaunay@wanadoo.fr
web www.manoirdulaunay.com

Manoir de Kerguéréon

Such wonderful, gracious hosts with a nice sense of humour: you feel you are at a house party; such age and history in the gloriously asymmetrical château: tower, turrets, vast fireplaces, low doors, ancestral portraits, fine furniture; such a lovely garden, Madame's own work. Once you have managed the worn spiral staircase you find bedrooms with space, taste, arched doors, a lovely window seat to do your tapestry in, good bathrooms; and the great Breton breakfast can be brought up if you wish. An elegant welcome, intelligent conversation, delightful house – and their son breeds racehorses on the estate.

rooms	2 twins.
price	€85 for two. Minimum stay 2 nights.
meals	Choice of restaurants 7-10km.
closed	November-Easter
directions	From N12 exit Bég Chra & Plouaret (bet. Guingamp & Morlaix); at Plouaret D11 for Lannion; after 5.5km left at x-road for Plounilliau & St Michel en G., D30; over r'way, on for 3km; left at Kerguéréon sign, 100m left again to end.

M & Mme Gérard de Bellefon
Manoir de Kerguéréon,
22300 Lannion,
Côtes-d'Armor
tel +33 (0)2 96 38 91 46
fax +33 (0)2 96 38 91 46

L'Ancien Presbytère

Inside an enclosed courtyard, a charming village presbytery. Walled gardens and an orchard for picnics complete the peaceful, private mood. The comfy, lived-in rooms are stuffed with personal touches; the biggest is the lightest, high and stylish with an amazing, 1950s-Deco bathroom. The cosy, cottagey, low-beamed attic rooms have very small shower rooms. Madame, easy and approachable, loves gardening and her two elderly cats, and knows the area "like her pocket". She has itineraries for your deeper discovery of secret delights, so stay awhile. You may eat here but make sure your dinner booking is firm.

rooms	3: 1 double, 2 twins.
price	€55 for two.
meals	Dinner with wine €20, book ahead.
closed	Rarely.
directions	From Guingamp N12 for Morlaix, exit Louargat. From Louargat church, D33 to Tregrom (7km). House in village centre opp. church & bell tower (blue door in wall).

Nicole de Morchoven
L'Ancien Presbytère,
22420 Plouaret,
Côtes-d'Armor
tel +33 (0)2 96 47 94 15
fax +33 (0)2 96 47 94 15
web tregrom.monsite.wanadoo.fr

Toul Bleïz

An art teacher in her other life, Julie takes people out painting while Jez, who once ran a vegetarian restaurant, does cook-ins where guests learn what to do with finds from the markets. Have breakfast sitting on a slab of granite in the courtyard of this traditional Breton cottage just listening to the birds going about their business or planning an expedition. What are these *allées couvertes* you are directed to follow? Ancient burial chambers. There are also standing stones, badgers and wild boar on the moors behind. Civilisation is a short drive away but you'd never need to know it.

rooms	2 doubles.
price	€43 for two.
meals	Dinner with wine €18, book ahead.
closed	Rarely.
directions	From N164 D44 for Gorges du Daoulas; left at junction for Allées Couvertes; past lay-by on right; Toul Bleïz next track on right.

Julie & Jez Rooke
Toul Bleïz,
22570 Laniscat,
Côtes-d'Armor
tel +33 (0)2 96 36 98 34
e-mail jezrooke@hotmail.com
web www.phoneinsick.co.uk

Manoir de Kerledan

Everyone loves Kerledan, its gargoyles, sophisticated theatrical décor and owners' enthusiasm. In 2002, they bought a neglected sadness. Peter, a builder and Penny, a designer, have made it stunningly original. Sit in the dining room with its great fire, lounge in the garden-in-progress (baroque courtyard, orchard, potager) or in your bedroom armchair. Natural colours of sisal and unstained oak, the odd dramatic splash of antique mirror or gilded *bergère* in fake leopard skin bring a calm, minimalist atmosphere; slate-floored bathrooms are perfect, candlelit dinners are legendary.

rooms	3: 1 double, 1 twin, 1 family room.
price	€60-€80.
meals	Dinner, 3 courses with wine, €25-€30, book ahead.
closed	January-February.
directions	From Boulevard Jean-Moulin (southern bypass of Carhaix); take small lane between Hotel des Impots & Disti-Centre. House signposted 250m on right.

Peter & Penny Dinwiddie
Manoir de Kerledan,
29270 Carhaix-Plouguer,
Finistère

tel +33 (0)2 98 99 44 63
e-mail pdin@wanadoo.fr

La Grange de Coatélan

Yolande is a smiling, helpful mother of five, Charlick the most sociable workaholic you could find. Having beautifully renovated their old Breton weaver's house, they are converting other ruins as well as running the small auberge that serves traditional dishes and meats grilled on the open fire. They are active, artistic (he paints) and fun. The rooms have clever layouts, colour schemes and fabrics and brilliant use of wood, all informed by an artist's imagination; they are superb in their rustic elegance. Deep in the countryside, with animals and swings for children's delight.

rooms	5: 2 doubles, 3 quadruples.
price	€42-€60 for two. Minimum stay 2 nights in summer.
meals	Dinner €18, book ahead; wine €10-€15.
closed	Christmas-New Year.
directions	From Morlaix D9 south to Pougonven; at 2nd r'bout D109 to Coetélan. House on right. Signposted.

Charlick & Yolande de Ternay
La Grange de Coatélan,
29640 Plougonven,
Finistère

tel +33 (0)2 98 72 60 16
fax +33 (0)2 98 72 60 16
e-mail la-grange-de-coatelan@wanadoo.fr
web www.lagrangedecoatelan.com

Manoir de Roch ar Brini

Crow's Rock Manor: sounds wild? It is wonderfully civilised. Built in the 1840s and admirably restored by your young and sociable hosts, who have three young children, it breathes an air of old-style, refined yet understated luxury in big, lofty-ceilinged, antiqued and chandeliered rooms with superb views of the generous grounds. The drawing-room parquet alone is worth the visit; bed linen is exceptionally luxurious; from one super bathroom you can gaze out to the fields or into a vast mirror; another has tapestries of… baths. Breakfast may include *far breton* and fresh fruit salad. *Horse riding possible.*

rooms	2 doubles.
price	€60-€70 for two. Minimum stay 2 nights July & Aug.
meals	Bistro 1km.
closed	Rarely.
directions	From Port Morlaix follow right bank of river N for Le Dourduff; 2nd right at Ploujean sign (hairpin bend) 500m. Right for Ploujean; house 3rd on right.

Étienne & Armelle Delaisi
Manoir de Roch ar Brini,
29600 Morlaix Ploujean,
Finistère
tel +33 (0)2 98 72 01 44
fax +33 (0)2 98 88 04 49
e-mail rochbrini@aol.com
web www.brittanyguesthouse.com

Kernévez

Squarely planted in its Breton soil, this is totally a family house open to guests, not a purpose-converted affair. The children run the farm and the Gralls, genuine Breton-speaking Bretons, have time for visitors. After a blissful night – rooms have warm traditional décor, excellent mattresses, family pieces – and a bucolic awakening to birdsong in the fields, come down to Madame's homemade crêpes or Breton cake at the long table. She's a lovely lady dressed in Breton dress, the perfect hostess. Prepare your own meals in the guest kitchenette, eat out in the garden that looks down to the sea.

rooms	2: 1 twin, 1 family room.
price	€42 for two. Minimum stay 2 nights July & Aug.
meals	Restaurant 2.5km.
closed	Rarely.
directions	From St Pol de Léon D10 W to Cléder, right at 2nd r'bout. Arriving in Cléder, take road to sea for 2km; left following signs to Ferme de Kernévez.

François & Marceline Grall
Kernévez,
29233 Cléder,
Finistère
tel +33 (0)2 98 69 41 14
web www.kernevez.fr.fm

Domaine de Rugornou Uras

The two most memorable things here are Marie-Christine's smile as she talks about her native Brittany, and the crispness of the décor. Guest rooms are in the old cider-press – pretty and fresh with skylight windows and country antiques, and shower rooms immaculate. Breakfast, perhaps with Breton music in the background (to make the Breton costumes dance?), is prepared in the guest dayroom and eaten at the refectory table, with views of the garden and books all around. Dinner is at an auberge run by Madame's daughter, a walk away. It is quiet and comfortable and you can be quite independent.

rooms	2: 1 double, 1 triple.
price	€44 for two.
meals	Dinner with wine €17, book ahead. Restaurants nearby.
closed	Rarely.
directions	From Morlaix D785 for Quimper, approx. 35km. 800m before Brasparts, right (on bend) & follow signs.

Marie-Christine Chaussy
Domaine de Rugornou Uras,
29190 Brasparts, Finistère
tel +33 (0)2 98 81 47 14
(0)2 98 81 46 27
fax +33 (0)2 98 81 47 14
e-mail marie-christine.chaussy@wanadoo.fr

Domaine du Guilguiffin

Guilguiffin is a powerful, unforgettable experience. The bewitching name of the warring first baron (1010), the splendidness of the place, its opulent, ancestor-hung, Chinese-potted rooms and magnificent grounds, are utterly seductive. Built with stones from the 11th-century fortress, it is a jewel of an 18th-century château, inside and out. Passionate about furniture and buildings, especially his ancient family seat, your host applies his intelligent energy to restoring his estate, nurturing thousands of plants and, with Madame's help, converting visitors to his views. Bedrooms are big and sumptuous.

rooms	6: 4 doubles, 2 suites.
price	€130-€150 for two. Suite €170-€210.
meals	Choice of restaurants nearby.
closed	Rarely; book ahead in winter.
directions	From Quimper D765 W for 5km; left D784 for Landudec 13km; left & follow signs.

Philippe Davy
Domaine du Guilguiffin,
29710 Landudec, Finistère
tel +33 (0)2 98 91 52 11
fax +33 (0)2 98 91 52 52
e-mail chateau@guilguiffin.com
web www.guilguiffin.com

Kerloaï

Here is a Breton house with naturally hospitable Breton owners, Breton furniture and a huge Breton brass pot once used for mixing crêpes. Madame is welcoming and chatty (in French), Monsieur has a reassuring earthy calmness; they love having children to stay. The large, light, country-style rooms are all merrily painted in sunny yellow, fresh green, orange or pink. Copious breakfasts include those crêpes (though not mixed in the brass pot) and home-grown kiwi fruit in season. An authentic rural haven between Armor, the land by the sea, and Argoat, the land of the woods.

rooms	4: 3 doubles, 1 twin.
price	€42 for two.
meals	Restaurant 4km.
closed	Occasionally.
directions	From Scaër, D50 for Coray Briec; after 3km, left at 'Ty Ru' & follow signs for Kerloaï.

Louis & Thérèse Penn
Kerloaï,
29390 Scaër,
Finistère
tel +33 (0)2 98 59 42 60
fax +33 (0)2 98 59 42 60
e-mail ti.penn@skaer.com

Kervren

The view from all six rooms across fields and wooded hills is perfectly wonderful. In a stone outbuilding separate from the owners' house, each small, neatly modern room, each impeccable, has a double-glazed door-window onto the long terrace where chairs await. Breakfast, with crêpes or croissants, is in a big modern veranda room where a richly carved Breton wardrobe takes pride of place. Madame is efficient, full of information about Breton culture, and very purposeful. *Only suitable for older children who can sleep alone. Small pets welcome.*

rooms	6: 4 doubles, 2 twins.
price	€42 for two. Minimum stay 2 nights July & August.
meals	Choice of restaurants, 10km.
closed	February.
directions	From Quimper D765 for Rosporden. At St Yvi left to Kervren; to end of lane (2.5km).

Odile Le Gall
Kervren,
29140 St Yvi,
Finistère
tel +33 (0)2 98 94 70 34
fax +33 (0)2 98 94 81 19

Kerambris

Madame is a darling: quiet, serene and immensely kind, she really treats her guests as friends. The long, low, granite house has been in the family for all of its 300 years, enjoying the peace of this wind-blown, bird-sung spot just five minutes from the sea and that gorgeous coastal path. And standing stones in the garden! Most of the building is gîtes; the *chambres d'hôtes* are tucked into the far end – small, impeccably simple, like the dining room, with some handsome Breton furniture. With charming Port Manech and good beaches nearby, it is a wonderful holiday spot.

rooms	4: 2 doubles, 2 twins.
price	€42 for two.
meals	In village, within walking distance.
closed	Rarely.
directions	From Pont Aven, D77 for Port Manech; right just before sign Port Manech; 1st left. Follow Chambres d'Hôtes signs.

Yveline Gourlaouen
Kerambris,
29920 Nevez,
Finistère
tel +33 (0)2 98 06 83 82
fax +33 (0)2 98 06 83 82

Le Rhun

Family-friendly, easy-going, this lovely German couple have done a high-class renovation job on their cluster of buildings, creating a thoughtful guest house in the old stables with living room, dining room and kitchen – just for B&B guests. Up the outside staircase are two well finished bedrooms, their slightly minimalist style lifted by colourful quilts, pretty rugs and one red rocking chair. Clouds move past the roof windows, cows graze next door (you can watch the milking), the lake attracts birds, ball games attract children and there's a sauna. Simple country pursuits, shared with a number of gîte guests.

rooms	2 twins.
price	€42-€45 for two. Minimum stay 2 nights.
meals	Dinner with wine €11, book ahead. Restaurant 3.5km.
closed	Winter.
directions	From Pontivy D768 south; exit to Pluméliau. In Pluméliau church square left D203 at sign for Gîtes du Rhun, 2.5km.

Eva & Jurgen Lincke
Le Rhun,
56930 Pluméliau, Morbihan
tel +33 (0)2 97 51 83 48
fax +33 (0)2 97 51 83 48
e-mail eva.lincke@wanadoo.fr
web www.lerhun.de

Lezerhy

A heavenly spot, cradled in a quiet hamlet 200 yards from the river in deepest Brittany. Delightful people: Martine looks after old folk and young Melissa, Philippe pots and teaches aikido; both have lots of time for guests. In an outbuilding, you have your own sitting/breakfast room and kitchen and two big, superbly converted, uncluttered attic rooms, decorated with flair in subtle pastels and fitted with good shower rooms. Birds sing; the cat is one of the best ever; the dog will love you. A genuine welcome and possibly a different kind of cake for breakfast every day. Readers' letters are full of praise.

rooms	2 twins.
price	€40 for two.
meals	Wide choice of restaurants in St Nicolas 3km; self-catering.
closed	November-Easter, except by arrangement.
directions	From Pontivy D768 S for 12km; exit to St Nicolas des Eaux; right immediately after bridge; follow signs for Chambres d'Hôtes & Poterie for 3km.

Martine Maignan
& Philippe Boivin
Lezerhy,
56310 Bieuzy les Eaux, Morbihan

tel	+33 (0)2 97 27 74 59
fax	+33 (0)2 97 27 73 11
e-mail	boivinp@wanadoo.fr
web	perso.wanadoo.fr/poterie-de-lezerhy/

Map 3 Entry 282

Le Ty-Mat Penquesten

The yellow mansion is a bit surprising in this remote setting of magnificent trees and tumbledown buildings, its renovation as impressive as the house. The Spences were respectful of origins during this huge job: the slightly wormy old staircase has great character; they laid the parquet in the grand drawing room, then put down fine Turkey carpets; they limewashed the walls and hung portraits beneath the high ceiling. Play with the animals, try the grand piano or admire the park from the deep windows. Soft blue and cream bedrooms are done in simple, unfussy luxury and Catherine, who's French, is charming.

rooms	4: 3 doubles, 1 twin.
price	€54-€64
meals	Crèperie 3km, restaurant 6km.
closed	Rarely.
directions	From N165 for Inzinzac-Lochrist. At Lochrist, right immediately after 2nd bridge onto D23. After 4km, Ty-Mat on left.

Catherine Spence
Le Ty-Mat Penquesten,
56650 Inzinzac-Lochrist,
Morbihan

tel	+33 (0)2 97 36 89 26
fax	+33 (0)2 97 36 89 26
e-mail	ty-mat@wanadoo.fr
web	pro.wanadoo.fr/ty-mat/

Map 3 Entry 283

Keraubert

Dreams drift over Keraubert, the pond mirrors the dragonflies' precious dance, a semi-tropical Breton gardens luxuriates. Your hosts create a welcoming, relaxed atmosphere, Bernard's paintings grace many walls and he and Jacqueline quickly convey their refreshing optimism and warm delight in the place. Each pretty but untwee guest room has a garden door with iron table and chairs for two. The very pink room is small and cosy with garden views, the garage at the end is being converted into a suite. All is to be revived with a new lick of paint. Unashamedly homey, with lovely owners and a special garden.

rooms	2: 1 double, 1 suite.
price	€50-€65 for two. Minimum stay 2 nights in suite.
meals	Dinner €15, book ahead. Restaurants 6km.
closed	Rarely.
directions	From Rennes N24 for Lorient, exit Baud & Auray; D768 for Vannes 4km; D24 right for Landevant 10km; entrance on left between Lambel & Malachappe.

Bernard & Jacqueline Belin
Keraubert,
56330 Pluvigner,
Morbihan
tel +33 (0)2 97 24 93 10
fax +33 (0)2 97 24 93 10

Lann Kerguy

What a find! Deep in the woods, this pale stone cottage sits private and secluded in 12 acres of land and a near-tropical garden. Your friendly, artistic hosts have incorporated a superb sloping extension for the limewashed, stone-walled, pine-ceilinged garden bedroom, there are patchwork and lace, painted headboards and delightful quirks such as newspaper cuttings varnished onto mirror mounts, new and unusual bathrooms. It's all done in soft colours, simple, fresh and amusing yet functional. The light, open-plan living area epitomises Chantal and René's sense of hospitality; they are excellent company.

rooms	2: 1 double, 1 family suite for 4.
price	€42-€48 for two.
meals	Restaurants nearby.
closed	Rarely.
directions	From Baud south for Auray; D24 right for Landevant; at Malachappe right for Lann Kerguy 2.5km. House in woods on left.

René & Chantal Le Jonny
Lann Kerguy,
56330 Pluvigner,
Morbihan
tel +33 (0)2 97 50 99 36
fax +33 (0)2 97 50 90 11
e-mail r.le.jonny@wanadoo.fr

Chaumière de Kerreo

Gérard loves his cooking, garden and house passionately and shares them generously. The B&B is all his, Nelly works in town. Once a chef for the wealthy and the deprived (château-hotels then schools for troubled youth), he has revived the old bread oven in the deliciously lush little garden and renovated the 'cottage' with flair and faithfulness, naming the rooms after Breton fairies – they are enchanting. He is quietly welcoming and the whole family is deeply Breton, doing an annual *Fest-Noz* with costumes, dances, pipes and songs, plus a dash of exotic in the odd moonlit game of boules or darts.

rooms	5: 4 doubles, 1 twin.
price	€50-€54 for two. Minimum stay 2 nights.
meals	Dinner with wine or cider €20, book ahead.
closed	Rarely.
directions	From Lorient N165 E 39km; exit D24 N 8km; left at sign Chaumière de Kerreo: thatched house, fuschia paintwork at hamlet crossroads.

Gérard Grevès & Nelly Le Glehuir
Chaumière de Kerreo,
56330 Pluvigner,
Morbihan
tel +33 (0)2 97 50 90 48
fax +33 (0)2 97 50 90 69

Kerimel

The standing stones of Carnac are minutes away, beaches, coastal pathways and golf course close by. Kerimel is a handsome group of granite farm buildings in a perfect setting among the fields. The bedrooms are beauties: plain walls, some panelling, patchwork bedcovers and pale blue curtains, old stones and beams, sparkling shower rooms and fluffy towels. The dining room is cottage perfection: dried flowers hanging from beams over wooden table, tiled floor, vast blackened chimney, stone walls. Gentle, generous, elegant people... "We talked of flowers", wrote one guest.

rooms	4 twins/doubles.
price	€65-€70 for two.
meals	Good restaurants 3km.
closed	Rarely.
directions	From N165 exit for Quiberon & Carnac on D768, 4km; right to Ploemel; D105 W for Erdeven; sign on right, 1.5km.

Babeth & Pierre Malherbe
Kerimel,
56400 Ploemel,
Morbihan
tel +33 (0)2 97 56 84 72
fax +33 (0)2 97 56 84 72
e-mail elisabeth.malherbe@wanadoo.fr
web kerimel.free.fr

Kernivilit

Bang there on the quayside, an oyster farm! Bedrooms touch the view – you may want to stay and capture that lovely, limpid light on canvas while drinking coffee on the balcony, smelling the sea and listening to the chugging of fishing boats. Madame worked in England, Germany and the USA before coming to Brittany to help François farm oysters – she never looked back. He'll take you out there too, if you ask. Hospitable and generous, alert and chatty, she hangs interesting paintings in her rooms, lights a fire on cool days and serves a good French breakfast. Unusual and very welcoming.

rooms	2 + 1: 1 twin, 1 triple; 1 apartment for 3.
price	€50-€65 for two.
meals	Restaurant 500m.
closed	Rarely.
directions	From Auray D28 & D781 to Crach & Trinité sur Mer.; right at lights before bridge for La Trinité sur Mer; house 400m along on left, sign 'François Gouzer'.

Christine & François Gouzer
Kernivilit,
56470 La Trinité sur Mer, Morbihan
tel +33 (0)2 97 55 17 78
fax +33 (0)2 97 30 04 11
e-mail fgouzer@club-internet.fr
web www.geocities.com/thetropics/cabana/8913/

Locqueltas

In a gem of a setting, the modern house looks over the ever-changing blue-green gulf and its islands. The three well-furnished garden-level rooms have eyes to the sea and loos in the corridor. A carved four-poster reigns imposingly in the room upstairs that leads to an even more startling dayroom with billiard table, books galore, oak altar, 1950s juke box, telescope, baby Louis XV armchair – all neatly arranged as if in a stately home – and the loo. Madame, brisk and practical, has a style that features marked contrasts – you will warm to her – and there's a little beach at the end of the garden for shallow bathing.

rooms	4: 1 double; 3 doubles with basin & bidet sharing 2 showers; all sharing 6 separate wcs.
price	€50-€65 for two.
meals	Restaurants in Larmor Baden, 1.5km.
closed	Mid-July & August.
directions	From Auray D101 S for Baden; D316 S for Larmor Baden; through village N/NE for Locqueltas; sign on right, house 10m on right.

Mme M C Hecker
Locqueltas,
56870 Larmor Baden,
Morbihan
tel +33 (0)2 97 57 05 85
fax +33 (0)2 97 57 25 02

photo Michael Busselle

western loire

Le Deffay

After a long dark (elf-filled?) wood, the drive explodes onto an impressive 19th-century château set among superb trees and 12 whole acres of dreamy lake (is that heron really a long-haired nymph?). Wild animals from forest to table (some stuffed for the entrance hall), lepers treated in a special pool, Romans guarding camp – so much history. No wonder your friendly young hosts are passionate about their family domain, holding it for their three little children. Inside, the château is pleasantly comfortable: you will sleep well. *Daily children's activities at the discreet camping site in summer.*

rooms	3: 2 doubles, 1 suite.
price	€46-€77 for two.
meals	Restaurant 1km.
closed	Rarely.
directions	From Nantes N165 exit for Herbignac; D33 through Le Calvaire; for Ste Reine de Bretagne. Château signposted on right.

Xavier & Thaïs de la Villesboisnet
Le Deffay B.P. 18,
44160 Pontchâteau,
Loire-Atlantique
tel +33 (0)2 40 45 65 60

Map 4 Entry 290

Château de Coët Caret

Come for a taste of life with the French country aristocracy – it's getting hard to find. Properly formal breakfast (at 9am sharp, a touch of old-fashioned primness about table manners) your hosts are cultured company and rightly proud of their château and grounds. Bedrooms are serenely big and beautiful; *Saumon* is softly carpeted under the eaves, the rest have old polished floorboards. Bathrooms are equally fine. There's a lake and 100 hectares of superb parkland... all within the Brière Regional Park where water and land are inextricably mingled and wildlife abounds.

rooms	3: 2 doubles, 1 twin.
price	€90-€100 for two. Minimum stay 2 nights.
meals	Excellent auberges nearby, 2km.
closed	Rarely.
directions	From N165, exit 15 D774 for La Baule to Herbignac, 10km; fork left D47 for St Lyphard for 4km; house on right.

François & Cécile de La Monneraye
Château de Coët Caret,
44410 Herbignac, Loire-Atlantique
tel +33 (0)2 40 91 41 20
fax +33 (0)2 40 91 37 46
e-mail coetcaret@free.fr
web coetcaret.com

Map 4 Entry 291

La Mercerais

These are the sweetest people, even if their somewhat kitschy taste is not everyone's cup of tea! They really do "treat their guests as friends". Madame, bright and sparkling, is proud to show you her decorated books, musical scores and hats with the dried flower and gold spray touch; Monsieur is a retired farmer, quiet, friendly, attached to this place. The house is warm (log fire in winter), cosily country-furnished, the smallish rooms (mind your head on the way up) are as pink as can be. In the immaculately tended garden, a summer kitchen. Breakfast is served in pretty little baskets at the long table.

rooms	3: 2 triples; 1 family room with bath & separate wc.
price	€48 for two; €62 for three.
meals	Good restaurant 3km; self-catering in summer.
closed	Rarely.
directions	From Rennes N137 for Nantes 63km. Exit at Nozay N171 for Blain 8km. At bottom of hill, left at roadside cross; sign.

Yvonne & Marcel Pineau
La Mercerais,
44130 Blain,
Loire-Atlantique
tel +33 (0)2 40 79 04 30

Map 4 Entry 292

Le Manoir des Quatre Saisons

This is a family venture. Jean-Philippe, his mother and sister, who spends six months of the year in Greece, are engaging hosts and attentive, providing not only robes but drinks beside the pool. Early bird and sleeper-in will both be happy: breakfast, complete with eggs and bacon as well as local choices, is served from really early (6am) till pretty late (11am). You can see the sea from upstairs where bedrooms are colourful without being overpowering – Jean-Philippe went to art school and has an eye for detail. Plenty to see and do nearby but children will love just mucking around in the big garden.

rooms	5: 3 doubles; 1 suite for 2, 1 suite for 4, both with kitchen.
price	€54-€84 for two. Minimum stay 2 nights July & Aug.
meals	Restaurants 1.5km.
closed	Rarely.
directions	From Guérande for La Turballe; just before town D333 right; at x-roads 'Café des 4 Routes' straight on; house 600m on right.

Jean-Philippe Meyran
Le Manoir des Quatre Saisons,
44420 La Turballe,
Loire-Atlantique
tel +33 (0)2 40 11 76 16
fax +33 (0)2 40 11 76 16
web www.manoir-des-quatre-saisons.com

Hello

Map 9 Entry 293

La Guérandière

Backed against the fortifications of beautiful, medieval Guérande, this Breton house with original mosaic and parquet floors, huge granite fireplace and wide wooden staircase feels older than its 140 years. Valérie's superb sense of colour, choice of fabrics and fine attention to detail blend its traditional solidity with contemporary lightness – her bedrooms are breathtaking. In the green and tranquil garden, breakfast in the company of 100-year-old trees and entertaining modern sculpture. Smiling and friendly, Valérie, who lives mostly in another house, sells local produce and crafts from a shop on the ground floor.

rooms	6: 4 doubles, 1 triple, 1 suite for 4.
price	€75-€105 for two.
meals	Good restaurants within walking distance.
closed	Rarely.
directions	From Nantes & Vannes follow signs to Guérande; enter through La Porte Vannetaise (north town gate), 1st house on right.

Valérie Lauvray
La Guérandière,
44350 Guérande,
Loire-Atlantique
tel +33 (0)2 40 62 17 15
fax +33 (0)2 51 73 04 17
e-mail valerie.lauvray@laguerandiere.com
web www.laguerandiere.com

Château de La Rousselière

The gutsy Scherers bought a "challenge in ruins" five years ago: the work they have done on the old château and its fabulous 19th-century-listed park (camellias, 100 types of geranium, great pond, miles of walks through woods and fields) is impressive too. Inside, there's space and space: for guests to have their own entrance, log-fired sitting room, billiard room, stuccoed breakfast room, big parquet-floored bedrooms done for family-style comfort with some antiques and Madame's paintings and stencilling. The whole village worships in the chapel twice a year. Great people – may they flourish.

rooms	3: 1 double, 1 family suite (1 double, 1 twin).
price	€75 for two. Minimum stay 2 nights in winter.
meals	Restaurant 3km.
closed	Rarely.
directions	From Nantes D723 for Paimbœuf; near Frossay left following signs to château.

Catherine Scherer
Château de La Rousselière,
44320 Frossay,
Loire-Atlantique
tel +33 (0)2 40 39 79 59
fax +33 (0)2 40 39 77 78
e-mail larouss@club-internet.fr
web www.larousseliere.com

Le Relais de La Rinière

A palm tree grows in the courtyard; a grassy garden big enough to satisfy the liveliest child stretches endlessly across vineyards of crisp Muscadet grapes. Madame is as full of fun and energy as ever and Monsieur, who is shyer and a retired baker, provides delicious cakes for breakfast on the terrace. The guest rooms in the main house are comfortable and very French with their fine carved armoires and fabric flowers. The other two, up steep outside stone stairs, are bright and cheerful, one a daring pink and yellow, the other bright blue, each with a kitchenette and sparkling bathroom.

rooms	5: 4 doubles, 1 twin.
price	€42 for two.
meals	Choice of restaurants 6km; self-catering in annexe.
closed	Rarely.
directions	From Nantes N249 for Poitiers, exit Vallet for Loroux Bottereau & Le Landreau, 5km; 600m before Le Landreau right; signs to La Rinière.

Françoise & Louis Lebarillier
Le Relais de La Rinière,
44430 Le Landreau,
Loire-Atlantique

tel	+33 (0)2 40 06 41 44
fax	+33 (0)2 51 13 10 52
e-mail	riniere@netcourrier.com
web	www.riniere.com

Map 9 Entry 296

Château de la Sébinière

When she was expecting her twins, Anne drew the house of her dreams and this is it: a small 18th-century château in a 12-hectare park and an unusually harmonious home. Walls are white or red-ochre, ceilings beamed, bathrooms a perfect blend of old and new. There's a delightful attention to detail – a pewter jug of old roses by a mirror, a contemporary wicker chair on an ancient, exquisite terracotta floor. You have your own entrance and the run of the sitting room, log-fired in winter. Anna serves real hot chocolate at breakfast, maybe a glass of Muscadet on arrival. A dream of a place.

rooms	3 doubles.
price	€74-€100 for two.
meals	Choice of restaurants in Clisson.
closed	Rarely.
directions	From Nantes N249 for Poitiers; 2nd exit N149 for Le Pallet; through village, 1st right, signposted.

Anne Cannaferina
Château de la Sébinière,
44330 Le Pallet,
Loire-Atlantique

tel	+33 (0)2 40 80 49 25
fax	+33 (0)2 40 80 49 25
e-mail	info@chateausebiniere.com
web	www.chateausebiniere.com

Map 9 Entry 297

Château Plessis-Brezot

The lofty dining room has massive beams, a massive table, massive old flags; the panelling took 500 hours to restore, fine period furniture gleams – Monsieur, a wine merchant, is passionate about buildings and an avid auction-goer (he buys old wells!). Bedcovers are bold-striped or floral and an air of Renaissance nobility pervades, except in the bathrooms, which are modern and white. Madame seems charmingly eccentric and, under daughter Gaëlle's management, the estate produces a Muscadet from the surrounding vineyards; book in a visit. There are bikes to spin off on and a big bue pool.

rooms	5 doubles.
price	€77-€107 for two.
meals	Good restaurants 5-8km.
closed	November-March, except by arrangement.
directions	From Nantes N249 for Poitiers; right N149 for Le Pallet; 1km before Le Pallet D7 right to Monnières; left for Gorges; château 1km on left.

Annick & Didier Calonne
Château Plessis-Brezot,
44690 Monnières,
Loire-Atlantique
tel +33 (0)2 40 54 63 24
fax +33 (0)2 40 54 66 07
e-mail a.calonne@online.fr
web www.chateauplessisbrezot.com

Château du Plessis-Atlantique

History-loaded Le Plessis belonged to the Roche family who crossed with William in 1066. The Belordes had it in 1632, kept it for centuries, lost it, bought in back 30 years ago. Pure château, it has velvet curtains and high-backed chairs in the salon, silver coffee pots and fresh orange juice at breakfast, 3,000 rosebushes in the garden and bedrooms of huge antique personality. Madame's father was in London with de Gaulle; she loves the English and enjoys cosmopolitan conversation. Expensive but special – enter another world.

rooms	3: 1 twin, 1 family room, 1 suite for 2-4.
price	€100-€160 for two; €185-€205 for three; €210-€220 for four. Singles €75-€105. Minimum stay 2 nights.
meals	Restaurant 800m.
closed	Rarely.
directions	From Nantes leave A83 ringroad on D85 past airport. At T-junc. at Champ de Foire left through Pont St Martin & follow signs to Le Plessis.

M & Mme Belorde
Château du Plessis-Atlantique,
44860 Pont St Martin,
Loire-Atlantique
tel +33 (0)2 40 26 81 72
fax +33 (0)2 40 32 76 67
e-mail chateauduplessis@wanadoo.fr
web monsite.wanadoo.fr/belorde.leplessis

Logis de Richebonne

Monsieur's parents bought this old *logis Vendéen* when he was six. Years later, researching the history of the house, he found his family first owned it in 1670! Madame's family tree, framed in the hall, goes back to the 14th century. But they are both warm and welcoming, not at all grand, and the house is full of personal touches: Madame painted the breakfast china and embroidered the beautiful tablecloth. Bedrooms are vast, with peaceful views and lots of fresh and dried flowers. The suite, and huge grounds, would be ideal for a family but very small children would need watching near the two pretty ponds.

rooms	3: 2 doubles, 1 suite for 5.
price	€55-€60 for two.
meals	Restaurants in nearby village.
closed	Rarely.
directions	From Nantes through Legé for Challans & Machecoul; on leaving village left after restaurant Le Paradis; Logis 150m left.

Mme de Ternay
Logis de Richebonne,
44650 Legé,
Loire-Atlantique
tel +33 (0)2 40 04 90 41
fax +33 (0)2 40 04 90 41
e-mail adeternay@wanadoo.fr

Le Verger

The Broux' new project is reviving this fine cluster of granite buildings for their family farm and the guests they welcome so well. One small ancient house of low heavy beams and big stones is the new guest quarters: two divans in the sitting area, double room upstairs, hand-painted furniture, loads of personality. Across the yard in the big square family house where noble stone, timber and terracotta also reign, Annick prepares meals at the long bright table – come and chat with her. Outside, horse and goats graze in the field, ducks and geese dabble in the pond, hens and turkeys squabble. Families love it.

rooms	1 suite for 2-4.
price	€38 for two.
meals	Dinner with wine €15, book ahead.
closed	Rarely.
directions	From Tiffanger D753 for Montaigu 1km; third road on right, signed.

Annick & Marc Broux
Le Verger,
85530 La Bruffière,
Vendée
tel +33 (0)2 51 43 62 02
e-mail annick.broux@wanadoo.fr
web perso.wanadoo.fr/laberangeraievendee

L'Hubertière

Hurry! Here is a lovely quiet farming family with cows that they know by name and a love of the land that is becoming rare. Michelle does the B&B, Gérard and their son run the farm. The hub is the huge tile-floored living room, while the bedrooms, all small, are comfortable in French country style. If you want a bit of extra space there is an upstairs sitting room for guests to use. The two rooms in the separate old sheepfold make up the family room, and the big garden has games for children as well as an immaculate potager. Good, down-to-earth B&B – and wonderful hosts.

rooms	5: 2 doubles, 2 triples, 1 family room.
price	€43 for two; €54 for three; €83 for five.
meals	Restaurants nearby.
closed	November-April.
directions	From Challans D948 to St Christophe du Ligneron; opposite baker's right D2 for Palluau for 4km; left at sign for house.

Michelle & Gérard Loizeau
L'Hubertière,
85670 St Christophe du Ligneron,
Vendée

tel	+33 (0)2 51 35 06 41
fax	+33 (0)2 51 49 87 43
e-mail	michelle.loizeau@terre-net.fr
web	www.vendee.com/hubertiere

La Fraternité

The lovely, lively Pikes and their two sets of identical (almost-grown-up) twin sons – *la fraternité* – brim with optimism and pleasure in their adopted country where they grow game birds. Their simple, old-fashioned, easily-renovated 1900s farmhouse has a big garden where children play and adults barbecue and, up the outside stairs in the former apple loft, two fresh, comfortable rooms for restful seclusion, all details cared for. Ian manages the farm, Janty helps with the eggs, they all love guests (gîte as well as B&B) and will point you towards the hidden treasures of the area they have come to love.

rooms	2: 1 double, 1 twin.
price	€43-€45 for two.
meals	Good restaurant 3km.
closed	Mid-September-mid-June, out of season by reservation.
directions	From La Roche sur Yon D948 (25km) through Aizenay; 4km after lake, D94 left for Commequiers, 1km (signs to La Fraternité); left for Maché, house immediately on right.

Janty & Ian Pike
La Fraternité,
85190 Aizenay,
Vendée

tel	+33 (0)2 51 55 42 58
fax	+33 (0)2 51 60 16 01
e-mail	janet.pike@wanadoo.fr
web	www.chez.com/lafraternite/

Le Rosier Sauvage

Eleanor of Aquitaine was born across the road in the exquisitely cloistered abbey – something of the serenity and simplicity of the convent permeates the immaculate bedrooms. The largest is in a splendidly converted loft with the original massive oak door, timbered ceiling, terracotta-tiled floor and simple red-checked fabrics. The breakfast room is the old stable, complete with manger, while the old laundry, with vast stone washtub, is now a sitting room. Guests can picnic in the walled garden, overlooked by the abbey. It's a family affair and when Christine is busy with her twins, her parents look after guests.

rooms	4: 1 double, 1 twin, 2 triples.
price	€45-€48 for two.
meals	Restaurant & crêperie 100m.
closed	October-April.
directions	From Niort N148 for Fontenay le Comte 20km (or A83 exit 9); after Oulmes right to Nieul sur l'Autise to Abbey: house just beyond on left.

Christine Chastain-Poupin
Le Rosier Sauvage,
85240 Nieul sur l'Autise,
Vendée

tel +33 (0)2 51 52 49 39
fax +33 (0)2 51 52 49 46
e-mail rosier.sauvage1@tiscali.fr

Map 9 Entry 304

69 rue de l'Abbaye

Pure serendipity: Madame's laughing eyes and infectious enthusiasm will lift the spirits of the world-weariest as she steps through the door. Choose from the old rocking chair in the conservatory, the chess set, books and a long monastery table in the sitting room, the vast garden where nature and man live happily side by side – mulberry trees, a wisteria-hung pergola, a punt to drift you into the mysterious Marais. Bedrooms are traditionally furnished with creaky polished parquet and fine family furniture, one with a four-poster bed, and the pretty garden room is in the converted hen-house.

rooms	5: 3 doubles, 1 triple, 1 twin.
price	€63 for two. Minimum stay 2 nights.
meals	Restaurants in village.
closed	Rarely.
directions	From Fontenay le Comte N148 for Niort 9km; right D15 to Maillezais; follow signs for Abbaye; house on left; signposted.

Mme Liliane Bonnet
69 rue de l'Abbaye,
85420 Maillezais, Vendée

tel +33 (0)2 51 87 23 00
fax +33 (0)2 51 00 72 44
e-mail liliane.bonnet@wanadoo.fr
web www.marais-poitevin.com/heberg-ch/bonnet/bonnet.html

Map 9 Entry 305

Massigny

A stone's throw from the house, the River Vendée winds sleepily through this secret valley. The steep sloping garden, where hoopoes nest, is full of hidden shady corners to linger in. For rainy days there is a sunny sitting room with videos and books about this unique marshy corner of France known as "Green Venice". The comfortable, immaculate bedrooms are beautifully decorated in a stylish mix of old and new. Marie-Françoise, an attentive and intelligent hostess, makes delicious and unusual jams from garden fruit and flowers, and Jean-Claude teaches cabinet-making. A perfect place to unwind.

rooms	2: 1 double, 1 family room.
price	€45 for two.
meals	Choice of restaurants 3-10km.
closed	November-March.
directions	From A83 exit Fontenay le Comte D938ter for La Rochelle 3km; right at small sign to Massigny; 1st house on left entering hamlet.

Marie-Françoise & Jean-Claude Neau
Massigny,
85770 Velluire, Vendée
tel +33 (0)2 51 52 30 32
fax +33 (0)2 51 52 30 32
e-mail neau.family@wanadoo.fr

Map 9 Entry 306

Demeure l'Impériale

A rare survivor of Cholet's imperial past, when the whole town flourished on making handkerchiefs, this elegant townhouse was the orangery of a long-gone château. Nothing imperial about Édith though, who loves to make guests feel at home. The bedrooms are light and beautiful with fine period furniture and gleaming modern bathrooms. Two give onto the quiet street, the suite looks over the rose-filled, tree-shaded garden. There are two pretty salons and a glass-roofed dining room in the sunken courtyard – excellent dinners here. French style and hospitality at its best.

rooms	3: 2 doubles, 1 suite for 4.
price	€61-€76 for two. Suite €120 for four.
meals	Dinner €23, book ahead; wine list. Restaurants 50m.
closed	Rarely.
directions	Rue Nationale is one-way street through Cholet centre. No.28 200m down on right.

Édith & Jean-René Duchesne
Demeure l'Impériale,
49300 Cholet, Maine-et-Loire
tel +33 (0)2 41 58 84 84
fax +33 (0)2 41 63 17 03
e-mail demeure.imperiale@wanadoo.fr
web demeure-imperiale.com

Map 9 Entry 307

Le Mésangeau

The Migons, who couldn't be nicer, have expertly renovated their unusual, long-faced house with its barn-enclosed courtyard, two towers and covered terrace. Big, north-facing bedrooms are elegant and comfortable behind their shutters. In the reception rooms: contemporary leather sofas and a suit of armour; blue and green painted beams over antique dining-room furniture; two billiard tables, a piano, a set of drums in the games room. Monsieur collects veteran cars and plays bass guitar – promises of entertaining evenings. Superb grounds with a fishing pond and an 'aperitif gazebo'.

rooms	6: 4 doubles, 1 twin, 1 suite for 3.
price	€70-€100 for two.
meals	Dinner with wine €28-€30, book ahead.
closed	Rarely.
directions	From A11 exit 20 on D923. Cross Loire to Liré on D763; right D751 to Drain; left D154 for St Laurent des Autels. In Drain, house 3.5km after church on left.

Brigitte & Gérard Migon
Le Mésangeau,
49530 Drain, Maine-et-Loire
tel +33 (0)2 40 98 21 57
fax +33 (0)2 40 98 28 62
e-mail le.mesangeau@wanadoo.fr
web www.anjou-et-loire.com/mesangeau

Demeure des Petits Augustins

History speaks from every cranny: from 16th-century convent to courtier's residence to police station, it became a B&B, keeping its superb stone staircases. The Suite Blanche is orange… and white and has beams, tiles, mirrors, fireplaces, carved armoires. Other rooms are big too, and inviting. It's a bit like staying in a beloved granny's house. The glorious living room with its mystifying high-level old bread oven, beamed ceiling and original built-in cupboards is worth the visit by itself. Monsieur restored antiques – his house speaks well of his skill; Madame is gentle and efficient; renovation continues.

rooms	3: 2 suites, 1 triple with kitchenette (very occasionally sharing bath or shower).
price	€58 for two.
meals	Choice of restaurants in town or self-catering.
closed	November-February.
directions	From Saumur, D147 for Poitiers. In Montreuil Bellay, follow signs to Les Petits Augustins; entrance to house near chapel; left at Café.

Monique & Jacques Guézénec
Demeure des Petits Augustins,
49260 Montreuil Bellay,
Maine-et-Loire
tel +33 (0)2 41 52 33 88
fax +33 (0)2 41 52 33 88
e-mail moniqueguezenec@minitel.net

L'Estaminet de la Fosse

The flattish countryside round the oldest house in the village gives little inkling that under your feet are quarries and caves, transformed by this delightful family into a maze of terraced gardens and courtyards. One cave is now a kitchen for guests and another a gallery for Carole's colourful and imaginative glass light fittings and paintings. Three bedrooms open onto the sunny courtyard, the others look down onto a sunken garden with pool. All are simply, attractively decorated, while mouthwateringly vibrant colours give an exotic feel to the dining room. A fascinating place. *Children over seven welcome.*

rooms	5: 4 doubles, 1 suite.
price	€48-€62 for two.
meals	Use of kitchen; Monsieur runs restaurant in village.
closed	Rarely.
directions	From Saumur D960 to Doué la Fontaine; 1st right D214 to Forges. Through village; fork left at crucifix. House on left, sign.

Carole Berréhar & Michel Tribondeau
L'Estaminet de la Fosse,
Meigné sous Doué,
49700 Forges, Maine-et-Loire
tel +33 (0)2 41 50 90 09
e-mail info@chambrehote.com
web www.chambrehote.com

La Mascaron

On the banks of the Loire broods old Saumur. Deep inside hides a miniature medieval 'palace' with courtyard and balcony worthy of those eternal star-cross'd lovers. A successful blend of old and contemporary is a rare surprise but the architect-owner – inspired, committed – has achieved it in his large, relaxing private suite. Beams, shutters, curtains and bedlinen are highly original in colour and design; the fireplace, furniture, pictures and tapestries in the sitting room are of such quality and interest that one feels "This could not have been done better". Juliets (and others) will not forget their stay here.

rooms	1 suite.
price	€100 for two.
meals	Samur is full of restaurants.
closed	November-March.
directions	From Tourist Office to Église St Pierre; in Place St Pierre, Rue Hte St Pierre on right opp. church.

Marie & Marc Ganuchaud
La Mascaron,
49400 Saumur,
Maine-et-Loire
tel +33 (0)2 41 67 42 91

La Closerie

Nothing pretentious about this quiet village house but a genuine welcome from nature-loving Carmen, a sprightly retired English teacher, and ex-chef Hervé who cooks excellent traditional French dinners. Bedrooms in the old farmhouse in the shady courtyard, two of them with their own entrances, are simply but pleasantly decorated with small shower rooms. One has a magnificent stone fireplace; another, up outside stairs, has old beams, stone walls and pretty yellow and white fabrics. Trees almost engulf the house and the sunny conservatory dining room looks over a bosky garden.

rooms	4: 2 doubles, 1 triple, 1 quadruple.
price	€43-€49 for two.
meals	Dinner with wine €21, book ahead.
closed	Rarely.
directions	From A85 exit 2 (Longué); then N147 for Saumur; at Super U r'bout D53 to St Philbert. House on right in centre of village.

Carmen & Hervé Taté
La Closerie,
49160 St Philbert du Peuple,
Maine-et-Loire

tel	+33 (0)2 41 52 62 69
e-mail	carmenhervetate@aol.com

Map 10 Entry 312

Château de Salvert

This highly-sculpted neo-Gothic folly is home to a couple of charming, unselfconscious aristocrats and lots of cheerful children. The baronial hall is properly dark and spooky, the dining room and salon elegant and plush with gilt chairs and ancestors on the walls. In the vast suite, a sitting area and a library in an alcove. The double has the shower in one turret, the loo in another (off the corridor). Both are well decorated with fine French pieces and modern fabrics. The park is huge, wild boar roam, spring boarlets scamper. Madame plays the piano and holds concerts. What a place!

rooms	2: 1 double, 1 suite for 2-5.
price	€90 for two. Suite €230.
meals	Dinner €55, book ahead; wine €22-€35.
closed	Rarely.
directions	From A85 exit 'Saumur' on D767 for Le Lude. After 1km, left on D129 to Neuillé. Signposted.

Monica Le Pelletier de Glatigny
Château de Salvert,
49680 Neuillé, Maine-et-Loire

tel	+33 (0)2 41 52 55 89
fax	+33 (0)2 41 52 56 14
e-mail	info@salvert.com
web	www.chateau-de-salvert.fr

Map 10 Entry 313

Château du Goupillon

The whole place sings this lovely lady's independent, artistic and nature-loving personality and her sensitive approach to interiors domestic and human. The suite is superb in dramatic red, white and blue, the children's room deeply child-friendly, the bathroom fetchingly jungly. The light pours in and you bask in the harmony of warm, authentic comfort: stripped woodwork, richly-clothed walls (all Madame's work), old but not wealthy furniture. Outside the rambling 19th-century château lies a lush magical haven, a 10-acre oasis of semi-wild vegetation where endangered flora and fauna take refuge. Out of this world.

rooms	3: 2 doubles, 1 suite for 5.
price	€65-€100 for two. Suite €160 for five.
meals	Good restaurants in Saumur, 9km.
closed	In winter, except by arrangement.
directions	From Saumur N147 for Longué to La Ronde; D767 for Vernantes; left D129 for Neuillé; 1km before Neuillé follow Fontaine Suzon; signposted.

Mme Monique Calot
Château du Goupillon,
49680 Neuillé,
Maine-et-Loire
tel +33 (0)2 41 52 51 89
fax +33 (0)2 41 52 51 89

House and hostess achieve the perfect balance of refinement and relaxed welcome. Once the servants' quarters of the château (they housed their servants grandly in those days...), it is in a deep, secluded valley, right on the GR3 long-distance path and the Loire Valley walk. Big, warm bedrooms are under the high exposed roof beams, elegantly and discreetly done with good antiques, matching wallpaper and flowery English-style fabrics, impeccable bathrooms and loos. Breakfast is beautifully served – linen table napkins and silver teapot – and you can prepare a light meal to take to the garden later if you wish.

rooms	2: 1 double, twin.
price	€68 for two. Singles €54.
meals	Restaurant nearby.
closed	Rarely.

House sold at time of going to press

Chambres d'Hôtes

Serenity and rural peace are the hallmarks here. Not the most spectacular countryside but the house is tranquil in its hamlet and for excitement Monsieur will guide beginners in the art of billiards. Quiet and kind, Madame is spontaneously welcoming and properly proud of her house. The lovely sitting room, dominated by the hearth beneath the old beams, mixes comfort and antiques; immaculate, unfussy bedrooms have pastel colours, oriental rugs, old rafters and stones; country-fresh breakfast can be in the garden on fine mornings. You can picnic there too or bicycle down to the banks of the Loire.

rooms	3: 2 doubles, 1 triple.
price	€46 for two; €60 for three.
meals	Dinner with wine €21, book ahead.
closed	Rarely.
directions	From Angers N761 for Brissac & Doué. At Les Alleuds left on D90 for Chemellier. Hamlet 3km on left. Sign on right, house immed. left.

Éliette Edon
Chambres d'Hôtes,
49320 Maunit Chemellier,
Maine-et-Loire

tel +33 (0)2 41 45 59 50
fax +33 (0)2 41 45 01 44
web perso.club-internet.fr/sevefrem/site

Le Haut Pouillé

This conversion of farm and outbuildings is impeccably done and Mireille's sense of style and attention to detail are everywhere: perfectly coordinated colour schemes with her own stencilling, new beds, good linen, nice big towels and a living area with fridge and microwave for guests. Wonderful meals, in tune with the season, and well-chosen wines, are served on the patio in summer. The Métiviers love to chat and are fascinating about local history and the environment; but they'll fully understand if you prefer to eat alone. Fantastic value, a lovely garden, and all utterly restful. *Children under two free.*

rooms	2 family rooms, 1 with separate wc.
price	€49 for two.
meals	Dinner with wine €16, book ahead.
closed	2 weeks in summer.
directions	From Angers N147 for Saumur; 3km after Corné D61 left for Baugé for 2km past dairy & agricultural co-op; 2nd left at sign. House 1st on right.

Mireille & Michel Métivier
Le Haut Pouillé,
49630 Mazé,
Maine-et-Loire

tel +33 (0)2 41 45 13 72
fax +33 (0)2 41 45 19 02
e-mail labuissonniere@mageos.com
web www.labuissonniere.fr.st

La Chouannière

It's a charming 16th-century house complete with the old *pigeonnier* and its resident owl – he may woo you in from his impressive quarters next to the huge guest dining room: they are about three feet across with a ceiling which can be pulled back to show the ancient carpentry. Your smiley, generous hosts converted the stables leaving its original beauties in view, all exposed brickwork and tiled floors. Antique French country pieces that they restored themselves are buoyed up by colourful furnishings. Stay for dinner, then take a stroll around the fairytale woodland garden. Enchanting.
WWF Gîte Panda. Jacuzzi May-October.

rooms	4: 1 double, 1 twin, 1 triple, 1 family room.
price	€55 for two. Minimum stay 2 nights July & August.
meals	Dinner with wine €22, book ahead.
closed	Rarely.
directions	From Saumur N147 for Longué; right D938 for Baugé; in Jumelles left at church for Brion; signposted.

Patricia & Gilles Patrice
La Chouannière,
49250 Brion, Maine-et-Loire
tel +33 (0)2 41 80 21 74
fax +33 (0)2 41 80 21 74
e-mail chouanniere@loire-passion.com
web www.loire-passion.com

La Besnardière

Unusual, alternative and great for the informal. Joyce, a relaxed, welcoming aromatherapist, grows organic veg, cooks good veggie food, receives art, yoga and meditation workshops in her lovely meditation room and shares her comforting, lived-in space with generosity. Beams spring everywhere in the 500-year-old farmhouse – take care going to bed. One room has steps to the courtyard, the other looks over the pond where otters may be playing, both are earthy-coloured, in harmony with the old wood and stone. Old rural it feels, mature alternative it sings. Small camping site, lots of animals.

rooms	2: 1 double, 1 twin, sharing bath & wc.
price	€50 for two.
meals	Vegetarian dinner with wine €15, book ahead.
closed	Rarely.
directions	From Le Mans N23 to La Flèche; D37 to Fougeré; D217 for Baugé, 1.5km. House on left.

Joyce Rimell
La Besnardière,
49150 Fougeré,
Maine-et-Loire
tel +33 (0)2 41 90 15 20
fax +33 (0)2 41 90 15 20
e-mail rimell.joyce@wanadoo.fr

La Chalopinière

Michael and Jill are good talkers, good listeners and great fun; their two lively children, their guinea pigs, cats and ponies bring young cheer to the old French house. Bedrooms are big, bright and comfortable. The double, up characterfully creaky stairs, has a green 'marbled' fireplace, two deep armchairs and garden views; the family room, under the beamed roof and up a steeper stair, has red beds and rugs on parquet, a large sofa, a rocking chair and a small shower. Everything is clean and tidy without being oppressively so, and the garden is lovely: fruit trees and roses, tack room and stable.

rooms 2: 1 double with separate bath & wc; 1 family room.
price €56 for two.
meals Very good restaurants 2.5km.
closed 1 week in February & July.
directions From La Flèche D308 & D938 to Baugé; follow signs for Tours & Saumur; right at lights on D61 to Le Vieil Baugé. Sign after 2km.

Michael & Jill Coyle
La Chalopinière,
49150 Le Vieil Baugé,
Maine-et-Loire
tel +33 (0)2 41 89 04 38
fax +33 (0)2 41 89 04 38
e-mail rigbycoyle@aol.com

Le Point du Jour

Down-to-earth, fun-loving and decent, Madame is a splendid woman and hers is authentic farmhouse hospitality. Breakfast is in the cosy living room, alive with the desire to please. The attic has become three well-finished, honest guest rooms and a children's room with a fascinating original *lit de coin*. Great old roof timbers share the space with new beds and inherited armoires. It is simple and clean-cut with discreet plastic flooring, pastel walls, sparkling new showers. Your hosts are delighted to show you their grass-fed brown oxen, have two lively kids and provide toys, games and swings for yours.

rooms 4: 1 double, 1 twin, 1 triple, 1 children's room.
price €42 for two.
meals Choice of restaurants 5km.
closed Rarely.
directions From Angers N23 to Seiches sur le Loir; right D766 Tours, 9km; right into Jarzé D59 for Beaufort en Vallé. On left 700m after Jarzé.

Véronique & Vincent Papiau
Le Point du Jour,
49140 Jarzé, Maine-et-Loire
tel +33 (0)2 41 95 46 04
fax +33 (0)2 41 95 46 04
e-mail veronique.papiau@wanadoo.fr
web perso.wanadoo.fr/veronique.papiau

La Rousselière

A fine-columned terrace faces the serenity of an impeccably lovely garden, Monsieur's pride and joy; château-like reception rooms open one into another – glass doors to glass doors, billiards to dining to sitting – like an indoor arcade; family portraits follow you wherever you go; mass is still said in the private chapel on 16 August. But it's never over-grand, bedrooms are highly individual with their hand-painted armoires (Madame's artistic sister) and family antiques, bathrooms are charmingly dated and Madame is the most delightful smiling hostess and fine cook. A hymn to peace and gentle living.

rooms	5: 2 doubles, 1 family room, 1 family suite for 5.
price	€55-€75.
meals	Dinner with wine €27.50, book ahead.
closed	Rarely.
directions	From Anger N23 to Nantes; exit St Georges sur Loire; left at 1st r'bout for Chalonnes; left at 2nd r'bout for Chalonnes. Immediately before bridge left to Possonnière; 1.5km, left, signposted.

François & Jacqueline de Béru
La Rousselière,
49170 La Possonnière,
Maine-et-Loire
tel +33 (0)2 41 39 13 21
fax +33 (0)2 41 39 12 23
e-mail larousseliere@unimedia.fr
web www.anjou-et-loire.com/rousseliere

Prieuré de l'Épinay

Your hosts are happy, interested, interesting people, and meals are the greatest fun – chicken from the farm, asparagus, raspberries, salads from the potager... all is organic. Facing the larged grassed garden, the ancient priory has changed so little that the monks would feel at home here today – though the swimming pool, large and lovely, might be a surprise. Your hosts happily share their home and its history; lofty ceilings, 15th-century beams, a fascinating *cave*, a rare fireplace. The two-storey guest suites in the barn have simplicity and space, delicious breakfasts are served in the chapel.

rooms	3: 1 suite for 2, 2 suites for 4-5.
price	€70 for two.
meals	Dinner with wine €27, book ahead.
closed	15 September-April.
directions	From Angers N23 for Nantes 13km; through St Georges; cont. 1.5km; left after garage. Pass château; house on left. Park outside, walk through gate.

Bernard & Geneviève Gaultier
Prieuré de l'Épinay,
49170 St Georges sur Loire,
Maine-et-Loire
tel +33 (0)2 41 39 14 44
fax +33 (0)2 41 39 14 44
e-mail bernard.gaultier3@wanadoo.fr
web monsite.wanadoo.fr/epinay1/index.jhtml

Château de Montriou

The park will explode your senses: the waves of crocuses in spring; the tunnel of squashes, ravishing at summer's last flush. Equally magnificent, the 15th-century château has been lived in and carefully tended by the same family for 300 years. Now Régis and Nicole are bringing fresh energy to the house along with a passion for gardening. A very old stone staircase illuminated by a stained-glass chapel window leads to the properly formal bedrooms whose bold blues and oranges were interior design flavour of the period and wooden floors, thick rugs and antiques are only slightly younger. Remarkable.

rooms	3: 1 double; 1 double with kitchen; 1 suite for 4 with kitchen.
price	€75 for two. Suite €135 for four.
meals	Choice of restaurants nearby.
closed	Rarely.
directions	From Angers for Lion d'Angers; at Montreuil-Juigné right on D768 for Champigné; Montriou signposted between Feneu & Champigné at crossroads La Croix de Beauvais; D74 left for Sceaux d'Anjou, on for 300m.

Régis & Nicole de Loture
Château de Montriou,
49460 Feneu,
Maine-et-Loire
tel +33 (0)2 41 93 30 11
fax +33 (0)2 41 93 15 63
e-mail chateau-de-montriou@wanadoo.fr
web www.chateau-de-montriou.com

Malvoisine

Age-old peace and youthful freshness breathe from the old farmhouse, transformed from tumbledown dereliction to rural idyll for this cultured, artistic, unpretentious couple and their four children. Rooms are decorated with flair and simplicity with strong, warm colours, seagrass flooring and good fabrics. Wonderful meals – Regina's regional recipes are very sought after. A perfect retreat too for music, art and nature lovers. This is the family estate: join the Tuesday choir practice at the château, take singing lessons with Patrice's sister. A special place, a delightful hostess. *Cookery classes.*

rooms	3: 1 double, 1 twin, 1 triple.
price	€60 for two.
meals	Dinner with wine €25, book ahead.
closed	Rarely.
directions	From Angers for Lion d'Angers. At Montreuil Juigné right on D768 for Champigné. 500m after x-roads at La Croix de Beauvais right up drive to La Roche & Malvoisine.

Patrice & Regina de La Bastille
Malvoisine,
49460 Écuillé,
Maine-et-Loire
tel +33 (0)2 41 93 34 44
fax +33 (0)2 41 93 34 44
e-mail bastille-pr@wanadoo.fr
web www.malvoisine-bastille.com

Château de Montreuil

An 1840s neo-Gothic delight in a stork-nested, deer-roamed park, a river for swimming and rowing and a film set of an interior: the sitting room is splendidly 'medieval', the panelled salon pure 18th century, taken whole from a château, with superb hangings and immensely high doors. This was once a self-sufficient country estate with its own chapel, dovecote and mill (remains still visible). And a Bishop's Room, of course, where you can sleep; the corner room has a fine four-poster; all are a mixture of old and new with super river views. Your hosts are gracious and humorous, fascinating to listen to and utterly French.

rooms	4: 1 triple, 3 doubles.
price	€75-€90 for two.
meals	Dinner with wine €26-€30, book ahead.
closed	November-Easter.
directions	From Angers N23 to Seiches sur Loir; D74 for Châteauneuf sur Sarthe 5.5km. Château on right as you leave Montreuil village.

Jacques & Marie Bailliou
Château de Montreuil,
49140 Montreuil sur Loir,
Maine-et-Loire
tel +33 (0)2 41 76 21 03
e-mail chateau.montreuil@anjou-et-loire.com
web www.anjou-et-loire.com/chateau

Map 5 Entry 326

La Croix d'Étain

Sprightly red squirrels decorate the stone balustrade, the wide river flows past the lush garden: it feels like deep country yet this handsome manor has urban elegance in its very stones. Panelling, mouldings, subtly-muted floor tiles bring grace, traditional French florals add softness. It looks fairly formal but Madame, relaxed and communicative, adores having guests and pampers them, in their own quarters, with luxury. Monsieur is jovial, makes wine and jam and loves fishing! Plush, lacy-feminine, sunny bedrooms, three with river views, all with superb bathrooms. Walking and cycling paths are marked.

rooms	4: 2 doubles, 2 twins.
price	€65-€75 for two.
meals	Dinner €25, book ahead; wine €10. Crêperie 50m.
closed	Rarely.
directions	From Angers N162 for Lion d'Angers 20km to Grieul; right D291 to Grez Neuville. At church, Rue de l'Écluse towards river on left.

Jacqueline & Auguste Bahuaud
La Croix d'Étain,
49220 Grez-Neuville,
Maine-et-Loire
tel +33 (0)2 41 95 68 49
fax +33 (0)2 41 18 02 72
e-mail croix.etain@anjou-et-loire.com
web www.anjou-et-loire.com/croix

Map 4 Entry 327

Les Travaillères

You cannot fail to warm to Madame's easy vivacity and infectious laugh. She virtually lives in her beloved garden – or in her kitchen in the house opposite, making pastries in the old bread oven. The lovingly-preserved Segré farmhouse with its deep roof and curious *outeau* openings (some would have put in modern dormers), has great beams, a big fireplace, exposed stone and new country furniture. Attic bedrooms are neatly rustic: crochet, terracotta, pine, with bathrooms cunningly sneaked in among the rafters. The woods are full of birdlife, cows graze in the field outside one bedroom's window.

rooms	3: 1 double, 2 suites for 4.
price	€36-€38 for two.
meals	Choice of restaurants 2-5km; kitchen available; picnic in garden possible.
closed	Rarely.
directions	From Angers N162 to Lion d'Angers; on for Rennes & Segré on D863 3km; right at Chambres d'Hôtes & La Himbaudière sign; under main road; 1km along on left.

Jocelyne & François Vivier
Les Travaillères,
49220 Le Lion d'Angers,
Maine-et-Loire
tel +33 (0)2 41 61 33 56
mob +33 (0)6 77 86 24 33

Map 4 Entry 328

Manoir du Bois de Grez

An old peace lingers over the unique fan-shaped yard, the old well, the little chapel: this place oozes history. Your doctor host, who also loves painting, and his friendly chatty wife, much-travelled antique-hunters with imagination and flair, set the tone with a bright red petrol pump and a penny-farthing in the hall. Generous bedrooms hung with well-chosen exotic pieces or paintings are done in good strong colours that reflect the garden light. You share the big sitting room with your charming, interesting hosts, lots of plants and a suit of armour. *Watch children with unfenced pond.*

rooms	2: 1 double, 1 twin.
price	€62-€71 for two.
meals	Light supper €10-€15.
closed	Rarely.
directions	From Angers N162 to Laval; exit Grieul D291 to Grez Neuville; exit village via Sceaux d'Anjou road; 900m right Allée du Bois de Grez.

Marie Laure & Jean Gaël Cesbron
Manoir du Bois de Grez,
49220 Grez-Neuville,
Maine-et-Loire
tel +33 (0)2 41 18 00 09
fax +33 (0)2 41 18 00 09
e-mail cesbron.boisgrez@wanadoo.fr
web www.boisdegrez.com

Map 4 Entry 329

Château de Chambiers

Another marvellous family château, this one surrounded by a forest of wild boar. Smiling Madame speaks perfect English, is proud of her gardens fronted by topiaried sheep and her big, beautiful rooms; she is an original and talented designer. Bedrooms have delicious antiques, one a French-Caribbean mahogany bed (the family owned a banana plantation), floors are 18th-century oak with *terre cuit* borders – exquisite; baths, washstands and fittings are period originals. There's a panelled, fresh-flowered *salon de thé* for breakfast and dinner, and vegetables from the potager. French heaven.

rooms	5 family rooms.
price	€80-€130 for two.
meals	Dinner €25, book ahead; wine list from €15.
closed	Rarely. Book ahead in winter.
directions	From Angers, N23 to Durtal; r'bout, 1st exit to Bangé; after 150m, right to Jarzé; château on left after 3km.

Anne Crouan
Château de Chambiers,
49430 Durtal, Maine-et-Loire
tel +33 (0)2 41 76 07 31
fax +33 (0)2 41 76 04 28
e-mail info@chateauchambiers.com
web www.chateauchambiers.com

La Ruchelière

Through the door in the wall, under the tunnel of greenery and lo! a fine presbytery rises from the lawns, fairly well sheltered from the road. The Ruches have done their classic French house in thoughtful, unusual fashion: a taffeta theme throughout with draperies and florals, collections of glass, china, dolls (the Indian puppets on the dining room walls are a joy) and modern paintings under high beautifully beamed ceilings, a piano by the great sitting-room fireplace and a convivial table for breakfast. These are fun, generous people (he's a pilot) with a talent for interior design and a desire to please.

rooms	4 doubles.
price	€50-€115 for two.
meals	Dinner with wine €22-£33, book ahead. Restaurants in village.
closed	Rarely.
directions	From Le Mans A11 exit 11; D859 for Châteauneuf sur Sarthe; D89 for Contigné; house opp. church, signposted.

Carole & Oliver Ruche
La Ruchelière,
49330 Contigné, Maine-et-Loire
tel +33 (0)2 41 32 74 86
fax +33 (0)2 41 32 76 84
e-mail rucheliere@wanadoo.fr
web www.anjou-bnb.com

Le Rideau Miné

The old country values are at home here: Madame has extended her house with deep respect for the 17th- and 18th-century shapes and materials of her lovely old millhouse (the Mayenne runs through the garden), she grows most of her own fruit and vegetables, delights in preparing local recipes for dinner and a fresh breakfast cake every day, sees that her pretty, beamed, many-windowed bedrooms with their good sitting areas are always spotless. Her sense for softened primary colours on white is remarkable: gentle but not timid. She is an unintrusive but caring hostess, rightly proud of her house and garden.

rooms	3: 1 double, 1 twin; 1 double with separate bathroom.
price	€53 for two.
meals	Dinner with wine €22, book ahead.
closed	Rarely.
directions	From Angers for Rennes N162; after Lion d'Angers D770 for Chamigne; after river Mayenne over bridge; D287 left for Chambellay; left after 500m. Signposted.

Dany Fabry
Le Rideau Miné,
49220 Thorigné d'Anjou,
Maine-et-Loire
tel +33 (0)2 41 76 88 40
e-mail lerideaumine@yahoo.fr
web www.lerideaumine.com

Map 4 Entry 332

Le Frêne

Unbroken views of the countryside, and not a whisper of the 21st century. The austere topiaried spinning-tops flanking the drive belie the warm, sunny rooms ahead – this house breathes books, music and art. Richard, who once had a book shop in Angers, is charming and funny; Florence runs art courses from home. Built on the ramparts of the old fortified village, the house has a 'hanging' garden whose beds are themed with colour. More in the house: crushed raspberry, lime green, sunny yellow. The attic suite, ideal for families, is big enough to hold a Russian billiard table – and Florence's charming watercolours.

rooms	4: 1 double, 2 twins, 1 suite for 4.
price	€50 for two. Suite €80 for four.
meals	Dinner with wine €17, book ahead.
closed	Rarely.
directions	From Angers N162 to Le Lion d'Angers; D863 to Segré; D923; left D863 to l'Hôtellerie de Flée; D180 to Châtelais. 1st left on entering village.

Richard & Florence Sence
Le Frêne,
49520 Châtelais, Maine-et-Loire
tel +33 (0)2 41 61 16 45
fax +33 (0)2 41 61 16 45
e-mail lefrene@free.fr
web lefrene.online.fr

Map 4 Entry 333

Château de Craon

Such a close and welcoming family, whose kindness will extend to include you, too. It's a magnificent place, with innumerable expressions of history, taste and personality, and Loïk and Hélène, the younger generation, are gracious and treat you like friends. A salon with sofas and a view of the park, an Italianate hall with sweeping stone stair, classic French bedrooms in lavender, blue, cream… an original washstand, a canopied bed, a velvet armchair. Everywhere a feast for the eyes, paintings, watercolours, antiques; outside, 40 acres of river, meadows and lake, and a potager worth leaving home for.

rooms	6: 2 doubles, 1 twin, 2 singles, 1 suite. Extra space for children.
price	€120-€160 for two. Suite €240 for two-three.
meals	Restaurants in village.
closed	Mid-December-mid-March.
directions	From Château Gontier, N171 to Craon; clear signs as you enter town. 30km south of Laval.

Loïk & Hélène de Guébriant
Château de Craon,
53400 Craon, Mayenne
tel +33 (0)2 43 06 11 02
fax +33 (0)2 43 06 05 18
e-mail chateaudecraon@wanadoo.fr
web www.chateaudecraon.com

La Gilardière

The old stairs wind up through the subtly-lit interior to fairly sophisticated rooms with lovely furniture, beams and low doorways, plenty of sitting areas, rooms off for your children or your butler. The French-Irish Drions' beautiful restoration of this ancient priory, mostly 14th and 15th century, is a marvel (famous people get married in the chapel). They are a friendly, humorous couple of horse and hunting enthusiasts who greatly enjoy their B&B activity. The huge grounds lead to open country unspoilt by 20th-century wonders, that big pond is full of carp for keen fishers and there's a tennis court.

rooms	4: 2 doubles, 2 family rooms.
price	€55-€100 for two.
meals	Dinner with wine €25, book ahead.
closed	16 October-April.
directions	From Château Gontier D28 for Grez en Bouère; at Gennes right D15 for Bierné; in St Aignan right before church; house 2km on left.

Ghislain & Françoise Drion
La Gilardière,
53200 Gennes sur Glaize,
Mayenne
tel +33 (0)2 43 70 93 03
fax +33 (0)2 43 70 93 03
e-mail ghislain.drion@wanadoo.fr

Château de Mirvault-Azé

Here beside the fast-flowing river reigns the easy atmosphere of genuine class – you are welcomed by Madame's gentle intelligence and Monsieur's boundless energy. The house has been much added to since the family arrived 400 years ago but each object, antique and picture has a tale to tell. Bedrooms are full of interest and comfort, some overlooking the rushing river, others a well-rabbitted field. The large, formal sitting room is pure 'château' while across the hall/piano room there's an elegant dining room with separate tables for breakfast – or your own, self-prepared supper. A happy family house.

rooms	2: 1 double, 1 family suite for 4.
price	€76 for two.
meals	Restaurants nearby.
closed	Rarely.
directions	In Château Gontier N162 N for Laval. Entrance on left 50m after last r'bout as you leave town.

Brigitte & François d'Ambrières
Château de Mirvault-Azé,
53200 Château Gontier, Mayenne
tel +33 (0)2 43 07 10 82
fax +33 (0)2 43 07 10 82
e-mail chateau.mirvault@worldonline.fr
web www.bienvenue-au-chateau.com

Le Chêne Vert

That aristocratic 18th-century look (graceful gazebo and diminutive chapel included) belies the dynamic and original talent let loose on the bedrooms. *Orientale* is orange and ornamented, Moroccan-style, with a dazzling royal blue mosaic shower room; *Tropicale* has all sorts of bamboos, even live ones, to stupendous effect, *Safari* has more colour and mosquito netting. Caroline looks after her house and her little girl single-handedly with shimmering artistic enthusiasm, her husband runs his wine business. Breakfast is in sunny yellow dining-room elegance or salon cosiness or sweeping gazebo parkland. A great find.

rooms	5: 1 double, 2 triples, 1 family room, 1 suite.
price	€70 for two.
meals	Dinner with wine €20, book ahead.
closed	Rarely.
directions	From Château Gontier D20 for Segré; after 1km, house signposted on left.

Caroline Heron
Le Chêne Vert,
53200 Château Gontier, Mayenne
tel +33 (0)2 43 07 90 48
fax +33 (0)2 43 07 90 48
e-mail caroline.heron@wanadoo.fr
web www.chateau-chene-vert.com

Le Rocher

Being the Richecours' only guests means free run of Madame's delightful conversation (travel, history, houses, gardens, people), her lovingly-designed garden, the old house that they have restored and furnished with care and imagination (she collects antique doors). Your room is in the 17th-century part above the old kitchen, so attractive in its wealth of fitted cupboards and slabs of slate. Character fills the big guest room: original tiles, iron bed, great old timbers (duck!). The meadow sweeps down to the river, the family boat and the little restaurant on the opposite bank awaits. Peaceful elegance and great warmth.

rooms	1 double.
price	€90 for two.
meals	Choice of restaurants within 7km.
closed	Rarely.
directions	From Château Gontier N162 for Laval, 4km; left for St Germain de l'Hommel; immediately right; on to village; left, signposted 'no through road', after 500m second house called Rocher.

Mme de Richecour
Le Rocher,
53200 Fromentières,
Mayenne
tel +33 (0)2 43 07 06 64
fax +33 (0)2 43 06 51 55

Le Logis du Ray

All who stay at the Logis du Ray are sure to be wonderfully looked after – the dozen or so fine draught horses by Jacques, B&B guests by Martine. From their previous life in Paris as antique dealers comes a love of beautiful things to add to their natural hospitality, but if you can tear yourself away from the lovely welcoming bedrooms, the homely sitting room or the delightful cottage garden, there are riverside walks and unspoilt countryside to explore on foot or by pony and trap (your hosts run a carriage-driving school). Our readers love it.

rooms	3: 1 twin, 2 triples.
price	€68 for two; €99 for three.
meals	Good restaurant in village.
closed	Rarely.
directions	From Sablé sur Sarthe D309 & D27 for Angers; entering St Denis, 1st left at 'Renov' Cuir' sign. House 100m along; signposted.

Martine & Jacques Lefebvre
Le Logis du Ray,
53290 St Denis d'Anjou,
Mayenne
tel +33 (0)2 43 70 64 10
fax +33 (0)2 43 70 65 53

Villeprouvé

Of vast age and character – and an ancient, leaning stair – this farmhouse is home to a humorous and talented couple who juggle cattle, children and guests. Delicious dinners end with a flaming presention of *grog maison* to guarantee deep sleep. In the big, soft rooms, every bed is canopied except the single box-bed which is carved and curtained to a tee. There are nooks, crannies and crooked lines, terracotta floors, half-timbered walls, antiques, books on art, tourism, history – and pretty new bathrooms. Ducks paddle in the pond, cows graze, the wind ruffles the trees, apples become cider – bucolic peace.

rooms	4: 2 doubles, 1 triple, 1 family room.
price	€42-€46.50 for two.
meals	Dinner €13, book ahead; wine €8.
closed	Rarely.
directions	From Laval N162 for Château Gontier 14km; right through Villiers Charlemagne to Ruille Froid Fonds; left C4 for Bignon 1km. Signposted.

Christophe & Christine Davenel
Villeprouvé,
53170 Ruille Froid Fonds,
Mayenne

tel +33 (0)2 43 07 71 62
fax +33 (0)2 43 07 71 62
e-mail christ.davenel@wanadoo.fr

Le Bas du Gast

In the heart of the town, here are chambres d'hôtes on the grandest of scales: a splendid mansion, a little park with 84 trimmed box hedges, and wonderful, courteous hosts. Monsieur is the showman, Madame quietly spoken, and both adore house, garden and guests. The magnificently châteauesque rooms are large and light, each in individual inimitably French style. There's an easy opulence in the cavernous bathrooms, marble fireplaces and beautiful panelling, some of it delicate blue against striking yellow curtains and bedcovers. Exceptional position, style and attention to detail.

rooms	4: 3 doubles, 1 suite.
price	€100-€110. Suite €200.
meals	Breakfast €13-€18. Restaurants within walking distance.
closed	December-January.
directions	In Laval follow signs to Mairie then brown signs to Le Bas du Gast - opp. 'Salle Polyvalente' & 'Bibliothèque' (1km from Mairie).

M & Mme François Williot
Le Bas du Gast,
53000 Laval,
Mayenne

tel +33 (0)2 43 49 22 79
fax +33 (0)2 43 56 44 71

Le Cruchet

This unusual and proudly restored 15th-century manor has a staircase tower to the upstairs bedroom to lend an air of mystery. Downstairs are the bread oven and a fine dining room where breakfast is served to the chiming of the church clock. The Nays' old family home is well lived in and they love sharing it with guests. Rooms are elegant with antiques and decent bathrooms. Your welcoming and unintrusive hosts can teach you French, weave baskets or make music. A wonderful atmosphere in delectable countryside – readers have loved the "real character of the place".

rooms	2: 1 double, 1 triple.
price	€38-€40 for two.
meals	Restaurants in village or 3km.
closed	Rarely.
directions	From Laval N157 for Le Mans; at Soulgé sur Ouette D20 left to Evron; D7 for Mayenne. signposted in Mézangers.

Léopold & Marie-Thérèse Nay
Le Cruchet,
53600 Mézangers,
Mayenne
tel +33 (0)2 43 90 65 55
e-mail bandb.lecruchet@wanadoo.fr

La Rouaudière

Prize-winning cows in the fields, prize-winning owners in the house. They are an exceptionally engaging, relaxed couple and their conversation is the heart and soul of this marvellous place. Breakfast is a feast at which you help yourself to eggs, cheese, fresh fruit juices, homemade jams and lashings of coffee. You get a warm fire in the salon, pretty chairs in the garden, and redecorated bedrooms that are straightforward and simple: plain walls, a few antiquey bits and bobs and pretty window boxes. Madame cannot do enough for her guests, and readers have been full of praise.

rooms	3: 1 double, 1 twin, 1 triple.
price	€45-€50 for two.
meals	Good choice of restaurants nearby.
closed	Rarely.
directions	From Fougères N12 east for Laval 15km; farm sign on right.

Maurice & Thérèse Trihan
La Rouaudière,
53500 Ernée, Mayenne
tel +33 (0)2 43 05 13 57
fax +33 (0)2 43 05 71 15
e-mail therese-trihan@wanadoo.fr
web www.chambresdhotes-auxportesdelabretagne.com

Garencière

The door stands open to welcome all comers or for waving excitedly to the little steam train. This happy, active couple look after three teenagers and a farm and keep a truly hospitable house, he the handyman, she the decorator and mosaic-layer (superb pool in a converted barn). Dinner is a lengthy, gregarious, joyful affair – wonderful for lovers of French family cooking. The endearingly French guest quarters in the outbuildings may show signs of the passing of time, and of the family cats… but you will like the Langlais a lot. And Madame's 150 egg cups. *Well-behaved pets with watchful owners only.*

rooms	5: 2 doubles, 1 twin, 1 triple, plus 1 suite in 'La Petite Maison'.
price	€48-€49 for two.
meals	Dinner with wine or cider €19, book ahead.
closed	One week at Christmas.
directions	From Alençon N138 S for 4km; left D55 through Champfleur for Bourg le Roi; farm sign 1km after Champfleur.

Denis & Christine Langlais
Garencière,
72610 Champfleur, Sarthe

tel	+33 (0)2 33 31 75 84
fax	+33 (0)2 33 27 42 09
web	monsite.wanadoo.fr/garenciere

Map 5 Entry 344

Château de Monhoudou

Your hosts are the nicest, easiest of aristocrats, determined to keep the ancestral home alive in a dignified manner – 19 generations on. A jewel set in rolling parkland, sheep grazing under mature trees, horses in the paddock, swans on a bit of the moat, peacock, deer, boar… it has antiques on parquet floors and modern beds; bathrooms and loos in turrets, cupboards, alcoves; an elegant dining room with family silver, a sitting room with log fire, family portraits, a small book-lined library – and do ask to see the chapel upstairs. Hunting trophies, timeless tranquillity, genuine, lovely people.

rooms	6: 4 doubles, 1 twin, 1 suite for 3.
price	€85-€140 for two.
meals	Dinner with wine €37, book ahead.
closed	Rarely.
directions	From Alençon N138 S for Le Mans about 14km; at La Hutte left D310 for 10km; right D19 through Courgains; left D132 to Monhoudou; signposted.

Michel & Marie-Christine de Monhoudou
Château de Monhoudou,
72260 Monhoudou, Sarthe

tel	+33 (0)2 43 97 40 05
fax	+33 (0)2 43 33 11 58
e-mail	monhoudou@aol.com
web	www.monhoudou.com

Map 5 Entry 345

Éporcé

You may think yourself as lucky to stay in this relaxedly luxurious place as the owner and his young family to have inherited it, so fine and genuine inside and out. Pure 17th century with a magnificent avenue of trees, moat, lofty beamed ceilings, three salons for guests, it brims with antiques, books and atmosphere yet never overwhelms. First-floor rooms are proper château stuff, upstairs they are cosier, less grand, sharing the loo and those pretty oval mansard windows. If you choose the gourmet dinner, your host will set out the family silver and Wedgwood as well as unforgettable food. Wholly delightful.

rooms	6: 4 doubles, 2 suites.
price	€75-€150 for two.
meals	Dinner with wine €30, book ahead.
closed	Rarely.
directions	From A11 exit 8, N157 for Laval; D28 for La Quinte; left by church for Coulans; 1km, wayside cross, fork right; entrance on left.

Rémy de Scitivaux
Éporcé,
72550 La Quinte,
Sarthe

tel +33 (0)2 43 27 70 22
fax +33 (0)2 43 27 89 29
e-mail eporce@wanadoo.fr

Château de Montaupin

Following her family's tradition, Marie is a good, helpful hostess while Laurent is in motor racing: buffs flock for Le Mans. Theirs is so French a château, not overwhelming, just peaceful loveliness with farmland and woods beyond. Some rooms look onto an amazing 400-year-old cedar, others have gorgeous garden views, all have interesting furniture and are being redone (50 windows to replace!). The long panelled sitting room feels like the inside of an old ship and it is all unpretentious with some gratifyingly untidy corners, small, pretty shower rooms and much unselfconscious good taste. A heated pool, too.

rooms	5: 2 family rooms, 3 suites for 4-6; 2 separate wcs.
price	€55-€60 for two; €70-€75 for three. Suite €300-€500.
meals	Dinner with wine €20, book ahead.
closed	Occasionally, please book ahead.
directions	From Le Mans N23 for La Flèche to Cérans Foulletourte; D31 to Oizé; left on D32; sign to right.

Laurent Sénéchal & Marie David
Château de Montaupin,
72330 Oizé,
Sarthe

tel +33 (0)2 43 87 81 70
fax +33 (0)2 43 87 26 25
e-mail chateaudemontaupin@oreka.com

Le Perceau

A happy house, part farm, part *maison bourgeoise*, where the smell of baking may greet you and the delicious results be on the table in the morning: fabulous pastries, breads and cakes. Your easy, amusing hosts have three young children – yours are welcome too and there's space indoors for little ones to run their socks off when they tire of the garden. Then it's up the spiral staircase to a cassis-and-orange bedroom (it works); or try the purple room in the old farmhouse kitchen. All very rural and river-viewed, yet pretty Malicorne, with its château and *faienceries*, market and restaurants, is a few minutes' meander.

rooms 2: 1 double, 1 room for 4.
price €47 for two.
meals Excellent restaurants in Malicorne, 800m.
closed Rarely.
directions From Le Mans N23 for La Flèche; at Fontaine St Martin, D8 for Malicorne sur Sarthe; D23 for Le Mans; house last on left, signposted.

Catherine & Jean Paul Beuvier
Le Perceau,
72270 Malicorne,
Sarthe
tel +33 (0)2 43 45 74 40
e-mail leperceau@libertysurf.fr

Le Moulin du Prieuré

It's a brilliantly converted old watermill, this couple's labour of love, down to the smooth cogwheels that turn in the great kitchen. Marie-Claire is so relaxed, such good company, such fun and unflappably efficient that it's hard to believe she has four young children – other kids love it here. The double-height sitting room bursts with books and videos for all; simple, attractive rooms have good beds, old tiled floors, bare stone walls. The atmosphere embraces you, the country sounds of stream, cockerel and Angelus prayer bells soothe, the unsung area brims with interest.

rooms 5: 4 doubles, 1 family room.
price €50 for two. Family room €75.
meals Restaurant opposite.
closed Rarely.
directions From Tours N138 for Le Mans 35km to Dissay sous Courcillon; left at lights; mill just past church.

Marie-Claire Bretonneau
Le Moulin du Prieuré,
72500 Dissay sous Courcillon,
Sarthe
tel +33 (0)2 43 44 59 79
e-mail moulinduprieure@wanadoo.fr

Le Prieuré

Bushels of history from the beams and vaulted ceilings of the moated priory, snug beneath its old church: built in the 12th, extended in the 16th, it had monks into the 20th century. Christophe loves telling the history, Marie-France does the decorating, brilliantly in keeping with the elegant old house: oriental rugs on old tiled floors, pale-painted beams over stone fireplaces, fine old paintings on plain walls and good modern beds under soft-coloured covers. They are attentive, intelligent hosts, happy to share their vaulted dining room and peaceful garden, and the road is not an inconvenience.

rooms	4: 1 twin, 2 doubles, 1 suite for 3.
price	€90-€120 for two. Suite €130 for three.
meals	Auberge opposite & restaurants nearby.
closed	November-February, unless booked in advance.
directions	From Le Mans A28 for Tours; exit Ecommoy; N138 to Dissay sous Courcillon; signposted in village.

Christophe & Marie-France Calla
Le Prieuré,
72500 Dissay sous Courcillon,
Sarthe

tel	+33 (0)2 43 44 09 09
fax	+33 (0)2 43 44 09 09
e-mail	ccalla@club-internet.fr

photo Michael Busselle

loire valley

Chambre d'hôtes

This was Roger and Dagmar's country cottage until they left Paris to settle here. She left her native Germany and adopted France many moons ago, he's a retired chef; readers tell us the food is wonderful. Your hosts join you for breakfast (hot croissants, homemade jams, smoked salmon, farm butter) and dinner. The cottage garden is cherished and, if you time it right, every old wall is covered with roses. One bedroom is wood-panelled, the other more typical with sloping rafters; fabrics are flowered and the varnished wooden floors are symmetrically rugged. Cosy, friendly and great fun.

rooms	2: 1 double, 1 suite for 3.
price	€46-€54 for two.
meals	Dinner with wine €20, book ahead.
closed	January-February.
directions	From Verneuil sur Avre D939 for Chartres; in Maillebois left on D20 to Blévy; follow signs to Chambres d'Hôtes.

Roger Parmentier
Chambre d'hôtes,
28170 Blévy,
Eure-et-Loir
tel +33 (0)2 37 48 01 21
fax +33 (0)2 37 48 01 21
e-mail parti@club-internet.fr
web www.bab-blevy.com

Maison JLN

The whole world comes to enjoy this gentle, polyglot family and the serene vibes of their old Chartrain house. Up two steep spirals to the attic, across the family's little prayer room (your sitting room), past the stained-glass window, the lovely bedroom feels a bit like a chapel with beds. Lots of books; reminders of pilgrimage, just beneath the great cathedral; Madame knowledgeably friendly, Monsieur a charmer who enjoys a chuckle, their children, interested in your travels: they're all happy to sit and talk when you get back. An unusual and welcoming place in a timeless spot.

rooms	1 twin with separate shower & wc on floor below.
price	€45 for two.
meals	Choice of restaurants on your doorstep.
closed	Rarely.
directions	Arriving in Chartres follow signs for IBIS Centre; park by Hotel IBIS (Place Drouaise); walk 20m along Rue de la Porte Drouaise to Rue Muret (approx. 100m car to house).

Jean-Loup & Nathalie Cuisiniez
Maison JLN,
28000 Chartres,
Eure-et-Loir
tel +33 (0)2 37 21 98 36
fax +33 (0)2 37 21 98 36
e-mail jln.cuisiniez@wanadoo.fr
web monsite.wanadoo.fr/maisonjln/

20 rue Pierre Genet

Caroline has cleverly organised the old 200-year-old farmhouse for herself and her animals to share easily with guests, who have the stable wing: the atmosphere is relaxed and informal, modern comfort and spirit in a deeply French rural husk. She is multi-lingual, having worked with Unesco, makes her own honey, does a lot of the restoration herself, weeds her pretty, crazy-paved garden and still finds time for art and literature. Bedrooms are big and airy, with pretty rugs and super bathrooms. Up the outside steps, the double has exposed beams and subtle lighting from rooflight and window. Very special.

rooms 2: 1 triple, 1 double.
price €60 for two.
meals Dinner with wine €30, book ahead.
closed 16-31 December.
directions From Paris A1 exit Thivars; N10 to Châteaudun. At 3rd r'bout with garage on left, left for Blois 5km; left for Le Mée 5km, left again for Le Mée. In village right opp. café. On 100m to No 20; turn into passage just after wall; into courtyard.

Caroline Vidican
20 rue Pierre Genet,
28220 Le Mée,
Eure-et-Loir
tel +33 (0)2 37 44 13 77
e-mail mcvidican@aol.com
web www.loire-bedandbreakfast.com

18 rue de la Grolle

The original 16th-century house huddles up to a cluster of only slightly younger siblings: the result is a charmingly higgledy-piggledy family, mothered by your delightful, easy-going and unintrusive hostess. Since the Moutons arrived here 30 years ago, the outskirts of Orléans have crept out to meet them but the country sounds still win through. Crunch along the drive to the split-level suite with masses of books and a bright new sofabed, sleep beneath the steeply-pitched roof and under Provençal fabrics, then repair to the huge breakfast room with its massive fireplace and the bust of a moustachioed *grand-père*.

rooms 3 doubles.
price €45 for two.
meals Plenty of restaurants nearby.
closed 1 November-31 March.
directions In Chaingy N152; left at lights from Blois; right at light from Orléans, Rue des Fourneaux 300m; left Rue de la Grolle. Signposted.

Ursula Mouton
18 rue de la Grolle,
45380 Chaingy,
Loiret
tel +33 (0)2 38 80 65 68
e-mail ulimout@yahoo.fr
web titmar.free.fr/Chambreshotes.htm

Les Charmettes

This robust 18th-century canalside townhouse has inherited an expansive atmosphere from its wine merchant builders. They were loading their wine onto barges on the canal which flows under the windows until the 1930s. So much for the past. For the present: you will dine with your refined hosts in the chandeliered dining room, sleep in good, very individual rooms (a bath in one bedroom), breakfast off ravishing Gien china with fruit from the garden, meet Lucia the labrador who helps her owner welcome guests over a glass of white wine. Madame is happy to arrange visits to wine growers.

rooms	1 + 2 apartments: 1 triple; 1 apartment for 4, 1 apartment for 5 with bath, wc downstairs.
price	€60 for two.
meals	Dinner with wine €25, book ahead.
closed	Rarely.
directions	From Orléans N60 E for Montargis & Nevers, exit to Fay aux Loges; through Fay, cross canal, left D709; house first on left arriving in Donnery.

Nicole & Jacques Sicot
Les Charmettes,
45450 Donnery,
Loiret
tel +33 (0)2 38 59 22 50
e-mail nsicot@club-internet.fr

Domaine de Sainte Hélène

Sologne used to be the hunting ground of kings and your bubbling, smiling hostess is a huntswoman, hence horses and dogs outside, horns and antlers in. Hers is a typical Solognote house with great beams and lovely flagstones, the talking telly in contemporary contrast. The double room is brilliantly done, small but cosy, with steeply sloping ceilings – no good for the over-stretched; the suite is larger (60m^2); both are differently furnished – this is very much a family house. Madame, genuinely eager to please, cooks only occasionally but will happily drive you to and from the restaurant.

rooms	2: 1 double, 1 suite for 4.
price	€60-€80 for two. Minimum stay 2 nights.
meals	2 auberges 1km; self-catering possible.
closed	Rarely.
directions	From Orléans N60 E to Jargeau; over bridge through town centre; left on D951 for Tigy; D83 through Vannes; house about 2km on right.

Agnès Célèrier
Domaine de Sainte Hélène,
45510 Vannes sur Cosson, Loiret
tel +33 (0)2 38 58 04 55
fax +33 (0)2 38 58 28 38
e-mail celerierloiret@hotmail.com
web monsite.wanadoo.fr/hotes.loiret

Les Vieux Guays

If secluded is what you want, this house sits in 200 acres of woods, its grassy garden – larder to legions of fearless rabbits – rambling down to the lake and a constant show of water fowl. Sandrine and Alvaro, a tennis professional, returned from Chile to open her family home to guests. They are a poised and friendly couple easily mixing old and modern, bright and dark, happy for guests to sit in their vast, colourful, galleried salon and breakfast at their long dining table before the bucolic lake view. In another wing, bedrooms are high-quality too: antiques, excellent new bedding, plain walls and floral fabrics.

rooms	5: 2 doubles, 2 twins, 1 family suite for 4.
price	€75 for two.
meals	Restaurant 2km.
closed	Rarely.
directions	From Paris de Gien by A6; A77 exit Gien; D940 Argents-Sauldre; D948 to Cerdon; D65 for Clémont; immed. right after level-crossing; 1.5km left onto track beside lake on left; straight on.

Sandrine & Alvaro Martinez Porte
Les Vieux Guays,
45620 Cerdon du Loiret,
Loiret
tel +33 (0)2 38 36 03 76
fax +33 (0)2 38 36 03 76
e-mail alydrine@aol.com

Map 6 Entry 357

Domaine de la Thiau

A vast estate by the Loire, a 19th-century house for the family, a 17th-century one for guests, exotic pheasants and peacocks strutting around the splendid garden. Your welcoming young hosts – he is a busy vet, she looks after the house, small children and you with natural elegance – make it feel friendly despite the grand appearance. Guest bedrooms with high ceilings are carefully decorated with carved bedsteads and papered walls – snug, exclusive, peaceful. Breakfast and dinner are served in the guests' house, or on the flowered terrace that borders the château's large, rambling garden.

rooms	3: 2 doubles; 1 suite for 3 with kitchen.
price	€45-€58 for two.
meals	Dinner with wine €14, book ahead. Good restaurants in Briare or Gien 4km; self-catering in suite.
closed	Rarely.
directions	From A6 onto A77 for Nevers, exit Briare; D952 for Gien. Between Briare & Gien: sign by nurseries.

Mme Bénédicte François
Domaine de la Thiau,
45250 Briare, Loiret
tel +33 (0)2 38 38 20 92
fax +33 (0)2 38 38 06 20
e-mail lathiau@club-internet.fr
web perso.club-internet.fr/lathiau

Map 6 Entry 358

La Brissauderie

Utter peace… this 1970s farmhouse is cradled in tumbling woodland and wrapped in birdsong. Goats softly bleat on the farm below. Madame is chatty and genuine, she still helps out with the animals and can arrange goaty visits for children. The downstairs double is functional, the upstairs suites perfect for families: all have stencilled furniture, some good family pieces, tongue-and-groove pine. Walls, ceilings and doors are filled with fun murals: sunflowers shine, bees bumble and butterflies flutter by. Your tasty breakfast comes with honey from a friend's bees and, of course, goat's cheese.

rooms	3: 1 double, 1 suite for 3-5, 1 suite for 4-6.
price	€32 for two; €69 for six.
meals	Choice of restaurants nearby.
closed	Rarely.
directions	From Sancerre D923 for Jars & Vailly sur Sauldre; 2km before Jars right on track into wood, house at end of track, signposted.

Madeleine & Philippe Jay
La Brissauderie,
18260 Jars, Cher
tel +33 (0)2 48 58 74 94
fax +33 (0)2 48 58 74 94
e-mail madeleine.jay@wanadoo.fr
web www.labrissauderie.com

La Verrerie

Fantastic bedrooms: in a pretty outbuilding, the double, with a green iron bed, old tiled floor and bold bedspread, look onto the garden from the ground floor; the twin has the same tiles underfoot, beams overhead and high wooden beds with an inviting mix of white covers and red quilts. The Count and Countess, who manage forests, farm and hunt but are relatively new to B&B, are charming and thoroughly hospitable. If you would like to eat in, you will join them for dinner in the main house. Members of the family run a vineyard in Provence, so try their wine.

rooms	2: 1 double, 1 suite for 2-4.
price	€75-€99 for two; €145 for four. Reduction for children under five.
meals	Dinner with wine €15-€28, book ahead; self-catering possible.
closed	Rarely.
directions	From Paris A6 to A77 exit 19 for Gien. From Bourges D940 to Chapelle d'Angillon; D12 to Ivoy le Pré. At church left D39 for Blancafort, Oizon, Château de la Verrerie for 2.5km; gate on right.

Étienne & Marie de Saporta
La Verrerie,
18380 Ivoy le Pré,
Cher
tel +33 (0)2 48 58 90 86
fax +33 (0)2 48 58 92 79
e-mail m.desaporta@wanadoo.fr

La Reculée

A marriage of 18th-century stones and 20th-century design have created ideal guest quarters in the stables. Pale timber clothes the space with clever features such as the vast staircase leading to the tree-house-like top bedroom. The breakfast/sitting room combines new wood, contemporary artists' work and antiques; bedrooms are all different, the twins on the ground floor: Japanese-style doors and shutters, modern fabrics, lacy linen, crocheted covers. The garden, where guests have a terrace, is full of green and flowery things. Meals are delicious – thanks to chic, gracious Madame.

rooms	5: 3 doubles, 2 twins.
price	€48 for two.
meals	Dinner with wine €20, book ahead.
closed	15 November-February.
directions	From Sancerre D955 for Bourges for 16km; D44 left to Montigny & 5km beyond; signposted.

Élisabeth Gressin
La Reculée,
18250 Montigny, Cher
tel +33 (0)2 48 69 59 18
fax +33 (0)2 48 69 52 51
e-mail e.gressin@wanadoo.fr
web www.pays-sancerre.sologne.com/c99

La Grande Mouline

Your hosts came to this rustic haven, where the natural garden flows into woods and fields, deer roam and birdlife astounds, to bring up their new family. Jean is a kindly young grandfather, proud of his efforts in converting his outbuildings for *chambres d'hôtes*. Bedrooms reflect his travels to distant places: Indian rugs, Moroccan brasses, a collection of fossils in an old chemist's cabinet and lots of old farmhouse stuff, nothing too sophisticated. Breakfast is in the main house where family life bustles busily. Return after contemplating Bourges to meditate in this corner of God's harmonious garden.

rooms	4: 2 triples, 1 quadruple, 1 family room.
price	€40 for two.
meals	Restaurant 2.5km.
closed	Rarely.
directions	From Bourges D944 for Orléans. In Bourgneuf left at little r'bout; immed. right & follow signs 1.5km.

Jean Malot & Chantal Charlon
La Grande Mouline,
18110 St Éloy de Gy,
Cher
tel +33 (0)2 48 25 40 44
fax +33 (0)2 48 25 40 44

Domaine de l'Ermitage

Deepest Berry, the heartland of rural France, where this articulate husband-and-wife team run their beef and cereals farm, taxi their children to school, make their own jam and still have time for their guests. Laurence is vivacious and casually elegant and runs an intelligent, welcoming house. The big, simple yet stylishly attractive bedrooms of her superior 18th-century farmhouse are of pleasing proportions – one of them in an unusual round brick-and-timber tower, others have views over the peaceful park. Guests may use the swimming pool, set discreetly out of sight, at agreed times.

rooms	5: 2 doubles, 1 twin, 1 triple, 1 quadruple.
price	€55-€58 for two; €76-€78 for three; €96-€98 for four.
meals	Restaurants in village or choice 6km.
closed	Rarely.
directions	From Vierzon N76 for Bourges through Mehun sur Yèvre; D60 right to Berry Bouy & beyond for about 3km; farm on right.

Laurence & Géraud de La Farge
Domaine de l'Ermitage,
18500 Berry Bouy,
Cher

tel +33 (0)2 48 26 87 46
fax +33 (0)2 48 26 03 28
e-mail domaine-ermitage@wanadoo.fr

Les Bonnets Rouges

Cross the secret garden courtyard and step into this venerable 15th-century guesthouse. Beyond the dining room, where ancient timbers and niches have been exposed in all their mixed-up glory, the knight in shining armour beckons you up the staircase. Bedrooms are elegant with antique beds and new mattresses, marble fireplaces and a claw-footed bath; in the attic, the pretty double is festooned with beams. Your charming hosts live just across the courtyard with their two small daughters. Add the privilege of sleeping beneath that unsurpassed cathedral and it feels like a gift from the angels.

rooms	4: 2 doubles, 2 suites for 3-4.
price	€58-€75 for two.
meals	Great choice of restaurants within walking distance.
closed	Rarely.
directions	In Bourges towards Cathedral; Rue des 3 Maillets; Rue Bourbonnoux. Park in yard if space permits.

Olivier Llopis
Les Bonnets Rouges,
18000 Bourges, Cher

tel +33 (0)2 48 65 79 92
fax +33 (0)2 48 69 82 05
e-mail bonnets-rouges@bourges.net
web bonnets-rouges.bourges.net

Domaine de la Trolière

The beautifully proportioned house in its big shady garden has been in the family for over 200 years. The salon is a cool blue-grey symphony, the dining room smart yellow-grey with a rare, remarkable maroon and grey marble table: breakfast is in here, dinner *en famille* is in the big beamed kitchen. Each stylishly comfortable room has individual character and Madame has a fine eye for detail. She is charming, dynamic, casually elegant and genuinely welcoming. Visitors have poured praise: "quite the most beautiful house we've ever stayed in", "a unique experience of French hospitality and taste".

rooms — 3: 1 double; 2 twins both with separate wc.
price — €47-€55 for two.
meals — Dinner with wine €19, book ahead.
closed — Rarely.
directions — From A71 exit 8; at r'bout D925 W for Lignières & Châteauroux. Sigposted 500m on right.

Marie-Claude Dussert
Domaine de la Trolière,
18200 Orval,
Cher
tel +33 (0)2 48 96 47 45
fax +33 (0)2 48 96 07 71

La Serre

The two Claudes inspire remarks like: "I learned heaps about Art Deco and gardening", "a wonderful lanky couple full of life, laughter and intelligence", "lovely, artistic, wacky". Conversation flows effortlessly over glass and ashtray. Their 1940s manor is entirely Art Deco with an eclectic collection of modern art. You find good beds in the rooms, can learn how to make a properly formal French garden, have breakfast when you want. Dine until the small hours beneath the huge collage in the congenial, bohemian, fun-loving atmosphere created by your down-to-earth hosts. Out of the ordinary – we love it.

rooms — 3: 2 doubles, 1 twin.
price — €69-€84 for two.
meals — Dinner with wine €23-€35, book ahead.
closed — Rarely.
directions — From St Amand Montrond, D951 for Sancoin & Nevers. At Charenton Laugère, D953 for Dun sur Auron; house 300m on left.

M & Mme Claude Moreau
La Serre,
18210 Charenton Laugère,
Cher
tel +33 (0)2 48 60 75 82
fax +33 (0)2 48 60 75 82

La Chasse

This delightful and hard-working English couple came to farm in France, with their two boys, and cattle, too, and invite you to drive 2km down a bumpy track through pretty woods to their comfortable farmhouse. There's a dining room in the sitting room, some old beams still and a stone fireplace, and bedrooms that are big, pale-floored and attractively simple and peaceful: pilgrims to Compostela often stay here. Alison will take wonderful care of you and Robin may tell you tales of shearing French sheep or where to gaze on rare orchids. Argenton, 'Venice of the Indre', is a must.

rooms	3: 1 double; 1 double, 1 family room, sharing bath & separate wc.
price	From €52 for two.
meals	Dinner with wine €22, book ahead.
closed	January-March.
directions	From Châteauroux A20 exit 16 to Tendu; 1st left in village. Pass Mairie, fork left at church for Chavin & Pommiers for 1.5km; left up 2km track.

Robin & Alison Mitchell
La Chasse,
36200 Tendu,
Indre
tel +33 (0)2 54 24 07 76
fax +33 (0)2 54 24 07 76

Château de la Villette

A gem – grand hunting lodge rather than château, it stands in acres of parkland before a vast private lake (boating and safe swimming). Karin lovingly tends every inch of it, including the vast picture window that seems to bring the lake into the sitting room. A great staircase leads to the 'Austrian baroque' room with its sloping ceilings, gorgeous rugs and super-luxy bathroom. The pretty 'modern' room on the ground floor has yellow walls and masses of cupboards. And nothing is too much trouble for Karin, a wonderful hostess. *German, Spanish and Dutch also spoken.*

rooms	2 doubles.
price	€60-€65 for two.
meals	Dinner with wine €22, book ahead.
closed	Rarely.
directions	From Châteauroux D943 to Ardentes; left on D14 for St Août 8km; left at château sign 400m; entrance on right.

Karin Verburgh
Château de la Villette,
36120 Ardentes,
Indre
tel +33 (0)2 54 36 28 46

Carrefour de l'Ormeau

Extravagant minimalism by Alain, a musical, artistic craftsman, cultivator of the senses, and Isabelle, lovely, warm, serene person – and superb cook. In bedrooms of almost monastic simplicity, nothing distracts from the natural warmth of old tiles and Alain's beautiful local-wood furniture: all is light, space, harmony. The magnificent room under the rafters is used for recitals and furniture display. Isabelle's vegetable garden centres on a lily pond and there's a little path through the 'wild' wood beyond: this house is a meeting of market place and wilderness where people grow.

rooms	4: 1 double, 2 triples, 1 suite for 5-6.
price	€47 for two; €62 for three; €92 for four.
meals	Dinner with wine €21, April-September, book ahead.
closed	November-Easter.
directions	From Le Mans N157 for Orléans 52km; left D921 to Mondoubleau; Carrefour de l'Ormeau is central village junction; house on corner opp. Ford garage.

Alain Gaubert & Isabelle Peyron
Carrefour de l'Ormeau,
41170 Mondoubleau, Loir-et-Cher
tel +33 (0)2 54 80 93 76
fax +33 (0)2 54 80 93 76
e-mail i.peyron1@tiscali.fr
web www.carrefour-de-lormeau.com

Les Bordes

With its sweeping farmyard, its pond and such a spontaneous welcome, it is, as one reader wrote, "a little gem of a B&B". You can see for miles across fields filled with lark song and cereals. The owners are a smiling couple who give you their time without invading your space but are delighted to show you their immaculate farm, orchard and vegetable garden if you're interested. Their rooms have gentle colours, soft materials and firm mattresses. The furniture is simple and rustic, the bedrooms and bathrooms are deeply raftered, the old farmhouse breathes through its timbers. It is peaceful, pretty and a place for picnics.

rooms	3: 1 double; 2 doubles sharing bath & wc.
price	€38-€41 for two.
meals	Dinner with wine €15, book ahead. Restaurant 6km.
closed	Rarely.
directions	From Vendôme D957 for Blois 6km. Right to Crucheray & Chambres d'Hôtes. 4km from turning; signposted.

Élisabeth & Guy Tondereau
Les Bordes,
41100 Crucheray,
Loir-et-Cher
tel +33 (0)2 54 77 05 43
fax +33 (0)2 54 77 05 43

La Mulotière

A big wall guards house and courtyard from the village street; at the back, a garden, then fields. Gentle Fabienne is a charming hostess who wants you to get the most out of your stay. A lot of the decorative detail is hers and the bedrooms are named after the flowers she loves and tends. Bright, light and full of birdsong, they have spotless parquet and hand-painted furniture picking up the pinks, whites and creams. Light floods in through the big dining room windows and there's always homemade jam and cake for breakfast. Fabienne may go with you on local walks or bike rides to make sure you don't miss a thing.

rooms	3: 2 doubles, 1 twin/double.
price	€40-€42 for two.
meals	Good restaurant in Pont de Braye, 2km.
closed	November-March.
directions	From Vendôme, D917 for Montoire & Trôo. Sougé 4km after Trôo. On left at entrance of village.

Fabienne & Alain Partenay
La Mulotière,
41800 Sougé sur Braye,
Loir-et-Cher

tel	MOB+33 (0)6 80 33 72 55
fax	+33 (0)2 54 72 46 97
e-mail	fabienne.lamulotiere@wanadoo.fr
web	www.gite-lamulotiere.com

9 rue Dutems

An old townhouse with a country feel, a lovely walled garden, a majestic chestnut and miniature trees at the bottom to screen the outbuildings. Guests sit at separate tables in a room full of brocante and wonderful pictures collected, and framed, by Joëlle; Claude, a farmer, serves and animates the whole affair. Up the characterful sloping-treaded stairs to light, simple bedrooms and bathrooms decorated in ephemeral greys, whites, creams and yellows – understated and beautiful. There are beams, polished parquet and tiles, billiards in the sitting room and a kitchenette for guests. A fun place to stay.

rooms	5: 1 twin/double, 3 triples, 1 suite.
price	€48-€68 for two.
meals	Choice of restaurants in Mer.
closed	January.
directions	N152 to Mer; park by church. House short walk up main street; entrance in picture-framing shop on left. (Car access details on arrival.)

Joëlle & Claude Mormiche
9 rue Dutems,
41500 Mer,
Loir-et-Cher

tel	+33 (0)2 54 81 17 36
fax	+33 (0)2 54 81 70 19
e-mail	mormiche@wanadoo.fr
web	www.chambres-gites-chambord.com

Le Moulin de Choiseaux

Beyond the security gates, a blissful, informal garden – lakes and bridges, nooks and ducks, even a Gingko biloba, the hardiest tree on earth – rambles round the old millhouse (a mill stood here in 1455). Inside, a warmly sensitive atmosphere radiates from beautiful old floor tiles, timbered ceilings, lovely family furniture. Your hosts are gently caring about your well-being. Madame uses her innate feeling for history to advise on visits; Monsieur restored the old mill wheel; there are myriad teas for breakfast – and bedrooms, all different, are big, harmonious in fabric and colour and lit by the garden sky.

rooms	5: 2 doubles, 2 triples, 1 suite.
price	€54-€76 for two.
meals	Excellent choice of restaurants within 7km.
closed	Rarely.
directions	From A10 exit 16 N152 for Blois. 3.5km after Mer, right for Diziers - follow Chambres d'Hôtes signs.

Marie-Françoise & André Seguin
Le Moulin de Choiseaux,
41500 Suèvres,
Loir-et-Cher

tel +33 (0)2 54 87 85 01
fax +33 (0)2 54 87 86 44
e-mail choiseaux@wanadoo.fr
web www.choiseaux.com

L'Échappée Belle

A house of style, originality and lovely surprises, with fascinating people. Madame, an art historian, talks exuberantly and creates beauty with her hands – patchwork, sculpture... Monsieur has a great sense of fun too, yet the house hums with serenity. Rooms are period-themed with family pieces: the 1930s has an old typewriter, a valve radio and an authentic, garish green bathroom; the 1900s has a splendid carved bed. The garden is a mixture of French geometric and English informal, the house set back enough for the road not to be a problem and the Loire a short step from the garden gate.

rooms	4: 1 double, 1 twin, 1 triple, 1 single.
price	€65 for two.
meals	2 restaurants in village.
closed	November-March, except by arrangement.
directions	From A10 exit 16 for Chambord; cross Loire river at Mer; after bridge right D951; house on right at end of village.

Francis & Béatrice Bonnefoy
L'Échappée Belle,
41500 St Dyé sur Loire,
Loir-et-Cher

tel +33 (0)2 54 81 60 01
e-mail fbonnefoy@libertysurf.fr
web perso.libertysurf.fr/fbonnefoy

La Villa Médicis

Why the Italian name, the Italianate look? Queen Marie de Médicis used to take the waters here in the 17th century: the fine garden still has a hot spring and the Loire flows regally past behind the huge old trees. Muriel, a flower-loving perfectionist of immaculate taste, has let loose her decorative flair on the interior. It is unmistakably yet adventurously French in its splash of colours, lush fabrics and fine details – fresh flowers too. Carved wardrobes and brass beds grace some rooms. The suite is a great 1930s surprise with a super-smart bathroom. You will be thoroughly coddled in this elegant and stylish house.

rooms	6: 2 doubles, 2 twins, 1 triple, 1 suite.
price	€68 for two.
meals	Dinner with wine €32, book ahead.
closed	In winter, except by arrangement.
directions	Macé 3km north of Blois along N152 for Orléans. In village follow signs; 500m on right before church.

Muriel Cabin-Saint-Marcel
La Villa Médicis,
41000 St Denis sur Loire,
Loir-et-Cher
tel +33 (0)2 54 74 46 38
fax +33 (0)2 54 78 20 27

Le Chêne Vert

A house of endless happy discoveries, an architectural dream marrying 16th-century roots with an ultra-modern, marble-floored open-plan spave and a glass walkway 5 metres overhead. Easy-going Marie-France and her husband live in an oasis of sophisticated rusticity with a few sheep and hens and egg hunts for children. They love the garden, too. The house has a soft, attractive feel and a gorgeous woodsy valley view. A cylindrical shower amazes in the centre of one room, a billiard table awaits above another, the suite has a full kitchen; a sense of texture and fabric inhabits them all. And your hosts are a great couple.

rooms	3: 2 doubles, 1 family suite for up to 8.
price	€64-€90 for two. Suite €224 for 8. Minimum stay 2 nights for suite.
meals	Good restaurants 3-7km.
closed	Rarely, but please book ahead.
directions	From Blois D751 to Candé, left after bridge for Valaire; pass memorial to Pontlevoy; right at fork; left for Le Chêne Vert; house on left after small bridge.

Marie-France Tohier
Le Chêne Vert,
41120 Monthou sur Bièvre,
Loir-et-Cher
tel +33 (0)2 54 44 07 28
fax +33 (0)2 54 44 17 94
e-mail tohier@sci-le-chene-vert.com
web www.sci-le-chene-vert.com

La Rabouillère

Monsieur built the Solonge farmhouse himself. This, and his first project, the delicious little cottage next door, bring together traditional style and modern comfort. Madame, who is charming, furnished the interiors delightfully, and the first-floor suite of the main house is particularly splendid and spacious, with fine views over woodland and park. All the rooms are immaculate and serene, some on ground-floor level. Old family pieces decorate the cottage, with its two bedrooms, kitchenette and rustic feel. Breakfasts are served at tables laid with English china, and include eggs from the farm and homemade jam.

rooms	6: 4 doubles, 1 suite, 1 cottage for 2-5.
price	€59-€90 for two. Cottage €107-€135.
meals	Good restaurants 3-10km.
closed	Rarely.
directions	Leave A10 at Blois for Vierzon, D765; D102 for Contres; after 6km sign for La Rabouillère on left.

Martine & Jean-Marie Thimonnier
La Rabouillère,
41700 Contres, Loir-et-Cher
tel +33 (0)2 54 79 05 14
fax +33 (0)2 54 79 59 39
e-mail rabouillere@wanadoo.fr
web www.larabouillere.com

Le Saint Michel

The original owner had royal connections and built a tower in one corner of his five-acre estate, an orchard (fruits for breakfast), a pool – now dry – with urns and statues. The impressive wooden dining room fireplace crawls with royal symbols and the odd carved joke. Rooms, two large, two smaller and named after royal women, are vibrant with colour and highly original bedheads for brand new mattresses. Having managed hotels for years, Marie-Paule knows her stuff and enthuses about her new life. It must be fun to eat with her and Dominique in that impressive room. Beautiful library too.

rooms	4 doubles.
price	€75-€90 for two.
meals	Dinner with wine €32-€50, book ahead.
closed	Rarely.
directions	From Paris A10 south; exit 17 to Blois; for Châteauroux to Cellettes; in Cellettes D77 right to Seur & Les Montils; in Les Montils right at stop sign. House on left opp. Crédit Agricole bank.

Marie-Paule Rondepierre & Dominique Couvreur
Le Saint Michel,
41120 Les Montils, Loir-et-Cher
tel +33 (0)2 54 44 12 84
fax +33 (0)2 54 44 12 84
e-mail lesaint.michel@laposte.net
web www.lestmichel.com

Les Chambres Vertes

Sophie left theatre management in Paris to devote her energy to B&B, simple living and *cuisine bio*. Breakfast breads are from the organic bakery and her dinners are wonderfully imaginative. The house is bathed in light, separated from the village street by a rose-climbed courtyard, with a pretty garden at the back. Bedrooms come simply furnished with the odd antique and an artistic touch – upstairs yellows and oranges, downstairs sands and cream. Paintings adorn the walls, including sketches of Sophie's mother, a dancer. Cultivated Sophie loves her English-speaking guests. *Spanish & German also spoken.*

rooms	5: 3 doubles, 1 twin, all with shower & separate wc; 1 twin.
price	€45-€55 for two.
meals	Dinner with wine €20, book ahead. Wednesdays & Saturdays at local restaurant.
closed	Occasionally.
directions	From Blois D764 to Montrichard for 18km. In Sambin, house up lane between church & grocer's.

Sophie Gélinier
Les Chambres Vertes,
41120 Sambin,
Loir-et-Cher

tel	+33 (0)2 54 20 24 95
fax	+33 (0)2 54 20 24 95
e-mail	sophie.gelinier@libertysurf.fr
web	www.chambresvertes.net/en

Prieuré de la Chaise

It's a delight for the eyes: stunning ancient buildings outside, Madame's decorating flair inside. The 13th-century chapel, still used on the village feast day, and the newer manor house (1500s), drip with history, 16th-century antiques, tapestries and loveliness – huge sitting and dining rooms, smallish cosy bedrooms. One has a large stone fireplace, painted beams and successful Laura Ashley fabrics. The setting is superb, fine mature trees shade the secluded garden and you can put your horse in the paddock. You can't fail to like your hosts and their estate wine and they can arrange tastings for you.

rooms	3: 2 doubles, 1 suite for 4.
price	€60-€70 for two. Suite €140 for four.
meals	Wide range of restaurants locally.
closed	Rarely.
directions	St Georges is between Chenonceau & Montrichard on N76. In town centre, up hill to 'La Chaise' (signs); on up Rue du Prieuré. No. 8 has heavy wooden gates.

Danièle Duret-Therizols
Prieuré de la Chaise,
41400 St Georges sur Cher,
Loir-et-Cher

tel	+33 (0)2 54 32 59 77
fax	+33 (0)2 54 32 69 49
e-mail	prieuredelachaise@yahoo.fr
web	www.prieuredelachaise.com

Le Moutier

The artist's touch and Jean-Lou's paintings vibrate throughout this house of tradition and originality where you are instantly one of the family: Hector the gentle giant hound, Persian Puss, a bright and friendly little girl, her congenial artist father and her linguist mother. Rooms – two in the main house, two in the studio – are subtle-hued with good family furniture and bold bathrooms. An Aubusson tapestry cartoon too, and understated elegance in the sitting and dining rooms. A joy of a garden, interesting, fun-loving hosts and a welcoming table in the evening.
Painting and French courses.

rooms	4 doubles.
price	€55 for two.
meals	Dinner with wine €25, book ahead.
closed	Rarely.
directions	From Blois D956 to Contres; D675 to St Aignan; over bridge; D17 right to Mareuil sur Cher. House on left in hamlet La Maison des Marchands (just before cat breeder sign) before main village.

Martine & Jean-Lou Coursaget
Le Moutier,
41110 Mareuil sur Cher,
Loir-et-Cher

tel +33 (0)2 54 75 20 48
fax +33 (0)2 54 75 20 48
e-mail lemoutier.coursaget@wanadoo.fr
web perso.club-internet.fr/vilain/lemoutier

Map 10 Entry 381

20 rue Pilate

In the lovely Loir valley where the intimate and romantic reign, you have the little house in the garden to yourselves. It has a kitchen and a bathroom downstairs, two bedrooms upstairs and its own piece of flower-filled garden for private breakfasts. Or you can join Madame at the long check-clothed table in her light and cheerful kitchen, baskets hanging from the beams. She is friendly, cultivated and dynamic, involved in tourist activities so an excellent adviser, will cook you refined dinners and is a great maker of jams. It's not luxurious, but elegantly homely, quiet and welcoming.

rooms	2 doubles in cottage, sharing bath; only let to same group.
price	€50 for two; €90 for four.
meals	Dinner with wine €20, book ahead.
closed	November-March.
directions	From Tours & La Membrolle N138 for Le Mans. At Neuillé Pont Pierre D68 to Neuvy le Roi. House on road D2; blue front door, opp. turning to Louestault.

Ghislaine & Gérard de Couesnongle
20 rue Pilate,
37370 Neuvy le Roi,
Indre-et-Loire

tel +33 (0)2 47 24 41 48
e-mail de-couesnongle-neuvy@caramail.com

Map 5 Entry 382

La Louisière

Simplicity, character and a marvellous welcome make La Louisière special. Madame clearly delights in her role as hostess; Monsieur, who once rode the horse-drawn combine, tends his many roses and they are both active in their community – a caring and unpretentious couple. The traditional rooms have subtle, well-chosen colour schemes and sparkling bathrooms; touches of fun, too. Breakfast in the dining room is homemade jams, flaky croissants and crusty bread. Surrounded by chestnut trees, the house backs onto the gardens of the château and is wonderfully quiet. Tennis to play, bikes to borrow.

rooms	3: 1 twin, 1 triple, 1 suite for 5.
price	€42-€45 for two.
meals	Auberge 300m.
closed	Rarely.
directions	From Tours D29 to Beaumont la Ronce. Signs to house in village.

Michel & Andrée Campion
La Louisière,
37360 Beaumont la Ronce,
Indre-et-Loire
tel +33 (0)2 47 24 42 24
fax +33 (0)2 47 24 42 24

Le Clos du Golf

All this in one place? There are 14 hectares of heron and duck, wild boar and deer – and three tame mallards; *and* a nine-hole golf course. Mark, a gallicised Englishman, and Katia, an anglicised French woman, great travellers come to rest, are so enthusiastic about their new life here. The old farmhouse is done, naturally, with a mix of English and French: pleasing antiques, crisp bright bedrooms beneath old beams, dinners of fresh seasonal things such as gentle local asparagus. Swimming, tennis and the splendours of the Loire lie just down the road.

rooms	4: 3 doubles, 1 single.
price	€45-€80 for two.
meals	Dinner with wine €28, book ahead.
closed	December-January.
directions	From A10 exit 18 on D31 for Amboise to Autrèche; left D55 to Dame Marie les Bois; right D74; 1st house on left after woods.

Mark & Katia Foster
Le Clos du Golf,
37530 Cangey-Amboise,
Indre-et-Loire
tel +33 (0)2 47 56 07 07
fax +33 (0)2 47 56 82 12
e-mail closdugolf@wanadoo.fr

Les Hauts Noyers

This garden is intriguing: in Paris, Madame decorated interiors but here she and her husband win prizes for a triumph of living outdoor design. Still full of energy and enthusiasm, they enjoy explaining how they pollarded trees for sculpture, collected their antique watering cans, created the vegetable garden. Each guest room has its own secluded patch of garden. In the fresh blue and white bedroom hang framed pieces of antique lace; in the large suite, white beams bring harmony to the grey and yellow décor, Madame's painted eggs intrigue and her lamps made with brocante pieces are most original.

rooms	2: 1 double, 1 suite for 4.
price	€58 for two. Minimum stay 2 nights.
meals	Restaurants nearby.
closed	Rarely.
directions	From Amboise D751 until Mosnes; right opposite church for Vallière les Grandes; on for 1.5km; straight over small crossroads to 'Hauts Noyers'. Last house on left.

Simone Saltron
Les Hauts Noyers,
37530 Mosnes,
Indre-et-Loire

tel +33 (0)2 47 57 19 73
fax +33 (0)2 4757 60 46

Château de Nazelles

Even the pool is special: a 'Roman' bath hewn out of the hillside with a fountain and two columns, set on one of several garden levels that rise to the crowning glory of vines where grapes are grown by natural methods. The young owners brim with enthusiasm for their elegant, history-laden château, built in 1518 to gaze across the Loire at Amboise. Every detail has been treated with taste and discretion. Rooms, two in the main house, one smaller in the adorable old *pavillon*, are light and fresh with lovely wooden floors – and there's a big living room with books, internet and games.

rooms	4: 3 doubles, 1 troglodyte suite for 4.
price	€90-€110 for two.
meals	Choice of restaurants in Amboise.
closed	Christmas Day & New Year's Day.
directions	From A10 exit 18 for Amboise 12km; right D1 to Pocé & Cisse & Nazelles Négron; in village centre, narrow Rue Tue la Soif between Mairie & La Poste.

Véronique & Olivier Fructus
Château de Nazelles,
37530 Nazelles,
Indre-et-Loire

tel +33 (0)2 47 30 53 79
fax +33 (0)2 47 30 53 79
e-mail info@chateau-nazelles.com
web www.chateau-nazelles.com

Manoir de la Maison Blanche

Your 17th-century manor sits in blissful seclusion yet you can walk into the centre of old Amboise. Annick has bags of energy and enthusiasm and gives you two comfortable, fine-sized bedrooms in a converted outbuilding. The downstairs room is tiled and beamed with a small patio overlooking the garden; the upstairs one, under the eaves, is charming, beamy and reached via an outdoor spiral stair. The carefully-landscaped young garden is full of promise and bursting with roses and irises. Look out for the 16th-century pigeon loft – a historical rarity.

rooms	2 doubles.
price	€80 for two.
meals	Choice of restaurants in Amboise.
closed	Rarely.
directions	From Place du Château in Amboise for Clos Lucé; round park; straight on at 1st stop sign, right at 2nd stop sign, 1st left. Signs.

Annick Delécheneau
Manoir de la Maison Blanche,
37400 Amboise,
Indre-et-Loire

tel	+33 (0)2 47 23 16 14
e-mail	annick.delecheneau@wanadoo.fr
web	www.lamaisonblanche-fr.com

Map 10 Entry 387

7 Chemin de Bois Soleil

High on a cliff above the Loire, it looks over the village across the vines and the valley to a château. It may be modern imitating old, but we chose it for Madame's superb, generous, five-star hospitality. The house is immaculate and meticulously kept; one room is repro Louis XIV, plus orangey carpet and flowery paper. There is a big living area with tiled floor and rugs, an insert fireplace and views over the large sloping garden; the oldest bit, a troglodyte dwelling, lies beneath the lawn! Giant breakfasts, wonderful welcome, great value for the Loire.

rooms	3: 2 doubles, 1 suite for 4.
price	€52 for two. Suite €83 for four.
meals	Several restaurants in village, 1km.
closed	Rarely.
directions	From Tours A10 for Paris; cross Loire; exit 20 to Vouvray. In Rochecorbon left at lights & right up steep narrow lane; signposted.

Mme Jacqueline Gay
7 Chemin de Bois Soleil,
37210 Rochecorbon,
Indre-et-Loire

tel	+33 (0)2 47 52 88 08
e-mail	jacqueline.gay2@wanadoo.fr
web	perso.wanadoo.fr/hautes-gatinieres

Map 10 Entry 388

Les Mazeraies

Intriguing, this thoroughly contemporary mansion on the old château foundations: in the Garden of France, the wisteria will soon grow to soften its new face as the (sculpted) sheep graze the lawn and the superb trees – giant cedars, age-old sequoias – stalk the splendid grounds. Humour, intelligence and love of fine things inhabit this welcoming family and their guest wing is unostentatiously luxurious in rich fabrics, oriental and modern furniture, good pictures and lovely, scented, cedar-lined bathrooms. Ground-floor rooms have a private terrace each, upstairs ones have direct access to the roof garden.

rooms	4: 1 double, 2 twins, 1 suite for 3.
price	€90 for two.
meals	Good choice of restaurants locally.
closed	Rarely.
directions	From Tours D7 for Savonnières; 3km before village left after Les Cèdres restaurant; 800m on left.

Marie-Laurence Jallet
Les Mazeraies,
37510 Savonnières,
Indre-et-Loire

tel +33 (0)2 47 67 85 35
e-mail lesmazeraies@wanadoo.fr
web www.lesmazeraies.com

Le Chat Courant

Traditional materials – soft Touraine stone, lime render, wood – and old furniture, pale colours and lots of light make the slate-topped house a stylish welcoming haven by the Cher where the birdsong drowns out the trains. Here live Anne, Éric, their four children and various animals. They have lots of local lore for you, and concoct wonders from their miniature-Villandry garden. Anne adores looking for new recipes, new bits of antiquery (your bedhead in the guest room is an adapted Breton *lit clos*) and attends lovingly to every detail. Flowers inside and out – exceptional. *Spanish spoken.*

rooms	1 double with extra beds available.
price	€55 for two; €95 for four.
meals	Dinner with wine €18, book ahead.
closed	Rarely.
directions	From Tours D7 to Savonnières; right across bridge; left for 3.5km; on right.

Anne & Éric Gaudouin
Le Chat Courant,
37510 Villandry,
Indre-et-Loire

tel +33 (0)2 47 50 06 94
e-mail info@le-chat-courant.com
web www.le-chat-courant.com

Château du Vau

Delightful philosopher Bruno and Titian-haired Nancy have turned his family château into a stylish refuge for travellers. The demands of children to be taken to dancing lessons and guests needing sustenance are met with quiet good humour. Generations of sliding young have polished the banisters on the stairs leading to the large, light bedrooms, freshly decorated round splendid brass bedsteads, with seagrass and family memorabilia. Dinners of estate produce, eggs, roast duck and, on summer evenings, gastronomic buffets you can take to a favourite corner of the vast grounds (with new pool).

rooms	5: 4 doubles, 1 triple, 1 family room.
price	€99-€108 for two.
meals	Dinner with wine €25-€39, book ahead.
closed	Occasionally.
directions	From Tours A85 (Saumur); 1st exit for Ballan Miré; signs for château de vau & golf course at motorway exit. Entrance opp. golf course.

Bruno & Nancy Clément
Château du Vau,
37510 Ballan Miré,
Indre-et-Loire

tel	+33 (0)2 47 67 84 04
fax	+33 (0)2 47 67 55 77
e-mail	chateauduvau@chez.com
web	www.chez.com/chateauduvau

Map 10 Entry 391

Château du Grand Bouchet

An elegant château, its big windows fore and aft let in floods of light. Guest rooms are large, well-proportioned, airy; there are no unnecessary frills, just a few good quality pieces of furniture, parquet floors, pretty floral curtains, attractive quilts and good beds. The attentive and very knowledgeable Devants have lived in Touraine for ever, are passionate environmentalists and enjoy this gracious house. A motley collection of 18th and 19th-century armchairs summons you to the fireside in the guest salon, there are billiards and board games next door, and a tree-rich garden that is their pride and joy.

rooms	4: 2 doubles, 2 suites for 2-4.
price	€98 for two.
meals	Dinner with wine €39, book ahead.
closed	January.
directions	From Tours D7 for Savonnières & Villandry; turning to house on left 3km after exit from by-pass west of Tours.

M & Mme Devant
Château du Grand Bouchet,
D7 Routes des Vallées,
37510 Ballan-Miré, Indre-et-Loire

tel	+33 (0)2 47 67 79 08
fax	+33 (0)2 47 67 79 08
e-mail	grandbouchet@wanadoo.fr
web	perso.wanadoo.fr/grandbouchet

Map 10 Entry 392

Le Pavillon de Vallet

When she moved to this little valley, charming, chatty Astrid had no B&B plans at all – "it happened" and she loves it, taking huge care over the rooms (new beds in all) and breakfast (delicious) – she and her pilot husband are escapees from Paris. The *tuffeau* stone is light and bright, the walled garden runs down to the Cher, country quiet fills the patios. Guests have an antique-furnished living room full of lightness and well-being. The lovely ground-floor bread-oven bedroom is sweet in its flowery wallpaper and painted beams; in another, an enormous four-poster looms beneath its canopy of joists.

rooms	3: 1 double, 2 triples.
price	€60-€70 for two.
meals	2 restaurants 4km.
closed	Rarely.
directions	From Tours N76 for Bléré; pass sign for Athée sur Cher, continue to Granlay; immed. left to Vallet; on down lane; left at bottom of hill; last house on right.

Astrid Lange
Le Pavillon de Vallet,
37270 Athée sur Cher,
Indre-et-Loire
tel +33 (0)2 47 50 67 83
fax +33 (0)2 47 50 68 31
e-mail pavillon.vallet@wanadoo.fr
web perso.wanadoo.fr/lepavillondevallet/

Le Belvédère

From plain street to stately courtyard magnolia to extraordinary marble-walled spiral staircase with dome atop – it's a *monument historique*, a miniature Bagatelle Palace, a bachelor's folly with a circular salon. The light, airy, fadingly elegant rooms, small and perfectly proportioned, are soft pink and grey; lean out and pick a grape from the vine-clad pergola. Monsieur was a pilot and still flys vintage aircraft. Madame was an air hostess and English teacher and is casually sophisticated and articulate about her love of fine things, places and buildings. Wonderful, and a stone's throw from Chenonceaux.

rooms	3: 2 double, 1 suite for 4.
price	€86 for two. Suite €140 for four.
meals	Excellent restaurant opposite, book ahead.
closed	Occasionally.
directions	From Amboise D31 to Bléré through Croix en Touraine; over bridge (Rue des Déportés opp. is one-way): left, immed. right, 1st right, right again. OR collection from private airport 5km.

Dominique Guillemot
Le Belvédère,
37150 Bléré,
Indre-et-Loire
tel +33 (0)2 47 30 30 25
fax +33 (0)2 47 30 30 25
e-mail jr.guillemot@wanadoo.fr
web thebelvedere.free.fr

La Lubinerie

Built by Elisabeth's grandfather a hundred years ago, its typical brick and tile face still looking good, this neat townhouse is done in an attractive, spirited mixture of modern and nostalgic: strong colour juxtapositions against family furniture, delicate muslin as a backdrop to a fascinating collection of paintings, prints, old cartoons and teapots. Elisabeth lived for years in England, collected all these things and calls her delicious rooms Earl Grey, Orange Pekoe, Darjeeling. She and Jacques, who is more reserved with a subtle sense of humour, love sharing their stories and knowledge with guests.

rooms	3: 1 double, 1 suite for 4; 1 double with separate shower room.
price	€65-€100 for two.
meals	Dinner with wine €20, book ahead. Restaurants 3km.
closed	Rarely.
directions	A10 exit 23 for Loches & Châteauroux; N143; carry straight on to 2nd r'bout; exit for Esvres sur Indre; in village left at stop sign; house opposite school.

Élisabeth Aubert-Girard
La Lubinerie,
37320 Esvres sur Indre,
Indre-et-Loire
tel +33 (0)2 47 26 40 87
e-mail lalubinerie@wanadoo.fr
web www.lalubinerie.com

Les Moulins de Vontes

Pure magic for all *Wind in the Willows* and other watermill fans. Three old mills side by side on an unspoiled sweep of the Indre, a boat for messing about in, wooden bridges to cross from one secluded bank to another, a ship-stern view of the river from the terrace as you share a civilised dinner with your amusing, well-travelled hosts. The airy, elegant, uncluttered rooms have stunning river views (the sound of rushing water is limited to a gentle murmur at night), in various styles – Empire, oriental – and bathrooms sparkle. You may swim, but watch little ones. Sophisticated, magical, fun.

rooms	3: 2 doubles, both with shower & separate wc; 1 twin.
price	€120 for two.
meals	Dinner with wine €30, book ahead.
closed	October-March.
directions	From Tours N143 for Loches for 12km; 500m after Esso garage, right D17 for 1.3km; left to Vontes; left to Bas-Vontes. At end of road.

Odile & Jean-Jacques Degail
Les Moulins de Vontes,
37320 Esvres sur Indre,
Indre-et-Loire
tel +33 (0)2 47 26 45 72
fax +33 (0)2 47 26 45 35
e-mail info@moulinsdevontes.com
web www.moulinsdevontes.com

Moulin de la Follaine

Follaine is a deeply serene place and feels as old as the hills (actually the Middle Ages: the background farm was used as a hunting lodge by Lafayette). Ornamental geese adorn the lake, the neatly-tended garden has places to sit, colourful bedrooms have antique furniture and lake views, and one opens to the garden. Upstairs, a lovely light sitting room. Amazingly, the old milling machinery in the breakfast area still works – ask and Monsieur will turn it on for you – and there are other relics from the old days. Your hosts, once in the hotel trade, are absolutely charming.

rooms	4: 2 doubles, 2 suites.
price	€60 for two.
meals	Good auberge in village, 500m.
closed	Rarely.
directions	From Tours N143 for Loches; left D58 to Reignac; D17 to Azay sur Indre; left opp. restaurant; at fork, left (over 2 bridges); mill below fortified farm on right.

Mme Danie Lignelet
Moulin de la Follaine,
37310 Azay sur Indre,
Indre-et-Loire

tel +33 (0)2 47 92 57 91
fax +33 (0)2 47 92 57 91
e-mail moulindelafollaine@wanadoo.fr
web www.moulindefollaine.fr.st

La Chapelle

'Tis no lie, this is a Gothic chapel transformed into a traditional family house, an unselfconscious witness of things past, a place to live in serenity. Up a winding stair in the little tower, the pretty guest rooms owe their marble fireplaces to an earlier conversion, their fine well-sat-in furniture to past generations, their good watercolours to friends and relations, their art books to Dominique himself. A well-travelled artist, he came home when he inherited the house; he is cultured, amusing, very good company and an excellent cook. A place to dawdle in and soak up the timeless charm.

rooms	2 doubles sharing bath, only let to same party.
price	€60 for two.
meals	Dinner with wine €20, book ahead.
closed	November-March.
directions	From A10 exit 18; D31 to Bléré; D58 to Cigngné; D83 to Tauxigny. Rue Haute on D82 to St Bauld. House on corner.

Dominique Moreau-Granger
La Chapelle,
37310 Tauxigny,
Indre-et-Loire

tel +33 (0)2 47 92 15 38
fax +33 (0)2 47 92 15 38

Le Moulin de Montrésor

Do you dream of living in a watermill? Your charming young hosts have converted theirs, near the magnificent château of Montrésor, in properly stylish and simple good taste: a wooden staircase leading to the coconut-matted landing, super colours, good linen. It's welcoming, very warm, with lots of original features... and quiet flows the water over the wheel beneath the glass panel in the dining room – wonderful! Madame is cultured and well-travelled, her family has had the château for 200 years but no-one stands on ceremony and there's a sense of timeless peace here, miles from anywhere.

rooms	4: 1 double, 1 twin, 2 triples.
price	€52-€57 for two; under 4s free.
meals	Choice of restaurants within 5km.
closed	Rarely.
directions	From Loches D760 to Montrésor; left for Chemillé; mill on left; signposted.

Sophie & Alain
Willems de Ladersous
Le Moulin de Montrésor,
37460 Montrésor, Indre-et-Loire
tel +33 (0)2 47 92 68 20
fax +33 (0)2 47 92 74 65
e-mail alain.willems@wanadoo.fr

Le Moulin L'Étang

As brilliant as ever, Sue with her unbeatable eye for colour and decorative detail, Andrew with his kitchen conjuring and dry wit, have turned another old mill into an exceptional B&B. You feel instantly at home – even if yours doesn't stretch to golden salamander stencils or angels-wing curtains, draped bedheads or lacquered chairs. The overgrown garden is being tamed, the pool is naturally filtered. Do dine with them: superb food and sparkling conversation vye for pride of place. A remarkable couple, their place basks in character. *Watch children with unfenced water.*

rooms	4: 3 doubles, 1 family room.
price	€65-€75 for two.
meals	Dinner with wine €30, book ahead.
closed	December.
directions	From Loches N143 for Tours; left before Chamboney sur Indre on road signposted L'Étang; 1 mile, left at T-junction; house on right.

Andrew & Sue Page
Le Moulin L'Étang,
37600 Chanceaux près Loches,
Indre-et-Loire
tel +33 (0)2 47 59 15 10
e-mail moulinletang37@aol.com
web www.moulinletang.com

La Métairie des Bois

Monsieur grew up in a château and some fine family pieces have followed him here, including a rare Napoleon III billiard table, one of only two in France. The small 16th-century farmhouse has been beautifully extended to incorporate an old barn for guest rooms, each one with private access to a patio and a bank of pink roses. Your hosts, charming and friendly, are proud of their finely comfortable house with its tranquil garden and pool. The estate stretches as far as the eye can see and has its own lake. Help yourself to boats and fishing rods or visit the cathedral and market of medieval Loches.

rooms	2 doubles.
price	€60 for two.
meals	Dinner with wine €25, book ahead.
closed	Rarely.
directions	From Loches D760 for Ste Maure de Touraine; left D95 for Vou; 1st right at sign 'La Métairie des Bois'.

M & Mme Jean-Claude Baillou
La Métairie des Bois,
37240 Vou,
Indre-et-Loire
tel +33 (0)2 47 92 36 46
fax +33 (0)2 47 92 36 46
e-mail baillou@wanadoo.fr

La Tinellière

A pretty farmhouse in a hamlet, a gentle goose wandering the garden, a glass of homemade *épine*. Éliane is a welcoming and enthusiastic hostess who loves talking to people about their interests and her own, and is constantly looking for ideas to improve her rooms: the ground-floor, mezzanined quadruple (with ladder steps), and the other larger room in the converted stable. Parts of the house are 17th century with massive beams, good mixes of new and old furniture, wild and dried flowers, colours and fabrics. The sitting/dining room is darkish, beamed and cosy, the guests' kitchenette brand new.

rooms	2 quadruples.
price	€41-€44 for two.
meals	Auberge nearby.
closed	Rarely.
directions	From A10 exit Ste Maure de Touraine; N10 for Tours 6km; right to Ste Catherine de Fierbois; D101 for Bossé; - house 3km.

Mme Éliane Pelluard
La Tinellière,
37800 Ste Catherine de Fierbois,
Indre-et-Loire
tel +33 (0)2 47 65 61 80

Les Bournais

Cats, a small dog and Sébastian the pheasant who hobnobs with six ponies – your horse-loving hosts encourage you to ride. Philippe and Florence are a great team: friendly, open, multi-talented. Their old farm, lovingly restored, is set round a pretty courtyard and the bedrooms are in the stables, upstairs and down. Each has brocante finds and striped drapes, sofabeds and armchairs, character, charm and space; spotless floors are black and white tiled, showers are walk-in. Traditional dinners with innovative touches are served round a rustic table and breakfasts are moveable feasts. Special.

rooms	4 doubles, each with extra bed.
price	€55 for two.
meals	Dinner with wine €22, book ahead.
closed	Rarely.
directions	Leave A10 at Ste Maure de Touraine; D760 to L'Ile Bouchard; cross river; D757 for Richelieu. Les Bournais signposted left just before entering Brizay.

Philippe & Florence Martinez
Les Bournais,
37220 Theneuil,
Indre-et-Loire

tel	+33 (0)2 47 95 29 61
e-mail	les.bournais@club-internet.fr
web	www.lesbournais.net

Domaine de Beauséjour

Dug into the hillside with the forest behind and a panorama of vines in front, this wine-grower's manor successfully pretends it was built in the 1800s rather than 20 years ago. Expect venerable oak beams and stone cut by troglodyte masons; the atmosphere is one of comfortable rusticity. In stylish, sophisticated rooms are carved bedheads, big puffy eiderdowns and old prints; bathrooms are spotless and elegant. There's a terraced pool with a view, a grassy hillside garden at the back, a functional guest sitting room, and wine to taste and buy. Exuberant Marie-Claude looks after you beautifully.

rooms	3: 1 suite for 3-4 in main house, 2 doubles in pool-side cottage.
price	€61-€84 for two; €107 for four. Minimum stay 2 nights.
meals	Choice of restaurants 5km.
closed	Rarely.
directions	From Chinon, D21 to Cravant les Côteaux. On towards Panzoult; house on left after 2km.

Marie-Claude Chauveau
Domaine de Beauséjour,
37220 Panzoult, Indre-et-Loire

tel	+33 (0)2 47 58 64 64
fax	+33 (0)2 47 95 27 13
e-mail	info@domainedebeausejour.com
web	www.domainedebeausejour.com

La Maison

When a diplomat's wife with impeccable taste and a flair for design is let loose on an austere 18th-century townhouse, the result is a treat. The family's antique furniture blends with pieces of art, sculpture and rugs from Africa and the Near East; tall windows, storied terracotta floors and an oval oak staircase are the grand backdrop; bedrooms are traditional and sumptuous, overlooking, via window and balcony, a walled formal garden which ends in a semi-wild area of bamboo. All is peace: even the fine chime of the church clock over the wall falls bashfully silent at night. The best house in Richelieu? Yes.

rooms 4: 2 doubles, 2 twins.
price €90 for two.
meals Ask Mme for recommendations.
closed Mid-October-mid-April.
directions From A10, exit Ste Maure de Touraine; left D760 for Noyant; left D58 for Richelieu; in town, cross over la Place des Religieuses, 1st left, signposted.

Mme Michèle Couvrat-Desvergnes
La Maison,
37120 Richelieu, Indre-et-Loire
tel +33 (0)2 47 58 29 40
fax +33 (0)2 47 58 29 40
e-mail lamaisondemichele@yahoo.com
web www.lamaisondemichele.com

Map 10 Entry 405

84 quai Jeanne d'Arc

The ochre and maroon sitting room – deep chairs round gleaming brass coffee table – calls for intelligent, convivial conversation; the dining alcove brings gasps of delight; the bedrooms have huge beautiful personalities, each detail lovingly chosen to honour this 19th-century town house by the stately River Vienne – *Iris*: her name and blue-and-yellow décor inspired by turret windows, *Loriette*: essential pink married to creamy quilt and magnificent old writing desk. Jean sings in the choir, Jany does ceramics, they are an articulate, music-, cat-, art-loving couple and the nicest possible, most caring hosts.

rooms 3: 2 doubles, 1 single.
price €56-€65 for two. Singles €39. Minimum stay 2 nights.
meals Good choice of restaurants within walking distance.
closed 15 October-April.
directions Entering Chinon on D751 from Tours, along river past bridge & Rabelais statue. House just after Post Office.

Jany & Jean Grosset
84 quai Jeanne d'Arc,
37500 Chinon,
Indre-et-Loire
tel +33 (0)2 47 98 42 78
fax +33 (0)2 47 98 42 78

Map 10 Entry 406

Logis de la Chèneraie

It is bucolic: this converted stone farmhouse with its new garden (1,000 shrubs, roses and trees) that runs down the hillside to the wooded valley, the George Sand landscape (the Indres was her patch), the peace. Now these friendly, perfectionist owners have turned their holiday home into stylish, sophisticated B&B. A light and lofty sitting room whose glass doors glide open to a rose-hedged pool, breakfasts an elegant profusion of fruits, brioche, jams, honeys and delicious breads, and softly serene bedrooms – painted beams, flowers, fine antiques – upstairs. New and special.

rooms	1 double, 1 family room.
price	€70 for two; €85 for three.
meals	Good restaurant 7km.
closed	Rarely.
directions	From Chateauroux D943 to La Châtre; D943; D917 to Ste Sévère; 2km along to Sazeray; left to Pouzoult. Signposted.

Michèle & Jacky Mechin
Logis de la Chèneraie,
36160 Sazeray,
Indre
tel 02 54 30 59 23
e-mail michele.mechin@wanadoo.fr
web www.michele.mechin.free.fr

Le Clos de Ligré

This solid wine-grower's house sings in a subtle harmony of traditional charm and contemporary chic under thoroughly modern Martine's touch. Terracotta sponged walls, creamy beams and colourful modern fabrics breathe new life into rooms with old tiled floors and stone fireplaces. Windows are flung open to let in the light and the stresses of city living are forgotten in cheerful, easy conversations with your hostess. There is a baby grand piano in the elegant sitting room for the musical, a pool for the energetic and wine-tastings at the vineyard next door. A great place.

rooms	3 doubles.
price	€90 for two.
meals	Dinner with wine €27, book ahead.
closed	Rarely.
directions	From Chinon D749 for Richelieu; 1km after r'bout D115 right for 'Ligré par le vignoble' 5km; left to Le Rouilly; left at Dozon warehouse; house 800m on left.

Martine Descamps
Le Clos de Ligré,
37500 Ligré,
Indre-et-Loire
tel +33 (0)2 47 93 95 59
fax +33 (0)2 47 93 06 31
e-mail martinedescamps@hotmail.com
web www.lesclosdeligre.com

La Renaudière

This low, gloriously-proportioned 17th-century stable block has all the elegance of a château with none of the pomposity; the same goes for your youthful hosts! They moved recently from Paris with sundry children and pets and have lovingly restored the house to reveal its innate glory of stone and timber-work. Guests are made to feel at home yet well-protected from the hurly-burly of family life. The unusual half-timbered bedrooms are decorated with stylish simplicity and a copious breakfast is served in the sunny dining room with its enormous double-bread-ovened fireplace. A great place.

rooms	4: 2 doubles, 1 twin, 1 family suite.
price	€80-€100 for two.
meals	Choice of restaurants nearby; cold supper €15.
closed	Rarely.
directions	From A85 exit Bourgueil for Chinon; just before Chinon right at r'bout for Loudun; at La Roche Clermault right D24 through Lerné; at end of road on leaving village.

Marie-Claire & André Geoffroy
La Renaudière,
37500 Lerné,
Indre-et-Loire
tel +33 (0)2 47 95 91 77
fax +33 (0)2 47 95 87 67
e-mail larenaudiere@wanadoo.fr
web perso.wanadoo.fr/larenaudiere

Les Coqueries

Down in a valley where time has stood still, Anne's house is camouflaged under its blanket of creeper and roses. The two pretty and freshly redecorated guest rooms (one with a fine old carved wedding bed) are just across the courtyard looking out onto the hillside garden – a magical blend of the work of (wo)man and nature. Gutsy, green-fingered Anne is a great source of wisdom about things to see and do in this bounteous corner of Touraine, and will show the way to walk in the footsteps of Eleanor of Aquitaine up the valley and through the forest to the nearby Abbey of Fontevraud.

rooms	2 doubles.
price	€47 for two.
meals	Wide choice of restaurants within 5km.
closed	Rarely.
directions	From Saumur D947 for Chinon to Montsoreau; D751 through Candes & St Germain sur Vienne. 500m after church, at Goujon Frétillant restaurant, right; follow signs for 1.5km.

Anne Dubarry
Les Coqueries,
37500 St Germain sur Vienne,
Indre-et-Loire
tel +33 (0)2 47 95 96 45

La Balastière

Antoinette indulges two loves, bringing people together and caring for nature, in her old vine-surrounded farmhouse on this environmentally-sensitive spit of land. Loire and Vienne meet nearby and the air tingles with watery prisms, spring flowers fill the meadow behind the house, shady trees and tall hollyhocks provide private corners in the large walled courtyard. There are delicious homemade jams for breakfast in the cool, stone-walled, low-beamed dining room with its huge 15th-century fireplace and there is a well-equipped guests' kitchen. Pleasant, comfortable rooms complete the picture. *Gîte Panda.*

rooms	5: 3 doubles, 1 twin, 1 suite for 3.
price	€42-€56 for two.
meals	Good restaurants nearby.
closed	January.
directions	From Chinon D749 for Bourgueil; Beaumont r'bout 3rd exit for La Roche Honneur; left at sign to Grézille & continue La Balastière.

Antoinette Degrémont
La Balastière,
37420 Beaumont en Veron,
Indre-et-Loire
tel +33 (0)2 47 58 87 93
fax +33 (0)2 47 58 82 41
e-mail balastiere@infonie.fr
web perso.infonie.fr/balastiere

Map 10 Entry 411

Chevire

Guests at Chevire stay in the well-converted stable block of an elegant stone house in a quiet little village, all a-shimmer in the Loire's inimitable limpid light – welcome to the protected wetlands between the rivers Loire and Vienne. Your quarters have ancient beams, stone walls, new floors, space to sit or cook, a little terrace; the uncluttered, sizeable rooms show the same happy mix of old and new with some fine pieces. Your hospitable, gentle hosts, proud of their house and area, will direct you to less obvious places of interest. "Very clean, very friendly, very good breakfasts", say our readers.

rooms	3: 1 double, 2 triples.
price	€38-€46 for two.
meals	Self-catering possible. Auberge 1km.
closed	15 December-15 January.
directions	From Chinon D749 for Bourgueil 6km; left to Savigny en Véron; in village follow 'Camping'; house 1km after campsite on right.

Marie-Françoise & Michel Chauvelin
Cheviré,
37420 Savigny en Véron,
Indre-et-Loire
tel +33 (0)2 47 58 42 49
fax +33 (0)2 47 58 42 49

Map 10 Entry 412

La Chancellerie

The Scarlet Pimpernel would feel at home in this elegant 18th-century house. In front: the formal courtyard with fountain playing; on either side: 15th-century outhouses where guests stay; behind: swimming pool, informal garden, barbecue. Madame has decorated the rooms with easy-going chic and charm, converting their artisan origins into the luxury of warm yellow fabrics, prints and tiles. The suite has corridors, alcoves, stained-glass windows and a tiny oratory – the peace of the convent here. And over your welcome drink, you hostess will regale you with tales of her world travels.

rooms	3: 2 doubles, 1 suite.
price	€85-€90 for two. Minimum stay 2 nights July & Aug.
meals	Auberge in village. Restaurants in Chinon, 8km.
closed	Rarely.
directions	From D751 north of Chinon D16 to Huismes; 1st left on entering village, sign 'L'Étui'; house ahead on small junction.

Anne-Claude Berthelot
La Chancellerie,
37420 Huismes,
Indre-et-Loire
tel +33 (0)2 47 95 46 76
fax +33 (0)2 47 95 54 08
web www.lachancellerie.com

Le Clos Saint André

The old rambling wine-grower's house on the edge of the village buzzes with activity and guests. Monsieur – wine grower, antique dealer, energetic host – and delightful Madame speak good English and organise memorable gourmet and wine-tasting evenings. A hotch-potch of bedrooms have old marble fireplaces, floor tiles, the odd antique: a small, chintzy one; another large, elegant and blue-grey; two under the fine old roof (hot in summer). The sitting room is shabbily comfortable, the courtyard has barbecue and boules. Lovely new pool, orchard, chicken run... Utterly welcoming.

rooms	6: 2 doubles, 3 triples, 1 family room.
price	€53-€60 for two.
meals	Dinner €20, book ahead; wine €7.
closed	November-March.
directions	From Langeais N152 for Saumur 7km; right D35 for Bourgeuil 5km; in Ingrandes right D71 Rue de l'Ouche d'or; 2nd right Rue St André.

Michèle & Michel Pinçon
Le Clos Saint André,
37140 Ingrandes de Touraine,
Indre-et-Loire
tel +33 (0)2 47 96 90 81
fax +33 (0)2 47 96 90 81
e-mail mmpincon@club-internet.fr

3 rue du Moulin de Touvois

The brook gently flows and soothes – so relaxing. Myriam and Jean-Claude are interesting and energetic and have renovated their old miller's house with a blend of styles: original stonework, beams and terracotta floors and some funky modern furniture. The Moroccan tiled table with wrought-iron legs works well with the old stone fireplace in the dining room. Simple, pleasantly-decorated bedrooms have parquet floors, good bedding and stylish modern lighting. The garden is a delight with its wide-planked bridge, fruit trees and dessert grapes and Jean-Claude is happy to arrange visits to local wine-growers.

rooms	5: 1 double, 3 twins/doubles, 1 triple.
price	€50-€57 for two.
meals	Dinner with wine €18, book ahead.
closed	Mid-December-mid-January.
directions	From A85 exit Saumur; D10 & D35 to Bourgueil; at r'bout on Bourgueil ringroad (north), D749 for Gizeux 4km; right immed. before restaurant; 200m on left.

Myriam & Jean-Claude Marchand
3 rue du Moulin de Touvois,
37140 Bourgeuil,
Indre-et-Loire

tel	+33 (0)2 47 97 87 70
fax	+33 (0)2 47 97 87 70
e-mail	moulindetouvois@wanadoo.fr
web	www.moulindetouvois.com

La Butte de l'Épine

A happy marriage of rustic French manor house and immaculate 'English' garden, surrounded by forest. Madame, caring, creative, soignée, is passionate about her flowers, inside and out, and the house has a harmonious feel despite being built so recently... in 17th-century Angevin style with old materials from the château next door. Terracotta tiles, polished oak, big vases of flowers – all is well-ordered peace and harmony in this unusual and refreshingly natural place. Bedrooms are carefully and prettily decorated; the pigeon loft with half-timbered walls and round window is enticing. *Children over 10 welcome.*

rooms	3: 1 double, 2 twins, all with shower (1 behind curtain) & wc.
price	€57 for two.
meals	Restaurants 2-5km.
closed	20 December-5 January.
directions	From Bourgueil; D749 to Gizeux; D15 to Continvoir; left on D64; signposted.

Michel & Claudette Bodet
La Butte de l'Épine,
37340 Continvoir,
Indre-et-Loire

tel	+33 (0)2 47 96 62 25
fax	+33 (0)2 47 96 07 36

photo Michael Busselle

poitou-charentes

L'Aumônerie

If walls could speak... this old hospital priory beside the original moat (now the boulevard bringing newer neighbours) has eight drama-packed centuries to tell. The L'Haridons have put back several original features and alongside picture windows the old stone spiral leads up to the suite (big warm sitting room, low oak door to fresh beamed bedroom with extra bed); the charming cottage-like double feels really old. Madame is well-travelled, loves history, old buildings and gardens and is a most interesting and considerate hostess who also has a passion for patchwork. Loudun has restaurants aplenty.

rooms	2: 1 double/twin, 1 suite for 2-3.
price	€43-€47 for two.
meals	Good restaurants within walking distance.
closed	Rarely.
directions	From Fontevraud, take Loudun Centre; cross traffic lights; at r'bout (Hotel de la Roue d'Or on right) take 1st exit for Thouars. Entrance 200m on right opp. Cultural Centre.

Christiane L'Haridon
L'Aumônerie,
86200 Loudun,
Vienne
tel +33 (0)5 49 22 63 86
fax +33 (0)5 49 22 63 86
e-mail chris.lharidon@wanadoo.fr

Le Bois Goulu

Set proudly at the end of its drive, the finely-proportioned 18th-century manor is a farming family's house. Five generations of Picards have lived here serenely, where Madame, intelligent, feisty and down to earth, will welcome you as family. Overlooking the chestnut-treed garden, the generous bedrooms have handsome wardrobes, good firm mattresses and slightly faded wallpapers. Sunlight streams onto the well-matched beams, white walls and terracotta floor of the huge sitting room, breakfast is in the yellow dining room or on the leafy terrace and there are simple cooking facilities for guests.

rooms	2: 1 double, 1 suite.
price	€43 for two.
meals	Restaurant 600m; self-catering possible.
closed	Rarely.
directions	From Richelieu D58 towards Loudun for 4km; right into drive lined with lime trees.

Marie-Christine Picard
Le Bois Goulu,
86200 Pouant,
Vienne
tel +33 (0)5 49 22 52 05
fax +33 (0)5 49 22 52 05

Le Bourg

After 20-odd years of B&B, your hosts still enjoy their guests enormously so come and experience daily life in a small hilltop village with a fine 12th-century church. He, a jovial retired farmer (their son now runs the farm), who knows his local lore; she smiling quietly and getting on with her cooking in the big homely kitchen – they are the salt of the earth. Up the superb old solid oak staircase to bedrooms clean and bright with good beds and curtained-off showers. A warm and generous welcome is guaranteed plus masses of things to do and see. Old-fashioned, authentic *chambres d'hôtes*.

rooms	3: 2 doubles, 1 family room, all with separate wc.
price	€42 for two.
meals	Dinner with wine €15, book ahead.
closed	Rarely.
directions	From Loudun for Thouars; D60 for Moncontour. From Mouterre Silly church, house 50m for Silly, signposted Chambres d'Hôtes.

Agnès & Henri Brémaud
Le Bourg,
86200 Mouterre Silly,
Vienne
tel +33 (0)5 49 98 09 72
fax +33 (0)5 49 98 09 72

Château de la Motte

Nothing austere about this imposing, lovingly-restored, 15th-century fortified castle. A wide spiral stone staircase leads to the simply but grandly decorated and high-ceilinged rooms where old family furniture, vast stone fireplaces and beds with richly textured canopies, finely stitched by your talented hostess, preserve the medieval flavour, while bathrooms (also generous) are state of the art. There is an elegant dining room and a huge, lofty, light-filled sitting room for enlightened conversation with your cultured and charming hosts.

rooms	4: 1 twin, 1 triple, 2 suites.
price	€65-€110 for two.
meals	Dinner with wine €23, book ahead.
closed	Rarely.
directions	From Paris A10 exit Châtellerault Nord; at r'bout after toll for Usseau 5km; D749 for Richelieu; D75 to Usseau.

Jean-Marie & Marie-Andrée Bardin
Château de la Motte,
86230 Usseau, Vienne
tel +33 (0)5 49 85 88 25
fax +33 (0)5 49 85 88 25
e-mail chateau.delamotte@wanadoo.fr
web www.chateau-de-la-motte.net

La Grenouillère

You will be mollycoddled by these delightful, good-humoured people. One room in a converted woodshed has beams, pretty curtains, blue and yellow tiled floor and view over the large, rambling garden with its meandering frog pond (hence *Grenouillère*), all show remarkable attention to detail. Two rooms are upstairs in a house across the courtyard where Madame's mother, a charming lady, lives and makes a phenomenal collection of jams. Pleasant, comfortable rooms, a most attractive group of buildings, meals on the shaded terrace in summer and messing about in the small rowing boat.

rooms	5: 3 doubles, 2 triples.
price	€42-€48 for two.
meals	Dinner with wine €20, book ahead.
closed	Rarely.
directions	From Tours N10 S for Châtellerault 55km. In Dangé St Romain, right at 3rd traffic lights, cross river, keep left on little square. House 200m along on left; signposted.

Annie & Noël Braguier
La Grenouillère,
86220 Dangé St Romain,
Vienne
tel +33 (0)5 49 86 48 68
fax +33 (0)5 49 86 46 56
e-mail lagrenouillere86@aol.com

19 rue Jacquard

An utterly delightful couple who cannot do enough for you. Monsieur once resuscitated cars – he now takes far more pleasure in reviving tired travellers; Madame cares for every detail. Their house is on the old ramparts and the pretty garden looks directly over the boulevard below where you would expect a moat (quiet enough at night). The neat, blue-carpeted bedroom has surprising big-flower paper on wall and ceiling, and a prettily tiled shower room. Breakfast is on high-backed chairs at the long table in the converted stables beneath the old hay rack. An authentic, unpretentious, very French home.

rooms	1 twin.
price	€39 for two.
meals	Restaurants in village.
closed	Rarely.
directions	From Châtellerault D725 for Parthenay 30km. In Mirebeau, left immed. after Gendarmerie traffic lights; no.19 about 50m on right.

Jacques & Annette Jeannin
19 rue Jacquard,
86110 Mirebeau,
Vienne
tel +33 (0)5 49 50 54 06
fax +33 (0)5 49 50 54 06

La Pocterie

A "passionate gardener" is how Martine describes herself, with a soft spot for old-fashioned roses: they ramble through the wisteria on the walls and gather in beautifully tended beds. The L of the house shelters a very decent pool while furniture is arranged in a welcoming spot for picnics. Martine works but will see you for breakfast or in the evening: she's the one with the big smile.
A peaceful, welcoming retreat with the Futuroscope literally minutes away. You can hire bikes nearby, or play tennis and there's a huge range of day trips to choose from.

rooms	3: 2 doubles, 1 triple.
price	€43-€45 for two; €55-€57 for three.
meals	Several restaurants 3km.
closed	Rarely.
directions	From Châtellerault D749 for Chauvigny & Limoges about 13km (through Vouneuil); follow sign on left 750m; left, house down track.

Michel & Martine Poussard
La Pocterie,
86210 Vouneuil sur Vienne,
Vienne
tel +33 (0)5 49 85 11 96

Château de Labarom

A great couple in their genuine family château of fading grandeur – mainly 17th century, it has a properly aged face. From the dramatic hall up the superbly bannistered staircase, through a carved screen, you reach the salon gallery that runs majestically through the house. Here you may sit, read, dream of benevolent ghosts. Bedrooms burst with personality and wonderful old beds. Madame's hand-painted tiles adorn a shower, her laughter accompanies your breakfast in the splendid family living room; Monsieur tends his trees and is a fund of local wisdom. A warm, authentic place.

rooms	3: 2 twins, 1 suite; extra children's room.
price	€61-€69 for two.
meals	Auberge nearby; good choice 10km.
closed	Rarely.
directions	From A10 Futuroscope exit D62 to Quatre Vents r'bout; D757 to Vendeuvre; left D15 through Chéneché. Labarom 800m on right after leaving Chéneché.

Éric & Henriette Le Gallais
Château de Labarom,
86380 Chéneché,
Vienne
tel +33 (0)5 49 51 24 22
fax +33 (0)5 49 51 47 38
e-mail chateau.de.labarom@wanadoo.fr

Chambres d'Hôtes

This charming young couple, frank, sociable and good company, will spend time with guests after dinner when their young children allow. They have converted a fine big barn into guest quarters – older than the main house, it has been well done, muted colour schemes and ethnic rugs in dark and pleasant rooms, a good dayroom with an open fireplace, a superb cobbled terrace inviting you to sit on balmy evenings and gaze across the wide landscape while the wind plays in the poplars. With a nature reserve on the doorstep – dragonflies a speciality – here is a little-known corner waiting to be discovered.

rooms	2: 1 double, 1 triple.
price	€50 for two.
meals	Dinner with wine €20, book ahead.
closed	Rarely.
directions	From Châtellerault D749 to Vouneuil sur Vienne; left in church square & follow Chambres d'Hôtes signs. Last house on right in hamlet of Chabonne.

Florence & Antoine Penot
Chambres d'Hôtes,
Chabonne,
86210 Vouneuil sur Vienne,
Vienne
tel +33 (0)5 49 85 28 25
fax +33 (0)5 49 85 22 75

La Ferme du Château de Martigny

Madame, vivacious and dynamic, is delighted for you to enjoy her simple, pretty rooms in the converted outbuilding and hugely generous breakfast in the creeper-clad patio or dining room (you can ask for doggy bags). The two rooms sharing kitchen and sitting room are traditional French-furnished. Off the games room, the delightful, two-storey suite has 'rustic' rooms and an intriguing window layout. So close to lovely old Poitiers, even closer to the high-tech Futuroscope, yet only the ping-pong of a little white ball or the splish-splosh of swimmers disturbs the hush of the tiny village.

rooms	3: 1 double, 1 triple, 1 suite for 4-5.
price	€42-€49 for two; €55-€60 for three; €68-€85 for four-five.
meals	Choice of restaurants 3km; self-catering in double & triple.
closed	Rarely.
directions	From A10 exit 28 on D18 for Avanton 2km. Signs in hamlet of Martigny.

Annie & Didier Arrondeau
La Ferme du Château de Martigny,
86170 Avanton, Vienne
tel +33 (0)5 49 51 04 57
fax +33 (0)5 49 51 04 57
e-mail annie.arrondeau@libertysurf.fr
web www.lafermeduchateau.fr

La Demeure de Latillé

A quiet village, a fine 18th-century coaching inn, a charming courtyard, large garden and mature trees: an oasis of green peace. Attractively restored by Monsieur and his vivaciously welcoming English/French wife, the rooms are airy, light, lovely: Spring – very French with its old cherrywood bed; Summer – brass four-poster and pretty wicker; Winter – snow-white canopied bed; Four Seasons – almost English with old-style pine and sweet children's room; and a peach-pink double on the ground floor. Immaculate bathrooms and a sitting room in the old stables. *Babysitting available.*

rooms	5: 1 double, 3 triples, 1 suite for 5.
price	€46-€56 for two.
meals	Good restaurant 7km.
closed	Mid-November-February.
directions	From Poitiers N149 W for Nantes 14km; at Vouillé left D62 to Latillé (24km). House largest in main village square.

Maryanne Broquerault
La Demeure de Latillé,
86190 Latillé, Vienne
tel +33 (0)5 49 51 54 74
fax +33 (0)5 49 51 56 32
e-mail latille@chez.com
web www.chez.com/latille

Château de Masseuil

In the big flagstoned kitchen of the crag-perched château, friends and family chat over the jam-making. Hunting trophies, family portraits, including a mob-capped great-grandmother, adorn the sunny breakfast room; comfortable, fresh bedrooms have old family pieces, a shower each, new beds; charming, unstuffily aristocratic hosts are hugely knowledgeable about local Romanesque art and tell stories of monks and brigands. Medieval castles didn't have en suite loos: there are chamber pots in case you can't face the stairs! Wonderful. *The simple suite can be turned into a gîte.*

rooms	3: 1 twin/double, 1 double, sharing wc; 1 suite.
price	€65 for two.
meals	Restaurants 3km.
closed	Rarely.
directions	From A10 exit Poitiers Nord N149 for Nantes 12km; at bottom of hill left for Masseuil.

Alain & Claude Gail
Château de Masseuil,
86190 Quinçay,
Vienne
tel +33 (0)5 49 60 42 15
fax +33 (0)5 49 60 70 15

Logis du Château du Bois Doucet

Naturally, unstiltedly, aristocratically French, owners and house are full of stories and character: a fine jumble of ten French chairs, bits of ancient furniture, pictures, heirlooms, lamps in the stone-flagged salon, a properly elegant dining room; there are statues indoors and out; large bedrooms bursting with personality; bathrooms too. Monsieur's interests are history and his family, Madame's are art and life – they are a delightful combination of unselfconscious class and flashes of Mediterranean non-conformism. You are very much part of family life in this people- and dog-friendly house.

rooms	3: 2 doubles, 1 twin.
price	€70 for two.
meals	Dinner with wine €30, book ahead.
closed	Rarely.
directions	From A10 exit Poitiers Nord, N10 for Limoges 7km; left to Bignoux; follow signs to Bois Dousset.

Vicomte & Vicomtesse Hilaire de Villoutreys de Brignac
Logis du Château du Bois Doucet,
86800 Lavoux,
Vienne
tel +33 (0)5 49 44 20 26
fax +33 (0)5 49 44 20 26

Siouvre

The humble bee reigns royal here where honeys and bee products are made and sold. It's a great place for families, with a child-friendly garden, and Jacky and Charline such fun. She is excellent at explaining (in French) the ancient complicity between man and insect over breakfast in the guest building. You get a cheerful dayroom, fronted by great banks of lavender, and two rooms in the converted pigsty: a big, cool, darkish double, and, up steep steps, a suite, with low skylights, colourful décor, sitting space and kitchenette. The third room is behind the main house – small, with its own tiny garden. Great fun.

rooms	3: 2 doubles, 1 family suite for 5.
price	€43 for two.
meals	Restaurant in St Savin. BBQ available.
closed	15 October-15 March.
directions	From Chauvigny, N151 for St Savin. 2km before St Savin, left to Siouvre; signposted.

Charline & Jacky Barbarin
Siouvre,
86310 St Savin, Vienne
tel +33 (0)5 49 48 10 19
fax +33 (0)5 49 48 46 89
e-mail charline.barbarin@wanadoo.fr
web www.lafermeapicole.com

Le Haut Peu

This delightful farming family are rooted in village life, including the local drama group. Monsieur also shares his time with mayoral duties and his dream of restoring the 12th-century Villesalem priory. Madame, somewhat shyer, embroidered the exquisite samplers. Both enjoy sharing their simple, stylish, much-loved house with cultured, like-minded guests. The suite is in the old coach house, its kitchen in the bread oven. Finely-decorated bedrooms blend with the garden and woodlands (golden orioles, hoopoes, wild orchids…). Visit the goats, watch the cheese-making or fish in their big lake.

rooms	3: 2 doubles, 1 suite for 4-5 with kitchen/diner. Extra room for children.
price	€52 for two.
meals	Dinner with wine €17, book ahead.
closed	Rarely.
directions	From Poitiers N147 SE to Lussac les Châteaux; D727 E for 21km; left D121 to Journet. There, N for Haims; house 1km on left.

Jacques & Chantal Cochin
Le Haut Peu,
86290 Journet,
Vienne
tel +33 (0)5 49 91 62 02
fax +33 (0)5 49 91 22 01

Château des Bruyères

Kim carries a parrot on her shoulder and a pair of scissors, ready to topiary a wayward plant into shape. With unquenchable energy, a zany sense of humour and deep love of animals, she has also made a mini English garden and a Treasure Island Beach, skeleton and all. Beyond, her husband grows organic cereals and seeds. Inside, this war-torn rebuilt château is unpretentiously elegant with some original faux panelling and stonework, big airy rooms up a staircase fit for Fred and Ginger, good French antiques and bathrooms where Kim's sense of fun explodes in colour and classical quotations.

rooms	2: 1 double, 1 twin.
price	€65 for two.
meals	Restaurants 12-18km.
closed	Rarely.
directions	From Le Blanc D10 to Belâbre; D15 to Les Hérolles; just before village at crossroads right on D10 for Thollet; road for Les Bruyères, 1km on right after crossroads.

Kim Blythen
Château des Bruyères,
86290 Thollet,
Vienne
tel +33 (0)5 49 83 02 82
fax +33 (0)5 49 83 02 82
e-mail kim.blythen@wanadoo.fr

Les Écots

The Salvaudons are educated, intelligent farmers, he energetic and down-to-earth, she gentle and smiling, who are committed to the natural way, like swapping travellers' tales and sharing simple, lasting values while providing decent guest rooms in a relaxed and genuine house. There is indeed "more here than the Futuroscope". The farm is fully organic: don't miss Madame's Limousin specialities – lamb, chicken cooked in honey, vegetable pies – round the family table. The sheep pastures lie in rolling, stream-run country beloved of fisherfolk and Monsieur will take children to meet the animals.

rooms	2 doubles, both with shower & basin, sharing wc.
price	€34 for two.
meals	Dinner with wine €14, book ahead.
closed	Rarely.
directions	From Poitiers D741 to Civray; D148 east & D34 to Availles; D100 for Mauprévoir, 3km; signposted.

Pierre & Line Salvaudon
Les Écots,
86460 Availles Limousine,
Vienne

tel	+33 (0)5 49 48 59 17
fax	+33 (0)5 49 48 59 17
e-mail	pierre.salvaudon@wanadoo.fr

Map 10 Entry 433

Le Bourg

Jean-Louis, a genial twinkly man, used to farm but now sticks to vegetables, chickens and a role in numerous local events; Geneviève is a perfectionist. Their traditional Poitevin farmhouse, rendered a sunny ochre, has a modern conservatory running the width of the house and rooms opening off either side. You come to it from the back, up a long tree-lined drive, so will be surprised to find it is in the middle of the village. Rooms are fresh and immaculate, with great colours, furniture is suitably old: the canopy over the double bed was made for Madame's great-grandmother's wedding. Real and comforting. *Heated pool.*

rooms	2: 1 twin with shower & separate wc; 1 family room.
price	€48-€50 for two.
meals	Dinner with wine €11.50-€15, book ahead.
closed	Rarely.
directions	From A10 exit Poitiers Sud N10 for Angoulême to Vivonne; 2nd exit D4 to Champagne St H. & Sommières du C.; right D1 for Civray 8km; left to Champniers; signposted.

Geneviève & Jean-Louis Fazilleau
Le Bourg,
86400 Champniers,
Vienne

tel	+33 (0)5 49 87 19 04
fax	+33 (0)5 49 87 96 94
e-mail	jeanlouis.fazilleau@free.fr
web	chambres-hotes-poitou-charente.ifrance.com

Map 10 Entry 434

5 rue des Petites Justices

Conversation is easy with your engaging hosts as you linger over homemade rosemary wine and dinner prepared by Michel – a Father Christmas look-alike whose speciality is pigeon (he used to breed them), while Marie-Claude teaches English at a local school. This fine house is in a rambling churchless village (but with a museum of Protestantism: this was the heart of Huguenot country). The second-floor suite is a happy mix of contemporary and traditional ideas; the others in a converted barn are simply but stylishly decorated; each has its own kitchen and sitting room and can be self-catering.

rooms	3: 2 suites for 4, 1 triple.
price	€45 for two; €57 for three; €67 for four.
meals	Dinner with wine €17, book ahead.
closed	Rarely.
directions	From A10 exit Niort Centre or A83 Niort Est for La Mothe St Héray 8km; right for Prailles. Sign on left entering village; continue & then left to house.

Michel & Marie-Claude Duvallon
5 rue des Petites Justices,
79370 Prailles, Deux Sèvres
tel +33 (0)5 49 32 84 43
e-mail m_c_d@club-internet.fr

Château de Tennessus

It's all real: moat, drawbridge, dreams. Two stone spirals to "the biggest bedroom in France": granite windowsills, giant hearth, canopied bed, shower snug in the old *garde-robe*; high in the keep, the medieval family room: vast timbers, arrow slits and real windows. Furniture is sober and fires are always laid, as in olden times, and you breakfast under the guardroom vault, feet on 14th-century flagstones. Indeed, the whole place is brilliantly authentic, the magnificent gardens glow from loving care and Pippa is eager and attentive – flowers, bubbly, fishing in the moat – all on the house! *Children over six welcome.*

rooms	2: 1 double, 1 family room.
price	€115-€140 for two.
meals	Restaurant 4km; choice 9km.
closed	Christmas-New Year.
directions	From A10 exit 29 on N147; N149 W to Parthenay; round Parthenay northbound; on N149 for Bressuire; 7km north of Parthenay right at sign for château.

Nicholas & Philippa Freeland
Château de Tennessus,
79350 Amailloux, Deux Sèvres
tel +33 (0)5 49 95 50 60
fax +33 (0)5 49 95 50 62
e-mail tennessus@csi.com
web www.tennessus.com

68 rue Élise Lucas

Madame is proud of her pretty breakfast table and the old family house down by the riverside where she was born. Monsieur, who is most knowledgeable about the fascinating Marais area, will take you out in his boat (at reasonable rates). Once the trippers have gone, the evening peace descends and the old-world atmosphere of house and garden takes over. Rooms are crammed with a lifetime's collection of objects, solid repro furniture and Madame's own tapestries. They are fun with a dry sense of humour but no English. Families welcome, preferably without toddlers (unfenced water).

rooms	2: 1 double, 1 triple.
price	€43-€48 for two.
meals	Restaurants within walking distance.
closed	Rarely.
directions	From Coulon centre, D23 for Irleau. At end of village, immed. left along bank of River Sèvre which is Rue Élise Lucas.

Ginette & Michel Chollet
68 rue Élise Lucas,
79510 Coulon,
Deux Sèvres
tel +33 (0)5 49 35 91 55/42 59

43 rue du Marais

The old farmhouse, lovingly restored and decorated, is simple, pristine, with biggish, comfortable rooms overlooking a pretty garden where you may picnic (there's a guest kitchen too). They are an interesting couple of anglophiles. Madame knows about nutrition and serves generous breakfasts with homemade jam, cheese, yogurt and cereals, all on local pottery. Monsieur teaches engineering in beautiful La Rochelle: follow his hints and discover the lesser-known treasures there. They love children of any age – there's some baby kit, table tennis and country peace. Good value. *No pets in rooms.*

rooms	2: 1 room for 2-4, 1 suite for 6.
price	€50-€57 for two.
meals	Dinner with wine €20, occasionally available, book ahead. Restaurants within 5 minutes' drive.
closed	Rarely, but please book ahead.
directions	From La Rochelle N11 E for 11km; north on D112 to Longèves; in village, right at 'bar-pizzas', 1st left, past Mairie; 700m on left.

Marie-Christine & Jean-Francis Prou
43 rue du Marais,
17230 Longèves,
Charente-Maritime
tel +33 (0)5 46 37 11 15
fax +33 (0)5 46 37 11 15
e-mail mcprou@wanadoo.fr
web www.alombredufiguier.com

Le Clos de la Garenne

In this lovingly-restored grand old 16th-century house lives a lively young family: three children to entertain young visitors, and sophisticated parents, avid collectors, to decorate with elegance and eclectic flair, cook with exotic inspiration and organics, and talk with passion. Old and modern rub happy shoulders: traditional armoires and new beds, a collection of scales and disabled facilities in the newer-style cottage, antique treasures and a tennis court. The air is full of warm smiles, harmony breathes from walls and woodwork, your hosts are endlessly thoughtful, families are positively welcome.

rooms	2 + 1: 1 triple, 1 suite for 6; 1 cottage for 5.
price	€63-€65 for two. Minimum stay 3 nights July & Aug.
meals	Dinner with wine €24-€25, book ahead.
closed	Rarely.
directions	From Surgères Gendarmerie & fire station, D115 for Marans & Puyravault 5km, following signs.

Brigitte & Patrick François
Le Clos de la Garenne,
17700 Puyravault,
Charente-Maritime

tel +33 (0)5 46 35 47 71
fax +33 (0)5 46 35 47 91
e-mail info@closdelagarenne.com
web www.closdelagarenne.com

Chambres d'Hôtes

Behind its modest, wisteria-covered mask, this 17th-century former wine-grower's house hides such a pretty face and a magnificent garden that flows through orchard and potager into the countryside – freshest fruit and veg for your 5-course dinner. Outstanding bedrooms too: light, airy and immaculate, they are beautifully done with luxurious bathrooms. The room for disabled guests is the best we have ever seen. Your hosts, recently retired from jobs in agriculture and tourism, have given their all to make house and garden as near perfect as possible and you will find them wonderfully attentive.

rooms	3: 2 doubles, 1 suite for 4.
price	€46-€50 for two.
meals	Dinner with wine €20, book ahead.
closed	Rarely.
directions	From A10 exit 34 on D739 to Tonnay Boutonne; left D114 to Archingeay; left for Les Nouillers; house just after turning, with hydrangea at door.

Marie-Thérèse & Jean-Pierre Jacques
Chambres d'Hôtes,
17380 Archingeay,
Charente-Maritime

tel +33 (0)5 46 97 85 70
fax +33 (0)5 46 97 61 89
e-mail jpmt.jacques@wanadoo.fr
web www.itea1.com/17/5114/

Les Grands Vents

In a lovely sleepy village in the heart of *pineau* and cognac country, this farm once produced *pineau*, a Charentes wine distilled with cognac. You have your own entrance here you and can be as private as you like – but Valérie and Nicolas are generous hosts and happy for you to have the run of the house.. Bedrooms, with views onto a young garden, are large, light and catch the morning sun. Décor is French-traditional; mattresses and sheets top-of-the-range. There's space to roam, an outdoor pool and dinners are relaxed, four-course affairs full of laughter and conversation. A real find for families.

rooms	2: 1 double, 1 suite for 4.
price	€50 for two.
meals	Dinner with wine €20, book ahead.
closed	Rarely.
directions	From A10 exit 33 E601 to Mauzé sur le Mignon; D911 to Surgères; D939 12km, right to Chervettes; behind iron gates.

Valérie & Nicolas Godebout
Les Grands Vents,
17380 Chervettes,
Charente-Maritime

tel	+33 (0)5 46 35 92 21
fax	+33 (0)5 46 35 92 21
e-mail	godebout@club-internet.fr
web	www.les-grands-vents.com

Les Moulins

A wonderful old house and dear hosts who grow endives – what more could one ask? Built in 1600, renovated in 1720, the house stands in a garden of mature trees reaching to the River Boutonne (lovely for swimming). In clean, fresh bedrooms are good beds and big armoires; in the huge guest sitting room, antiques, armchairs and a French billiards table. French country food is served in ample proportions, breakfast brioche is scrumptious. You might be staying with your favourite granny, though Monsieur has a wicked sense of humour. Spin off on bike trails, visit fabulous Romanesque churches.

rooms	2: 1 twin/double, 1 suite for 4.
price	€46 for two.
meals	Dinner with wine €17, except July-August, book ahead.
closed	Rarely.
directions	From Gendarmerie in St Jean d'Angély, D127 NE for Dampierre, 8km. In Antezant, 1st right.

Pierre & Marie-Claude Fallelour
Les Moulins,
17400 Antezant,
Charente-Maritime

tel	+33 (0)5 46 59 94 52
fax	+33 (0)5 46 59 94 52

Le Clos du Plantis

Your hostess brazenly indulges her passion for old buildings in this area of vast architectural wealth. She'll teach you stone wall restoration, the intricacies of the Romanesque style or how to garden beautifully – the creamy local stone is a perfect foil for flowers and the veg is organic. In the old cognac press, the cool, light garden bedrooms are big and uncluttered, effective in their pale colours with a few well-chosen pieces each and exquisite bathrooms. Cognac nearby, the island beaches not too far and such a delightful, intelligent couple, full of fun and sparkle, make this a very special place to stay.

rooms	3: 2 doubles, 1 twin, (family suite with double).
price	€52-€55 for two; €85 for four.
meals	Dinner with wine €17, book ahead.
closed	Rarely.
directions	From A10 exit 34 for St Jean d'Angély. East on D939 to Matha (20km); right for Thors; follow signs; left before entering Thors; Le Goulet on right.

Frédérique Thill-Toussaint
Le Clos du Plantis,
Le Goulet,
17160 Sonnac,
Charente-Maritime

tel	+33 (0)5 46 25 07 91
e-mail	auplantis@wanadoo.fr
web	www.auplantis.com

Map 10 Entry 443

Château Mouillepied

A truly delightful pair, Martine and Pierre rescued Mouillepied ('wet feet'; today's stream-fed moat is mostly dry) and are restoring house and grounds. Large airy bedrooms are charming and uncluttered, with original wooden floors or new boards suitably wide; walls are white, curtains cotton. Breakfast – stewed fruit, croissants, all the coffee or tea you'd like – is in the vast orangery overlooking the gardens. Seek out the fascinating old laundry in the grounds, the pigeon house, bread oven and wine store, pick up a fishing licence at the bakery, stroll along the banks of the Charente. Deeply atmospheric.

rooms	8: 4 doubles, 3 triples, 1 suite for 4.
price	€64-€103 for two.
meals	Dinner, with wine €15, book ahead. Restaurant 2km
closed	Rarely
directions	From A10 exit 35 at Saintes. N137 to Rochefort, right to Ecurat D119. Right for Taillebourg D236, D127 to Saint James. Right to Saintes D128, right after 300m. Signposted.

Martine & Pierre Clément
Château Mouillepied,
17350 Port d'Envaux,
Charente-Maritime

tel	+33 (0)5 46 90 49 88
fax	+33 (0)5 46 90 36 91
e-mail	chateau-mouillepied@voila.fr
web	www.chateaumouillepied.com

Map 9 Entry 444

Le Logis de l'Épine

It's an enormous, intriguing old château with dark walls, weapons on the walls, fabulous antiques – and lots of light: it's just one room thick. Your hostess, a beautiful, laughing extrovert, has lived here for decades, knows the history deeply and is addicted to receiving guests. Appropriately old-fashioned bedrooms are furnished with taste and flair (plumbing a bit old-fashioned too) and the open-fired original kitchen, where you step over and under priceless objects, is a gem, ideal for cold-weather breakfast. Artists and musicians love the long thin house and its fine gardens; Madame is unforgettable for all.

rooms	4: 1 double, 1 triple; 2 twins sharing shower & wc.
price	€53-€60 for two. Minimum stay 2 nights.
meals	At neighbouring farm; restaurants 5-12km; picnic possible.
closed	November-March.
directions	From Saintes N137 for La Rochelle 10km; D119 to Plassay; house on right on entering village, signposted.

Alix Charrier
Le Logis de l'Épine,
17250 Plassay,
Charente-Maritime
tel +33 (0)5 46 93 91 66

La Jaquetterie

Arrive at La Jaquetterie and step back in time: the old virtues of having time for people and living at a gentler pace are here in this well-furnished, old-fashioned house, and it is so comfortable. These kindly farmers are really worth getting to know: Madame keeps a good home-produced table; Monsieur organises outings to distilleries and quarries; both enjoy their guests, especially those who help catch escaping rabbits. Great old armoires loom in the bedrooms, lace covers lovely antique sleigh beds, and one of the bathrooms is highly modern-smart. An authentic country experience with genuinely good, kind people.

rooms	2: 1 triple, 1 suite for 2-4.
price	€47 for two; €65 for three; €80 for four.
meals	Dinner with wine €17, book ahead.
closed	Rarely.
directions	From A10 exit Saintes N137 for Rochefort & La Rochelle, 11km; D119 to Plassay. House on left on entering village.

Michelle & Jacques Louradour
La Jaquetterie,
17250 Plassay,
Charente-Maritime
tel +33 (0)5 46 93 91 88
fax +33 (0)5 46 93 48 09
e-mail louradour-denis@aviva-assurances.com

Domaine de la Chasse

The communal table stretching the length of the huge dining hall may look monastic but the food served in this converted stable is not frugal: Thierry's the designer, Catherine shares the cooking, both are lively, artistic and delight in their house and guests. They take good care of house and gîte dwellers alike. The four bedrooms are full of colour, one bright wall each, original North African paintings, small carvings, luminous fabrics and modern furniture – alive, individual, uncluttered. Outside, the soft calm of the Marais throngs with birds. Thierry gives painting and pottery courses – heaven.

rooms	4: 3 doubles, 1 twin.
price	€68. Suite €84. Minimum stay 2 nights.
meals	Dinner with wine €25, book ahead.
closed	Rarely.
directions	A10 from Paris. Exit Rochefort. D123 for Marennes; at lights in Marennes right onto D341 for Brouage; on leaving Le Breuil right at sign for chambre d'hôtes; 2km house on left.

Catherine & Thierry Corbeau
Domaine de la Chasse,
17320 Marennes,
Charente-Maritime
tel +33 (0)5 46 85 52 82
fax +33 (0)5 46 85 52 82
e-mail catherine.corbeau@wanadoo.fr
web www.domaine-de-la-chasse.com

La Rotonde

Stupendously confident, this city mansion seems to ride the whole rich story of lovely old Saintes from its Roman glory days. Soft blue river light hovers into high bourgeois rooms to stroke the warm panelling, marble fireplaces, perfect parquet. The Rougers love renovating their guest house. Marie-Laure, calm and talented, has her own sensitive way with classic French furnishings: appropriately grand, they are feminine yet not frilly, rich yet gentle, just ornate enough. Superb linen and bathrooms, too, little extras and always that elegance. *Two plainer self-catering studios on 2nd floor.*

rooms	5: 2 doubles, 2 twins, 1 suite.
price	€96 for two.
meals	Restaurants in town centre.
closed	Rarely
directions	A10 exit Saintes; straight ahead to Charante river.

Marie-Laure Rouger
La Rotonde,
17100 Saintes,
Charente-Maritime
tel +33 (0)5 46 74 74 44
fax +33 (0)5 46 74 74 45
e-mail larotonde@fr.st
web www.larotonde.fr.st

Les Hauts de Font Moure

The grand house lords it over a tiny hamlet surrounded by walking country and tantalising views. Dinah is English and tends a beautiful garden; Claude's ravishing collection of ornaments and antiques is on display in every room. Inside all is serenity and space; big bedrooms, one of which has a fabulous ormolu wardrobe, are magnificently decorated and scattered with oriental rugs; bathrooms are terrific. Look at the floor tiles in the salon: they were left to dry outside in the woods where they collected imprints of the feet of badgers and birds, before being laid in a church. Delicious pool, too.

rooms	4: 2 doubles, 1 twin, 1 family suite.
price	€66-€73 for two. Family suite €83.
meals	Dinner with wine €25, book ahead.
closed	Occasionally.
directions	From A10 exit 37 for Mirambeau. At r'bout pass 'Marché U'; D254 1st right to St Georges des Agoûts; right at church D146; 1st junc. left & follow Chambres d'Hôtes signs.

Dinah & Claude Teulet
Les Hauts de Font Moure,
17150 St Georges des Agoûts,
Charente-Maritime

tel	+33 (0)5 46 86 04 41
fax	+33 (0)5 46 49 67 18
e-mail	cteulet@aol.com
web	www.fontmoure.com

La Font Bétou

Both former market researchers, Londoner Gordon and Parisienne Laure thoroughly enjoy people. Laure cooks because she loves it and breakfast is a spread. The two big, spotlessly clean rooms in the annexe are pretty and welcoming with tea-making stuff and plenty of stone and wood. Sit by the hosts' sitting-room fire or by the pool; the kitchen door is always open. Once a modest inn for train travellers, the house still overlooks the old station, now another house, and there's a pond with thousands of frogs behind. As the owners say, this is not a place that pretends to be anything, it just is.

rooms	2: 1 split-level double, 1 twin, both with sitting space downstairs.
price	€60 for two. Minimum stay 4 nights July & Aug.
meals	Dinner with wine €25, book ahead.
closed	January.
directions	From Angoulême N10 S for 45km; left D730 for Montguyon. 1km after Orignolles, right to house, signposted.

Laure Tarrou & Gordon Flude
La Font Bétou,
17210 Orignolles,
Charente-Maritime

tel	+33 (0)5 46 04 02 52
fax	+33 (0)5 46 04 02 52
e-mail	tarrou@club-internet.fr
web	www.fontbetou.com

Le Chiron

There's an old-fashioned, well-lived-in, much-loved air to this interesting house. The bedrooms have parquet floors, old-style wallpapers, pretty old beds with new mattresses; bathrooms have been modernised. Madame's regional cooking is highly appreciated and dinner is worth coming back for. A conservatory has been built to seat more people round a bigger table where your hosts stay and chat if not too busy serving you. They'll also show you the fascinating old cognac still and on winter weekends you may be able to help with the distilling process. It's a blissful spot, too. *Camping possible.*

rooms	6: 2 doubles, 1 twin, 2 triples, 1 family suite for 4.
price	€40 for two. Suite €70 for four.
meals	Dinner with wine €15, book ahead.
closed	Rarely.
directions	From A10 Pons exit D700 for Barbezieux Archiac. After Echebrune D148 (1st left) for Lonzac-Celles; right D151 & follow signs.

Micheline & Jacky Chainier
Le Chiron,
16130 Salles d'Angles,
Charente

tel	+33 (0)5 45 83 72 79
fax	+33 (0)5 45 83 64 80
e-mail	mchainier@voila.fr

Map 10 Entry 451

Le Chatelard

This is a gem of a place to stay, both grand and intimate. Béatrice inherited the exquisitely French neo-Gothic château and she lovingly protects it from the worst of modernisation (though the hurricane took its toll in the garden and trees have had to be replanted). Sleep between old linen sheets, sit in handsome old chairs and wallow in a superb bathroom. The sitting room has that unusual quirk, a window over the fireplace, the dining room a panelled ceiling studded with plates. Béatrice, a teacher, and Christopher, a lecturer in philosophy, are interesting, cultured hosts who enjoy eating with their guests.

rooms	4: 2 doubles, 1 twin, 1 family suite, all with bath or shower, sharing 2 wcs on guest room floor & 1 downstairs.
price	€50 for two.
meals	Dinner with wine €15, book ahead.
closed	Rarely.
directions	From A10 exit 36 to Pons, Archiac & Barbezieux; D731 for Chalais 12km. After Passirac, 1st right at roadside cross; up leafy drive.

Mme Béatrice de Castelbajac
Le Chatelard,
16480 Brossac,
Charente

tel	+33 (0)5 45 98 71 03
fax	+33 (0)5 45 98 71 03
e-mail	c.macann@wanadoo.fr
web	www.lechatelard.tk

Map 10 Entry 452

La Grenouille

Do look up as you enter the guest house in the old stables: the hall ceiling is marvellous. Breakfast is served here if it isn't fine enough to sit outside. Rooms are good too: white paint and exposed stone make a stunning setting for fine antiques and old beds fitted with new mattresses. Madame, busy breeding horses (gorgeous foals in summer), is full of smiles and always has time to help arrange cognac-distillery visits or invite you to relax in a hammock after a bit of badminton. Monsieur may offer a local aperitif to guests of an evening. A peaceful wooded spot in a very special corner of France.

rooms	2: 1 double, 1 twin.
price	€48 for two.
meals	Good restaurants at St Adjutory.
closed	Rarely.
directions	From Angoulême, N141 to La Rochefoucauld; right at 3rd traffic light on D162 to St Adjutory; in village 2nd right & follow signs.

Sylviane & Vincent Casper
La Grenouille,
16310 St Adjutory, Charente
tel +33 (0)5 45 62 00 34
fax +33 (0)5 45 63 06 41
e-mail scasper@saint-a.com
web www.saint-a.com

Lesterie

Home to young English farmers, their family antiques, two bilingual children (small visitors positively welcomed) and three friendly dogs, this prosperous-looking country house has many original delights. From the panelled dining hall with its polished wood, soft colours and high doors, a splendid staircase sweeps up to simple rooms. The big one feels romantic with its stained-glass window over claw-footed bath; they are all airy and plainly furnished. Your hosts are busy but still happy to sit round the big table at informal, family meals. Real value and an excellent base for a few days exploring en famille.

rooms	4: 2 doubles, 1 twin; 1 double with shower & sharing wc.
price	€45 for two.
meals	Dinner with wine €18, book ahead. Choice of restaurants in Confolens.
closed	Rarely.
directions	From Confolens, D948 for Limoges for 4km; sign on road.

Stephen & Polly Hoare
Lesterie,
16500 Confolens,
Charente
tel +33 (0)5 45 84 18 33
fax +33 (0)5 45 84 01 45
e-mail polly.hoare@libertysurf.fr
web www.lesterie.com

Le Pit

What an interesting, unexpected place – heaven for walkers. And children, thanks to llamas, wallabies and deer. Pretty, fresh guest rooms are in a converted outbuilding, the larger one overlooking the lake. Dinner is unusual (ostrich pâté perhaps) and delicious, preceded by a chilled glass of homemade *pineau des Charentes*. Alex left hectic London for French farming with a difference (and a thriving farm shop); Hélène loves pergolas, and there are plenty of little corners of rustic charm and colour from which to enjoy the fascinating surroundings. Fun and hugely welcoming.

rooms	2: 1 triple, 1 quadruple.
price	€48 for two; €70 for three; €90 for four.
meals	Dinner with wine €20, book ahead. Auberge 2km.
closed	Rarely.
directions	From Poitiers D741 S for Confolens 50km. 10km after Pressac, left on D168 for St Germain de Confolens; sign after 2km.

Alex & Hélène Everitt
Le Pit,
16500 Confolens,
Charente
tel +33 (0)5 45 84 27 65
fax +33 (0)5 45 85 41 34
e-mail everitt16@aol.com

Meals, booking and cancelling

Dinner

Do remember that table d'hôtes is a fixed-price set menu that has to be booked. Very few owners offer dinner every day. Once you have booked dinner, it is a question of common courtesy to turn up and partake of the meal prepared for you. Dining in can be a wonderful opportunity to experience both food and company in an authentic French family atmosphere. Or it may be more formal and still utterly French. Some owners no longer eat with their guests for family and waistline reasons.

Rooms

We have heard of chambres d'hôtes hopefuls arriving unannounced at 7pm and being devastated to learn that the house was full. For your own sake and your hosts', do ring ahead: if they can't have you, owners can usually suggest other places nearby. But arriving without warning at the end of the day is asking for disappointment.

Cancelling

As soon as you realise you are not going to take up a booking, even late in the day, please telephone immediately. The owners may still be able to let the room for that night and at least won't stay up wondering whether you've had an accident and when they can give up and go to bed.

By the same token, if you find you're going to arrive later than planned, let your hosts know so that they won't worry unnecessarily or… let your room to someone else.

photo Michael Busselle

aquitaine

Cantemerle

From Brazil, New Zealand, the New Hebrides, the Sahara, Michèle came home to the hacienda-style house built when her family's old wine-growing farm crumbled away. The imitation zebra and tiger skins in the living room fit strangely well with all the memorabilia and African sculptures; bedrooms are good traditional, with fine views across oceans of vines. It is relaxed and exotic and Michèle, lively and intelligent, knows all there is to know about this area (ask her about the roses planted at the ends of the vines). Their own wine comes with dinner and the nearby ferry comes from Blaye and Royan.

rooms	3: 1 double, 2 twins.
price	€55-€60 for two. Minimum stay 2 nights.
meals	Dinner with wine €25, book ahead.
closed	Rarely.
directions	From Bordeaux bypass exit 7 on D1 to Castelnau; N215 through St Laurent; 4km, D104 to Vertheuil; abbey on right, over level crossing, house 1km on left.

Michèle Tardat
Cantemerle,
33180 Vertheuil Médoc,
Gironde
tel +33 (0)5 56 41 96 24
fax +33 (0)5 56 41 96 24
e-mail micheletardat@tele2.fr
web www.bbfrance.com

Le Luc

These people take extraordinary trouble to make each guest feel at home, so forget the suburban environment and enjoy delightful Philippe's deep wine knowledge and lively Monika's eagerness to please. She is German, once nursed in Vietnam and loves filling her space with crochet, danglers and soft toys; he's a retired cellar master who will prepare visits for individual guests. They are urbane, well-travelled polyglots who can obtain entry to most big wine châteaux for you. The mature trees and large fish-and-lily pond add a note of serenity. And the beach is just 20 minutes away.

rooms	3: 1 twin/double, 1 double, 1 suite.
price	€42-€65 for two.
meals	Ten restaurants 7km.
closed	Rarely.
directions	From Bordeaux ring road exit 7 N215 & D1 41km; right D104 to Cissac; right at War Memorial Rue du Luc; house 1km on left, after water tower.

Philippe & Monika Achener
Le Luc,
33250 Cissac Médoc,
Gironde
tel +33 (0)5 56 59 52 90
fax +33 (0)5 56 59 51 84
e-mail ph.achener@gmx.net
web www.achener.com

Domaine les Sapins

You couldn't be deeper into wine country than this. Alain is a wine broker and although he doesn't bring his work home, he could probably be persuaded to talk wine of an evening. Natalie's father was born in this house and it is very much a family home, despite its size. Alain and Natalie enjoy having an aperitif and a chat with their guests so they can plan the most congenial seating arrangement at dinner. The house is set back from the village road (ask for one of the quieter rooms) in a large garden with a big and breathtaking pool: jets can be set so it feels like swimming against the current.

rooms	6: 5 twins/doubles, 1 suite for 4.
price	€45-€140 for two.
meals	Dinner with wine €25, book ahead.
closed	Rarely.
directions	From Bordeaux A630 exit 7; D1 for Le Verdon sur Soulac; skirt around Castelnau; N215 for St Laurent 1km to Bouqueyran. Sign on left.

Alain & Natalie Genestine
Domaine les Sapins,
33480 Moulis en Médoc, Gironde
tel +33 (0)5 56 58 18 26
fax +33 (0)5 56 58 28 45
e-mail domaine-les-sapins@wanadoo.fr
web www.domaine-les-sapins.com

Château de la Grave

Here you will find three good and very big bedrooms, a stone entrance hall, a wrought-iron balcony terrace for a glass of the Bassereaus' own dry white Semillon wine, and decorative bantams all over the garden. They are a hard-working young couple in an 18th-century château without quite enough money to make it over-stylish, thank heavens. It is relaxed and easy – even busy – with three young children, and deer in the woods. Breakfast is on the terrace, wine-tasting in the magnificent *salle de dégustation*. The small pool is for evening dippers rather than sun-worshippers.

rooms	3: 1 family room, 2 triples.
price	€60-€76 for two; €106 for four.
meals	Choice of restaurants in Bourg.
closed	February & 1 week in August.
directions	From A10 exit 40a or 40b through St André de Cubzac; D669 through Bourg for Blaye; quickly right D251 for Berson for 1km; sign on right up lane.

M & Mme Bassereau
Château de la Grave,
33710 Bourg sur Gironde, Gironde
tel +33 (0)5 57 68 41 49
fax +33 (0)5 57 68 49 26
e-mail reservation@chateaudelagrave.com
web www.chateaudelagrave.com

83 rue de Patay

Martine may be new to B&B but she's used to making guests feel welcome: she owns a restaurant in the middle of the old town. Le Loup has been serving local specialities since 1932: you will probably want to pay a visit. This old stone townhouse is a welcome retreat after days visiting the city or those renowned vineyards. Martine has given it a light modern touch which works well. Your bedroom is approached up a curved stone staircase and you have the floor to yourselves. It overlooks a small courtyard garden and has a desk and other pieces stencilled by a friend.

rooms	1 twin/double.
price	€60 for two.
meals	Madame's restaurant near Cathedral.
closed	Rarely.
directions	Take Les Boulevards to Barrière de Pessac; 100m, 1st right, right again onto Rue de Patay.

Martine Peiffer
83 rue de Patay,
33000 Bordeaux,
Gironde

tel +33 (0)5 56 99 41 74
e-mail martine.peiffer@wanadoo.fr

Château le Baudou

Old tiles, a fine stone staircase, light colours, long windows, modern bathrooms and the joy of big bedrooms with plenty of space: to stow your luggage, sit in comfort, lounge on big beds (with new mattresses) and dream up your next move. The relaxed, welcoming Heftres have done a huge amount, from shifting stone to hunting antiques to running up curtains, and are proud of the results – the place feels loved but not over-smart. Ask Monsieur if you may play the piano; he does, and also occasionally leads tours of this rich wine-producing area. A fine old manor house, in unspoilt countryside.

rooms	4: 3 doubles, 1 triple.
price	€55-€75 for two.
meals	Choice of restaurants 1.5-4km.
closed	Rarely.
directions	From Coutras D10 towards Guitres; over river Dronne, 1.1km; 2nd house on right.

M & Mme Heftre
Château le Baudou,
33230 Coutras, Gironde

tel +33 (0)5 57 49 16 33
fax +33 (0)5 57 49 16 33
e-mail le.baudou@wanadoo.fr
web www.chateaulebaudou.com

La Closerie St Michel

Perfect for those who want to 'do' Bordeaux, a *maison vigneronne* 10km from St Émilion, presided over by viticulturist Monsieur (do taste the wines) and his wife, the delightful Marie-Christine. Your rooms are in two attractive 17th-century stone cottages and have top-quality furnishings, excellent showers, books, maps, magazines, space. Downstairs, a kitchen with washing and ironing room, salon, woodburner, table for cards and games. The garden is full of shady corners and window boxes are beautifully tended. It's polished, professional, friendly, and very French.

rooms	4: 2 doubles, 1 twin, 1 family.
price	€75-€85 for two.
meals	Self-catering possible. Choice of restaurants 3-12km.
closed	Rarely.
directions	From A10, exit 39a from north, 40b from south; D670 for Libourne; in St Michel de Fronsac, at post office, follow signs for Lariveau, 1.5km; signposted.

Marie-Christine Aguerre
La Closerie St Michel,
33126 St Michel de Fronsac,
Gironde
tel +33 (0)5 57 24 95 81
fax +33 (0)5 57 24 95 30
e-mail closeriesaintmichel@wanadoo.fr
web www.closeriesaintmichel.com

Château Monlot Capet

You appreciate good wine? Believe you can absorb the knowledge by osmosis? Then you will enjoy this coolly restrained, very beautiful manor among the vines. It has been in the family for nine generations, though the owners live in another Grand Cru château leaving nephew and pleasantly relaxed manager to run this one. They come every day and will invite you to taste the goods in the cellars – an easy if busy couple. Rooms, with plain sandstone or painted walls and simple antiques, offer sober quiet and the shrubby garden has an arch of trees that gives dappled shade as you walk towards the distant statue.

rooms	7: 5 doubles, 1 twin, 1 family room.
price	€65-€115 for two.
meals	Restaurants in St Émilion, 2km.
closed	Rarely.
directions	From A10 exit St André de Cubzac through Libourne for Bergerac; 3km after Bigaroux left D234E for St Laurent; right before railway for St Hippolyte; house on left.

Bernard & Béatrice Rivals
Château Monlot Capet,
33330 St Émilion,
Gironde
tel +33 (0)5 57 74 49 47
fax +33 (0)5 57 24 62 33
e-mail mussetrivals@belair-monlot.com
web www.belair-monlot.com

Château Millaud-Montlabert

Tradition has deep, proud roots here. Monsieur is a kind, gentle man, his big farmhouse has stood for three centuries, his vines, now tended by the next generation, are mature, his wine superb; the lovely linen, patchwork and lace are family heirlooms and the family has a strong, lively presence. The country-style, stone-walled, old-furnished bedrooms and their small bathrooms are immaculate, though great beams and attic ceilings may reduce your space. You have your own living room and kitchen (ideal if you're daunted by local restaurant prices). Superb breakfasts are served in the cosy family dining room.

rooms	5: 2 doubles, 2 twins, 1 triple.
price	€52-€55 for two; €70 for three.
meals	Choice of restaurants St Émillion; self-catering possible.
closed	15 January-15 February.
directions	From Libourne D243 for St Émilion; pass Château Girard Bassail on right; 3km before St Émilion left D245 towards Pomerol; house 300m on right.

Claude Brieux
Château Millaud-Montlabert,
33330 St Émilion,
Gironde
tel +33 (0)5 57 24 71 85
fax +33 (0)5 57 24 62 78

3 rue Abbé Bergey

Utterly quiet in its large walled garden where the shutters match the oleander flowers, the elegant townhouse has properly classy furnishings – superb antiques set off by unfussy fabric or grasspaper walls, beautiful rugs on polished floors, lustrous chests, paintings and prints of real quality and an astounding quantity of tapestry work done by Monsieur himself. The smallest (cheapest) room is fine enough, the others are sheer luxury. Your hosts, smart and highly hospitable retired professionals, can guide you round the local vineyards. A high-class house in an amazing, historic town.

rooms	3: 1 twin, 1 suite; 1 double with separate bath.
price	€70-€90 for two.
meals	Restaurants nearby.
closed	Christmas & New Year.
directions	From Libourne D243 to St Émilion; r'bout right to Hôtel de Ville. Park in square: Rue Abbé Bergey leads off this.

François & Élisabeth Musset
3 rue Abbé Bergey,
33330 St Émilion,
Gironde
tel +33 (0)5 57 24 70 12
fax +33 (0)5 57 24 70 12
e-mail francois.musset@wanadoo.fr
web sitestemilionhotes.monsitewanadoo.fr

Le Refuge du Peintre

Monsieur has lived all round the world and there are quantities of fascinating souvenirs to tell the tale but this immaculate and comfortable 1750s farmhouse was his family holiday home for years; Madame, pleasant and houseproud, is an artist who used to be a nursery school teacher; their combined conversation is stimulating. She does much to please her guests and we were naturally offered tea and cake on the terrace. Beautiful bedrooms, simple yet not stark, have white or clean stone walls, the suite has a bathroom big enough to hold a decent party in and the whole place is full of peace.

rooms	2: 1 twin/double, 1 suite for 2-4.
price	€55 for two; €89 for three; €95 for four. Minimum stay 2 nights.
meals	Auberge 300m.
closed	Rarely.
directions	From Bordeaux D936 E for 36km; 4km after Branne right D670 for Agen 1km; at Lavagnac left after 'Boucherie-Charcuterie'; 2nd house on left.

France Prat
Le Refuge du Peintre,
Lavagnac,
33350 Ste Terre, Gironde

tel	+33 (0)5 57 47 13 74
e-mail	france.prat@wanadoo.fr
web	perso.wanadoo.fr/france.prat

Domaine de Barrouil

As befits its calling, this old winegrower's house stands in a sea of vines whose liquid fruits you will taste and over which may wander re-enactment battlecries or summer fireworks. Inside this colourful and immaculate house, green, cream and red set off gilt-framed mirrors and bright modern bathrooms. Your hosts believe in big thick towels too. They have lived in French Guiana so Madame's classic French dinners, served in the beautifully tiled dining room, may bring echoes of more exotic lands. She is charming and chatty, a former English teacher; he is shyer but most interesting.

rooms	4: 2 doubles, 1 twin, 1 family suite for 4.
price	€50-€80 for two.
meals	Dinner with wine €23, book ahead, or wine list from €6-€9.
closed	Rarely.
directions	A10 exit St André de Cubzac to Libourne Bergerac. At Castillon, D17 south; left at x-roads with D126; 1st house on left.

Annie & Michel Ehrsam
Domaine de Barrouil,
33350 Castillon La Bataille,
Gironde

tel	+33 (0)5 57 40 59 12
fax	+33 (0)5 57 40 59 12
e-mail	m.ehrsam@sudouest.com

Château de Carbonneau

Big château bedrooms done in safe pastels over classic dados, a fine old bed in the beige room, huge bathrooms done with rich tiles – here is a quiet, self-assured family house where quality is natural, history stalks and there's plenty of space for four young Ferrières and a dozen guests. Visit Wilfred's winery and taste the talent handed down by his forebears. Jacquie, a relaxed dynamic New Zealander, does all the interior stuff, wields a canny paintbrush and has created a guest sitting room of comfortable furniture, old family pieces and modern lampshades. And they breed gorgeous Bearnaise dogs.

rooms	5: 2 twins/doubles, 1 double, 1 twin, 1 suite.
price	€65-€85 for two.
meals	Dinner €15, book ahead; wine €4.60-€6.50.
closed	November-March.
directions	D936 to Castillion la Bataille-Bergerac; from Réaux, right to Gensac, Pessac; at r'bout, D18 to Ste Foy le Gde; 2km on right.

Wilfred & Jacquie Franc de Ferrière
Château de Carbonneau,
33890 Pessac sur Dordogne ,
Gironde

tel	+33 (0)5 57 47 46 46
fax	+33 (0)5 57 47 42 26
e-mail	carbonneau@wanadoo.fr
web	www.chateau-carbonneau.com

Map 10 Entry 468

Le Prieuré

Arrive, soak up the serenity, and time will cease to matter – pilgrims have rested at this hospitable priory for 800 years. Breakfast in a courtyard on homemade jam, lie in a hammock under the walnut tree... let the fantails coo you into a blissful siesta, the nightingales serenade your dawn. Susie, a psychotherapist who also practices aromatherapy, simply loves her old stone house and rambling gardens and provides big inviting rooms done with a sophisticated combination of antique and modern pieces. The pool is shared with gîte guests as well as other B&Bers.

rooms	2 + 1: 2 doubles; 1 apartment with 2 doubles, sitting room & kitchenette.
price	€91 for two. Apartment €129 for two-four. Minimum stay 2 nights July-August.
meals	Restaurants 3-8km.
closed	Rarely.
directions	From Bordeaux D936 for Bergerac; 1.3km after St Quentin de Baron, sign on right then left, house at end of lane.

Susie de Castilho
Le Prieuré,
33750 St Quentin de Baron,
Gironde

tel	+33 (0)5 57 24 16 75
e-mail	stay@stayfrance.net
web	www.stayfrance.net

Map 10 Entry 469

Le Grand Boucaud

Food is the thing here, and your intelligent, very personable hosts are continually on the look out for wines that will marry well with their repertoire of dishes. Madame is a superb cook and Monsieur knows all about wine; they offer wine and cookery courses and vineyard trails. Set among fields and vineyards, the rose-covered farmhouse is dark inside but has space and a lovely feel. Beamed and English-wallpapered guest rooms are big and comfortable; the family room is particularly attractive, with its modern mezzanine and sitting area overlooking the garden.

rooms	3: 1 double, 1 triple, 1 family room.
price	€65 for two; €80 for three.
meals	Dinner €23-€34, book ahead; good wine list €14-€35.
closed	16 October-December.
directions	From Libourne D670 S for 31km; left D230 to Rimons; for Monségur; 1st left, on bend; signposted.

Dominique & Patrick Lévy
Le Grand Boucaud,
33580 Monségur,
Gironde
tel +33 (0)5 56 71 88 57
fax +33 (0)5 56 61 43 77
e-mail grandboucaud@free.fr
web grandboucaud.free.fr

Les Charmettes

Think it looks modest? Don't be fooled – go through the main buildings and splendour strikes. Discover delightful gardens and a great pool enclosed by charming guest quarters: your dynamic hosts, both full-time doctors, have converted the old stables brilliantly, keeping much of the original dark wood, adding elegant antiques and artefacts to each of the large, individual bedrooms, armoires lined with sophisticated fabrics matching curtains and wallpaper, good bathrooms. Superb breakfasts may be served by the housekeeper as your hosts are out by 9am. Luxurious but good value.

rooms	3: 2 doubles, 1 twin.
price	€75 for two.
meals	Restaurant 300m.
closed	Rarely.
directions	From Libourne D670 S 45km to La Réole; left N113 for Agen; house on left on edge of town opp. Automobile & Train Museum.

Christian & Danielle Henry
Les Charmettes,
33190 La Réole,
Gironde
tel +33 (0)5 56 71 09 23
fax +33 (0)5 56 71 25 13

La Tuilerie

Such a special place. Antoine, a cookery teacher, loves to whip up feasts in his sensational kitchen and offer good wines from his 'trade contacts'. Dinner is at a giant round table, made from an outsize wine barrel, in a 19th-century barn with a cantilevered gallery and a superb two-storey fireplace; good quality rooms are interestingly different. Children are spoilt: sandpit, climbing frame, huge shallow-ended pool, horses to feed, three Laborde children to play with. Canoeing, trips on the lovely Canal du Midi, fishing, riding, cycling are all possible. Readers write reams of praise.

rooms	5: 3 doubles, 1 triple, 1 twin.
price	€59 for two.
meals	Dinner with wine €25, book ahead.
closed	Last two weeks in February.
directions	From A62 exit 4 onto D9; left for Bazas-Grignols; over m'way bridge; 1st left, 250m after bridge; follow signs Chambres d'Hôtes 3km.

Claire & Antoine Laborde
La Tuilerie,
33190 Noaillac,
Gironde

tel	+33 (0)5 56 71 05 51
fax	+33 (0)5 56 71 05 51
e-mail	claire.laborde@libertysurf.fr
web	latuilerie33.com

Map 15 Entry 472

Maison Cameleyre

Tall pines guard the clearing, tall timbers support the 300-year-old buildings in a world of vertical wood on horizontal green with ancient oaks for shade and luscious mushrooms. Emma and Thierry's barn conversion is full of peace and natural country finishes (the farmhouse is their space) and has pride of place: lovely big rooms, soft textures, gentle light. Emma, a fitness trainer, loves cooking and gives Aga demos; do book your dinner. They run de-stress weekends, too – super people. An ideal country retreat for city-mad adults and families. *Also available for self catering.*

rooms	3 twins/doubles.
price	€61 for two.
meals	Dinner with wine €15, book ahead.
closed	Rarely.
directions	N10 Bordeaux & Bayonne exit 15 for Escource; at r'bout D44 to village; D63 for Mézos; house in Cameleyre on right, after 3km sign at entrance.

Emma & Thierry Bernabeu
Maison Cameleyre,
40210 Escource,
Landes

tel	+33 (0)5 58 04 22 02
fax	+33 (0)5 58 04 22 04
e-mail	tbernabe@club-internet.fr
web	www.cameleyre.com

Map 14 Entry 473

Moulin Vieux

A house to satisfy your soul: lost in a forest, its windows onto endless oaks and pines with mere and river beyond. Madame, a lovable person, joins you in the warm conservatory for deliciously organic meals. Bedrooms are small and simply furnished with a touch of Liliane's son's artistry in a marbled or frescoed wall; colours are harmonious, shower rooms basic. In the salon: a trompe l'oeil of the Enchanted Forest, a piano and masses of books, in the huge kitchen an open fire. The setting is tremendous and springtime walks yield birdsong and wildflower treasures.
German spoken too.

rooms	3: 1 double, 1 twin, 1 family room.
price	€35-€40 for two.
meals	Dinner with wine €14, book ahead.
closed	Rarely.
directions	From Mont de Marsan N134 NW to Garein; left D57 for Ygos & Tartas; follow signs: 1km of lane to house.

Mme Liliane Jehl
Moulin Vieux,
40420 Garein,
Landes
tel +33 (0)5 58 51 61 43
fax +33 (0)5 58 51 61 43

Domaine d'Agès

In an intriguing mixture of typical brickwork and colonial verandas, this noble manor stands among fabulous old hardwoods and acres of pines. Nature rejoices, cranes fly overhead, thoroughbreds grace the paddock (the Hayes breed horses), hens range free and Madame deploys boundless energy to ply you with exquisite food from the potager, myriad teas, lovely antique-filled, sweet-coloured bedrooms (with her own framed embroidery): she adores entertaining. Monsieur smiles while 15-year-old Jonathan is all discretion. A huge open fire, baby grand piano and panelled salon tell it perfectly.

rooms	3: 1 double, 1 twin, 1 family suite for 4.
price	€45-€50 for two.
meals	Dinner with wine €20, book ahead.
closed	Rarely.
directions	N10 Bordeaux & Bayonne exit Morcenx; D38 for Mont de Marsan; in Ygos right to Ousse Suzan; in Ousse pass 'Chez Jojo'; signposted Chambres d'Hôtes; up lane; Domaine 1.5km on left.

Élisabeth Haye
Domaine d'Agès,
40110 Ousse Suzan,
Landes
tel +33 (0)5 58 51 82 28
fax +33 (0)5 58 51 82 29
e-mail haye.eeb@wanadoo.fr
web www.hoteslandes.com

Château de Bezincam

An atmosphere of dream-like tranquillity wafts over this grand and appealing old French country house with its elegant doors and polished oak floors. Just outside the park gates is the beautiful River Adour, abundant in bird and wildlife – every 10 years or so it comes and kisses the terrace steps. Two of the gilt-mirrored bedrooms overlook the water and a great spread of meadows where animals graze. There is a vast choice for 'flexitime' breakfast on the terrace or in the rustic-chic dining room. Madame, an energetic and interesting hostess, was a publisher in Paris for many years. *Spanish spoken.*

rooms	3: 2 doubles, 1 triple.
price	€60-€70 for two.
meals	Wide choice of restaurants 2-5km.
closed	Rarely.
directions	From A63 exit 8 to St Geours de Maremne; D17 S for 5km to Saubusse; right just before bridge; château 800m on right.

Claude Dourlet
Château de Bezincam,
Saubusse les Bains,
40180 Dax,
Landes
tel +33 (0)5 58 57 70 27
fax +33 (0)5 58 57 70 27
e-mail dourlet.bezincam@tiscali.fr

Maison Capcazal de Pachioü

Fall asleep by a crackling fire – a lovely place for a weekend escape. Stay and be moved by this house, with prodigious original panelling (1610) and contents, accumulated by Colette's family for 14 generations. Portraits from the 12th century onwards, spectacular bedrooms with canopied antique beds, strong colours, luscious armoires, embroidered linen. One luminous bathroom has a marble-topped washstand. Dining room and salon are handsome, too: twin grandfather clocks, terracotta tiles and a huge stone fireplace. Colette is elegant, attentive, remarkable and resourceful. An exceptional place.

rooms	4 doubles.
price	€45-€65 for two.
meals	Dinner with wine €20, book ahead.
closed	Rarely.
directions	From Dax D947 for Pau & Orthez; from r'bout at end of town on for 10km; at crossroads on D947 ignore sign for Mimbaste; take next right C16; follow discreet yellow signs for 1km.

Colette Dufourcet-Alberca
Maison Capcazal de Pachioü,
40350 Mimbaste,
Landes
tel +33 (0)5 58 55 30 54
fax +33 (0)5 58 55 30 54

Château de Monbet

The miniature château in its secluded setting rejoices in a fine chestnut staircase, a veranda paved with rare Bidache stone, high ceilings, old prints, a glimpse of the Pyrenees and the call of a peacock. Madame is a gem, gracious and charming – she teaches yoga, paints, is a long-distance walker and a committed vegetarian; her husband is gently reserved. Children can roam the 20 hectares of parkland freely – they love it. The rooms, large and properly decorated, have gorgeous parquet floors and relatively little 'château' furniture. We think the smaller ones give better value.

rooms	3: 2 doubles, 1 twin.
price	€50-€80 for two.
meals	Good restaurant in village.
closed	November-March, except by arrangement.
directions	From A10 or A63 exit St Geours de Maremne to Saubusse & Orist. Or, from A64 exit Peyrehorade to Dax. In both cases, 10km to Monbet.

M & Mme Hubert de Lataillade
Château de Monbet,
40300 St Lon les Mines,
Landes

tel	+33 (0)5 58 57 80 68
fax	+33 (0)5 58 57 89 29
e-mail	chateau.de.monbet@wanadoo.fr
web	www.chateaudemonbet.com

Villa Ty Gias

Light, birdsong and ocean breezes whisper round this seductive modern house and its balmy garden so don't be daunted by the residential area or the steep drive. Up and down go the pale wooden decks connecting living spaces and levels – is it an earthbound ship or a Californian beach house? Waves of light wash over super contemporary furniture, natural colours, finishes and fabrics that are gentle on the eye and Madame's exotic pieces from Africa and the Far East. Straightforward and unpretentious, she revels in her house and guests' appreciation of their soft, clean-cut rooms and alfresco breakfasts.

rooms	2 + 1: 1 double, 1 twin; 1 apartment for 4.
price	€60-€75 for two. Apartment €110-€150.
meals	Choice of restaurants nearby.
closed	Rarely.
directions	From A63 exit 10 for St Vincent de Tyrosse & Seignosse; on for Golf 3km; over r'bout, 800m; left into Av. de Morfontaine, 200m, blue house, signposted.

Jean-Luc & Noëllie Annic
Villa Ty Gias,
40510 Seignosse,
Landes

tel	+33 (0)5 58 41 64 29
fax	+33 (0)5 58 41 64 29
e-mail	tygias@wanadoo.fr
web	perso.wanadoo.fr/tygias

Nun Obeki

Nun Obeki, a 1970s house, a comfortable mixture of American (the owners), French (the furnishings) and Basque (the house and this village). Rooms are elegant without being overpowering, done in soft pastels and florals with just the right amount of furniture and very decent bathrooms. In the living room, you will have breakfast on Louis XV chairs and lounge on a squashy sofa – an ideal mix of casual and classic. Delightful hosts, Richard laughing his rich deep laugh, Elyane a consummate painter of eggs, among her many talents. Do visit the lovingly-carved Basque church in this colourful village.

rooms	4: 3 doubles, 1 twin.
price	€55-€61 for two.
meals	Restaurant 100m.
closed	Rarely.
directions	From A63 exit 3, then left on RN10 for St Jean de Luz Nord for 1.5km. House signposted; look for bank & telephone booth at corner of rue Elie de Seze.

Richard & Elyane Mann
Nun Obeki,
64500 St Jean de Luz,
Pyrénées-Atlantiques

tel	+33 (0)5 59 26 30 71
fax	+33 (0)5 59 85 30 65
e-mail	nunobeki@nunobeki.com
web	www.nunobeki.com

Domaine de Silencenia

The house cornerstone, the magnificent magnolia, the towering pines were all planted on one day in 1881. The Mallor family's welcome is as generous as they: an enchanting couple with teenage children who have lived and fished in southern seas. Their deeply sensitive restoration includes a Blue Marlin room, canopied pine beds, modern fittings and respect for the original chestnut panelling. They know about good food and wine too: Krystel ran a restaurant, Philippe's cellar is brilliant – do dine with them. There's great walking, a sauna for afterwards and lots more. *Spanish spoken.*

rooms	5: 3 doubles, 2 triples.
price	€60-€70 for two.
meals	Dinner with wine €25, book ahead. Restaurants 800m.
closed	Rarely.
directions	From A63 exit on D932, on through Ustaritz & Cambo les Bains; left into Louhossoa; straight over crossroads. House 800m on left.

Krystel & Philippe Mallor
Domaine de Silencenia,
64250 Louhossoa,
Pyrénées-Atlantiques

tel	+33 (0)5 59 93 35 60
fax	+33 (0)5 59 93 35 60
e-mail	domaine.de.silencenia@wanadoo.fr
web	www.domaine-de-silencenia.fr.st

Bidachuna

Hear the electronic gate click behind you and 29 hectares of forested peace and quiet are yours with their fabulous wildlife. Draw your beautiful curtains next morning and you may see deer feeding; lift your eyes and feast on long, long vistas to the Pyrenean foothills; come down to the earthly feast that is Basque breakfast. Shyly attentive, Isabelle manages all this impeccably and keeps a refined house where everything is polished and gleaming, floors are chestnut, bathrooms marble, family antiques of high quality. A beautifully manicured haven – worth staying several days for serious cossetting.

rooms	3: 2 doubles, 1 twin.
price	€100-€110 for two.
meals	Restaurant 6km.
closed	Rarely.
directions	From Biarritz railway station to Bassussary & Arcangues; D3 for St Pée; 8km after Arcangues house on left; signposted.

Isabelle Ormazabal
Bidachuna,
64310 St Pée sur Nivelle,
Pyrénées-Atlantiques
tel +33 (0)5 59 54 56 22
fax +33 (0)5 59 54 55 07

Lacroisade

Sylvianne lives on a hill in a typical old Basque farmhouse full of timbers, pictures, carved country furniture and her own skillfully orchestrated patches of colour – she loves colour! Up the twisty old staircase, each super room has its strong chromatic vibration: *Pamplona* rippling blue and yellow with an open timber frame in the middle; *Seville* vigorously orange and green; *Cordoue* fresh blue and acid green; bits and bobs, bouquets and bows finish the effects and bathrooms are good. Downstairs, you will be generously received by your smilingly bright young hostess who knows the area and cooks very well.

rooms	4: 3 triples, 1 quadruple.
price	€57-€60 for two.
meals	Dinner with wine €25, book ahead.
closed	Rarely.
directions	From A64 exit 4 for Urt; right D123; through Labastide Clairence for St Palais for 3km. House on left on top of hill; signposted.

Sylvianne Darritchon
Lacroisade,
64240 La Bastide Clairence,
Pyrénées-Atlantiques
tel +33 (0)5 59 29 68 22
fax +33 (0)5 54 29 62 99
e-mail lacroisade@aol.com

Maison Marchand

A lovely face among all the lovely faces of this superb listed village, the 16th-century Basque farmhouse, resuscitated by its French/Irish owners, is run with well-organised informality. Dinners around the great oak table are lively; local dishes excellent. Rooms are big, light, well-decorated with hand-stencilling and pretty fabrics, beams and exposed wafer bricks, country antiques and thoughtful 'extras' such as good books and bottled water. Breakfast is on the terrace in warm weather. And Gilbert will laugh and teach you *la pelote basque*.

rooms	3: 2 doubles, 1 double with extra bed for 2 children.
price	€55-€65 for two; €15 extra per child.
meals	Dinner with wine €25, book ahead.
closed	Occasionally.
directions	From A64 junc. 4 for Urt & Bidache; right on D936, right on D123 at mini-island to La Bastide Clairence. House on main street, opp. bakery.

Valerie & Gilbert Foix
Maison Marchand,
64240 La Bastide Clairence,
Pyrénées-Atlantiques

tel	+33 (0)5 59 29 18 27
fax	+33 (0)5 59 29 14 97
e-mail	valerie.et.gilbert.foix@wanadoo.fr
web	perso.wanadoo.fr/maison.marchand

La Closerie du Guilhat

Guilhat is one of those sturdy Béarn houses with solid old furniture and traditional décor. Marie-Christine has added her own decorative touches – colourful bedroom wallpapers, small, modern bathrooms – and everything is immaculate. She is elegant and energetic, doing nearly all the work here herself and longing to show you her remarkable garden. It has huge old trees, magnolia, azalea, rhododendron, with benches discreetly placed for quiet reading... and the Pyrenees as a backdrop. There's table tennis and the new spa centre in Salies is good for swimming all year.

rooms	3: 1 double, 1 twin, 1 suite.
price	€50-€54 for two.
meals	Dinner with wine €20, book ahead.
closed	Rarely.
directions	From A64 exit 7; right for Salies '5 tonnes'; next right to Le Guilhat 1.8km; house on left beside nurseries at junction with Chemin des Bois.

Marie-Christine Potiron
La Closerie du Guilhat,
64270 Salies de Béarn,
Pyrénées-Atlantiques

tel	+33 (0)5 59 38 08 80
fax	+33 (0)5 59 38 31 90
e-mail	guilhat@club-internet.fr
web	www.holidayshomes.com/guilhat

Maison L'Aubèle

The Desbonnets completely renovated their grand 18th-century village house after finding it and this sleepy village in the Pyrenean foothills: both house and owners are quiet, elegant, sophisticated and full of interest, the furniture a feast for the eyes. Breakfast is a chance to pick their well-stocked brains about the region and do delve into their tempting library (she binds books). The light, airy bedrooms have more interesting furniture on lovely wooden floors. *La Rose* is very chic, *La Verte* is a dream – enormous and boldly coloured with views of the mountains and a 'waltz-in' bathroom.

rooms	2 doubles.
price	€60 for two.
meals	Restaurants 4-10km.
closed	Rarely.
directions	From Navarrenx D2 for Monein to Jasses; right D27 for Oloron Ste Marie; in Lay-Lamidou, left, 1st right, 2nd house on right.

Marie-France Desbonnet
Maison L'Aubèle,
64190 Lay-Lamidou,
Pyrénées-Atlantiques
tel +33 (0)5 59 66 00 44
fax +33 (0)5 59 66 00 44
e-mail desbonnet.bmf@infonie.fr
web www.ifrance.com/chambrehote/

Château d'Agnos

This exceptional couple, Heather, warmly communicative, Desmond, ex-architect with a great sense of fun, have brilliantly restored Agnos (and do all the cooking). There are high ceilings framing remarkable mirrors, paintings set into panelling, fine period furniture, a black marble dining room fountain, a medieval kitchen, an old prison... François I is said to have escaped by a (still secret) tunnel. Bedrooms are great: *Henri IV* has antique gilt beds, *François I*'s black and white bathroom has an antique cast iron bath. It's huge and you will feel completely at home. *Children over 12 welcome.*

rooms	5: 1 double, 1 twin, 3 suites.
price	€80-€140
meals	Dinner €22. Wine list from €10. Book ahead.
closed	Rarely.
directions	From Pau N134 for 35km to Oloron Ste Marie; through town; N134 towards Zaragoza 1km. In Bidos, right for Agnos.

Heather & Desmond Nears-Crouch
Château d'Agnos,
64400 Agnos,
Pyrénées-Atlantiques
tel +33 (0)5 59 36 12 52
fax +33 (0)5 59 36 13 69
e-mail chateaudagnos@wanadoo.fr

Maison Rancesamy

Landscape painters love this haven. From terrace and pool you can see for ever into the high Pyrenees – sunlit snowy in winter, all the greens in summer. Beside their 1700s farmhouse, the Brownes' remarkable barn conversion shelters refined, beamed and stone-walled bedrooms and a superb dining room – Isabelle's trompe-l'œil floor, huge carved table – an eclectic style reflecting their multinational origins (Polish, French, South African). They are a happy, relaxed and thoroughly integrated family. It is informal, easily friendly and, on windless, balmy, summer evenings, the food is deliciously garden-aromatic.

rooms	5: 1 double, 1 twin, 3 family rooms.
price	€52-€65 for two. Family room €72-€90. Minimum stay 2 nights July-August.
meals	Dinner with wine €32, book ahead.
closed	Rarely.
directions	From Pau N134 S for Saragosse to Gan; right at lights after chemist, D24 for Lasseube 9km; left D324. Follow Chambres d'Hôtes signs; cross 2 small bridges; house on left up hill.

Simon & Isabelle Browne
Maison Rancesamy,
64290 Lasseube,
Pyrénées-Atlantiques

tel	+33 (0)5 59 04 26 37
fax	+33 (0)5 59 04 26 37
e-mail	missbrowne@wanadoo.fr
web	www.missbrowne.com

Château de Cantet

Quintessentially French B&B is yours at this down-to-earth 17th-century manor-farm. Old pillared gates, smooth grass, glimpses of farm life – barns, thousands of ranging hens, tractors, sheep: it is instantly, warmly real. Your animated, extrovert hostess leads you, in good English, to big unflouncy bedrooms done in best French provincial style with opulent but unostentatious white bathrooms and views of meadows and woods. The family take you to their bosom: dine at their big dining table, swim in their lovely pool, play billiards, table tennis, croquet and, of course, boules and... eat their eggs for breakfast.

rooms	3: 1 double, 2 twins.
price	€56-€70 for two; €99 for four.
meals	Dinner with wine €23, book ahead.
closed	15 December-13 January.
directions	From Marmande right at 3rd r'bout for Samazan.

M & Mme de La Raitrie
Château de Cantet,
47250 Bouglon,
Lot-et-Garonne

tel	+33 (0)5 53 20 60 60
fax	+33 (0)5 53 89 63 53
e-mail	jbdelaraitrie@wanadoo.fr

Château de Rodié

Paul and Pippa did the triumphant restoration themselves, with two small children and a passionate commitment to the integrity of this ancient building: brash modernities are hidden (the telephone lurks behind a model ship). It is breathtaking: an elaborate *pisé* floor set in cabalistic patterns and lit only with candles, two stone staircases, patches of fresco, a vast hall with giant fireplace and table – and a welcome to match. The tower room is unforgettable, so is the pool. The family is veggie-friendly and Pippa cooks sumptuous organic dinners (home-reared lamb…) that last for hours.

rooms	5: 3 doubles, 2 suites.
price	€70-€100 for two.
meals	Dinner with wine €18, book ahead.
closed	Rarely.
directions	From Fumel D102 to Tournon; D656 for Agen 300m; left to Courbiac, past church, right at cross for Montaigu 1km; house on left.

Paul & Pippa Hecquet
Château de Rodié,
47370 Courbiac de Tournon,
Lot-et-Garonne

tel +33 (0)5 53 40 89 24
fax +33 (0)5 53 40 89 25
e-mail chateau.rodie@wanadoo.fr
web www.chateauderodie.com

Manoir de Roquegautier

In a beautful park with rolling views, the fairytale château is wondrously French. Drapes, swags and interlinings – all done, but never overdone, by Madame – and the rooms in the old tower truly memorable with their own entrance and spiral stone stair. There are claw-footed baths and huge old basins and taps, and each top-floor suite has one round tower room. There are swings and games room, a discreet pool, gazebos around the garden and mature trees to shade your picnic lunches. Delicious food fresh from the family farm and shared with your hosts – such gentle, friendly people that you'll wish you could stay for ever.

rooms	4: 2 doubles, 1 family suite for 3, 1 family suite for 4.
price	€68 for two. Suites for €102-€109 three-four.
meals	Dinner with wine €23, July-August, book ahead.
closed	October-April.
directions	From Villeneuve sur Lot N21 north for Cancon, 15.5km. Manoir signposted on left 3.5km before Cancon.

Brigitte & Christian Vrech
Manoir de Roquegautier,
47290 Cancon,
Lot-et-Garonne

tel +33 (0)5 53 01 60 75
fax +33 (0)5 53 40 27 75
e-mail roquegautier@free.fr
web roquegautier.free.fr

Colombié

With infectious energy and fluent English, Madame tells her love of her house, land and gently cropping horses. Hawks and owls nest outside the old-style *pigeonnier* where one bold-coloured, kempt bedroom sits above the other, plus tiny children's attic, minute kitchen and log-fired living room. Throw open the shutters, smell the freshness, behold the Pannetier empire of paddocks, pool and lake (for fishing and boating) up to distant hills. After breakfast at the family table, on the terrace or in your dayroom, launch into this area's endless riches. Children fully provided for.

rooms	2 twins/doubles (1 with mini-kitchen).
price	€55 for two.
meals	Dinner with wine €18, book ahead. Self-catering €10 per day.
closed	Rarely.
directions	From Villeneuve sur Lot D676 to Monflanquin; D272 towards Monpazier. 1.5km beyond x-roads to Dévillac, left before bridge; 3rd house on right.

Michel & Maryse Pannetier
Colombié,
47210 Dévillac,
Lot-et-Garonne

tel +33 (0)5 53 36 62 34
fax +33 (0)5 53 36 04 79
e-mail colombie@wanadoo.fr
web perso.wanadoo.fr/colombie

Château de Péchalbet

Having lived vibrantly on the Riviera, the Peyres moved here in search of rural peace, then chose to share their love of the place. Glorious public rooms have high rafters, splendid furnishings and sensuous old terracotta tiles. Bedrooms are on the ground floor, off a rag-rolled hall: one with a metalwork four-poster, another bluebell walls and a terrace. Children get bunk beds in an ancient tower. Then there's the fine old kitchen for breakfast, a formal terrace for dining and a view of the lake (illuminated at night). Highly civilised casualness in both house and owners – and acres of wildlife to discover.

rooms	3: 1 family suite, 1 double, 1 twin.
price	€70-€85 for two.
meals	Dinner with wine €23, book ahead.
closed	November-March.
directions	From Bergerac D933 for Marmande. 1.5km after Eymet left C1 for Agnac-Mairie; 500m on left.

Françoise & Henri Peyre
Château de Péchalbet,
47800 Agnac,
Lot-et-Garonne

tel +33 (0)5 53 83 04 70
fax +33 (0)5 53 83 04 70
e-mail pechalbet@hotmail.com
web pechalbet.free.fr

Domaine des Rigals

A many-gloried 17th-century family château with 15 fabulous hectares of garden and woodland: red squirrels and deer cavort, wild orchids glow, the Babers nurture 400 new trees. Their furniture from Scotland sits graciously in the French rooms, white carpeting spreads deep luxury in the lovely suite, family antiques grace the guest sitting room and they love you to share their welcoming manor. Breakfast generously in the huge kitchen or on the terrace then roam, relax or play: there's a carp lake for fishing, a tennis court, a 16m child-friendly pool. Great hosts, rooms, local markets, restaurants and wines.

rooms	3: 2 doubles, 1 family suite.
price	€90-€125 for two.
meals	Several good restaurants in Castillonnès.
closed	Christmas & New Year.
directions	From Bergerac N21 for Villeneuve. 1.5km after Castillonnès, pass 'Terres du Sud' on left. After 50m, sign on right before crest of hill.

James Petley,
Patricia & David Baber
Domaine des Rigals,
47330 Castillonnès, Lot-et-Garonne
tel +33 (0)5 53 41 24 21
fax +33 (0)5 53 41 24 79
e-mail babersrigals@wanadoo.fr
web www.domainedesrigals.com

Map 15 Entry 494

La Maison de la Halle

Eighteenth-century elegance in a lovely hilltop village... there are a walled garden, two geranium-ed terraces (the lower with a pool), breathtaking views and "sunsets to die for". Fiona is Scottish, Leif, a wonderful raconteur, is Danish; their background: cosmopolitan in film and design; their house: full of paintings, antiques, props from film and theatre productions. Bedrooms, one upstairs, two down, overlook the peaceful old market square, and beige and white luxury reigns – white-painted floors, sumptuous raw linen, a fine polished armoire. Guests have praised the supremely comfortable beds!

rooms	3: 2 doubles, 1 twin.
price	€65-€80 for two.
meals	Dinner with wine €40, book ahead.
closed	Rarely.
directions	From Marmande D708 for Duras 17km to Lévignac; bear left; head for Centre Ville; house on left behind market hall: two bay trees & white front door.

Leif & Fiona Pedersen
La Maison de la Halle,
47120 Lévignac de Guyenne,
Lot-et-Garonne
tel +33 (0)5 53 94 37 61
fax +33 (0)5 53 94 37 66
e-mail maison.de.la.halle@wanadoo.fr
web www.lamaisondelahalle.com

Map 15 Entry 495

Manoir de Levignac

Walk through the entrance hall into the handsome country kitchen and thence into the grounds with nature reserve, pond, pool, pines and views. Or stay and dine, in this room with big fireplace, pottery pieces and beautiful carved cupboard doors. In the sitting room, terracotta tiles, kilim rugs, and grand piano give a comfortably artistic air. Adriana is Swiss-Italian, Jocelyn South African; they are warm and lovely and do everything well. You get a lush bedroom with rural views, a sitting room and an immaculate bathroom. Table tennis and space outside, attention to detail within, delicious food.

rooms 1 suite.
price €70-€80 for two.
meals Dinner with wine €20, book ahead.
closed Rarely.
directions From A10 exit St André de Cubzac to Ste Foy La Grande; D708 to Duras; 4km after Duras left C1 to St Pierre.

Jocelyn & Adriana Cloete
Manoir de Levignac,
47120 Duras,
Lot-et-Garonne
tel +33 (0)5 53 83 68 11
fax +33 (0)5 53 93 98 63
e-mail cloete@wanadoo.fr

Le Branchat

Waltz in the marble halls of this magnificent manor, sophisticate in its fine new bathrooms, go natural with Richard's ark of roaming animals and gorge on his home-grown fruits. He knows his mushrooms too, and can take you picking. He and Isabelle, happily out of the tourist industry and fervent B&B believers, will share their imaginative cooking with you if you are a small group (book ahead). Simple white bedrooms with plain beds and Richard's excellent paintings are a calm contrast to the opulence below but the pool area is wickedly tempting. Luxury, enthusiasm, efficiency all make this special.

rooms 7: 2 doubles, 2 twins, 1 triple, (2 connect for family use); 2 suites in separate building.
price €53-€69 for two. Minimum stay 2 nights July & August.
meals Dinner €20-€25, book ahead; wine €9-€19.
closed 15 October-7 November & 5 January-1 April.
directions From Périgueux D710 S for Belvès. At r'bout stay on D710 500m then left; signposted. House 600m on left.

Richard & Isabelle Ginioux
Le Branchat,
24170 Belvès,
Dordogne
tel +33 (0)5 53 28 98 80
fax +33 (0)5 53 28 90 82
e-mail info@lebranchat.com
web www.lebranchat.com

La Guérinière

Once a charterhouse, this good-looking Périgord house sits squarely in 10 hectares of parkland and peace, a tribute to the rich, sober taste of the area. Inside reflects outside: the same dark timbers against pale stone and the new owners have redecorated the bedrooms most charmingly. They are gradually replacing the modern furniture with country antiques and the feel is warmly authentic. And moreover, they used to run a restaurant – do eat in. Sitting at the big table for house guests, you may find more gourmets in the beamed dining room: a few outsiders are occasionally allowed. A gem.

rooms	5: 1 double, 2 twin, 1 triple, 1 quadruple.
price	€75-€90 for two.
meals	Dinner €21, wine €15, book ahead.
closed	2 November-March.
directions	From Sarlat D46 to Cénac St Julien. At end of village on for Fumel. House 3rd turning on right.

Brigitte & Christophe Demassougne
La Guérinière,
24250 Cénac et St Julien,
Dordogne
tel +33 (0)5 53 29 91 97
fax +33 (0)5 53 30 23 89
e-mail contact@la-gueriniere-dordogne.com
web www.la-gueriniere-dordogne.com

Château de Puymartin

Neither dream nor museum, Puymartin is a chance to act the aristocrat for a spell, survey the trippers from your own wing. The fireplace in the tapestried baronial dining room would take a small tree, painted beams draw the eye, the carved stone staircase asks to be stroked, the furniture is authentic 17th-century Perigordian, history oozes from every corner (possibly a ghost). Bedrooms are vastly in keeping – twin four-posters, a loo in a turret, thick draperies. The ever-elegant Comtesse is friendly and very French; her son helps in the château and speaks good English; both are delightful.

rooms	2: 1 twin, 1 family suite.
price	€115 for two.
meals	Good restaurant 5km; choice in Sarlat.
closed	November-March.
directions	From Sarlat D47 for Les Eyzies 8km. Château signposted regularly.

Comte & Comtesse de Montbron
Château de Puymartin,
24200 Sarlat la Canéda,
Dordogne
tel +33 (0)5 53 59 29 97
fax +33 (0)5 53 29 87 52
e-mail xdemontbron@wanadoo.fr

La Licorne

In a tiny, peaceful hamlet in a particularly lovely area, La Licorne is three old buildings with a stream bounding the courtyard. Claire and Marc are from the Alps – she teaches skiing, he works in tourism and is an experienced cook – and are keen to make their new home a relaxing place to be. Clutter-free rooms, one in the 13th-century barn overlooking the nut trees and garden, are small, white, with modern furniture and the occasional old carved cupboard door. The dining room is superb with its big fireplace and gallery at each end; food is light and vegetable-orientated. *Arrivals from 5pm.*

rooms	3: 2 doubles, 1 suite for 4.
price	€55-€58 for two. Minimum stay 2 nights.
meals	Dinner with wine €20, book ahead. Restaurants 500m-6km.
closed	November-Easter.
directions	From Montignac D65 south for 6km; left on minor road to Valojoulx. House in centre of hamlet, left of Mairie.

Claire & Marc Bosse
La Licorne,
24290 Montignac Lascaux,
Dordogne

tel	+33 (0)5 53 50 77 77
fax	+33 (0)5 53 50 77 77
e-mail	licornelascaux@free.fr
web	www.licorne-lascaux.com

Château de Mombette

Built in the 1600-1700s by the same family, it has the simple, harmonious elegance that natural style brings to an organically-grown house; from its hilltop perch, it gazes across to the splendid medieval fortifications of Domme. Madame is fittingly welcoming and easy, has travelled a lot, especially to North Africa, and may even join you for a game of bridge. The character of her house is made of fine, generous spaces and good regional antiques, an attractive library and very lovely gardens. Rooms are comfortable, light and airy and you are within reach of all the delights of the Dordogne. Most relaxing.

rooms	3: 1 double, 1 twin, 1 triple.
price	€90-€95 for two.
meals	Restaurants within walking distance.
closed	15 November-1 April.
directions	From Sarlat D46 to Cénac & St Julien; D50 right for St Cybranet for 300m; left signposted.

Mme Michèle Jahan
Château de Mombette,
24250 Cénac et St Julien,
Dordogne

tel	+33 (0)5 53 28 30 14
fax	+33 (0)5 53 28 30 14
e-mail	michele.jahan@wanadoo.fr

Le Relais de Lavergne

Enter the creeper-climbed courtyard through the old arch: looks a touch sophisticated? Francine and Odile will reassure you – they are funny, extrovert, intelligent, and wonderful company. Browse in their library, seize the chance to share their genuine pleasure in their house and guests. The curvy roof, wafer bricks and ancient timbers may be familiar friends but the long-drop privy is a fascinating rarity. Splendid main rooms combine simplicity and taste, antique and modern; smaller, tempting bedrooms have hand-stencilled doors and the playroom has table tennis, telly and tea kitchen. Marvellous!

rooms	5: 3 doubles, 1 twin, 1 family suite.
price	€58 for two.
meals	Dinner with wine €20, book ahead.
closed	Rarely.
directions	From Bergerac D660 for Lalinde & Sarlat; right over R. Dordogne at Pont de Couze (still D660); at Bayac right D27 for Issigeac 2km; house on left at top of hill.

Francine Pillebout
& Odile Calmettes
Le Relais de Lavergne,
24150 Bayac,
Dordogne

tel +33 (0)5 53 57 83 16
fax +33 (0)5 53 57 83 16
e-mail relaisdelavergne@wanadoo.fr

Map 10 Entry 502

Les Chambres de Toutifaud

The intriguing new house opens big eyes to rolling paddocks and woods, the garden glides past in soft lines and curves, terraces parade before spectacular sunsets. Your enthusiastic hosts have married one of humanity's oldest businesses – breeding horses – to a sure sense of modern design. Travellers hoping for peace and uncluttered style will appreciate the mood created by books, restful fabrics and fine fittings. Rooms face south or onto the terraces. The Simon children only use the pool when you're out and Madame will make you comfortable without invading your privacy. Appealing in all aspects.

rooms	3 doubles.
price	€70 for two.
meals	Choice of restaurants 1.5-5km.
closed	Rarely.
directions	From Bergerac D660 19km to Port Couze; cross Dordogne to Couze; after Mairie left up hill; sharp right; sharp left; past cemetery, 2nd right, 50m house on left.

Anne & Denis Simon
Les Chambres de Toutifaud,
24150 Couze St Front,
Dordogne

tel +33 (0)5 53 57 28 55
fax +33 (0)5 53 57 28 55
e-mail contact@chambres-hotes-perigord.com
web www.chambres-hotes-perigord.com

Map 10 Entry 503

Le Moulin Neuf

Robert or Stuart's greeting is the first line of an ode to hospitality written in warm stone and breathtaking gardens, set to the tune of the little stream hurrying by to the lake. Freshly flowery, the immaculate rooms in the guest barn are comfortingly filled with excellent beds; bathrooms are utter luxury. The breakfast room has pretty tables and tea-making kit: have your succulent fruit salad here or on the vine-shaded terrace. All is lovingly tended, in perfect peace; nearby is unspoilt Paunat with its huge church – the whole place is a delight. *Ask about pets; children over 10 welcome.*

rooms	6 twins/doubles.
price	€80-€85 for two. Minimum stay 3 nights in winter.
meals	Good restaurant 1km.
closed	Rarely.
directions	From Le Bugue D703 & D31 through Limeuil. Past viewpoint to x-roads; D2 for Ste Alvère; after 100m fork left; house 2km on left at small crossroads.

Robert Chappell & Stuart Shippey
Le Moulin Neuf,
24510 Ste Alvère,
Dordogne
tel +33 (0)5 53 63 30 18
fax +33 (0)5 53 63 30 55
e-mail moulin-neuf@usa.net
web www.the-moulin-neuf.com

Domaine des Blanches Colombes

Yellow stone walls of rustic grandeur, large, light, 400-year-old rooms, wonderful kitchen where Clare and Steven both cook at the great Aga, observed by their new baby. Instantly likeable, young and optimistic, they are finding their new life of visitors (gîters and B&Bers) great fun. Clare loves funky colours so her simply furnished white rooms have patches of bold life against stone walls and wooden floors, calico curtains billowing in the breeze. New bathrooms have the same feel, plus heated rails. The pool and games barn are for all inhabitants, the secret garden for B&B guests only. A happy set-up.

rooms	2: 1 double with separate shower, 1 twin. 4 gîtes also available for B&B.
price	From €45 for two.
meals	Dinner with wine €25, book ahead.
closed	Rarely.
directions	From Bergerac D936 1st exit at r'bout, next r'bout straight on; 3rd left. 1st turn for Lalinde. 3rd exit over railway, right at junc. D32 to St Alvere. Right D8 for Grand Castang, 3km, left. Right after village, follow signs.

Clare Todd
Domaine des Blanches Colombes,
24150 Grand Castang,
Dordogne
tel +33 (0)5 53 57 30 38
e-mail clare.todd@quality-gites.co.uk
web www.quality-gites.com

La Barabie

This deeply-united family honours tradition: the recipes for hand crafting pâtés and foie gras are their heirlooms, the wiggly roof tiles original, the wallpapers timelessly French. Wonderful Marie-Jeanne shares the B&B tasks with her son, a poultry breeder, and daughter-in-law, a brilliant (non-vegetarian) cook. She'll welcome you with her natural, vigorous humour, settle you into your pure French Rustic room, let you admire the view, then drive you across the Dordogne to her son's lovely old house for a memorable dinner. Exceptionally genuine French country people – all power to them.

rooms	2: 1 twin, 1 family room.
price	€47 for two. Minimum stay 2 nights.
meals	Dinner with wine €20, book ahead.
closed	1 November-15 March.
directions	From Bergerac D32 for Ste Alvère for 10km then look for signpost 'Périgord - Bienvenue à la Ferme'.

Marie-Jeanne & Marie-Thérèse Archer
La Barabie,
24520 Mouleydier,
Dordogne
tel +33 (0)5 53 23 22 47
fax +33 (0)5 53 22 81 20
e-mail regis.archer@wanadoo.fr

Les Hirondelles

Carine, half-Greek, energetic and fun, makes you feel very welcome in the sunny kitchen of her restored farmhouse on the top of a hill. She enjoys cooking French and international dishes, sometimes organises barbecues round the big pool and makes amazing walnut jam. Each new-bedded, newly-decorated, modern-bathroomed bedroom in the converted barn has its own terrace onto the shady garden (the pool is far enough away not to disturb your siesta). Spend two or three nights and get to know this beautiful village and the whole area; Carine knows the best places to go.

rooms	4: 2 doubles, 2 twins.
price	€46-€49 for two. Book at least 1 day ahead in winter.
meals	Dinner with wine €15, book ahead.
closed	January.
directions	From Le Bugue go to Ste Alvère; at main x-roads there, D30 for Trémolat. House 2nd right, 500m after sign Le Maine at top of hill.

Carine Someritis
Les Hirondelles,
24510 Ste Alvère,
Dordogne
tel +33 (0)5 53 22 75 40
fax +33 (0)5 53 22 75 40

La Petite Auberge

The whole family are involved: Madame has handed the daily management of auberge and B&B to her two daughters, Monsieur runs the mixed farm producing fruit, vegetables, poultry and wine, and they all thrive. The two bedrooms, in Grandmother's old house over the road from the auberge, are simple and good, perfect for two couples travelling together who could have the whole house. People come quite a way to eat here, the food is so good (open every day for lunch – leave time for a siesta afterwards – and dinner). With a brand new pool in the kempt little garden, it's a real bargain.

rooms	2 doubles.
price	€40 for two. Minimum stay 2 nights.
meals	Dinner with wine €15-€24, book ahead.
closed	October-April.
directions	From Périgueux N21 for Bergerac. 4km after Bordas left to St Maime; on for Vergt & immediately left for Castagnol. Follow Auberge signs.

Laurence & Ghislaine Gay
La Petite Auberge,
24380 St Maime de Péreyrol,
Dordogne

tel +33 (0)5 53 04 00 54
fax +33 (0)5 53 04 00 54

Map 10 Entry 508

Les Rocailles de la Fourtaunie

Your Belgian hosts know their adopted region "like their pocket" and are keen that you discover hidden treasures not just the oversubscribed star sights. Their fine set of Périgord buildings sits high on a wooded, hawk-hunted hill and the big, solar-heated pool is a decent distance from the beautifully restored house – the garden is taking shape too. In the biggest room, you sleep under a soaring timber canopy – a hymn to the carpenter's art – supporting a crystal chandelier. Easy décor, good furniture, a friendly welcome and the run of the kitchen. You may even be able to paint your own souvenir tile.

rooms	3: 1 double, 1 triple, 1 quadruple.
price	€42-€60 for two.
meals	Auberge 2km; choice of restaurants in Bergerac, 9km; use of kitchen possible.
closed	Rarely, but please book ahead in winter.
directions	From Bergerac N21 for Périgueux. 4km after Lembras, Les Rocailles sign on right.

Marcel Vanhemelryck
& Nicole Denys
Les Rocailles de la Fourtaunie,
24520 Lamonzie Montastruc,
Dordogne

tel +33 (0)5 53 58 20 16
fax +33 (0)5 53 58 20 16
e-mail rocaille@infonie.fr

Map 10 Entry 509

Le Domaine de Foncaudière

Sumptuous, the champagne breakfast with salmon and possibly truffle omelette; opulent, the bright and simple luxury of the big suites; unmissable, the discovery trail through 100 acres of history, caves, fountains, great trees. The warm, leafy, many-eyed face of the lovely old manor draws you in: take time to absorb all the beautiful things inside, carved in wood or stone, wrought in iron or wool, against the calm uncluttered backdrop of vast cut stones. Marcel and his partner care passionately about their guests and their new venture: you will be remarkably well looked after.

rooms	2 suites for 3-4.
price	€150-€175 for two; €185-€210 for three; €220-€245 for four. Minimum stay 2 nights.
meals	Restaurants 3km.
closed	Rarely
directions	From Bergerac N21 for Périgueux 3.5km; left D107 for Maurens 5km; left for Maurens; entrance 300m on right.

Marcel Wils
Le Domaine de Foncaudière,
24140 Maurens,
Dordogne
tel +33 (0)5 53 61 13 90
fax +33 (0)5 53 61 03 24
e-mail info@foncaudiere.com
web www.foncaudiere.com

Domaine de la Mouthe

The hilltop site, with wide rural views, was carefully chosen to transplant this lovely old barn – once the garden has matured, you'll think it's been here for centuries. Marie-Ange and Philippe's country furniture looks just right on the old floor tiles beneath the old oak beams; ancient wood and new glass marry beautifully, and the small but fresh bedrooms have views, stylish fabrics and a piece of patio each. Soaps and towels are luxurious. Loll by the heavenly new pool, or contemplate a spot of fishing – they have their own lake. There's riding, too: another member of this charming family runs stables nearby.

rooms	3: 2 doubles, 1 twin.
price	€54 for two.
meals	Good choice of restaurants 3km.
closed	Rarely.
directions	From Libourne A89 exit Monpon Ménestérol; right D708 for Ste Foy la Grande 8km. Right in St Rémy, opp. Le Pressoir, D33 for St Martin & Villefranche; follow signs.

Marie-Ange Caignard
Domaine de la Mouthe,
24700 St Rémy sur Lidoire,
Dordogne
tel +33 (0)5 53 82 15 40
fax +33 (0)5 53 82 15 40
e-mail lamoutheperigord@wanadoo.fr

Le Moulin de Leymonie du Maupas

The Kieffers did the brave and utterly successful restoration of their old Dordogne mill themselves, their professional gardening past speaks softly in the herb-scented patio and the little brook trembles off past grazing horses to the valley. Inside, levels juggle with space, steep stairs rise to smallish rooms of huge character with wood walls, brilliantly chosen colours, rich rugs and selected antiques. Your sitting room is seductive with its logs on the fire and a forest overhead. Add a relaxedly bubbly welcome, delicious home-grown organic dinners, homemade bread and jams for breakfast, and you have excellent value.

rooms	2: 1 double, 1 twin; child's room available.
price	€50 for two.
meals	Dinner €16, book ahead; bottle of wine €9.
closed	Rarely.
directions	In Mussidan, at church, for Villamblard 4km; follow blue signs left for St Séverin 2km, blue sign on right.

Jacques & Ginette Kieffer
Le Moulin de Leymonie du Maupas,
24400 Issac,
Dordogne
tel +33 (0)5 53 81 24 02
e-mail jacques.kieffer2@wanadoo.fr

Le Vignoble

Long views down the hamlet-studded valley and a graceful restoration by owners who swapped London for deepest Dordogne. Fine bedrooms have big beds, white walls and fresh flowers, coired floors and sylvan views. Two of them share an enchanting lavender-panelled bathroom with a swish shower. Snug up on the landing sofa with a book, seek out a private corner in the elegantly simple garden where the hidden pool is heated to West Indian temperatures – Sue was brought up in Trinidad. Seven hectares for walkers and wild orchids, delightful civilised people, superb food. Worth a proper stay.

rooms	3: 1 twin; 2 doubles sharing bath & wc.
price	€55 for two.
meals	Dinner €18, book ahead; wine €6.
closed	Rarely.
directions	From Ribérac D708 for Verteillac; over bridge; D99 right to Celles; through village leaving church on right. House sign 2nd right after Peugeot garage.

Sue & Nick Gild
Le Vignoble,
24600 Ribérac,
Dordogne
tel +33 (0)5 53 90 26 60
e-mail nsgild@compuserve.com

Pauliac

The overflowing stone plunge pool in the green, tumbling terraced garden is unforgettable (OK for children too). John and Jane's talent is a restful atmosphere, their conversion a brilliant marriage of cottage simplicity – simple décor with sparks from African throws and good paintings – and contemporary style. Delightful, energetic Jane offers superb, imaginative food in the new veranda or the bright, rustic dining room with its limed walls and ticking chair covers, and early supper for children. And John "is a joy to be with". Lovely people and a house of taste in a tranquil view-drenched spot.

rooms	5: 2 doubles, 1 twin; 1 suite, 1 twin sharing bath & wc.
price	€60 for two.
meals	Dinner €20, book ahead; wine €10.
closed	Rarely.
directions	From Angoulême D939 for Périgueux 29km; right D12 for Ribérac to Verteillac; left D1 for Lisle 5km; right D99 for Celles for 400m; sign to left.

Jane & John Edwards
Pauliac,
24600 Ribérac,
Dordogne
tel +33 (0)5 53 91 97 45
e-mail info@pauliac.fr
web www.pauliac.fr

La Fournière

Your hostess, painter, flautist, French teacher, shares her library and, drawing on a long and interesting life, her talent for good conversation. Come to her long-viewed cottage among bird-filled woods and fields for cultural and rural peace. Furnished with interesting Belgian pieces and exceptional paintings, it has a split-level sitting room opening to the terrace, unfussy bedrooms, open fires and a big heated pool. Single visitors are welcome for week-long rest cures, French language immersion and excellent guided tours of the area – enquire about full-board terms.

rooms	2: 1 double, 1 twin, sharing bath, shower & wc (2nd wc on ground floor). Only let to same party.
price	€55 for two; €100 for four. Minimum stay 2 nights.
meals	Dinner with wine €17, book ahead.
closed	Rarely.
directions	From Angoulême D939 S 29km; right D12 & D708 22km to Bertric Burée; D106 for Allemans 3km; right for Chez Marty 1km, left at junction; last house to left at end of lane.

Anne Hart
La Fournière,
24320 Bertric Burée,
Dordogne
tel +33 (0)5 53 91 93 58
fax +33 (0)5 53 91 93 58

La Roche

Such a gorgeous garden on several levels – you breakfast at shaded tables or under a pergola draped in honeysuckle and vines. A convinced vegetarian, Alison produces her own (organic) vegetables, eggs, honey and jams. Two spotless bedrooms, with sloping ceilings, big beams and modern windows, are in a converted barn where they share a comfortable living room furnished with books and hand-crafted furniture. Bathrooms, too, are a good size. It's a marvellous place for children, with donkeys, goats, cats, hens, table tennis and a fenced pool that looks out over heavenly countryside.

rooms	2: 1 double, 1 twin.
price	€65 for two.
meals	Restaurants 12km.
closed	Christmas Day.
directions	From D675 (Nontron to Brantôme), D98 east. La Roche on right about 3km from D675.

Alison Coutanche
La Roche,
24530 Champagnac de Belair,
Dordogne

tel	+33 (0)5 53 54 22 91
e-mail	allisons@club-internet.fr
web	perso.club-internet.fr/allisons/

Domaine d'Essendieras

A panorama of apple orchards, river, lakes and two châteaux captures the visitor's eye on this 360-hectare estate. In a modernized outbuilding, each stylish bedroom has an original colour scheme, immaculate wooden floors, the odd country antique and a splendid bathroom with 21st-century shower. You will share breakfast, a sumptuous affair, with the Dutch owners or, in their absence, with charming Véronique. There's so much to do you may never leave: a vast heated pool with sauna and bar, three pool tables and an antique juke box in the baronial hall, cycling and fishing on the estate. A magnificent place.

rooms	5: 3 doubles, 2 twins.
price	€79-€110 for two.
meals	Dinner with wine €17.50, book ahead.
closed	Rarely.
directions	From Limoges D704 for St Yrieix; 60km right on D705 for Excideuil; 1km, house on right.

Ellen & Jeroen Bakker
Domaine d'Essendieras,
24160 St Médard d'Excideuil,
Dordogne

tel	+33 (0)5 53 52 81 51
fax	+33 (0)5 53 52 89 22
e-mail	info@essendieras.fr
web	www.essendieras.fr

photo Michael Busselle

limousin

Château de Sannat

The serene 18th-century château stands proud for all to see on the site of an ancient fort – oh, the panorama! Bedrooms are mostly vast, traditionally furnished, regally wallpapered, modern bathroomed; breakfast is seriously good. Madame, full of warmth and enthusiasm, has restored the exceptional, part-hanging gardens, and organises cookery courses. The atmosphere in the spectacular west-facing dining room, with its pale blue and yellow panelling, high-backed tapestried chairs and antique table may be informal, but the surroundings impose civilised dressing for dinner. *Golf nearby.*

rooms 4: 3 doubles, 1 twin.
price €115 for two.
meals Dinner with wine €35, book ahead.
closed Rarely.
directions From Poitiers N147 towards Limoges, through Bellac; left D96 for St Junien les Combes. 1st left in village for Rançon for 1km.

Comte & Comtesse Aucaigne de Sainte Croix
Château de Sannat,
87300 Bellac, Haute-Vienne
tel +33 (0)5 55 68 13 52
fax +33 (0)5 55 60 85 51
e-mail labeljack@aol.com
web www.chateausannat.com

Thoveyrat

Plain, simple and real French value, Thoveyrat is an organic meat farm (sheep and pigs) run by a sweet young couple who delight in their French country cooking, done with home-grown vegetables, lamb, duck, pigeon and rabbit (delicious pâtés). Myriam cares for their baby and guests while Pierre looks after the farm and sees to house improvements. The 18th-century farmhouse has lots of dark old wood – a sturdy great staircase, beams and timber framing – family clutter, fireplaces, peaceful, functional bedrooms and a garden full of toys.

rooms 4: 1 double, 1 triple, 2 family rooms, all with shower & basin, 3 wcs in corridor.
price €40 for two.
meals Dinner with wine €13, book ahead.
closed Rarely.
directions In Bellac follow signs to Limoges; just before leaving Bellac D3 right for Blond 4km to Thoveyrat. House sign on left.

Pierre & Myriam Morice
Thoveyrat,
87300 Blond,
Haute-Vienne
tel +33 (0)5 55 68 86 86
fax +33 (0)5 55 68 86 86
e-mail chambrehote@freesurf.fr

Château du Fraisse

For 800 years the Monstiers have adapted their château to family needs. It is now mainly a Renaissance gem by the great Serlio, whence warm limestone and a discreetly elegant portico, a Henry II staircase, an astonishing fireplace in the vast salon; a mix of grand and rustic. Your cultured hosts will greet you with warmth, happily tell you about house and history and show you to your room: fine furniture, paintings and prints, traditional furnishings; one bathroom has a fragment of a 16th-century fresco. If you return late at night you must climb the steep old spiral stair to your room as the main door is locked.

rooms	7: 1 double, 3 twins, 1 suite for 3, 2 suites for 4.
price	€92-€114 for two; €145 for three; €154 for four.
meals	Auberge 3km.
closed	Christmas.
directions	From A20 exit 23 to Bellac; Mézières sur Issoire; left to Nouic; château on left.

Comte & Comtesse des Monstiers Mérinville
Château du Fraisse,
87330 Nouic, Haute-Vienne
tel +33 (0)5 55 68 32 68
fax +33 (0)5 55 68 39 75
e-mail jfdesmon@aol.com
web www.chateau-du-fraisse.com

Les Chênes

Among lovely Limousin lakes and woods, here is a nature-loving, chemical-free house where natural materials triumph: wood outside and in (have you perchance strayed into the Alps?), cork insulation, organic food that includes meat and homemade bread, and they've been doing it for 30 years! The central heating is carried by steam ducts leading from the cooking-pot over the open fire. Lorenzo's paintings decorate the big airy rooms; Édith made all the upholstery, bedheads and patchworks; rooms have soothing colour schemes and more wood. And there are more fabulous colours, and walks, to be found outside.

rooms	3: 2 doubles, 1 triple.
price	€50 for two. Minimum stay 2 nights July & Aug.
meals	Dinner with wine €17, book ahead.
closed	Rarely.
directions	From A20 exit 25 D44 for St Sylvestre; left D78 for Grandmont & St Léger la Montagne; through Grandmont; right for Les Sauvages, 200m.

Lorenzo & Édith Rappelli
Les Chênes,
87240 St Sylvestre,
Haute-Vienne
tel +33 (0)5 55 71 33 12
fax +33 (0)5 55 71 33 12
e-mail les.chenes@wanadoo.fr
web www.leschenes-st-sylvestre.com

Niolet

A paradise of activity and fun for all: Marie was and Franck still is a sports teacher, they are gentle and educated, very involved in the community, live in a perfect old hamlet in the Périgord nature park and encourage guests to walk, ride and explore their lovely area. Their house is full of arts and crafts, there's a tepee for adventurous children, a sitting room packed with books and toys, special kids' cereals for breakfast as well as Marie's jams. The pretty bedrooms aren't huge but the welcome is and "Marie's chicken, sage and chestnut casserole was to die for" (an enthusiastic reader).

rooms	2: 1 double, 1 family suite for 4.
price	€42 for two.
meals	Dinner with wine €15, book ahead.
closed	Rarely.
directions	From Limoges N21 for Perigueux; at Sereillac D34 right to St Laurent.

Marie & Franck Robert
Niolet,
87310 St Laurent sur Gorre,
Haute-Vienne
tel +33 (0)5 55 48 21 50
fax +33 (0)5 55 48 21 50
e-mail niolet@9online.fr
web www.niolet.fr.fm

La Roche

It's homely yet exciting with Michel's works as artist and handyman everywhere: his sculptures lead you magically through the big, unusual garden; in the old stables, his iron balustrade and carved door frames open onto an abundance of ceiling and bed coverings in generous, painting-hung bedrooms. These are Josette's work, as are the opulent curtains, wall fabric and tented ceiling in the salon. An interesting, likeable couple of ex-Parisians, Michel has a fascinating studio/gallery, Josette loves cooking for vegetarians. The beautiful forested valley alone is worth the visit.

rooms	2 doubles.
price	€53 for two.
meals	Dinner with wine €17, book ahead.
closed	January-March.
directions	From Eymoutiers D30 for Chamberet. House in village of La Roche, 7km beyond Eymoutiers.

Michel & Josette Jaubert
La Roche,
87120 Eymoutiers,
Haute-Vienne
tel +33 (0)5 55 69 61 88
web clos.arts.free.fr

Moulin de Marsaguet

The nicest possible people, they have done just enough to this proud old building so it looks as it did 200 years ago when it forged cannon balls. The farm is relaxed and natural, they keep animals (including Lusitanian horses), three small children and a super potager, make pâtés and *confits* by the great mill pond and hang the *magrets* and hams to dry over the magnificent hearth in their big stone sitting room with its tatty sofa. Relish the drive up past tree-framed lake (boating possible) and stone outbuildings and the prospect of dining on home-grown ingredients. It's glorious. *Ask about pets when booking.*

rooms	3 doubles.
price	€39 for two.
meals	Dinner with wine €17, book ahead.
closed	October-15 April; Sundays July-August.
directions	From A20 exit 39 to Pierre Buffière; cross river D15 & D19 for St Yrieix for 15km. At Croix d'Hervy left D57 for Coussac Bonneval; mill on left after lake (7km).

Valérie & Renaud Gizardin
Moulin de Marsaguet,
87500 Coussac Bonneval,
Haute-Vienne
tel +33 (0)5 55 75 28 29
fax +33 (0)5 55 75 28 29

La Souvigne

Jacquie, half-French, and Ian, half-Hungarian, are fervent Francophiles who know the local people, history, flora and building regs. intimately and will tell you all. Indeed, aperitifs and dinner en famille, even breakfast in the separate guest house, are intensely stimulating occasions – not for shrinking violets. A professional chef, Ian serves superb food with a flourish and wines from his cellar. Their clever renovation of the little old village house makes for a communal kitchen, a biggish downstairs room and two cosy rooms under the rafters with Laura Ashley-style décor and some nice furniture.

rooms	3: 2 doubles, 1 twin.
price	€34-€37 for two.
meals	Dinner with wine €17, book ahead.
closed	Rarely.
directions	From Tulle N120 for Argentat Aurillac. Left into main square with Mairie on right, park in square on left of church.

Ian & Jacquie Hoare
La Souvigne,
19380 Forgès,
Corrèze
tel +33 (0)5 55 28 63 99
fax +33 (0)5 55 28 65 62
e-mail info@souvigne.com
web www.souvigne.com

Le Prézat

The Lardners were born to do B&B: interested in others, they genuinely love having visitors, their enthusiasm for their adopted area is infectious, Anne's cooking is superb – good wine too. The kitchen is a wonderful place, full of farm things and Anne's sunny presence – she delights in texture, smell and colour and her cooking reflects her pleasure. Their house restoration, done under Jim's caring guidance, is a form of perfection. Many local farmers are friends and visits can be arranged, proof of thorough integration among the rolling hills of rural France. Deep peace and really excellent value.

rooms	2 twins. Extra children's room.
price	€42 for two.
meals	Dinner with wine €21, book ahead.
closed	Rarely.
directions	From Argentat N120 for Tulle; left D921 for Brive. After 4km, left to Le Prézat; through hamlet; house on right with lawn.

Anne & Jim Lardner
Le Prézat,
19380 Albussac,
Corrèze
tel +33 (0)5 55 28 62 36
fax +33 (0)5 55 28 62 36
e-mail jlardner@libertysurf.fr

Hello

Map 11 Entry 526

La Poulvelarie

An accomplished architect who taps into unseen energies, vibrant Dorota offers far more than a luxurious bed in a cream-carpeted room. Her brilliantly converted old farm buildings are a rich tapestry of possibility: to every nook an exotic memento, to every cranny an art object, up and down levels into the computer studio or the home cinema (200 films), out into the gorgeous garden for the dreamlike hilltop view, a dip in the UV-purified pool or a picnic in the woods. Then back to the caring sharing house for meditation and talk, painting and massage, cosmopolitan cuisine in the convivial kitchen. Magic.

rooms	2 doubles.
price	€100-€150 for two.
meals	Dinner with wine €30; lunch €20; book ahead.
closed	Rarely.
directions	In Altillac left past ecomarché; for La Poulelaire; left opp. grey bins. House on right.

Dorota Katelbach
La Poulvelarie,
19120
Beaulieu sur Dordogne/Altillac,
Corrèze
tel +33 (0)5 55 91 50 91
fax +33 (0)5 55 91 06 26
e-mail info@betweenthedreams.com
web www.betweenthedreams.com

Hello

Map 11 Entry 527

Saulières

The delightful Madame Lafond was born in the area and will never move away – you will soon understand why. With rooms in a modern extension, Saulières is no ancient monument but it's a picture of genuine French rural style, blissfully quiet in its conservation area. Ideal for families, it has masses of space, lots of grass for playing on, a guest kitchen and big, log-fired living room with good old armchairs, magazines and games, plus some fabulous places to visit. The superbly 'family, friends and farming' atmosphere created by this highly likeable couple has been much praised.

rooms	4: 1 double, 1 twin, 1 triple, 1 quadruple.
price	€40 for two; €65 for four.
meals	Self-catering possible; good choice of restaurants, 2km.
closed	Rarely.
directions	From A20 exit Brive. A89 exit Tulle. N120 to Argentat; D12 along R. Dordogne for Beaulieu, past Monceaux to Saulières (6km from Argentat).

Marie-Jo & Jean-Marie Lafond
Saulières,
19400 Argentat, Corrèze
tel +33 (0)5 55 28 09 22
fax +33 (0)5 55 28 09 22
e-mail info@chambredhotes-saulieres.com
web www.chambredhotes-saulieres.com

La Farge

The stone hamlets take you back to another, slower France as you drive through these rugged valleys. The Archibalds have adopted the stones and the peace, updating them with their English sense of fine finish: an ancient cart carefully restored before being set alight with flowers, old windows fitted with the latest fly screens against sometime bugs, first-class showers. Pretty pastel rooms have honey-boarded floors and a teddy each; modern pine mixes with antique oak; the kitchen's solid farmhouse table, wood-burning stove and super food are the heart of this welcoming house.

rooms	3: 2 doubles; 1 twin with separate bath.
price	€50 for two.
meals	Dinner with wine €25, book ahead.
closed	Rarely.
directions	From Argentat D12; D83E1 for Le Vialard & Moustoulat; 3km right for La Farge; right again; 2nd house on right in village with black gates.

Keith & Helen Archibald
La Farge,
19400 Monceaux sur Dordogne, Corrèze
tel +33 (0)5 55 28 54 52
e-mail archi-at-lafarge@wanadoo.fr

L'Abbaye du Palais

Everything here is big, beautiful, generous: each marvellous wood-floored bathroom has a rolltop tub and a walk-in shower; high, square bedrooms have comfortable old furniture and fine embroidered linen; there are two pianos, some stupendous linden trees and so much heartfelt friendship. Martijn and Saskia left powerful jobs to bring their three young children to a life of nature and creativity in this exceptional old Cistercian abbey. With endless energy and delight, they'll share its wonders with you. And a sprig of rosemary on your pillow for sweet dreams – who cares about a worn blanket or two?

rooms	5: 1 double, 2 twins, 2 suites for 4.
price	€65-€95 for two.
meals	Dinner with wine from €30 (not on Wednesdays), book ahead. Picnic baskets can be arranged.
closed	Rarely.
directions	From Limoges N141 east through Bourganeuf for Pontarion; just after Bourganeuf, left onto D940A. Abbaye with blue gates 5km on right.

Martijn & Saskia Zandvliet-Breteler
L'Abbaye du Palais,
23400 Bourganeuf, Creuse
tel +33 (0)5 55 64 02 64
fax +33 (0)5 55 64 02 63
e-mail abbayedupalais@wanadoo.fr
web www.abbayedupalais.com

Les Montceaux

Brigitte-Marie's house is a breath of fresh air, a place of organised chaos where paintings by friends old and new, carvings from Borneo, antiques from her native Belgium and Bauhaus armchairs sing together in artistic harmony: objects of interest are everywhere. Bedrooms are vast, inviting and full of yet more original works – the two scenes of life in Zimbabwe are wonderful. Even the bathrooms are full of stylish character. Brigitte-Marie, a fabric designer, travelled a lot with her husband and is happy to be receiving appreciative guests in this old 1800s wine merchant's house which was the first in a land of cider.

rooms	2 doubles.
price	€40-€46 for two.
meals	Dinner with wine €16, book ahead.
closed	Rarely.
directions	From A20 exit 23 to Guéret; N145 to Gouzon; D997 to Boussac; D11 for Clugnat 4km; D13 for Domeyrot; 1.4km left D77. At 'Les Montceaux' on hill, right before chestnut tree. 1st house on right.

Brigitte-Marie Van de Wege
Les Montceaux,
23600 Toulx Ste Croix,
Creuse
tel +33 (0)5 55 65 09 55
e-mail brigitte.van-de-wege@wanadoo.fr
web perso.wanadoo.fr/chez.brigitte

La Courtepointe

Some habits die hard: this delightful, genuine, scatty couple were in haute couture so Daniel still wears a thimble on his thumb and Françoise teaches teddy-making. Their quirky 18th-century house is a collector's treasure chest where bouncy dog and exquisite patchwork contrast with fading wallpaper; cluttered terrace and double room have stunning views of medieval Boussac castle; you wade through dolls, teddies and scent bottles to the good chairs in the lovely, haphazard salon; bedrooms glory in fine furniture and handmade curtains. A totally French experience, an ideal touring base.

rooms	3: 1 double, 1 twin, 1 suite (double + bunk beds).
price	€48 for two.
meals	5 restaurants 500m.
closed	October.
directions	From A71 exit 10 on D94 W for 15km; right D916 to Boussac; in main square, road to left of Mairie; left again at butcher's; on right.

Françoise Gros & Daniel Colsenet
La Courtepointe,
23600 Boussac, Creuse

tel	+33 (0)5 55 65 80 09
fax	+33 (0)5 55 65 80 09
e-mail	courtepointe@wanadoo.fr
web	perso.wanadoo.fr/courtepointe

Some False Friends

Biologique and Organic

If you want organically-grown, chemical-free food in France, ask for items *de culture biologique*, called *bio* for short. If you talk about *organique*, people may think you're having trouble with your organs.

Donjon: medieval keep, all above ground, unlike an English dungeon.
Compote: Stewed fruit.
Marmelade: Well-stewed fruit.
Marmalade: *Confiture d'oranges amères* (bitter-orange jam).
Mousse (la): Mousse, as in lemon; or foam, lather, froth, as on sea, soap, beer; or foam rubber; or moss; or (*le mousse*) ship's boy.
Offrir: To give (for free), to offer; *offert*: free.
Prune: Plum; *pruneau*: prune.
Pomme de pin: fircone. Pineapple: *ananas*. *Pamplemousse*: grapefruit.
Grappe: bunch, cluster – *Grappe de raisins*: bunch of grapes.
Raisin: Generic term for the fruit of the vine: 'grapes'; one grape is *un grain de raisin*.
Raisins de Corinthe: currants; *raisins de Smyrne*: sultanas; *raisins secs*: raisins!
Une pie: Magpie – *La Pie Voleuse*: The Thieving Magpie; *une pie volante*: a flying magpie.
Tourte: a savoury pie with pastry on top.
Un pis (pronounced like pie): udder of any milking animal.
Scotch: Whisky or adhesive tape – context will tell...
Soldes: Sales, i.e. reduced-price goods, not yet sold.
Tartine: Usually half a baguette sliced lengthwise and buttered; *tartine grillée*: the same, toasted before being buttered.
Trouble: Cloudy, murky (liquid, story) – you can send that bottle back.
Troublé: Troubled, disturbed.
À la manière de... In the manner of...

photo Michael Busselle

auvergne

Manoir Le Plaix

Thick, thick walls, great old stones and timbers: the immense age of this gloriously isolated house, once a fortified manor, is evident but it has been beautifully restored. Big, cosy, subtly-lit rooms, lovingly decorated with family antiques and memorabilia, are reached by a treat of a spiral staircase. The family's cattle graze safely in the fields which surround the house – here, you can walk, fish and hunt mushrooms in season. Easy and good-natured, Madame Raucaz opens her heart, her intelligence and her dining table to all (excellent-value dinners). Relax and feel at home.

rooms	4: 2 doubles, 1 twin, 1 triple.
price	€45 for two.
meals	Dinner with wine €16, book ahead.
closed	Rarely.
directions	From Nevers N7 S 22km; right D978a to Le Veudre; D13 then D234 to Pouzy Mésangy. Signed.

Claire Raucaz
Manoir Le Plaix,
03320 Lurcy Levis,
Allier

tel	+33 (0)4 70 66 24 06
fax	+33 (0)4 70 66 25 82
e-mail	leplaix@yahoo.fr

Map 11 Entry 533

Demeure d'Hauterive

Opulent are those gilded curlicues, marble fireplaces and ornate mirrors; light pours in through the tall salon windows, bouncing off the glowing floor; even the games room is panelled. A fine mansion, built by a devout family whose bricks were refused for a church, it is now owned by a descendent of Corot and there's good art in every room as well as a small gallery. Lovely knowledgeable hosts who also have an excellent eye for colour. Their rooms are good enough for the glossies yet it remains an unpretentiously welcoming family house.

rooms	5: 2 doubles, 1 triple, 1 triple, 1 suite for 4.
price	€67-€73 for two.
meals	Dinner with wine €17-€23, book ahead.
closed	Rarely.
directions	From Moulins N9 S 20km; in Châtel de Neuvre left to La Ferté Hauterive; house on right.

Jérôme & Annick Lefebvre
Demeure d'Hauterive,
03340 La Ferté Hauterive,
Allier

tel	+33 (0)4 70 43 04 85
fax	+33 (0)4 70 43 00 62
e-mail	j.lefebvre@demeure-hauterive.com
web	www.demeure-hauterive.com

Map 11 Entry 534

Cognet

Billowing hilly pastures surround the hamlet with sensuality. Here, built in 1886 as a rich man's summer place, is a generous, sophisticated house, informed by Madame's broad cultural interests, her father's paintings and her superb Provençal furniture that sits so well by original panelling and wide fireplace. Alone up steep shiny stairs, the guest space is a sweep of pine floor and ceiling; light floods in past royal blue curtains, big pine bed, old chest; a proud tree shades the splendid shower room. Deep rest, super breakfast and conversation, Romanesque jewels to visit – a must. *Not suitable for children.*

rooms	1 twin/double.
price	€60 for two; book ahead.
meals	Restaurant in village.
closed	November-February.
directions	From A75 exit Gannat to Vichy; over Allier; immed. right Bd JFK, left for Cusset; over railway; 5 traffic lights, D906 right for Ferrières; right D995 9km; left D121; bear right to Cognet 800m. House with iron gates.

Bénita Mourges
Cognet,
03300 La Chapelle,
Allier
tel +33 (0)4 70 41 88 28
e-mail andre.mourges@wanadoo.fr

8 route de la Limagne

A generous and handsome family house: the volcanoes gave their lava for dining room and staircase floor slabs; ancestors gave their names for bedrooms where their faded photographs and intricate samplers hang on the walls. Others left some fine old *objets* and pieces of furniture and built the stupendous brick barns that shelter the garden; Élisabeth applied all her flair to the décor, marrying vital colour harmonies and soft fabrics. She is dynamic, intelligent and full of wry humour, once a trace of shyness has worn off, and serves her deliciously wholesome breakfast in the flower-decked garden in summer.

rooms	3 doubles.
price	€58-€64 for two.
meals	Good restaurants 9km.
closed	November-March, except by arrangement.
directions	From A71, Riom exit, N144 for Combronde & Montluçon. 2.5km after Davayat, right onto D122 to Chaptes.

Mme Élisabeth Beaujeard
8 route de la Limagne,
63460 Beauregard Vendon,
Puy-de-Dôme
tel +33 (0)4 73 63 35 62

Château de Vaulx

Is this real or a fairy tale? Creak along the parquet, pray in the chapel, swan around the salon, sleep in one tower, bath in another. It's been in the family for 800 years and room names are as evocative as furnishings are romantic – worthy of the troubadours who surely sang here. Breakfast of home-hive honey, brioche, yogurt, eggs, cheese, get to know your delightfully entertaining hosts, visit the donkey, admire the magnificent trees or, if you're feeling homesick, have a drink in Guy's evocatively vaulted cellar *pub* with its impressive collection of beer mats. A dream of a place.

rooms	2: 1 double, 1 triple.
price	€50-€70 for two.
meals	Auberge 3km.
closed	Rarely.
directions	From A72 exit 3 on D7 through Celles sur Durolle to Col du Frissonnet. Château 1st right after Col du Frissonnet.

Guy & Régine Dumas de Vaulx
Château de Vaulx,
63120 Ste Agathe,
Puy-de-Dôme

tel +33 (0)4 73 51 50 55
fax +33 (0)4 73 51 50 55

Domaine de Ternant

Ternant is *grand style* – marble, mouldings, gilt frames – with modern touches to prevent any stiffness, Madame's astoundingly beautiful patchwork hangings to make it utterly personal and the scent of beeswax hovering. All is pure Auvergne: owners, house, original porcelain basins, fabulous breakfasts. Bedrooms have antique beds – brass, carved, delicious 1930s – on polished parquet with good rugs and, of course, Madame's artistic needle. The dining room is elegant, the salon sophisticated, the billiard room a library. An interesting couple who have lived in foreign lands and enjoy their guests.

rooms	4: 1 double, 1 twin, 2 suites for 4.
price	€82-€86 for two.
meals	Good choice of restaurants 3-10km.
closed	15 November-15 March.
directions	From A71 for Clermont Ferrand; exit Riom for Volvic & Puy de Dôme; at Le Cratère, left for Clermont; right for Chanat, 3km Ternant, signposted.

Catherine Piollet
Domaine de Ternant,
63870 Orcines,
Puy-de-Dôme

tel +33 (0)4 73 62 11 20
fax +33 (0)4 73 62 29 96
e-mail domaine.ternant@free.fr
web domaine.ternant.free.fr

Sailles

Perched above Saint Nectaire with views of almost endless forest and mountain, it's the farmhouse in the perfect setting. Inside lives Monique, enthusing her guests with descriptions of the Auvergne in perfect English. She does not pretend to provide luxury, just cosy comfort and the feeling of being in a real home. You stay in an attached but independent cottage and have a kitchen area of your own, but breakfast in Monique and Daniel's vaulted dining room, full of exposed beams and stone; eat copiously and enjoy the humour and zest of a couple who were born to hospitality.

rooms	1 double.
price	€42 for two.
meals	Restaurants in St Nectaire. Guests' kitchen available.
closed	December-January.
directions	From A75 exit 6 to St Nectaire; at church D150 for 1.5km; left D643. Last house 300m.

Monique Deforge
Sailles,
63710 St Nectaire,
Puy-de-Dôme
tel +33 (0)4 73 88 40 08
e-mail daniel.deforge@wanadoo.fr

La Closerie de Manou

What is B&B perfection? Spring water running from the taps of a huge walk-in shower? La Closerie, a typical old stone-walled and shingled house, sits among the ancient volcanoes of Auvergne where great rivers rise and water is pure. Françoise, called Manou, is a delight, sprightly and elegant, as generous with her time as with her scrumptious embroidered-napkin buffet breakfast, served in the impressive dining room or the garden. Bedrooms are perfect, hung with silk, hairdryers hide in bathrooms; in short, every modern comfort against a timeless backdrop of drama and character. *Book ahead.*

rooms	5: 2 doubles, 1 twin, 2 triples.
price	€60-€70 for two.
meals	Several good restaurants in village.
closed	15 November-February.
directions	From A71 & 75 exit 2 on D799 to Bordeaux; N189, 23km; left D983 to Le Mont Dore by Col du Gery; in Mont Dore right for Murat le Quaire; pass Mairie, 3km to Le Genestoux. House signposted.

Françoise Larcher
La Closerie de Manou,
63240 Le Mont Dore,
Puy-de-Dôme
tel +33 (0)4 73 65 26 81
fax +33 (0)4 73 65 58 34
e-mail lacloseriedemanou@club-internet.fr
web www.auvergne.maison-hotes.com

Le Chastel Montaigu

The solid reality of this magical tower is deeply moving. Michel's skill in renovation (well, reconstruction from near-ruin), Anita's decorating talent, their passionate dedication, have summoned a rich and sober mood that makes the 15th-century *chastel* throb with authenticity: only 'medieval' materials; magnificent deep-tinted fabrics, many designed by Anita; antique tapestries, panelling and furniture – nothing flashy, all simply true to the density of the place. Spectacular bedrooms, amazing bathrooms of antique-faced modern perfection and a generous breakfast – this is a treat.

rooms	3 doubles.
price	€87-€125 for two. Minimum stay 2 nights.
meals	Auberge & traditional restaurants 1-4km.
closed	December-February.
directions	From A75 exit 6 for St Nectaire; through Champeix to Montaigut le Blanc; follow signs up to château.

Anita & Michel Sauvadet
Le Chastel Montaigu,
63320 Montaigut le Blanc,
Puy-de-Dôme
tel +33 (0)4 73 96 28 49
fax +33 (0)4 73 96 21 60
web www.le-chastel-montaigu.com

Château de Pasredon

Whichever of the splendid rooms is yours – we loved the yellow *Louis Philippe* – you will feel grand: here a canopied bed, there an exquisite little dressing room, everywhere shimmering mirrors, fabulous views of acres of parkland, ancient trees, the Puy-de-Dôme. The vast, panelled, period-furnished drawing and dining rooms are quite dramatic. A perfect hostess, Madame makes you feel immediately at ease and helps you plan your day over a delicious breakfast. She will show you the 14th-century vaulted chapel, the walled garden and how to make lace (*dentelle du Puy*). Really very special.

rooms	5: 3 doubles, 1 twin, 1 suite.
price	€65-€90 for two.
meals	Excellent restaurants 2-8km.
closed	15 October-15 April.
directions	From Clermont Ferrand A75 exit 13 to Parentignat; D999 for St Germain l'Herme 6km; sign on right. (8km from A75 exit.)

Henriette Marchand
Château de Pasredon,
63500 St Rémy de Chargnat,
Puy-de-Dôme
tel +33 (0)4 73 71 00 67
fax +33 (0)4 73 71 08 72

Ma Cachette

Pierre is the gardener, Johan the cook and Frederick a brilliant handyman. All South African, your charming hosts left the film and television world for this aqua-shuttered village house in the heart of the Regional Park. A few steps from the romantic, private garden, lush with roses, ancient fruit trees and well-tended vegetables, will find you walking some of the most stunning and unspoilt trails through the Massif Central. Rooms have Persian carpets and garden flowers; a stylish living room is for guests. And do have dinner: you'll enjoy the conversation as much as the *confit de canard*.

rooms	4: 3 doubles, 1 twin.
price	€50-€55 for two.
meals	Dinner with wine €23, book ahead.
closed	Rarely.
directions	From A72 exit 2 for Thiers (west); D906 for Ambert & Le Puy en Velay; 67km, signs on entering Arlanc; close to Roman church on left.

Johan Bernard, Pierre Knoesen & Frederick Bezuidenhout
Ma Cachette,
63220 Arlanc, Puy-de-Dôme
tel +33 (0)4 73 95 04 88
fax +33 (0)4 73 95 04 88
e-mail cachette@club-internet.fr
web www.ma-cachette.com

La Jacquerolle

Built on the ramparts of the ancient town, just below the medieval Abbey whose August music festival draws thousands, the old house has been lovingly filled with flowers in every fashion and form – carpets, curtains, wallpaper, quilts. It is a soft French boudoir where mother and daughter, quietly attentive, welcome their guests to sleep in cosy, pine-slatted bedrooms with firm-mattressed divan beds and good little bathrooms (some with wonderful views out to the hills) and enjoy true Gallic cuisine enhanced by bone china and bohemian crystal before the huge stone fireplace.

rooms	4: 1 double, 1 twin, 2 triples.
price	€55-€58 for two.
meals	Dinner with wine €22, book ahead.
closed	Rarely.
directions	From Brioude D19 to La Chaise Dieu. Head for Centre Ville; facing Abbey, right to Place du Monument. Park here; house is off square: bottom right-hand corner then down on left.

Jacqueline & Carole Chailly
La Jacquerolle,
43160 La Chaise Dieu,
Haute-Loire
tel +33 (0)4 71 00 07 52
e-mail lajacquerolle@hotmail.com

Le Bourg

Simple, unaffected people and keen walkers love Rosa, her somewhat dated décor and her fabulous home-grown, homemade food which oozes genuine natural goodness. A real old soldier, she manages the flock of milk-producing sheep, is surrounded by grandchildren and welcomes all-comers with a 'cup of friendship' before her great granite hearth. The house is warm, the rooms basic but perfectly adequate, the meals good, the hostess unforgettable. And walkers can join a circuit here and walk from B&B to B&B in this superbly unspoilt area; or cross-country ski through it in winter.

rooms	3: 1 double, 1 twin, 1 triple.
price	€36 for two.
meals	Dinner with wine €12, book ahead.
closed	November-February.
directions	From Le Puy en Velay, D589 to Saugues; D585 for Langeac, left onto D32 to Venteuges.

Rosa Dumas
Le Bourg,
43170 Venteuges,
Haute-Loire
tel +33 (0)4 71 77 80 66

Domaine de Luc

Such a heart-filled house, no wonder Olivia, with her husband's support, is battling to keep it in the family. Her ancestor built it in 1900 and grew hay for stagecoach horses. He also planted the lime tree walk to the lake – you can swim, row, fish and picnic all day long. The house is amiable, uncluttered, full of the charm of things imperfect: antique and modern pine beds in parquet-floored family-friendly rooms, big homely bathrooms, the warm kitchen or elegant panelled dining room for meals, lots of light from the rolling Cantal wilds, space for all and their mounts and real hospitality.

rooms	6: 1 suite; 1 family room & 1 double sharing separate bath; 2 doubles & 1 family room sharing separate bath.
price	€60-€75 for two.
meals	Dinner €20, book ahead; wine €5 or wine-list.
closed	Rarely.
directions	A75 exit 25; for St Poncy. Signposted.

Olivia Brunel
Domaine de Luc,
15500 St Poncy,
Cantal
tel +33 (0)4 71 23 06 79
fax +33 (0)4 71 23 06 79
e-mail ddeluc15@wanadoo.fr
web www.domaine-de-luc.com

Château de Lescure

On the slope of Europe's largest extinct volcano, where nine valleys radiate for fabulous walking, stands a rustic 18th-century manor guarded by an 11th-century tower where two vaulted bedrooms soar, one, up stairs for the nimble only, with four-poster. The elegant twin room has the right furbelows and in the glorious inglenook kitchen Sophie serves home-smoked ham and veg from her organic garden. She and Michel are cultured, bilingual hosts. You play an instrument? Bring it with you. Bridge? Bring your tricks. Or possibly volunteer for bread making, cooking, organic gardening, trail blazing...

rooms	3: 1 twin; 1 double with separate shower; 1 double with separate shower room downstairs.
price	€60-€65 for two. Minimum stay 2 nights in summer.
meals	Dinner with wine €23, book ahead. Super restaurant in Laguiole.
closed	Rarely.
directions	From Clermont Ferrand A75 to St Flour; up to old town; left D921 10km; right D990, through Pierrefort to St Martin. Right for Brezons; château 3km on right.

Michel Couillaud
& Phoebe Sophie Verhulst
Château de Lescure,
15230 Saint Martin Sous Vigouroux,
Cantal
tel +33 (0)4 71 73 40 91
fax +33 (0)4 71 73 40 84
e-mail michel.couillaud@wanadoo.fr
web www.multimania.com/psvlescure

Map 11 Entry 547

Lou Ferradou

Your young hosts escaped from heaving, stressful Paris to this rural paradise where their brilliant conversion of an old Cantal farmhouse has preserved the original scullery ledge and sink (vast slabs of stone), the beams, the inglenook. They now aim to convert their neighbours to better environmental (get the scrap metal off the hillside) and social (more respect for your woman?) attitudes. Bedrooms are country comfortable with big oak beds and white counterpanes, the meals are feasts, there are a games room, billiards and books, a sitting room in the barn, and the Balleux are a most interesting and happy couple.

rooms	5: 1 double, 1 suite; 2 suites, 1 double in cottage.
price	€42-€54 for two; half-board €34-€40.
meals	Dinner with wine €13, book ahead.
closed	Rarely.
directions	From Aurillac D920 to Arpajon; left on D990 for 10km (don't go to St Étienne de Carlat); left for Caizac; signposted.

Francine & Jacky Balleux
Lou Ferradou,
15130 St Étienne de Carlat,
Cantal
tel +33 (0)4 71 62 42 37
fax +33 (0)4 71 62 42 37
e-mail lou.ferradou@tiscali.fr
web www.louferradou.com

Map 11 Entry 548

Château de la Vigne

A rare treat, an experience from another age: the deliciously organic old château in pure Cantal style surveying the panorama has been in the family for ever and is utterly lavish. The courtroom panelled and dazzlingly painted; the fine and formal dining room (do dress for dinner); the Aubusson-hung, chandeliered salon; the Louis XV guest room with its lovely carved fireplace, the darkly four-postered Troubadour room, the bathrooms squeezed into impossible places... a remarkable Dinky Toy collection, and more. Stunning but not overbearing, and yours to share with these gentle, open, aristocratic hosts.

rooms	4: 2 doubles, 1 twin, 1 triple.
price	€122 for two.
meals	Dinner €25, book ahead, wine-list.
closed	November-Easter.
directions	From Clermont-Ferrand N89 for Tulle; left D922 to Bort les Orgues; D681 to Mauriac & Ally. Signs.

Bruno & Anne du Fayet de la Tour
Château de la Vigne,
15700 Ally, Cantal

tel	+33 (0)4 71 69 00 20
fax	+33 (0)4 71 69 00 20
e-mail	la.vigne@wanadoo.fr
web	www.chateaudelavigne.com

Château de Bassignac

Its front door wide open, Bassignac is real unposh family B&B run, for many years, by charming, active Annie with the support of her artist husband (come and paint with him). She was born in this 16th-century fortified manor built on 13th-century ruins beside what is now a fairly busy road and sold her Parisian furniture shop to come back and... furnish her guest rooms. They are big (two or three windows, fireplace) and small (invitingly womb-like), kempt and clear with Monsieur's watercolours and a dated chintzy charm that draws people back. Son and daughter-in-law run a delicious *ferme auberge* next door.

rooms	6: 4 doubles, 1 family room, 1 family apartment for 5.
price	€60-€130 for two.
meals	Dinner with wine €45, occasionally available, book ahead. Auberge next door.
closed	Rarely.
directions	D922 from Mauriac for Bort les Orgues Basignac; 16km on right.

Annie & Jean-Michel Besson
Château de Bassignac,
15240 Saignes,
Cantal

tel	+33 (0)4 71 40 82 82
fax	+33 (0)4 71 40 82 82
e-mail	chateau.bassignac@wanadoo.fr

photo Michael Busselle

midi-pyrénées

Manoir de Malagorse

Passionate eager hosts, a refined old manor in an idyllic setting, magnificent rooms, meals cooked by a master (in winter they run an alpine restaurant). Abel and Anna's restoration is caring and sophisticated, rooms and bathrooms are statements of simple luxury, the great kitchen, where cookery demonstrations and meals happen, is a dream, its cooker a wonder to behold, fireplace massive, ceiling vaulted. There is space for togetherness and privacy, your hosts are unintrusively present and Anna can offer a professional massage after Abel's demanding wine-tastings. You get more than you pay for – enjoy it to the hilt.

rooms	6 doubles.
price	€100-€125 for two.
meals	Dinner €36 book ahead; good wine list.
closed	Mid-October-May.
directions	From Souillac 6km; N20 for Cressensac, on dual carriageway 1st right to Cuzance, Église de Rignac; 1st right in Rignac, signposted.

Anna & Abel Congratel
Manoir de Malagorse,
46600 Cuzance,
Lot

tel	+33 (0)5 65 27 15 61
fax	+33 (0)5 65 27 15 61
e-mail	acongratel@manoir-de-malagorse.fr
web	www.manoir-de-malagorse.fr

Map 10 Entry 551

Moulin de Goth

Frogs and kingfishers enchant the pool, a 13th-century mill, brilliantly restored by its generous, welcoming Australian owners, guards a garden of peace and beauty, lily pads and lawns, willows and water – it is ineffably lovely. Coral sings like a bird (garden choir concerts in summer) and cooks like an angel; Bill, former marathon-runner, makes tables and intelligent conversation – do join him for billiards. Big, properly-raftered rooms have cast-iron beds, soft fabrics, antique chests. The dining room is anciently barrel-vaulted but meals are mostly in the glorious garden. *Children over 10 welcome.*

rooms	2: 1 double, 1 triple, both with separate baths.
price	€60 for two.
meals	Dinner with wine €20, book ahead.
closed	Rarely.
directions	From Martel on N140 D23 for Creysse. After 3km right fork for Le Goth, 1.5km; 1st house on right after stone bridge.

Coral Heath-Kauffman
Moulin de Goth,
46600 Creysse,
Lot

tel	+33 (0)5 65 32 26 04
e-mail	coral.heath@wanadoo.fr
web	www.moulindugoth.com

Map 10 Entry 552

Pouch

The old farmhouse is quaint and inviting with its steep roofs and light-coloured stone: the Bells' restoration has been a labour of love. The original character of beams, old floors and twisty corners has been preserved, furnishing is simple with cast-iron beds, original paintings and, in the huge living-kitchen, an open hearth and a closed stove. It's not smart, just family-comfortable and relaxed. Gavin, an artist and potter, and Lillian, an easy, open person, left South Africa to live with their young son in this quiet place. They'll give you a great welcome – and you can picnic if you want.

rooms	2: 1 double, 1 double & bunks.
price	€50 for two.
meals	Restaurants 2km.
closed	Rarely.
directions	From Brive N20 S 10 km; N140 for Rocamadour; D673 to Alvignac, through town, right after glassblower, follow signs for Pouch.

Gavin & Lillian Bell
Pouch,
46500 Rignac,
Lot

tel	+33 (0)5 65 33 66 84
fax	+33 (0)5 65 33 71 31
e-mail	lilianbel@aol.com
web	www.bellfrance.com

Map 11 Entry 553

La Buissonnière

The converted 18th-century barn with its great Lot views feels instantly like home. Madame spent years in America (she's bilingual), loves ceramics and patchwork, uses her creative touch everywhere, including the terrace and garden with its secluded spots, and is a fount of historical and cultural lore. The open-plan living room, where old skylights deliver splashes of sky, is full of artistic character with oak floors, old stove and pretty antiques beneath paintings of all periods. The airy ground-floor guest room has its own antique writing table, watercolours and a glazed stable door to the garden.

rooms	1 twin/double with separate bath; extra room for children.
price	€52 for two.
meals	Dinner with wine €16, book ahead.
closed	Rarely.
directions	From Gramat N140 for Figeac; left for 'Le Bout du Lieu' after sign for Thémines; house, 200m on left; signposted.

Élisabeth de Lapérouse Coleman
La Buissonnière,
46120 Thémines,
Lot

tel	+33 (0)5 65 40 88 58
fax	+33 (0)5 65 40 88 58
e-mail	edelaperouse.coleman@wanadoo.fr

Map 16 Entry 554

Mas de la Feuille

Charles cooks – the huge kitchen is his domain – and meals, French or Franco-Japanese, are memorable. Kako paints – even the wooden coat hangers bear her flowers. The house is French and spotless. All bedrooms, in the older, lower part of the house, have an exceptionally tranquil rolling view, superb mattresses and lush bathrooms; the oldest has an ancient stone fireplace and the original stone sink. They are delightful people, a multi-talented, cosmopolitan couple who keep house here in the summer and live in Japan in the winter. And Figeac is said to be one of the best-renovated towns in Europe.

rooms: 3; 2 twins, 1 suite for 3.
price: €50 for two.
meals: Dinner with wine €25, book ahead.
closed: November-March
directions: From Gramat N140 for Figeac 17km; through Le Bourg, sharp left immediately after small bridge on edge of village. Sign on left, 1km.

Kako & Charles Larroque
Mas de la Feuille,
46120 Le Bourg,
Lot
tel: +33 (0)5 65 11 00 17
fax: +33 (0)5 65 11 00 17
e-mail: larroquecharles@club-internet.fr

La Maison Jaune

The whole house has a light, happy feel and Gisèle, a much-loved B&B owner, is making guests feel utterly at home again in this brand-new, architect-designed house. It is horseshoe-shaped: owners' and guests' wings flank a fine big kitchen/living area with a clever mix of modern and antique furniture, some good Art Deco ornaments and a wall of window onto the pool terrace. Bedrooms, Apricot and Raspberry, are prettily done in pine and comfort with super bathrooms. And Gisèle still cooks with delight, including her organic jams. An exceptional place. *Will drop walkers with no car at the next B&B.*

rooms: 2: 1 twin, 1 family suite for 4-5.
price: €48 for two; €71 for four.
meals: Dinner with wine €16, book ahead.
closed: Rarely.
directions: From Gourdon D673 for Fumel; to Salviac; from Crédit Agricole bank straight ahead & follow signs to Bertrand Joly.

Gisèle & Alain Hauchecorne
La Maison Jaune,
46430 Salviac,
Lot
tel: +33 (0)5 65 41 48 52
fax: +33 (0)5 65 41 48 52
e-mail: lamaisonjaune@wanadoo.fr
web: perso.wanadoo.fr/lamaison.jaune/

Valrose - Le Poujal

The Italian ambassador, homesick for Florence, built this house and its balustraded terrace overlooking the river in 1805. It has a beautiful garden and a swimming pool in a flowery corner of the lawn (for guests in the mornings) but inside, the first word that comes to mind is 'dramatic'. The library is raspberry with a zebra throw over the black leather sofa while the big, white beamed dining room – once the kitchen perhaps? – is dominated by a vast fireplace, bold still-lifes and red and white checks. A teacher, who loves to talk to people, Claude is due to retire soon and finds B&B the perfect solution.

rooms	2 doubles.
price	€50 for two.
meals	Choice of restaurants nearby.
closed	Rarely.
directions	From Cahors D8 to Pradines; right at roundabout; house 100m down on right through big gates.

Claude Faille
Valrose - Le Poujal,
46090 Pradines,
Lot
tel +33 (0)5 65 22 18 52
e-mail claude.faille@libertysurf.fr
web valrose.chez.tiscali.fr/

Flaynac

A heart-warming and very French experience, staying with this lovely cheerful couple who are always ready for a drink and a chat (in French) – their love of life is infectious. Use the peaceful terrace where your hosts are happy for you to sit all day over your breakfast, revelling in the setting, the vast views and the flowering garden. The décor – floral papers and family furniture – is in keeping with the old farmhouse. No dinner but lots of home-grown wine and aperitif, fruit from their trees and *gâteau de noix* (walnut cake) with their own honey – flowing as in paradise.

rooms	1 double with curtained-off shower & wc.
price	€45 for two.
meals	Good restaurant 2km.
closed	Rarely.
directions	From Cahors D8 for Pradines 8km; at sign for Flaynac, follow Chambres d'Hôtes sign on right, then right & right again.

M & Mme Jean Faydi
Flaynac,
46090 Pradines,
Lot
tel +33 (0)5 65 35 33 36

Maison Rouma

Dr Rouma, a distinguished local figure and Consul General, built the house in the 1850s. It was almost a ruin before the Arnetts found it on their return from Japan and restored it, keeping as much of the original as possible, including the wallpaper in the hall where the winding staircase is such a delight. The décor has an oriental tendency, particularly in the enormous dining room. The setting just couldn't be better; there are stunning views over the river and the pretty old town – famous for its medieval music festival which climaxes, by the way, with the "largest firework display in France".

rooms	3: 2 doubles, 1 twin.
price	€50 for two.
meals	Choice of restaurants nearby.
closed	Rarely.
directions	From Cahors D911 for Fumel & Villeneuve sur Lot. At Puy l'Évêque take Rue du Dr Rouma to bridge: house last on right before bridge.

Bill & Ann Arnett
Maison Rouma,
46700 Puy l'Évêque,
Lot

tel	+33 (0)5 65 36 59 39
fax	+33 (0)5 65 36 59 39
e-mail	williamarnett@hotmail.com
web	www.puyleveque.com

Mondounet

The golden Lot stone glows, there are stunning views over two valleys, the pool is solar-heated and salt-purified, so what matter if rooms are smallish with limited storage and the atmosphere sometimes a little chaotic. The Scotts labour ever on at their little empire, restoring the 17th-century farmhouse and outbuildings to their original character and adding modern comforts. Zoé will charm you, see you have a good time, serve breakfast at any time. Dinner, sometimes a poolside barbecue, is fun, relaxed and informal and Peter plays the guitar. There is a pool-house kitchen for lazy picnic lunches.

rooms	1 double.
price	€43-€55 for two.
meals	Dinner with wine €18, book ahead.
closed	Rarely, please book ahead.
directions	From Cahors for Toulouse; at r'bout D653 for Agen 16km; at junc. right D656 for 14km; through Villesèque, Sauzet, Bovila; after Bovila, 3rd left; signposted.

Peter & Zoé Scott
Mondounet,
46800 Fargues,
Lot

tel	+33 (0)5 65 36 96 32
fax	+33 (0)5 65 31 84 89
e-mail	scotsprops@aol.com
web	www.mondounetholidaysandhomes.com

Domaine de Lacombe

The elegant, flamboyantly decorated great barn living room reveals Michèle's sense of adventure, the books and baby grand tell of her earlier life as a bookseller and her love of music, the variegated bedrooms in the converted pigsties and stables, from modern simplicity to traditional florality, speak of her eclectic taste. Some have their own patios, one has the original spring welling up behind glass, all have space, privacy and fine bathrooms. Michèle bubbles with delight, encouraging guests to come chat while she prepares a superb family meal to be shared sitting on rainbow chairs at the deep red table.

rooms: 4: 1 double, 1 triple, 1 family room, 1 suite for 4.
price: €60-€92 for two.
meals: Dinner with wine €23, book ahead; restaurants in Castelnau.
closed: Rarely.
directions: From Paris A20 to Cahors Nord, exit 52; N20 to Montauban Toulouse; right for Castelnau-M., in Castelnau D19 right to Lauzerte Moissac; 2km, left 100m after brick barn. Lacombe 2nd left

Michèle Lelourec
Domaine de Lacombe,
46170 Castelnau Monratier,
Lot
tel: +33 (0)5 65 21 84 16
fax: +33 (0)5 65 21 84 49
e-mail: michele.lelourec@free.fr
web: www.domaine-lacombe.com

Map 15 Entry 561

Mas de Guerre

Walkers with a taste for magnificent bathrooms and rare orchids (Gary's delight), this is for you. Food lovers too: Sheila always aims to produce a feast – traditional with a twist. They left city jobs for these wild spaces, did a superb restoration of this old house with huge attention to detail and now... B&B: a certain formality still hangs in the air. The big guest rooms in the old stables could scarcely be bettered: original stone flags, white-painted stone walls, classically comfortable new furniture, gorgeous old tiles in the bathrooms. Your attentive hosts do expect you to be out between 11am and 4pm.

rooms: 4 doubles.
price: €55-€60 for two.
meals: Dinner €18-€20, book ahead.
closed: Rarely
directions: From Cahors, D911 to Limogne-en-Quercy; D24 to Beauregard; right next to rack containing Buta gas canisters & follow signs.

Sheila & Gary Tucknott
Mas de Guerre,
46260 Beauregard,
Lot
tel: +33 (0)5 65 24 32 86
e-mail: masdeguerre@freesurf.fr
web: www.masdeguerre.com

Map 16 Entry 562

La Grange

Tranquillity itself. The 19th-century house and its wonderful converted barn for guests are enchanting and Colette's garden adds to the magic, a little paradise with every cranny a carefully unmanicured, flower-filled delight. Breakfast in a shady arbour, while away the afternoon in a steamer chair, sink into a deep sofa with a good book before the open fire. Charming, stylish and utterly welcoming, Colette pours as much enthusiasm into looking after her guests as her garden. Inviting, spotless bedrooms, done with refined simple taste, tempt the weary with their garden views. A true find for peace seekers.

rooms	3 doubles.
price	€56 for two.
meals	Restaurants in Parisot, 2km.
closed	Rarely.
directions	From Caylus D926 for Villefranche de Rouergue; pass Parisot; left for Belvésé; signposted.

Mme Colette Norga
La Grange,
82160 Parisot,
Tarn-et-Garonne
tel +33 (0)5 63 67 07 58
fax +33 (0)5 63 67 07 58

Ferme du Gendre

"Her smile is fabulous." And Le Gendre is pure rural Frenchness, a working farm where fowl and pigs roam. Lively and empathetic, these people share their home easily, without fuss: rustic, cluttered living room with an open fire; simply-furnished, spotless bedrooms with slightly old-fashioned patterns and good beds; breakfast coffee in a bowl and, with that lovely smile, Madame taking you in as family. Her dogs and cats are as friendly as she is. Go lightly on lunch: dinner is uncompromisingly, deliciously 'farmhouse' with portions suitable for a hard-working farmer – she loves feeding her guests.

rooms	2: 1 double, 1 suite for 4.
price	€38 for two.
meals	Dinner with wine €14, book ahead.
closed	Rarely.
directions	N20 S from Cahors to Caussade; left D926 to Septfonds; 3km beyond, left for Gaussou. Farm 1km on; signposted.

Françoise & Jean-Louis Zamboni
Ferme du Gendre,
82240 Lavaurette,
Tarn-et-Garonne
tel +33 (0)5 63 31 97 72

Domaine de Canals

Monsieur is passionate about the garden of his old family home which is a dream of trees, shrubs, lilypond and rare plants (their daughter is a botanist): a pergola awaits the contemplative guest, a maze summons the adventurous. Inside, the suite's gentle country décor is coloured with memories of Egypt, Mexico, India as well as Madame's hand-painted furniture. Opening onto the courtyard, the more old-fashioned double room has its own tapestry-hung hall and a wood-burning stove. More tapestries hang in the antique-filled dining room, the atmosphere is safe and friendly, the conversation full of interest.

rooms	2: 1 double, 1 suite for 6.
price	€45-€75 for two; €105-€125 for six.
meals	Dinner with wine €15-€22, book ahead.
closed	Rarely.
directions	At Nègrepelisse D64 to Bioule; left after Bioule on D78 for Realville; at La Bouffière house on right after cemetery.

M & Mme Auréjac
Domaine de Canals,
82800 Bioule,
Tarn-et-Garonne
tel +33 (0)5 63 64 21 07
fax +33 (0)5 63 64 21 85
e-mail aurejac.arnaud@wanadoo.fr
web domaine-de-canals.fr.st

Maison des Chevaliers

The door opens onto the bricks and beams of the hall of this huge old house – you're in for a treat. Fascinating proofs of the owners' lives abroad steal your eyes at every turn, their conversation sparkles with anecdotes and interest, their house oozes taste and style. Bedrooms are big, all differently charming with antiques from Spain and Portugal, stencilled wood, superb paint finishes, old lace – it's endlessly, originally beautiful. The courtyard calls for summer breakfast, the secluded pool for cooling dips, the library for contemplation. The crowning glory? Madame once owned a restaurant.

rooms	4: 2 doubles, 2 suites.
price	€65 for two.
meals	Dinner with wine €20, book ahead.
closed	Rarely.
directions	From Castelsarrasin for Toulouse, RN113; exit Escatalens; to 'centre du village'; house next to church.

Claudine Choux
Maison des Chevaliers,
82700 Escatalens,
Tarn-et-Garonne
tel +33 (0)5 63 68 71 23
fax +33 (0)5 63 30 25 90
e-mail claude.choux@wanadoo.fr
web www.maisondeschevaliers.com

Las Bourdolles

The Quercy light glides through deep window reveals to dapple the creamy old stones, dark beams and warm floorboards of this 17th-century farmhouse: the pilgrims' welcome cockleshell on the eaves is still deserved; nature-loving walkers and culture vultures flock here. Linda and Erica use a light touch, mixing old and new, cooking with delight, be it hearty game dinners or plum jam. The bedroom is soft and simple, colours pale, the great stone fireplace marvellous in winter. Having thrown over the pinstripe business life they are happily growing vegetables and welcoming visitors to peace.

rooms	1 suite.
price	€60-€90 for two.
meals	Dinner with wine €25; lunch €15, book ahead.
closed	Christmas.
directions	A62 exit 8; D953 to Golfech & Lauzerte. Before Lauzerte, right onto D34 to Castelnau-Montratier. At church x-roads, straight on; D57 to Tréjouls. After 1km, sign on left.

Linda Hilton & Erica Lewis
Las Bourdolles,
82110 Tréjouls,
Tarn-et-Garonne

tel +33 (0)5 63 95 80 83
e-mail erica.lewis@wanadoo.fr
web www.frenchbedbreakfast.com

La Marquise

Quiet Gilbert will take you egg-hunting or goose-feeding of a morning – if you wish. Soft, smiling and big-hearted, Michèle loves doing B&B, has won prizes for her recipes, invents sauces and makes her own aperitif. The quaintly old-fashioned rooms are comfortable (beware waist-low beams) but food is definitely the priority here. Fishing rods on loan for use in the pond; footpaths out from the gate; proper hiking trails a bit further away; the treasures of Moissac, lovely villages, caves, all within easy reach. This is exceptional farm B&B. *Small pets welcome.*

rooms	4: 2 doubles, 2 twins.
price	€41-€42 for two. Singles €39.
meals	Dinner with wine €17-€18, book ahead. Restaurant 5km.
closed	Rarely.
directions	From Moissac D7 for Bourg de Visa about 14km; before Brassac, just before bridge, right for Fauroux; farm 2km; signposted.

Gilbert & Michèle Dio
La Marquise,
82190 Bourg de Visa,
Tarn-et-Garonne

tel +33 (0)5 63 94 25 16
fax +33 (0)5 63 94 25 16
e-mail mglamarquise@infonie.fr

Tondes

Warm country people, the Sellars left a big Sussex farm for a smallholding in deepest France to breed sheep, goats and poultry naturally, traditionally: no pesticides, no heavy machines, animals roaming free. Their enthusiasm and guts – it's hard work – have earned them great respect locally and their recipe for a simple, rewarding life includes receiving guests happily under the beams, by the open hearth, in pretty-coloured, country-furnished rooms. Julie will welcome you to her wonderful farmhouse kitchen, where she creates feasts of organic veg and homemade marvels. Even the geese are friendly.

rooms	2: 1 double, 1 family room.
price	€45 for two.
meals	Dinner with wine €17, book ahead.
closed	Rarely.
directions	From A62 exit 8 for Golfech. Right on Rn113. Left for Cahors on D953 at r'bout. Before Fourquet left at sign Chambres d'Hôtes 2km.

Julie & Mark Sellars
Tondes,
82400 Castelsagrat,
Tarn-et-Garonne
tel +33 (0)5 63 94 52 13

Cap du Pech

Fabulous Auvillar, one of 'France's most beautiful villages', a feast of pink brick and old cobbles, is five minutes' walk from this modern villa whose secluded grounds and shrubberies hide the neighbours well. Your hosts are the sweetest couple, loving guests of all ages (family photographs abound), chatting happily about local treasures with real warmth. They offer documents and offers galore for perusing in deep sofas, a welcoming open-plan kitchen/diner with comfortable furniture, pretty pale guest rooms where old-style beds grace pine floors and lace hangs at the windows. Deliciously French.

rooms	3: 2 doubles, 1 family room.
price	€40 for two.
meals	Restaurant 400m.
closed	Rarely.
directions	Take exit RN113 to Auvillar. Up to La Gendarmerie; left; go past La Poste, right, 400m, house on left.

Jacques & Annick Sarraut
Cap du Pech,
82340 Auvillar,
Tarn-et-Garonne
tel +33 (0)5 63 39 62 45
fax +33 (0)5 63 39 71 02

Au Village

As lovingly restored as the dreamy hamlet with its wonderful church, this 19th-century stone farmhouse is owned by a Franco-Dutch couple who enjoy sharing their summers here. Madame teaches Spanish, is extrovert and energetic, Monsieur is calm, diplomatic and in business and they offer delicious dinners at their long, convivial table – regional and exotic dishes and an excellent cheeseboard. The honeysuckled courtyard and tall-treed garden are lovely, the rooms are fresh and light with good prints, local art, old wardrobes, terracotta tiles – a happy marriage of old and new. *Only open July-August.*

rooms	2: 1 double, 1 suite for 2-4.
price	€47 for two.
meals	Dinner with wine €16, book ahead.
closed	September-June.
directions	From A62 exit 8 for Gramont; follow signs to Lachapelle; entering village, house on right.

M & Mme Van den Brink
Au Village,
82120 Lachapelle, Tarn-et-Garonne
tel +33 (0)5 63 94 14 10
(0)1 39 49 07 37
e-mail lachapelle_vdb@hotmail.com
web lachapelle-vdb.monsite.wanadoo.fr

Casteyre

Sophie came from England and took over a group of three old sheepfolds brilliantly converted into one beautiful big *mas*: the biggest bungalow in the Gers? Her sophistication, superb family furniture, paintings and whatnots have done the rest: it is top-class aristo-rustic. She is composed and outgoing, delighted to have visitors to share the house, the view, the peace. Rooms are extravagantly, comfortable in either Trad English or Trad French style but always perfect and pleasing. Bathrooms too, of course. Guests have their own big well-furnished drawing room but the terrace is where one wants to be.

rooms	4: 2 doubles; 1 double, 1 single both with shower & sharing wc.
price	€100-€120 for two.
meals	Dinner with wine €25, book ahead.
closed	October-Easter.
directions	From Agen N21 south; D7 west for Condom; at junc. on for Marsolan; right for Lagard-Fimarlon; 1st house on right.

Sophie Allington Lepage
Casteyre,
Marsolan,
32700 Marsolan, Gers
tel +33 (0)5 62 68 95 72
fax +33 (0)5 62 68 95 73
e-mail sophieallington@wanadoo.fr

Les Colombiers

No splashing, no screaming – no pool! Peace reigns in the big garden; the gently rolling, wooded and brooked countryside beckons; wild orchids and woodpecker thrive in the clean air. Once a professional cook, Rosie still loves cooking, knows about vegetarian as well as local cuisine and uses virtually organic veg and eggs from Sam's fine potager. The late 19th-century house has wood-burning stoves and comfortable, relaxing furniture; bedrooms have polished wooden floors, big windows and impeccable bathrooms. And the area bursts with temptation for the gourmet and the *sportif*.

rooms	3: 1 twin, 2 family rooms.
price	€60 for two.
meals	Dinner with wine €18, book ahead.
closed	Rarely, but book ahead.
directions	From Agen D931 to Condom; D15 to Castelnau; right for 'Centre Village'; right at crossroads D43 for St Pé & Sos about 5km; house on left before bridge.

Rosie & Sam Bennett
Les Colombiers,
32440 Castelnau d'Auzan, Gers
tel +33 (0)5 62 29 24 05
e-mail rabennett@talk21.com

Domaine du Glindon

Set about with tubs and decorative scarecrows, the old timbers and stones glow under the Duchênes' caring attention. Their clever renovation has exposed the fine 300-year-old structural timbers, ideal for dividing living from dining areas in their magnificent salon. Guests have their own excellent dayroom; pretty bedrooms are colourful Provençal, strongly modern, chintz-and-plush traditional. Dynamic Brigitte does it all, tirelessly, cooking great meals every day; genial Daniel longs to please and his local knowledge is inexhaustible: there is a wealth of interest in the area; they are always around to help.

rooms	3: 1 double, 2 family rooms.
price	€55 for two.
meals	Dinner with wine €20, book ahead.
closed	
directions	

STOP PRESS: HOUSE SOLD

Setzères

An 18th-century Gascon manor, square and generous in its large lush garden – boules, badminton, tranquil pool. Beautifully restored, decorated with English antiques and oriental mementoes, breathing charm and peace, it has heart-stopping views to the Pyrenees. Christine is well travelled, her local dishes are made with fresh ingredients and dinner conversation on the star-lit terrace is both cosmopolitan and fun. This is hidden France: old stone hamlets scattered across wide empty countryside, fascinating architecture, fabulous food. A highly civilised place to stay. *Children over 12 welcome.*

rooms	3: 1 double, 1 twin, 1 suite for 4.
price	€110 for two.
meals	Dinner €40, book ahead; good wine list €5-€30.
closed	2 weeks December-January.
directions	From Auch N124 for Vic Fézenac 5km; left D943 to Barran, Montesquiou, Bassoues (32km); D943 left for Marciac, sign for Scieurac & Flourès; in village left by church; house on right.

Christine Furney
Setzères,
32230 Marciac,
Gers
tel +33 (0)5 62 08 21 45
fax +33 (0)5 62 08 21 45
e-mail setzeres32@aol.com
web www.setzeres.com

Jautou

Way out in the beautiful Gersois wilds, this happy young English family welcome visitors with open arms to their gorgeous 1760s courtyard farmhouse. Life centres on the lively, relaxed family kitchen but there's also a long cool ancient-timber, modern-pink dining room with shady terrace for guests. The ground-floor bedroom is splendidly French and opens onto the privacy of the back lawn; upstairs, the suite is cosy, rustic and has super country views. Scottish Laura, vivacious and talented, is a subtle cook; thoughtful Andrew, a builder/renovator, is every ready to help. *Pool available 4-7pm.*

rooms	2: 1 double, 1 family suite for 4.
price	€50-€70 for two; €100 for four. Minimum stay 2 nights.
meals	Dinner with wine €25, book ahead.
closed	Occasionally in winter.
directions	N21 from Mirande for Tarbes; 9km D16 right for Tillac; right; D564 left; past lake; right at T-junction; signposted.

Laura & Andrew Gardener
Jautou,
32230 Blousson Serian / Marciac,
Gers
tel +33 (0)5 62 09 35 87
e-mail gardener@wanadoo.fr
web www.gasconbreaks.com

Lieu Dit Fitan

In 1999, this was just another derelict barn in the glorious Gers countryside. Dido's restoration is inspired: at the door, the whole superb space opens before the eyes, English antiques gleam, the fine modern kitchen sparkles (available for a small fee). Upstairs, one luscious room: raw stones punctuate the soft white wall, patchwork cheers, books tempt. Downstairs, an impeccable full-disabled room. Delightful Dido wants to provide a holiday space for all, loves cooking, has travelled thousands of miles and is highly cultured. A corner of paradise, it even smells heavenly.

rooms	2: 1 double, 1 twin.
price	€65-€68 for two.
meals	Dinner with wine €25, book ahead. Use of kitchen €8.
closed	Rarely.
directions	From Marciac D134 north; cross D946, continue to Louslitges church, 2nd right, Fitan 3/4 up on right. Pale green shutters.

Dido Streatfeild-Moore
Lieu Dit Fitan,
32230 Louslitges,
Gers
tel +33 (0)5 62 70 81 88
e-mail deedoenfrance@aol.com
web www.chezdeedo.com

Maison de la Porte Fortifiée

The house in the ramparts still welcomes pilgrims, the luxury pilgrims of today, and peace flows in from ancient stone walls and plunging country views. Interior designers, friendly outgoing Carsten and his shyer friend, who also cooks divinely, have clothed these medieval bones in Art Deco by Louis XVI out of Bauhaus with exquisite taste and consummate success: it is sensual and stunning, be it winter by the fire in the cosy study or summer on the terrace with The View. Big light bedrooms are simply lovely, pale with colour splashes, lavish touches, clever little shower rooms, one with a superb bathroom.

rooms	4: 2 doubles, 2 twins. Smaller overflow room for 2.
price	€79-€110 for two.
meals	Dinner €29, book ahead; wine from €7.50.
closed	Rarely.
directions	From Auch N21 for Tarbes. At le Trouette D2 to l'Isle de Noé; D943 to Montesquiou. Drive to top of village; park opp. church; house on right near fortified tower.

Carsten Lutterbach
Maison de la Porte Fortifiée,
32320 Montesquiou,
Gers
tel +33 (0)5 62 70 97 06
fax +33 (0)5 62 70 97 06
e-mail maison@porte-fortifiee.de
web www.porte-fortifiee.de

Domaine de Peyloubère

The sober buildings give no inkling of the explosion inside: 80 years ago, an Italian painter spread his heart and love of form and colour over ceilings and doors. 'His' suite has vast space, fine antiques, a dream of a great bathroom and dazzling paintings. Theresa and Ian fell for the romantically wild house and glorious park and left high-pressure London jobs to save the whole place from dereliction – their enthusiasm and sensitive intelligence show in every room. And the waterfall, the Italian garden, the wild bit – there's no other place like it. Wonderful for an anniversary treat.

rooms	2 suites.
price	€72-€100 for two.
meals	Dinner with wine €20, book ahead.
closed	Rarely.
directions	From Auch N21 south 3km; left D929 for Lannemezan; in Pavie, left after Mairie, cross old bridge, 1st right, signposted Auterrive; house 1km on left.

Theresa & Ian Martin
Domaine de Peyloubère,
32550 Pavie,
Gers
tel +33 (0)5 62 05 74 97
fax +33 (0)5 62 05 75 39
e-mail martin@peyloubere.com
web www.peyloubere.com

La Garenne

Youthful and enthusiastic, outgoing and warm-hearted, Mireille is an inspired cook and a delight to be with; Olivier is less ebullient but just as warm a presence and those rolling bird-filled spaces beyond the wooden terrace outside your window are his wheat and sunflower crops. Together, they fill their cosy house with antique plates, prints, pictures and furniture. Their guest room is as family-comfortable, warm-furnished as the rest. Theirs is a relaxed and happy family home with the essential dogs and cats plus a swimming pool by the gîtes. Perfect for children.

rooms	1 double (+ 1 small room for 1 child).
price	€50 for two.
meals	Dinner with wine €15, book ahead. Auberge 4km.
closed	Rarely.
directions	From Auch N21 for Tarbes 2km; left D929 for Lannemezan; in Masseube, left for Simorre 4km; left for Bellegarde; 1st left, before church & castle.

Mireille & Olivier Courouble
La Garenne,
32140 Masseube,
Gers
tel +33 (0)5 62 66 03 61
fax +33 (0)5 62 66 03 61
e-mail ocourouble@wanadoo.fr
web www.visitorama.com/32/la-garenne.html

Château de Sombrun

A flourish of oval lawn as you arrive, six handsome horses and 200 years of charm: Sombrun can entertain all ages. In the vast hall, billiards and an electric piano; in the pool house, more games; in the sitting room, squishy sofas and telly. Gillian, young and sociable, leads you up the generous original staircase to a colourful, antique-filled room, or out to the barn annexe with its own sitting room and more casual bedrooms. She and Jeffrey enjoy having guests, though he's a bit shyer. Breakfast will be in the fine dining room, out on the terrace, or in the cosier kitchen with its great fireplace and table.

rooms	5: 2 doubles, 1 twin, 2 family suites for 3-4.
price	€75-€96 for two.
meals	Dinner with wine €34, book ahead.
closed	24-26 December.
directions	From Pau NE on D943 through Morlaas & Lembeye for Maubourguet. 2km before Maubourguet D59 left to Sombrun; house in village near church & Mairie.

Gillian Quirk
Château de Sombrun,
65700 Sombrun,
Hautes-Pyrénées
tel +33 (0)5 62 96 49 43
fax +33 (0)5 62 96 01 89
e-mail gillian@sombrun.com
web www.sombrun.com

Jouandassou

Standing in rolling farmland on the Gers border – a wildlife haven an hour from the mountains – this is the most relaxed house you could wish for: 18th-century bones, 20th-century flesh. Dominique's decorative talent runs to cleverly-used bright colours, fantasy patchwork and great flair at auction sales. Nick cooks with French, Thai, Latin American flourishes and is a great entertainer. They have three teenage children, are a well-travelled, thoughtful couple, involved in the local music festival, concerned with the countryside – evenings on the terrace can be stimulating. Great walks, super food, easy living.

rooms	3: 2 doubles, 1 triple.
price	€55 for two. Minimum stay 2 nights.
meals	Dinner with wine €20, book ahead.
closed	Christmas & New Year.
directions	From Tarbes D632 to Trie sur Baïse; through village onto D939 for Mirande 1km; house up little road sign on left.

Nick & Dominique Collinson
Jouandassou,
65220 Fontrailles,
Hautes-Pyrénées
tel +33 (0)5 62 35 64 43
fax +33 (0)5 62 35 66 13
e-mail dom@collinson.fr
web www.collinson.fr

Namaste

The Hindu greeting *namaste* is the name; slightly exotic is the feel of this comfortable 18th-century farmhouse. The Fontaines restored it, polished the floors and created a lasting air of harmony. One of the ground-floor rooms has a fine big shower room and doors onto a semi-secluded corner of the garden. The rooms upstairs are ideal for yoga, dance or art workshops. In cold weather, enjoy the huge open fire in the comfortable salon and make the most of Jean's dinners at the long table: he's a dab hand at vegetarian food and likes to use organic ingredients. *Pool open summer 2005.*

rooms	2: 2 doubles, 1 triple, 2 quadruples.
price	€48-€50 for two.
meals	Dinner with wine €18, book ahead.
closed	Rarely.
directions	From A64 exit 16 on D939 through Lannemezan to Galan; from village square & church, Rue de la Baïse for Recurt; house 500m on left.

Jean & Danielle Fontaine
Namaste,
65330 Galan,
Hautes-Pyrénées

tel	+33 (0)5 62 99 77 81
fax	+33 (0)5 62 99 77 81
e-mail	namaste_65@libertysurf.fr
web	www.namaste-pyrenees.com

Domaine de Jean-Pierre

Madame is gracefully down-to-earth and her house and garden an oasis of calm where you may share her delight in playing the piano or golf (3km) and possibly make a lifelong friend. Built in Napoleon's time, her house has an elegant hall, big, airy bedrooms and great bathrooms, while fine furniture and linen sheets reflect her pride in her ancestral home – a combination of uncluttered space and character. The huge quadruple has space to waltz in and the smallest bathroom; a beautifully presented breakfast comes with civilised conversation. Come to unwind – you may never want to leave.

rooms	3: 1 double, 1 triple, 1 quadruple.
price	€48 for two.
meals	Good restaurants 3-7km.
closed	Rarely.
directions	From A64 exit 16 to Lannemezan; there, N117 for Toulouse 5km; at Pinas church D158 for Villeneuve. House on right 1km.

Mme Marie-Sabine Colombier
Domaine de Jean-Pierre,
65300 Pinas,
Hautes-Pyrénées

tel	+33 (0)5 62 98 15 08
fax	+33 (0)5 62 98 15 08
e-mail	marie@domainedejeanpierre.com
web	www.domainedejeanpierre.com

La Souleillane

Fabienne and Jean-Luc are working wonders, undoing some rather ruthless decorating left by their predecessors. Rooms are huge and bright, the cheery yellow family room in the house, the other two in the barn, one a restful white and blue, the other pink *toile de Jouy*. Having two little boys of their own, Fabienne and Jean-Luc make children very welcome and give them the run of the walled garden. Fabienne enjoys cooking typical local meals and chatting round the table while Jean-Luc, Pyrenean born and bred, is a source of great mountaineering stories. Don't miss St Bertrand de Comminges, 12 km away.

rooms	3: 2 doubles, 1 quadruple.
price	€47 for two; €57 for three; €67 for four.
meals	Dinner with wine €16, book ahead.
closed	Rarely.
directions	From Toulouse A64, exit 17; D938 west, 7km; signposted. 8km from Lannemezan station.

Fabienne & Jean-Luc Garcia
La Souleillane,
65150 St Laurent de Neste,
Hautes-Pyrénées

tel	+33 (0)5 62 39 76 01
e-mail	info@souleillane.com
web	www.souleillane.com

Maison de L'Évêque

You could weep, this valley is so beautiful; so are the house, its story, garden, owners. A doctor built it (see the caduceus on the great newel post), then fostered one Bishop Laurence, who 'proved' Bernardette's miracles and set Lourdes up for glory. Arlette, a miracle of industry and human warmth, decorates prettily, cooks simply and brilliantly (you'll never want to eat out) and still finds plenty of time for guests. Quiet and attentive, Robert will take you hiking and fishing in that gorgeous valley (Pyrenean high-mountain trout are the best, naturally). A very special place.

rooms	4: 3 doubles, 1 triple.
price	€41-€48 for two.
meals	Dinner with wine €20-€28, book ahead. Restaurants in Lourdes.
closed	Rarely.
directions	From Lourdes N21 S for 2km; left at bridge; immediately left again D26 to Juncalas; house in village centre on right.

Arlette & Robert Assouère
Maison de L'Évêque,
65100 Juncalas,
Lourdes,
Hautes-Pyrénées

tel	+33 (0)5 59 62 42 02 04
fax	+33 (0)5 62 94 13 91
e-mail	robert.assouere@wanadoo.fr

Eth Berye Petit

A couple of Basques from either side of the Pyrenees: Henri, whose family have lived here for over 1000 years, is home at weekends, Ione is a gently hospitable mother of two and there's Valdo, the little dog who smiles. The fine old house with its wonderful four-sided roof and grand staircase looks from its mountain niche over amazing scenery. Family-comfortable pastel bedrooms, one with the balcony, have antique French sheets; the living room, where a fire roars and dinner is served on winter weekends, is a great space to come back to after a day's white-water rafting, skiing, falconing… And really sweet people.

rooms	3: 1 twin, 2 suites for 3.
price	€45-€54 for two.
meals	Dinner with wine €15, November-April, book ahead. Restaurants within walking distance.
closed	Rarely.
directions	From Lourdes for Argelès-Gazost; 10km, left at r'bout for Beaucens, follow Vielle signs.

Henri & Ione Vielle
Eth Berye Petit,
65400 Beaucens,
Hautes-Pyrénées
tel +33 (0)5 62 97 90 02
fax +33 (0)5 62 97 90 02
e-mail contact@beryepetit.com
web www.beryepetit.com

Chambres d'Hôtes

From the lovely dining room you see straight across to a great snowy peak, a spectacular view for breakfast. Expressionist André Derain hid here during the war, understandably. Inside are pretty fabrics and your hosts' own works (from July to September they stage a special exhibition). Goan Teresa was educated in England and paints; Alpine-born, Paris-educated Bernard is an expert on water mammals, sculpts and draws. A very special couple. And this tiny village (pop. 60) feels almost Alpine. *Children over five and babes in arms only (ladder to mezzanine).*

rooms	2: 1 double, 1 single.
price	€45 for two. Singles €43. Minimum stay 2 nights.
meals	Good restaurants within 5km.
closed	Rarely.
directions	From A64 exit 20 to St Girons; right D618 for Castillon 12km; tiny D404 on left to Cescau. Park below church on left. Phone & owners will meet you at 1st farm in village.

Teresa & Bernard Richard
Chambres d'Hôtes,
09800 Cescau,
Ariège
tel +33 (0)5 61 96 74 24
fax +33 (0)5 61 04 98 24
e-mail tizirichard@caramail.com

La Baquette

The tiny hamlet has spectacular views up to the mountains and across miles of fields, farms and forests – ineffably lovely. Nick, a fauna and flora guide who really knows his stuff, lists 200 different birds and over 50 orchids; he also cooks a mean fish pie, served with salad from the garden. He and Julie, who's a nurse, are a thoroughly likeable pair, genuinely welcoming, helpful and interesting. Their simple, pretty renovated house has small bedrooms and a big cosy family living room: this is family B&B *par excellence*, where you stay in their house, occupy their sofa, share their lives. Great people, great value.

rooms	3: 1 double, 2 twins.
price	€37 for two.
meals	Dinner with wine €15, book ahead.
closed	November-April.
directions	From St Girons D117 E for 7km; just before fork for Mas d'Azil left at Chambres d'Hôtes sign; up tiny, metalled track for 2km.

Nick & Julie Goldsworthy
La Baquette,
09420 Lescure,
Ariège
tel +33 (0)5 61 96 37 67
fax +33 (0)5 61 96 37 67
e-mail goldsnj@aol.com

Madranque

After years of renovation your delightful weaver hosts have made this rural idyll what it is today. Samples of their work, using only natural dyes from local plants, are everywhere and fit well with the exposed stone and wood of the old house tucked into the valley. Bedrooms are rustic-warm with good views. Dine en famille in a room where the village dances were held; or rustle up your own snack in the dayroom – brilliant for families. Perfect for summer walking and winter cross-country skiing: the tiny hamlet is perched 900m up on the side of a National Park valley and the valley above is virtually unpopulated.

rooms	2 doubles.
price	€45 for two.
meals	Dinner with wine €16, book ahead.
closed	Rarely.
directions	From Foix D17 for Col des Marrous 15km; do not follow for Le Bosc on left: 'Hameau de Madranque' sign on right.

Birgit & Jean-Claude Loizance
Madranque,
09000 Le Bosc,
Ariège
tel +33 (0)5 61 02 71 29
fax +33 (0)5 61 02 71 29
e-mail birgit.loizance@libertysurf.fr
web www.lavalleeverte.net

Route de Cabus

Once you've reached this typical old stone mountain house, you won't need wheels again: 80km of hiking trails, from easy to tough, lead from the front door into a paradise for botanists, bird-watchers and tree insect fanatics, and your kindly hosts know them intimately. A paradise of rest for the weary heat-drenched traveller too: Layrole's most memorable features are the greenery, the riot of flowers all round the south-facing terrace, the babbling brook. Your room has an immaculate new bed, a mass of books and many personal touches; the Orient Express loo will appeal to train buffs and dinners are good homely fare.

rooms	1 double with shower & sharing wc.
price	€38 for two.
meals	Dinner with wine €16, book ahead.
closed	Mid-October-mid-April.
directions	From Foix N20 S to Tarascon; D618 for St Girons; 2.5km after café & bar at Saurat, right up steep road for Cabus; house 700m on right.

Roger & Monique Robert
Route de Cabus,
09400 Saurat,
Ariège
tel +33 (0)5 61 05 73 24

Les Carcis

Bring your hiking boots to this magical valley where nails were once made. Beds are softer but don't expect silver or lace: it is simple and honest, the semi-basement guest room is white and pine with a sitting corner, the bathroom is small. There are two adorable furry-eared donkeys to delight young and old, and rushing water for trout (in season), which will lull you to sleep after that great walk. Your hospitable hosts, who love to chat but don't flutter, will gladly harness a horse for a day in the foothills with a picnic lunch. You have a private kitchen; breakfast is *à la française*. Small is beautiful.

rooms	1 twin. Kitchenette available.
price	€35-€40 for two.
meals	Good restaurant in St Pierre de Rivière, 2km.
closed	January.
directions	From Foix D21 to Ganac. After 5km towards Micou 'Les Carcis'; right just after small bridge.

Sylviane & Guy Piednoël-Drouet
Les Carcis,
09000 Ganac,
Ariège
tel +33 (0)5 61 02 96 54
fax +33 (0)5 61 02 96 54
e-mail lescarcis@aol.com

Le Poulsieu

Bring the kids and leave them to it: Mieke and Hans have had six, still love 'em and provide games galore – trampoline, basketball, a gated pool; holiday times are full. In quieter seasons, on this remote edge of the world in the breathtaking Pyrenean foothills, you will find a thoughtful couple who have led interesting lives and now wax poetic about their gîte and B&B ventures. The rooms are pretty cramped but it's all simple and beamed, there's a kitchen for guests to use, and communal life and dinners are lived on the veranda, or in the garden, under the eye of those blissful serene views.

rooms	5: 2 doubles, 1 twin, 1 triple, 1 quadruple (summer only).
price	€45-€55 for two.
meals	Dinner with wine €20, book ahead.
closed	Rarely.
directions	From Foix D17 towards Col de Marrous 9km; in La Mouline left at Chambres d'Hôtes sign for 1.5km, right C6, tiny but easy track, to house.

Mieke van Eeuwijk & Hans Kiepe
Le Poulsieu,
09000 Foix,
Ariège

tel	+33 (0)5 61 02 77 72
fax	+33 (0)5 61 02 77 72
e-mail	le.poulsieu@wanadoo.fr
web	www.ariege.com/le-poulsieu

La Genade

Up in her beloved mountains with the wild streams splashing and an unbroken view of 13th-century Lordat, Meredith loves sharing her new-found heaven. A passionate climber and skier, she has rebuilt her ruined auberge: old stones and new wood, craggy beams and precious furniture make it rustic-warm and elegant-formal. Under truly American care, rooms have beautiful fabrics, oriental rugs and books, nooks and crannies. The ensuite bathrooms are gorgeous, the welcome is exuberant and genuine. Stay a week: Meredith can reveal some fabulous visits and walks. *Children over seven welcome.*

rooms	3 doubles.
price	€40-€60 for two.
meals	Dinner with wine €18-€23, book ahead. Summer local auberge 2 minutes' walk.
closed	Rarely.
directions	From Toulouse-Montpellier autoroute; E9 for Andorra. 4-lane route ends in Tarascon, becomes E9 & N20; south to Luzenac There, left for Château de Lordat, D20. After Lordat left, Axiat 1km, 1st house on left, facing church.

Meredith Dickinson
La Genade,
09250 Axiat,
Ariège

tel	+33 (0)5 61 05 51 54
e-mail	meredith.dickinson@wanadoo.fr

L'Impasse du Temple

Down on the Cathar Trail, how about breakfast in a Protestant temple? Well, remains of, turned into a pretty patio by twinkling, down-to-earth John and lively, sociable Lee-anne – Australians restoring this elegant mansion and loving it. Graciously high ceilings, a sweeping spiral staircase, lovely great windows: it's a fine and formal house in an oasis of ancient, stream-kissed oaks made relaxed and welcoming by your hard-working, fun-loving hosts. Guest rooms are generous too, in pastels and with just enough antiques; one even has the vast original claw-footed bath.

rooms	5: 2 doubles, 2 triples, 1 suite for 4.
price	€61-€66 for two. Suite €93-€98 for four.
meals	Dinner €20, book ahead; wine €6-€15; restaurant 200m.
closed	Rarely.
directions	From Toulouse A61 for Montpellier; exit 22 at Bram to Mirepoix on D4; D119; D625 to Lavelanet, 11km; at Aigues-Vives left for Léran D28.

John & Lee-anne Furness
L'Impasse du Temple,
09600 Léran,
Ariège
tel +33 (0)5 61 01 50 02
fax +33 (0)5 61 01 50 02
e-mail john.furness@wanadoo.fr
web www.chezroo.com

L'Oustal

Enchanting: spectacular setting, fine fireplaces, antique chests, elegant airy bedrooms, good snug bathrooms. Michel, twinkly and teasing, the finest chef around, takes inspiration from the market and loves talking about cooking (try him on the Cathars); he may even let you into his sanctum. Simone is all grace and refinement. Choose your space for the season: perched glass porch, devouring armchairs, summer dining room with enamelled lava table... And moreover, the church next door is an early Romanesque jewel – people fight for the room with the bell-tower view. *Children over five welcome.*

rooms	2: 1 double, 1 triple.
price	€64 for two.
meals	Dinner with wine €28, book ahead.
closed	Rarely.
directions	From Foix N20 S 33km through Tarascon to Luzenac; left D2; follow signs to Unac; 2nd entrance to Unac; house just down from church, 100m on right.

Michel & Simone Descat
L'Oustal,
09250 Unac,
Ariège
tel +33 (0)5 61 64 48 44

Gratia

Luscious texture combinations of original floor tiles discovered virgin in the attic, stupendous beam structures – loving hands crafted this place in the 1790s, flair and hard work brought it back from ruin in the 1990s. Jean-Paul's motto 'less is more' informs the wonderful uncluttered bedrooms with their pretty beds and linens; Florence, chic and charming, will do physiotherapy in the great attic studio – mats, music, massage; the ethos is 'polished and cool'. Chill out on the manicured lawn by the saltwater pool, dine in the great kitchen, converse delightfully, depart thoroughly renewed.

rooms	3 doubles.
price	€65-€70 for two.
meals	Dinner with wine €20, book ahead. Restaurant 5km.
closed	October-April.
directions	A64 exit 28; at St Sulpice, D919 to Foix; at Lézat-sur-Lèze left onto D19b to Esperce. 200m after Lèze metal bridge, take small road directly in front of you. Gratia at top of hill.

Florence Potey
& Jean-Paul Wallaert
Gratia,
09210 Lézat sur Lèze,
Ariège
tel +33 (0)5 61 68 64 47
e-mail ferme.gratia@wanadoo.fr
web www.ariege.com/gratia/

La Cazalère

A Parisian composer came to save a piece of country heritage and did it most deftly. With energy and imagination, from ancient hermitage to monastery to 17th-century manor, Isabelle has tracked the details; her highly personal restoration is sometimes fun, never stiff, even if doors must be five foot high. Each floor has its snug salon-library with piano, 'cinema' with television and real cinema seating. The gently monastic *Yaïch* bedroom with a desk in the tower is hung with a friend's paintings, *Purcell* has graceful furniture and green views, the great attic is for rainy games and artists. Tremendous.

rooms	3: 1 double, 1 suite, 1 suite for 5.
price	€80-€90 for two.
meals	Dinner with wine €19, book ahead.
closed	Rarely.
directions	From A64 for Tarbes; after Muret péage exit 21 on N11 for Bousens; at r'bout left for Nazères & Roquefort. Through Roquefort; 4km left at tiny x-roads for Belbezes & Ausseing; left. House above village with square tower.

Isabelle Pérusat
La Cazalère,
31260 Ausseing,
Haute-Garonne
tel +33 (0)5 61 97 04 50
e-mail lacazalere@ifrance.com

Les Pesques

A quiet lane, a happy family, an old manor decorated in peaceful good taste: it's a delight. Every antique, including cupboard doors, is the right one, bed linen is pretty, most rooms have a gentle blue and white valentine theme; the beautiful new room is in warm yellows, as cheerful as Brigitte's personality and done with her very special feel and an exquisite bathroom. All is soft, mellow, uncluttered; she is smiling, enthusiastic, young; her daughters are adorable and helpful. A dreamy, comfortable, joyful house where you appreciate the skill of Bruno the hard-working kitchen gardener when you sit down to dinner.

rooms	3: 1 double, 1 twin sharing shower & wc; 1 double.
price	€45 for two.
meals	Dinner with wine €15, book ahead.
closed	Last week in August & Christmas week.
directions	From Toulouse N117 SW for about 50km; exit S D6 to Cazères; over River Garonne, 1st right D7, right D62; house 2nd left after Camping.

Brigitte & Bruno Lebris
Les Pesques,
31220 Palaminy,
Haute-Garonne
tel +33 (0)5 61 97 59 28
fax +33 (0)5 61 98 12 97

Le Moulin

Steve a wonderful cook and Kris a man of the theatre have achieved a splendid restoration of their remote old mill whose stream now feeds their fully-fledged organic smallholding: kitchen garden, sheep, poultry, all for your dinner delight. They are deeply involved in the local environment, preserving trees and wildlife and helping farmers. Inside, the fire roars, French country furniture glows, rugs are oriental, colours simple and they still dream of a turbine to make heat from the river (so rooms may be a little chilly in winter). They are a wonderfully friendly pair, it's great value and the Pyrenees are so near.

rooms	4: 1 double, 2 triples; 1 triple sharing shower & wc.
price	€43 for two.
meals	Dinner with wine €16, book ahead.
closed	Rarely.
directions	From Toulouse A64 to Boussens, exit 21; D635 to edge of Aurignac; right D8 for Alan 3km; left past Montoulieu to Samouillan D8, 7km; left on D96; signs.

Stephen Callen
& Kris Misselbrook
Le Moulin,
31420 Aurignac,
Haute-Garonne
tel +33 (0)5 61 98 86 92
fax +33 (0)5 61 98 60 77
e-mail kris.steve@free.fr
web www.moulin-vert.net

En Tristan

Gérard taught philosophy, Chantal taught English and they love music, too. The old farmhouse still has its hay loft, well and bread oven and you will gape, astounded, at the scale of the inglenook fireplace with all its attendant oak beams plus a nail where Grandmère used to hang her money among the washing. Sizeable bedrooms are bright and welcoming, bathrooms beautifully done. A terrace overlooks the hills (kites available), a vine-covered pergola gives shade, a grassy courtyard has a barbecue and table tennis. No antiques, but we loved it for its unpretentious simplicity and engaging hosts.

rooms	4: 3 triples, 1 family room.
price	€39-€44 for two; €52-€56 for three.
meals	Restaurants 5-6km.
closed	Rarely.
directions	From A68 exit 3 to Montastruc; D30 for Lavaur for 5km; left D30c to Azas; continue 2km; sign for Garrigue (D22g).

Chantal & Gérard Zabé
En Tristan,
31380 Azas,
Haute-Garonne
tel +33 (0)5 61 84 94 88
fax +33 (0)5 61 84 94 88
e-mail gerard.zabe@free.fr
web en.tristan.free.fr

La Bousquétarié

Madame Sallier is delightful, running her family château with boundless energy and infectious *joie de vivre*, serving breakfast in her big kitchen in order to chat more easily to you, loving everyone, especially children. Charming bedrooms still have their original personality, and one rare 1850s wallpaper, and turning walk-in cupboards into showers or loos was a stroke of brilliance; antique-filled sitting rooms are totally French; the little reading room holds hundreds of books; even the fresh roses are old-fashioned. It's all comfortably worn around the edges with a tennis court you're welcome to use.

rooms	4: 1 double, 1 twin, 2 family suites.
price	€60-€75 for two.
meals	Dinner with wine €19-€22, book ahead.
closed	Rarely.
directions	From Revel D622 for Castres for 9km; left D12 to Lempaut; right D46 for Lescout; house on left.

Monique & Charles Sallier
La Bousquétarié,
81700 Lempaut,
Tarn
tel +33 (0)5 63 75 51 09
fax +33 (0)5 63 75 51 09
web www.chateau.bousquetarie.com

Les Abélias

Geneviève moved here from Alsace for more sun and a slower pace of life. As soon as you enter the courtyard and see the mellow old house with little angels guarding the steps you will want to be one of her returning guests, all welcomed as old friends. The chapel in the garden is dedicated to Our Lady of the Angels. One room is soft green with a muslin canopy and more angels round the walls. The family room is white with rosebuds. Both rooms are Geneviève's own work and utterly appealing. Breakfast is on a sunny terrace under the lime trees looking at the garden and fields. Possibly dinner, too.

rooms	2: 1 double, 1 family room.
price	€56 for two.
meals	Dinner with wine €16, book ahead.
closed	Rarely.
directions	From Revel D84; right V10 for Lamothe; follow signs 'Les Abélias'.

Geneviève Millot
Les Abélias,
81700 Blan,
Tarn

tel	+33 (0)5 63 75 75 14
fax	+33 (0)5 63 75 75 14
e-mail	lesabelias@libertysurf.fr
web	lesabelias.chez.tiscali.fr

La Bonde-Loupiac

Genuine human warmth and refined luxury are the keynotes of this beautifully restored house and its superb gardens. Forty-three big ebony beams (brought from Madagascar in the family's repatriation luggage...) went into the renovation. The atmosphere is happily, humorously family with many traces of those years on exotic shores – in the cooking as well as the bathrooms. The large, pretty bedrooms are immaculate, and the cultured, people-loving owners are most unusual, both refined and down-to-earth, country-comfortable and artistic. A wonderful place.

rooms	2: 1 double, 1 twin.
price	€55 for two. Minimum stay 3 nights.
meals	Dinner with wine €18, on day of arrival, book ahead. Plenty of restaurants 6km.
closed	Mid-December–mid-January.
directions	From Rabastens D12 for Coufouleux; cross River Tarn; left at lights D13 for Loupiac. Just before village right by cemetery; skirt cemetery, fork right, follow signs for La Bonde 1km.

Maurice & Bernadette Crété
La Bonde-Loupiac,
81800 Rabastens,
Tarn

tel	+33 (0)5 63 33 82 83
fax	+33 (0)5 63 33 82 83
web	www.labonde81.com

Mas de Sudre

George and Pippa are ideal B&B folk – relaxed, good-natured, enthusiastic about their corner of France, generous-spirited and adding lots of little extras to make you comfortable. Sudre is a warm friendly house with beautiful furniture, shelves full of books, big inviting bedrooms. Wine-tastings can be arranged and there's a large shady garden set in rolling vineyards and farmland where you can sleep off any excesses. The more energetic may leap to the pool, boules, bikes or several sorts of tennis and you are genuinely encouraged to treat the house as your own.

rooms	4: 2 doubles, 2 twins.
price	€60 for two.
meals	Good choice of restaurants nearby.
closed	Rarely.
directions	From Gaillac for Cordes; over railway; fork imm'ly left D964 for Castelnau de Montmiral. 1km; left D18 for Montauban 400m; right D4 1.5km; 1st left, 1st house on right.

Pippa & George Richmond-Brown
Mas de Sudre,
81600 Gaillac,
Tarn
tel +33 (0)5 63 41 01 32
fax +33 (0)5 63 41 01 32
e-mail masdesudre@wanadoo.fr

8 place St Michel

Come for an absolutely fabulous French bourgeois experience: a wide stone stair deeply worn, high ceilings, southern colours, antique doors and gorgeousness at every turn. Add the owners' passion for Napoleon III furniture, oil paintings and ornate mirrors and the mood, more formal than family, is unmistakably French. Bedrooms, some with cathedral, some with rooftop views, are antique-furnished and very comfortable; breakfast is on the terrace overlooking the cathedral square. It's good to be in a town with utterly French people. Madame is a sweetheart and it's very good value for money.

rooms	6: 4 doubles, 1 twin, 1 suite.
price	€48 for two.
meals	Restaurants within walking distance.
closed	Rarely.
directions	In centre of Gaillac, directly opposite St Michel abbey church as you come in across bridge from A68 Toulouse-Albi road.

Lucile Pinon
8 place St Michel,
81600 Gaillac,
Tarn
tel +33 (0)5 63 57 61 48
fax +33 (0)5 63 41 06 56

Les Buis de Saint Martin

The dogs that greet you are as friendly as their owner, she has exquisite taste, and the banks of the Tarn can be reached from the garden – it's a dream place. Madame has lived here for 25 years and is delighted to please you and practise her English. You will love the softest mushroom hues and white in her bedrooms and bathrooms, the quilting on the high-quality beds, the good paintings on the walls and the floaty muslin at the windows that look over the garden. Meals are served in the luminous white dining room – gleaming antiques on old terracotta tiles – or on the lovely teak-furnished patio.

rooms	2 doubles.
price	€80 for two. Minimum stay 2 nights in summer.
meals	Dinner €29, book ahead.
closed	Rarely.
directions	From A68 exit 11 to Marssac; for Lagrave, right after level-crossing; 2nd right chemin du Rougé; 2nd right rue St Martin; right at red transformer; left at fork, signposted.

Jacqueline Romanet
Les Buis de Saint Martin,
81150 Marssac-sur-Tarn,
Tarn
tel +33 (0)5 63 55 41 23
fax +33 (0)5 63 53 49 65
e-mail jean.romanet@wanadoo.fr
web perso.wanadoo.fr/les-buis-de-saint-martin/

La Barthe

Your Anglo-French hosts welcome guests as friends to their deeply converted farmhouse. The pastel-painted, prettily-stencilled rooms are smallish but beds are good, the hospitality is great and it's a deliciously secluded place to stay and walk or bike out into the country. The Wises grow their own vegetables and summer dinners happen on the terrace overlooking the lovely Tarn valley, a largely undiscovered part of France where birds, bees and sheep will serenade you. Watch the local sheep farmers milking for Roquefort and don't miss Albi, with that fascinating red-brick Cathedral – it's no distance at all.

rooms	3: 1 double, 1 family room; 1 twin sharing bath.
price	€40 for two.
meals	Dinner with wine €18, book ahead.
closed	Rarely.
directions	From Albi D999 for Millau 25km; at La Croix Blanche left to Cambon du Temple, up to La Barthe on D163; right; house on left.

Michèle & Michael Wise
La Barthe,
81430 Villefranche d'Albigeois,
Tarn
tel +33 (0)5 63 55 96 21
fax +33 (0)5 63 55 96 27
e-mail labarthe@chezwise.com
web www.chezwise.com

Saint Marcel

Way off the beaten track, 30km from Albi, this young couple have recreated the past in their brilliantly authentic restoration of a crumbled old farmhouse. Sylvie's kitchen is a poem: cooking area in the farmer's old fireside bed, shelves groaning with jars of goodies from Pierre's garden. She adores cooking, he loves to chat, has an excellent sense of humour and good English. They have put their heart into their house with its natural garden, intriguing collection of country antiques and sweetly rustic guest rooms full of beams, armoires, Provençal prints – plus super shower rooms. Exceptional.

rooms	2: 1 double, 1 quadruple.
price	€46-€50 for two.
meals	Dinner with wine €15, book ahead.
closed	Rarely.
directions	From Albi for Ambialet to Valence d'Albigeois; left D53 to Tanus 5.5km; left towards St Marcel for 1.5km; Chambres d'Hôtes sign; opposite church (with no bells!).

Sylvie & Pierre Dumetz-Manesse
Saint Marcel,
81340 Valence d'Albi,
Tarn

tel +33 (0)5 63 76 38 47

Château de Mayragues

A child's dream become an adult's paradise of history, culture and peace: inside those stern walls you climb old stone stairs to the open sentry's gallery, enter your chamber and gasp at the loveliness of the room and the depth of the view. Beyond the fine old timbers and stonework, glowing floor, furniture and fabrics, your eyes flow out over luscious gardens and woods. Alan is a softly-spoken Scot, Laurence a charming Parisienne, both are passionate about their prize-winning restoration – original materials, expert craftsmen – and they hold musical evenings and produce excellent wine. Quite a place.

rooms	2: 1 double, 1 twin.
price	€75 for two.
meals	Restaurants within 5km.
closed	20 December-February.
directions	From Gaillac D964 for Castelnau de Montmiral; at junc. D15 to Château de Mayragues, signposted.

Laurence & Alan Geddes
Château de Mayragues,
81140 Castelnau de Montmiral,
Tarn

tel +33 (0)5 63 33 94 08
fax +33 (0)5 63 33 98 10
e-mail geddes@chateau-de-mayragues.com
web www.chateau-de-mayragues.com

La Croix du Sud

A fantastic base for touring the bastide towns or just basking in the garden beneath stunning hilltop Castelnau – even picnics can be arranged. Catherine runs her 19th-century manor farmhouse with quiet sophistication and gentle humour: she wants you to love this place as much as she does. It has table tennis, *pétanque*, a discreetly hidden pool; immaculate rooms with pretty colours, good bedding, scintillating bathrooms; meals in the bright, pleasant dining room or on the terrace. And further afield: fascinating Albi, the Grésigne forest, great walks and a lake complex with all those water sports.

rooms	5: 3 double, 2 triples.
price	€60 for two.
meals	Dinner with wine €20, book ahead.
closed	Rarely.
directions	From Gaillac D964 to Castelnau de Montmiral, right at bottom of village 100m; right at sign Croix du Sud; fork left for Mazars; on left.

Catherine Sordoillet
La Croix du Sud,
81140 Castelnau de Montmiral,
Tarn
tel +33 (0)5 63 33 18 46
fax +33 (0)5 63 33 18 46
e-mail catherine@la-croix-du-sud.com
web www.la-croix-du-sud.com

Maison Barbacane

Climb the cobbles, reach the ramparts, sit in the little garden/terrace and watch the spreading landscape as you would have done 800 years ago. This is Gilles and Donna's third venture in Cordes: they already have two little children, a small hotel and are planning a small restaurant. Food's the thing here (Donna is an exquisite cook), dynamic and hard-working are the words: they are delightful. Each big, light and clearly individual bedroom has its own entrance, wrought-iron bed, colour splashes in keeping with its name (Cornflower, Tuscany,...), an uncluttered, stylish bathroom and space for easy chairs.

rooms	4: 1 double, 3 suites for two.
price	€75-€110 for two.
meals	Dinner €25, book ahead; wine-list.
closed	Rarely.
directions	Halfway up to Cordes sur Ciel, park at Trésor; walk few hundred metres to house. Gilles will help with bags.

Gilles Thacker
Maison Barbacane,
81170 Cordes sur Ciel,
Tarn
tel +33 (0)5 63 56 88 95
e-mail gillesrace@aol.com
web www.maisonbarbacane.com

Aurifat

Good furniture, books and paintings are thoroughly at home in this seriously old, history-laden house (the watchtower is 13th century) and all is serene and inviting. Each freshly decorated room has its own private entrance, balcony or terrace and stupendous views. The house is on the southern slope of hilltop Cordes (only 10 minutes from both the top and the bottom), the lovely pool is big enough for real exercise and there's a barbecue and summer kitchen. Cosy in winter too. Enough to entice you to stay a while and try the special three-day deal? Nothing is too much trouble for these lovely hosts.

rooms	4: 1 double, 3 twins.
price	€62-€70 for two. Minimum stay 3 nights July & August.
meals	Wide choice of restaurants in Cordes, within easy walking distance. BBQ & kitchen available.
closed	17 December-17 February.
directions	From Albi D600 to Cordes; up 'Cité' road on right of 'Cordes Presse' for 600m; fork left for Le Bouysset; 350m, left at hairpin bend marked Rte de St Jean; 200m on right.

Ian & Penelope Wanklyn
Aurifat,
81170 Cordes sur Ciel,
Tarn
tel +33 (0)5 63 56 07 03
fax +33 (0)5 63 56 07 03
e-mail aurifat@wanadoo.fr
web www.aurifat.com

Les Tuileries

The magnificent hallway and sweeping staircase carry you with billows of French character to fine, airy rooms that abound in old fireplaces, beams, interesting pictures, super views of Cordes and beautiful furnishings (matt satin and very fitting prints). A gentle couple with a keen dry sense of humour, your hosts warm up over dinner – most of which they'll proudly tell you they produced themselves. Children are welcome: there are games, a little park for picnics, Léonard the beloved donkey and Géant his pony friend. The whole place glows with sensitive, loving care – a small corner of delight beneath the sky.

rooms	5: 2 doubles, 1 twin, 1 triple, 1 quadruple.
price	€54-€62 for two.
meals	Dinner with wine €20, book ahead.
closed	Rarely.
directions	From Albi D600 to Cordes; there follow signs 'Parking 1 & 2'; signposted.

Annie & Christian Rondel
Les Tuileries,
81170 Cordes sur Ciel,
Tarn
tel +33 (0)5 63 56 05 93
fax +33 (0)5 63 56 05 93
e-mail christian.rondel@wanadoo.fr

Les Vents Bleus

You'll know you will love it here as you drive into the crunchy gravel courtyard. Palest stone, topped with sun-mellowed tiles, Les Vents Bleus is as inviting as its name. Isabelle and Laurent have restored the house – and outbuildings as gîtes – so well that nothing looks 'done up'. Rooms are large, airy with lots of cream and white, set off by confident touches of colour. The smell of figs warming in the sun wafts across the courtyard at breakfast, while Isabelle can provide a feast most evenings. Great for children too, with a safe pool, sandpit and huge enclosed garden.

rooms	5: 2 doubles, 2 twins, 1 family room.
price	€80-€105 for two.
meals	Restaurants nearby 5km.
closed	November-March.
directions	From Gaillac, D622 for Cordes; 5km after Cahuzac sur Vère, right D33 to Donnazac; pass village church, house on left, signposted.

Isabelle & Laurent Philibert
Les Vents Bleus,
Donnazac ,
81170 Cordes sur Ciel, Tarn
tel +33 (0)5 63 56 86 11
fax +33 (0)5 63 56 86 11
e-mail lesventsbleus@free.fr
web www.lesventsbleus.com

Montarsès de Tayrac

The rambling farmhouse in the hills is utterly charming; so are its owners. Jacques and Jo love having guests and he is a fountain of knowledge re wildlife and walks (and what walks they are!). Fields, woods, a lake, two donkeys and views that merit several hours of gazing; this swathe of southern Auvergne is sensational. Bedrooms have cream walls, stripped floors, old beams, bathrooms have fluffy towels, and the suite is brilliant for families (two bedrooms, a small salon/dining room, a kitchenette, fresh fabrics). In the living room: logs in the stone fireplace and deep chairs. Marvellous.

rooms	2: 1 double, 1 family suite.
price	€45 for two; €75 for four.
meals	Restaurant in village, 4km.
closed	Rarely.
directions	From Villefranche de Rouergue for Rodez D911; exit Rieupeyroux for Rodez 2km; right D85 to Tayrac. At La Rode right for La Salvetat Peyralès; towards Montarsès, signs.

Jo & Jacques Rieben
Montarsès de Tayrac,
12440 La Salvetat Peyralès,
Aveyron
tel +33 (0)5 65 81 46 10
fax +33 (0)5 65 81 46 10
e-mail chantelouve@club-internet.fr
web www.ifrance.com/aveyronvacances

Monteillet-Sanvensa

A lovely, old stone mini-hamlet in the calm green Aveyron where there is so just much space. Two compact rooms, each with a nice little terrace, look out over a typical medieval château. One guest room is white and yellow with a walk-in shower, the other washed-pink and white, with a super bathroom and a small kitchenette. The garden is full of flowers, the rolling views stupendous, and Monique is eager to please. Relax in one of the many shady areas in summer with a drink or a book and enjoy the birdsong. *Well-behaved children and pets welcome.*

rooms	2 doubles.
price	€46 for two.
meals	Dinner with wine €19, book ahead. Restaurant 8km.
closed	2 weeks in September.
directions	From Villefranche D922 for Albi; at entrance to Sanvensa, follow signs on right to Monteillet Chambres d'Hôtes.

Monique Bateson
Monteillet-Sanvensa,
12200 Villefranche de Rouergue,
Aveyron
tel +33 (0)5 65 29 81 01
fax +33 (0)5 65 65 89 52

Joany

A dream, both house and garden, in the post-industrial waste of this old mining area. Mireille is a dear, deeply interested in art and furniture, loves decorating her beamy old house with style and poise that reflect her personality, and is a genius with a needle. Her garden of plenty has three secret sitting corners and many fruit trees, a stream runs at the bottom, forests march along the edge, and you are æons away from the ugliness down the road. Bedrooms are painted white with colour trimmings, lots of wood (beams, floors, country antiques) and beautiful soft furnishings. One even has its own little terrace.

rooms	3: 1 twin, 2 doubles.
price	€45 for two.
meals	Light supper with wine €10. Restaurant 1km.
closed	Rarely.
directions	From A20 or N20, N140 for Figeac & Decazeville; just before Decazeville right to Viviez; over railway; sign.

Mireille Bernard
Joany,
12110 Viviez,
Aveyron
tel +33 (0)5 65 43 42 90
fax +33 (0)5 65 43 42 90
web www.joany.org

Le Château de Marcenac

The sunny enthusiasm comes from your enchanting, talented hosts, the history that hangs in the air oozes from the château and its former occupants. Globetrotters and linguists, Tony the architect – his renovation is faultless and deeply alive – and Fiona the chef – freshness, subtlety and flavour mark her table – are fulfilling a dream here and invite you to join them. This means vaulted ceilings, sweeping stone stairs up to vast dramatic bedrooms full of charm and romance, exceptional food from an organic potager, stimulating company, glorious vistas. Who needs more?

rooms	2: 1 double, 1 suite.
price	€90 for two. Suite €140 for two.
meals	Dinner €28, book ahead; wine list €5-€20.
closed	Rarely.
directions	Before Livinhac le Haut, immediately after bridge right; straight on past pharmacy; follow signs for Marcenac & 1km into château gardens.

Tony Archibold & Fiona Cantwell
Le Château de Marcenac,
12300 Livinhac le Haut,
Aveyron
tel +33 (0)5 65 64 54 38
fax +33 (0)5 65 64 54 38
e-mail reservations@chateaumarcenac.com
web www.chateaumarcenac.com

Quiers

Vast pastures slope away, a castle towers on a rock: it's ideal for outdoors lovers – orchids to hunt, canoeing, climbing, hang-gliding to practise. Bedrooms are a short walk away – bring the umbrella! – up a steepish track. Sitting snugly in the converted 16th-century *bergerie*, they vary in size, have shiny terracotta floors, old beams, fresh white walls and simple pine beds crafted by Jean, your friendly farmer host. In the main house are tapestries and antiques smelling of years of polish; here Véronique serves excellent meals of home-grown organic meat and veg. Worth staying some time.

rooms	6: 2 twins, 2 doubles, 1 triple, 1 family room.
price	€45 for two.
meals	Dinner €17-€19, book ahead. Good choice of restaurants in Millau.
closed	Mid-November-March.
directions	From Millau N9 to Aguessac; on way out, D547 right to Compeyre; left in village, follow signs for 2km.

Jean & Véronique Lombard-Pratmarty
Quiers,
12520 Compeyre, Aveyron
tel +33 (0)5 65 59 85 10
fax +33 (0)5 65 59 80 99
e-mail quiers@wanadoo.fr
web www.ifrance.com/quiers

Montels

The house is modern and rather dark, the rolling Languedoc hills are wild and very ancient. You can put on your wings and join the paragliders launching off the nearby cliff, or you can watch them from the safety of your breakfast table in the garden, enjoying Madame's *lafloune*, a local sheep's-milk cake. It matters little that she speaks no English: she is kind and welcoming and you can get a long way with smiles and sign language while Monsieur tends his sheep. The immaculate, simply and attractively furnished bedrooms include a suite which is perfect for a family. A simple unpretentious home.

rooms	2: 1 double, 1 suite for 4.
price	€37-€40 for two.
meals	Choice of restaurants Millau, 3km.
closed	Rarely.
directions	From Millau D911 for Cahors. Just after leaving city limits right after 'Auberge' x-roads. Signposted. Follow small road for about 2km.

Mme Henriette Cassan
Montels,
12100 Millau,
Aveyron
tel +33 (0)5 65 60 51 70

La Grande Combe

An energetic, lovable couple live in this astonishing old place, built on a hillside before a heart-stopping view. You go from level to delightful level: the ancient timber frame holds brilliantly restored rooms done in a simple, contemporary style that makes the old stones glow with pride. The emphasis is on communal living, of course – superb dining and sitting rooms with original paving, huge organic potager, great atmosphere – but there are little terraces and a library for quiet times. Lovely guest rooms are big (except the singles), pale or bright. An exceptional place.

rooms	7: 5 twins; 2 singles with shower & separate wc.
price	€70 for two.
meals	Dinner with wine €22, book ahead.
closed	Rarely.
directions	From Millau D992 & D999 for Albi; at St Pierre D902 right for Réquista; 4.5km after Faveyrolles left through Salelles; signposted.

Hans & Nelleke Versteegen
La Grande Combe,
12480 St Izaire, Aveyron
tel +33 (0)5 65 99 45 01
fax +33 (0)5 65 99 48 41
e-mail grande.combe@wanadoo.fr
web www.la-grande-combe.nl

photo Michael Busselle

languedoc–roussillon

La Maison de Marius

Fascinating Quézac: a pilgrimage 'street-village' with a Black Virgin and a lovely old bridge over the Tarn. Amazingly, Marius is a new house: it fits in perfectly with its old stones, beams and doors and its warm, lived-in feel, all light and fresh. Genuine locals, Dany and Pierre adore embellishing their home – delightful country fabrics, hand-painted furniture and murals – and spoiling their guests with homemade and home-grown delicacies from their superb veg patch. Their speciality? *Gâteau de noix* made with their own walnuts. Lovely terrace and rose garden where only birds, water and wind are to be heard.

rooms	5: 4 doubles, 1 family suite.
price	€50-€65 for two.
meals	Dinner with wine €25, book ahead.
closed	Rarely.
directions	From A75 exit 39 on N88 E for 25km; right N106 for Alès 25km; at Ispagnac right to Quézac; signs in village.

Danièle Méjean & Pierre Parentini
La Maison de Marius,
48320 Quézac,
Lozère
tel +33 (0)4 66 44 25 05
fax +33 (0)4 66 44 25 05
web www.chez.com/maisondemarius

Château Massal

Sit in the château's drawing room where a dozen French chairs open their arms. Or wander into the rambling, many-terraced garden with its views across river and red-roofed town. Up a spiral stone stair to big beautiful bedrooms with a château feel; walnut parquet floors and strong-coloured walls set off family furniture to perfection; one has a bathroom in the tower and is enchanting. Madame, one of an old French silk family who have been here for several generations, is as elegant and charming as her house; a fine cook, too. She will show you where to find really good walks, exciting canoeing, and wildlife.

rooms	3: 2 doubles, 1 twin.
price	€68-€88 for two.
meals	Dinner with wine €26, book ahead.
closed	Rarely.
directions	From Millau S on N9 for 19km to La Cavalerie; left D7 for Le Vigan about 50km to Bez; before bridge, sign on left.

Françoise du Luc
Château Massal,
30120 Le Vigan,
Gard
tel +33 (0)4 67 81 07 60
fax +33 (0)4 67 81 07 60

Mas de l'Amandier

Sheep and silk worms are part of the story of this atmospheric old house that looks out over the Cévennes; children, who still know the value of simplicity, spend hours in the splash pool or playing with the two dogs; adults feel the loving energy of fine linen and one beautiful piece of furniture, appreciate the handmade bathroom tiles, the natural materials. Nothing has been overdone or overplushed, Sophie's designer eye and taste for the right thing has given white vaulted rooms with terracotta floors a painted alcove or an elegant table decoration. And she cooks beautifully. A real B&B where caring counts.

rooms: 4: 3 family rooms, 1 family suite for 6.
price: €80-€95; suite €120 for 6
meals: €35; wine list.
closed: Rarely
directions: South of Alès N110 for Montpellier; right on D910 for Anduze; 50m left for Lézan. For Ribaute.

Sophie Lasbleiz
Mas de l'Amandier,
30720 Ribaute les Tavernes,
Gard
tel +33 (0)4 66 83 87 06
fax +33 (0)4 66 83 87 69
e-mail mas.amandier@free.fr

Mas Cassac

Reached through aromatic banks of thyme, lavender and juniper, set among hills and woods, here is a place for potters and walkers. Monsieur is a talented *potier* – the house is dotted with lovely pieces and there's a little gallery – and runs international pottery courses which bring an informal, creative atmosphere and lots of interesting people. Madame is delightful and an excellent cook. The guest room, separate from the main house, is simply furnished, meals (dinner on request) are served on the terrace or in the log-fired living room and the summer brings masses of festivals and happenings.

rooms: 1 double.
price: €48.50 for two.
meals: Dinner with wine €15.50, book ahead.
closed: Rarely.
directions: From Alès D16 through Le Saut du Loup. 7 km after Le Saut D241 left for St Julien de Cassagnas; sign.

Michel & Françoise Simonot
Mas Cassac,
30500 Allègre,
Gard
tel +33 (0)4 66 24 85 65
fax +33 (0)4 66 24 80 55
e-mail mas.cassac@wanadoo.fr
web www.ceramique.com/Mas-Cassac

Le Mas Escombelle

An 18th-century silkworm farm, the rambling house has old stones, arched terraces, a lovely courtyard and is done in the owners' own friendly, informal image. Delightful Isabelle is an artist, her warm sensitivity evident in her imaginative treatment of space, with African artefacts and original paintings indoors, a lovely orchard and shrubby pool area outside. Delicious breakfast is taken on the shady terrace in summer. You dine here, too, on Isabelle's cosmopolitan creations – meals are good fun (booking essential). This is genuine B&B, nothing hotelly, the three children join in and the road shouldn't impinge.

rooms	4: 2 twins, 1 triple, 1 quadruple.
price	€55 for two.
meals	Dinner with wine €18, book ahead.
closed	Rarely.
directions	From Alès D16 & D579 NE through Barjac for Vallon Pont d'Arc; 300m after Gendarmerie, house on right, arched doorway.

Antoine & Isabelle Agapitos
Le Mas Escombelle,
30430 Barjac,
Gard
tel +33 (0)4 66 24 54 77
fax +33 (0)4 66 24 54 77
e-mail mas-escombel@wanadoo.fr
web perso.wanadoo.fr/mas-escombel/

Pont d'Ardèche

An ancestor of Madame's built the fine old fortified farmhouse 200 years ago: it still stands, proudly worn, by the Ardèche River and has its own beach. Inside, in sudden contrast, is the magic of imagination and originality. Madame paints furniture, doors, friezes, ceilings, anything, brilliantly; rooms have all been redone; there's the superb stone staircase, the much-painted ruined bridge, the squirrelly, tall-treed park where shade invites summer lingerers, the delicious oval pool. Monsieur can accompany you on canoe trips (you may spot an otter) – an attractive, sociable couple who enjoy their guests.

rooms	5: 2 doubles, 1 twin, 1 triple, 1 quadruple.
price	€60 for two; €75 for four.
meals	Good restaurants in village.
closed	Rarely.
directions	From A7 Bollène exit D994 to Pont St Esprit; N86 for Bourg St Andéol; sign before bridge across river.

Mme de Verduzan
Pont d'Ardèche,
30130 Pont St Esprit,
Gard
tel +33 (0)4 66 39 29 80
fax +33 (0)4 66 39 51 80
e-mail pontdardeche@aol.com
web www.pont-dardeche.com

Le Clos de la Fontaine

The earthy, goldy colours of the south glow at every turn of this beautifully restored old house beneath the ancient fort: red-gold stone, soft limewashed walls, terracotta tiles; the blue light filters in through garden greenery, smelling of lavender and wax, to highlight an old picture frame here, a stencilled detail there, a beam, a fireplace, a lovely flower bowl. Madame has a highly creative approach to décor, and enjoys cooking too. Both love opening their home to visitors, sharing the care and the pleasure, and no comfort is neglected. *La Jasse*, the garden room, is ideal for the less mobile.

rooms 4 twins/doubles.
price €80-€85 for two.
meals Dinner €23, book ahead; wine from €8.
closed 15 December-15 February.
directions From Uzès D23 for St Quentin la Poterie; for St Laurent la Vernède.

Marie & Albert Henninger
Le Clos de la Fontaine,
30330 St Laurent la Vernède,
Gard
tel +33 (0)4 66 72 95 85
fax +33 (0)4 66 72 95 71
e-mail albert.henninger@wanadoo.fr
web www.closdelafontaine.com

La Magnanerie

This happy, artistic couple welcome guests to their open, light-filled, authentically-renovated old Cévenol silk farm, splashed with colour and *objets*. Flashes: pretty ochre-coloured plates, a long wooden table on the uneven stone floor of the huge kitchen, the old stone sink opposite; beams twisting through the house, glimpses of sky through little windows, a ravishing courtyard, big, uncluttered, attractive bedrooms, a roof terrace looking over Provence. Michèle manages tranquilly and adores cooking, Michel knows his wines and the local community, their talk is deeply cultural and enriching.

rooms 3: 2 doubles, 1 suite.
price €50-€55 for two.
meals Dinner with wine €18, book ahead.
closed Rarely.
directions From Alès D6 E 27km; left D979 beyond Lussan for Barjac 1km; left D187 to Fons sur Lussan; right at fountain; up on left by church.

Michèle Dassonneville
& Michel Genvrin
La Magnanerie,
30580 Fons sur Lussan,
Gard
tel +33 (0)4 66 72 81 72
e-mail la-magnanerie@wanadoo.fr

Les Marronniers

They are a delightfully open couple, in love with their life and their 19th-century *maison de maître*, who welcome guests with exuberant gaiety. John is a joiner with a fine eye for interior design while Michel, quieter, softer, does the cooking. From the classic black and white tiles of the entrance hall to the carefully-planned lighting in the bedrooms, every detail counts. A very generous breakfast is served under the chestnut trees or by the pool; afterwards you can wander off to join in lazy Provençal village life or visit Avignon, Uzès or nearby Lussan, the fortified Cévenol village. *Heated pool.*

rooms	4: 2 doubles, 2 twins.
price	€90-€105 for two.
meals	Dinner with wine, aperitif & coffee €39, book ahead.
closed	Rarely.
directions	From A9 exit 23 W to Uzès 19km; D979 N 7.5km; right D238 to La Bruguière. House on big square next to Mairie (vast Micocoulier tree in front).

John Karavias & Michel Comas
Les Marronniers,
30580 La Bruguière,
Gard
tel +33 (0)4 66 72 84 77
fax +33 (0)4 66 72 85 78
e-mail les.marronniers@12stay.co.uk
web www.les.marronniers.12stay.co.uk

Mas Vacquières

Your bit has the pink shutters, the owners' has yellow. They have restored these lovely old buildings with a sure touch, white walls a perfect foil for southern-toned fabrics and materials. The little vaulted room is intimate and alcoved, the big one smartly four-postered. Also a big soft living room, tables on the terrace under the great leafy tree and a lawn sloping down to the river bed – brilliant spots for silent gazing. You may share the pool in its roofless barn with your charming hosts who will also have coffee with you after dinner. Very pretty, if a touch detached from the owners' quarters.

rooms	3 doubles.
price	€65-€90 for two.
meals	Dinner €25, book ahead; good wine list from €5.50-€30.
closed	Rarely.
directions	From Alès, D6 for 12km; right on D7; in St Just, left for Vacquières, pink signs to house.

Thomas & Miriam van Dijke
Mas Vacquières,
30580 St Just et Vacquières,
Gard
tel +33 (0)4 66 83 70 75
fax +33 (0)4 66 83 74 15
e-mail info@masvac.com
web www.masvac.com

Mas d'Oléandre

Lovely, long stone buildings enfold the two-tier courtyard, great trees give generous shade, the Cévennes hillsides march away behind. It is enchanting. Your young and welcoming Dutch hosts have created a beautiful and unpretentious place to stay; the garden, the lawn around the pool, the glowing old furniture inside. Bedrooms, light and white with splashes of colour, feel separate from each other round the courtyard. Esther really loves cooking – make the most of good regional dishes on the covered terrace, or in the delightful dining room. *Painting courses in April & October.*

rooms	3 doubles.
price	€60-€110 for two. Minimum stay 2 nights in winter.
meals	Dinner €25, book ahead; wine list €5-€15.
closed	Rarely.
directions	From Uzès D981 to Montaren for 6km; right on D337 to St Médiers; in village continue up & around to right. House on left.

Léonard Robberts
& Esther Küchler
Mas d'Oléandre,
30700 Montaren et St Médiers,
Gard

tel	+33 (0)4 66 22 63 43
fax	+33 (0)4 66 03 14 06
e-mail	info@masoleandre.com
web	www.masoleandre.com

Map 17 Entry 633

La Maison

Christian's flair and human touch has revived the grand old stones with beautiful Indonesian furniture and hangings, soft lighting and a gentle golden sandy colour – he and Pierre are delighted with their new Maison. Beneath the old church of lovely Blauzac (daytime chimes), the lush garden and ancient tower look over wavy red rooftops to blue hills, bedrooms bask in ethnic fabrics and relaxed good taste, the stunning suite has its own roof terrace. Plus masses of books, a long long breakfast table in the library and good sofas in the salon. Superb. *Watch children with unfenced water.*

rooms	5: 4 doubles, 1 suite for 4.
price	€95-€180 for two.
meals	2 bistros in village.
closed	Rarely.
directions	From Nîmes, D979 for Blauzac 16km; after Pont St Nicolas, left for Blauzac; enter village, house behind church.

Christian Vaurie
La Maison,
30700 Blauzac,
Gard

tel	+33 (0)4 66 81 25 15
fax	+33 (0)4 66 81 02 18
e-mail	lamaisondeblauzac@wanadoo.fr

Map 17 Entry 634

Les Bambous

Circles of delight: the Provençe of vines and umbrella pines, a peaceful typical village, a lovely converted barn and glowing little house, a warm, affectionate couple who genuinely enjoy having guests. Joël paints and Michèle is a keen and good cook. Meal times are flexible, the atmosphere relaxed, the sheltered, well-tended courtyard or cosy dining room conducive to lingering chat. Cottagey, beamed bedrooms have good solid furniture, wooden floors, patchwork, plants and sensible bathrooms. An easy place to be, 10 minutes from Avignon, and in excellent rosé wine, olive and fruit country.

rooms	1 double.
price	€48 for two.
meals	Dinner with wine €18, book ahead.
closed	Rarely.
directions	From Avignon & Villeneuve N580 for Bagnols & Cèze; right on D377 & D177 to Pujaut. House opp. town hall; large metal door.

Joël & Michèle Rousseau
Les Bambous,
30131 Pujaut,
Gard
tel +33 (0)4 90 26 46 47
fax +33 (0)4 90 26 46 47
e-mail rousseau.michele@wanadoo.fr
web lesbambous.monsite.wanadoo.fr

Saba'ad

Helen and Jacques met in Africa – she a nurse, he an agriculturist – and are an interesting, committed couple (10% of their B&B income goes to development projects). Come and share their simple life in this little old village house with all its stairs, African mementos and pine furniture. There's space in your white-vaulted, red-curtained suite and you won't hear much traffic in enchanting Pujaut. The pretty, peaceful, terraced garden has a summer kitchen for guests but is not really suitable for adventurous toddlers. Super folk with whom to share good conversation over delicious suppers and a village worth exploring.

rooms	1 suite.
price	€45 for two.
meals	Dinner with wine €15, book ahead.
closed	Rarely.
directions	From Avignon N580 for Bagnols & Cèze; right D377 & D177 to Pujaut. In village head for Mairie; house 300m into old village from Mairie & church.

Helen Thompson
& Jacques Sergent
Saba'ad,
30131 Pujaut,
Gard
tel +33 (0)4 90 26 31 68
fax +33 (0)4 90 26 31 68
e-mail sergent.thompson@wanadoo.fr

La Terre des Lauriers

A path through the woods leads from the house to the river by the Pont du Gard – the setting is special. The house is less historic, and its décor idiosyncratic – a net canopy over one of the beds, hanging hats, splayed fans, silk flowers, etc. Bedrooms are themed, fresh and spotless; one has a connecting room with bunk beds and soft toys. Monsieur works in Nîmes but gives all his remaining time to welcoming and caring for his guests. You get a salon with games for the children, bedrooms with air conditioning and a lovely garden that slopes down to a pool. A reader describes breakfasts as "stupendous".

rooms	5: 2 doubles, 2 twin, 1 suite.
price	€98 for two.
meals	Choice of restaurants within 3km.
closed	Never.
directions	From Remoulins follow signs for Pont du Gard 'Rive Droite'. Sign on right.

Gérard Cristini
La Terre des Lauriers,
30210 Remoulins,
Gard
tel +33 (0)4 66 37 19 45
fax +33 (0)4 66 37 19 45
web www.laterredeslauriers.com

Les Écuries des Chartreux

A village or not a village? It feels like one and is a perfect place to stay when Avignon itself is heaving with people. A former stable block next door to a beautiful 13th-century monastery, the house is cool and light inside, its bedrooms polished and appealing with nice touches and a perfect little kitchen for guests. Pascale runs the Écuries as a B&B though in fact you have a fully-equipped studio, so can opt to be independent. But don't think she doesn't want you! She is on hand with breakfast, information and magazines you can borrow, and an aperitif before you head out for the evening.

rooms	3: 2 doubles, 1 suite.
price	€70-€125 for two.
meals	Good choice of restaurants nearby.
closed	Rarely.
directions	From Avignon cross Rhône for Nîmes & Villeneuve lès Avignon. Just after bridge right for Villeneuve centre, Rue de la République. House next to La Chartreuse.

Pascale Letellier
Les Écuries des Chartreux,
30400 Villeneuve lès Avignon,
Gard
tel +33 (0)4 90 25 79 93
fax +33 (0)4 90 25 79 93
e-mail ecuries-des-chartreux@wanadoo.fr
web www.ecuries-des-chartreux.com

Hôtel de l'Orange

At his *hôtel particulier* (private mansion), Philippe receives with warm refinement. Each very private room, named after a different local luminary (including our own Lawrence Durrell), is in traditional Provençal style: polished floors, warm-painted walls, white bedcovers, a different and beautiful wall hanging over each bed, super big bathrooms. The magic secluded terrace garden with gasping views over the roofs of the old town is where you swim; breakfast, which to Philippe is *the* moment of the day, is in the old-style dining room or the gorgeous courtyard. Grand, elegant – but utterly lovable.

rooms	6: 4 doubles, 1 twin, 1 triple.
price	€68-€152 for two.
meals	Dinner with wine €25, book ahead.
closed	Rarely.
directions	From Nîmes D40 W 28km to Sommières; from town centre for centre historique; from Post Office follow street up to château; signposted.

Philippe de Frémont
Hôtel de l'Orange,
30250 Sommières,
Gard

tel	+33 (0)4 66 77 79 94
fax	+33 (0)4 66 80 44 87
e-mail	hotel.dorange@free.fr
web	hotel.delorange.free.fr

26 boulevard Saint Louis

A Moorish tang colours Marion's 17th-century town house and garden: a fountain in the wall of the deliciously cool walled garden; candlelit dinners that taste of Provence and North Africa; adventurous colours and lovely fabrics; a sunken bath in the open-plan suite; beautiful pieces of furniture and paintings placed just where they enhance the generous proportions. It isn't grand, just simply elegant. This talented lady is a wonderful hostess who adores having guests, serving breakfasts of cold meats, cheese and local *fougasse* (a soft delicate bread) then pointing them to the cultural riches of the area. Very special.

rooms	4: 3 doubles, 1 suite.
price	€75-€110 for two.
meals	Dinner with wine €25, book ahead.
closed	Rarely.
directions	From A9 exit 26 Aimargues Centre. Cross r'bout with fountain down plane tree lane 300m. Entrance opp. Carli Immo, Rue de la Violette (3 cypresses behind garden wall).

Marion Escarfail
26 boulevard Saint Louis,
30470 Aimargues,
Gard

tel	+33 (0)4 66 88 52 99
fax	+33 (0)4 66 88 52 99
e-mail	marionmais@aol.com
web	members.aol.com/marionmais

Mas de Barbut

Smart, imaginative and decorated with great flair. Bedrooms are Mexican, Mandarin and Provencale: the first vibrant with chunky ethnic touches, the second aesthetically pure with clean lines, the third gracefully, flowingly comfortable. Outstanding bathrooms have fabulous tiles. The Gandons are great travellers, and have brought together fascinating things in a strikingly harmonious way. They also love cosseting guests. The traditional farmhouse protects you from the summer heat; there's a cool pool and a lovely spot for drinks on the river bank. Fifteen minutes from beaches, miles from worldly bustle.

rooms	3: 2 doubles, 1 triple.
price	€90-€102 for two.
meals	Dinner €30, with wine (Monday, Wednesday, Friday book ahead). Restaurants within 6km.
closed	Rarely.
directions	From A9 exit 26 for Gallargues. D979 for Aigues Mortes, 12.5km. Right at 7th r'bout for Le Vidourle, 2km. House on right.

Danielle & Jean-Claude Gandon
Mas de Barbut,
30220 St Laurent d'Aigouze, Gard
tel +33 (0)4 66 88 12 09
fax +33 (0)6 64 14 28 52
e-mail gandon.barbut@club-internet.fr
web www.masdebarbut.com

Map 17 Entry 641

La Ciboulette

The sun-drenched village street with its arched doorways and shuttered windows leads you to the gates of a fine old house where bull-fighting posters hang in the hall. At the back, your eye leaps straight into the parallel vines and uneven hills – a festival of flaming colour in autumn. Monsieur is English; Madame is French, an artist and good company. She has done her house with great sympathy for its original spaces and stone floors. Her works are a bonus on the walls. It is a privilege to be her only guests, enjoy the big unfussy bedroom onto the garden and step out into the morning light for homemade fig jam.

rooms	1 double.
price	€58 for two.
meals	Choice of restaurants 5km.
closed	Rarely.
directions	From A9 exit 27; D34 Sommières; left to St Christol; right of post office for Cave Coop.; left at r'bout (before small bridge) 800m, left Av. des Bruyères; Rue de l'Église.

Monique Sykes-Maillon
La Ciboulette,
34400 St Christol,
Hérault
tel +33 (0)4 67 86 81 00
e-mail happy@stchristol.com
web www.stchristol.com

Map 17 Entry 642

Castle's Cottage

On the edge of a wild, unspoilt forest, in a green oasis flooded with mimosa, hibiscus and iris where 46 tortoises roam freely, it's hard to believe you're a short bus ride from lively Montpellier. The house is recent, built with old materials, the vegetation lush, the swimming pool set among atmospheric stone 'ruins'. You sleep in smallish rooms full of family furniture and colour, sharing a very good shower room, and opening onto the terrace. Your hostess, once a city girl in public relations, loves this place and her many tortoises passionately, talks easily and generously shares her fireside and living space.

rooms	2 doubles, sharing shower & separate wc.
price	€78-€95 for two.
meals	Montpellier 3km.
closed	Rarely.
directions	From Mairie in Castelnau le Lez take Rue Jules Ferry; 5th left Chemin de la Rocheuse; last house on left.

	Dominique Carabin-Cailleau
	Castle's Cottage,
	34170 Castelnau le Lez, Hérault
tel	+33 (0)4 67 72 63 08
fax	+33 (0)4 67 72 63 08
e-mail	dpcc@libertysurf.fr
web	www.multimania.com/castlecottage

La Missare

A vast and lovely stone winery is the guest wing on this old family property. Your host's sensitive conversion uses old tiles, doors and beams; simple, stylish bedrooms are designed for comfort and privacy, each with an excellent shower room, antique embroidered linen and French windows onto the well-caressed garden courtyard. Jean-François and his mother happily share their living space: go through the big hall, hung with some fine prints, to generous breakfast in the living room where a cabinet of treasures will intrigue. Outside, a discreet pool glimmers under a vast umbrella pine.

rooms	4 doubles.
price	€60-€70 for two.
meals	Restaurants 3-12km.
closed	Rarely.
directions	From Clermont L'Hérault N9 r'bout D4 for Brignac 3.5km; house on right entering village.

	Jean-François Martin
	La Missare,
	34800 Brignac,
	Hérault
tel	+33 (0)4 67 96 07 67
e-mail	la.missare@free.fr
web	la.missare.free.fr

Domaine du Pélican

A perfect B&B on a superb estate with mulberry-lined drive, hills, vineyards and a real family atmosphere: simplicity, peace, fine big rooms and a charming welcome. The owners have four children of their own and run an inn in their beautifully restored old family house. In a separate building, guest rooms have soft-coloured walls, beds on mezzanines, pretty shower rooms. The dining room has old honey-coloured beams – a dream – and gives onto the terrace and rows of vines beyond: just the place for authentic, and delicious, auberge dinner. New: a lovely guest sitting room and saltwater pool.

rooms	4: 1 double; 1 double with fold-out bed; 1 twin with fold-out bed; 1 suite for 4.
price	€61-€66 for two; €83-€88 for four.
meals	Dinner with wine €20, book ahead. Pizzeria & brasserie 3-5km.
closed	Last week in October.
directions	From Gignac east towards Montpellier; at edge of town bust stop Pelican on right; right & follow signs for 3km.

Isabelle & Baudouin Thillaye de Boullay
Domaine du Pélican,
34150 Gignac, Hérault

tel	+33 (0)4 67 57 68 92
fax	+33 (0)4 67 57 68 92
e-mail	domaine-de-pelican@wanadoo.fr

Map 16 Entry 645

La Genestière

Madame's work upon the walls (she's an artist and sculptor), Monsieur's fine horse in the paddock – the modern house has lots of atmosphere and your hostess is an open, fun person who loves getting to know you, even teaching you to sculpt (do enquire). Rooms are big and simply furnished, each with a few lovely things, good fabrics and a private outside space onto the green garden with a summer kitchen. All in a fabulous spot protected by umbrella pines by the magnificent Salagou lake for sailing and swimming on long, hot summer's days, great biking, walking, riding in winter. Definitely worth staying longer.

rooms	2 doubles.
price	€50-€60 for two. Minimum stay 2 nights.
meals	2 restaurants 3.5km.
closed	Rarely.
directions	A9 exit 34 on D13 N 10km; N9 to Clermont l'Hérault; D156 left for Lac du Salagou 3km; left to Liausson; 700m along last house on right before woods.

M & Mme Neveu
La Genestière,
34800 Clermont l'Hérault,
Hérault

tel	+33 (0)4 67 96 30 97
fax	+33 (0)4 99 91 08 89
e-mail	lagenestiere@free.fr
web	www.mediatisse.com/Lac-du-Salagou/genestie/genestie.htm

Map 16 Entry 646

7 Grand Rue

Villeneuvette is a special village, built under Louis XIV to produce red cloth for soldiers, and its surrounding wall and workers' cottages, cobbled streets and giant plane trees are still intact. Swedish Anna is a special person doing real B&B in this phase of her interesting life. A travel guide, acupuncturist, gatherer of arts and crafts, she is quiet and welcoming. Her living room floods with morning light, crackles with winter logs, glows with plants, paintings and books. Looking over rooftops to the hills, your bedroom is uncluttered and lovely: Tibetan hangings, one antique chest, a few stunning colours.

rooms	1 double with separate shower.
price	€50-€60 for two.
meals	Restaurant in walking distance, several more 3km away.
closed	Rarely.
directions	From Clermont Littérault for Bédarieux; 3km, right to Villeneuvette; enter village 2nd last house on right.

Anna Samson
7 Grand Rue,
34800 Villeneuvette,
Hérault
tel +33 (0)4 67 96 96 67
e-mail anna.samson@tiscali.fr

Château de Grézan

An amazing, 19th-century, neo-medieval château built in a troubadour style, with towers, turrets and castellated walls. Yet a very simple welcome from Marie-France – a remarkable, generous lady, a member of the champagne family who organises her own 'taste travels'. Crystal chandeliers, grand piano, original wallpapers, cavernous rooms… you'll forgive the odd imperfect corner. Bedrooms are big and absolutely château, bathrooms fittingly old-fashioned. The evocative inner courtyard is lush with camellias and cyclamen, the gardens are lovely, the swimming pool lies beneath the palms.

rooms	3: 2 doubles, 1 twin.
price	€90-€110 for two. Suite €170 for four.
meals	Restaurant in château grounds.
closed	Rarely.
directions	From A75 exit 35 Béziers N112 NW 10km; right D909 for Bédarieux 17km; right to Grézan.

Mme Marie-France Lanson
Château de Grézan,
34480 Laurens,
Hérault
tel +33 (0)4 67 90 28 03
fax +33 (0)4 67 90 05 03
e-mail chateau-grezan.lanson@wanadoo.fr

Château de Murviel

The château is perched right on top of the town. From the windows, ancient mellow rooftops give way to vineyards and more hills. Soft, plastered walls, honey-coloured floorboards or pale, nearly white stone floors and bleached linen curtains around beds give a wonderful feeling of light – unexpected in such an old building. Breakfast is in an enclosed courtyard, dotted with lemon trees and white oleander and guests can cook supper in their own kitchen. Whether you are interested in wine or the Cathars, want to cycle along the Canal du Midi or swim from a river beach – this is just the place.

rooms	4: 1 double, 2 triples, 1 suite for 3.
price	€80-€100 for two. Whole house per week €1,950-€3,900. Minimum stay 2 nights in high season.
meals	Restaurants nearby; self-catering possible.
closed	Rarely.
directions	From A9 exit 35 for Centre Ville; at 1st & 2nd r'bouts: for Bédarieux; 3rd r'bout: for Corneilhan & Murviel; in Murviel centre, next to Mairie.

Yves & Florence Cousquer
Château de Murviel,
34490 Murviel lès Béziers,
Hérault

tel +33 (0)4 67 32 35 45
fax +33 (0)4 67 32 35 25
e-mail chateaudemurviel@free.fr
web www.murviel.com

La Cerisaie

The shyly friendly Dutch owners of the elegant Cerisaie came to visit, fell in love with it and bought it, lock, stock and furniture. At a long outdoor table with green wicker chairs, Honorah serves a fabulous buffet from 12 till 5pm. She also makes jam from the big old cherry trees in the garden, and has decorated the uncluttered, classically-proportioned rooms with her attractive paintings.
A proud old staircase mounts to the bedrooms which are just right – light, roomy, marble-fireplaced, old-furnished, double-glazed against the road (though there is some noise), with super views of hills and the truly lovely garden.

rooms	6: 3 doubles, 2 twins, 1 suite with kitchenette.
price	€70-€80 for two. Minimum stay 2 nights.
meals	Dinner €22 Wednesdays, book ahead; wine €10-€17; lunch à la carte. Good restaurant nearby.
closed	October-May
directions	From A9 exit Béziers Ouest; D64; N112 for Castres, Mazamet & St Pons; 1km before St Pons right D908 to Riols; house on left leaving Riols.

Honorah & Albert Jan Karsten
La Cerisaie,
34220 Riols,
Hérault

tel +33 (0)4 67 97 03 87
fax +33 (0)4 67 97 03 88
e-mail cerisaie@wanadoo.fr
web www.cerisaie.net

La Métairie Basse

In these wild, pastoral surroundings with great walking and climbing trails, you bathe in simplicity, stream-babble and light. Your hosts, hard-working walnut and chestnut growers, have converted to 'bio' and sell delicious pureés and jams. The guest barn is beautifully tended: country antiques, old lace curtains, new bedding and blue tones relax the eye, and there's a fireplace and a full kitchen too. Monsieur has a real, friendly handshake, Madame is gentle and welcoming, and breakfast on the shady terrace includes cheese or walnuts or honey. The wonderful Cathar city of Minerve is a 40-minutes drive.

rooms	2 doubles.
price	€48 for two.
meals	Restaurants 3-4km.
closed	October-March, except by arrangement.
directions	From A9 exit Béziers Ouest; D64; N112 to Mazamet; N112 for St Pons de Thomières. At Courniou, right to Prouilhe; farm on left.

Éliane & Jean-Louis Lunes
La Métairie Basse,
34220 Courniou,
Hérault

tel	+33 (0)4 67 97 21 59
fax	+33 (0)4 67 97 21 59
e-mail	info@metairie-basse.com
web	www.metairie-basse.com

La Bastide des Corbières

The big inviting bedrooms – called Syrah, Chardonnay… to reflect Jacques' passion for his wild and wonderful Cathar country and its wines – have a superb feeling of space and light. Divine smells rise from the kitchen where Françoise bakes cakes to be served for tomorrow's breakfast on the stone terrace that leads to the garden. She so clearly loves having guests to cook for and chat to. Wide stone stairs, old pieces of furniture and soothing colours make this house most comfortable and welcoming. "A little corner of Paradise", one guest wrote to tell us – and good value.

rooms	5: 4 doubles, 1 twin.
price	€70-€84 for two. Minimum stay 3 nights July-August.
meals	Dinner with €29, book ahead.
closed	Rarely.
directions	From A61 exit 25 for Lézignan; D212 for Fabrezan (back over A61); D106 to Ferrals les Corbières; D161 to Boutenac; signposted in village.

Françoise & Jacques Camel
La Bastide des Corbières,
11200 Boutenac,
Aude

tel	+33 (0)4 68 27 20 61
fax	+33 (0)4 68 27 62 71
e-mail	bastide.corbieres@wanadoo.fr
web	www.bastide-corbieres.com

Château de Donos

History upon history, stone upon stone: ruined medieval fortress, Romanesque church, austere 17th-century fortified manor (where guests live) and 200-year-old château (where owners live) are all here, owned astonishingly by just two families in 1,300 years. Bedrooms and bathrooms, huge and beautiful, ooze class; the vineyards give superbly. In the grounds is a delightful lake where you may swim among the fishes (but watch children at all times). Monsieur, whose heart is at Donos, will tell you heroic tales of his forebears. Shyly gracious, Madame is generous to a fault. Both are endlessly interesting.

rooms	6: 4 doubles, 2 family suites for 4.
price	€80-€105 for two.
meals	Restaurant 3km.
closed	October-April.
directions	From Carcassonne for Narbonne exit Lezignan-Corbières. For Ferrals les Corbières; for Villerouge la Crémale; for Thézan des Corbières; D611 through Thézan; 3km, 3rd entrance on right.

M & Mme Chardigny
Château de Donos,
11200 Thézan des Corbières,
Aude
tel +33 (0)4 68 43 32 11
fax +33 (0)4 68 43 32 11
e-mail reservations@chateaudonos.com
web www.chateaudonos.com

La Marelle

What a lovely, starry-eyed team, so young, so enthusiastic about their new venture beneath the château in the middle of this pretty village. They have taken on La Marelle as it was: simple décor in light comfortable rooms (the pale pink 'family' room is very appealing), same huge living room in the old school refectory. Work on bathrooms is in progress. They are both wonderful cooks, she with her Polish influence, he with memories of his grandmother's French farm kitchen; she also makes essential oils and natural soaps; there's a really interesting collection of (French) books in their library.

rooms	5: 4 doubles, 1 family room.
price	€53 for two.
meals	Dinner with wine €21, book ahead.
closed	Rarely.
directions	Exit A61 at Carcassone Est; D610 for Marseillette & Puichéric; 23.5km, left for La Redorte; after green bridge left; house behind big green iron fence on right.

Philippe & Anna Lizé
La Marelle,
11700 La Redorte,
Aude
tel +33 (0)4 68 91 59 30
e-mail la-marelle11@wanadoo.fr
web perso.wanadoo.fr/lamarelle/

Le Vieux Relais

With all her energy, Sally has turned her 17th-century coaching inn into a balanced marriage of solid old French base and modern inspiration. Having lived in England and America, where she was an interior designer, she then adopted France and her sense of style permeates the old house in a comfortable mix of antique and contemporary. She is also a superb cook, making delicious Mediterranean-inspired dishes with the best local produce, provides all possible goodies in her big, well-furnished bedrooms and loves to share her passion for history and travel. *Children over 12 welcome.*

rooms	3: 2 doubles, 1 suite for 4.
price	€61 for two. Suite €106. Minimum stay 2 nights June-Sept.
meals	Dinner with wine €30, book ahead.
closed	Rarely.
directions	From Carcassonne N113 to Trèbes; left D610 to Marseillette & Piuchéric; left D910 to Olonzac; follow signs to Pépieux; next to church.

Sally Worthington
Le Vieux Relais,
11700 Pépieux,
Aude

tel +33 (0)4 68 91 69 29
fax +33 (0)4 68 91 65 49
e-mail sally.worthington@wanadoo.fr
web perso.wanadoo.fr/carrefourbedbreakfast/

L'Ancienne Boulangerie

In the history- and legend-laden north Minervois, Caunes is one of France's most beautiful medieval towns. Quiet too: the twisting lanes make speed impossible. This house baked bread from 1500 to 1988. Its new American owners, easy, interesting people, have kept the steep narrow stairs and the old floors, made five good, cosy guest rooms – antique beds, new mattresses – and a tiny first-floor terrace for summer breakfasts. Diminutive ground floor, but hugely good conversation – they organise an annual exhibition with artists from San Francisco (Terry was a reporter there). And all that exploring to do.

rooms	5: 2 doubles; 1 double, 1 triple, sharing shower & wc; 1 family suite.
price	€41-€61 for two.
meals	Restaurant opposite.
closed	Christmas.
directions	From Carcassonne D620 to Caunes Minervois; cross river & follow to Mairie; house behind Épicerie opp. Place de la Mairie.

Terry & Lois Link
L'Ancienne Boulangerie,
11160 Caunes-Minervois,
Aude

tel +33 (0)4 68 78 01 32
e-mail ancienne.boulangerie@free.fr
web www.caunes-minervois.com

Domaine Saint Pierre de Trapel

Coming in from the magnificent gardens, you catch a wonderful smell of herbs as you walk through the house. The charming owners, educated and well-travelled, moved here from east France for a more relaxing way of life and climate. Using exquisite taste, they have combined original 18th-century elegances with new necessities in big bedrooms and bathrooms of pure luxury, each with its own lovely colour scheme. Best in the summer, with relaxing outdoor spots for all, a superb 150-year-old cedar, olive trees, a swimming pool surrounded by roses and a lovely covered terrace. A place of great beauty.

rooms	5: 1 twin, 3 doubles, 1 suite for 4.
price	€85-€145 for two.
meals	Restaurants in Carcassonne.
closed	November-March.
directions	From A61 exit 23 for Mazamet; at r'bout D620 for Villalier; after 1.5km, towards Villedubert; on right, through wrought-iron gates.

Christophe & Catherine Pariset
Domaine Saint Pierre de Trapel,
11620 Villemoustaussou,
Aude

tel	+33 (0)4 68 77 00 68
fax	+33 (0)4 68 77 01 68
e-mail	cpariset@trapel.com
web	www.trapel.com

Domaine des Castelles

There are space and air galore in this 19th-century gentleman-farmer's house. The freshly decorated bedrooms – with own entrance – are vast, comfortably furnished (plus good mattresses), pine-floored and impeccably clean; the restful gardens cover one whole hectare. Madame, open and welcoming, willingly chats to guests over breakfast – on the terrace in fine weather – and enjoys their travellers' tales. You are in the country yet so near the buzz of Carcassonne (and the airport!), while the dreamy Canal du Midi and the vineyards offer their seductively parallel alternatives.

rooms	3: 1 double, 1 triple, 1 suite for 5.
price	€60-€65 for two.
meals	Choice of restaurants nearby.
closed	Rarely.
directions	On A61 exit Carcassonne-West to Salvaza airport; stay on D119 for approx. 4km more. Sign on left.

Isabelle Clayette
Domaine des Castelles,
11170 Caux et Sauzens,
Aude

tel	+33 (0)4 68 72 03 60
fax	+33 (0)4 68 72 03 60

Ferme de la Sauzette

Beautifully converted Sauzette, resplendent in huge beams, open fireplace and impeccable taste, has five pretty rooms (one for disabled), utter quiet to relax into and wonderful walks around. Chris and Diana, warm and attentive, are great cooks; meals, served outside in summer, are hugely enjoyable affairs (they have been known to run late). Your hosts revel in the area, its birdlife, wild flowers, history and wine. They have lovely children (and well-behaved large dogs) and give language courses in winter. All this 5km from Carcassonne, 10km from an 18-hole golf course.

rooms	5: 3 doubles, 1 twin, 1 triple.
price	€62-€73 for two. Minimum stay 2 nights May-September.
meals	Dinner with wine €28, book ahead.
closed	January & November.
directions	From Carcassonne D142 to Cazilhac. Left opp. Mairie D56 for Villefloure (bear left at cemetery); follow signs for 2km; left at Sauzette sign.

Chris Gibson & Diana Warren
Ferme de la Sauzette,
Cazilhac ,
11570 Palaja, Aude
tel +33 (0)4 68 79 81 32
fax +33 (0)4 68 79 65 99
e-mail info@lasauzette.com
web www.lasauzette.com

Villelongue Côté Jardins

Romantics, painters, poets – here be paradise. One room looks onto the lush-wild, magic-exotic park watered by 17th-century monastic hydraulics, the other over the great courtyard, where the donkey may call you, to the ruined Cistercian abbey. Rooms are big, beamy and simply refined in their white cotton and fine old armoires. Sisters Renée and Claude, earthy and generous, were born here, are renovating with loving care on a shoestring, will take you to meet each great tree and provide extravagantly elegant dinners with family linen and silver. There are four retired horses... and so much more. It's incomparable.

rooms	2 doubles.
price	€55 for two.
meals	Dinner with wine €18, book ahead. Auberge 100m.
closed	Rarely.
directions	From A61 exit Bram; D4 through Bram & St Martin le Vieil; right on tiny D64 3km to Abbey. Caution: Go to Côté Jardins B&B not Abbey B&B next door.

Claude Antoine
Villelongue Côté Jardins,
11170 St Martin le Vieil,
Aude
tel +33 (0)4 68 76 09 03
e-mail avillelongue@free.fr
web avillelongue.free.fr

Château de Saint Michel de Lanes

Your admirable hosts have saved this utterly romantic place, a near-ruin of an ancestral château, by dint of sheer crusading aristocratic grit, intelligent research and hard manual work. The Viscount, a self-taught master builder, even regilded the lofty baroque ceilings. There are 40 rooms and four ghosts; Madame can recount pre-Revolutionary family lore for hours; every piece of furniture tells a tale; the cedars are regal, the river peaceful, breakfast luxurious with grandmama's fine silver. Guests have the privilege of the best renovations: two fine salons, huge, elegant bedrooms. Exceptional.

rooms	3: 1 double, 1 twin; 1 double with separate bath & wc.
price	€95-€145 for two.
meals	Restaurant 50m.
closed	Christmas holidays.
directions	A61 for Carcassone; exit Villefranche de Lauragais for Gardouch; cross Canal du Midi; left D625, 10km. In St Michel left cross bridge; château on left.

Vicomte & Vicomtesse Vincent de La Panouse
Château de Saint Michel de Lanes,
11410 St Michel de Lanès,
Aude

tel +33 (0)4 68 60 31 80
e-mail chateausaintmichel@tiscali.fr
web www.chateausaintmichel.com

Map 16 Entry 661

Domaine de Couchet

It's a joy to see this great old farmhouse imbued with new blood: Belgian Justine and Scottish Alan left high-flying high-pressure Brussels to indulge their love of nature, local markets and good food (they both cook) at Couchet, in heavenly meadows and woodland, and long to share it with others. The bedrooms are already enjoying their soft human touch and new beds, bathrooms have been renovated, the wraparound garden is ever glorious and produces wonders for pot and table, their French and English library is for all to share and they will be the most charming, intelligent hosts.

rooms	3: 2 doubles, 1 triple; children's room available.
price	€56-€68 for two. Minimum stay 2 nights July & Aug.
meals	Dinner with wine €25, book ahead.
closed	Rarely.
directions	From Limoux D620 for Chalabre 7km; fork right D626 for Mirepoix to Peyrefitte. Signs from village.

Justine Wallington & Alan Lynch
Domaine de Couchet,
11230 Peyrefitte du Razès,
Aude

tel +33 (0)4 68 69 55 06
fax +33 (0)4 68 69 55 06
e-mail justine.wallington@wanadoo.fr
web www.domainedecouchet.com

Map 16 Entry 662

Sanglier Lodge

Jan, a larger-then-life photographer, came from Zimbabwe seeking a peaceful refuge, was charged by a wild boar and promptly bought the two old hillside houses. He and Margaret, a lively doctor, have created a cottagey atmosphere with exotic overtones: Zimbabwean teak chairs and an antique Spanish table on rough chestnut floors, cast-iron beds on old tiles, original oils on rough white walls. The old bakery bedroom has the bread oven and the baker's licence, showers are like dinner plates. In an exceptionally beautiful area, it has a wonderful plunge pool, the river Tech below the house and much more.

rooms	5: 3 doubles, 1 twin, 1 family room.
price	€70 for two.
meals	Restaurant nearby.
closed	Nov-March
directions	From Perpignan-Barcelona motorway south exit Le Boulou & Céret. Follow signs for Céret & Arles sur Tech; for Prats le Mollo & La Preste, 12km. Park in village square, go left of post office, Sanglier Lodge is No. 6.

Jan Teede
Sanglier Lodge,
66230 Le Tech,
Pyrénées-Orientales

tel	+33 (0)4 68 39 62 51
fax	+33 (0)4 68 39 62 51
e-mail	info@sanglierlodge.com
web	www.sanglierlodge.com

Map 16 Entry 663

La Châtaigneraie

The Bethells have created a haven of Pyrenean-Scottish hospitality among some of Europe's wildest, remotest landscapes just 15 minutes' walk from lively Céret. In the magical, lush garden, the family parrot may flit with you among the intimate sitting areas where views dazzle up to snowy Canigou or down to the sea. Super, romantic rooms have original works of art and bright scatter cushions, two even promise the bliss of a private terrace for breakfast, delivered by Kim – a very warm and lovely person. And for dinner, there's the famous Terrasse au Soleil. *Watch children with unfenced pool.*

rooms	6: 3 doubles, 1 twin/double, 2 suites.
price	€80-€163 for two.
meals	Excellent restaurant 400m or choice in village; BBQ available.
closed	December-January.
directions	A9 to Spain, last exit before border; into Céret for Centre Ville then for Hôtel La Terrasse au Soleil. House 400m after hotel, on left.

Kim & Gill Bethell
La Châtaigneraie,
66400 Céret,
Pyrénées-Orientales

tel	+33 (0)4 68 87 21 58
fax	+33 (0)4 68 87 77 86
e-mail	gillandkim@ceret.net
web	www.ceret.net

Map 16 Entry 664

photo Michael Busselle

rhône valley–alps

Quartier Versailles

The high-walled garden is a dream where hibiscus, oleander, mallows and vines rampage, nothing is too kempt and statues can take you by surprise. It has secret corners and a perfect breakfast terrace with splendid pots against the pale stone wall. Indoors, Madame plays soothing classical music so the antics of Ivan the dachshund don't impinge. A gently friendly hostess, she brought her children up here and creates a family atmosphere. The guest room's fireplace can be lit to make the fine red and blue tiled floor cosier, its antique bookshelves are stuffed with books, the spot of damp is due for repair. A good hideaway.

rooms	1 double.
price	€48 for two.
meals	Dinner with wine €17, book ahead. Good auberge in village.
closed	November-March.
directions	From A7 exit Bollène to Pont St Esprit; N86 for Bourg St Andéol; in St Just, Rue de Versailles opposite church; house with big gates 100m on right.

Jacqueline Crozier
Quartier Versailles,
07700 St Just d'Ardèche,
Ardèche
tel +33 (0)4 75 04 60 52

Map 17 Entry 665

Le Couradou

Diana, bright and gifted, and Jos, a shy geologist, came from cool populous Belgium to empty rustic Ardèche, fell in love with the ghost of a silk worm and set about transforming this fine big silk-farm house into a warm home. Outside, vineyards and the distant Cévennes, inside, wonderful vaulted 15th-century ceilings, split-level living spaces and six super guest rooms. All different, they are simply done with the local gifts of stone walls, country antiques, Provençal patterns and wrought iron. Each room has an armchair or a sofa, bright cushions, all the comforts. They will welcome you like friends.

rooms	6: 2 doubles, 2 twins, 1 quadruple, 1 family room.
price	€78-€121 for two. Minimum stay 2 nights in high season.
meals	Dinner with wine €25, book ahead.
closed	November-February
directions	From N86 Bourg St Andeol; D4 to Vallon Pont d'Arc; D579 left for Baryac, 4km; D217 left for Labastide.

Diana Little
& Jos Vandervondelen
Le Couradou,
07150 Labastide de Virac,
Ardèche
tel +33 (0)4 75 38 64 75
fax +33 (0)4 75 38 68 26
e-mail infos@lecouradou.com
web www.lecouradou.com

Map 17 Entry 666

La Petite Cour Verte

The drive up is spectacular – go gently. Once there, gasp at the view, and unwind among the flower-tumbled terraces. The 400-year-old house, a haven of unpretentious cosmopolitan elegance hugging its courtyard, has super old/new, light-filled, balconied rooms, a fine vaulted salon, good art, a small indoor pool, solarium and sauna and fabulous walking. Henri and Jacote have spared nothing to renovate their amazing house; relaxed and interesting hosts who love sharing their space, they provide excellent food – sorbets to die for – with real conversation. Oh, and 20 jams for breakfast.

rooms	6: 2 doubles, 2 twins, 2 family rooms.
price	€69-€75 for two.
meals	Dinner with wine €20, book ahead.
closed	December-April, except by arrangement.
directions	From Joyeuse D203 for Valgorge. At Pont du Gua cross bridge; narrow paved road up hillside to La Roche (10 hairpins in 3km!).

Henri Rouvière
La Petite Cour Verte,
07110 La Roche Beaumont,
Ardèche
tel +33 (0)4 75 39 58 88
fax +33 (0)4 75 39 43 00
e-mail henri.rouviere@wanadoo.fr
web www.lapetitecourverte.com

Les Roudils

A piece of paradise. The climate: Mediterranean. The setting: high, rural, hidden, silent, in the nature-rich Monts d'Ardèche park. The views: long, of mountain peaks, inspiring. The house: of stone, and wood from the surrounding chestnut forests, lovingly restored, light, open. Bedrooms: sunny, just right. Food: organic, home-grown, imaginative, lots of honey. Your hosts warm, trusting are quickly your friends. Marie sings; Gil makes beautiful furniture – see their monumental dining table – and keeps bees; music plays. There's lots more: come up the long narrow road to walk, talk, and believe us.

rooms	3: 1 double, 1 triple, 1 suite for 5.
price	€48 for two.
meals	Dinner-Restaurant 4km
closed	November-Easter
directions	From Aubenas N102 for Le Puy 8.5km. At Lalevade left to Jaujac centre. By Café des Loisirs cross river & follow signs 4km along narrow mountain road.

Marie & Gil Florence
Les Roudils,
07380 Jaujac,
Ardèche
tel +33 (0)4 75 93 21 11
fax +33 (0)4 75 93 21 11
e-mail le-rucher-des-roudils@wanadoo.fr
web www.le-rucher-des-roudils.fr

Il Fut Un Temps

Once upon a time, Anne-Marie found her fairy-tale house in a deep undiscovered corner between the Auvergne and the Loire. Now her son Julien and his partner Trudi have joined the dream, kept the charm and added their own youthful mark. Lively dinners before a crackling log fire are a seductively rustic mix of modern and traditional; the beer and fruit wine are homemade, the cookery courses are a treat (courses in French language, art, relaxation too...). Be seduced by rooms that are cosy and enticing (pretty fabrics, new art, rafters and rough stone walls) and shower rooms that sparkle.

rooms	5: 1 double, 2 twins, 2 quadruples.
price	€58-€75 for two.
meals	Dinner with wine €22, book ahead.
closed	Rarely.
directions	From A72 exit 4 D53 E to Champoly. D24 E to St Marcel d'Urfé; D20 S for St Martin la Sauveté & follow signs.

Famille Hauck-Perbet
Il Fut Un Temps,
42430 St Marcel d'Urfé,
Loire

tel	+33 (0)4 77 62 52 19
fax	+33 (0)4 77 62 53 88
e-mail	ilfutuntemps@wanadoo.fr
web	www.ilfutuntemps.com

Map 12 Entry 669

Domaine de Champfleury

A charmingly typical Napoleon III manor, square and confident in its five acres of superb parkland and the famous Troisgros restaurant nearby make this a place to stay some time. A tennis court and great walking (all levels) create an appetite for the local gastronomy. You are guests in a family home, your antique-furnished bedroom is relaxedly formal, the bath is a claw-footed marvel (plenty of towels and bathrobes go with it) and Madame a gentle, generous widow. She loves sharing a welcome cup and guiding one to the hidden delights of this lovely area. *Ask about pets.*

rooms	2: 1 double; 1 suite for 3-4.
price	€72 for two. Suite €108 for three.
meals	Choice of restaurants within 3km; Trois Gros at Roanne, 8km.
closed	15 November-15 March.
directions	From Roanne D53 for 8km. Right into village & follow signs.

Mme Gaume
Domaine de Champfleury,
42155 Lentigny,
Loire

tel	+33 (0)4 77 63 31 43
fax	+33 (0)4 77 63 31 43

Map 12 Entry 670

Château de Bachelard

Lake and Loire fill the air with liquid magic for the deer, duck and fish that flourish here – but the full-size lion of Bachelard drank African waters before being culled by Hervé's father. Daniéla and he are city people, sophisticated and entertaining, one vivacious, the other discreet, and very welcoming. Rooms, smallish to plain vast, have some fine big antiques, rich but simple draperies and colourful carpets. An artist friend let loose in the Painter's room left wrap-around exotica and a painted ceiling – extraordinary. Add a huge living room, log fire, relaxed mood, and you have unstinting generosity.

rooms	4: 3 doubles, 1 suite for 6.
price	€90 for two.
meals	Dinner with wine €23, 2km, book ahead.
closed	Rarely.
directions	From Roanne by-pass on N7 exit 68 to Comelle Vernay & Le Coteau; D43 & D56 to château.

Hervé & Daniéla Noiard
Château de Bachelard,
42120 Commelle Verney,
Loire
tel +33 (0)4 77 71 93 67
fax +33 (0)4 77 78 10 20
e-mail bachelard@worldonline.fr
web www.accueil.com/bachelard

Le Bayard

On a clear day you can see the snow. This marvellous place is clear every day in intention and presence. Gentle people, they have renovated their little old farmhouse with love, different woods (his hobby), pretty lamps. There's sitting space and a woodburner in the barn guest room, plus two big beds, one on a platform. Delicious, healthy breakfast is at a long table in Marie-Odile's enchanting, light kitchen or on the terrace in their nature garden. She loves all things natural, the house smells of wax and fresh wild flowers, the peace is palpable and you can be as private as you wish.

rooms	1 double.
price	€50 for two.
meals	Restaurants 5km.
closed	Rarely.
directions	South of Lyon leave A7 at Pierre Benits; A45 for Brignais; in Thuris Bourg; for St Martin du Haut; D122 for Yzeron; right at Loiy Première. Signposted.

Marie-Odile Lemoine
Le Bayard,
69510 Thurins,
Rhône
tel +33 (0)4 78 19 10 83
e-mail mo-lemoine@wanadoo.fr

Autrefois St Fortunat

In a strangely Italianate village minutes from the cultural treasures of Lyon, this big 1830's house has the softness and wisdom of honey-coloured stones, pale beams and hand-made floors, clothed by Karine in gentle pale fabrics and beautiful oriental rugs. She loves being at home with her little girl while amateur musician father is at work, welcoming guests to their big, creamy rooms on the floor below (separate entrances). Designer bathrooms vie for attention with well-polished old furniture and iron beds. Discreet sophistication, a couple of patios, city delights so near. Marvellous.

rooms	2 doubles.
price	€105-€140 for two.
meals	Good choice of restaurants within walking distance.
closed	Rarely.
directions	A6 exit Limonest le Bourg; for Les Monts d'Or - St Didier; right for Gendarmerie; 4km left; right at r'bout for St Fortunat. In village turn right; on right.

Karine Laurent-Rault
Autrefois St Fortunat,
Hameau de St Fortunat,
69370 St Didier au Mt d'Or,
Rhône

tel +33 (0)4 78 35 52 38
fax +33 (0)4 78 35 52 38
e-mail contact@autrefois-saintfortunat.com
web www.autrefois-saintfortunat.com

Château de Longsard

Orange trees in the *orangerie*, an obelisk amid the topiary chessmen, two spectacular Lebanon cedars, wine from the estate, beautiful 17th-century beams to guard your sleep. Your Franco-American hosts, sophisticated, multi-lingual, are genuinely keen to share their enthusiasm for the area and its wines (and will organise tastings, including their own). Bedrooms, pure château from pastel to bold with hints of modernity, some with fine carved door frames, are eclectically furnished. Dinner is certainly worth booking. If you want to sample *le grand style*, this is for you.

rooms	5: 3 doubles, 2 suites.
price	€102-€122 for two.
meals	Dinner with wine €34, book ahead.
closed	Rarely.
directions	From north A6 exit 'Belleville'; N6 for Lyon 10km; right D43 to Arnas. Through village; château on right after 1.5km.

Alexandra & Olivier du Mesnil
Château de Longsard,
69400 Arnas,
Rhône

tel +33 (0)4 74 65 55 12
fax +33 (0)4 74 65 03 17
e-mail longsard@wanadoo.fr
web www.longsard.com

Château de Pramenoux

It took 150 tons of tiles to restore the two towers and tons of loving care from charming young Emmanuel, whose partner Jean-Luc works in town, to restore the brilliantly intricate parquet floor. One of the bedrooms is panelled in cherrywood; all are generous and uplifting, each with a fireplace and a big jacuzzi bathroom, another with a royal blue baldaquin flecked with golden fleur-de-lys. And just enough of just the right furniture. Built between the 10th and 16th centuries with fairy-tale turrets in a natural clearing and views down the valley, it is so peaceful a place that it might almost be an hallucination.

rooms	4 doubles.
price	€120-€135 for two.
meals	Dinner with wine €35, book ahead.
closed	Rarely.
directions	From A6 exit Belleville D37 for Beaujeu to St Vincent; left D9 to Quincié, Marchampt, Lamure; at end of Lamure, lane opp. 'terrain de sport' for Pramenoux.

Emmanuel Baudouin
& Jean-Luc Plasse
Château de Pramenoux,
69870 Lamure sur Azergues,
Rhône

tel	+33 (0)4 74 03 16 43
fax	+33 (0)4 74 03 16 28
e-mail	pramenoux@aol.com
web	www.chateau-de-pramenoux.com

Les Pasquiers

Come and join this family's charming, authentically aristocratic life: no prissiness (two screened-off bathrooms) in their big townhouse, just unselfconscious style. The richly-decorated golden salon has a piano, books and open fireplace. The richly-stocked garden has a pool, a summerhouse, a large terrace, 150 species of trees, an organic vegetable garden and a statue of *Grand-père*. Madame is too busy cooking to eat with guests but welcomes company as she's preparing dinner. Children love it – there are toys and the hosts' own children to play with.

rooms	4: 2 doubles, 2 twins.
price	€80 for two.
meals	Dinner with wine €25, book ahead.
closed	Rarely.
directions	From A6 exit Macon Sud or Belleville; N6 to Romanèche & Lancié. In village for Fleurie into Square Les Pasquiers.

Jacques & Laurence Gandilhon
Les Pasquiers,
69220 Lancié,
Rhône

tel	+33 (0)4 74 69 86 33
fax	+33 (0)4 74 69 86 57
e-mail	ganpasq@aol.com

Manoir de Marmont

An amazing avenue of plane trees takes you to this exceptional house and hostess. Madame is a live wire, laughing, enthusing, giving – unforgettable; her house is as elegantly colourful as she is. Climb the grand stairs to your splendid château-style room, revel in Persian carpets, trompe-l'œil walls, antiques, fresh flowers. Beside Shakespeare and the candles, Madame pours tea from silver into porcelain and artfully moves the breakfast butter as the sun rises; at night she'll light your bedside lamp, leaving a book open at a carefully chosen page for you to read after a game of (French) Scrabble. Inimitably fine...

rooms	2 doubles.
price	€79 for two.
meals	Good restaurant 3km.
closed	Rarely.
directions	From Bourg en Bresse N83 towards Lyon. At Servas right D64 towards Condeissiat 5km; left at sign Le Marmont: plane-tree avenue. Don't go to St André.

Geneviève & Henri Guido-Alhéritière
Manoir de Marmont,
01960 St André sur Vieux Jonc,
Ain

tel +33 (0)4 74 52 79 74

Map 12 Entry 677

La Ferme du Champ Pelaz

It was love at first sight so three generations of Smiths came to the gentle land where distant peaks tantalise, to repair and pamper the 19th-century farmhouse for all: Michael and Linda at one end, daughter Katey and her children at the other, guests to be warmly, privately in between. They are spontaneously hospitable, know all about the area, and will even bus groups here and there for some of the many delights on offer. Bedrooms are big, light and softly comfortable without any fuss, ideal for families. The big log fire and the deep green sofas in the dayroom are perfect come the evening cool.

rooms	4: 3 doubles, 1 triple.
price	€66-€86 for two.
meals	Dinner with wine €25, book ahead.
closed	Rarely.
directions	A41 exit Annecy south; off N508 for Bourg en Brouse. D17 through Sillingy; D38 through Combe de Sillingy to Thusy; house on right in Pesey.

Michael, Linda & Katey Smith
La Ferme du Champ Pelaz,
74150 Thusy,
Haute-Savoie

tel	+33 (0)4 50 69 25 15
fax	+33 (0)4 50 69 25 15
e-mail	champ-pelaz@wanadoo.fr
web	www.champ-pelaz.com

Map 12 Entry 678

La Bécassière

The light, harmonious air in this old Savoyard farmhouse is created by stone and wood, white paint, dried flowers and country antiques – and it matches Madame's delightful, energetic presence. Now virtually retired from farming, Monsieur happily shares his great knowledge of the area, wines and mushrooming; they will do anything for you. Your sitting room has a half-moon window at floor level (the top of the old barn door), your big light bedrooms have antique, new-mattressed, lace-covered beds and spotless showers. A revelation to those who expect farms to be a bit scruffy.

rooms	3: 1 double, 2 twins, all with shower & wc (1 behind curtain).
price	€62-€64 for two.
meals	Savoyard restaurant 3-4km.
closed	December-27 February.
directions	From Annecy N201 for Geneva. 1km after Cruseilles, left D27 through Copponex; left at cemetery; signs to Chambres d'Hôtes Châtillon. House on left.

Suzanne & André Gal
La Bécassière,
74350 Copponex,
Haute-Savoie
tel +33 (0)4 50 44 08 94
fax +33 (0)4 50 44 08 94

Le Châlet

Anne-Marie, outgoing and a delight to talk to, makes this place – come if you want to bathe in genuine French mountain hospitality. She speaks English, keeps horses, organises treks to the Alpine pastures. The mood here is rustic and characterful; the triple is in the converted cellar and don't expect spick or span. Exceptional walking: you may see chamois and marmots if you go far enough. Dinner (served late to allow you time to settle) is eaten at the long wooden table, with grand-mama's delicious recipes cooked on a wood-fired stove – and the half-board formula includes absolutely everything.

rooms	5: 1 triple; 4 doubles sharing 2 showers & 2 wcs.
price	Half-board only: €36.50 per person.
meals	Dinner with wine included in price.
closed	Rarely.
directions	From Thonon les Bains, D26 for Bellevaux. House 2km before Bellevaux on left; sign.

Anne-Marie Félisaz-Denis
Le Châlet,
74470 Bellevaux,
Haute-Savoie
tel +33 (0)4 50 73 70 13
fax +33 (0)4 50 73 70 13

Fleur Sauvage

The clean air of the Swiss borderlands is brilliantly evident at Fleur Sauvage: a spotless, uncluttered, modern chalet that Peter, an excellent carpenter, has finished most professionally and that Evelyn has decorated in coordinated colours set off by big windows and white walls. They are an interesting, friendly couple, have been posted to many parts of the world, are very active in local life and are now happy to share their delight in their adopted village. In a wonderful centre for walking and watery activities, this house welcomes families and couples with equal warmth.

rooms	3: 1 double, 2 twins, each with shower & sharing 2 separate wc.
price	€60-€65 for two.
meals	Dinner with wine €21. Book ahead.
closed	October-January.
directions	From Thonon les Bains N5 for Evian; opp. Evian ferry terminal D21 & D52 right. On descent into Bernex left at tabac, Rue de Trossy; right fork, past boulangerie; left into lane. House 1st right.

Evelyn & Peter Weston
Fleur Sauvage,
74500 Bernex,
Haute-Savoie
tel +33 (0)4 50 73 26 80
e-mail eanpweston@hotmail.com

Chalet Odysseus

The village has great character; Chalet Odysseus has much besides. Find comfort in soft sofas, check curtains, bright rugs and open fire, and swishness in sauna and small gym; a French chef who waves his wand over the dining table once a week in winter, and relaxed English hosts to spoil you (Madame also is a fine cook). They have the ground floor of this brand-new chalet; you live above. Cheerfully pretty bedrooms come with the requisite pine garb, two have balconies that catch the sun, the tiniest comes with bunk beds for kids. Marvellous for a family break, whatever the season.

rooms	5: 3 doubles, 1 twin, 1 room with 1 set of bunk-beds.
price	€90 for two.
meals	Dinner with wine €40 six nights a week, book ahead; full-board €100 p.p.
closed	Rarely.
directions	After Cuses N205; left D106; 7km before Les Carros red & white-shuttered chalet on left; signposted.

Kate & Barry Joyce
Chalet Odysseus,
74300 Les Carraz d'Araches,
Haute-Savoie
tel +33 (0)4 50 90 66 00
fax +33 (0)4 50 90 66 01
e-mail chaletodysseus@wanadoo.fr
web www.chaletodysseuslachat.com

Proveyroz

Madame has boundless energy, is a great walker, adores her mountain retreat in this lovely valley and cooks very well indeed. Her chalet rooms, all wood-clad of course, are bright and welcoming in blue, white and orange; they have unusually high ceilings, good storage and plenty of space. The open-plan living area has huge windows – opening to a small sun-soaked terrace and little garden – and the mixture of old and modern furniture plus bits and pieces of all sorts gives the whole place a comfortable, family feel. Paragliding is the big thing round here, Annecy is close and Geneva an hour away.

rooms	2 doubles.
price	€42 for two.
meals	Dinner with wine €18, book ahead. Restaurant 800m.
closed	Rarely.
directions	From Annecy D909 to Thones; D12 for Serraval & Manigod; 200m after 'Welcome to Manigod' sign, left at cross; chalet on left.

Josette Barbaud
Proveyroz,
74230 Manigod,
Haute-Savoie
tel +33 (0)4 50 44 95 25
fax +33 (0)4 50 44 95 25

Les Murailles

The Brownes have built a hymn to sweet-smelling pine: the new chalet, warm and reassuring, is delightfully furnished – and has panoramic views south across the valley to rising green pastures and great rocky mountains. The guest room is spacious and private, with doors to the garden and that view. Your hosts, retired contented travellers, she a great cook, are fun, energtic and enthusiastic about their house, the 135km of marked mountain trails, and their lovely labradors. Delightful Annecy is a few bends away and the skiing's great, Manigod teaming up with La Clusaz in winter.

rooms	1 twin.
price	€60 for two. Minimum stay 2 nights.
meals	Dinner with wine €20, book ahead.
closed	Rarely.
directions	From Annecy, D909 to Thônes. Then D12 for Serraval & Manigod &, soon after, D16 to Manigod. Through village, 1st left past garage, house 4th on right.

Colin & Alyson Browne
Les Murailles,
74230 Manigod,
Haute-Savoie
tel +33 (0)4 50 44 95 87
fax +33 (0)4 50 44 19 42
e-mail colin.browne@wanadoo.fr

Chessine

Overlooking the valley, vineyards and distant peaks, the 18th-century house, once the château's cottages and stables, has been a country cottage for years. Simone and Henry did some sensitive renovation, using old materials and recreating an authentic atmosphere, then opened for B&B. They are still feeling their way, learning how much contact or privacy their guests expect, hunting for little tables and pieces of character to add to their sparklingly clean, mezzanined guest rooms – each has a small sitting area. Breakfast is in the pretty courtyard garden in summer. Excellent hosts and good value.

rooms	2: 1 double, 1 twin.
price	€76 for two. Minimum stay 2 nights.
meals	Good choice of restaurants 2-10km.
closed	November-Easter.
directions	A41 exit Aix les Bains D991 to Viuz; D56 right for Ruffieux; at r'bout head for Chessine & Chambres d'Hôtes.

Simone & Henry Collé
Chessine,
73310 Ruffieux,
Savoie
tel +33 (0)4 79 54 52 35
fax +33 (0)4 79 54 52 35
e-mail chessine@chessine.com
web www.chessine.com

La Touvière

Mountains march past Mont Blanc and over into Italy, cows graze in the foreground – perfect for exploring this walkers' paradise. Myriam, bubbly and easy, adores having guests with everyone joining in the lively, lighthearted family atmosphere. In their typical old unsmart farmhouse, the cosy family room is the hub of life. Marcel is part-time home improver, part-time farmer (just a few cows now). One room has a properly snowy valley view, the other overlooks the owners' second chalet, let as a gîte; both are a decent size, simple but not basic, while shower rooms are spotless. Remarkable value.

rooms	2 doubles.
price	€40 for two.
meals	Dinner with wine €15, book ahead.
closed	Rarely.
directions	From Albertville N212 for Megève for 21km; after Flumet, left at Panoramic Hotel & follow signs to La Touvière.

Marcel & Myriam Marin-Cudraz
La Touvière,
73590 Flumet,
Savoie
tel +33 (0)4 79 31 70 11

Yellow Stone Chalet

Perched on the edge of a mountain, you have sensational views of peaks above and villages below, be you in your room, in the jacuzzi, or rolling in the snow post-sauna. Blazing fires, natural wood, big rooms, luxury bathrooms, a convivial table: a treat. Take a book from the galleried library above the lounge, fit in a pre-dinner dip in the indoor pool-with-a-view. After a hearty breakfast your Franco-American hostess will help you map out your itinerary – hiking, mountain-lake fishing in summer, skiing in winter (from the door). For off-piste adventurers, the baby of the Savoyard ski resorts is unsurpassed.

rooms	6: 3 doubles, 3 suites for 4.
price	€110-€165 for two.
meals	Dinner €29, book ahead; wine list €10-€55.
closed	Rarely.
directions	From Bourg St Maurice D902 for Val d'Isère through Ste Foy Tarentaise. After La Thuile left for Ste Foy Station & follow signs.

Nancy Tabardel & Jean Marc Fouquet
Yellow Stone Chalet,
73640 Ste Foy Tarentaise, Savoie
tel +33 (0)4 79 06 96 06
fax +33 (0)4 79 06 96 05
e-mail yellowstone@wanadoo.fr
web www.yellowstone-chalet.com

Maison Coutin

A year-round Alpine dream. In summer it's all flowers, birds and rushing streams… in winter you can ski cross-country, snow-walk or take the ski lift, just 500m away, to the vast ski field of Les Arcs. La Plagne and Val d'Isère are quite close too. Cooking takes place in the outside wood oven and the food is delicious. Your dynamic and friendly young hosts cater for children with early suppers, son Boris and daughter Clémence may be playmates for yours, and Claude will babysit in the evening. Guests have their own comfortable dayroom with a refrigerator. *Discount on ski hire and passes.*

rooms	2: 1 double with extra bed available, 1 suite for 4.
price	€50 for two; €62-€65 for three. Suite €74-€100.
meals	Dinner with wine €17, book ahead.
closed	Rarely.
directions	From Albertville N90 to Moutiers; on for Bourg St Maurice. Right D87E to Peisey Nancroix; left to Peisey centre; follow green arrows. 9km from main road to house.

Claude Coutin & Franck Chenal
Maison Coutin,
73210 Peisey Nancroix,
Savoie
tel +33 (0)4 79 07 93 05
fax +33 (0)4 79 04 29 23
e-mail maisoncoutin@aol.com
web www.maison-coutin.fr.st

Le Traversoud

Flowers, ponies and poultry grazing, climbing, tumbling all over courtyard and garden – you can tell the Garniers love living things. Now retired, Albert gardens and plans to be a potter. Jean-Margaret, who is English, grows all her own veg, loves cooking, collects dolls from their worldwide treks, and paints furniture. An interesting, accomplished couple, they welcome you delightedly to their farmhouse, guide you up the outside stairs to colourful, comfortably feminine bedrooms – pretty linen, spotless bathrooms – before serving you excellent French food in their dining room. Sauna and massage shower, too.

rooms	3: 1 twin, 2 triples.
price	€50 for two.
meals	Dinner with wine €20, book ahead.
closed	Rarely.
directions	From A43 exit La Tour du Pin left to N6; right at r'bout for Aix les Bains; left at lights at St Clair de la Tour. 3km for Dolomieu; Chambres d'Hôtes signposted.

Jean-Margaret & Albert Garnier
Le Traversoud,
38110 Faverges de la Tour,
Isère

tel	+33 (0)4 74 83 90 40
fax	+33 (0)4 74 83 93 71
e-mail	garnier.traversoud@free.fr
web	www.le-traversoud.com

Map 12 Entry 689

Longeville

There is a gentle elegance about this house and the people who live in it, including several sleek cats. Originally Scots and Irish, the Barrs have spent their adult years in France and now run a wooden toy business. Their love for this 1750s farmhouse shows in their artistic touch with decorating, their mix of old and modern furniture, their gorgeous big bedrooms done in soft pale colours that leave space for the soaring views coming in from the hills. A high place of comfort and civilised contact where dinner in the airy white living room is a chance to get to know your interesting, relaxed hosts more fully.

rooms	2 twins/doubles.
price	€48-€60 for two.
meals	Dinner with wine €23, book ahead.
closed	September-December.
directions	From A43 exit 8, N85 through Nivolas. Left D520 for Succieu. After 2km, left D56 through Succieu for St Victor; 3km; sign for Longeville on right; farm at top of steep hill.

Mary & Greig Barr
Longeville,
38300 Succieu,
Isère

tel	+33 (0)4 74 27 94 07
fax	+33 (0)4 74 92 09 21
e-mail	mary.barr@wanadoo.fr

Map 12 Entry 690

Domaine de Gorneton

The most caring and endearing of B&B owners: he, warmly humorous and humble about his excellent cooking; she, generous and outgoing. Built in 1646 as a fort, high on a hill beside a spring that still runs through the shrubby garden, their superb old house is wrapped round a green-clad courtyard. Inside, levels change, staircases abound, vast timbers span the dining room, guest rooms have separate entrances and floral papers, plush chairs and country antiques, impeccable bathrooms – and a bedhead from Hollywood in the best room. Deep country 15 minutes from Lyon.

rooms	4: 3 doubles, 1 suite for 4.
price	€93-€120 for two.
meals	Dinner with wine €33, book ahead.
closed	Rarely.
directions	From A7, A46 or A47 exit Chasse & Rhône; through large Centre Commercial; under railway; left for Trembas. (Will fax map or guide you to house.)

M & Mme Fleitou
Domaine de Gorneton,
38670 Chasse sur Rhône,
Isère

tel +33 (0)4 72 24 19 15
fax +33 (0)4 78 07 93 62
e-mail gorneton@wanadoo.fr
web www.gorneton.com

Map 12 Entry 691

La Cabane Bleue

No worries about finding your accommodation in even the remotest parts of France! Just stop your car, get out your mobile phone and ring. Your fully mobile chambre d'hôte will arrive within hours. Skilfully designed to cope with the roughest terrain, your accommodation will appear accompanied by your personal flock of mountain sheep. Beds are comfortable in a primitive sort of way, and covered with fleece (or was it fleas?). Breakfast consists of fresh ewe's milk and not-always-so-fresh cheese. An unforgettable experience!

rooms	1 double with wc en plein air; frequent showers. Your room has a mini-baa.
price	Negotiable, includes evening perfomances by the Folies Bergères.
meals	Dinner served on a catch-it-yourself basis.
closed	Most of the year.
directions	Take a sheepdog to help you locate your chambre.

M & Mme Berger
La Cabane Bleue,
Mouton dans les Montagnes,
Isère

tel field line only
fax best by pigeon-post
web www.moutonnoir

Map Entry 692

Château de Paquier

Old, mighty, atmospheric – yet so homely. Hélène teaches cookery and spit-roasts poultry in the huge dining room fireplace, then joins you for dinner. Her modernised 17th-century tower kitchen (wood-fired range, stone sink, cobbled floor) is where she makes her bread, honey, jams and walnut aperitif. Wine is from the Rossis' own vineyard near Montpellier. Enormous rooms, high heavy-beamed ceilings, large windows with sensational valley views; terraced gardens and animals; bedrooms (handsome wardrobes, underfloor heating) up an ancient spiral staircase that sets the imagination reeling.

rooms	5: 2 doubles, 2 twins, 1 family room.
price	€60 for two.
meals	Dinner with wine €20, book ahead. Self-catering possible.
closed	Rarely.
directions	From Grenoble A51 or N75 for Sisteron 25km to r'bout; follow signs to St Martin de la Cluze. Château signs in village.

Jacques & Hélène Rossi
Château de Paquier,
38650 St Martin de la Cluze, Isère
tel +33 (0)4 76 72 77 33
fax +33 (0)4 76 72 77 33
e-mail hrossi@club-internet.fr
web chateau.de.paquier.free.fr

Le Marais

Opt for the simple country life at this friendly farm which has been in the family for over 100 years and has returned to organic methods; Madame calls it "acupuncture for the land". Four horses, a few hens, and – when there's a full house – meals of regional recipes served family-style, with home-grown veg and *vin de noix* aperitif. Monsieur collects old farming artefacts and Madame, although busy, always finds time for a chat. The bedrooms are in a separate wing with varnished ceilings, antique beds and candlewick covers; baths are old-fashioned pink. At the foot of the Vercors range, utter peace.

rooms	4: 1 twin, 1 double, 1 triple, 1 family room.
price	€41-€46 for two.
meals	Dinner with wine €16, book ahead. Restaurants 3km.
closed	Rarely.
directions	From Romans D538 for Chabeuil. Leaving Alixan left by Boulangerie for St Didier; left again, Chambres d'Hôtes St Didier signs for 3km; farm on left.

Christiane & Jean-Pierre Imbert
Le Marais,
26300 St Didier de Charpey,
Drôme
tel +33 (0)4 75 47 03 50
e-mail imbert.jean-pierre@wanadoo.fr
web perso.wanadoo.fr/les-marais/

La Pineraie

A good stopover, this 1970s villa in something of a time warp, high above the valley outside Valence: dark floral paper in hall, stairs and bedrooms, animal skins on floors and sofas, interesting modern sculptures in many corners. Your hostess is chatty (in French), enthusiastic and welcoming, a gift inherited from Armenian parents. Enjoy breakfast with homemade organic jam on the terrace and admire the magnificent chalk escarpments of the Vercors range (beyond less attractive Saint Marcel). Little traffic noise can be heard. *Careful: this is the B&B on the left-hand side of the road. Secure parking.*

rooms	2: 1 twin, 1 double.
price	€48-€53 for two.
meals	Restaurants in village, 500m.
closed	Rarely.
directions	From A7 exit Valence Nord; through Bourg lès Valence; left N532 for Grenoble; exit to St Marcel; Place de la Mairie left; over Stop, under bridge, up hill (total 400m); house on LEFT round hairpin.

Marie-Jeanne Katchikian
La Pineraie,
26320 St Marcel lès Valence,
Drôme
tel +33 (0)4 75 58 72 25
fax +33 (0)4 75 58 72 25
e-mail marie.katchikian@minitel.net

Les Péris

Here is the grandmother we all dream of, a delightful woman who cossets her guests, and puts flowers, sweets and fruit in the bedrooms. This old stone farmhouse facing the Vercors mountains is definitely a family home and good meals of regional dishes with local wine, prepared by daughter Élisabeth, can be very jolly with family, friends and guests all sharing the long table in the kitchen. And there's a *menu curieux* using ancient forgotten vegetables! The roomy, old-fashioned bedrooms with walnut armoires breathe a comfortable, informal air. Great for kids, and a duck pond good for splashing in.

rooms	3 triples.
price	€45 for two.
meals	Dinner with wine €16, book ahead.
closed	Rarely.
directions	From A7 exit Valence Sud on D68 to Chabeuil. There, cross river; left on D154 for Combovin 5km; signposted, on left.

Mme Madeleine Cabanes
Les Péris,
26120 Châteaudouble,
Drôme
tel +33 (0)4 75 59 80 51
fax +33 (0)4 75 59 48 78

Chambedeau

Madame's kindliness infuses her home, one that at first glance is coy about its age and charms. Her eventful life has nourished a wicked sense of humour but no bitterness and she is a natural storyteller (she'll show you the photographs too) – she alone is worth the detour. The slightly fading carpets and small shower rooms become incidental after a short while. Enjoy, instead, the pretty bedrooms, the peace and birdlife of the lush leafy garden which shelters the house from the road and relish breakfast – organic honeys, homemade jams and cake, cheese – where the table is a picture in itself.

rooms	3: 2 twins, 1 single.
price	€47-€49 for two. Singles €42.
meals	Restaurants 2-7km.
closed	Rarely.
directions	From A7 Valence Sud exit A49 for Grenoble. Exit 33 right D538a for Beaumont, 2.6km; right at sign Chambres d'Hôtes & Chambedeau; 800m on right, tarmac drive.

Mme Lina de Chivré-Dumond
Chambedeau,
26760 Beaumont lès Valence,
Drôme

tel	+33 (0)4 75 59 71 70
fax	+33 (0)4 75 59 75 24
e-mail	linadechivredumond@minitel.net

Les Volets Bleus

Your heart will lift at the view over oak forests to the distant foothills; your body will revive with the Gauberts' creative Mediterranean food, all organic, lots grown in their huge kitchen garden. These are charming, talented people – photographers, restaurateurs, house restorers – with a gentle sense of colour, a taste for beautiful things, books, musical instruments, and one young son. The dayroom, opening onto the grassy garden, is inspiring and restful; there's a ping-pong barn; the delightul themed bedrooms are smallish but neat and simple in their different colours with occasional echoes of Africa or the sea.

rooms	6: 4 doubles, 1 family room, 1 triple.
price	€59-€65 for two.
meals	Dinner with wine €26, book ahead.
closed	Rarely.
directions	From Dieulefit for Crest; D192 left for Truinas. Signposted.

Sophie & Serge Gaubert
Les Volets Bleus,
26460 Truinas, Drôme

tel	+33 (0)4 75 53 38 48
e-mail	lesvolets@aol.com
web	www.guideweb.com/provence/chambres_hotes/volets-bleus

La Joie

Francis has renovated the house with huge care, giving new life to old beams and tiles – the (spotlit) stone cross-vaulting in the dining room is wonderful. Jackie is immediately likeable too, an artist who goes out of her way to make you feel at home. Food is bought locally for superb, mostly organic meals, and lemonade is homemade. Bedrooms are simple, with tiled floors and Provençal prints; bathrooms are functional. Lively and charming people living in lovely countryside, a courtyard in which passing musicians may play and a garden with swings.

rooms	4: 1 double, 1 twin, 2 triples.
price	€55-€65 for two.
meals	Dinner €20, book ahead; good wine list from €6-€10.
closed	Occasionally.
directions	From Montélimar D540 E to La Batie Rolland (10km). In village left onto D134 for 2km for St Gervais; sign on right.

Francis & Jackie Monel
La Joie,
26160 La Batie Rolland,
Drôme

tel	+33 (0)4 75 53 81 51
fax	+33 (0)4 75 53 81 51
e-mail	f.monel@infonie.fr
web	www.lajoie.fr

Villa Mary

Thrilled with their new life in this handsome yet ungrand house, your hosts welcome guests with joyous pleasure all year and run Provence-lore courses in winter. They want the house to be full of like-minded people and local craftsmen, Norbert indulging his passion for cooking, Marie-José making pastries, gentle Orion, the shiny dog, loving everybody. In big light-filled rooms where parquet gleams, you will sleep as you would *chez grand-mère* in gentle elegance. Lavender and honey waft, lawns slope to woods, the pool mountain-gazes, high windows open onto an ancient collection of trees.

rooms	5: 4 doubles, 1 family room.
price	€80-€105 for two. Minimum stay 3 nights July & Aug.
meals	Dinner €25, book ahead; wine €18.
closed	Rarely.
directions	From A7 exit Montélimar Nord for Dieulefit. House on left as you enter village.

Marie-José Mancel
& Norbert Schulz
Villa Mary,
26220 Dieulefit, Drôme

tel	+33 (0)4 75 46 89 19
fax	+33 (0)4 75 46 30 23
e-mail	villa-mary@club-internet.fr
web	www.guideweb.com/provence/bb/villa-mary

photo Michael Busselle

provence–alps–riviera

L'henge en Pierre

Thrilling – a chance to sleep in an original neolithic dwelling, a near-perfect exemplar. We fought long and hard to persuade the owners to join in with us, and bear the cudgel wounds to this day. It is about as Spartan as one can find, entirely devoid of comfort. But there is an exquisite pleasure to be had from such close contact with nature and history – a pleasure that many B&B owners seek to provide, and fail dismally. There are no roads, no light pollution, no noise – just Provence at its most surreally lovely.

rooms	(Room, actually). One compact half single with narrow but far-reaching views across surrounding valley. Bring your own bed if needed.
price	3 copper nuggets or an animal hide.
meals	Self-catering - in its purest form.
closed	Always - bring a friend to help with opening it.
directions	From Gap, follow road to nearest Alp, then go up until nearing summit. L'henge (as it is known locally) sits on a western plateau.

M Pierre L'henge
L'henge en Pierre,
Champ de la Poussière,
00000 Ailleurs,
Alpes-de-Haute-Provence

tel	1 0 1 0 1 0 1
fax	0 1 0 1 0 1 0
e-mail	pierre.l'henge@about3000.bc
web	www.about3000.bc/l'henge-en-pierre

Mas Saint Joseph

Come for the view of row upon row of peaks fading into the distance, the walking, the welcome. Hélène and Olivier bought the *mas* as a holiday home 17 years ago, restored it with loving care. then moved here and began taking guests. Olivier is a walker and can arrange a spectacular circuit, with a donkey carrying your stuff, from one B&B to the next. One bedroom has an ancient brick bread oven in a corner; another, once a stable, has a manger to prove it. Breakfast and dinner are on the terrace in warm weather or in the fine old barn, and you can use the biggish pool behind the house.

rooms	4: 1 double, 1 triple, 2 suites.
price	€47 for two; €63 for three; €79 for four.
meals	Dinner with wine €16.50, book ahead. Children under 10 €10. Good restaurant 5km.
closed	Mid-November-March.
directions	From Châteauneuf Val St Donat 1.5km for St Étienne les Orgues; house on bend, on right above road; steep 100m drive to house.

Hélène & Olivier Lenoir
Mas Saint Joseph,
04200 Châteauneuf Val St Donat,
Alpes-de-Haute-Provence

tel	+33 (0)4 92 62 47 54
e-mail	lenoir.st.jo@wanadoo.fr
web	provenceweb.fr/04/st-joseph

Montsalier

Venerable stones in the remote thyme-wafted air of a hillside village: an apparently modest old house unfolds into a place of grandeur with a vast flourish of a dining hall, a tower, a pigeon loft and well-travelled, fascinating hosts with a fine mix of shyness and humour for company. The courtyard is wisteria-clad, the garden sheltered, the food superb. Two rooms on the 17th-century lower level charm with their simple ancientness, the canopy bed lies in splendour below serried beams; they overflow with character, gentle colours, antique wardrobes. There are two lovely terraces, and hot-air ballooning nearby.

rooms	3 doubles.
price	€80-€90 for two.
meals	Dinner with wine €40-€45, book ahead.
closed	Rarely.
directions	From Forcalquier N100 for Apt; at 1st r'bout D950 right to Banon; D51 to Montsalier; house at entrance of village beside Mairie; signposted.

Mme Karolyn Kauntze
Montsalier,
04150 Banon,
Alpes-de-Haute-Provence

tel	+33 (0)4 92 73 23 61
fax	+33 (0)4 92 73 23 61
e-mail	montsalier@infonie.fr
web	maison.karolyn.chez.tiscali.fr

Château d'Esparron

Castellanes built Esparron in the 1400s, both have been pivots of Provençal history. The superb stone stairs lead to vastly luscious bedrooms: plain walls and fresh flowers, tiles and gorgeous fabrics, family antiques with tales to tell. The garden is small but perfect. Slender Charlotte-Anne and her two beautiful children come straight from a Gainsborough portrait. She attends to everyone: family, staff, guests. Bernard, a mine of information with suntan and real manners, adds a touch of 1930s glamour. Wonderful family, splendiferous house, vast breakfast in the cavernously cosy kitchen.

rooms	5: 3 doubles, 1 twin, 1 suite.
price	€130-€200 for two.
meals	Restaurant 5 minutes' walk.
closed	November-March.
directions	From Aix en Provence A51 exit 18 on D907; D82 to Gréoux les Bains; follow on D952 & D315 to Esparron. Stop & ring at gates (once past, it's impossible to turn).

Bernard & Charlotte-Anne de Castellane
Château d'Esparron,
04800 Esparron de Verdon,
Alpes-de-Haute-Provence

tel	+33 (0)4 92 77 12 05
fax	+33 (0)4 92 77 13 10
e-mail	chateau@esparron.com
web	www.esparron.com

Ferme de Felines

Southern energies, wild evergreen hills and strong light push in through big architect's windows to meet the sober cool of black-white-grey northern design in a thrilling encounter. Small, wiry and full of laughter, Rita has a passion for this house, her land and the wildlife she fights to preserve. She may adorn your space of purity with one perfect flower in a glass cylinder, some fruit and a candle. Linen, beds, taps and towels are all top quality, her generosity is warm, her dog and six cats beautiful, her vast living room a treat. Breakfast at a marble table, then walk straight out to the lovely lake. Quite a place!

rooms	3 doubles with shower & separate wcs.
price	€110 for two. Minimum stay 2-3 nights.
meals	Restaurants in Mounstiers.
closed	Rarely.
directions	From Aix A51 exit Manosque for Gréoux; D952 to Riez, Monstiers; D952 for Castellane, 6km black sign on right.

Rita Ravez
Ferme de Felines,
04360 Moustiers Ste Marie,
Alpes-de-Haute-Provence
tel +33 (0)4 92 74 64 19
fax +33 (0)4 92 74 61 39
e-mail ferme-de-felines@wanadoo.fr
web www.ferme-de-felines.com

Richarnau

Sincere, charming, animated hosts: Monsieur is a keen cook and prepares fresh Provençal dishes while Madame makes the desserts and also gives Feldenkrais ('conscious movement') sessions. Their 19th-century farmhouse, built around a courtyard shaded by a spreading lime, is encircled by a sea of lavender and vast views. The family living/dining room is homely and warm with a large table and a fireplace for cooler weather; the kitchen has a fridge for guests' use. Bedrooms are decorated in an unpretentious manner, the newest in Provençal yellows and greys. Stay long enough to taste all these pleasures.

rooms	5: 1 double, 1 twin with extra bed available, 1 family room, 1 suite for 2-3, 1 suite for 2-4, all with separate bath.
price	€70-€85 for two; €100-€110 for three; €120 for four. Minimum stay 2 nights.
meals	Dinner €22, book ahead; good wine list €10-€15.
closed	January-February.
directions	From Carpentras, D941 & D1 to Sault, 41km; D942 for Aurel. Just before Aurel, left at sign.

Christian & Visnja Michelle
Richarnau,
84390 Aurel,
Vaucluse
tel +33 (0)4 90 64 03 62
fax +33 (0)4 90 64 03 62
e-mail richarnau@free.fr
web richarnau.free.fr

L'Évêché

Narrow, cobbled streets lead to this fascinating and very beautifully furnished house that was once part of the 17th-century Bishop's Palace. The Verdiers are charming, cultivated people – he an architect/builder, she a teacher – with a keen interest in antiques and modern art. There's an impressive poster collection in the cosy guest sitting room, and the serene bedrooms – whitewashed beamed ceilings, terracotta floors – have a Provençal feel. Well-presented breakfasts on the terrace come complete with French and English newspapers and, best of all, long, magnificent views to the Roman bridge.

rooms	5: 3 doubles, 2 suites for 3.
price	€70-€80 for two. Suite €105-€140 for three.
meals	Good choice of restaurants in Vaison.
closed	2 weeks in November.
directions	From Orange, D975 to Vaison. In town, follow 'Ville Médiévale' signs.

Aude & Jean-Loup Verdier
L'Évêché,
84110 Vaison la Romaine,
Vaucluse
tel +33 (0)4 90 36 13 46
fax +33 (0)4 90 36 32 43
e-mail eveche@aol.com
web eveche.free.fr

L'École Buissonnière

A stone jewel set in southern lushness and miles of green vines and purple hills. Country furniture (a particularly seductive choice of Provençal chairs) is polished with wax and time; big, luminous bedrooms are prettily uncluttered: moss-coloured Birds sings to the tune of the aviary outside; Elephant has Indian fabric and... elephants; Camargue, in the mezzanined old barn, has a balcony and a *gardian's* hat. John rightly calls himself a Provençal Englishman, Monique is warmly welcoming too – theirs is a happy house, where German is also spoken.

rooms	3: 2 doubles, 1 family room.
price	€50-€57 for two.
meals	Restaurant in village. Self-catering possible.
closed	Mid-November-Easter.
directions	From A7 exit Bollène for Nyons D94; D20 right for Vaison & Buisson; cross River Aygues; left for Villedieu & Cave la Vigneronne D51 & D75 for 2.2km.

Monique Alex & John Parsons
L'École Buissonnière,
84110 Vaison La Romaine,
Vaucluse
tel +33 (0)4 90 28 95 19
e-mail ecole.buissonniere@wanadoo.fr
web www.guideweb.com/provence/bb/ecole-buissonniere

Les Airs du Temps

Michael's handsome, rambling old house sits in prime walking and cycling country. The mood inside is relaxed and comfortable, every room rich and warm: fresh colours, polished and be-rugged parquet, interesting brocante and paintings by an artist friend. Fireplaces are original; some period baths and basins, too. You breakfast at nine on local bread and homemade jam – under leafy trees in summer, with vineyard and mountain views. Your host is well-travelled and an artist in the kitchen: he cooks Asian and Mediterranean, and roasts lamb and bakes delicious pizza in the old bread oven.

rooms	4: 3 doubles, 1 suite for 4.
price	€70-€73 for two. Minimum stay 2 nights.
meals	Dinner with wine €30, book ahead.
closed	November-March.
directions	From Vaison la Romaine D938 N for Nyons, 5km; right at r'bout on D46 for Buis les Baronnies, 4km. On entering Faucon, on right at crossroads with D205 (blue gate).

Michael Berry
Les Airs du Temps,
84110 Faucon,
Vaucluse

tel +33 (0)4 90 46 44 57
fax +33 (0)4 90 46 44 57
e-mail michaelaberry@hotmail.com

Map 17 Entry 709

Domaine du Bois de la Cour

A great spot for exploring Provence. The big old house, surrounded by its vineyards and within harmless earshot of a road, is very handsome and Madame brings it to life with her special sparkle and enthusiasm for what she has created here. The decoration is all hers – more 'evolved French farmhouse-comfortable' than 'designer-luxurious'. She loves cooking, herbs and flowers; you may be offered her elderflower aperitif and have homemade cakes at breakfast. Nothing is too much trouble – walkers' luggage can be transferred, picnics can be laid on, or wine, or honey tastings...

rooms	5: 2 doubles, 1 triple, 1 suite for 4, 1 suite for 6.
price	€84 for two.
meals	Dinner with wine €23, book ahead.
closed	Rarely.
directions	A9 exit Bollène for Carpentras 18km; leaving Cairanne, head for Carpentras 1.5km; house on right-hand turn.

Élisabeth & Jerry Para
Domaine du Bois de la Cour,
84290 Cairanne, Vaucluse

tel +33 (0)4 90 30 84 68
fax +33 (0)4 90 30 84 68
e-mail infos@boisdelacour.com
web www.boisdelacour.com

Map 17 Entry 710

Les Convenents

For this delightful English couple, refugees from spinning plates in London, welcoming visitors in their haven is as natural as breathing. Five former workers' cottages have become a relaxing Provençal *mas* where space and simplicity leave old stones and timbers to glow and there's a vine-shaded terrace. Small explosions of cushions and paintings bring fresh white walls and fabrics alive; more modernity in good clean bathrooms and superb finishes – Ian's domain. Sarah, who was in catering, rules in the kitchen. They support the local economy, use the village shops, enjoy their community.

rooms	2 doubles.
price	€80-€85. Singles €75-€80.
meals	Dinner €23 with wine, Monday & Friday, book ahead. Wide choice of restaurants nearby.
closed	November-March (available on special request)
directions	From Orange D976 to Gap & St Cécile les Vignes; D11 left to Uchaux; through village, 3km. Les Covenants on left. Signposted.

Sarah Banner
Les Convenents,
84100 Uchaux, Vaucluse
tel +33 (0)4 90 40 65 64
fax +33 (0)4 90 40 65 64
e-mail sarahbanner@wanadoo.fr
web www.lesconvenents.com

La Ravigote

Madame and her house both smile gently. It's a simple, authentic Provençal farmhouse that has escaped the vigorous renovator, its courtyard shaded by a lovely lime tree. Madame, who grows chemical-free vegetables and fruit, considers dinners with her guests, in dining room or courtyard, as the best part of B&B – her meals are showcases for local specialities. The interior is a bright version of traditional French country style with old family furniture and tiled floors. Set among vineyards below the Montmirail hills, it has soul-pleasing views across the surrounding country and unspoilt villages.

rooms	4: 1 double, 2 twins, 1 family room.
price	€43 for two. Minimum stay 2 nights.
meals	Dinner with wine €17, book ahead. Restaurants in village 3km.
closed	November-March.
directions	From Carpentras D7 N through Aubignan & Vacqueyras; fork right (still D7) for Sablet; right 500m after 'Cave Vignerons Gigondas'; signposted.

Sylvette Gras
La Ravigote,
84190 Gigondas,
Vaucluse
tel +33 (0)4 90 65 87 55
fax +33 (0)4 90 65 87 55
e-mail info@laravigote.com

Le Mas de Miejour

These are young hosts, with a passion for wine and a fine display of Frédéric's pottery, who've escaped from their city pasts. Their guest bedrooms in this converted farmhouse are all different, all serene: one with a white appliquéd bedcover made in Thailand, another with Senegalese bedspreads, a family room with a big brass double bed; on a separate floor are three singles for children. The land here is flat with a high water table so the garden, sheltered by trees and waving maize in summer, is always fresh and green; with its lovely pool, an idyllic retreat after a hard day's sight-seeing.

rooms	3: 1 double, 1 twin, 1 family room.
price	€75-€125.
meals	Choice of restaurants 6km.
closed	November-March, except by arrangement.
directions	From A7 exit 23; after toll right at r'bout for Carpentras & Entraigues; 1st exit to Vedène D6 to St Saturnin lès Avignon; left to Le Thor D28 for 2km; right Chemin du Trentin.

Frédéric & Emmanuelle Westercamp
Le Mas de Miejour,
84250 Le Thor, Vaucluse
tel +33 (0)4 90 02 13 79
fax +33 (0)4 90 02 13 03
e-mail mas.miejour@free.fr
web www.masdemiejour.com

La Ferme des Trois Figuiers

Turning a fortress-like face to the Mistral when it tears down the valley, the old house is a blessed refuge from wind or heat. Sunshine yellows and soft greens, fresh flowers and natural stone inside are partnered by a shade-dotted garden and views of the Lubéron. The Gouins are real Provençal fruit-growers and Madame a renowned cook. Breakfast may see her *galette de pommes*, dinners under the spreading plane tree are outstanding. The apartment (3 rooms, jacuzzi!) is ideal for teenage families. Simply arrive, absorb and wonder what on earth you did to deserve this gem. *Children over 12 welcome.*

rooms	5 + 1: 2 doubles, 2 quadruples, 1 suite; 1 apartment for 6 (minimum stay 2 nights).
price	€92-€122 for two. Apartment €182.
meals	Dinner with wine €25, book ahead.
closed	Rarely.
directions	From Avignon N7 E then D22 for Apt (approx. 29km total). After Le Petit Palais, sign on right.

Isabelle & Rolland Gouin
La Ferme des Trois Figuiers,
84800 Lagnes,
Vaucluse
tel +33 (0)4 90 20 23 54
fax +33 (0)4 90 20 25 47
e-mail lestroisfiguiers@wanadoo.fr
web wwwlestroisfiguiers.fr

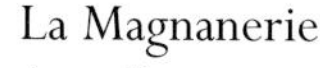

Villa La Lèbre

Madame is an absolute dear and she and Charles genuinely love doing B&B – they offer an open-hearted welcome and a real guest room in a real home. The comfy room has its own dressing room, an extra mezzanine single and a newly-tiled shower; you have use of a fridge and are welcome to picnic. This is a modern house built of old stone in traditional local style and surrounded by hills, woods and vineyards with lovely views across the valley towards Goult and the Lubéron. The Lawrences worked overseas for 40 years and the house is packed with trinkets from far-flung places. Great value.

rooms	1 triple.
price	€50 for two.
meals	Good choice of restaurants 5km.
closed	Rarely.
directions	From Avignon N100 towards Apt. At Coustellet, D2 for Gordes. After Les Imberts right D207 & D148 to St Pantaléon; pass church; D104 for 50m; left small hill; 3rd drive on right.

Pierrette & Charles Lawrence
Villa La Lèbre,
84220 Gordes,
Vaucluse

tel +33 (0)4 90 72 20 74
fax +33 (0)4 90 72 20 74

Map 17 Entry 715

La Magnanerie

A totally revamped 18th-century silkworm farm, it's a handsome building with a clever mix of old and new: big, country-elegant bedrooms, gnarled beams, old stonework and armoires, then modern touches – glass-topped tables and good bedding, linen and bathrooms. In the stylish guest sitting room you can enjoy an open fire, comfy sofa, books, games and bits of Provençalia – bunches of dried lavender, candles... Add superb breakfasts – plenty of choice – great views from the pool, a boules court and a terraced garden with a backdrop of cherry trees.
A professional and personal delight.

rooms	5: 2 double, 1 twin, 2 triples.
price	€80-€90 for two. Minimum stay 2 nights.
meals	3 Provençal restaurants 6-12km.
closed	15 November-15 December; 5 January-February.
directions	A7 exit Cavaillon for Apt through Robion; D3 right for Menerbes. Before entering village & at the foot of the hill, take D103 for Bonnieux for 3km; house 200m, signposted.

Natalie & Vincent Rohart
La Magnanerie,
84560 Ménerbes,
Vaucluse

tel +33 (0)4 90 72 42 88
fax +33 (0)4 90 72 39 42
e-mail magnanerie@aol.com
web www.magnanerie.com

Map 17 Entry 716

Villa Saint Louis

Stepping into this typical Provençal town house from the busy street one enters a magical oasis, a refined, elegant and colourful cocoon of lived-in gentility and old-world charm where period furniture – to each room its style – and a throng of objects create an intrinsically French *demeure*, unchanged since Balzac. Affable, attentive and cultured, Madame runs the B&B with her daughter, a fluent English-speaker whose children bring sparkle to the old house. Guest quarters, including breakfast room, are self-contained on the top floor, there's a patio with summer kitchen and a cool, fragrant garden for everyone below.

rooms	5: 2 doubles, 3 twins.
price	€60-€70 for two.
meals	Restaurants nearby.
closed	Rarely.
directions	From Aix en Provence N96 & D556 to Pertuis; D973 to Cadenet; D943 for Bonnieux to Lourmarin.

Mme Lassallette
Villa Saint Louis,
84160 Lourmarin,
Vaucluse
tel +33 (0)4 90 68 39 18
fax +33 (0)4 90 68 10 07
e-mail villasaintlouis@wanadoo.fr
web www.style-luberon.com/heberg_stlouis.htm

La Louveterie

Stone wolves at the gate, two real ones (superbly stuffed) in the salon, flowers pouring over arch, tower and well: this astounding 17th-century house drips with character, its wealth of history beseiges you, it lacks only the sound of an idly-plucked lute. Artist Véronique's culture and courtesy will enchant you: her Greek admiral ancestress (*louve des mers*), her ode to the house, her flair for marrying cosmopolitan mementos with local materials and colours, peaceful, unfussily elegant rooms, breakfast exquisitely laid in patio or dining room. An exceptional experience. *Children over 12 welcome.*

rooms	4: 1 double, 1 twin, 2 suites.
price	€99-€129 for two. Minimum stay 2 nights.
meals	Wide choice of restaurants.
closed	Rarely.
directions	From A51 exit 15 to Pertuis; left D973 to Lauris r'bout; follow to Puyvert; house on main street opposite Mairie.

Véronique Pfeiffer
La Louveterie,
84160 Puyvert,
Vaucluse
tel +33 (0)4 90 08 76 50
fax +33 (0)4 90 08 76 51
e-mail info@lalouveterie.com
web www.lalouveterie.com

Mas de Bassette

Sophisticated simplicity is here: white walls and pale fabrics, old beds and cupboards that glow venerably in the sunlight filtering through the greenery outside – an ethereal picture of pure Provence. Your hosts are as quiet and charming, gentle and generous as their 15th-century *mas* and its magical great garden where the pool hides among big potted plants and wooden furniture. Big bedrooms are perfect: one picture and one framed text chosen by Marie for each, old terracotta tiles and wicker chairs, thick towels and soap in a basket. Superb value, utter peace.
Air-conditioning in bedrooms.

rooms: 2 doubles.
price: €95 for two.
meals: Good restaurants 5-20km.
closed: Rarely.
directions: In Barbentane for Abbaye St Michel du Frigoulet; at windmill for tennis club; house entrance near club; signposted.

Marie & François Veilleux
Mas de Bassette,
13750 Barbentane,
Bouches-du-Rhône
tel: +33 (0)4 90 95 63 85
fax: +33 (0)4 90 95 63 85
e-mail: bassette@club-internet.fr
web: www.masdebassette.com

Le Mas Ferrand

Pure 19th century: house, décor, furniture, all authentic in a slightly chaotic assemblage, all imbued by Jean-Paul's love of life and people, his dedication to his magical wild garden – you will fall beneath the spell. Christine bakes three sorts of bread and croissants each morning, 'Grannie' is part of the equation, you can talk to them about anything, feel at home without trying, leave with new friends to write to.
At night, they leave the place to their guests, with two comfortably old-fashioned rooms and a big simple bathroom at each end of the house let as suites. A place for free spirits.

rooms: 5: 2 double, 1 family suite for 2-3, 2 family suites for 2-4.
price: €55 for two.
meals: Restaurants nearby, 200m-1km.
closed: Rarely
directions: Between Avignon & Tarascon & Arnles N570. At r-bout take CD28 to Châteaurenard, direction Graveson. Property 300m on right.

Jean-Paul & Christine Ferrand
Le Mas Ferrand,
13690 Graveson,
Bouches-du-Rhône
tel: +33 (0)4 90 95 85 29
fax: +33 (0)4 90 95 86 51
e-mail: le-mas.ferrand@wanadoo.fr
web: www.le-mas-ferrand.fr

24 rue du Château

On a medieval street near one of the loveliest châteaux in France, two *maisons de maître* joined by an ochre-hued courtyard and a continuity of taste. It's an impeccable renovation that has kept all of the soft patina of stone walls and tiles. No garden, but a courtyard for candlelit evenings and immaculate breakfasts. Calming, gracious bedrooms have fine old furniture and beams, perfect bathrooms, crisp linen. While you can be totally independent, your courteous hosts receive guests in the most relaxed, friendly way and thoroughly enjoy the contact. Ineffably Mediterranean, deeply atmospheric.

rooms	5: 3 doubles, 2 twins.
price	€70-€85 for two. Minimum stay 2 nights July-August.
meals	Choice of restaurants in town.
closed	November-20 December, except by arrangement.
directions	In Tarascon centre take Rue du Château opposite château (well signposted). No. 24 is on right.

Yann & Martine Laraison
24 rue du Château,
13150 Tarascon,
Bouches-du-Rhône
tel +33 (0)4 90 91 09 99
fax +33 (0)4 90 91 10 33
e-mail ylaraison@wanadoo.fr
web www.chambres-hotes.com

Le Mas D'Arvieux

The elegant manor is enhanced by Marie-Pierre's refined, pastel, almost baroque décor. She is passionate about art and books, Christian loves music and making furniture, both were journalists travelling the world before settling here and they organise concerts in the barn and painting classes. The stylish, well-furnished bedrooms, one in the tower wing, one with carved mezzanine, all with great personality, have beams and stone walls, fine old armoires and polished floors, excellent bathrooms and wonderful views of the Provençal hills beyond. A flower-bordered pool, memorable breakfasts, much peace.

rooms	5: 2 doubles, 1 triple, 1 suite.
price	€95-€115 for two.
meals	Dinner with wine €29, book ahead.
closed	Rarely.
directions	From Avignon D570 to Tarascon; leave road to Arles to left; now on D970: under bridge; 2km beyond, left on humpback bridge through white gate.

Marie-Pierre Carretier
& Christian Billmann
Le Mas D'Arvieux,
13150 Tarascon, Bouches-du-Rhône
tel +33 (0)4 90 90 78 77
fax +33 (0)4 90 90 78 68
e-mail mas@arvieux-provence.com
web www.arvieux-provence.com

Mas Shamrock

A manicured farmhouse whose interior is as southern cool as the welcome from its owners is sincerely Franco-Irish – John is big and relaxed, Christiane is trim and efficient. Natural stone, oak beams, terracotta floors and cool colours give a wonderfully light and airy feel to the house while bedrooms are carefully elegant with small, functional shower rooms. Outside, a delectable garden, centuries-old plane trees, a vine tunnel, three hectares of cypresses and horses (why not head for the Alpilles mountains?) add to the magic. An oft-tinkled piano is there for you to play.

rooms	5: 3 doubles, 2 twins.
price	€92-€115 for two.
meals	Choice of restaurants in St Rémy.
closed	November-Easter.
directions	From St Rémy D571 for Avignon; over 2 r'bouts, left before 2nd bus stop (Lagoy), opp. 2nd yellow Portes Anciennes sign, Chemin de Velleron; house 6th on right.

Christiane & John Walsh
Mas Shamrock,
13210 St Rémy de Provence,
Bouches-du-Rhône
tel +33 (0)4 90 92 55 79
fax +33 (0)4 90 92 55 80
e-mail mas.shamrock@wanadoo.fr

Map 17 Entry 723

7 boulevard Marceau

This little old stone townhouse, built into the 500-year-old ramparts of history-gorged St Rémy, is Vanessa's new hideaway, a refuge from the West Country, where you are invited to share her pretty Provençal dining room, the tiny two-person courtyard and the cosy sitting room. The high-ceilinged bedrooms are furnished in a satisfying mix of local, ethnic and English and hung with interesting pictures. It all has a secret atmosphere, closed in upon itself inside its exposed stone walls, and the hurly-burly of this lively town seems dim and distant, yet you are within walking distance of all its treasures.

rooms	2: 1 double, 1 twin.
price	€80-€95 for two. Minimum stay 2 nights.
meals	Restaurants in town.
closed	1 November-1 March open by arrangement only.
directions	One way system in St Rémy town. 7 bd Marceau close to L'Amandier museum on left side of one-way system; before church opposite main square. Car park.

Vanessa Maclennan
7 boulevard Marceau,
13210 St Rémy de Provence,
Bouches-du-Rhône
tel +33 (0)4 90 92 15 73
e-mail vanessamaclennan@hotmail.com

Map 17 Entry 724

Mas de la Miougrano

Float in the pool and watch the sun set over the Alpilles, join Saïd for a game of *pétanque*, share a pastis under the planes. Built by great-grandfather in 1897, up a quiet lane, surrounded by fields and fruit trees, this *mas* blends modern with rustic Provence. Discreetly decorated rooms with colourful local fabrics open onto terrace and garden, ideal with wrought-iron furniture and useful summer kitchen. Madame, a former teacher, will help you choose the perfect walk or restaurant, or you can use the guest kitchen/dining/reading room or the pretty veranda. Breakfasts are a feast.

rooms	2: 1 double, 1 suite for 4.
price	€63-€68 for two. Suite €97-€105 for four.
meals	Good restaurants nearby; self-catering available.
closed	Rarely.
directions	From Avignon, N7 for Aix-Marseille, exit for Plan d'Orgon - Cavaillon. House shortly before church on left (arrow signposts).

Magali & Saïd Rodet
Mas de la Miougrano,
13750 Plan d'Orgon,
Bouches-du-Rhône
tel +33 (0)4 90 73 20 01
fax +33 (0)4 90 73 20 01
e-mail lamiougrano@net-up.com
web perso.net-up.com/lamiougrano

Mas de la Rabassière

Fanfares of lilies at the door, Haydn inside and Michael smiling in his chef's apron. La Rabassière means 'where truffles are found' and epicurean dinners are a must: vintage wines and a sculpted dancer grace the terrace table. Cookery classes with olive oil from his trees, jogging companionship, airport pick-up are all part of the unflagging hospitality, aided by Théri, his serene assistant from Singapore. Big bedrooms and drawing room are classically comfortable in English house-party style: generous beds, erudite bookshelves, a tuned piano, Provençal antiques. Charmingly generous and individual.

rooms	2 doubles.
price	€125 for two. Singles €70.
meals	Dinner with wine €35, book ahead.
closed	Rarely.
directions	From A54 exit 13 to Grans on D19; right on D16 to St Chamas; just before r'way bridge, left for Cornillon, up hill 2km; house on right before tennis court. Map sent on request.

Michael Frost
Mas de la Rabassière,
13250 St Chamas,
Bouches-du-Rhône
tel +33 (0)4 90 50 70 40
fax +33 (0)4 90 50 70 40
e-mail michaelfrost@rabassiere.com
web www.rabassiere.com

Mas Sainte Anne

On its hilltop on the edge of pretty Peynier, the old *mas* stands in glory: pull the cowbell, pass the wooden doors and the solid red-shuttered mass surges up from beds of roses. Beautifully restored, it once belonged to painter Vincent Roux and memories of Vincent and his friend Cézanne live on. The Roux room (the best) has a delicious garden view, beams, terracotta tiles, a fantastic ochre/green bathroom down the hall. The others are good too, if more functional, and the salon is a lovely spot. We have heard much praise for the atmosphere created by your gracious hostess. *Older children welcome.*

rooms	2 doubles.
price	€65-€72 for two. Minimum stay 2 nights.
meals	Restaurants in village; summer kitchen available for lunches.
closed	First three weeks in August.
directions	From Aix on D6, 4km before Trets, right D57 to Peynier; up hill to Trets & Aubagne road; left D908; right between Poste & Pharmacie. House 50m.

Mme Jacqueline Lambert
Mas Sainte Anne,
13790 Peynier, Bouches-du-Rhône
tel +33 (0)4 42 53 05 32
fax +33 (0)4 42 53 04 28
e-mail stanpeynier@tele2.fr

La Royante

The Bishop of Marseille once resided in this delicious corner of paradise and you may sleep in the sacristy, wash by a stained-glass window, nip into the chapel/music room for a quick midnight pray. Your brilliant hosts, a cosmopolitan mix of talent, fantasy and joy – their conversation alone is worth the price – have got every detail right without a hint of pedantry. The stupendous big bedrooms throng with original features and Bernard's beloved antiques (the more old-fashioned St Wlodek is reached through its bathroom) and his leisurely breakfast is fit for a bishop with time to talk about everything.

rooms	4 doubles.
price	€85-€137 for two.
meals	Good restaurant 1km.
closed	Rarely.
directions	From Aix A8 for Nice; A52 Aubagne & Toulon, do not exit at Aubagne; A50 Marseille; exit 5 La Valentine; stay right; for Le Charrel 3km; after 'Legion Etrangere' building on left, 1st left D44a for Eoures; 1st right after bridge, signposted 'Maison de Retraite: Kaliste'; 800m to La Royante.

Xenia Saltiel
La Royante,
13400 Aubagne en Provence,
Bouches-du-Rhône
tel +33 (0)4 42 03 83 42
fax +33 (0)4 42 03 83 42
e-mail xbsaltiel@aol.com
web www.laroyante.com

Les Cancades

Madame lavishes equal amounts of loving care on her guests and her spectacularly beautiful Mediterranean garden with its tall trees, flowering shrubs and manicured lawn. Indeed, the whole place, designed by Monsieur 20 years ago as a big luxurious family villa with thoughtfully concealed pool, is thoroughly manicured. Comfortable Provençal-style rooms have Salernes bathroom tiles; one has its own piece of garden. Monsieur is shyly welcoming, Madame smilingly efficient; you've the hills full of medieval villages and wine estates to explore. Or make a picnic in the summer kitchen and just laze.

rooms	3: 2 doubles, 1 suite for 4.
price	€70 for two.
meals	Restaurants in village.
closed	Rarely.
directions	From Toulon N8 for Aubagne; in Le Beausset cross 2 r'bouts; right opp. Casino supermarket; immediately left by boulangerie, right Chemin de la Fontaine 1.5km; sign on left.

Charlotte & Marceau Zerbib
Les Cancades,
83330 Le Beausset, Var

tel	+33 (0)4 94 98 76 93
fax	+33 (0)4 94 90 24 63
e-mail	charlotte.zerbib@wanadoo.fr
web	www.les-cancades.com

Le Vallon

This young house, informed by the natural charm and taste of an old-established family, stands in a haven of green peace. The three rooms off the cool patio are good, simple and restful with a modern feel, the odd fine antique, fluffy white towels on heated rails and little gates onto the lawn. Your host, a former French forestry commissioner, loves all growing things; his charming and kind-hearted wife loves people and... dogs (three live here); they and their daughter, a nurse, will give you a sparkling welcome. In the fine big garden, a *promenade botanique*, a summer kitchen and a delicious, discreet pool.

rooms	3 twins/doubles.
price	€70 for two.
meals	Restaurants 2-4km.
closed	Rarely.
directions	A50 exit 11 for Le Beausset & La Cadière d'Azur; in Beausset N8 for Toulon; left at 1st r'bout; signs for Baro Nuecho.

Élisabeth & Frank
Guibert de Bruet
Le Vallon,
83330 Le Beausset, Var

tel	+33 (0)4 94 98 62 97
fax	+33 (0)4 94 98 62 97
e-mail	le-vallon@beausset.com
web	www.beausset.com

Bastide de la Roquette

Mosquito nets and honey walls soften the southern light flooding these lovely simple bedrooms with their modern touches of colour in the old bastide. It stands proudly at the end of the valley, jasmine and honeysuckle scent the air beneath the pergola, Jean, ever the perfect gent, takes guests up to the Big Rock for a glass of wine and a gasp at the view, Michèle is a lot of fun and soon gets everyone laughing: they are an elegant, well-travelled, cultured and happy couple creating a tender atmosphere and sharing their stunning treasures from Africa and the East with lucky guests. Genuine heartfelt B&B.

rooms	3: 1 twin, 1 double; 1 double with shower & separate wc.
price	€75-€90 for two.
meals	Dinner with wine €30, book ahead.
closed	Rarely.
directions	A8 exit St Maximin for Toulon; don't turn for Tourves; next turning for la Roque Bursanne & Toulon; 5km for Tourves; right at r'bout; immediately right on small road; at stadium left; signposted.

Michèle & Jean Jérusalemy
Bastide de la Roquette,
83170 Tourves, Var
tel +33 (0)4 94 78 81 92
fax +33 (0)4 94 78 81 92
e-mail bastidedelaroquette@hotmail.com
web www.bastidedelaroquette.com

La Cordeline

The Counts of Provence lived here in the 1100s: they had style; so does Michel Dyens, a civilised, sociable gentleman. Panache too. The house lies in the quiet heart of the old town, the châteauesque side over the little street, the other over the walled garden, trees and fountain; it feels almost colonial. Enter to original honeycomb tiles under a grand, arched, embossed ceiling. The elegant comforts of your big, beautifully furnished bedroom include headed paper with the house's 17th-century front door logo. In winter you can snuggle down by a log fire and read in peace.

rooms	5: 3 doubles, 1 twin, 1 triple, all with bath/shower & separate wc.
price	€65-€98 for two.
meals	Dinner with wine €25, book ahead. Restaurants in Brignoles.
closed	Rarely.
directions	From A8 exit Brignoles; over river for Centre Ville, immediately right for Hôtel de Claviers; round Pl. Palais de Justice; right Av. F. Mistral; Rue des Cordeliers on left.

Michel Dyens
La Cordeline,
83170 Brignoles, Var
tel +33 (0)4 94 59 18 66
fax +33 (0)4 94 59 00 29
e-mail lacordeline@ifrance.com
web www.lacordeline.com

Bastide de la Fave

The Muselets fell in love with this old sheep farm and its 57 secret acres (all vines and lavender), then opened for B&B. Bedrooms, freshly pale, have glazed doors for windows, opening to an expanse of gravel stylishly dotted with tables and chairs, guarded by an ancient oak. Three times a week pre-dinner drinks, conducted by Monsieur, are followed by house-party meals dreamt up by Madame. Breakfasts are served on the terrace in summer. The Muselets strive for perfection in all they do; the pool is sun-trapped, the stone-floored dining room elegantly airy, the atmosphere civilised and friendly.

rooms	5: 3 doubles, 2 twins.
price	€65-€85 for two.
meals	Dinner with wine €23, book ahead.
closed	5 November-mid-March.
directions	Leave A8 exit St Maximin la Ste Baume; D560 for Barjols 8km; right D35 for Bras 3km; left before bridge 1km; signposted.

Jean-Patrick & Cécile Muselet
Bastide de la Fave,
83119 Brue Auriac,
Var

tel	+33 (0)4 94 69 94 43
fax	+33 (0)4 94 69 94 43
e-mail	bastide-de-la-fave@wanadoo.fr
web	bastide-de-la-fave.com

Domaine de la Blaque

Out here among the wild flowers, oak forests and rolling hills you will find a dedication to the genuine, a particular sense of place. Your hosts have that artistic flair which puts the right things together naturally, palest pink-limed walls with white linen, old-stone courtyard walls with massed jasmine and honeysuckle, yoga groups and painters with wide open skies. Indeed, Jean-Luc is passionate about astronomy, Caroline is a photographer, they produce olives, truffles and timber, organise courses and love sharing their remote estate with like-minded travellers. Each pretty, private room has its own little terrace.

rooms	2: 1 double, 1 twin, both with kitchenette.
price	€59-€69 for two.
meals	Restaurants nearby.
closed	Rarely.
directions	A8 exit St Maximum; D560 before Barjols; at Brue-Auriac D35 to Varages; sign on left as leave village for Tavernes; follow signs, dirt track part way.

Caroline & Jean-Luc Plouvier
Domaine de la Blaque,
83670 Varages,
Var

tel	+33 (0)4 94 77 86 91
fax	+33 (0)4 94 77 86 91
e-mail	ploublaque@hotmail.com
web	www.lablaque.com

Domaine de Saint Ferréol

Readers write: "Armelle is wonderful". Breakfast is the highlight of her hospitality: she full of ideas for excursions, and Monsieur happily sharing his knowledge of the area. Theirs is a warm, lively family – a cultivated couple, four lovely children – and their working vineyard has a timeless feel. Glorious views to Ponteves Castle from the first-class, authentically Provençal bedrooms; they and the breakfast room (with mini-kitchen) are in a separate wing but, weather permitting, breakfast is on the terrace. Peace and privacy in a beautiful old house, superb walking and seriously good value.

rooms	3: 2 twins/doubles, 1 suite for 4.
price	€56-€64 for two. Suite €84 for four.
meals	Self-catering; good restaurant 1.6km.
closed	November-March.
directions	From A8 exit St Maximin & Ste Baume D560 to Barjols; D560 2km for Draguignan; entrance opp. D60 turning for Pontevès.

Guillaume & Armelle de Jerphanion
Domaine de Saint Ferréol,
83670 Pontevès, Var

tel	+33 (0)4 94 77 10 42
fax	+33 (0)4 94 77 19 04
e-mail	saint-ferreol@wanadoo.fr
web	www.domaine.de.saint.ferreol.fr

Mas Saint Maurinet

Simply welcoming, your hosts were born in this unspoilt part of the Var where beautiful, distant views of the Pre-Alps – and genuine human warmth – await you at their modernised farmhouse with 19th-century foundations. The smallish bedrooms have typical Provençal fabrics and antiques and personal touches such as dried-flower arrangements; one has its own big terrace. On the verdant veranda Madame brings you breakfast of wholemeal bread, local honey and homemade jams. Plan a day away or make yourselves at home: you get picnic tables under the linden tree, an excellent summer kitchen and a good pool.

rooms	2: 1 double, 1 twin.
price	€55-€60 for two.
meals	Restaurants 1-3km. BBQ available.
closed	Rarely.
directions	From Aups, D9 & D30 to Montmeyan; D13 for Quinson. On left of road, 1km along; signposted.

Dany & Vincent Gonfond
Mas Saint Maurinet,
83670 Montmeyan,
Var

tel	+33 (0)4 94 80 78 03
fax	+33 (0)4 94 80 78 03
web	www.st-maurinet-moslyy

Alegria

Belgian Cindy and Dieter, an attractive couple, have performed a masterly French renovation among the gnarled grey olive groves (they press their own). With simplicity and flair, intense colours and minimal furniture, Moroccan lights and repolished brocante, they have created a house of atmosphere, vibrant warmth and easy living. Bedrooms are inspired: light and lots of white, pools of colour, total attention to detail, originality (some bathrooms behind bedhead walls, some pure Marrakech). Their enthusiasm is boundless, their breakfast gorgeously Flemish, their food finely fusional.

rooms	5: 4 doubles, 1 suite for 4.
price	€110-€140 for two. Minimum stay 2 nights July-Aug.
meals	Dinner with wine €35, book ahead; good restaurant 400m.
closed	January.
directions	From Aups take road for Salernes; left opposite Gendarmerie. Signposted.

Dieter & Cindy Ruys
Alegria,
83630 Aups,
Var

mobile	+33 (0)6 32 20 15 37
fax	+33 (0)4 94 70 00 41
e-mail	alegria-aups@wanadoo.fr
web	www.alegria.tk

Domaine de Nestuby

Bravo Nathalie! The children are growing, the guest rooms refreshed, and she's still in calm, friendly control of this gorgeous, well-restored 18th-century bastide. One whole wing is for guests: yours the light, airy, vineyard-view bedrooms, pastel-painted and Provençal-furnished with a happy mix of antique and modern, yours the big bourgeois sitting room (little used: it's too lovely outside), yours a swim in the great spring-fed tank. Gently confident, Jean-François runs the vineyard, the tastings and the wine talk at dinner with sweet-natured ease. Utterly relaxing and very close to perfection, we thought.

rooms	4: 1 double, 1 twin, 1 triple, 1 family room, 1 suite.
price	€65-€80 for two. Minimium stay 3 nights July & Aug.
meals	Dinner with wine €22, book ahead.
closed	November-February.
directions	From A8 Brignoles exit north D554 through Le Val; D22 through Montfort sur Argens for Cotignac. 5km along left; sign.

Nathalie & Jean-François Roubaud
Domaine de Nestuby,
83570 Cotignac, Var

tel	+33 (0)4 94 04 60 02
fax	+33 (0)4 94 04 79 22
e-mail	nestuby@wanadoo.fr
web	www.sejour-en-provence.com

Bastide des Hautes Moures

Colours rich with Mediterranean sunshine and heat, a sure eye for stunning touches: this lovely house is a celebration of your young hosts' love of colour and brocante. And flawless workmanship. Those delectable bathrooms by North African craftsmen: Moroccan hammams? Roman baths? Bedrooms: there's space to dance round the easy chairs and Catherine's brilliant mix of furniture – into the walk-in wardrobe and out. Dinner? Antoine is an accomplished chef. Butterflies dance to the call of the cicadas beneath the 300-year-old oaks. The wealth of Provence is here. *Children welcome for specific weeks.*

rooms	3 doubles.
price	€80-€110 for two.
meals	Dinner with wine €27, book ahead.
closed	Rarely.
directions	From A8 exit Le Luc & Le Cannet des Moures for Le Thoronet. Right on D84 for Vidouban. 4.5km to Les Moures, right & 800m onto house.

Catherine Jobert
& Antoine Debray
Bastide des Hautes Moures,
83340 Le Thoronet, Var

tel	+33 (0)4 94 60 13 36
fax	+33 (0)4 94 73 81 23
e-mail	jobertcatherine@aol.com
web	www.bastide-des-moures.com

La Canal

Built in 1760 as a silkworm farm, this delicious old manor house still has mulberry trees shading the wonderful terrace that gives onto a mature walled garden. Plus a meadow area with children's games, a summer pool and a stupendous view to the distant hills. Inside it is just as authentic: old tiles with good rugs, beams, white walls and simple, comfortable antique furniture. Organised, warm-hearted Nicola cannot be here for every month of the year but has arranged for a friendly, alternative helper to be there for you on the occasions when she is away.

rooms	4: 1 double, 1 twin; 1 double, 1 twin, sharing shower/bath & wc.
price	€95 for two. Minimum stay 2 nights.
meals	Wide choice of restaurants within walking distance.
closed	Rarely.
directions	From A8 exit 13 on N7 E to Vidauban; left D48 to Lorgues. In main street, post office on right: right, right again; at T-junction left Pl. Arariso. Leave square on left into Rue de la Canal; house on left.

Nicola d'Annunzio
La Canal,
Quartier le Grand Jardin,
83510 Lorgues, Var

tel	+33 (0)4 94 67 68 32
fax	+33 (0)4 94 67 68 69
e-mail	lacanallorgues@aol.com
web	www.lacanal-lorgues.com

21 chemin des Marguerites

The warm-hearted, tireless Didiers seem to have been born to run a happy and hospitable B&B and they do so, enthusiastically, in their quiet 1960s villa with its backdrop of vineyards and hills. Two spotlessly clean bedrooms with real attention to comfort – good cupboards and bedside lights, for example – share the modern shower room and are hung with Amélie's fine paintings. The guest dining room leads to a private outside terrace and thence to the peaceful, beautiful garden; ideal for relaxing after the day's visit, maybe by boat to one of the Îles d'Hyères.

rooms	1 suite for 4 (double & twin).
price	€70 for two; €110 for four.
meals	Simple restaurants nearby; choice in Le Lavandou.
closed	Rarely.
directions	From Le Lavandou D559 E to La Fossette. Arriving in village, left Av. Capitaine Thorel, left again Chemin des Marguerites. If lost, phone for help!

Robert & Amélie Didier
21 chemin des Marguerites,
83980 Le Lavandou, Var
tel +33 (0)4 94 71 07 82
fax +33 (0)4 94 71 07 82
e-mail ra-didier@tele2.fr
web www.ra-didier.tk

45 boulevard des Pêcheurs

Looking from this perch past umbrella pines out over the town to the marina and the amazing bay is a tonic in itself, served on your private terrace: your delicous many-windowed space feels like a lookout tower, fittingly done in blue and white with a new parquet floor and good bathroom. Breakfast is served under the trumpet vine on the main terrace in the luxuriant garden. The salon, wide, welcoming and uncluttered, has windows to let the view in, old ship's binoculars to look out, nice old French furniture. Danielle is active and attentive, Jean used to work in boats and they are helpful yet unintrusive hosts.

rooms	1 double.
price	€70-€79 for two.
meals	Restaurants nearby.
closed	Rarely.
directions	Into Lavandou centre; left up hill at 2nd lights; 1st left ave Bir-Hakem; Ave des Champs Fleuries; Boulevard des Pêcheurs.

Claudine & Serge Draganja
45 boulevard des Pêcheurs,
83980 Le Lavandou, Var
tel +33 (0)4 94 71 46 02
e-mail draganja@wanadoo.fr
web www.draganja-maison-hote.tk

Le Petit Magnan

Georges is retired and runs the B&B with great efficiency, keeping the house and its surprising touches of colour and imagination immaculately. The bedrooms are indisputably pretty; one, the much larger of the two, has floral curtains on a brass rod, peach-coloured 'dragged' walls and a painted bed. Hard to imagine anyone not liking it, especially the doors onto the private terrace. Half a mile up a rough stoney track, it is all immensely peaceful, there's a splendid pool, a woodland of ancient corks, views across tree-laden countryside and generous windows to let the Provençal light stream in.

rooms	2 doubles.
price	€80 for two.
meals	Good restaurants nearby.
closed	Rarely.
directions	From A8 exit Le Muy for Ste Maxime & St Tropez. About 5km before Ste Maxime right D74 to Plan de la Tour; entering village left D44 for Grimaud.

M & Mme Georges Ponselet
Le Petit Magnan,
83120 Plan de la Tour, Var
tel +33 (0)4 94 43 72 00
fax +33 (0)4 94 43 72 00
e-mail lepetitmagnan@worldonline.fr
web www.lepetitmagnan.fr.st

Les Trois Cyprès

What a view! Sit here, gazing past palms and pool to the plunging sea and enjoying Yvette's speciality of the day (tart, crumble...). She is a wonderful woman, sprightly and endlessly caring; Guy, a gentle and invaluable member of the team, collects the fresh bread and helps you plan your stay; they have travelled lots and simply love people. All three pretty, pastel guest rooms lead off a delightful bright, Moroccan-touched landing – brass lamps, hand-painted mirror – and have lovely rugs on honeycomb-tile floors. The biggest room is definitely the best. And a sandy beach is 10 minutes down the cliff.

rooms	3: 2 doubles, 1 twin.
price	€75-€105 for two. Minimum stay 2 nights.
meals	Restaurants in Les Issambres.
closed	October-May.
directions	From Ste Maxime N98 E through San Piere; after Casino supermarket, 4th left Av. Belvédère; right Av. Coteaux; left Corniche Ligure; house on junction.

Yvette & Guy Pons
Les Trois Cyprès,
83380 Les Issambres, Var
tel +33 (0)4 98 11 80 31
fax +33 (0)4 98 11 80 31
e-mail gyjpons@mac.com
web homepage.mac.com/gyjpons/TOC.html

L'Hirondelle Blanche

Monsieur Georges is passionate about painting, music, wine and old houses and has renovated and decorated this typical palm-strewn 1900s Riviera villa all by himself. Each appealing room has a personal touch – a big red parasol over a bed, a fishing net on a wall; some have little balconies for private aperitifs. His own paintings hang in the cosy salon, wines appear for the evening tasting (you can buy them), the beach is just over the road. Despite the nearby road, you don't need a car: fly in, train in, just take a taxi, or come by bike. A caring couple with two young children in a highly convivial house. *Most bedrooms with air-conditioning.*

rooms	6: 2 doubles, 1 twin/double, 1 family suite for 4; 2 doubles with shower & separate wc.
price	€57-€157 for two.
meals	Dinner €23 in July & August, book ahead; wine list from €5.50.
closed	Rarely.
directions	Autoroute A8 exit 38 Frejuis & St Raphael for Saint Raphael town centre; from old port follow sea front for 900m after Casino de Jeux heading for Cannes.

Florence Methart
L'Hirondelle Blanche,
83700 St Raphaël, Var
tel +33 (0)4 98 11 84 03
fax +33 (0)4 98 11 84 04
e-mail kussler-methout@wanadoo.fr
web www.hirondelle-blanche.fr

Les Suanes

If you crave a moment of utter tranquillity on your journey down the river of life, then Les Suanes is a perfect green mooring to tie up to for a few days: the views of sliding hills, woods and pastures from the patio and bedroom are wonderfully restful. Fiona is charming. English, yet a fluent French speaker, she has decorated her house and garden with great care. The bedroom has an antique chest of drawers, pastel walls, good linen and tall windows that open onto a pretty old tiled balcony. There are masses of books, so why not pick one and snuggle down to read after a day discovering the local delights?

rooms	1 double.
price	€60 for two.
meals	Good restaurant 2km.
closed	October-March & August.
directions	Exit A8 at Fréjus; D4 north to St Paul en Forêt; D55 left for Claviers & Draguignan, 2km; over bridge, 50m; right at Hurrell postbox.

Fiona Hurrell
Les Suanes,
83440 St Paul en Forêt,
Var
tel +33 (0)4 94 76 32 39
fax +33 (0)4 94 76 32 39
e-mail fiona.hurrell@wanadoo.fr

La Guillandonne

These lovely, civilised people, former teacher of English and architect, have treated their old house with delicacy and taste. Standing so Italianately red-ochre in its superb *parc* of great old trees by a stream, it could have stepped out of a 19th-century novel yet the interior speaks for your hosts' caring, imaginative approach (polished cement floors, stunning bathrooms). Bedrooms of fine personality, elegant and colourful, are antique, modern and 'ethnic' (heirlooms beside prison-made pieces). After the madding expats in town, you find here a taste of the peace that was the hallmark of inland Var.

rooms	4: 2 doubles, 2 twins.
price	€60 for two.
meals	Restaurants 1.5km.
closed	Rarely.
directions	A8 'Les Adrets' exit 39 for Fayence; at intersection with D562 (after lake) left for Fayence/Tourrettes; D219 right uphill for Tourrettes, Chemin du Pavillon, 200m. Entrance signposted on right.

Marie-Joëlle Salaün
La Guillandonne,
83440 Tourrettes,
Var

tel +33 (0)4 94 76 04 71
fax +33 (0)4 94 76 04 71

Chemin de la Fontaine d'Aragon

On an ancient hillside studded with rows of gnarled, sentry-like olives, this generous modern house is an oasis of cool peace between sophisticated Monte Carlo and the wild Verdon gorges. The sheer pleasure your hosts find in giving hospitality fills the serene place and its comfortable new and 'medieval' furnishings. Monsieur will tell you about everything (in French) and may take you walking in the 'red' Esterel hills; Madame is quieter with the sweetest smile; both are wonderfully attentive. The excellent double room – good storage and lighting – shares a big pink shower room with the small twin.

rooms	2: 1 double, 1 twin, sharing bath & wc.
price	€49 for two; €96 for four.
meals	Restaurant short walk or choice in Montauroux, 4.5km.
closed	Rarely.
directions	From A8 exit 39 on D37 N for 8.5km; cross D562; continue 200m; house on right; signposted.

Pierre & Monique Robardet
Chemin de la Fontaine d'Aragon,
83440 Montauroux,
Var

tel +33 (0)4 94 47 71 39
fax +33 (0)4 94 47 71 39
e-mail p.robardet@wanadoo.fr

Villa Panko

A thorough riot of colour: the sheltered (no-smoking) garden has clumps of orange, mauve and scarlet flowers; real and fake flowers invade the living room and fight with the cheerful pictures that cover the variegated walls; upstairs are rainbow sheets, patchwork bedcovers, painted furniture and *objets* galore, fine big towels and myriad toiletries; big outdoor breakfasts are served on colourful china. Madame's energy drives it all – she'll organise your stay to a tee, galleries and museums a speciality. It is quiet, exclusive, six minutes from several small beaches – superb!

rooms	2 twins/doubles.
price	€100-€115 for two. Minimum stay 3-5 nights depending on season.
meals	Good choice of restaurants 10 minutes' walk.
closed	Christmas, New Year, 2 weeks August.
directions	From Antibes for Cap d'Antibes; palm-tree r'bout for 'Cap d'Ant. Direct'; next junc. for Cap d'Ant.; 1st right Ch. du Crouton; 1st left cul-de-sac; at end, left on drive; at No. 17, 2nd house on right.

Clarisse & Bernard Bourgade
Villa Panko,
06160 Cap d'Antibes,
Alpes-Maritimes
tel +33 (0)4 93 67 92 49
fax +33 (0)4 93 61 29 32
e-mail capdantibes.panko@wanadoo.fr
web www.villapanko.com

Villa Maghoss

Blushes of pelargonium and cascades of bougainvillea tumble over this 1930s villa, and grapes dangle into your hand at breakfast. From the pretty garden you enter your delightful little sitting room with its country antiques, then through a basic shower room to a rather cramped bedroom. But your hosts are so genuinely, generously welcoming – fresh flowers in the rooms, delicious breakfast – and take such great care of you that this is a minor thorn among the roses. Although this is a quiet, dull piece of suburbia, sweet old seaside Antibes is only a 20-minute walk away – or borrow the bikes.

rooms	1 double with small sitting room.
price	€70 for two. Minimum stay 2 nights.
meals	Wide choice of restaurants in Antibes.
closed	Rarely.
directions	In Antibes centre from Place de Gaulle take Rue Aristide Briand; left at r'bout, follow railway 600m; right Impasse Lorini with barrier marked 'Privé'; at end on right.

Martine & Pierre Martin
Villa Maghoss,
06600 Antibes,
Alpes-Maritimes
tel +33 (0)4 93 67 02 97
fax +33 (0)4 93 67 02 97
e-mail maghoss@voila.fr

Mas du Mûrier

The paradise of a garden, blending into the pine-clothed hillside, is a lesson in Mediterranean flora, æons away from the potteries and madding fleshpots of nearby Vallauris, and Madame makes marmalade with the oranges. The Roncés restored this old building on a terraced vineyard: such peace. Pamper yourself by the pool, relax to the sound of chirruping cicadas. The bedrooms – one large, with kitchenette, one small, with garden view – have in common their comfort and cheery fabrics. Your hosts may seem rather distant – is it shyness or a desire not to intrude? *Italian spoken.*

rooms	2: 1 double, 1 twin.
price	€75-€85 for two.
meals	Good bistro walking distance; choice in town.
closed	Rarely.
directions	From A8 Antibes exit to Vallauris; D135 Rte de Grasse; over 2 r'bouts, slow after hairpin bend; left down track signposted Mas du Mûrier. Telephone if lost.

M & Mme G. Roncé
Mas du Mûrier,
06220 Vallauris,
Alpes-Maritimes
tel +33 (0)4 93 64 52 32
fax +33 (0)4 93 64 52 32
e-mail fcwh.ronce@libertysurf.fr

Le Cheneau

This very appealing Provençal-type villa is a happy marriage of modern technique and traditional design; the setting is entrancing, with umbrella pines, palms, the southern skies and Mediterranean heat. In the cool interior all is well-ordered and smart. Your charming, efficient and enthusiastic hosts have created old out of new, paved their generous terrace with lovely old squares, and furnished the rooms with a mix of the antique and the contemporary – and big beds. There is a dayroom/kitchen for guests and a beautifully tended garden with breakfast terrace – and 10 golf courses within a three-mile radius!

rooms	3: 2 twins/doubles, 1 double.
price	€60-€80 for two.
meals	Two excellent restaurants 300m.
closed	Rarely, please book ahead.
directions	From A8 exit for Antibes D103; over Bouillides r'bout for Valbonne village 3km; 100m after Bois Doré restaurant on right, before Petite Ferme bus stop, ring at iron gate No. 205; up lane, on left at top.

Alain & Christine Ringenbach
Le Cheneau,
06560 Valbonne,
Alpes-Maritimes
tel +33 (0)4 93 12 13 94
fax +33 (0)4 93 12 13 94
e-mail ringbach@club-internet.fr

L'Olivier Peintre

Breakfast in heaven on Michelle's finely-laid spread before a vast and magic sea view, birdsong thrilling from the lush subtropical vegetation and Beethoven from the house. The terraced garden drops down to the sheltered pool, the house is done with antiques and taste. Your hosts, a devoted couple who adore children, make all who come near them feel happier: he, a partially blind former soldier, makes olive-wood carvings and fascinating conversation; Madame, a management consultant of charm and intelligence, is now Cultural Attachée to the Mairie. Wonderful hosts and super dog, Oomba.

rooms	4: 1 twin/double, 2 doubles, 1 family suite.
price	€90-€110 for two; under 10s free. Minimum stay 2 nights.
meals	Dinner €15, book ahead; wine €3. Restaurants in village.
closed	Occasionally in winter.
directions	From A8 exit St Laurent du Var; over r'bout for Zone Ind.; over 2nd r'bout; 3rd r'bout left D118 to St Jeannet; through village to top, Rue St Claude. (Owners will send map.)

Guy & Michelle Benoît Sère
L'Olivier Peintre,
06640 St Jeannet,
Alpes-Maritimes
tel +33 (0)4 93 24 78 91
fax +33 (0)4 93 24 78 77
e-mail mbenoitsere@aol.com

13 Montée de la Citadelle

Both Alain and Michelle, a delightfully happy and enthusiastic couple, are rightly proud of this very pretty and lovingly renovated old house. It has an ideal setting on the upper fringe of a very pretty village, with the woods behind and wild boar who snuffle into the garden at night. The charming bedrooms, each with its own terrace onto the garden, and the suite on two floors, are separate from yet cleverly integrated with the rest of the lovely, white, uncluttered space. Dinners are amazing, with delicious wines and patisserie by Alain; breakfast is under the plum tree.

rooms	2: 1 double, 1 suite.
price	€60-€70 for two. Minimum stay 2 nights.
meals	Dinner with wine €20, book ahead.
closed	October-February.
directions	From Cagnes sur Mer centre D18 to La Gaude; left 100m after Cupola; left into Place des Marronniers; walk up behind grocer's Rue des Marroniers to house. (Alain will fetch luggage.)

Alain & Michelle Martin
13 Montée de la Citadelle,
06610 La Gaude,
Alpes-Maritimes
tel +33 (0)4 93 24 71 01
fax +33 (0)4 93 24 71 01

Un Ange Passe

Serenity, forests and views. The Deloupys used to have a Special Place in Nice Old Town, now they've moved from the hum of the city to the jingle of goats' bells and the splash of the stream. The old sheepfold is palm-lush on the outside, freshly modern within: open-stone walls, polished terracotta, plants, cushions, gliding glass doors to a flood-lit pool. Light, airy, air-conditioned bedrooms have tree-top views, showers have delicious towels. You are on the edge of the village, five minutes from St Paul de Vence, and your hosts are cosmopolitan people who delight in sharing their knowledge of the area.

rooms	5: 2 doubles, 2 suites, 1 family room.
price	€65-€130 for two. Minimum stay 2 nights.
meals	Restaurants 1km.
closed	Rarely.
directions	From La Colle sur Loup for Bar sur Loup by-pass; at sports stadium right; 1st left after pharmacy; follow Chambres d'Hôtes signs.

Bernard & Martine Deloupy
Un Ange Passe,
06480 La Colle sur Loup,
Alpes-Maritimes

tel	+33 (0)4 93 32 60 39
fax	+33 (0)4 93 32 63 64
e-mail	martine@deloupy.com
web	www.un-ange-passe.com

Map 18 Entry 755

Le Castel Enchanté

Way up above Nice and the lowly quarters (the drive up is part of the adventure), drowned in bougainvillea, the great Italianate villa stands in a veritable jungle of scented garden – the 'enchanted' tag is not usurped. Your hosts are new to B&B, enthusiastic, attentive and enjoying it lots. Rooms, all big, one very big with its own veranda, are almost lavish in their rich Provençal colours, excellent furnishings and bathrooms unmatched by many hotels. Served on the sunny terrace, a brilliant breakfast includes cheese, cereals and fresh fruit salad. And a super pool to finish the picture.

rooms	3: 2 doubles, 1 suite for 4.
price	€100 for two.
meals	Vast choice in town, 2km (walk down, taxi back?).
closed	Rarely.
directions	From Pl. St Philippe, under expressway, left Av. Estienne d'O. 600m, over level crossing, after sharp right-hand bend, hard back left private track climbing to house.

Mme Martine Ferrary
Le Castel Enchanté,
06000 Nice, Alpes-Maritimes

tel	+33 (0)4 93 97 02 08
fax	+33 (0)4 93 97 13 70
e-mail	contact@castel-enchante.com
web	www.castel-enchante.com

Map 18 Entry 756

La Tour Manda

Such engaging hosts – nothing is too much trouble. Set well back from the dual carriageway, the house is conveniently near both airport and town. And what a classic Côte d'Azur setting: look from your elegant bedroom over immaculate lawns and palms imported from Egypt. Inside, light, space and heaps of southern style – family antiques, Persian carpets, gorgeous paintings, pristine bathrooms yet not the least intimidating. "Super inside, super outside and super people" – and do visit the Fondation Maeght in hilltop St Paul de Vence for fabulous modern art. *Open by request during carnival.*

rooms	3: 1 double; 1 suite, 1 double sharing bath.
price	€80-€110 for two. Suite €160-€175 for four. Minimum stay 2 nights.
meals	Restaurants in Nice.
closed	Rarely.
directions	From Nice airport for Digne Grenoble; past centre commercial Carrefour; right on small road just before 'Cuisine Mol'.

Jean-Claude & Brigitte Janer
La Tour Manda,
06200 Nice, Alpes-Maritimes
tel +33 (0)4 93 29 81 32
fax +33 (0)4 93 29 81 32
e-mail latourmanda@wanadoo.fr
web www.bb-tourmanda.com

Villa L'Aimée

In one of the most authentic parts of Nice, a short bus ride from the city's rich culture (buses stop virtually at the gate), L'Aimée is a typical 1890s villa and Toni's decoration has restored its wonderful shapes and details to their original Belle Époque opulence. Warm, cultured and much-travelled – one of her lives was in the art world, she's an exceptional cook – she has created delightful bedrooms in soft subtle colours of damask and silk, good antiques, fine linen, tulle canopies, exuding an atmosphere of old luxury. The Blue Room's original parquet is breathtaking. *Children over 10 welcome.*

rooms	3: 2 twins/doubles, 1 twin.
price	€100-€125 for two.
meals	Restaurants 8-15 minutes' walk.
closed	December-January.
directions	From A8 exit 54 Nice Nord for Nice & centre ville; left Ave du Ray; r'bout right; over 2nd r'bout; Place Alex Medicin left; left into Ave Henri Durant; 1st left at Garage Auto Bilan; immed. right Vieux Chemin de Gairaut; 1st right Ave Piatti.

Toni Redding
Villa L'Aimée,
06100 Nice, Alpes-Maritimes
tel +33 (0)4 93 52 34 13
fax +33 (0)4 93 52 34 13
e-mail bookings@villa-aimee.co.uk
web www.villa-aimee.co.uk

151 route de Castellar

Delightful Paul and English Dorothy have been here since the 60s and have made the most of every square inch of the steep site (not for the infirm or elderly!). He is proud of his handiwork, his latest creation being a bridge over the water garden. The views – of wooded valley leading to distant sea – are stupendous and make it entirely worth braving the narrow approach roads through the outskirts of Old Menton. Bedrooms open off a south-facing terrace, have satin bedspreads, simple furniture and good bathrooms. Breakfast may be on that pretty shaded terrace and it's breezy by the pool in summer.

rooms	4 doubles.
price	€60 for two. Minimum stay 2 nights.
meals	Wide choice of restaurants in Menton, 2km.
closed	December-January, except by arrangement.
directions	From Autoroute exit Menton; for Centre Ville & Hotel de Ville; right for Castellar; up narrow road; 151 on left.

M & Mme Paul Gazzano
151 route de Castellar,
06500 Menton,
Alpes-Maritimes
tel +33 (0)4 93 57 39 73
e-mail natie06@yahoo.fr
web www.chezgazzano.com

Domaine du Paraïs

Set in gentle isolation just a dramatic drive up from hot Riviera vulgarity, the slightly faded Italianate mansion is home to a trio of highly cultured, artistic, English-fluent people who have re-awakened its 19th-century magic. No clutter, either of mind or matter, here. Breakfast is in the atmospheric old kitchen. White bedrooms have pretty fabrics, simple antiques and views of trees where birds burst their lungs and Marcel Mayer's superb sculptures await you. Come for dreamy space, natural peace, intelligent conversation. And ride a horse into the hills for a day.

rooms	4: 3 doubles, 1 triple.
price	€55-€75 for two.
meals	Several restaurants in Sospel, 2km.
closed	Rarely.
directions	From Menton D2566 to Sospel; at entrance to village left for Col de Turini 1.9km; left for 'La Vasta' & 'Campings'. Paraïs 1.3km along, hard back on right after ranch & sharp bend.

Marie Mayer & Marcel Mayer
Domaine du Paraïs,
06380 Sospel,
Alpes-Maritimes
tel +33 (0)4 93 04 15 78
fax +33 (0)4 93 04 15 78
e-mail domaine.du.parais@wanadoo.fr

Villa Nyanga

Looking east over the yacht-studded bay, south over the onion domes of a *fin de siècle* Persian palace, here is a warmly human refuge from the fascinating excesses that are Monaco. Michelle's sober, white-painted flat is decorated with wood, marble and lots of contemporary art, her own and her friends'. Living room: arched doors, little fireplace, little breakfast table, wide balcony; guest room: white candlewick bedcover, big gilt-framed mirror, sea view; bathroom: gloriously old-fashioned beige. Space everywhere, and Michelle is as good a hostess as she is an artist.

rooms	1 twin/double.
price	€90 for two.
meals	Wide choice of restaurants in Monaco.
closed	August.
directions	From A8 exit 56 Monaco for centre (tunnel); past Jardin Exotique; on right-hand bend (pharmacie on corner) left; left at end Malbousquet; park opposite no. 26 to unload.

Michelle Rousseau
Villa Nyanga,
98000 Principauté de Monaco,
tel (00) 377 93 50 32 81
fax (00) 377 93 50 32 81
Please note this includes code for Monaco.
e-mail michelle.rousseau@mageos.com
web www.bbfrance.com/rousseau.html

Meals, booking and cancelling

Dinner

Do remember that table d'hôtes is a fixed-price set menu that has to be booked. Very few owners offer dinner every day. Once you have booked dinner, it is a question of common courtesy to turn up and partake of the meal prepared for you. Dining in can be a wonderful opportunity to experience both food and company in an authentic French family atmosphere. Or it may be more formal and still utterly French. Some owners no longer eat with their guests for family and waistline reasons.

Rooms

We have heard of chambres d'hôtes hopefuls arriving unannounced at 7pm and being devastated to learn that the house was full. For your own sake and your hosts', do ring ahead: if they can't have you, owners can usually suggest other places nearby. But arriving without warning at the end of the day is asking for disappointment.

Cancelling

As soon as you realise you are not going to take up a booking, even late in the day, please telephone immediately. The owners may still be able to let the room for that night and at least won't stay up wondering whether you've had an accident and when they can give up and go to bed.

By the same token, if you find you're going to arrive later than planned, let your hosts know so that they won't worry unnecessarily or... let your room to someone else.

French words & expressions

French words and expressions used in this book

Table d'hôtes Dinner with the owners of the house: fixed price set menu, that must be booked ahead.

Types of houses:

Gîte Panda May be either a chambre d'hôtes or a self-catering house in a national or regional park; owners provide information about flora and fauna, walking itineraries, sometimes guided walks and will lend you binoculars, even rucksacks.

Château A mansion or stately home built for aristocrats between the 16th and 19th centuries.

Bastide Has several meanings: it can be a stronghold, a small fortified village or, in Provence, it can simply be another word for mas.

Bergerie Sheep fold, sheep shed.

Longère A long, low farmhouse made of Breton granite.

Maison bourgeoise/Maison de maître Big, comfortable houses in quite large grounds built for members of the professions, captains of industry, trade, etc.

Maison vigneronne Vine-worker's cottage.

Mas A Provençal country house, usually long and low and beautifully typical in its old stone walls, pan-tiled roof and painted shutters.

Moulin A mill – water or wind.

Other words and expressions:

Armoire Wardrobe, often carved.

Brocante Secondhand furniture, objects, fabric, hats, knick-knacks.

Confît Parts of goose or duck preserved in their own fat then fried.

Châtelain/e Lord/lady of the manor.

Clafoutis Fruit flan.

Garrigue Typical scrub vegetation on Mediterranean hillsides.

Boules, pétanque Bowling game played with metal balls on a dirt surface.

Lavoir Public washing place.

Lit clos Old-fashioned panel-enclosed box bed.

Marais Marsh or marshland.

Maquis Wild scrubland.

Objets/objets trouvé Objects, bric-a-brac, ornaments, finds (lost property).

Paysan Not peasant in the English sense but smallholder, modest farmer.

Pelote Basque ball game, with similarities to squash.

Potage/potager Vegetable soup/vegetable garden.

Pressoir Press for olives/grapes/apples.

Salle de chasse Gun room.

Salon Sitting or drawing room.

Photo Christine Buxton

Phonecard
If you are not wedded to a mobile phone buy a phonecard (*télécarte*) on arrival; they are on sale at post offices and tobacconists'.

Public holidays
Be aware of public holidays; many national museums and galleries close on Tuesdays, others close on Mondays (eg. Monet's garden in Giverny) as do many country restaurants, and opening times may be different on the following days:
New Year's Day (1 January)
May Day (1 May)
Liberation 1945 (8 May)
Bastille Day (14 July)
Assumption (15 August)
All Saints (1 November)
Armistice (11 November)

Movable feasts in 2005 & 2006
Easter Sunday 27 March 2005 (16 April 2006)
Ascension Thursday 5 May 2005 (25 May 2006)
Whit Sunday & Monday (Pentecost) 15 & 16 June 05 (4 & 5 June 2006)

Beware also of the mass exodus over public holiday weekends, both the first and last days.

Medical & emergency procedures
If you are an EC citizen, have an E111 form with you for filling in after any medical treatment. Only part of the sum will subsequently be refunded, so it is advisable to take out private insurance.

French emergency services are: the public service called SAMU or the Casualty Department – Services des Urgences – of a hospital; the private service is called SOS MÉDECINS.

Other Insurance
It is probably wise to insure the contents of your car.

Roads & driving
Current speed limits are: motorways 130 kph (80 mph), RN national trunk roads 110 kph (68 mph), other open roads 90 kph (56 mph), in towns 50 kph (30 mph). The road police are very active and can demand on-the-spot payment of fines.

One soon gets used to driving on the right but complacency leads to trouble; take special care coming out of car parks, private drives, one-lane roads and coming onto roundabouts.

The French drive towards a destination and use road numbers far less than we do. Thus, to find your way *à la française*, know the general direction you want to go, ie. the towns your route goes through, and when you see *Autres Directions* or *Toutes Directions* in a town, forget road numbers, just continue towards the place name you're heading for or through.

Avoiding cultural confusion

En Suite

'En suite' is not used in France to describe bathrooms off the bedroom and to do so can lead to confusion. To be clear, simply ask for a room *avec salle de bains et wc.*

Greetings and forms of address

We Anglo-Saxons drop far more easily into first-name terms than the French. This reluctance on their part is not a sign of coldness, it's simply an Old National Habit, to be respected like any other tribal ritual. So it's advisable to wait for the signal from them as to when you have achieved more intimate status.

The French do not say *Bonjour Monsieur Dupont* or *Bonjour Madame Jones* – this is considered rather familiar. They just say *Bonjour Monsieur* or *Bonjour Madame* – which makes it easy to be lazy about remembering people's names.

Breakfast

À table

In simple houses there may be only a bowl/large cup and a teaspoon per person on the table. If so, you are expected to butter your bread on your hand or on the tablecloth using the knife in the butter dish, then spread the jam with the jam spoon.

A well-bred English lady would never dream of 'dunking' her croissant, toast or teacake in her cup – it is perfectly acceptable behaviour in French society.

Lunch/dinner

Cutlery is laid concave face upwards in 'Anglo-Saxon' countries; in France it is proper to lay forks and spoons convex face upwards (crests are engraved accordingly). Do try and hold back your instinctive need to turn them over!

To the right of your plate, at the tip of the knife, you may find a knife-rest. This serves two purposes: to lay your knife on when you are not using it; to lay your knife and fork on (points downwards) if you are asked to *garder vos couverts* (keep your knife and fork) while the plates are changed eg. between starter and main dish.

Cheese comes before pudding in France. Cut a round cheese as you would cut a round cake – in triangular segments. When a ready-cut segment such as a piece of Brie is presented, the rule is to 'preserve the point', ie. cut it at an angle which removes the existing point but makes another one.

Photo Sara Allan

National Parks

General De Gaulle signed the initial legislation for the creation of its National and Regional Parks in 1967. Forty national and regional nature parks in France now represent 11% of its landmass. Most are off the beaten track and are often missed by the foreign visitor. The motorway network is such that one swishes by huge patches of beautiful countryside without even realising it. The National and Regional Parks charter promotes:

- Protection and management of natural and cultural heritage
- Participation in town and country planning and implementation of economic and social development
- Welcoming and informing the public, raising environmental awareness

There is a ban on hunting, camping, building and road construction in the six national parks: Cévennes, Ecrins, Mercantour, Port-Cros, Pyrénées and Vanoise. Access can be difficult but the rewards are considerable.

There are regional parks to be found in the mountains of Queyras (Hautes Alpes), the plains of Vexin (Ile de France), along the coast of Camargue (Provence), in the woodlands in the Northern Vosges (Alsace-Lorraine), in the wetlands of Brière (Western Loire) and off-shore in Port-Cros (Côte d'Azur). All are ideal for rambles. Serious walkers can choose from the sentiers de Grandes Randonnées (GRs for short) which range through the parks and all park offices can provide maps of local walks. There are grottos and museums to visit along with animal parks roaming with bison, yak, greater kudu and a pack of wolves. Activities include: horseriding, cycling and bike rentals, canoeing and kayaking, canal boating, sailing, fishing, spa treatments, wine tours, bathing, rock climbing, hangliding, ballooning. There are packhorses in Livradois-Forez (Auvergne) and donkeys for hire in Haut-Languedoc (Languedoc). A range of activities make them ideal for children and a multitude of crafts are to be observed: clog making, silk weaving, glass working, stone working in the Morvan (Burgundy), cheese making and pipe making in the Haut Jura (Franche Comté).

www.parcs-naturales-regionaux.tm.fr
This central web site links to all the other parks. All have English language versions.

Photo Sara Allan

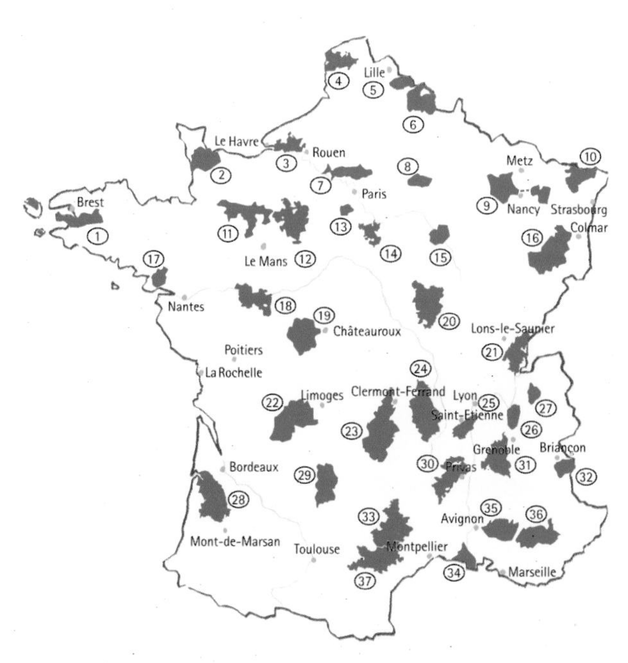

1. Armorique
2. Marais du Cotentin et du Bessin
3. Boucles de la Seine Normande
4. Caps et Marais d'Opale
5. Scarpe-Escaut
6. Avesnois
7. Vexin français
8. Montagne de Reims
9. Lorraine
10. Vosges du Nord
11. Normandie-Maine
12. Perche
13. Haute-Vallée de Chevreuse
14. Gâtinais français
15. Forêt d'Orient
16. Ballons des Vosges
17. Brière
18. Loire-Anjou-Touraine
19. Brenne
20. Morvan
21. Haut-Jura
22. Périgord Limousin
23. Volcans d'Auvergne
24. Livradois-Forez
25. Pilat
26. Chartreuse
27. Massif des Bauges
28. Landes de Gascogne
29. Causses du Quercy
30. Monts d'Ardèche
31. Chartreuse
32. Queyras
33. Grands Causses
34. Camargue
35. Luberon
36. Verdon
37. Haut-Languedoc

Cycling in France

Two and a half times the size of the UK, France offers rich rewards to the cyclist: plenty of space, a superb network of minor roads with little traffic, and a huge diversity of landscapes, smells and terrains. You can chose the leafy forests and gently undulating plains of the north, or the jagged glacier-topped mountains of the Alps. Pedal through wafts of fermenting grapes in Champagne, resinous pines in the Midi, or spring flowers in the Pyrenees. You can amble slowly, stopping in remote villages for delicious meals or a café au lait, or pit yourself against the toughest terrains and cycle furiously.

You will also be joining in a national sport: bikes are an important part of French culture and thousands don their lycra and take to their bikes on summer weekends. The country comes to a virtual standstill during the three-week Tour de France cycling race in July and the media is dominated by talk of who is the latest *maillot jaune* (literally 'yellow jersey' – the fellow in the lead). Cycling stars become national heroes and heroines with quasi-divine status.

Mountain bikes are becoming increasingly popular. They are known as VTTs (vélos tout terrain) and there is an extensive network of VTT trails, usually marked in purple.

When to go

Avoid July and August, if possible, as it's hot and the roads are at their busiest. The south is good from mid-March, except on high ground which may be snow-clad until the end of June. The north, which has a similar climate to Britain's, can be lovely from May onwards. Most other areas are suitable from April until October.

Getting bikes to and through France

If you are using public transport, you can get your bicycle to France by air, by ferry or via the Channel Tunnel. Ferries carry bikes for nothing or for a small fee. British Airways and Air France take bikes free. If you are travelling by Eurostar, you can store your bike in one of the guards' vans which have cycle-carrying hooks, with a potential capacity of up to eight bikes per train. To do this you need to reserve and pay extra.

A few mainline and most regional trains accept bikes free of charge and you can place them in the guard's van. These trains are indicated by a small bike symbol in the timetable. In the Paris area, you can take bikes on most trains except during rush hours. Certain central RER stations forbid the mounting of bikes onto trains. In the Rhône-Alps region, all local trains accept bikes free of charge. However, some trains limit the number of bikes to three.

Maps

The two big names are Michelin and the Institut Géographique National (IGN). For route-planning, IGN publishes a map of the whole of France showing mountain-biking and cycle tourism (No. 906). The best on-the-road reference maps are Michelin's Yellow 1:200,000 Series. IGN publishes a Green Series at a scale of 1:100,000. For larger scale maps, go for IGN's excellent 1:25,000 Top 25 and Blue Series (which you will also use for walking). You can buy maps at most Maisons de la Presse newsagents in France, or at Stanfords in the UK.

Repairs and spare parts

Bike shops are at least as numerous as in Britain and you should be able to get hold of spare parts, provided you don't try between noon and 2pm, when shops close for the all important business of lunching. Prices are often lower than in Britain and the US. However, if you have a non-French bike with non-standard metric wheels, it's advisable to carry spare tyres.

Some useful contacts

Fédération Française de la Randonnée Pédestre (FFRP)
www.ffrp.asso.fr
Leading organisation for walkers and ramblers. Many of their guide books have been translated into English.

Fédération Française de Cyclotourisme
www.ffct.org
As before, for cyclists and mountain bikers.

SNCF (French Railways)
www.sncf.com
Cycles are available for hire at most SNCF stations (useful as you can drop them off at another). Some accept bikes free of charge, others require you to buy your bike a ticket and travel separately. Check insurance.

Maison Roue Libre
www.rouelibre.fr (0)1 44 76 86 43
Affiliated to Paris's public transport system RATP; initiated the opening up of bus lanes to cyclists. Bike rental.

FatTire Bike Tours
www.fattirebiketoursparis.com
(0)1 56 58 10 54
Bike tours designed with the English-speaking tourist in mind; day and night tours of Paris; day trips to Versailles and Monet's Garden at Giverny. Also organise Segway (self-balancing motorized scooter) tours of Paris and Nice.

Mieux se Déplacer à Bicyclette
www.mdb-idf.org (0)1 42 60 66 55
Cycle tours to Versailles, the hidden corners of Paris and up to 80km beyond.

Paris Tourist Office
www.paris-touristoffice.com
Click on 'roller' for details of roller-blading tours (Fridays and Sundays).

Walking in France

With over 60,000km of clearly marked long distance footpaths, or *sentiers de Grandes Randonnées* (GRs for short), and a fantastic variety of landscapes and terrains, France is a superb country in which to walk. Hike in the snow-topped glaciers of the Northern Alps, walk through the lush and rugged volcanic 'moonscapes' of the Auvergne, or amble through the vineyards of Burgundy, Alsace or Provence.

Stroll for an afternoon, or make an odyssey over several months. Some long-distance walks have become classics, like the famous GR65, the pilgrim road to Santiago de Compostela, the Tour du Mont Blanc, or the 450km long GR3 Sentier de la Loire, which runs from the Ardèche to the Atlantic. Wild or tamed, hot or temperate, populated or totally empty: France has it all.

Wherever you are staying, there will almost certainly be a GR near you. You can walk a stretch of it, then use other paths to turn it into a circular walk. As well as the network of GRs, marked with red and white parallel paint markings, there's a network of *Petites Randonnées* (PRs), usually signalled by single yellow or green paint stripes. In addition, there are sentiers de *Grandes Randonnées de Pays* (GRPs), marked by a red and yellow stripe, and any number of variants of the original GR route which eventually become paths in their own right. Paths are evolving all the time.

The paths are lovingly waymarked and maintained by the Fédération Française de la Randonnée Pédestre (FFRP), which was founded in 1947 under another name. The federation is also responsible for producing the topo-guides, books for walkers containing walking directions and maps (see under Books).

The great reward for walkers is that you'll penetrate the soul of rural France in a way you never could from a car. You'll see quaint ruined châteaux, meet country characters whom you'll never forget, and last but not least, you'll encounter a dazzling variety of flora and fauna if you look for it. France has a remarkably rich natural heritage, including 266 species of nesting birds, 131 species of mammal, and nearly 5,000 species of flowering plants. Look out for golden eagles, griffon vultures and marmots in the Alps and Pyrenees, red kites and

Photo Sara Allan

lizard orchids in the Dordogne, and fulmars and puffins off the rocky Brittany coast. There's no room for complacency, however, as hundreds of species are threatened with extinction: 400 species of flora are classed as threatened and about 20 species of mammals and birds are vulnerable or in danger of extinction.

When to go

The best months for walking are May, June, September and October. In high mountain areas, summers are briefer and paths may be free of snow only between July and early September. In the northern half of France July and August are also good months; southern France is ideal for a winter break, when days are often crisp and clear.

Maps

As mentioned in the cycling section, the two big names for maps are IGN (Institut Géographique National) and Michelin. IGN maps are likely to be of most use for walkers. A useful map for planning walks is the IGN's France: Grande Randonnée sheet No. 903 which shows all the country's long distance footpaths. For walking, the best large-scale maps are the IGN's 1:25,000 Serie Bleue and Top 25 series. Also look out for IGN's 1:50,000 Plein Air series which includes GRs and PRs, plus hotels and campsites. Unfortunately they cover only limited areas.

Books

The FFRP produces more than 180 topo-guides – guidebooks for walkers which include walking instructions and IGN maps (usually 1:50,000). Most of these are now translated into English so it's worth buying one of these before you leave.

The Code du Randonneur

Love and respect nature • Avoid unnecessary noise • Destroy nothing • Do not leave litter • Do not pick flowers or plants • Do not disturb wildlife • Re-close all gates • Protect and preserve the habitat • No smoking or fires in the forests • Stay on the footpath • Respect and understand the country way of life and the country people • Think of others as you think of yourself

Clothing and equipment

This obviously depends on the terrain, the length of the walk and the time of year, but here's a suggested checklist:
Boots, sunhat, suncream and lip salve, mosquito repellent, sunglasses, sweater, cagoule, stick, water bottle, gaiters, change of clothing, phrase book, maps, compass, sense of humour, field guides to flora and fauna, waterproof daypack, camera and spare film, Swiss Army knife, whistle (for emergencies), spare socks, binoculars, waterproof jacket and trousers, emergency food, first-aid kit, torch.

A week in the life of an inspector

A call from the Bristol office: "Can you do some extra last-minute inspections?" A quick check of my diary then "OK, no problem" and before long I'm in my little hire car heading off to Provence, a heap of books on the back seat, a well-worn Michelin map beside me and a long list of potential Special Places.

A week later, weary but satisfied, I arrive home with a heavy file of reports and a boot full of gifts – bottles of olive oil, fresh lavender, homemade jams.

Two thousand kilometres of magic. I have lived in France for over 30 years and still marvel at the vast areas of unspoilt land, forests, fields, mountains and river gorges. Old villages hanging off cliff edges, barns and bridges – all witnesses to a rich history and, more often than not, still alive, used and inhabited.

On this trip, I visited a very varied mix of Special Places in town and country, on the coast and in the hills. Hosts ranged from the retired couple wanting to keep their house full and buzzing now the children have left, to the farmer needing to make ends meet, to Dutch immigrants starting a new life in France and restoring an abandoned farm. I invariably met warmth and kindness, was often invited to join in a meal – "You can't go off on an empty stomach"; Monsieur always eager to open a good bottle of wine! – and share the stories of the guests who come through their doors in all their diversity.

Setting off early one morning I saw the sun rise over lavender hills and was almost drowned by a flock of 900 sheep being taken up to the summer slopes, my little car surrounded, bells ringing. It was breathtaking. Waiting for me an hour later were fresh orange juice and croissants, homemade bread and hot coffee on a terrace shaded by trumpet vines and wisteria.

My next overnight hosts welcomed me at 9.30 pm with delicious homemade pâté and local goat's cheese. I joined them and their Swiss guests in the lovely drawing room to watch the World Cup – France against Switzerland. The atmosphere was electric and hilarious, all barriers down as we hooted and applauded, the wine flowed and Swiss chocolate followed.

I am full of admiration for the work 'our' hosts do running their houses and providing such comfort and pleasure to their guests. Wanting to share their lovely homes and truly enjoying people are the basic ingredients for successful B&B. Guests should feel they are Guests, not Clients.

Diana Harris

Flight routes to France from the UK

Destination	UK/Ireland airports
Bergerac	Southampton, Stansted
Biarritz	Stansted
Bordeaux	Birmingham, Dublin, Gatwick
Brest	Stansted
Carcassonne	Stansted
Chambery	Gatwick
Clermont-Ferrand	Gatwick, Stansted
Dinard	Stansted
Grenoble	Gatwick
La Rochelle	Stansted
Limoges	Stansted
Lyon	Birmingham, Edinburgh, Heathrow, Manchester, Stansted
Marseille	Gatwick
Montpellier	Gatwick, Stansted
Nantes	Cork, Gatwick
Nice	Birmingham, Bristol, Cork, Dublin, E. Midlands, Edinburgh, Gatwick, Glasgow, Heathrow, Leeds, Bradford, Liverpool, Luton, Manchester, Stansted, Teesside
Nîmes	Stansted
Paris Beauvais	Dublin, Glasgow Shannon
Paris CDG	Aberdeen, Belfast City Birmingham, Bristol, Cardiff Cork, Dublin, E. Midlands, Edinburgh, Gatwick, Glasgow, Heathrow, Leeds, Bradford, London City, Liverpool, Luton, Manchester, Newcastle, Southampton, Teesside
Paris Orly	London City
Pau	Stansted
Perpignan	Stansted
Poitiers	Stansted
Reims	Stansted
Rodez	Stansted
St Etienne	Stansted
Strasbourg	Gatwick, Stansted
Toulon	Gatwick
Toulouse	Belfast City, Birmingham, Bristol, Cardiff, East Midlands, Edinburgh, Gatwick, Glasgow, Heathrow, Manchester, Southampton
Tours	Stansted

Photo Sara Allan

French Holiday Homes

The B&Bs below also have self-catering accommodation in our French Holiday Homes guide (£11.99).

The North 3
Picardy 41 • 46 • 58
Champagne - Ardenne 66
Burgundy 97 • 99 • 110
Paris - Île de France 139
Normandy 159 • 197 • 201 • 208 • 210 • 219 • 223 • 225 • 231
Brittany 262 • 263 • 267 • 270
Western Loire 296 • 320 • 340 • 354 • 365 • 397
Loire Valley 414
Poitou - Charentes 443 • 444
Aquitaine 466 • 487 • 488 • 490 • 494 • 497 • 505 • 510 • 517
Limousin 530
Auvergne 534 • 539
Midi - Pyrénées 553 • 559 • 567 • 575 • 579 • 607 • 610 • 612 • 613 • 616 • 617 • 622
Languedoc - Roussillon 635 • 637 • 648 • 649 • 657
Provence - Alps - Riviera 711 • 713 • 739 • 747

Wheelchair-accessible

These places have full and approved wheelchair facilities.

Alsace 82
Burgundy 122
Normandy 170 • 181 • 243
Western Loire 293 • 298 • 318 • 346
Poitou - Charentes 421 • 439 • 440 • 444
Aquitaine 472 • 502
Midi - Pyrénées 577 • 612
Languedoc - Roussillon 625 • 659
Rhône Valley - Alps 676 • 699

Limited Mobility

Need a ground-floor bedroom and bathroom? Try these.

The North 3 • 5 • 7 • 9 • 17 • 21 • 22 • 23 • 24 • 25 • 27 • 33 • 36
Picardy 40 • 43 • 46 • 47 • 48 • 50 • 51 • 52 • 54
Champagne - Ardenne 65 • 66 • 71 • 73
Lorraine 77 • 80
Franche Comté 87 • 89 • 90
Burgundy 92 • 94 • 98 • 100 • 113 • 114
Paris - Île de France 127 • 128 • 131 • 138 • 139 • 143 • 144 • 147
Normandy 158 • 165 • 172 • 174 • 175 • 178 • 179 • 188 • 196 • 197 • 198 • 201 • 209 • 211 • 214 • 216 • 218 • 220 • 222 • 226 • 228 • 229 • 235 • 242
Brittany 249 • 251 • 255 • 256 • 257 • 266 • 275 • 279 • 280 • 284 • 285
Western Loire 292 • 297 • 300 • 302 • 305 • 308 • 309 • 310 • 312 • 316 • 317 • 323 • 325 • 328 • 329 • 331 • 334 • 342 • 344 • 347 • 348 • 349
Loire Valley 353 • 354 • 356 • 357 • 358 • 359 • 361 • 362 • 363 • 364 • 369 • 373 • 375 • 376 • 379 • 381 • 384 • 389 • 393 • 394 • 395 • 397 • 400 • 401 • 402 • 403 • 404 • 408 • 410 • 411 • 413 • 415
Poitou - Charentes 417 • 419 • 423 • 425 • 426 • 427 • 429 • 430 • 437 • 443 • 446 • 455
Aquitaine 458 • 464 • 467 • 468 • 473 • 474 • 477 • 480 • 489 • 492 • 493 • 495 • 496 • 497 • 499 • 501 • 504 • 506 • 509 • 516

Photo Sheila Clifton

Cookery courses available

Photo Paul Groom

Language courses available

These places offer French language courses.

Well-being

These places offer massage or yoga.

Midi - Pyrénées 594 • 601
Languedoc - Roussillon 623 • 648
Provence - Alps - Riviera 706 • 732 • 755

Art courses available

Painting or sculpture courses available.

Picardy 58
Franche Comté 91
Burgundy 120 • 123
Normandy 190 • 197 • 233
Brittany 267 • 271 • 277 • 281 • 282
Western Loire 317 • 331 • 333
Loire Valley 371 • 381 • 395 • 398
Poitou - Charentes 420
Aquitaine 466
Limousin 518 • 523
Midi - Pyrénées 553 • 601
Languedoc - Roussillon 626 • 630 • 633 • 648
Provence - Alps - Riviera 734 • 737

Places with good public transport or where owners will collect

Owners of these B&Bs have told us they live within 16km of an airport or train station, and they can organise a lift or a taxi. Dinner is available at these places or there is a restaurant within 1km.

The North 3 • 4 • 10 • 12 • 14 • 25 • 27 • 34 • 35 • 38
Picardy 41 • 42 • 50 • 52 • 54 • 58 • 61 • 62
Champagne - Ardenne 67
Lorraine 78 • 81
Franche Comté 86
Burgundy 97 • 98 • 100 • 102 • 106 • 107 • 109 • 112 • 114 • 115 • 117 • 120 • 123 • 124
Paris - Île de France 127 • 150 • 153
Normandy 158 • 170 • 178 • 180 • 194 • 196 • 197 • 198 • 201 • 228 • 233 • 237
Brittany 248 • 251 • 256 • 257 • 258 • 259 • 266 • 272 • 276 • 284 • 288
Western Loire 290 • 305 • 307 • 319 • 326 • 330 • 337 • 341 • 342 • 346 • 348
Loire Valley 353 • 354 • 355 • 356 • 362 • 365 • 370 • 374 • 378 • 388 • 393 • 395 • 396 • 401 • 403 • 408 • 414

Photo Phillipa Gibbon

Quick reference indices

Good Gardens

Wine tasting

Organic produce

These places serve at least 90% organic produce

These places have swimming pools

Photo Las Bourdolles, entry 567

The Little Earth Book

Edition 4, £6.99

By James Bruges

A little book that has proved both hugely popular – and provocative. This new edition has chapters on Islam, Climate Change and The Tyranny of Corporations.

The Little Food Book

Edition 1, £6.99

By Craig Sams, Chairman of the Soil Association

An explosive account of the food we eat today. Never have we been at such risk - from our food. This book will help understand what's at stake.

The Little Money Book

Edition 1, £6.99

By David Boyle, an associate of the New Economics Foundation

This pithy, wry little guide will tell you where money comes from, what it means, what it's doing to the planet and what we might be able to do about it.

www.fragile-earth.com

Six Days

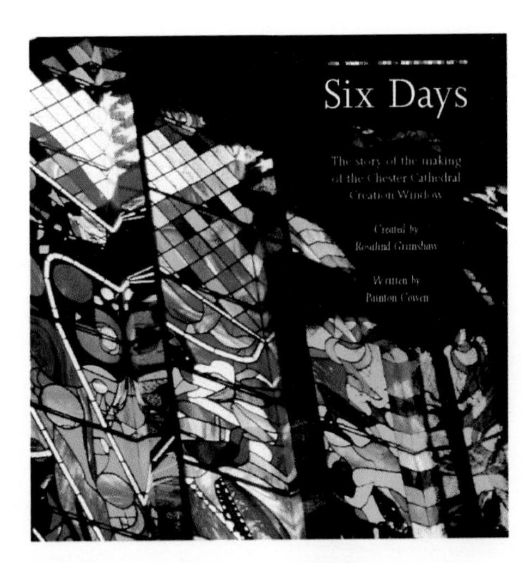

Celebrating the triumph of creativity over adversity.

An inspiring and heart-rending story of the making of the stained glass 'Creation' window at Chester Cathedral by a woman battling with debilitating Parkinson's disease.

"Within a few seconds, the tears were running down my cheeks. The window was one of the most beautiful things I had ever seen. It is a tour-de force, playing with light like no other window ..."
Anthropologist Hugh Brody

In 1983, Ros Grimshaw, a distinguished designer, artist and creator of stained glass windows, was diagnosed with Parkinson's disease. Refusing to allow her illness to prevent her from working, Ros became even more adept at her craft, and in 2000 won the commission to design and make the 'Creation' Stained Glass Window for Chester Cathedral.

Six Days traces the evolution of the window from the first sketches to its final, glorious completion as a rare and wonderful tribute to Life itself: for each of the six 'days' of Creation recounted in Genesis, there is a scene below that is relevant to the world of today and tomorrow.

Heart-rending extracts from Ros's diary capture the personal struggle involved. Superb photography captures the luminescence of the stunning stained glass, while the story weaves together essays, poems, and moving contributions from Ros's partner, Patrick Costeloe.

Order Form

All these books are available in major bookshops or you may order them direct. Post and packaging are FREE within the UK.

British Hotels, Inns & Other Places	£13.99
Bed & Breakfast for Garden Lovers	£14.99
British Holiday Homes	£9.99
Pubs & Inns of England & Wales	£13.99
London	£9.99
British Bed & Breakfast	£14.99
French Bed & Breakfast	£15.99
French Hotels, Châteaux & Inns	£13.99
French Holiday Homes	£11.99
Paris Hotels	£9.99
Ireland	£12.99
Spain	£13.99
Portugal	£8.99
Italy	£12.99
Mountains of Europe	£9.99
Europe with courses & activities	£12.99
India	£10.99
Morocco	£10.99
The Little Earth Book	£6.99
The Little Food Book	£6.99
The Little Money Book	£6.99
Six Days	£12.99

Please make cheques payable to Alastair Sawday Publishing. Total £ __________

Please send cheques to: Alastair Sawday Publishing, The Home Farm Stables, Barrow Gurney, Bristol BS48 3RW. For credit card orders call 01275 464891 or order directly from our web site www.specialplacestostay.com

Title First name Surname

Address

Postcode Tel

FBB9

If you do not wish to receive mail from other like-minded companies, please tick here ☐
If you would prefer not to receive information about special offers on our books, please tick here ☐

Report Form

If you have any comments on entries in this guide, please let us have them. If you have a favourite house, hotel, inn or other new discovery, please let us know about it. You can e-mail info@sawdays.co.uk, too.

Existing entry:

Book title: ____________________

Entry no: ____________________ Edition no: ____________________

New recommendation:

Country: ____________________

Property name: ____________________

Address: ____________________

____

____

____

Tel: ____________________

Comments: Report:

____

____

____

____

____

____

____

Your name: ____________________

Address: ____________________

____

____

Tel: ____________________

Please send completed form to ASP, The Home Farm Stables, Barrow Gurney, Bristol BS48 3RW or go to www.specialplacestostay.com and click on 'contact'. Thank you.

Index by place name

Index by place name

Index by place name

Index by place name

Index by place name

Index by surname

Index by surname

Index by surname

Index by surname

Index by surname

Photo opposite Sara Allan

Burgundy

Cabalus

❶ Was it Cabalus that made Monsieur the character he is? Or has he made it? It's a case of perfect osmosis. Ancient and atmospheric, this old pilgrims' hospice stands in the shadow of the revered Basilica. A gallery of quietly intriguing, tempting objects and a much-loved coffee shop occupy the 12th-century vaulted hall but guests have that vast fireplace to themselves for breakfast. Rooms are simple, authentic, with good beds. Eccentric, Swiss and slightly shuffling, Monsieur Cabalus is the perfect gentleman with a fine sense of humour, Madame a most welcoming artist. An inimitable house.

❷	rooms	4: 2 doubles; 2 doubles, both with shower, sharing wcs.
❸	price	€75 for two.
❹	meals	Dinner with wine €20, book ahead.
❺	closed	Rarely.
❻	directions	In Vézelay centre take main street up to Basilica. Park, walk down main street, ring at 2nd door on right.

M Cabalus
Cabalus,
Rue Saint Pierre,
89450 Vézelay, Yonne

tel	+33 (0)3 86 33 20 66
fax	+33 (0)3 86 33 38 03
e-mail	contact@cabalus.com
web	www.cabalus.com

❼ 

❽ Map 11 Entry 120

Burgundy

Le Moulinot

The handsome millhouse, surrounded by herons, kingfishers and a rushing river, is reached via a narrow, private bridge. Wander the beautiful grounds or settle yourself in the most inviting sitting room, complete with roaring log fire when it's cold. Leigh and Cinda are charming hosts who delight in sharing their watery world. There's a canoe and a lake where Leigh has sunk a brilliant natural-looking swimming pool; and balloon flights can be arranged. The big, light bedrooms are freshly decorated with good bathrooms and the mill race is generally noisier than the road. Wonderful. *Children 8 and over welcome.*

rooms	6: 5 doubles, 1 twin.
price	€55-€80 for two.
meals	Restaurants close by.
closed	Rarely.
directions	From Auxerre N6 for Avallon, 22km; just before Vermenton village sign, sharp right, double back & over bridge.

Leigh & Cinda Wootton
Le Moulinot,
89270 Vermenton, Yonne

tel	+33 (0)3 86 81 60 42
fax	+33 (0)3 86 81 52 21
e-mail	lemoulinot@aol.com
web	www.moulinot.com

Map 6 Entry 121

explanation

❶ write-up
Written by us, after inspection.

❷ rooms
If no mention is made of bathrooms, assume they are 'en suite'.
If a room is not en suite we say 'with separate bath' or 'sharing bath': the former you will have to yourself, the latter may be shared with other guests or family members; both will have a wc, basin and either a bath or a shower.

❸ price
The price shown is the one-night price for two sharing a room with breakfast. A price range incorporates room/seasonal differences.

❹ meals
Prices are per person.
Lunch and dinner must be booked in advance.

❺ closed
When given in months, this means for the whole of the named months and the time in between.

❻ directions
Use as a guide; the owner can give more details.

❼ symbols
See the last page for a fuller explanation:

- wheelchair facilities
- easily accessible bedrooms
- all children welcome
- no smoking in house
- credit cards accepted
- good vegetarian dinner options
- guests' pets can sleep in room
- owners' pets live here
- farm
- pool
- bike hire from premises
- tennis on the premises
- good walks from the house
- English spoken

www.specialplacestostay.com

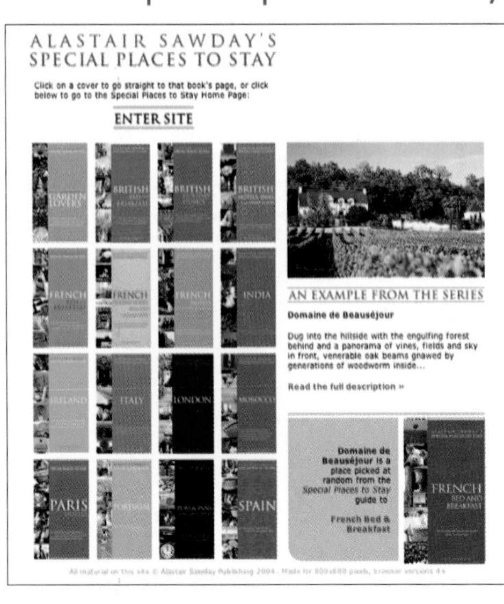

- Britain
- France
- India
- Ireland
- Italy
- Morocco
- Portugal
- Spain...

all in one place!

On the unfathomable sea of online accommodation pages, those who have discovered www.specialplacestostay.com have found it to be an island of reliability. Not only will you find a database full of trustworthy, up-to-date information about all of the places in the series, but also:

- Links to their web sites
- Colourful, clickable, interactive maps
- The opportunity to make most bookings by e-mail
- Online purchasing of our books, securely and cheaply
- Regular, exclusive special offers
- The latest news about future editions and future titles
- Special offers and news from our owners
- News and updates about our books, sent to you by e-mail

Keep an eye out for news and special features that won't appear anywhere else but in our window on the worldwide web.

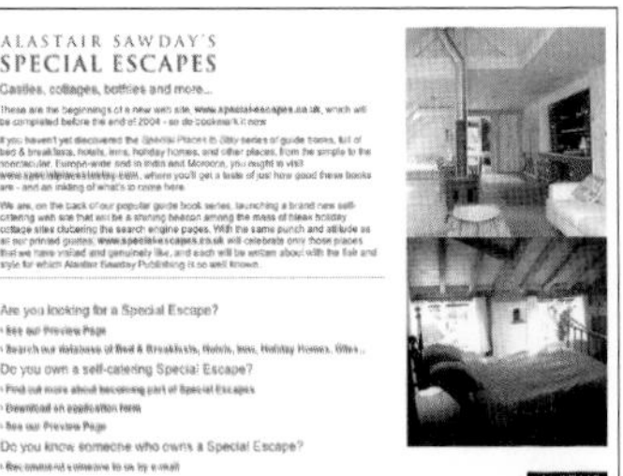

www.special-escapes.co.uk

Discover your perfect self-catering escape in Britain...

We have launched a brand new self-catering web site. With the same punch and attitude as all our printed guides, www.special-escapes.co.uk celebrates only those places that we have visted and genuinely like – castles, cottages, bothies and more...

Russell Wilkinson, Web Site Manager
website@specialplacestostay.com